AF600108

ANGLES ON A KINGDOM

East Anglian Identities from Bede to Ælfric

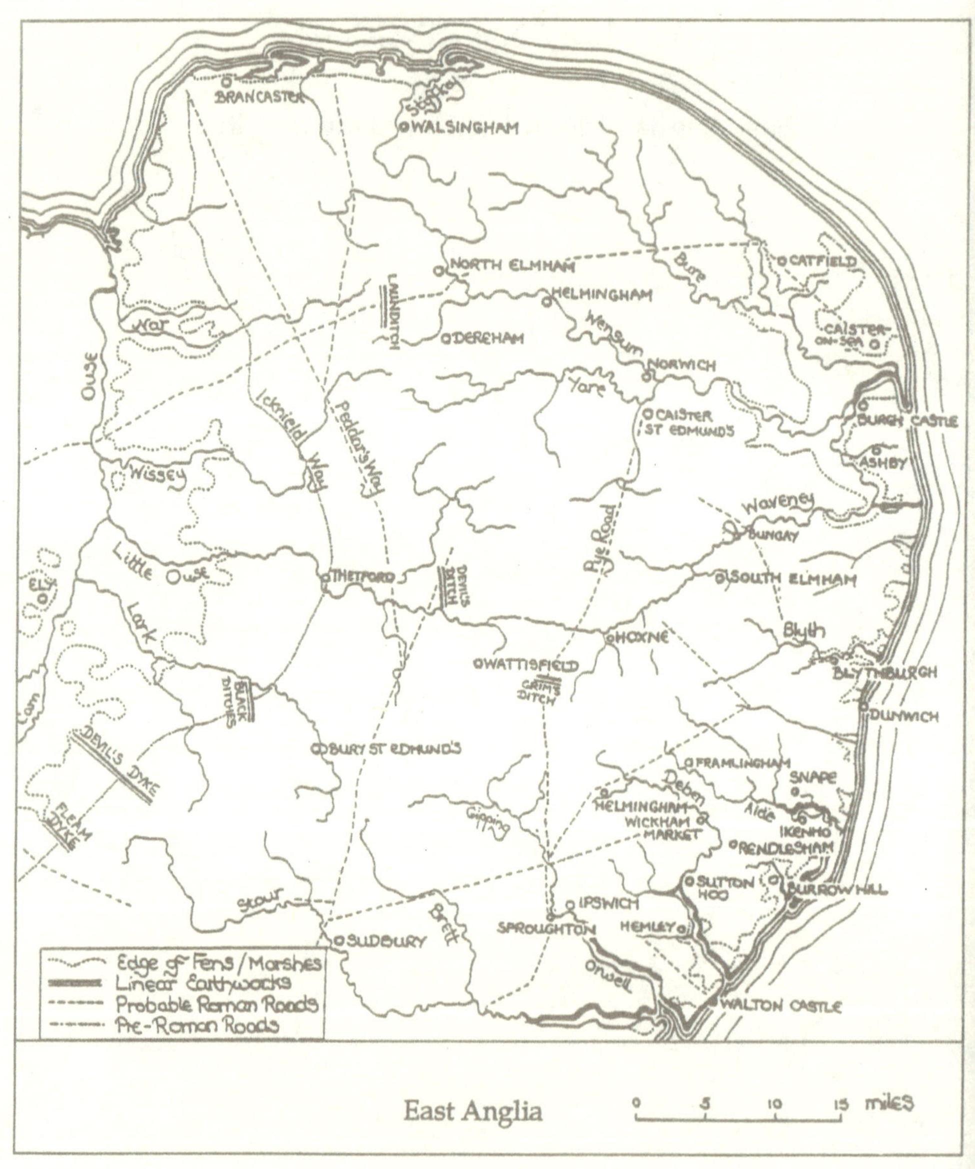

Map of East Anglia.

Angles on a Kingdom

East Anglian Identities from Bede to Ælfric

JOSEPH GROSSI

UNIVERSITY OF TORONTO PRESS
Toronto Buffalo London

Toronto Buffalo London
utorontopress.com

ISBN 978-1-4875-0573-8 (cloth)
ISBN 978-1-4875-3257-4 (EPUB)
ISBN 978-1-4875-3256-7 (PDF)

Library and Archives Canada Cataloguing in Publication

Title: Angles on a kingdom : East Anglian identities from Bede to Ælfric / Joseph Grossi.
Names: Grossi, Joseph L., 1968– author.
Description: Includes bibliographical references and index.
Identifiers: Canadiana (print) 20210145897 | Canadiana (ebook) 20210146052 | ISBN 9781487505738 (cloth) | ISBN 9781487532574 (EPUB) | ISBN 9781487532567 (PDF)
Subjects: LCSH: English literature – Old English, ca. 450–1100 – History and criticism. | LCSH: East Anglia (England) – In literature.
Classification: LCC PR173 .G78 2021 | DDC 829/.09 – dc23

This book has been published with the help of a grant from the Federation for the Humanities and Social Sciences, through the Awards to Scholarly Publications Program, using funds provided by the Social Sciences and Humanities Research Council of Canada.

University of Toronto Press acknowledges the financial assistance to its publishing program of the Canada Council for the Arts and the Ontario Arts Council, an agency of the Government of Ontario.

Canada Council for the Arts | Conseil des Arts du Canada

Funded by the Government of Canada | Financé par le gouvernement du Canada | Canada

To my family: Marina Bettaglio, Anna Grossi, and Thomas Grossi, and in memory of my parents, Joseph Grossi (1932–2003) and Norma Quirk Grossi (1936–2019)

Contents

Acknowledgments ix

List of Abbreviations xiii

Introduction 3

1 Rædwald's Unhappy Realm: Bede's Mixed Views of East Anglian *Imperium* 35

2 Æthelthryth in a Virgin Wilderness 69

3 Solace for a Client-King: Felix's *Vita sancti Guthlaci* 102

4 Made in Wessex: Danish East Anglia and the Alfredian Court 127

5 Edmund, East Anglia, and England 171

Conclusion 210

Notes 219

Bibliography 325

Index 375

Acknowledgments

In an ideal world, the path from first idea to published monograph would be as straight and as straightforward as one of the ancient Roman roads that neatly slice their way through eastern England. In reality, the path is often tortuous, and the present book's journey has seemed to me like a slog through the labyrinthine Fens of the eighth-century monk Felix's *Vita sancti Guthlaci*: the project has by turns dragged, stumbled, slipped, lurched, staggered, and finally waded (if not waddled) its way towards a clearing, now losing itself in false methodological turns, now struggling in the mire of grant applications, now sinking neck-deep after the collapse of ill-conceived and ramshackle causeways of argumentation. I am grateful for the frequent encouragement I have received, whether in the form of tips about conferences (or articles or books, sometimes gifted), patient and generous readings, astute questions posed at key moments, or wishes of good luck or at least "good luck with that."

With a view to capaciousness, then, I warmly thank, in alphabetical order, the following persons: John Archibald, Meredith Bacola, Nina Belmonte, John Black, Virginia Blanton, Adrienne Williams Boyarin, Shamma Boyarin, Andrew Breeze, Tom Bredehoft, Julio Burgo, Christa Canitz, Hélène Cazes, Alison Chapman, Catherine A.R. Clarke, Fran Cudlipp and Trevor Hancock, Misao Dean, Siân Echard, Gordon Fulton, Jay Paul Gates, Jeanne and Ted St. Michel, Alison Gulley, Joel Hawkes, Melanie Hibi, Iain McLeod Higgins, Lloyd Howard, Matt Huculak, Giovanni Iamartino, Henry Ansgar Kelly, Erik Kwakkel, Stephanie Lahey, Rodrigo Pérez Lorido, Kathryn Lowe, Robert Miles, Marcus Milwright and Evanthia Baboula, J. Allan Mitchell, Ruben Valdés Miyares, Lynnea Ness, Michael Nowlin, Emma Nuding, Brian O'Camb, Richard van Oort, Merridy Peters, Kevin Rea and Jennifer Rhoads, Michael Reed, Jane Roberts, Robert Rouse, Stephen Ross, Connie Rousseau, Bob

Shepherd and Lori Mathis, Matt Simeone, Monica Rydygier Smith, Ken Streutker, Alan Thacker, John Tucker, Christine Voth, Andrew Wareham, Carl Watson, Sarah and Scott White, and Gernot Wieland. They have my sincere thanks, and I apologize to anyone whose name I may have forgotten. Any errors, oversights, or absurdities are mine alone.

I also express my profound gratitude to Suzanne Rancourt, Terry Teskey, Leah Connor, Stephanie Mazza, Breanna Muir, and their colleagues at the University of Toronto Press, and to a number of anonymous readers who have guided this project along at various stages over the years and signalled the many reasons it was not yet sea-worthy. Although I have delved relatively little into palaeography and codicology, I would have learned a great deal less about the manuscript environments of literary texts if not for the generous assistance of librarians at the University of Victoria, the British Library, the Bodleian Library of the University of Oxford, Cambridge University Library, the University of Glasgow Library, and the Widener Library of Harvard University; I am grateful to them all, and to the University of Victoria again for providing funding in the form of travel and research grants. I also thank Eva Oledzka, Chris Fletcher, and Colin Walker for permission to quote from manuscripts held in the Bodleian, and Sandra Powlette for permission to quote from manuscripts held in the British Library.

Special acknowledgment is reserved for the medievalists who patiently taught and mentored me: the late Rodney Delasanta, of Providence College; Lisa Kiser, of Ohio State University; and the late Christian Zacher and Nicholas Howe, also of Ohio State. My efforts to reinvent myself as a student of pre-Conquest English literature began too late for me to seek Nick's advice about sense of place, regional identities, and much else, but I continue to learn much from his writings. Finally, my deepest thanks go to my wife, friend, soulmate, and colleague Marina Bettaglio, Italo-Hispanist scholar *straordinaria,* who remains for me a model of erudition whose regional sensibilities have deeply informed my own; and to our two children, apprentice culture critics Anna Grossi and Thomas Grossi, who may yet glimpse the connection between their love of British cult comedies and the anecdotes they've heard far too many times about the exploits of Rædwald, Æthelthryth, Guthlac, Edmund, and many another glorious champion of early East Anglian lore.

This book has been published with the help of a grant from the Federation for the Humanities and Social Sciences, through the Awards to Scholarly Publications Program, using funds provided by the Social Sciences and Humanities Research Council of Canada. An early version of chapter 1 was published as "A Place of 'Long-Lasting Evil and

Unhappiness': Rædwald's East Anglia in Bede's *Ecclesiastical History*," in *New Medieval Literatures* 15 (2013). A version of chapter 3 appears in *Guthlac: Crowland's Saint*, edited by Jane Roberts and Alan Thacker (Donington, UK: Shaun Tyas, 2020), a book that gathers together the contributions to the co-editors' conference "Guthlac of Crowland: Celebrating 1300 Years," held at the University of London on 10–11 April 2014. I happily express my gratitude to Drs. Roberts and Thacker and to Mr. Tyas, as well as to Ms. Elisabeth Walczuk of Brepols Publishers for permission to use revised forms of those essays here. Some ideas in chapter 3 were also adumbrated in "Barrow Exegesis: Quotation, Chorography and Felix's *Life of St. Guthlac*," in *Florilegium* 30 (2013); I thank Christa Canitz for her permission to revisit and build upon those ideas, and Gernot Wieland for his original invitation to submit that article for inclusion in his guest-edited issue of that journal. I am also grateful to Boydell and Brewer and to Sam Newton for permission to reproduce the map of East Anglia in Dr. Newton's book *The Origins of* Beowulf *and the Pre-Viking Kingdom of East Anglia* (Cambridge: D.S. Brewer, 1993). Bits and pieces of other chapters of the present study have been presented in conference panels at Leeds, Glasgow, Kalamazoo, Victoria, and Vancouver, and I thank the organizers of those panels and venues as well.

Abbreviations

AGT	Alfred-Guthrum Treaty
ASC	Anglo-Saxon Chronicle
ASC	*Anglo-Saxon Chronicle*, trans. M. Swanton
ASE	*Anglo-Saxon England* (journal)
ASSAH	*Anglo-Saxon Studies in Archaeology and History*
BAR	British Archaeological Reports
Bosworth-Toller	Joseph Bosworth, with supplement by Thomas Northcote Toller, *Anglo-Saxon Dictionary Online*
DOE	*Dictionary of Old English*
DMLBS	*Dictionary of Medieval Latin from British Sources*
EETS	Early English Text Society
EHR	*English Historical Review*
Electronic Sawyer	*The Electronic Sawyer Online Catalogue of Anglo-Saxon Charters*, Centre for Computing in the Humanities, King's College, University of London; and KEMBLE website, University of Cambridge, https://esawyer.lib.cam.ac.uk/about/index.html
HE	Bede, *Historia ecclesiastica gentis Anglorum*, ed. and trans. Colgrave and Mynors as *Ecclesiastical History of the English People*
JEGP	*Journal of English and Germanic Philology*
LE	*Liber Eliensis*
LSE	Abbo of Fleury, *Passio sancti Eadmundi*, ed. M. Winterbottom as *Life of St. Edmund*
MGH	Monumenta Germaniae Historica
N.S.	New Series
OE	Old English
O.S.	Original Series

PASE	Prosopography of Anglo-Saxon England (database; http://www.pase.ac.uk)
SEKM	Ælfric of Eynsham, *Life of St. Edmund*, ed. G.I. Needham as *St. Edmund, King and Martyr*
S.S.	Supplementary Series
SS rer. Germ.	Scriptores rerum Germanicarum
SS rer. Mero.	Scriptores rerum Merovingicarum
TRHS	*Transactions of the Royal Historical Society*
VSG	Felix, *Vita sancti Guthlaci*, ed. Bertram Colgrave as *Felix's Life of Saint Guthlac*

ANGLES ON A KINGDOM

East Anglian Identities from Bede to Ælfric

Introduction

Comprising chiefly the English counties of Norfolk and Suffolk, the region of East Anglia usually conjures up scenes of flat landscapes at the mercy of a coastline-hungry North Sea, or perhaps images of a rapidly vanishing agrarian way of life whose stolid practitioners have been as much scarred as shaped by its demands.[1] The district's perceived isolation from the rest of England may come to mind; although this diminishes as London's commuter belt expands, East Anglia's reputation for being out of the way has persisted well into modernity. Malcolm Bradbury remarked that his adoptive Norfolk was

> defined by its geography (cut off on three sides by the sea and the fourth by British Rail, is what they always used to say when we still had a British Rail), and shaped by its very distinctive history. Before the fens were drained, and routes to the Midlands opened (still only to a point), it felt truly islanded: open by land only to the south, but by water everywhere.[2]

Even the county of Suffolk, the "fourth" side of Norfolk to which Bradbury alludes, was once considered well off the beaten track despite being nearer to the metropolis.[3] Suffolk forester and Labour activist David Collyer, a semi-fictional character in Ronald Blythe's beloved *Akenfield* (1969), reflects that "London can remain a foreign country, although it is only ninety miles away," because "East Anglia is a nation, which makes it different"[4] – different, that is, from "The Shires."[5] One wonders how long this sense of difference has induced the East Anglian "nation" to judge itself, and to be judged, an odd fit within England.

Modern maps encourage such curiosity by showing the region as a prominent bulge in eastern England that is seemingly being pulled across the North Sea by some irresistible gravitational force emanating from mainland Europe (Brexit notwithstanding). To assert that early

East Anglia was torn between two worlds, between the British Isles on one hand and the Continent and Scandinavia on the other, would be to overdramatize matters; but it is fair to say that it was shared by those worlds, each highly complex and subject to frequent interaction with the other in what has come to be called the larger North Sea Zone or North Sea Province. Much scholarship over the past two decades has illuminated the early medieval societies composing that maritime milieu; archaeological evidence in particular has blurred the lines between a variety of categories – e.g. Insular and Continental, pagan and Christian – that once were held to be clear-cut.[6] Eighth- to early eleventh-century authors were responsible for establishing such rigidly demarcated concepts in the first place: where they saw intermingling, be it of cultural groups or of religious practices, they often reacted with disdain if not with horror, declaiming against heathenism in favour of Christian orthodoxy (the latter itself an ideological not merely religious position), and preferring visions of unity to the spectacle of diversity.

The focus of this book is early medieval East Anglia, from time to time the source of various threats to a cohesive "Englishness" that was imagined to exist by some early medieval writers as a feature either of an evolving Insular Christian Church or of a developing society of kings, queens, and courts. "Anglo-Saxon" is the phrase conventionally used by modern scholars to describe the nation as it was before the Norman Conquest in 1066, but the phrase is generally avoided in these pages because of its increasingly frequent use by nationalists and white supremacists. Academics often employ it as a convenient, strictly taxonomic shorthand within certain well-established fields such as art history and numismatics; nevertheless, the controversy surrounding its use is relevant throughout the English-speaking world and has persuaded me to forgo it.[7] Another reason I avoid the term "Anglo-Saxon," albeit a far less urgent one, is that it implies a steady, organized process of late ninth- and tenth-century political amalgamation that is likely to have been slower, more fitful, indeed more contested than what is suggested by writings produced during the reigns of King Alfred, his sons, and his grandsons. The textual representation of East Anglia from the eighth century to the turn of the millennium highlights the unique love-hate relationship that the region enjoyed with centralizing powers in the early English nation. My fastidious approach to terminology also leads me to distinguish between the "East Angles" of Bede's day and the "East Anglians" of Alfred's, because after 869 the latter people comprised significant numbers of Danes and others from Continental Europe as well as the descendants of the original "East Angles" known to Bede.

As noted above, the place of East Anglia was and is regarded chiefly as the union of Norfolk and Suffolk, for centuries considered to be the district's heartlands. In the twelfth century Geoffrey of Wells believed, or at least wished his readers to believe, that the district's dual composition was well established: "regio uero illa que estengle dicitur … continens in se duas prouincias famosas Norfulchiam atque sudfulchiam" ("[n]ow that region which is called East Anglia … contains within its limits two famous provinces, Norfolk and Suffolk").[8] Internal differences between the region's halves nevertheless existed and will be considered below. Some but not all modern writers would widen the geographical scope of discussion by including the county of Essex and the Fens of north-eastern Cambridgeshire and southern Lincolnshire.[9] Care is needed, however, to prevent a too-expansive idea of the historical East Anglia from encroaching on Middle Anglia, which, though smaller than its eastern neighbour, was once a kingdom in its own right. It will receive further comment in chapter 3.

Blurred and contested boundaries, geographical as well as ideological, form one of East Anglia's principal historical traits; the question of "fit" alluded to above – specifically, how the region troubled larger literary programs of national or ecclesiastical identity or of international harmony – was what prompted me to write this book in the first place. Early East Anglia disturbed some writers by displaying too much cultural or political hybridity; in response to this unsettled state, those writers then promoted or fabricated the region's full integration with an imagined English whole. The texts that disclose the vexed problem of assimilation most intriguingly are the Venerable Bede's *Historia ecclesiastica gentis Anglorum* (*HE*), the monk Felix's *Vita sancti Guthlaci* (*VSG*), the peace treaty between King Alfred and the Anglo-Danish ruler Guthrum (the so-called "Alfred-Guthrum Treaty" [AGT]), entries from various recensions of the Anglo-Saxon Chronicle (ASC), Abbo of Fleury's *Passio sancti Eadmundi* (*LSE*, abbreviating the edition as titled by Michael Winterbottom), and Ælfric of Eynsham's *Life of St. Edmund, King and Martyr* (*SEKM*). These texts, though penned mostly by outsiders to the region, occupy the foreground of this study not only because they refer frequently to East Anglia but also, and more importantly, because they treat it as a distinct place, on one hand integral and desirable to a unified England because of its strategic location and its contributions to ecclesiastical culture, on the other hand dangerous to England because of its vulnerability to Scandinavian and Continental influences, chiefly "pagan" raiders and "paganism" in general (as the texts in question construct those categories). Scholars who see precocious early English "national" identity going back to at least King Alfred's time, if not the Venerable Bede's, have tended to privilege product over process, often playing down the persistence of regional identities and the strain they placed on the unifying agendas of larger political programs and of literary visions aligned with those programs. This book accepts the existence of those pan-English agendas but seeks to gauge the pressure on them exerted by an occasionally wayward region.

East Anglia's distinctness within England can, I admit, be difficult to pinpoint. Touted often by archaeologists, historians, and travel writers,[10] that distinctness fascinates like a will-o'-the-wisp; it inspires so much confidence in its own tangibility that many an authority navigates by it.[11] To seize upon what East Anglia's identities might have conjured up in the minds of early medieval writers, I have found it necessary to think about very disparate fragments of a long-vanished culture: annals in conjunction with lyres (if only briefly); saints' lives in tandem with earthen ramparts; treaties alongside tumuli. The present study has been informed by the findings of landscape historians and archaeologists even as it primarily deals with textual perceptions of East Anglia as a simultaneously vital and volatile part of England.

The vitality is not in question, especially as regards the region's importance within the early English church. In the middle of the seventh century the East Anglian king Sigeberht encouraged the local missionary activity of Felix, the first bishop of the East Anglian diocese, and of the Irish hermit Fursey (or Fursa); their efforts helped to consolidate Christianity in the early kingdom. The royal abbess Æthelthryth, leader of a religious community for women and for men at Ely in the last quarter of the seventh century, added further lustre to the church both in and out of East Anglia. Shortly thereafter, the Mercian aristocrat Guthlac established a hermitage at Crowland and, between the 720s and the 740s, was claimed in effect as an honorary East Anglian by King Ælfwald. The region's most illustrious saint was, of course, King Edmund, killed by "vikings"[12] in 869 and subsequently culted as a virgin martyr in yet another triumph for English no less than regional hagiography. These several regional saints contributed much to what a turn-of-the-millennium scholar like Ælfric of Eynsham regarded as England's national culture.

Yet East Anglia had also been judged a volatile threat to broader cultural and political stability, both in the south-east and beyond. In the early seventh century, King Rædwald, though a converted Christian, refused to renounce the paganism of his forebears; whatever his contemporaries in East Anglia might have thought about his intransigence in this regard, Bede in Northumbria in the 730s deemed it dangerous to the overall health of Christianity in England. In the late ninth century, the former viking leader Guthrum, who had renounced paganism at least outwardly before becoming de facto king of East Anglia, nevertheless aided pagan Scandinavian plunderers, much to the chagrin of the West Saxon king Alfred and his court. Early East Anglia was, then, a hybrid land, now adapting to "heathen" Continental and Scandinavian influences, now asserting its pre-eminence as a bulwark of Christianity and sometimes even over-extending itself in this latter regard at the expense of its neighbours, as hinted at in Felix's *VSG* and in Ælfric's *SEKM*. Between the late ninth and middle tenth century the region fell under Danish rule, though idiosyncratically; afterwards, it elicited yet partly resisted West Saxon military takeover.[13] By the time Wulfstan of Winchester wrote his *Vita sancti Æthelwoldi* in ca. 996, East Anglia had known sufficient vicissitudes and cultural estrangement to seem alien to a West Saxon perspective; Wulfstan could identify the Ely of St. Æthelthryth only by saying that it lay "in remotis Britanniae partibus" ("in remote parts of Britain").[14] The hybridities the region assumes in early English texts endangered but also stimulated contemporary ideals of what a unified England and its church should be, and motivated writers north of the Humber and west of the Fens to try to compensate for a perceived lack in the *gens Orientalium Anglorum*, whose territory was sometimes suspected of being insufficiently "English" and "Christian" and indeed of lying on the front lines of the foreign.

Towards a Methodology

In exploring textual representations of the place and people of early East Anglia, I have been guided by several interrelated critical formulations. "Ethnic identity," John Hines writes, "is a certain form of attributed membership of a group of people. As *attributed*, it is distinctly a product of ideology, although this may be an ideological response to social and economic factors."[15] In a similar vein, and in defence of his own treatment of literary texts as meaningful sources of history in their own right, Ian Wood explains in his *Merovingian North Sea* that "[t]he tribal geography envisaged here is that demanded by the Merovingian sources, reflecting the Franks' view of their neighbours, even if it does not reflect reality."[16] More recently, and with a view to blurring the boundaries between "historical" and "literary" analysis, Paul Strohm has defended what he calls "an extratextual and material history measurable in its textual effects";[17] his critical practice, like those of Hines and Wood, simultaneously respects agents, events, and the written words used to narrate the former's actuation of the latter. My focus, then, is on the chiefly textual attributions of ethnic, ethical, and aesthetic identities; but I also attend to those features of "extratextual and material" reality that would have conditioned those attributions qua "textual effects." Recovering early verbal depictions of East Anglia requires a dual perspective.

Angles on a Kingdom analyses what might be called the developing literary "chorography" of East Anglia, that is, Old English and Anglo-Latin descriptions or figurations of a region, the root *choro-* deriving from the Greek word for "place," "space," "region," or "district." Chorography, as a branch of Greco-Roman geography, pertained specifically to the representation of territorial parts, that is, of regions or localities. The science was exemplified in the works of Strabo and Ptolemy in particular, as Alfred Hiatt and Darrell Rohl have shown with regard to the spatial sensitivities of *Beowulf* and of Enlightenment-era Scottish antiquaries.[18] Where the classical tradition had presupposed a link between chorography and cartography, between verbal and visual representations of regions, the early English approach to conjuring up space relied chiefly on words, as has been demonstrated by Hiatt, Nicholas Howe, Fabienne Michelet, Kathy Lavezzo, and Nicole Guenther Discenza, who in different and fascinating ways have examined the cultural work performed by rhetorical as opposed to pictorial evocations of place and space in pre-Conquest texts.[19] Writings projected a mental map of the environments in which contests for regional pre-eminence unfolded; for this reason, phrases like "mental map" and "social map" are not inapposite to this context.[20]

Precisely because this book traces the textualization of a single region, it bears in mind the larger national context, more specifically what Kathleen Davis has called "the ideological production of England" between the early eighth and the late tenth century.[21] "Regional" and "national" (or, better, "regnal")[22] sensibilities developed in tandem with one another, sometimes overlapping, at times overstepping; attending to their interrelatedness can helpfully disabuse one of the assumption that nations and national feeling arise unproblematically, as if guided along by some benevolent destiny that conveniently erases antagonisms between regions, provinces, or city-states. Hugh Thomas has pointed out that "[b]efore and after 1066 local identities could easily coexist with broader ones," and that "far from competing with or detracting from the strength of attachment to England, and thereby undermining Englishness, local feeling may well have fed into and strengthened the constructs of England and Englishness."[23] Thorlac Turville-Petre has discerned an acrimonious form of this dynamic in late thirteenth- to mid-fourteenth-century literary representations of Norfolk's relationship to the rest of the country;[24] but interregional tensions ran especially high in pre-Conquest England, which had not yet acquired the same national status or national aspirations that would be articulated in the Angevin and Plantagenet periods. The Mercians in the seventh and eighth centuries, the Danes in the ninth,[25] and the West Saxons in the tenth needed to confront the persistent problem of what to do with pre- and post-Scandinavian East Anglia, how to absorb it into larger political configurations that were as yet only groping their way towards cohesion, let alone achieving hegemony. "The history of the East Anglians," it is safe to say with Alice Sheppard, "is particularly associated with the question of kingship in Anglo-Saxon England"[26] and indeed with the question of what it meant to be English. The very ideas of "England" and "the English" were works in progress throughout the pre-Conquest centuries;[27] those ideas stimulated and were stimulated by robust regionalism in East Anglia, and examining this dialectical relationship will, I hope, serve as a useful corrective to any lingering belief that the early English "nation" was a uniquely productive source of identity for the people who lived in it. In considering the interplay between region and nation, between part and whole, I follow the lead of David Rollason, Jacqueline Stodnick, Michelle Brown and Carol Farr, Robert Barrett, Virginia Blanton, and Rebecca Pinner, all of whom have written eloquently about the cultural meanings of specific regions, districts, or localities within their larger geopolitical Insular contexts.[28]

Northumbrians, Mercians, Danes, and West Saxons variously had political designs on East Anglia, and individual authors put literary constructions upon those designs. If at times those authors' textual portraits bear only a dubious resemblance to reality, it's in part because many of them were composed far from the land and people they describe. Even the name "East Anglia," Bede's *provincia Anglorum Orientalium* ("kingdom of the East Angles"), likely originated elsewhere, probably in Canterbury where the earliest archbishops would have found it convenient to organize their several English dioceses according to cardinal taxonomy.[29] From Bede to Ælfric, writers who commented on East Anglia from outside such rarefied bureaucratic climes had their own didactic, moralizing, and sometimes propagandistic agendas, which inhibited a strictly disinterested chorography and instead made possible a variety of highly partisan angles on a kingdom.

Such textual dynamism enhanced what was doubtless an already charged cultural and political landscape, and recent work by social scientists yields insights that can be adapted, with caution and in a general vein, to account for the textual formation of early medieval East Anglia. Fredrik Söderbaum and Björn Hettne, for example, have observed that regions are "processes ... in the making (or un-making)" that owe their form to discourse itself insofar as they "come to life as we talk and think about them."[30] This insight felicitously complements studies by Steven Bassett, John Hines, Barbara Yorke, William O. Frazer, John Moreland, Stephen Harris, Sarah Foot, and David Dumville, all of whom see similar fluidity in early Insular kingdoms.[31] In general, the ethical imperative to discern the constructed nature of identities – sometimes self-generated, at other times attributed or even fabricated by outsiders – has been underscored by writers as varied as David Newman, Chris Rumford, David Rollason, Gloria Anzaldúa, Walter Mignolo, Thomas King, Daniel Boyarin, Tim Ingold, Walter Pohl, Elaine Treharne, Lindy Brady, and Kelley Wickham-Crowley, all of whom have explored the complexities inherent in understanding borders between regions, between countries, and even between mentalities. Their contributions allow us to perceive boundaries for what they really are: imposed physical lines of demarcation as well as processual zones of interaction and mutual influence.[32]

Some of the chorography surveyed in this book takes the form of "mere" observations about place seemingly made in passing. Bede notes that the Isle of Ely is surrounded by water; the monk Felix observes that the Fens are vast; Abbo of Fleury tells us that East Anglia's soil is fertile.[33] Rather than remarks about territory for its own sake, however, these asides are embedded in texts imbued with ideological concerns that obviate "realism" as we understand it; far from obscuring the place of East Anglia, those concerns made it possible for East Anglia to be spoken of in the first place. From the very beginning of the literary record, the region's character was shaped largely by a specifically Christian and often monastic didacticism; this was the ideological angle that allowed the region to come into view. Bede's *HE*, for example, promotes a unified Catholic Church and occasionally employs hagiography for this purpose; Felix's *VSG* and Abbo's *LSE* are entirely hagiographic in nature, their descriptions of place composing a sacred chorography concerned at least as much with literary tropes and pastoral exhortation as with actual fens, rivers, and pastures. The present book necessarily adopts a flexible approach to place description that remains attuned to the pedagogical agendas that inform attitudes towards landscapes.

A further, related methodological caveat – again regarding the ethical concerns surrounding regional study – has to do with early English authors' interest in illustrious individual personages as the human foci of chorography. In the texts analysed in the following chapters, East Anglian kings, queens, monks, and bishops embody their land as agents of wide-ranging spiritual reform or stagnation, or as bearers of political stability or upheaval. Prosopography comes with the territory and often characterizes it. Although the term "prosopo-chorography" is too rebarbative to warrant its use beyond this one coinage, it would (if it existed) describe what I am up to in this book, for the authors considered here often describe places by identifying their rulers, courts, and prelates; by accounting for the processes of governance and evangelization; and by attending to elite networks of power. As Nicole Guenther Discenza observes,

> [e]xploring the geography of the Anglo-Saxons reminds us that space is always constructed and situated, in place and in time. They regarded it pragmatically, creating word-pictures of places populated and full of history. Geography conveys psychological meaning more than a sense of physical reality.[34]

The various characterizations of East Anglia surveyed in this book all point to similarly pragmatic constructions of regional space, the underlying concern of their authors having been to promote a social order that could be implemented only by the figures occupying the highest echelons of society. Today we would probably not describe a place by first considering the social networks of its leading inhabitants, but the writers considered here did so because they believed that countries and their constituent districts were made primarily by those who governed them and secondarily by those who lived in them as subjects.[35] The preoccupation with social elites will be discussed further in the following section, while the conflation of geographical territory with personal and social loyalties will be considered in the section entitled "Vocabulary of Governance."

The Problem of Social Class

There is no way to avoid the "classism" of early representations of East Anglia. A seventh-century cowherd from the region may well have composed songs like the *Trinklieder* shunned by his or her famous counterpart at Hild's monastery of Whitby; but if such songs ever existed, and if they contained colourful references to local life, they have not survived. Even if they had done, we might have gleaned no more of their content than what we can learn about secular folk music from Bede's story of Cædmon. Nor – to pose another hypothetical scenario – are we likely to know how a Cambridgeshire peasant family in the 890s might have gauged the personal relevance to them of labels like "Danish" and "English," governed as their lives were by the more abiding realities of food rents, harvests, and droughts.[36] One could speculate at length about the many lost perspectives on East Anglia once held by, say, eighth-century precursors to the nineteenth-century Suffolk poets

Robert Bloomfield and George Crabbe, or by the distant ancestors of Mary Chamberlain's Fenwomen.

Some of those perspectives may have been entertained by the people named in one of the earliest extant East Anglian charters, a deed of 962 in which King Edgar grants *Ceorleswyrðe* (Chelsworth in Suffolk), valued at seven hides, to his stepmother Æthelflæd of Damerham.[37] The deed warrants consideration here because of its dual spatial sensibility: it is local in that it concerns a Suffolk estate, yet foreign insofar as it was produced in a West Saxon milieu and records a grant of land by a West Saxon king. In general, early English diplomas have piqued the curiosity both of the landscape historian and of the student of early English mentalities, for as bilingual records of transactions that comprise Latin proems and Old English boundary clauses, they allow us to ask certain limited questions about their writers' complex sense of geography.[38] The Latin prefaces contain formulaic wording; the vernacular boundary clauses trace the perimeters of the estates concerned. "Although the diploma was produced in some sense centrally," as Kathryn Lowe observes, "the boundary details were necessarily local affairs, undertaken by those with knowledge of the area to be surveyed."[39] A charter presupposed collaboration between those who owned and those who toiled, between the powerful and the powerless living in overlapping spaces of activity. It also envisioned a role for the divine: its "boundary clause spoke not only to the legal ownership of a parcel of land but also to its ultimate place within God's creation."[40] The part of the text that delimited the estate may have evoked the back of beyond to almost everyone except the people who lived in the immediate area; by contrast, the charter's bombastic, rhetorically convoluted Latin portions appealed to the Great Beyond itself, turf claimed by king and cleric to enforce obedience to the deed.

This dual perspective and the diverse but complementary social attitudes it implies inform the Chelsworth charter. Its fourteen witnesses include four ealdormen and both archbishops; together with the two principal parties involved, the witness list reads almost like a Who's Who of mid-tenth-century England. Other people associated with the land come into view through the boundary markers, the *landgemæro*, which contain their names. These include the Manna and Asa referred to in the phrase "on mannan mearce and on asan" ("to Manna's boundary and Asa's boundary"), as well as the Oswyth and Eadwold who gave their names to "oswiðes mearce 7 eadwoldes" ("Oswyth's boundary and Eadwold's boundary"), and just perhaps a Cula associated with *culan fenne* ("Cula's Fen"?).[41] The estate's very name spurred the curial writers of the document, probably at Abingdon (Oxon), to acknowledge the non-elite community living in the area, for the Latin explains that the place "a ruricolis uulgariter CEORLESWYRÐE prolatum est" ("is commonly known by the country folk as Chelsworth").[42] It is thanks to their naming practices that the dwellers of the countryside come into royal view; they are credited with just enough agency to confer a form of identity upon an estate, a toponym that half-recalls a specific individual's ownership at some earlier time.

The Old English compound of *ceorles* and *wyrþ/worþ* means, at its most general, "a man's homestead," though it may be possible to classify the "man" in question as "a member of the lowest class of free men," "a tenant or proprietor of less than five hides of land," or "a layman" (as opposed to a clergyman).[43] Cyril Hart acknowledges the difficulty of ascertaining when the place-name might have arisen:

> Since the first element of the place-name Chelsworth is in the genitive singular, its origin may be manorial. ... The OE personal name *Ceorl* is found commonly from the seventh to the eleventh centuries. Ceorl's *worth* (homestead, enclosure) was probably so named before the Danish occupation of Suffolk in 879. The village settlement is most likely to have originated in the seventh century or earlier.[44]

Although the place-name resists easy dating, it is not therefore timeless. Intimating "society's unconscious,"[45] the name *Ceorleswyrð* binds together the *ceorl* who had first obtained the enclosed land and made his home thereupon; his local contemporaries, who recognized the act of acquisition and passed the place-name down to posterity; and the villagers who, in the year 962, supplied a peculiarly local way of referring to the estate that was picked up by the charter's authors and witnesses.

Moreover, as Nicholas Howe reflects, "stylistic differences suggest that a place is, at least in part, defined by the style one uses to write it."[46] The Chelsworth diploma "writes" its subject into being by means of two media, the everyday speech of the OE vernacular and the textual idiom of curial administrative Latin. Where the former associates landscape features with specific members of local communities (the *ceorl*, Asa, Manna, etc.), the latter suggests the distance between those communities and the West Saxon royal court, which asserted the power to dispose of properties from afar. The distance between locality and royal power is not necessarily unbridgeable, despite the geographical divide between East Anglia and Wessex; by referring (if only briefly) to the area's *ruricolae*, literally "those who till the earth,"[47] the diploma recognizes the unnamed denizens as the custodians of the vill's name. Though excluded from the transaction, they are nevertheless accorded a place in the transaction's wider life.

Provincial milieus are not always obliterated, then, by centralizing bureaucracies. As late as the 1930s Julian Tennyson, the poet laureate Alfred's great-grandson, could pronounce the modern village of Chelsworth to be "perfect ... because it [was] unmarred by discovery."[48] Perhaps the impact of discovery by outsiders depends on one's point of view; Chelsworth had, after all, been discovered by, and integrated into, a West Saxon economy of land-granting almost a millennium earlier. But the fact that it looked so pristine to an astute observer of Suffolk culture like Tennyson implies that something of the town's local character could still be defined as "unmarred" – that is, untouched by excessive outside influence – in a way not unworthy of the persistence of the names Manna, Cula, Asa, Eadwold, and Oswyth in the vill's tenth-century human geography. Edgar's grant to Æthelflæd typifies the oscillation between local culture and regnal authority characteristic of estate charters in general, but it also exemplifies textual images of East Anglia in that it permits Chelsworth's seven hides to stand out from their surroundings even as it documents their participation in a larger network of exchange. Æthelflæd was, as mentioned above, stepmother to a Cerdicing potentate;[49] but she was also "a representative of a wealthy East Anglian family whose extant wills record their religious patronage of Bury St. Edmunds and their own foundation at Stoke-by-Nayland in Suffolk."[50] Her receipt of Chelsworth from King Edgar suggests regnal intervention in the region but also a distinctly local influence on that intervention.

The Question of Distinctness

It is necessary to return to a point made earlier in this introduction, that East Anglia's distinctness is often attested by historians and archaeologists. Although the present study is chiefly about human *perceptions* of distinctness, it is important to acknowledge that such perceptions are grounded in landscapes that predate humanity. As Tim Pestell observes,

> East Anglia's cultural identity was in no small part a consequence of its topographical definition. Bounded by the sea to the north and east, the Fen basin formed a barrier to the west. To the south-west and south lay the less tractable and more densely wooded claylands, with the deep estuaries and river valleys of the Stour forming a final barrier to the south-east, dividing off Suffolk from Essex.[51]

As described by Pestell, its topography dictates that East Anglia proper will have enjoyed a degree of isolation from its English neighbours that fostered internal homogeneity. Roy Rainbird Clarke made an even bolder version of this claim when, adducing the region's relative nearness to the European mainland, he wrote that "East Anglia … looks out across the narrow seas to the continent, with which it is more intimately linked than with the rest of Britain."[52] This assertion, as extravagant as it may sound, is not wholly unfounded. Accessibility by sea had made the district attractive to outsiders at least as far back as the fifth century, when European migrants possibly made it their first destination in Britain.[53] Trade enabled links between East Anglia and the world beyond the Channel, from Scandinavia to Byzantium to North Africa, as evidenced by the myriad of grave goods excavated from the famous Sutton Hoo ship-burial, itself a foreign practice in its apparent association with what is today Sweden.[54] Furthermore, pottery unearthed at the extensive fifth- to sixth-century cremation cemetery at Spong Hill in North Elmham (Norfolk) resembles finds from an area around Stade on the Elbe River in modern-day Lower Saxony; from this evidence scholars infer "ongoing contact between communities on both sides of the North Sea, and the repeated sharing of material culture and depositional behaviours, rather than a single migration event at the start of the fifth century."[55] Even a less well-known East Anglian site like the assemblage of graves at Harford Farm near Caistor St. Edmund (Norfolk), some twenty-five miles south-east of Spong Hill, opens up broad vistas of cultural exchange thanks to the Kentish disc brooch, Byzantine pin-set, and Roman intaglio thereat unearthed.[56]

Early East Anglia, then, was defined in part by its involvement in far-flung trade networks. But by what else? Jack Ravensdale and Richard Muir, though ardent believers in its uniqueness, caution that "geographical regions, unlike counties and countries, do not have sharp boundaries but gradually merge into their neighbours."[57] Norman Scarfe highlights the same problem of definition when discussing the interior of East Anglia's southern half:

> Suffolk men have had to depend for the perpetuation of their boundaries on the few obvious natural features – rivers and streams, or prominent, long-living oak trees – and on existing man-made features such as earlier metalled roads, field-ditches and hedgerows. The rest they have created for themselves, usually from earth banks.[58]

On the other hand, the early East Angles sometimes moulded their landscape to enhance already discernible frontier zones. As Oliver Rackham points out, "[e]ven where there is a natural explanation for two regions, the boundary is often unexpectedly sharp; we suspect that human endeavour has removed what would naturally have been a transition zone."[59] Border areas between East Anglia and its neighbours are often more pronounced in texts than on the landscape, usually because the former testify to various forms of "human endeavour," specifically the carving out of zones of governance. A written place-name or demonym could reinforce relations or aggravate tensions between neighbours; the very naming of "East Anglia," "Mercia," "Wessex," "Northumbria," and other *regna* by Bede and subsequent writers likely strengthened existing perceptions of political difference and heightened sensitivities to transition zones. There was, however, only so much cultural work that even the most artful of literary productions could perform, because in the political context "borders appear to have been as fluid as the power exerted by rival kingdoms, which ebbed and flowed."[60] The close ties to Europe that Rainbird Clarke perceives in East Anglia's history and pre-history did not preclude other English polities from trying to impose their own will upon the region. When the East Angles eventually entered the larger English political community, they did so because of pressures brought to bear upon them, not because of any essential kinship they might have felt with the Mercians, East Saxons, West Saxons, or Northumbrians.[61]

Those pressures are discernible in early texts and in the landscape itself, where signs of cultural contact and conflict antedate even Bede's time. Recently, Robert W. Barrett Jr. has located the beginnings of the medieval and early modern chorography of Cheshire in the monk Lucian's *De laude Cestrie* (ca. 1195), in which "[t]ext and context explicitly fuse in Cheshire's medieval monastic writing: the foundation of the county's literary tradition is simultaneously the foundation of its local identity."[62] Unearthing East Anglia's literary character requires expanding the search for context to include the material remains of the kingdom's past, a task that necessitates bringing the work of landscape historians and archaeologists into dialogue with philological study.[63] For example, in the late tenth century, Abbo of Fleury conceded that the East Angles had needed to construct earthworks because their western frontier area had always been *pervia*; enemies had always managed to find "a way through" it.[64] Abbo's remark, however fleeting, anticipates Scarfe's insight into Suffolk's scarce natural boundaries and the local need to compensate for them by means of dykes.

Martin Carver has pointed to the combination of texts and artefacts in early East Anglia's multimedia campaign to proclaim and protect the very distinctness we now take for granted:

> The territory of the East Angles, with its estuaries, fens and long coastline, is geographically distinct, then as now. Provoked by the anxieties of the age, leaders emerged, from prominent families, who were to protect the

> people's perceived interests. These leaders soon found it necessary to acquire the conceits of kingship: genealogies, regalia and monumental burial mounds. This defining moment took place within the political context of the communities of the North Sea.[65]

The "defining moment" to which Carver refers might be thought of as a series of self-definitions over time, in essence *performances* of distinctness.[66] The "monumental burial mounds" that still exist at Sutton Hoo in Suffolk announced the importance of their occupants; the regalia once deposited in those mounds (surviving in the British Museum) testified to the singularity of East Anglian monarchical power;[67] the dynastic genealogies – preserved, in different versions, in Bede's *HE* and in London, British Library, MS. Cotton Vespasian B.vi – asserted the bond between land, people, and royal lineage.[68] All of these cultural artefacts were used to supplement porous frontier districts and provisional loyalties. In their own ways Bede, Felix, Abbo, Ælfric, and the court annalists of the Anglo-Saxon Chronicle shaped the performance of East Anglian identities; they created what might be called "conceits of regionalism" with their accounts of kings, queens, hermits, missionaries, and (from the late ninth century onwards) marauders and settlers.

Surviving material evidence suggests that the performance of distinctness could be dramatic even if it enjoyed only limited success in maintaining regnal autonomy. The burial complex at Sutton Hoo and the various prehistoric dykes of Cambridgeshire (about which more later) are cases in point and contrast with the famous Offa's Dyke on the old Mercian-Welsh border. D.J. Tyler has argued that the latter expressed not "ineffectuality or wishful thinking" on the part of the Mercian king Offa but instead "strong, centralising kingship asserting its power in a newly integrated region";[69] in other words, it may have celebrated ascent rather than concealing decline. Things seem to have been different in the Fens. In the late seventh and eighth century East Anglia was much weaker than Mercia, so the former's affirmations of identity – its saints' works no less than its earthworks – may well have signalled aspirations to authority that lacked the means to back them up. In the seventh century in particular, the "fluid … power exerted by rival kingdoms" to which Pestell alludes spilled over frequently from Mercia into East Anglia, usually to the great inconvenience of the latter. It was an indirect commentary on that realm's proneness that authors from Bede onwards should have enriched East Anglia's "cultural capital" as they did by playing up its illustrious rulers and saints.[70]

Of course, other kingdoms – the Mercians, the Northumbrians, the West Saxons – boasted their own important personages, their own "conceits of kingship." No evidence proves that the early East Angles and the later East Anglians were radically different from their neighbours. The term "Anglian" itself is used by archaeologists to cover a wide area of habitation that extended well beyond Norfolk and Suffolk and was characterized by certain kinds of grave goods.[71] East Anglia may be said to have been distinctive in embodying broader cultural traits in its own ways: for example, as John Hines has pointed out, "[i]n terms of the quality, quantity and diversity of known Early Anglo-Saxon archaeological sites, the region of East Anglia is second to none in England."[72] With regard to specifics, Graeme Lawson observes that five of the seven known finds of early English musical instruments, specifically traces of lyres, are associated with this region, in particular with north-eastern Suffolk and south-eastern Norfolk. Two similar sites have been found elsewhere in England, but the presence of five in East Anglia suggests "[s]ome degree of local specialization" and may even "provide ... direct archaeological links ... if not with the very creators of *Beowulf* itself, then at least with those directly responsible for the preservation and communication of the body of ancient traditions within which it was composed."[73] It would be otiose to till ground already worked so diligently by Sam Newton, who has situated *Beowulf* within an East Anglian royal milieu;[74] but it bears emphasizing that if the great Old English epic was produced therein, then East Anglia is to be associated with a specific textual culture – an author or authors as well as their audiences, real or imagined – that deemed centuries-old tales of Scandinavian heroes and battles especially relevant to its own communal self-perception.[75] Personally I find Newton's arguments plausible and have nothing to add to them; but even if we hold that *Beowulf* was produced elsewhere, for example in Mercia, as proposed recently by Richard North and Leonard Neidorf and conceded in passing by Newton himself,[76] then the imagined culture of the poem still gestures towards East Anglia because the latter offers the closest known parallels to the text's description of Scyld Scefing's ship-burial at sea. According to Frederick Klaeber, "[t]his custom was subsequently replaced by the ship-burial on land";[77] the only known English examples of Scandinavian-style boat inhumation lie on or near to the East Anglian coast: at Sutton Hoo, Burrow Hill (Butley, Suffolk), Snape (Suffolk), and Caister-on-Sea (Norfolk).[78]

What all of this means in the present context is that the proliferation of musical instruments and of ship-burials characterizes sixth- and early seventh-century East Anglia significantly even if not uniquely. Such artefacts reflected conscious strategies of cultural self-definition. Although the "body of ancient traditions" behind the genesis of *Beowulf* may well have conditioned aristocratic sensibilities throughout England, that body seems to have been very much at home among the East Angles. The *gens* of that land may even have perceived something of its own fragile independence in the poem's grim reminders of the eventual loss of Geatish autonomy.[79]

Deliberate cultural self-definition and collective performance in East Anglia may be inferred from the position of the mounds that originally contained the ship-burials obliquely recalled in *Beowulf*. These, and perhaps even the tumulus at the now-inland village of Snape, may have been intended to be seen from the North Sea or at least from the local rivers – the Deben in the case of Sutton Hoo, the Alde in the case of Snape.[80] As Howard Williams states, "while there is no categorical evidence for 'monument reuse' at Sutton Hoo, in scale, location and appearance the mounds may have been deliberately evoking associations with prehistoric barrow cemeteries in the environs."[81] The intended spectators of such evocations may have been visitors from far away. In response to Williams, Tom Williamson wonders just how visible Sutton Hoo would have been from the sea, and instead proposes the early utilization of different kinds of perspective;[82] he suggests that "[t]he view of the Sutton Hoo cemetery from the river was … less important than the view of the river from the cemetery."[83] Williamson affirms the strategic and symbolic importance of the River Deben as the route taken by northern European migrants in the fifth and sixth centuries:

> It was a highway which linked those living near its banks together, but which at the same time provided a gateway to places more distant. … [T]he location of the Sutton Hoo and Tranmer House cemeteries, together with the presence within some of the Sutton Hoo mounds of ships, may thus have referenced a lost origin-myth, describing how the people living in this area had first arrived here. In short, in innumerable ways the river would have been the centre of the imaginative and experienced world of those who dwelt beside it.[84]

It is as if the East Angles, or at least the peoples of the Deben, had wished to flaunt to would-be visitors a peculiar style of funeral commemoration and the world view informing it, or to keep at the forefront of their own collective imagination a remembered bond with the sea and with the European mainland.[85] Williamson's discussion of Sutton Hoo in its Deben Valley context builds upon Williams's insights into the conscious staging of funeral rites; the total picture is one in which mourners prepared or cremated bodies, arranged grave goods, and constructed tombs in deliberate ways, both to formalize death and to enact and perpetuate their society's values.[86] Although the siting of cemeteries within view of rivers was not unique to the East Angles, the prevalence of the practice in Norfolk and Suffolk suggests its importance in the cultural self-fashioning of the peoples who adopted that form of inhumation.[87] If Sutton Hoo's ship-burial, for example, reflects "the artificial contrivance of a creative mind; not so much an assemblage of finds, as a statement or text, composed of carefully selected symbols,"[88] then much the same thing can be said about the mound that housed it, along with the other tumuli in the complex. The emphasis on visibility suggests a performative dimension to the East Angles' elite burial customs, a display of ancestor veneration as itself a defining cultural trait, meant perhaps to broadcast enduring affinity between the Angles of England and the Angles of the Continental homelands within the larger "North Sea Province."

Cultural signalling of a different sort may have informed the earthworks dug into the western side of the region. Bran (or Heydon) Ditch, Brent Ditch, Fleam Dyke, High Ditch, and Devil's Dyke, all in southern Cambridgeshire, seem to have been defensive measures undertaken to protect the early East Angles from the Mercians, though the system is likely to have been built in several phases from late Roman times to the seventh century.[89] Advances from the west were not regarded in the east as a foregone, let alone wished-for, conclusion, despite the eighth-century monk Felix's sanguine depiction of Mercian overlordship in the *VSG*. East Anglians have long resisted encroachment on their borders, whether by Mercians in the 650s or by MPs in the 1970s; amalgamation can appear inevitable especially to those who stand to gain from it. Such gain seems not to have been immediately apparent to the peoples who lived to the east of the ancient Cambridgeshire dykes in the sixth and seventh centuries, for they relied on those earthen structures to assert the territorial integrity they believed it was their right to defend.

Before the East Angles

So much has been said up to this point about the East Angles and their defensiveness that it would be easy to overlook the peoples in eastern Britannia whose territory they had seized before becoming East Angles in the first place. If we are to take borders seriously in both their cultural and temporal dimensions, we should acknowledge East Anglia's Romanized substrate. This earlier layer of the region's identity was at least noted in passing by Bede and Felix, both of whom mentioned a small ruined fort or *castrum* in the western Fens that eventually became Cambridge. Before there were Insular "Angles" living in the areas corresponding to modern Norfolk and Suffolk, there were respectively the

Iceni and the Trinovantes, British tribes that had come under Roman control in the middle of the first century CE.[90] In the year 61 those peoples were inspired by Boadicea, or Boudicca, queen of the Iceni, to revolt against the ham-fisted administrators whom the Romans had placed over them. Her forces devastated London, Camulodunum (Colchester, Essex), and Verulamium (St. Albans, Herts) before Roman pacification eventually ensued. Subsequent centuries witnessed the prosperous Romanization of East Anglia, as evidenced by the famous Hoxne Hoard and Mildenhall Treasure, both preserved in the British Museum.[91]

This prosperity did not go unnoticed. Longstanding piratical "Saxon" raids necessitated the building of a system of coastal defences in the late third or fourth century; the task was said to have been entrusted to a "comes litoris Saxonici" ("Count of the Saxon Shore"), a title used in the perhaps fifth-century document known as the *Notitia dignitatum*.[92] This document gives us an early example of the longstanding use of misleading terminology to describe the new transmarine arrivals to Britain, for the word *Saxonici* was used to cover widely varying groups of people. By pausing at the slippage between ethnic names and ethnic realities in this context, we can see how, even before eastern Britannia became the land of the *Eastængle*, textual labelling had served to simplify complex migrations of peoples.

It was formerly held that Germanic mercenaries, "allied" (*foederati*) with the Roman legions but serving alongside them only as irregulars, had settled in Britain in the mid-fourth century. This assumption has been often questioned,[93] but Scandinavians were certainly present long before the first, ninth-century "Viking Age," as John Hines has shown.[94] At any rate, the heterogeneity of peoples already living in Britain would have been evident to those Continental newcomers – themselves highly heterogeneous – who arrived in the fifth century.[95] Bede, in *HE* I, famously categorized the latter as Angles, Saxons, and Jutes, and identified discrete European places of origin for all three peoples. In doing so he displayed only a general accuracy and seems to have oversimplified matters. In Book V he gives an alternative list that includes, among others, *Danai* or "Danes"; while still limited, this second list is more specific, more heterogeneous, and probably closer to the truth than the first.[96] Ian Wood has reminded us of "the amount of social and political diversity within these peoples,"[97] and his research leads one to suspect that Bede used the term "Anglian" not just to connect the Germanic immigrants to Angeln in present-day Germany[98] but also to homogenize and bring under control a potentially dizzying panoply of tribes who had been less unified than a manageable history of the church of the English peoples could easily deal with.[99]

The well-known phrase *adventus Saxonum* or "coming of the Saxons" similarly conceals ethnic and political complexity by reducing a long period of migration to a single event.[100] Bede, working from the *De excidio et conquestu Britanniae* by the British author Gildas (ca. 500–70), dated the *adventus* to the period 449–56, the reign of the co-emperors Marcian and Valentinian. During that time, Bede claims, a British chieftain named Vortigern invited Hengest and Horsa from overseas to fight on behalf of the Britons against the Picts from the north (*HE* I.15, pp. 48–51). The ASC follows Bede but narrows the time frame to the precise year 449.[101] Scholars today prefer a more general time frame in the early to middle fifth century, when the proto-East Angles are thought to have supplanted the ancient territories of the Romano-Celtic Iceni and Trinovantes. The *adventus* ushered in near-universal slaughter and genocide, or so it was long believed; influential in this regard were Gildas's *De excidio* and an anonymous early ninth-century compiler of the *Historia Brittonum*, formerly held to be the work of "Nennius," a Welsh monk.[102] According to Della Hooke, in some parts of Britain early Germanic migrants simply imposed their culture on native populations;[103] she and other scholars regard then-new territorial divisions in the Fens and elsewhere as having been layered atop pre-existing Romano-British units.[104] Susan Oosthuizen, however, has recently revived older views that Germanic newcomers to the Fenland assimilated to existing Romano-British culture, that the native Britons did not vanish from the scene, and that the Fens maintained continuity of resource management throughout the sub-Roman and early English periods rather than having been abruptly and largely depopulated after the fifth century.[105] On the basis of place-names, intercommoning, and agriculture in the Fenland, Oosthuizen argues that "[t]here is … no evidence to suggest a political takeover by 'Anglo-Saxons' of existing communities, or their foundation of new, different 'Germanic' kingdoms. Nor does the vividly apparent change in the material culture of the region indicate demographic, cultural or social upheaval."[106] More persuasive to my way of thinking, however, is the line of argument represented by Hooke, Williamson, Wood, Härke, and others; Wood, for example, believes that "some places saw rapid takeover with minimum disruption, others saw instances of carnage, and yet others saw a slow, destructive infiltration."[107] In any event, the texts examined in the present book will not be treated as realistic accounts of how the newcomers displaced, destroyed, or intermarried with the Romano-Britons; their thoroughgoing suppression of all, or almost all, references to East Anglia's pre-"Anglian" past indicates ignorance of or indifference to that past.

The Romans (as opposed to the Romanized Iceni and Trinovantes) were a different matter; their cultural legacy remained valuable to the newcomers, whatever the latter may have thought about the British bearers of that legacy. An eighth-century genealogy in London, British Library, MS. Cotton Vespasian B.vi traces King Ælfwald's pedigree back through his Wuffing forebears to Julius Caesar himself, an association thought to be unique to the East Anglian kings' sense of their own familial history. Furthermore, the Roman she-wolf who nurtured Romulus and Remus is paralleled in, and perhaps was deliberately appropriated by, the Wuffing dynasty's own totemic lupine figure; this appears on a variety of seventh- to tenth-century treasures unearthed in East Anglia and is associated with that land's *gens* and church.[108] Royal East Anglian identity possessed a Roman dimension, in its own way a culturally productive "conceit of kingship." Francis Young argues that Rædwald's adoption of the wolf symbol "was the means by which the dynasty could boldly assert its barbarian [i.e. Scandinavian] heritage while simultaneously claiming to be Romans, descendants of 'Caser,'" and that "[s]uch symbols and claims enabled East Anglia to project its 'soft power' as one of the cradles of Anglo-Roman Christianity even when it was politically at its weakest," between the times of Rædwald's and Edmund's deaths.[109] It is tempting to see, as Young does, the "'Englishness' of the Wuffing dynasty" as an early step in a process that eventually would lead to "English national unity."[110] It seems more prudent, however, to regard East Anglian royal identity – whether claimed by the area's kings or attributed to them by outsiders – as an attempt to proclaim the singularity of the *gens Orientalium Anglorum*, the "people/nation of the East Angles," for that people did not yet think of itself as "English" in our expanded sense of the word, let alone in the Mercians' or the West Saxons' expansionist sense of the word. The Wuffings first and foremost regarded their identities as local; only secondarily did they regard themselves as akin to other "English" peoples on the grounds of linguistic or cultural similarity.

Internal Diversity

So far, I have been talking about "conceits of kingship" (Carver) or "conceits of regionalism" in terms of East Anglia's relations with other districts or with its Romano-British predecessor tribal units. But the cultural work of homogenization in the textual record also vied with internal heterogeneity, a tension disguised by the very names "East Anglia" and "the East Angles." As Carl Sauer asserted long ago, "geography is based on the reality of the union of physical and cultural elements of the landscape";[111] both sets of elements compose East Anglian geography and point to its internal divisions, "a political homogeneity but a series of distinct regions."[112] The historical overview that follows is necessary to show just how much synthesis – not necessarily all of it peaceful, though some of it may have been – needed to occur to enable Bede, Felix, Abbo, Ælfric, and the anonymous contributors to the Anglo-Saxon Chronicle to make a discrete East Anglian kingdom knowable to early medieval textual audiences.

Although they will have effaced some ancient divisions in the Romano-British territory in which they settled, the Germanic migrants also created new ones. Just as internal diversity has been discerned in early Northumbria, Mercia, and the various "Saxon" kingdoms of the south,[113] so too has it been found in early East Anglia, if perhaps not to the same extent as in the polities to the north and west. The iconic Sutton Hoo offers a good starting point. Some scholars have argued for its link to the ancient East Saxons,[114] though the mound complex is usually understood to express the power of the early kingdom of the East Angles. (This, by the way, is the view adopted in the present book, as is the conventional, often reasserted, but still unproven claim that the person interred in Mound 1 was King Rædwald before the acidic soil dissolved his body.)[115] It is possible, however, that Sutton Hoo was the work of a much smaller society, restricted to that part of south-eastern Suffolk which overlooks the River Deben; early on, the *villa regia* of Rendlesham mentioned by Bede may have commanded only a very limited portion of East Anglia's political geography,[116] beyond which lived peoples who may not have welcomed expansionism emanating from the royal vill. One such people may have created the cemetery at Snape, also in south-eastern Suffolk.[117] A "mixed" elite and lower-status burial ground used between the fifth and seventh century, Snape lies only about ten miles from Sutton Hoo yet is now thought to have belonged to a social group distinct from and older than the creators of that more famous burial complex who eventually drew them into their orbit.[118] Complicating matters is the possibility that both tribes, and the East Saxons to boot, were related through common origins in the Sandlings district of south-eastern Suffolk.[119]

Further to the north but still in the eastern part of the county is Blythburgh, whose name may have originated with a tribe called the Blythingas.[120] This group likewise may have been presented with an offer it couldn't refuse. Its absorption into the East Anglian royal house is implied by a tradition recorded in the twelfth-century *Liber Eliensis* (*LE*) that identifies the ruins of Blythburgh Priory, near Holy Trinity Church, as the final resting place of King Anna, the pious Christian ruler killed by the pagan Mercian king Penda nearby at the Battle of Bulcamp in 654.[121] Bede claims that all of the East Anglian kings were known as Wuffingas from their descent from Wuffa (*HE* II.15, pp. 190–1), but he notes that Anna had been the son of Eni and was "de regio genere, uir optimus" ("an excellent man of royal descent"; *HE* III.18, pp. 268–9). One assumes that Anna was understood by Bede to have belonged to the line of East Anglian kings and therefore to have been a Wuffing; yet his father Eni appears nowhere else in the *HE*'s accounts of the East Angles, and his "royal descent" praised by Bede is not explicitly connected to the Wuffing line (though the connection is made plain in the genealogy preserved in London, British Library, MS. Cotton Vespasian B.vi).[122] The mother of Eni or of Anna himself may have married into the family from a smaller folk-group; perhaps on the maternal side the slain king's family had been Blythings before they became Wuffings.

Although the present book treats East Anglia as a cohesive kingdom, then, the question of discrete identities at the local level must be kept open. Even in its early heyday under Rædwald, the East Anglian *provincia* may have been as fractious and factitious as the most contrived of what Benedict Anderson would call "imagined communities."[123] As Tom Williamson has observed, the nascent kingdom may have amounted to little more than "a constellation of semi-autonomous territories which recognised [Rædwald] as overlord, and rendered him tribute, but which still retained their own ruling families and a measure of political independence."[124]

Post-Conquest differences of speech between Norfolk and Suffolk may reflect ancient cultural as well as linguistic disparities between East Anglia's two halves.[125] From the early seventh century East Anglia boasted not one but two bishoprics, at North Elmham in Norfolk and at *Domnoc* (present-day Walton Castle) in Suffolk, a fact that suggests to Barbara Yorke "a political division of much older origin" and supports Dorothy Whitelock's supposition of tribal heterogeneity.[126] Even if the two bishoprics' origins had nothing to do with existing folk divisions within East Anglia (a possibility put forward recently by Lucy Marten),[127] it is hard to believe that the eventually large seventh-century kingdom had always been socially homogeneous.[128] Such co-existence as eventually arose between Norfolk and Suffolk may have come about after a period of strife at a very early period, given that the document known as the *Tribal Hidage*, which distinguishes a considerable number of Middle Anglian subgroups living on the periphery of East Anglia, neglects to differentiate between what became the region's two major divisions.[129] The southerners may have moved outwards from their Deben stronghold at the expense of other Anglians dwelling near the

River Ouse.[130] On the other hand, consolidation may have happened peacefully, with the more northerly groups participating actively and early in a political fusion experiment initiated to the south.[131]

West Suffolk has long been recognized to be geographically unlike the east.[132] On the basis of archaeological finds, Tom Williamson has recently argued that Essex and the southern and south-western parts of Suffolk were different from the rest of Suffolk along with Norfolk: the former territorial grouping was aligned with London, the larger south-eastern quadrant of England, northern France, and what today corresponds to Belgium; by contrast, Norfolk and the northern and eastern parts of Suffolk were more decisively orientated towards "the North Sea World" and its Germanic and especially Scandinavian influences.[133] The Roman-Scandinavian synthesis that Francis Young sees in East Anglia's adoption of the wolf symbol may be the visible remnant of a more complex policy of cultural reconciliation. Williamson's image of a Janus-faced East Anglia, "always a divided world, looking both ways,"[134] accords with Ravensdale and Muir's claim that "there is a schizophrenic quality to East Anglian culture," a condition attributable to "the historical role of the region as a reception area for settlers, refugees and all manner of new ideas from the Continent" on one hand, and to the well-known tendency of East Anglia to be "introspective and characterised by a deep conservatism" on the other.[135] Given this dual quality, the region's character seems defined by a peculiar mix of opposing tendencies, but one that need not obviate synthesis. Again Tom Williamson: "East Anglia has always been a land divided between the North Sea World and the Channel-focused south-east of England. Yet this, paradoxically, in large part explains the fact that it *is* a recognizable entity: it owes its very existence to the peculiar advantages which its first rulers gained from living close to the junction of both."[136] The very trait of fissiparity that threatens to defy categorization is what makes the chorography of this region possible.

Writers from Bede onwards depicted a heterogeneous if not "schizophrenic" society, and did so by strategically representing its internally conflicting interests in relation to an overarching goal that they themselves imposed on East Anglia's relationship with the rest of England. One thinks, for example, of the tension said to have existed between King Rædwald, a convert to Christianity, and his queen and courtiers, defenders of traditional pagan worship: Bede's retrospective eighth-century account, written from a Northumbrian, pro-Roman, and monastic perspective, presupposes a clear-cut divide between two ideologies when the actual state of affairs in early seventh-century East Anglia may have been far less tidy (see below, chapter 1). Multiple and indeed conflicting "identities" can be detected beneath the synthesizing strokes of the scholar of Wearmouth-Jarrow. It is because of these complexities, and in keeping with the findings of scholars from across the disciplinary spectrum, that I often use the plural noun "identities" to treat the region's representation.[137] For economy's sake the singular noun "identity" sometimes slips in, and I plead guilty to the simplification that choice entails;[138] context occasionally requires me to zoom outwards to glimpse East Anglia's similarities to, or differences from, other regions or from England as an imagined whole.

Vocabulary of Governance

Before I conclude this introduction with summaries of the book's chapters, a final word needs to be said about the specific terminology available to writers of Anglo-Latin and OE texts when they contemplated individual kingdoms; and though not an East Anglian production, the OE translation of Bede's *HE* will be among those texts discussed in this section because it implies some change in the use of that terminology in the late ninth to early tenth century. Within Bede's Latin vocabulary of governance, the word *gens* is of great importance, denoting as it does the social elite of a realm rather than the "people" broadly.[139] A discrete *gens* was thought to inhabit and to rule a particular *provincia,* a noun that in the eighth century connoted political identity and separateness from other polities. As James Campbell points out, "[Bede's] normal word for what we think of as a kingdom is *provincia*: *provincia Merciorum* etc.; but he also uses it, if rarely, for lesser divisions: *provincia Gyruiorum.*"[140] Such correspondences can be only approximate, however, because as David Sturdy reminds us,

> [w]e should not imagine, as tidy-minded historians tend to, that any of these [Anglo-Saxon] kingdoms were cohesive areas with people of a single distinctive racial origin and culture within a trim and obvious boundary. They were casual agglomerations of territories brought together by conquest, inheritance, marriage and purchase. People at the nucleus of a kingdom probably considered most of the outlying provinces as having different customs from their own and being rather alien, as if all those parts of the kingdom were frontier lands, conquered territories, which in most cases they were.[141]

At any given time, the word *provincia* may have betokened a cohesion that was even more fragile than the government it was used to identify. Over the centuries the term's meaning changed with political circumstances. Bede in the 730s used it to refer to the East Angles' country as an independent kingdom, militarily weaker than Mercia but still boasting a royal dynasty of its own. When roughly 250 years later Abbo of Fleury used the same word to describe East Anglia, he had in mind an administrative district within a country rather than a proto-state in its own right – a province, or rather an "ealdormanry," one of several large divisions of tenth-century England ruled by royal appointees.[142] After Edward the Elder broke the Danes' military hold over East Anglia in 917, this is what the district became (though whether it fully embraced and accommodated West Saxon political imperatives is a question that will be taken up later). Abbo spent two years at the Fenland abbey of Ramsey, so he knew that the land on which the house stood had been given to Oswald, bishop of Worcester and later archbishop of York, by Æthelwine "Dei amicus" ("friend of God"), ealdorman of East Anglia.[143] When in the *LSE* Abbo excoriated the vikings for murdering Edmund, he did so with an eye to defending the integrity of an English "nation" that was exemplified but not obscured by the East Anglian "region." He was not seeking to promote a resurgent East Anglia as a rival to Cerdicing England, even if – as we shall see in chapter 5 – his English translator Ælfric may have suspected him of doing otherwise.

Old English had its own, evolving vocabulary of governance. Some debate exists over whether it referred to physical territory or to personal loyalty. It has to be conceded that Insular tribal identities always had to do less with geography, with being able to say "I am the product of that place," than with lordship, with being able to claim "I am the subject of that ruler."[144] Even as late as King Alfred's time, the demonym *Angelcynn* or *Ongolþeode* was the preferred term for "England," the toponym *Englalonde* or *Englaland* appearing only "by the late tenth or early eleventh centuries."[145] Yet geography was not therefore wholly irrelevant to perceptions of place. As Kathleen Davis, Janet Nelson, Scott Smith, and Ryan Lavelle have shown, early English rulers and subjects did recognize territory as a projection of authority, as the tangible space in which interpersonal relations developed over time.[146] Susan Oosthuizen has argued that the many smaller Fenland folk-units recorded in the *Tribal Hidage* reveal attachment to land – specifically intercommoning rights – as the basis of those folk-units' identities.[147] These findings confirm the wider applicability of Peter Hunter Blair's insight about the "political and geographical boundary, not … tribal or racial boundary" that had lain behind Bede's differentiation of the East Angles from the East Saxons.[148]

The ASC, AGT, and the OE translation of Bede's *HE* (to select only three examples) concentrate especially on peoples rather than on lands, in keeping with the general practice described above. When the "A" recension of the Chronicle mentions East Anglia in the annal for 823, it speaks of the "Eastengla cyning 7 seo *þeod*" ("king and … *nation* of the East Angles"),[149] where *þeod* literally signifies "people," not "nation" in the abstract sense that word has for us; and the genitive plural ending of *Eastengla* suggests "of the East Angles." We may find a slight redundancy in the construction "the people of the East Angles," but ninth- or tenth-century audiences likely did not, especially if they were familiar with the same structure in Latin, e.g. Bede's phrase *gentis Anglorum* (lit. "of the people of the English"). The same annal goes on to note that the East Anglian king Beornulf slew the *Miercna cyning*, which here means "king of the Mercians," not "king of Mercia."

There is room for variation. A slight shift of perspective away from people towards territory appears in the annal for 870 (*recte* 869), the topic of which is the Scandinavian invasion of eastern England: "Her rad se here ofer Mierce innan Eastengle 7 wintersetl namon æt Þeodforda. 7 þy wintra Eadmund cyning him wiþ feaht, 7 þa Deniscan sige namon 7 þone cyning ofslogon 7 þæt lond all geeodon" ("Here [i.e. in this year] the raiding-army rode across Mercia into East Anglia, and took winter-quarters at Thetford; and that winter King Edmund fought against them, and the Danish took the victory, and killed the king and conquered all that land").[150] *Mierce* means "Mercia" in the geographical sense; the word *Eastengle* sometimes means "East Angles," but the lack of the dative plural ending *–um* indicates that it is not a people being encroached upon but a place, "East Anglia." This impression is reinforced by the annalist's subsequent reference to the "land" that was overrun.

Even when a text clearly requires us to understand political areas in terms of peoples rather than geography, as in the case of the AGT, its wording need not preclude all concern with the latter.[151] The text emphasizes *ðēoda* ("peoples") in a way that indirectly speaks to the importance of the places they occupy: "Ðis is ðæt frið, ðæt Ælfred cyninc 7 Gyðrum cyning 7 ealles Angelcynnes witan 7 eal seo ðeod ðe on Eastænglum beoð ealle gecweden habbað 7 mid aðum gefeostnod for hy sylfe 7 for heora gingran[.]" Simon Keynes and Michael Lapidge translate this as follows: "This is the peace which King Alfred and King Guthrum and the councillors of all the English race and all the people who are in East Anglia have all agreed on and confirmed with oaths, for themselves and for their subjects[.]"[152] The phrase *on Eastænglum* is idiomatically rendered by Keynes and Lapidge as "in East Anglia," but literally "eal seo ðeod ðe on Eastænglum beoð" may mean "all the people who are among the East Anglians," the "people" being Guthrum's followers, who were involved in the oath-taking. Either way, Alfred stops short of identifying the Scandinavian newcomers to East Anglia with all the inhabitants of that district.[153] If Edward the Elder encouraged his subjects to purchase property in Guthrum's domains, to use legal transactions as the thin edge of the wedge of eventual West Saxon conquest,[154] he would not have been deterred by the AGT, which seems not to apply explicitly to the native East Angles. This subject is considered further in chapter 4.

Tim Pestell's remark about the fluidity of borders resulting from the ebb and flow of power has already been noted. In literary texts, the terminology used to denote nations can appear unstable both because of hegemonic mutability and because of the varying aims of individual writers. Alfred, for example, deployed terms like *Angelcynn*, *Eastænglum*, and *ðēod* with a view to shaping rather than merely accepting their significance. Authors who lacked a king's power to alter political realities could influence semantics, but they were more often obliged to use language that reacted to and accurately reflected those realities. Unlike Alfredian texts, the OE version of Bede's *Historia*, whose earliest manuscript has been dated by Sharon Rowley to ca. 883–930,[155] illuminated political change without apparently effecting it in its own time.[156] We read, for example, that Æthelberht, *cyning* of Kent, "hæfde rice oð gemæro Humbre streames" ("ruled a kingdom extending to the boundary of the river Humber").[157] In this passage, *rīce* corresponds to Bede's idea of *provincia* and signals both far-flung territorial power and widespread personal allegiance. But a somewhat different semantic scope is implied when the text notes the death of the East Anglian king Eorpwald, following which event Eorpwald's successor Sigeberht "Eastengla rice … fore wæs" ("ruled over the kingdom of the East Angles").[158] *Eastengla* is the genitive plural noun meaning "of the East Angles," so the emphasis here is indeed on people, *rīce* in this context referring to political subjects not landscape features.

The OE Bede is not absolutely consistent in this regard, though. The text perhaps suggests a certain diminishment of the East Anglian kingdom when it presents Bede's recollection of an old Northumbrian monk who knew a man who had seen the Irish missionary Fursey face-to-face; that encounter with Fursey is said to have taken place "in Eastengla mægðe." Thomas Miller took this phrase to mean "in the province of the East Angles";[159] unlike *rīce*, the noun *mǣgð* ("a tribe, subdivision of a people"; "a people, nation"; "province, country") may imply reduced political status, a lessening of autonomy not connoted by Bede's original phrase "in provincia Orientalium Anglorum" (*HE* III.19).[160] The choice of *mǣgð* indicates that the Old English translator either judged it necessary to depart from Bede's equation of *provincia* with "kingdom" or thought the Latin noun could denote regions as well as wholly autonomous polities.

In concluding this short digression on political terminology in the OE Bede, I concede that the vernacular translator may simply have regarded *mǣgð* and *rīce* as synonyms, a possibility implied in the OE rendering of Bede's well-known list of English kings who at one time or another wielded wide authority:

> Þa wæs ymb syx hund wintra 7 syxteno winter from Drihtnes menniscnesse … Æðelberht Contwara cyning æfter þæm willendlecan rice, þæt he syx 7 fiftig wintra wuldorlice hæfde, ond þa to þam heofonlican rice mid gefean astag. Wæs he se ðridda cyning in Ongolþeode cyningum þæt allum suðmægþum weold 7 rice hæfde oð Humbre stream.
>
> (Then about six hundred and sixteen years after the incarnation of our Lord … Æthelberht, king of Kent, after gloriously ruling the temporal kingdom for fifty-six years, now ascended with joy to the kingdom of heaven. He was the third among the kings of England who ruled over all the southern provinces and held sway as far as the river Humber.)[161]

Here *rīce* seems to mean the same thing as the element *mǣgþ* embedded in the word *sūðmǣgþum*, but it should be noted that in the first clause the word *rīce* is used twice for chiefly rhetorical effect. Although the noun is repeated, the adjectives *willendlecan* and *heofonlican* differentiate its use so as to dramatize the contrast Bede wished to draw between this world and the next. Within the second clause, *sūðmǣgþum* appears in a different, strictly temporal context; absent the need for rhetorical effect to exalt heaven over earth, the preference of *mǣgþ* over *rīce* may suggest the translator's awareness of an altered political map in the late ninth or early tenth century, when the East Angles and other Southumbrian peoples had lost their original autonomy. In sum, Anglo-Latin and OE political terminology changed in meaning from century to century, varied with the purposes of individual authors, and, perhaps because it was evolving rapidly, sometimes defies consistency within individual texts.

The topic of social and territorial understandings of space will be taken up again later, especially in chapter 4, but in general this study concurs with Fabienne Michelet that England emerges from OE texts as both a "place and [a] people" in its relationships with other nations, and that furthermore "[p]ossession and control of space are crucial issues in a mental outlook in which land grounds not only claims to power but also lays the foundations of a sense of identity."[162] The principle obtains on a smaller scale, too. East Anglia possessed territorial as well as social reality because its textual depiction projects yearnings and anxieties not only about lords and subjects but also about the places that both called home.

Summary of Chapters

Angles on a Kingdom proceeds roughly in chronological order, beginning with Bede's *HE* and ending with Ælfric's *SEKM*. This approach raises to high relief the ways in which later authors borrowed or departed from earlier authors' representations of East Anglia, but it does not presuppose that the region itself was destined to become part of a unified England. No uncomplicated trajectory of East Anglia's literary image can be plotted through eighth- to late-tenth-century texts like a line connecting points on the *x-y* axis of a school geometry assignment. When examined closely, East Anglian textual identities show intermittent bursts of centrifugal energy that stimulate commentators to try to harness the *provincia* and redirect it centripetally towards the whole it was thought to have been endangering. This capturing process differed from author to author and from century to century.

Chapter 1 centres on Bede's references to Rædwald, specifically on his place in the famous *imperium*-list in the *HE*, on his role in helping Edwin secure the leadership of the Northumbrians, on his behaviour after being chastised by his own queen, and on his unique status as a baptized ruler who mingled pagan with Christian religious practices. The chapter argues that Rædwald, though probably not unique, was so portrayed by Bede, who differentiates him from several East Saxon, Kentish, and Northumbrian kings represented either as having delayed before fully embracing the new faith or as having remained hostile to it without ever undergoing baptism. This idiosyncrasy establishes the foundational literary image of East Anglia as a land beset by an ideological ambivalence embodied by its most powerful ruler.

Chapter 2 focuses on Bede's representation of Æthelthryth in light of other holy women and men in the *HE* and argues that her uniqueness as virgin queen and former Northumbrian royal spouse lies behind her exemplification of East Anglian Christianity in Bede's history. The *Historia* plays down her secular authority as Northumbrian queen and so departs from Stephen of Ripon's *Life of Wilfrid*; yet although Bede sought to exalt Æthelthryth as a champion of the Church Universal, he also emphasizes her own self-identification as an East Angle. Without, therefore, labouring her connection to the Wuffing royal house, and despite her activities in Ely far from the known centres of East Anglian royal authority, Bede implicitly shows her redeeming the whole kingdom's reputation, her *Vita* an edifying distraction from the reprehensible transitional period Bede associated with Rædwald and his queen. The political foundations of conversion had been laid by Eorpwald, Sigeberht, and Anna; but their violent deaths at the hands of pagan Mercian aggression are merely noted in the *HE*, which derives from their killings surprisingly little in the way of Christian exemplification. It is rather Æthelthryth, Bishop Felix, and St. Fursey who, in Bede's telling, reincorporate East Anglia into the full community of the English church, with Æthelthryth receiving the most fervent accolades.

Chapter 3 considers the monk Felix's *VSG* as an attempt by the East Anglian royal house to claim the Mercian hermit Guthlac for itself as, in effect, the continuator of Æthelthryth's earlier success in spiritually reclaiming the Fens. By the 740s, when Felix wrote his work on commission from King Ælfwald, the East Angles could boast a formidable number of sainted personages.[163] The *VSG* seems poised to recruit Guthlac to that group. Yet the content of the text nearly undermines the cultural orientation of the commission, because Felix has included far more frequent and fulsome flattery of the Mercians than of the East Angles; indeed, he celebrates the then-reigning Mercian king Æthelbald as the cult's main sponsor. The chapter suggests that Felix was something of a double agent, trying to fulfil his royal commission while minding the proximity and power of the Mercians. It furthermore argues that the closeness to the East Anglian king made possible by his commission would have emboldened Felix to remind his patron of Æthelbald's political supremacy in eastern England and to propose Guthlac – a Mercian nobleman who had chosen the eremitic over the kingly life – as a model of saintly conduct for Ælfwald himself. On this reading, the *VSG* delimits East Anglian self-assertion by confronting its royal patron with the realities of Mercian cultural supremacy in the Fens.

Because this book explores the dynamics of East Anglia's early textual representation, it considers a variety of genres rather than surveying pre-Conquest East Anglian saints' Lives exclusively. The work of researching individual saints and their cults has already been done far better than I could hope to do by Alexandra Hennessey Olsen, Antonia Gransden, Susan Ridyard, Virginia Blanton, Anthony Bale, Rebecca Pinner, Rosalind Love, Tom Licence, Francis Young, and others.[164] Chapter 4 deliberately turns away from hagiography, then, to analyse the shape East Anglia's identities assume when framed by other genres' textual conventions. Such evidence as survives for East Anglian kingship after Ælfwald's death in 749 is relatively scant until the death of Edmund at viking hands in 869 and permits only a tentative regnal chronology.[165] By contrast, the rise of Scandinavian East Anglia, which formed a key part of the wider so-called Danelaw,[166] prompted a fair amount of written comment. Chapter 4 considers the Alfred-Guthrum Treaty and excerpts from different recensions of the ASC that pertain to East Anglia. It explores the implications of Cerdicing annalistic historiography as the framework within which King Edmund's death is contextualized and upon which the later *Vitae* of Abbo and Ælfric elaborate. The chapter then highlights the instability attributed to East Anglia after the erstwhile kingdom's takeover by a foreign people, and finally turns to the ASC to follow its struggle to make sense of a land that alternated between English and Scandinavian mastery.

Chapter 5 returns to saints' Lives. Though accorded only a brief mention in the ASC *s.a.* 870, Edmund's death became, at the hands of his late tenth-century hagiographers, a pivotal moment in the growth alike of the English church and of East Anglia's prestige. In telling Edmund's story, Abbo and Ælfric manifested different approaches to East Anglian regional identities. The former promoted the *provincia* as a virtual paradise with its centre at Bury St. Edmunds, which he judged uniquely holy in England even though his hosts at the much newer house of Ramsey had commissioned his work on the *Passio*. In translating his Latin source, Ælfric suppressed East Anglia's singularity and, to this end, derided and demonized the Jews as outsiders to distract his readers from persistent English interregional tensions. In Edmund's hagiography as well as in earlier writings, East Anglia appears as a source of centrifugal instability that only a factitious English oneness can contain.

1

Rædwald's Unhappy Realm: Bede's Mixed Views of East Anglian *Imperium*

In the *Historia ecclesiastica gentis Anglorum* (*HE*) Bede took up East Anglian themes on several occasions.[1] His larger purpose in recounting England's ecclesiastical history, of course, was to promote Christian orthodoxy; to that ideological end, he envisaged religious cohesion among all the various English kingdoms, the East Anglian *provincia* included.[2] An idealized whole will therefore have mattered far more to Bede than any one of its parts. Even so, his book, as A.H. Merrills has discerned, "is simultaneously a local and a universal history: the viewing of regional events through a wide-angled lens and the presentation of broad historical themes on a truncated geographical stage."[3] The "broad historical themes," of course, were constructed by Bede; by imposing them upon his accounts of events in specific kingdoms, he created histories and identities for those kingdoms that did not always correspond to local perceptions.

This is not to say that Bede objected to all forms of diversity within Britannia's 4,785 miles of coastline (*HE* I.1, pp. 14–15) but rather that he preferred to highlight and indeed emphasize commonalities in spite of it. For example, although the English, British, Irish, and Picts speak their own languages, they are all said to read the Bible in Latin (*HE* I.1, pp. 16–17). The English, for their part, compose one *gens* yet also comprise individual *gentes* (*HE* I.15, pp. 50–1).[4] Merrills sees "the geographical emphases of the *Historia Ecclesiastica* … not as an adjunct to Bede's historical programme, but as a central element within it";[5] the various English *provinciae* exist in spatial and political relationships with one another and, ultimately, with God.[6] Taking further the point about geographical specificity, Georges Tugène observes that it is precisely because "les nations se trouvent impliquées comme telles dans le processus de la conversion … que l'on peut dégager, d'un texte essentiellement centré sur la conversion, quelques idées sur la nation" ("nations find themselves involved as such in the process of conversion … that some ideas about the nation can be derived from a text essentially centred on conversion").[7] In Bede, a country's distinctness is defined partly by the extent and speed of its Christianization; "[f]or him, every physical place matters – whether a province accepting conversion, a newly founded monastery, or a bishopric receiving a new leader – because they all add to the spiritual achievements of the English church, demonstrating the work of divine providence."[8] In his view, East Anglia had impeded that work. Rædwald, though baptized, was irresolute in his Christianity; having kept pagan and Christian altars in the royal temple, he made religious dualism the defining trait of his reign and thus posed a grave spiritual danger to the entire East Anglian *provincia*, which for a time became a land of what Bede calls *infelicitas* ("unhappiness"). Because of its author's rigid notions of paganism, Christianity, syncretism, backsliding, and apostasy,[9] the *HE* proposes a moralized chorography, one that renders early seventh-century East Anglia as ambiguous territory, an object lesson in half-hearted conversion and thus a territorial threat to the church's overall coherence.

It should be admitted that the bias informing this chorography was of a piece with Bede's subjective and at times partisan stance on a range of issues.[10] Nor was this bias his uniquely. His information about East Anglia had come from influential figures in the church of his time: Albinus, abbot of St. Augustine's Abbey, Canterbury; Nothhelm, a future archbishop of Canterbury; the obscure East Anglian abbot Esi; and an early hagiographic account of St. Fursey.[11] To their shaping perspectives Bede added his own desire to impart ideological form to the stories that reached him.[12] Anthony D. Smith has reminded us that the "region" can be exploited by the "nation" and indeed "has often provided a powerful base for collective sentiments and for social and political action."[13] Though not quite a "region" in Smith's sense of the word, the East Anglia of the *HE* forms an important part of the whole that Bede imagined the English church to have been. Accordingly, it is characterized in such a way as to galvanize his readers' will to envisage unity and orthodoxy as that church's defining traits.

The fault line of Bede's East Anglia is Rædwald, the most prominent of the early Wuffingas. Bede, the first writer to speak of him at any length,[14] regarded him as at best a half-hearted convert to the "true" faith whose tolerance of pagan idols and practices was only gradually eliminated by his successors.[15] The East Anglian king becomes a scapegoat in the *Historia* for what in reality had been a complex and probably common intermingling of the Continental cultural heritage with newer Christian religious practices throughout England.[16] Bede does acknowledge this complexity elsewhere,[17] yet he aims to persuade his readers that Rædwald's effort to synthesize paganism with Christianity had been uniquely misguided among the English and all the more dangerous because of the expansive rule, or *imperium*, ascribed to Rædwald in Bede's well-known list of major kings in the *HE*'s first book.

The East Angles on Bede's Lists

However unprepossessing they may look to us, lists provided precious information to Bede and furnished him with foundational material for the East Anglian identities that can be pieced together from his work.[18] His own *imperium*-list names especially powerful rulers who had acquired military leadership over other peoples. Much debate has arisen over exactly what *imperium* meant to Bede and how he thought kings wielded it,[19] but it must suffice here to echo Simon Keynes's prudent conclusion that "all of the kings [in the list] may have been important figures in their different ways, and they were certainly important to Bede."[20] Rædwald stands out from this select group, but to fully understand why, we should turn first to an earlier list, which provides Continental origins for Rædwald's and all the other early English kingdoms.

Famous for its (suspiciously) tidy organization of the main peoples of the England familiar to Bede, that list is as follows:

> Aduenerant autem de tribus Germaniae populis fortioribus, id est Saxonibus, Anglis, Iutis. De Iutarum origine sunt Cantuari et Uictuarii, hoc est ea gens quae Uectam tenet insulam, et ea quae usque hodie in prouincia Occidentalium Saxonum Iutarum natio nominatur, posita contra ipsam insulam Uectam. De Saxonibus, id est ea regione quae nunc Antiquorum Saxonum cognominatur, uenere Orientales Saxones, Meridiani Saxones, Occidui Saxones. Porro de Anglis, hoc est de illa patria quae Angulus dicitur, et ab eo tempore usque hodie manere desertus inter prouincias Iutarum et Saxonum perhibetur, Orientales Angli, Mediterranei Angli, Merci, tota Nordanhymbrorum progenies, id est illarum gentium quae ad boream Humbri fluminis inhabitant, ceterique Anglorum populi sunt orti.
>
> (They came from three very powerful Germanic tribes, the Saxons, Angles, and Jutes. The people of Kent and the inhabitants of the Isle of Wight are of Jutish origin and also those opposite the Isle of Wight, that part of the kingdom of Wessex which is still today called the nation of the Jutes. From the Saxon country, that is, the district now known as Old Saxony, came the East Saxons, the South Saxons, and the West Saxons. Besides this, from the country of the Angles, that is, the land between the kingdoms of the Jutes

and the Saxons, which is called *Angulus*, came the East Angles, the Middle Angles, the Mercians, and all the Northumbrian race (that is[,] those people who dwell north of the river Humber) as well as the other Anglian tribes. *Angulus* is said to have remained deserted from that day to this. [*HE* I.15, pp. 50–1])

This brief gazetteer places the East Angles within a broader mytho-historical narrative of Continental migration, that *adventus Saxonum* which, as we have seen already, simplified a complex reality of multiple groups arriving over a long period of time. As Walter Pohl observes, Bede's *gentes*-list is "a rather opaque piece of ethnic rhetoric" in comparison with the *HE's* earlier enumeration of the five languages used in Britain (I.1, pp. 16–17). That is, it is "opaque" because it blurs the distinction between ethnicities and territories. Even as it does so, however, the *gentes*-list creates a verbal sociopolitical map that served Bede's purposes. As Pohl goes on to explain, "[e]thnic divisions among the newcomers, according to him, were territorial and on the whole corresponded to political entities. … Although the boundaries between the kingdoms shifted quite frequently and sometimes radically, these kingdoms were [to Bede] certainly the foci of politically meaningful ethnic identities."[21] The *gentes*-list in *HE* I.15 proved highly influential among later generations of pre-Conquest English writers and readers; it was more often noticed than the alternative origins-list that appears much later in the *HE*, when Bede reports that the missionary Ecgberct intended to convert the still-pagan *nationes* in Germania from whom he knew the Insular Angles and Saxons to have been descended: "Sunt autem Fresones, Rugini, Danai, Hunni, Antiqui Saxones, Boructuari" ("Now these people are the Frisians, Rugians, Danes, Huns, Old Saxons, and *Boruhtware* [Bructeri]," *HE* V.9, pp. 476–7). This curious list, John Hines suggests, reflects "Bede's knowledge of recent and projected missionary expeditions on the Continent, which *is* the immediate context of the list, not his interest in the details of the English settlements."[22] The lists in Books I and V function differently in context; but together they enabled Bede to connect the Insular Angles to their supposed European ancestors, to reduce a mass of plot threads to straightforward linear narratives of migration, and to highlight a few key protagonists.

The list in Book I went especially far towards establishing an English origin myth.[23] This migration account is sometimes thought to have been associated in Bede's mind with the Hebrews' journey to the Promised Land, with Britannia the divinely ordained goal of Continental peoples in the fifth and sixth centuries.[24] Some recent scholarship questions whether Bede really saw the *gens Anglorum* as latter-day Israelites uniquely blessed by God;[25] but even if he didn't, his Christian-exegetical cast of mind still led him to reject paganism as a worthless means of cultural self-identification for all the peoples who had crossed the sea. All were capable of Christian conversion, though Bede's remarks about the Angles suggest that he thought them advantaged in this regard.

Although Bede's list in *HE* I.15 does not yet single out the East Angles for special attention, instead emphasizing their commonalities with other peoples, it does imply that the larger population of Angles to which they belonged were unusual in having totally abandoned their homeland. The country of *Angulus* (Angeln or Anglia peninsula, modern-day Southern Schleswig) is said to have "remained deserted" ever since the various Anglian peoples left it; from this aside one infers Bede's belief in total population transfer, a willed dislocation from a place whose very name *Angulus* may have connoted to the *HE*'s readers a backwater, "retired place" or "outback."[26] The Angles' enterprising nature contrasts to the "segnitia Brettonum" ("slackness of the Britons," *HE* I.15, pp. 50–1), whom they encountered in Britain. According to Bede, sloth in arms and apathy of spirit cost the Britons their governance of the island, their just deserts for the pastoral indifference they had showed earlier in refusing to convert the pagan invaders (*HE* I.22, pp. 68–9). In contrast to the Britons, Bede's "Saxons, Angles, and Jutes" become the island's last and most successful possessors.[27] The Angles seem especially worthy of this honour because they in effect had gambled everything on the sea crossing; to their empty homeland of Angulus there apparently was no turning back, for they had effectively made their homeland a wasteland.[28] In the *HE* their place of origin has reverted to the spatio-temporal nothingness that exists before history.

The Angles have remade themselves in Britain, and Bede's *imperium*-list portrays Rædwald as a king singularly on the move even by the standards of his fellow Angles on the list. Even as the naming of peoples in *HE* I.15 hints at the Angles' special character, the *imperium*-list implies Rædwald's idiosyncrasy: where the Angles come into their own by leaving nothing behind in their original Continental homeland, Rædwald rises by throwing off the yoke of his Christian overlord. In *HE* II.15 he will be shown to cling to the pagan practices of his forebears; the *imperium*-list recounts the king's rise to power in a way that does not prepare us for the later revelation of the same king's alleged syncretism. After identifying Ælle of the South Saxons, Cælin (or Ceawlin) of the West Saxons, and Æthelberht of the people of Kent as the first three wielders of *imperium* (translated by Colgrave and Mynors as "sovereignty"), Bede explains that "quartus Reduald rex Orientalium Anglorum, qui etiam uiuente Aedilbercto eidem suae genti ducatum praebebat, obtenuit" ("the fourth was Rædwald, king of the East Angles, who, while Æthelberht was still alive, acted as the military leader of his own people"; *HE* II.5, pp. 148–9).[29] Calling the *East* Angles as such implies a sense of geography, a sense made explicit when Bede observes that "quintus Aeduini rex Nordanhymbrorum gentis, id est eius quae ad borealem Humbrae fluminis plagam inhabitat" ("the fifth was Edwin, king of the Northumbrians, the nation inhabiting the district north of the Humber"). The *imperium*-list, like the tribal origins list, imparts "politically meaningful ethnic identities" (Pohl) to the peoples who had achieved dominion in Britain. Specifically, it implicitly credits this or that *gens* with success in robbing other *gentes* of their autonomy.[30] The Angles are noteworthy in this regard: having depopulated *Angulus* itself, they crowd the *imperium*-list in the persons of Rædwald, Edwin, and, later (*HE* II.5, pp. 150–1), Edwin's fellow Northumbrians Oswald and Oswiu. Rædwald stands out even in this exalted company as an unusually ambitious warrior whose "overlordship" overlapped with that of his predecessor.

Much ink has been spilt over the passage quoted above referring to Rædwald's *ducatum* or "military leadership"; most commentators take it to mean that Rædwald won it by defeating Æthelberht.[31] The East Anglian *rex* is, then, distinguished not for having trounced other peoples such as the Britons, Picts, or Irish, but for having taken command of his own subjects at the expense of another, still-living *imperator*. This apparently is a noteworthy achievement. Only in Rædwald's case is a verb in the imperfect tense used: by writing that he "ducatum praebebat" (literally, "was providing [military] leadership"), Bede associates the East Anglian king's ambition with ongoing precociousness, albeit in the past. Rædwald was singularly active, moving through time and place to occupy the centre of early English political life on behalf of a *provincia* that Æthelberht of Kent had sought to relegate to marginality.

Rædwald's mobility characterizes East Anglia as a peculiarly dynamic place, one in which allegiance to one's Christian overlord need not have precluded one's own self-aggrandizement. Rædwald's master Æthelberht may have elicited Bede's sympathies; he had converted to Christianity and remained steadfast in that faith, going on to promote the earliest church in Canterbury (*HE* I.25–6, pp. 72–9). Yet the nature of the *imperium*-list qua list is to record the fact of rule without divulging very much about the how or the why; it is likely that Æthelberht had earlier coerced Rædwald to embrace the new faith.[32] As Wormald understands it, *imperium* entailed just such coercion, and a king forced to adopt another king's religion could be forgiven for chafing at the bit. Bede, we shall see, was less forgiving in this case, but he included

Rædwald in the roll of illustrious Southumbrian leaders not to register approval of the man as such but merely to acknowledge that even a rebel against his Christian overlord could shape the course of Insular history. Bede never attributes Rædwald's success to God's favour, but he does seem to understand *imperium* – no matter who wielded it – as a useful if impermanent precedent for the kind of broader, lasting political unity that one day might underpin enduring stability in the Roman Church. Georges Tugène argues that Bede understood full membership in that church to mean equality of participation among all peoples rather than the "elect" status of any one *gens*: "Comme nation missionnaire, la *gens Anglorum* participe aux côtés d'autres nations à un mouvement d'ensemble qui, guidé par Rome, suggère l'image d'une 'Église des nations'" ("As a missionary nation, the *gens Anglorum* participates alongside other nations in a movement of the whole that, guided by Rome, suggests the image of a 'Church of nations'").[33] If for Bede "overlordship" offered a foundation for eventual oneness of belief, then Rædwald's seizure of "imperial" powers from Æthelberht may well have seemed to him a necessary evil, a loss for the Christian king of Kent but a step towards long-term gain for an eventually Christian England.

The *imperium*-list shows Rædwald's dominion to have been followed by Edwin's. The baton is passed yet again, so however lacking the East Anglian king might have been as an individual, his performance had not jeopardized what Bede would have regarded as the eventual collective benefits of overlordship. The phenomenon of wide rule by one person could be and was repeated, and the Northumbrian king Edwin went on to become one of the shining secular lights of the entire English church. Edwin's *imperium*, and the stable Christianization resulting thence, owed much to Rædwald's help; yet in explaining that debt, Bede, as we shall see, places Rædwald in such an ambiguous light that early East Anglia itself is made to look like a land of irresolution. In this chorographic characterization Rædwald's queen plays no small role.

The East Anglian Queen as Spur to Honour

HE II.12 (pp. 174–83) supplements the *imperium*-list's account of Rædwald's rise to overlordship by explaining how the East Anglian king, after a period of doubt and apparent fear, resolved to help the Deiran prince Edwin in his bid to assume the Northumbrian throne, occupied then by a dangerous rival. The Bernician king Æthelfrith had sent Edwin into exile and continued to persecute him from afar; having discovered that his quarry had found shelter among the East Angles, he plied their leader Rædwald with offers of money, followed by threats, to make him hand over the refugee-pretender. Initially Rædwald thought it prudent to comply: "uel minis fractus uel corruptus muneribus cessit deprecanti, et siue occidere se Eduinum seu legatariis tradere promisit" ("being either weakened by [Æthelfrith's] threats or corrupted by his bribes, [he] yielded to his request and promised either to slay Edwin or to give him up to the messengers"; *HE* II.12, pp. 176–7). Not quite the doughtiness one would associate with an *imperator*, though under the circumstances discretion may have seemed the better part of valour. Yet Bede's loaded adjectives *fractus* and *corruptus* discourage even-handed evaluation. Both participles connote brokenness: *fractus* derives from the infinitive *frangere*, "to break, shatter, smash" and just perhaps also, in this context, "break down, exhaust, wear out" or even "to destroy [the] manly quality of"; and *corruptus* is the past participle of *corrumpere*, "to harm, disintegrate, spoil, rot," or "to affect (w. disease or sim.), infect."[34] Whatever majesty the East Anglian king may have gained from his inclusion in Bede's *imperium*-list looks fragile when contrasted to his actual behaviour, until the East Anglian queen saves the day by intervening on their Deiran guest's behalf and chiding her husband for his disloyalty and greed.

All along, Edwin had been despondent, fearing his betrayal by Rædwald to Æthelfrith; but a sympathetic messenger, whom Bede quotes (and who turns out to be Paulinus, a future bishop of York), is reported to have come to tell him that the queen herself "reuocauit eum illa ab intentione, ammonens quia nulla ratione conueniat tanto regi amicum suum optimum in necessitate positum auro uendere, immo fidem suam, quae omnibus ornamentis pretiosior est, amore pecuniae perdere" ("dissuaded [Rædwald] from it, warning him that it was in no way fitting for so great a king to sell his best friend for gold when he was in such trouble, still less to sacrifice his own honour, which is more precious than any ornament, for the love of money"; *HE* II.12, pp. 180–1). Until now Bede has given us scant evidence that Rædwald was in fact *tantus rex*, aside from the *imperium*-list itself and the hint it contains that the East Anglian ruler had risen up boldly against Æthelberht of Kent. Outside of that context, we depend for our knowledge of the king's high renown on the queen's reminding him of it, or rather on how Bede imagines her to have reminded him of it. The revelation serves to diminish the stature of Rædwald, for in scolding him as she does, the queen shows that the very stature as "great king" to which she appeals is being undermined by its holder's own pusillanimity.

Having thus required to be taught how to be *tantus rex* and, in effect, a proper wielder of *imperium*, Rædwald girded his loins, resolved to defend Edwin, and declared war himself against Æthelfrith. In a persuasive show of that *ducatus* or "military leadership" he had earlier won from his Kentish predecessor, Rædwald killed Edwin's Bernician foe at the battle of the River Idle (near modern Gainsborough, Lincs), thus securing Edwin's position as king of all the Northumbrians. The alliance cost Rædwald dearly, for his own son Rægenhere, who had joined him in battle against Æthelfrith's forces, died in combat (*HE* II.12, pp. 180–1). The East Anglian king must already have exercised great power to have been able to march through Middle Anglia and Lindsey to meet Æthelfrith at the Idle;[35] yet despite his control of a large swath of eastern England, Rædwald suffered tragic personal loss in the death of his son. In deferring to his queen's advice not to "fidem suam … perdere" ("sacrifice his own honour," *HE* II.12, pp. 180–1), he had been willing to risk much to defend Edwin; there seems no reason to think that Bede should have judged Rægenhere's death a blot on Rædwald's reputation as a leader.[36]

A real blot, fully intended by Bede, is the queen's critique of that reputation and her having to spur her husband to live up to it. When all due recognition is given to Rædwald for his success in making the East Angles an Insular superpower, it is the anonymous queen who must be credited with reviving his royal "honour" (*fidem suam*) and with reinforcing an image of East Anglia as a land where oaths matter more than rewards. Having pricked her husband's conscience, she is shown helping her realm to consolidate both its Southumbrian military dominion and its ethical stature. These outcomes benefited Northumbria too, because Rædwald's eventual show of courage led to Edwin's crowning and to his realm's subsequent glory. "The kingdoms of Bede's England," David Kirby has observed, "had evolved over a long time and continued to do so. The geography of power was in an almost continuous state of flux as more powerful principalities assimilated weaker neighbours"[37] or simply intervened in their neighbours' royal successions. In her own way, and despite the risks involved, the queen contributed to this flux and so raised East Anglia's own "geography of power" to especially high relief on the political and historiographical landscapes.

Rosalind Hill is surely right to identify in Rædwald's "nameless and remarkable wife" that devotion to "fidelity" which, in early England, underpinned one's loyalty to a secular lord as well as to one's religion, whether pagan or Christian.[38] Bede memorializes the queen as East Anglia's conscience, the agent of historical change who determined that Rædwald's military action would elevate the kingdom beyond purely local prominence. Rather than being relegated to the background of history or permitting her land to be so relegated, she appears front and centre as an irresistible, entirely laudable ethical force that compels Rædwald to lead the East Anglian *gens* out of its isolated corner of England to pursue the greater good of wide-ranging, altruistic overlordship. Although the queen's advice to Rædwald is not uniquely Christian, it does accord with the exhortation to spiritual over material values found elsewhere in the *HE* and, for example, in the *Letter to Ecgbert*.[39] In *HE* II.12, wise counsel creates a temporary space for East Anglia as an ideologically in-between polity, poised between the new faith and the old even as it asserts itself against Kent and Bernicia.

That space is, however, an unstable one. When we compare the queen's private counsels with the king's public behaviour, we find an East Anglia distinguished by two markedly different royal attitudes towards leadership: Rædwald's initial preference for *realpolitik* on one hand, his wife's insistence on magnanimity on the other. In the above-described scene from *HE* II.12, which is the first of Bede's two accounts of Rædwald and his queen, the "fidelity" identified by Rosalind Hill as a trait of the latter extends implicitly to her country, for it is the queen's virtue that allows Bede to establish East Anglia's literary reputation as the refuge for outsiders that, according to Jack Ravensdale and Richard Muir, has long been one of the region's characteristic features.[40] Rædwald's original instinct, however, had been to surrender Edwin to Æthelfrith, so the region's renown for sheltering newcomers can hardly be said to have been intrinsic; when it emerges in the *HE* as one of East Anglia's early defining traits, it is because Bede underscores the queen's success in persuading her husband to put duty and loyalty before greed and cowardice.

Rædwald's Divided Loyalties

This is as far as Bede is willing to go in fostering positive impressions of East Anglia in this early period of its history. Francis Young sees a transformation in the Rædwald of the *HE* from a "flawed hero," whose queen "shames him into fighting the Northumbrians," to (again with the queen's help) an "avenging and victorious ideal warrior" after his son Rægenhere's death.[41] As far as Bede's characterization of Rædwald's military exploits is concerned, Young's analysis is spot on; but the transformation does not apply to Bede's depiction of Rædwald qua baptized ruler. *HE* II.12 offers a generally positive portrayal of both king and queen in part because Edwin's ascent to the lordship of Northumbria is shown to depend on East Anglian military aid.

In a rather different story, told in *HE* II.15, Edwin is now shown to need nobody's help: no longer beholden to an East Anglian ruler, he governs Northumbria in his own right and eventually exercises enough influence outside his domains to compel Rædwald's successor, Eorpwald, to follow his lead in baptism.[42] It is when he explains why

Eorpwald's conversion had been necessary in the first place that Bede offers an account of Rædwald and his wife that differs radically from the story in the twelfth chapter of the *HE's* second book. In this later narrative, East Anglia comes into view not as an aid to Northumbrian stability but as a threat to the Gregorian mission to convert the English. As the source of this threat, Bede's Rædwald becomes the object of chorographic character assassination.

The criticism begins when Bede notes Edwin's wholesome influence over Eorpwald, a son of Rædwald who at the outset of his reign had followed in his father's footsteps: "Tantum autem deuotionis Eduini erga cultum ueritatis habuit, ut etiam regi Orientalium Anglorum Earpualdo filio Redualdi persuaderet relictis idolorum superstitionibus fidem et sacramenta Christi cum sua prouincia suscipere" ("so great was Edwin's devotion to the true worship, that he also persuaded Eorpwald, son of Rædwald and king of the East Angles, to abandon his idolatrous superstitions and, together with his kingdom, to accept the Christian faith and sacraments"; *HE* II.15, pp. 188–9). Eorpwald seems to have required little time to convert, probably because Edwin's influence on him was political rather than purely theological.[43] For his part Edwin himself had delayed baptism for eleven years after receiving counsel from Bishop Paulinus (*HE* II.12–14); even so, once he had accepted it he clung to it until the end of his life,[44] and Bede emphasizes the Northumbrian king's devotion as well as his skill as a teacher as the reasons Eorpwald renounced the old ways.

This short account of Eorpwald and Edwin, likely edifying in its own right to the *HE's* early readers, prefaces Bede's depiction of Rædwald as a lacklustre defender of the "true" faith. For although it was not their chief concern, seventh- and eighth-century kings were thought to have at least some duty to further orthodox Christian worship,[45] and Rædwald's own *imperium* would have entailed no small show of leadership in the matter of religion. The prestige of his rule is thus compromised when Bede attacks East Anglia's court ideology as mere paganism, and then associates it with those who had the power to sway the king's judgment. Before gaining *imperium* Rædwald had been converted to Christianity; but shortly thereafter he yielded to pressure from his own queen and counsellors: "Et quidem pater eius Reduald iamdudum in Cantia sacramentis Christianae fidei inbutus est, sed frustra; nam rediens domum ab uxore sua et quibusdam peruersis doctoribus seductus est, atque a sinceritate fidei deprauatus" ("Indeed his father Rædwald had long before been initiated into the mysteries of the Christian faith in Kent, but in vain; for on his return home, he was seduced by his wife and by certain evil teachers and perverted from the sincerity of his faith"; *HE* II.15, pp. 188–91). Nicholas Higham argues that the East Anglian court's willingness to conjoin the two religions resulted from a considered political strategy to preserve traditional culture:

> If the traditional world was to be fully restored ... [t]he obvious direction for Rædwald and his *doctores* to turn was the Baltic littoral whence the English believed, with good cause, that they had originally derived. There lay the heartland of Germanic paganism ... [and] the fount of English cultural and racial identity.[46]

The word "syncretic" then, used often by scholars who comment on the East Anglian experiment during Rædwald's reign, need not imply that the king had amalgamated two world views out of ignorance.[47] By showing their resolve to sustain the religious practices of their ancestors even while learning new ones, the East Anglian court synthesized ideologies out of deliberation, not desperation. Churchmen of Bede's stamp may have thought that this approach risked renouncing heaven itself; but in keeping a foothold in the religion of his forebears, Rædwald and his inner circle defended the culture that those forebears had tried to salvage during their North Sea exodus.[48] Bede ignores these considerations when he scapegoats the East Anglian king, queen, and "teachers" as sources of an especially pernicious spiritual unregeneracy. And although he expresses disappointment in Rædwald, he also blames his wife and court *doctores* for their influence upon him and for the temporary unmaking of Christian East Anglia that resulted. It is to their representation that I now turn.

Believing Husband, Unbelieving Wife

Like her name, the political life of the East Anglian queen in its full complexity has been lost to us, but something of her role may be surmised from the fact that, as Martin Carver has pointed out with regard to the Scandinavian context, "women, key spiritual agents in the pagan period, remained in charge during the conversion process. Only when Christianity became institutionalised within the political process of nation-building did women all over Europe surrender their spiritual authority."[49] Considered in this light, early East Anglia's reputation for calculated syncretism takes on a gendered character in Bede: the queen showed more backbone than Rædwald because she was obliged to uphold "spiritual authority" in her domains.[50] Bede's East Anglia stands out in the *HE* not only because its sole *bretwalda*, his wife, and their court fall short of the Edwin model of prudent deliberation and delay, and not merely because they remain in part pagan, but also because its queen insists upon these features of official East Anglian religious policy, perhaps to safeguard her role in this area against eventual interference from a local bishop eager to get her husband's ear.

The East Anglian queen challenged Bede's very notion of what a strong woman could and should be. Æthelthryth, the subject of chapter 2, was for him a better example. So too were Queen Æthelburh, wife of Edwin, whom Pope Boniface V had exhorted to encourage her converted husband to abandon his own lingering pagan practices (*HE* II.11, pp. 174–5),[51] and Bertha, the Frankish queen of Kent who had been instrumental in Æthelberht's conversion.[52] The *HE*'s portrayal of powerful women hints at the exegetical cast of mind that Judith McClure, Alan Thacker, Georges Tugène, and other scholars have discerned as a link between Bede's narrative history and his biblical commentaries.[53] For example, Bede's gloss on Proverbs 31 treats the *mulier fortis* allegorically, or rather typologically, as a prefiguration of the church itself.[54] Scripture thus defines the "valiant woman": "Consideravit agrum et emit eum. De fructu manuum suarum plantavit vineam" ("She hath considered a field and bought it. With the fruit of her hands she hath planted a vineyard"; Prov. 31:16).[55] Believing with his fellow Christian commentators that the church had a mission to cultivate minds and direct them heavenward, Bede held that Rædwald's queen had thwarted the mission of evangelization by sowing in her newly converted husband's mind seeds of doubt about the efficacy of Christian faith unaided by paganism.

As Damian Tyler has pointed out, "at least in Bede's view, Raedwald's wife was the motive force behind both his greatest triumph and his blackest sin."[56] The fact that Bede apparently concedes the queen's virtue in handling the Edwin crisis chimes with the church's willingness to recognize that even pagans might grope their way towards the "truth" if they had not yet encountered Christianity. This is why Bede was less troubled by strictly pagan rulers from England's past than by those kings who were only half-converted. As Alan Thacker has shown, the former at least could be likened to those virtuous Hebrews who had lived before Christ and presumably would have embraced his teachings had they been able to do so.[57] The latter, professing Christianity but practising paganism, struck Bede as being worse than thoroughgoing pagans because they threatened to undermine reform.

East Anglia differed from neighbouring *provinciae* whose Christianization Bede believed had been hampered by resurgences of paganism. In summing up his own analysis of pagan kings in Bede, Richard North observes that the East Anglian *rex* had tried to observe pagan and Christian practices without committing himself to either; for this reason, quite simply "Rædwald's lapse is different from the others."[58] Had such syncretism become entrenched among subsequent East Anglian rulers, the ecclesiastical health of England as a whole might have been endangered by the implication that *felicitas* or "happiness" could be enjoyed by kings regardless of conversion.[59] A realm's spiritual state depended on the king's convictions; what Bede perceived as Rædwald's lack of commitment to the new religion risked pulling East Anglia back into a heathenism that, in his view, ought to have been renounced once and for all. The *HE* contains only roughly comparable instances of what Bede regarded as pagan backsliding; none is quite like Rædwald's syncretism. Eadbald, king of Kent, is said to have succeeded to the throne in 616 as a pagan after the death of his father, the Christian Æthelberht (*HE* II.5). He remained a heathen for an additional year, though D.P. Kirby persuasively argues that the pagan interlude lasted at least five years and possibly eight, and "must have been an anxious time for the Gregorian mission."[60] Bede condemns Eadbald more harshly than he does Rædwald;[61] yet he also makes clear that once the former had been converted, he remained firmly committed to the new faith: "ecclesiae rebus, quantum ualuit, in omnibus consulere ac fauere curauit" ("[in all things] he promoted and furthered the interests of the Church to the best of his ability"; *HE* II.6, pp. 154–5).

Other early English kingdoms produced similar stories of individual one-way royal conversion, and these too differ from Bede's account of Rædwald's spiritual tergiversation. The Northumbrian king Edwin has already been mentioned in this regard. To the south, in the kingdom of the East Saxons, the death of the Christian king Sæberht had led to serious trouble because his surviving three sons "pagani perdurauerant" ("had all remained heathen," *HE* II.5, pp. 152–3). Yet this was not strictly a case of apostasy: the three sons had not publicly converted to Christianity along with their father and then renounced their formal entry into the new religion upon his death. Bede recounts that, before acceding to the kingship, they refrained from pagan practices, likely in deference to Sæberht's wishes; but on the evidence of Bede's narrative it is by no means clear that they had ever been baptized in the first place. All three died as unrepentant heathens in battle against the Gewisse or West Saxons, and their kingdom only eventually returned to the Christian fold, the Kentish king Eadbald's conversion prompting the Londoners and the rest of the East Saxons to toe the line. Bede clearly relishes narrating the three East Saxons' discomfiture, but their offence is still quite unlike Rædwald's. Although religious admixture can hardly have been unique to East Anglia, and although Bede will have known that – as John Blair has put it – "the skin-deep conversion of a king and his household was a shaky foundation at best,"[62] the monastic historian would have his readers believe that in seventh-century England only Rædwald and his kingdom had tried to reconcile different religious world views to one another. Bede told of other areas of seventh-century England that had seen revivals of paganism,[63] but he reacted to the East Anglian king's flexibility in the matter of religion as if it had posed unusual danger.

To be sure, despite being married to the Christian Bertha, even Æthelberht of Kent had exercised caution in welcoming the new creed. As he told the missionary Augustine, "Pulchra sunt quidem uerba et promissa quae adfertis; sed quia noua sunt et incerta, non his possum adsensum tribuere relictis eis, quae tanto tempore cum omni Anglorum gente seruaui" ("The words and the promises you bring are fair enough, but because they are new to us and doubtful, I cannot consent to accept them and forsake those beliefs which I and the whole English race have held so long"; *HE* I.25, pp. 74–5).[64] That Bede should have recorded this speech shows that even he acknowledged that tradition could legitimately hinder conversion.

Yet a converted king who had relapsed must have struck Bede as doubly culpable if he had also proved too pliable in the hands of an unbelieving queen. Examining Bede's representation of Rædwald and other early English kings in their domestic contexts, Stacy Klein compellingly argues that "increased proximity between husband and wife tends to be associated with apostasy," and that at the very least "the king's home space and domestic life appear as wholly inadequate sites for fostering spiritual change."[65] Certainly in Bede's East Anglia the queen's resolution contrasts vividly to the king's irresolution, both in governance and in conversion; the only development in the realm's spiritual life was regression. When he says that Rædwald had "in vain" been "initiated [*inbutus*] into the mysteries" of the new faith, Bede is not simply employing elegant periphrasis; he is reminding his audience of the public, ritual cleansing of "original sin" effected through baptism by water, which was to be followed by full imbuement of doctrine, both processes negated by the East Anglian king in deference to his spouse and court circle.[66] Such acquiescence is very different from the kind of royal passivity of which Bede approves, the act of being *imbutus* into the Christian faith. Richard North has pointed out that his use of the adjectives *seductus* and *deprauatus* to characterize Rædwald marks a king who is "not the subject but the object of heathen activity."[67] Similarly, the participial pairing "inbutus est … seductus est" underscores Rædwald's passive lordship by juxtaposing the king's earlier, admirable catechesis with his later about-face and surrender of true leadership to what Bede regarded as the forces of evil.[68]

Bede's East Anglia only incompletely resembles the picture provided by material evidence as studied by archaeologists.[69] The monastic historian's animus towards paganism and its defenders is well known, and the words "paganism," "Christianity," "syncretism," and "backsliding" fail to do justice to the complex intermingling of religions that obtained among many sixth- and early seventh-century English people.[70] What matters for present purposes is not that Bede misrepresented this state of affairs, which is not in doubt, but rather how and why he did so. East Anglia's material history shows that early seventh-century political realities had been fluid, more so than Bede could tolerate or even than our own modern conventional vocabulary could accommodate until recently. The Sutton Hoo ship-burial, for example, is usually classified as "heathen," but this perception "implies a much sharper divide between "pagan" and "Christian" burial practice than actually existed."[71] Principled opposition to (Frankish) Christian influence seems belied by the presence in the ship-burial of thirty-seven Frankish coins, no two from the same mint, as well as the (probably) Byzantine spoons engraved with the names "Paulos" and "Saulos," the latter inscription the work of a Frankish die-cutter. That person may or may not have known about Saul's road-to-Damascus conversion that led to his becoming Paul, but the placement of the two spoons in the tomb has been interpreted as a sign that mixed religious belief was attributed to the personage buried therein.[72] Such a hybrid assemblage of grave goods as that found at Sutton Hoo suggests a degree of flexibility in Tom Williamson's dichotomy between "Frankish" and "Scandinavian" cultures and thus between the diverse orientations of the "two" East Anglias.[73]

As far as Bede was concerned, such reconciliation between religions amounted to a betrayal of divine Providence itself. According to Stephen Harris, Bede's very use of the term *gens Anglorum* is informed by a deep conviction about the historical progress the "English people" ought to be making:

> The term *gens* forms a nexus between the language of tribal identity and the language of morality. Bede uses it to develop a supratribal, religio-political identity in apposition to localized notions of groups and belonging. Consequently, his implications in the *HE* as a whole develop from this historically instantiated identity such that those leaders who act against the logic of their tribe's own past by rejecting conversion suffer not only religious but also political failure.[74]

On this reading, the Northumbrian scholar's use of the word *gens* lies at the heart of an ethnography that, at most, meets the various *gentes* themselves only part way. Those peoples, Bede believed, differed from one another in dialect, geography, political structures, and royal genealogy; yet upon all of them the *HE* imposes a vision of divinely ordained purpose. For Harris this is Bede's logic of conversion, while for Nicholas Howe it is Bede's "logic of history" itself.[75] The East Angles emerge as composite in nature, their identity (really identit*ies*) a fusion of, on one hand, Bede's conviction that they ought to be steadfastly Christian, and on the other hand the Rædwaldian court's belief – just as tenacious – that they could legitimately retain, and indeed needed to retain, their ancestral pagan ways while recognizing new teachings.

Within the *HE*'s world view these combined identities risked leading the East Angles down a spiritual dead end. The queen and court advisers, however, can hardly be blamed for their intransigence on the matter. Theirs was a society that commemorated the illustrious dead with ship-burials housed in barrows, the aim of that practice being not only to evoke the spiritual passage between this world and the next, but also, perhaps, to signal an enduring bond between the East Angles' current home and the Continental and Scandinavian lands of their forebears (as was discussed in the present book's Introduction). The *doctores* who counselled adherence to paganism will have been "learned ones" within that cultural context. Not so for Bede, who uses the noun *doctores* to refer to the professionalized agents of unbelief whom he judged to have gripped Rædwald's East Anglia. Conor O'Brien has shown that Bede, in his Commentary on Genesis, discerned perverse learning behind the Tower of Babel but true wisdom embodied in the Jewish Temple: "As the Church has its teachers, the *doctores* and *magistri* so vital to it, so do these alternative structures have wicked teachers and preachers of error. The builders of the tower, like those of the temple, represent *doctores*, though *mali doctores*, and Bede even referred to pagan and schismatic *doctores*."[76] The *HE* almost always reserves use of the noun *doctor* to refer to exemplary Catholic Christian pastoral work.[77] The Northumbrian scholar was much exercised by those who had fallen short in this regard; "[he] shows particular anxiety that contemporary spiritual leaders, including members of both the ordained hierarchy and of the order of teachers and preachers, are not up to the task, because they are corrupt or ignorant and unskillful."[78] Bede's worries extended beyond badly trained missionaries; as evidenced in *HE* V, his familiarity with English evangelization in Frisia and Saxony shows that he thought Christianity was imperilled even when the missionaries themselves were competent.[79] Frequent too are his animadversions on heresy, which scholars of his work increasingly view as signs of engagement with contemporary realities, not as expressions of antiquarian interest. "Heretics and their doings," observes Thacker, "were generally referred to in the present tense; for Bede they were part of the here and now."[80] It is against this background that the reference to "quidam peruersi doctores" in East Anglia is properly seen, as those teachers represented the queen and, likely, the majority or an influential minority within the East Anglian court.[81]

A Shrine Divided

Their sense of duty compelled the queen and counsellors to insist that traditional belief should be represented in the royal temple. So forceful were they that they succeeded in convincing Rædwald to place a small altar or *arula* in it next to the Christian *altare*: "atque in eodem fano et altare haberet ad sacrificium Christi et arulam ad uictimas daemoniorum" ("in the same temple he had one altar for the Christian sacrifice and another small altar on which to offer victims to devils"; *HE* II.15, pp. 190–1). The temple with its two devotional structures embodies the East Anglian royal court's ideological manoeuvring. As Bede characterizes it, the *arula* enshrines the kingdom's then-dualistic outlook and co-animates and contaminates what should have been the kingdom's most sacred space.[82]

Scholars have debated whether Bede intended the noun *arula*'s diminutive ending (*-ula*) to convey something of the scorn he plainly expresses elsewhere about the king's reluctance to abandon his old ways. Dorothy Whitelock remarked that "the diminutive is probably contemptuous,"[83] but J.M. Wallace-Hadrill disagreed and inferred from it simply that "Redwald meant the pagan altar to be less prominent than his Christian altar."[84] Following Charles Plummer, Sam Newton has claimed (persuasively, I believe) that Bede's differentiation between *altare* and *arula* "is purely rhetorical, which means that Rædwald's altar to the old gods was not necessarily physically smaller or less important in its context than that to Christ."[85] Marilyn Dunn goes further; sensitively discussing several possible meanings of the *altare*-vs.-*arula* distinction, she concludes that "[i]t may be a mistake to read into Bede's elliptical comment any significance other than that of Christian diabolization of pagan deities."[86] Because Bede held both that "paganism" was absolutely distinct from Christianity and that he himself had a moral duty to polemicize against the former and uphold the latter, the ending of *arula* looks like an artful signal of contempt for a devotional object that the monastic historian believed to have been used "ad uictimas daemoniorum" ("to offer victims to devils"). It may matter that the diminutive ending of *arula* resembles that of the word *ciuitatula*, which Bede uses to refer to the "small deserted fortress" of *Grantacæstir* (Cambridge); formerly a pagan Romano-British site, it was where the monks of Ely are said to have discovered a marble sarcophagus that would fit the remains of St. Æthelthryth (*HE* IV.19, pp. 392–5). Also suggestive is Felix's use of the word *cellula* to describe Guthlac's hermitage in the Crowland fens; literally it means a "tiny cell,"[87] but as a hut (*tugurium*) built atop a reservoir-like *cisterna* attached to the side of a barrow (*tumulus*),[88] it is also associated with the Christian supersession of formerly heathen structures.[89]

Whether or not such diminutive endings are all meant to alert readers to underlying pagan cultural substrates (and I am not certain they are), the desinence of *arula* likely has that function in Bede's discussion of the East Anglian temple. It not only creates obvious contrast to the full- or at least fuller-sized Christian *altare* but also reflects on the pusillanimity of the royal house, which had allowed the smaller structure into the temple in the first place. Bede's unkind quip about devil worship reminds one of that lack of growth, indeed lack of hope, which some Christian writers ascribed to people who were prone to revert to heathenism in times of crisis; one thinks of the villagers around Melrose Abbey whom, according to Bede himself, St. Cuthbert was obliged to re-evangelize because they had revived their pagan customs (in vain) as protection against plague.[90] Furthermore, at the outset of the *HE*'s second book Bede praises Pope Gregory the Great because he delivered the English "de potestate Satanae" ("from the power of Satan") and because he "nostram gentem eatenus idolis mancipatam Christi fecit ecclesiam" ("made our nation, till then enslaved to idols, into a Church of Christ"; *HE* II.1, pp. 122–3). For these reasons, his noun *arula* does more than feature as part of a mini-diatribe against Rædwald's pointless sacrifice of animals;[91] it also gives tangible form to his sense that the East Anglian king had betrayed the Gregorian mission by, in effect, undoing his own conversion in Kent. When elsewhere in the *HE* Bede praises Hild's tenure as abbess of Whitby, he treats the *altare* as a synecdoche for the liturgy and for the correct training of the priests in "altaris officium" ("the service of the altar"; *HE* IV.23, pp. 408–11), in other words as a sign of responsible and disciplined teaching of the true faith. From Bede's point of view, a compromised *altare* such as existed in Rædwald's temple could hardly have provided royal support for such teaching in early East Anglia.

Small wonder that the scholar of Wearmouth-Jarrow should have lamented the East Anglian king's lapse. Rædwald was no mere villager; he was a ruler, and from Bede's perspective he had brought from Æthelberht's Christian Kent a new religion and the duty to spread it upon crossing back into pagan East Anglia. The physical frontier he traversed upon his homecoming goes unremarked in the text, like that of other geopolitical boundaries in the *HE*; but an ideological significance is clear in his straddling of a spiritual *limes* between Christian and heathen world views,[92] a border that becomes tangible in the contact between the *altare* and the *arula*. Rather than demarcating "before" and "after," the pagan-Christian divide compromises the temple by keeping two ideologies in constant dialogue with each other, refusing to let the new Word finally silence the old lore, as for example St. Paul wished had occurred in the city of Athens, where the coming of Christianity had initially resulted in confusion, an altar inscribed "Ignoto Deo" ("To the unknown God," Acts 17: 23) having been built – rather grudgingly, it would seem – among a myriad of idols to other, better-known deities.[93] The tone of the Bedan text is more critical than that of the passage from Acts, for Paul at least could intervene in person to proselytize the Athenian Jewish and pagan communities and teach them about the God they professed not to know. Although Rædwald had no Paul to correct his misbelief, he was a baptized Christian and could not very well have claimed that the Christian God had remained unknown to him.

Although the "little altar" is smaller in stature than its Christian counterpart, to Bede's way of thinking it must have overshadowed the rightful embodiment of the Gregorian mission in the royal temple. In this regard the *arula* is not unlike the queen herself, challenging the king's will despite possessing a nominally lesser power. A projection, perhaps, of the royal couple's own precarious symbiosis, the juxtaposed altars lie at the ideologically charged heart of Bede's chorography of East Anglia. Dual in its cultural orientation, the temple embodies the duality of the *provincia* itself.

The royal temple would have reminded Bede of what a house of correct worship ought to have been, a means whereby the souls of an English *gens* might be won for heaven, not lost to hell.[94] Material evidence suggests that there had been mutual influence, rather than sharp distinction, between pagan and Christian practices of site consecration in sixth- to seventh-century England;[95] yet Bede saw only the rigid polarization of possibilities, evil pitted against good. The degree to which Bede dichotomized right and wrong belief should not be underestimated for the cultural work it performed, nor should the dichotomy's long pedigree be taken for granted. Judith M. Lieu has seen in the Gospel accounts of Jesus's cleansing of the Temple the beginning of a conscious literary representation of Christianity's break with Judaism culminating in fourth-century commentaries on those texts. Building on her work, Daniel Boyarin has investigated overlap between the forms of self-identification used by early Jewish and Christian communities and has concluded that "orthodoxy/heresy came to function as a boundary marker, because the boundaries had indeed been blurred."[96] In the *HE*, East Anglia's regional character derives much from Bede's conviction that local Christian worship had failed to make a clean break with the pagan past; in this regard, too, the East Anglian royal family were different from their peers elsewhere in seventh-century England. Northumbria, by contrast, had had a proper temple-cleansing moment when Coifi, King Edwin's high priest who expected to thrive better under the Christian dispensation than he had done while serving his kingdom's pagan gods, took it upon himself to desecrate the heathen temple at Goodmanham by throwing a spear into it. Bede tells the story with gusto (*HE* II.13, pp. 182–7), relishing the moment when conversion might be shown to break decisively with paganism. In contrast to Northumbria, East Anglia produced no such dramatic rupture with the old traditions; Rædwald, unlike Edwin, neglected to advance the work done by Pope Gregory the Great himself, who "nostram gentem per praedicatores ... de dentibus antiqui hostis eripiens aeternae libertatis fecit esse participem" ("snatched our race from the teeth of the ancient foe and made them partakers of everlasting freedom by sending us preachers"; *HE* II.1, pp. 130–1).[97] If Bede had anything to say about it, the salvation of the English people would not be jeopardized by the misguided fence-straddling of the likes of Rædwald.[98]

His own sense of what it meant to be a Northumbrian Christian influenced how Bede regarded East Anglia. Rædwald's doctrinally flexible *imperium* had hindered ecclesiastical unity and thus warranted a reaction that to us looks highly partisan but is informed by Bede's awareness of the ideological fissures in his own native Northumbria, despite Edwin's eventual conversion and Coifi's dramatic performance at Goodmanham. As Alan Thacker has observed, "Bede's stress on the oneness of the English flows from a need to connect up the somewhat unsatisfactory history of the origins of his own people's Church with the blue-chip catholicity of the Church in Kent."[99] On this analysis, the ideologically homogenizing vision of the *HE* compensates for Northumbria's supposed deficiencies even as it underlies Bede's hostility towards the East Anglian royal *fanum*. The temple in question may have stood at Rendlesham in modern Suffolk, where Suidhelm of Essex was baptized (*HE* III.22, pp. 284–5);[100] but more important than its literal whereabouts is its place on the moralized "map" of East Anglia that can be reconstructed from the *HE*. As an official place of, in effect, state worship, the Wuffing temple may well have served Bede as a lightning rod for his dismay with his own *provincia*'s shortcomings; it certainly focused his disdain for ideological divisiveness, sinful syncretism, and fissiparity within the East Anglian kingdom. Stacy Klein regards Rædwald and his queen's fusion of pagan and Christian practices as evidence of the ideological division and political stasis characteristic of Bede's depiction of religiously mismatched royal couples: "Apparently convinced, or at least intent on convincing his readers, that queens were powerless to effect kingly conversions, Bede consistently figures spiritual division within marriage not as a catalyst for individual or national change but as an inert and static condition to be remedied only by the intercessory efforts of kings, or more typically, churchmen."[101] Within the East Anglian royal court itself, in the world outside Bede's narrative, things may have been quite dynamic; the experiment in compromise attempted by Rædwald may have added years to his political (and perhaps biological) life by appeasing the queen and counsellors' faction.[102] But Bede's *depiction* of the East Anglian royal couple does indeed suggest "an inert or static condition"; for the historian, anything short of progress towards the salvific unity of worship amounted to stagnation at best, death and decay at worst.

As Bede describes it, the health of the East Anglian realm seems positively to have worsened from the time the king compromised his own baptism. In a critical aside, he writes of Rædwald that "habuit posteriora peiora prioribus, ita ut in morem antiquorum Samaritanorum et Christo seruire uideretur et diis, quibus antea seruiebat" ("his last state was worse than his first. After the manner of the ancient Samaritans, he seemed to be serving both Christ and the gods whom he had previously served"; *HE* II.15, pp. 190–1). Bede has adapted Luke 11:26 to amplify his invective against Rædwald's religious dualism,[103] which for him was an enormity worse than thoroughgoing paganism.[104] Richard North observes that "Bede does not forgive Rædwald, comparing him with the Samaritans in a reference to the worship of rightful and unrightful gods" and associating him with the possessed man in Luke 11 from whom an unclean spirit is exorcised only to return to it accompanied by seven more demons.[105] Perhaps too the reader is meant to contrast the "bad" Samaritan who worshipped wrongly to the Good Samaritan who cared for a hapless stranger lying beaten and ignored by the inhabitants of Jericho (Lk. 10:25–37). Because Rædwald had himself played the Good Samaritan to Edwin, his seeming ambivalence about the altars may have struck Bede as doubly unconscionable.[106]

Furthermore, with regard to the *HE*'s adaptation of Luke 11, Bede may also have thought Rædwald akin to the unclean spirit itself rather than to the man it possessed. According to Scripture, Jesus dismissed as foolish his hecklers' charge that he enlisted Beelzebub's aid to drive out demons: "Omne regnum in se ipsum divisum desolabitur, et domus supra domum cadet" ("Every kingdom divided against itself shall be brought to desolation, and house upon house shall fall"; Lk. 11:17). Like the possessed victim whose "last state" of demonic possession was "worse than his first," East Anglia is shown to have been worse off than it had been before Rædwald's conversion. It too is a "kingdom divided against itself," because its ruler, by having permitted religious dualism, defeated the exorcistic purpose of baptism[107] and so introduced "long-lasting evil and unhappiness" into his realm.[108]

Fear of a Pagan East Anglia? Post-Rædwaldian Developments

Evidently the kingdom remained ideologically divided against itself for some time. Bede notes that "[q]uod uidelicet fanum rex eiusdem prouinciae Alduulf, qui nostra aetate fuit, usque ad suum tempus perdurasse, et se in pueritia uidisse testabatur" ("Ealdwulf, who was ruler of the kingdom up to our time, used to declare that the temple lasted until his time and that he saw it when he was a boy"; *HE* II.15, pp. 190–1). From this aside one infers that Rædwald's successors must have had their work cut out for them if they sought to abolish their traditional religion in favour of the new one. Assuming that the Council of Hatfield (Herts) took place in 679, "Alduulfo rege Estranglorum, anno septimodecimo regni eius" ("in the seventeenth year of the reign of Ealdwulf, king of the East Angles"; *HE* IV.17, pp. 384–5), we can date the beginning of Ealdwulf's reign to about 662.[109] That reign is usually said to have ended in 713, so Ealdwulf's boyhood may be supposed to have spanned the 630s and early 640s.[110] This estimate leaves anywhere between a mere handful of years and two whole decades for the continued existence of the pagan altar following the death of Rædwald himself in around 625.[111] Although even twenty years is not an inordinate amount of time for an early seventh-century kingdom to experiment with religion, Bede seems to have worried about the long-term prospects of the Christian church in East Anglia much as he did with regard to Europe in general. His own evidence shows such anxiety to have been unfounded and conversion eventually to have taken firm root everywhere in Britain; moreover, the *HE* has persuaded scholars that, following Rædwald's death, "the conversion of the East Angles [was] amongst the earliest in the country" and revealed "no suggestion of relapse or of persistence of pagan elements."[112] Yet Bede's glimpses of post-Rædwaldian history indicate that the new faith had struggled to gain traction.[113] The remainder of this chapter considers the chaotic middle decades of the seventh century and Bede's efforts to convince not only his readers but also himself that East Anglia could now be reckoned a reliable cornerstone of the early English church.

We know, because Bede tells us, that Eorpwald did not ascend to the throne a Christian but was converted through the agency of the Northumbrian king Edwin (*HE* II.15, pp. 188–91).[114] Bede praises the activity of the latter and, as we saw earlier, underscores his success in rescuing Eorpwald's kingdom; but in doing so he demonstrates that the path to East Anglia's Christianization was not as smooth as the passage in *HE* II.15 suggests. That Edwin's intervention was needed to secure the church's ideological influence in eastern England hints that, upon his accession, Eorpwald forwent baptism and carried on as his father had done before him, maintaining both altars but privileging old practices. Again a foreign potentate is shown meddling in East Anglian affairs, as Æthelberht of Kent had done with Rædwald. The intervention highlights the East Angles' vulnerability and may explain the subsequent broils within the ruling dynasty itself.

Although Bede tells us that Edwin secured the conversion of Eorpwald, he does not say just how pious the latter really was. Deeply converted or not, he would soon be killed by a pagan rival, Ricberht, whose usurpation temporarily decided East Anglia's ideological orientation in favour of tradition, or what Bede simply refers to as *error*: "tribus annis prouincia in errore uersata est" ("the kingdom remained in error for three years"; *HE*, II.15, pp. 190–1). What Bede represents as murder followed by relapse into misbelief may actually have been the culmination of long-simmering tensions, caused either by old rivalries within the Wuffing dynasty or by challenges to the dynasty's legitimacy from without; if the latter scenario, then suspicion falls upon the Mercians.[115] Yet even if that rival *gens* had nothing to do with Ricberht's rise to power, the end of that "erroneous" king's reign did not immediately lead East Anglia to embrace the kind of stable Christian adherence Bede held up as a *condicio sine qua non* of happy governance. "There was a very sizeable royal family," Ian Wood reminds us, "and … rulership was not necessarily confined to one member of it at a time."[116] Although Bede somewhat frustratingly leaves unexplained the reasons for this state of affairs, he shows clearly enough that royal authority in East Anglia was not always unitary or uncontested. Even the apparently peaceful (if temporary) co-reign in the 630s of Ricberht's successors Sigeberht and Ecgric hints at competition and compromise within the royal court.[117] As David Kirby has pointed out, Bede praises the Christian Sigeberht for his patronage of the church (*HE* III.18, pp. 268–9) but expresses no similar admiration for Ecgric, and "the probability is that Ecgric was and remained a pagan."[118] Such tensions, whether or not they led to bloodshed, reverberate beneath the straightforward-sounding demonym "East Angles" and perhaps suggest the presence of an early centre of East Anglian dynastic power vying with Rendlesham, possibly as far afield as Norfolk,[119] where Mercian encroachment and influence would have been easier. Or the tensions may have been purely social in origin, deriving from competition within the Wuffing family itself in the "Sandlings Province."

The fact that Bede is silent on these possibilities implies a wish to simplify and to polemicize. Nicholas Howe has shown that "demarcating the world as he knew it, designating it as Christian or pagan terrain, as converted or yet-to-be converted, was fundamental to Bede's sense of his work as a historian and as a biblical commentator in the cause of religious orthodoxy."[120] Rædwald is scapegoated as an enemy of orthodoxy who resisted ideological demarcation. For Bede's purposes, the crucial boundary in East Anglia was one that ran not between Norfolk and Suffolk, or between different districts of the one or the other, but between true Christian belief and wicked pagan "error." Anglian religion, like Anglian migration, entailed for Bede an all-or-nothing boundary crossing.

After chastising Rædwald for attempting to have it both ways in the matter of the two altars, Bede goes on to provide a partial genealogy of the East Anglian royal house: "Erat autem praefatus rex Reduald natu nobilis, quamlibet actu ignobilis, filius Tytili, cuius pater fuit Uuffa, a quo reges Orientalium Anglorum Uuffingas appellant" ("[Moreover, the aforesaid] Rædwald, who was noble by birth though ignoble in his deeds, was the son of Tytil, whose father was Wuffa, from whom the kings of the East Angles are called Wuffings"; *HE* II.15, pp. 188–91). It's a curious moment to add a regnal list. According to Higham, "[t]he literary device is a subtle one and far from accidental, serving to separate Rædwald as an individual from the inherent nobility which (as Bede was keen to emphasise) was the general condition of his dynasty."[121] The separation of which Higham speaks, however, ruptures the regnal list's very integrity, the "constructed continuity" that Walter Pohl discerns in "the rudimentary but highly structured narratives of genealogies."[122] Although Bede clearly concedes the East Anglian king's membership in an illustrious royal line, his opposition of *natu nobilis* to *actu ignobilis* actually detracts from that line's lustre.[123] After all, Rædwald's "ignoble deeds" included trying to keep alive the old ways practised by his forebears; it would be his successors who eventually exemplified the new and improved model of kingship. The fact that Rædwald's name is even revealed by Bede when it is omitted from the "Anglian List" in London, British Library, MS. Cotton Vespasian B.vi, fol. 110v, is itself significant; the acts of including and excising names from royal genealogies had a propagandistic function,[124] so when Bede prefaces a regnal list with harsh opinions about one of its members, he breaks the list's spell over the audience. One reads the other kings' names, remembers Bede's censure, and wonders if the completely pagan forebears of Rædwald are guilty of sin merely by association with him. Rædwald's conversion ought to have marked a new beginning, the efflorescence of Christianity among the East Angles; a medieval polity's sense of its own importance depended on the recording of such historical junctures, whether of royal lines or of ideological realignment with a new religion. If a genealogy acts as a lifeline of dynastic prestige, the mention of Rædwald's pedigree immediately after an attack on the king himself shows Bede going for East Anglia's jugular.

The fragmentary nature of the regnal list as Bede reproduces it may indicate that he was willing to acknowledge the importance of genealogies only as a way of reminding his readers that, at this point in the *HE*, his subject was a single kingdom's pre-Christian history. Yet Georges Tugène offers the fascinating insight that "Bède est prêt à faire état de la généalogie païenne d'un roi chrétien, mais uniquement lorsque la conversion de ce roi est récente, fragile ou superficielle. Cela signifierait alors qu'il voit une incompatibilité entre la signification traditionnelle des généalogies royales et le sens d'une adhésion véritable à la foi nouvelle" ("Bede is prepared to mention the pagan genealogy of a Christian king, but only when that king's conversion is recent, fragile, or superficial. This would mean that he sees an incompatibility between the traditional signification of royal genealogies and the meaning of true adherence to the new faith").[125] Perhaps it is for this reason that Bede describes post-Rædwaldian Christian evangelization in East Anglia not in relation to a regnal list, much less to an *imperium*-list, but rather in relation to individual pious kings, bishops, and missionaries who laboured to spread the faith. The importance of King Anna, St. Fursey, St. Botwulf, and especially St. Æthelthryth will be considered in the next chapter; but to convey a further sense of East Anglia's quirky religious development as Bede recounted it, I turn next to the *HE*'s portraits of King Sigeberht and Bishop Felix before concluding this chapter.

Sigeberht the literalist

Sigeberht, Ecgric's co-ruler, is shown to have gone above and beyond the call of duty to prove himself a devout Christian (and thus to compensate for Ecgric's probable paganism?). Likely a stepson of Rædwald, he had endured a period of exile in Gaul while the latter was king (*HE* III.18, pp. 266–9) and even during the three years of Eorpwald's reign (*HE* II.15, pp. 190–1). After securing his hold on power, he sponsored the missionary activity of Fursey, even going so far as to renounce royal rule altogether to become a monk. Unfortunately for him, the pagan Mercian king Penda had designs on the East Angles, and when he attacked their kingdom they insisted that Sigeberht renounce the tonsured life to defend his people. One may be forgiven for feeling somewhat nonplussed by the outcome as Bede relates it:

> [D]um [Orientales Angli] se inferiores in bello hostibus conspicerent, rogauerunt Sigberctum ad confirmandum militem secum uenire in proelium. Illo nolente ac contradicente, inuitum monasterio eruentes duxerunt in certamen, sperantes minus animos militum trepidare, minus praesente duce quondam strenuissimo et eximio posse fugam meditari. Sed ipse professionis suae non inmemor, dum opimo esset uallatus exercitu, nonnisi uirgam tantum habere in manu uoluit; occisusque est una cum rege Ecgrice, et cunctus eorum insistentibus paganis caesus siue dispersus exercitus.
>
> (As the East Anglians realized that they were no match for their enemies, they asked Sigeberht to go into the fight with them in order to inspire the army with confidence. He was unwilling and refused, so they dragged him to the fight from the monastery, in the hope that the soldiers would be less afraid and less ready to flee if they had with them one who was once their most vigorous and distinguished leader. But remembering his profession and surrounded though he was by a splendid army, he refused to carry anything but a staff in his hand. He was killed together with King Ecgric, and the whole army was either slain or scattered by the heathen attacks. [*HE* III.18, pp. 268–9])

According to Wallace-Hadrill, Sigeberht's religious devotion in trying circumstances elicited Bede's admiration;[126] certainly as an early medieval effort at *imitatio Christi* it is not easily surpassed. Yet although such conduct is more honourable than Rædwald's first instinct to hand over Edwin of Deira to Æthelfrith of Bernicia – more honourable, that is, in being more redolent of early medieval *fidelitas* to one's religion – it is hardly more laudable as a show of responsible kingship.

Bede himself seems to have been at a loss for words, remarkably so in light of the material he had to hand. In the late tenth century, as we shall see in chapter 5, Abbo of Fleury would have no difficulty weaving into hagiography the loose threads of history and legend about King Edmund's murder at Scandinavian hands. In the early seventh century, when the young and still-fragile Christian church in England depended on strong royal leadership, Sigeberht had benefited his realm neither militarily nor, it would seem, spiritually by abdicating his rightful *ducatus* to die a martyr's death; a hundred years later Bede neglected to applaud that choice. It is one thing to promote missionary work and establish schools, achievements for which Sigeberht earned Bede's unambiguous approval; it is quite another thing to choose invasion as the context in which to emulate Christ's last agonies on the cross. Susan Ridyard argues persuasively that Bede would have found such absolute renunciation of responsibility better suited to recluses than to kings, and that he would have judged Sigeberht, "although a good and religious man ... ultimately rather misguided."[127] Alan Thacker goes further, claiming that the most conspicuous admiration shown for kings in the *HE* is reserved for rulers like the Northumbrians Edwin and Oswald, who exemplified Christian piety while also using military force to defend church and country.[128] Sarah Foot goes furthest of all when she maintains that kings like Sigeberht who renounced the responsibilities of rulership or *ministerium* "were not fulfilling the divine will"; by forgoing their "paternal role," they "contrived to make orphans of their subjects."[129] By displaying pacifism before Penda's army, Sigeberht ensured the East Angles' defeat and risked the undoing of the evangelization efforts that he himself had undertaken.

Such uncompromising all-or-nothing orthodoxy is a world away from Rædwald's accommodative synthesis. Students of East Anglia's later medieval and early modern history will remember the dramatic swing in the region's spiritual tenor from the late medieval Catholicism of Julian of Norwich, John Lydgate, and even Margery Kempe (who, though idiosyncratic, still esteemed pilgrimages and relics) to the seventeenth-century iconoclasm of William Dowsing and his fellow Puritans. Bede, focusing as he does on the relationship between kings and the church from the seventh century to his own day, anchors East Anglia's penchant for astonishing oscillations of faith roughly a millennium before the final spoliation of the abbeys, and shows it emerging not over the course of centuries but within a mere couple of decades.

More to the point, Sigeberht's self-sacrifice resembles the kind of weak kingship that, in early medieval Eastern Europe and Scandinavia, the church sought to compensate for by promoting exemplary saint-kings. Susan Ridyard infers from the Polish historian Karol Górski's work on the subject the principle that "[w]here the political power of the Crown was weak, the church sought to bolster royal authority by the creation of the saint king; where the monarchy was strong, the saintly ruler was conspicuously – and deliberately – absent."[130] Ridyard, however, sees a more complex sociopolitical dynamic at work in the promotion of English royal saints' cults, and I do not wish to underestimate the complexity of this dynamic either in England or in Bede's thinking in particular. Even so, it is beyond doubt that the Northumbrian monk rejected pagan Continental "sacrality," which was attributed to kings while they were still alive; it also seems pretty clear that he refrained from crediting Sigeberht with posthumous "sanctity," a trait that the Roman Catholic Church recognized in Christian kings held to have been martyred.[131] Bede instead set much more store by Sigeberht's success at furthering pastoral work. After Rædwald's time, seventh-century East Anglian kingship no longer resulted in broad political *imperium* but did form part of the foundation for Bede's narrative about the church's wider, gradual conversion of England.[132] As such it became the basis for a reformed East Anglia in the story recounted in *HE* II.15 about that kingdom's first bishop, Felix.

Felix's Pious Cultivation

In the *HE*, East Anglia becomes a refreshed spiritual landscape at a time when conventional *imperium* is no longer possible. Although Sigeberht failed to shine as a military leader, he fulfilled his pastoral responsibilities by recruiting Felix to diffuse Christianity throughout his realm: "Felix episcopus, qui de Burgundiorum partibus, ubi ortus et ordinatus est, cum uenisset ad Honorium archiepiscopum, eique indicasset desiderium suum, misit eum ad praedicandum uerbum uitae praefatae nationi Anglorum" ("bishop [Felix], who had been born and consecrated in Burgundy, came to Archbishop Honorius, to whom he expressed his longings; so the archbishop sent him to preach the word of life to this nation of the Angles"; *HE* II.15, pp. 190–1). The event is dated 636 by the Parker manuscript of the ASC, which notes that "Felix biscep bodade Eastenglum Cristes geleafan" ("Bishop Felix preached the faith of Christ to the East Angles").[133] Felix is thought to have died in 647,[134] and Bede's remark that his death occurred seventeen years after the beginning of his episcopacy (*HE* III.20, pp. 266–7) places the latter event in ca. 630 or 631. Bede's diction, livelier than the annalist's, refers to the new faith as the "word of life" and, as we shall see, associates that life with the imagery of agricultural labour. The effect is to evoke responsible stewardship; East Anglia's spiritual rescue is figured as hard work on English soil, the Burgundian bishop having been identified as the only cultural import from the Continent.

At Archbishop Honorius's bidding, Felix is said to have successfully dismantled the culture of paganism encouraged by Rædwald, his queen, and his court counsellors, "quin potius fructum in ea multiplicem credentium populorum pius agri spiritalis cultor inuenit. Siquidem totam illam prouinciam, iuxta sui nominis sacramentum, a longa iniquitate atque infelicitate liberatam ... perduxit" ("for the devoted husbandman reaped an abundant harvest of believers in this spiritual field. Indeed, as his name signified, he freed the whole of this kingdom from long-lasting evil and unhappiness"; *HE* II.15, pp. 190–1). In asserting that East Anglia had been a land long dominated by *infelicitas* before Felix set to work, Bede has in mind an "unhappiness" or "unluckiness" opposed to the *felicitas* that fully converted rulers were expected to foster by combining Christian orthodoxy with good government.[135] Here it is a bishop who effects the "national salvation" normally entrusted to kings but forsaken by Rædwald.[136] The East Angles have finally got their Coifi, and then some; because Felix does the bidding of both the archbishop and Sigeberht, his evangelical impact goes well beyond even the Northumbrian high priest's dramatic rupture with the past.

As A.H. Merrills has noticed, the *HE* contains a didactic and spiritual geography resembling that found in the commentary on the Acts of the Apostles that Bede was writing contemporaneously with his great book on the English church. "In each case," Merrills observes, "reference to physical reality at crucial points of the narrative both provided a setting for the evangelical episodes described, and allowed these victories to be located within the wider Christian world."[137] Thanks to Felix, the "spiritual field" of East Anglia at last coalesces firmly despite its limited extent as literal territory. Eighth-century readers knowledgeable about this specific *provincia* would have known that it occupied a sea-girt corner of an island; that its bishopric was near to or faced the water at *Dommoc* (*HE* II.15, p. 190) or, more properly, *Domnoc*, recently identified as Walton Castle near Felixstowe on the Suffolk coast;[138] and that the site given by Sigeberht to the Irish Fursey for monastic use "[e]rat ... siluarum et maris uicinitate amoenum, constructum in castro quodam quod lingua Anglorum Cnobheresburg, id est Vrbs Cnobheri, uocatur" ("was pleasantly situated close to the woods and the sea, in a Roman camp which is called in English *Cnobheresburg*, that is the city of Cnobhere (Burgh Castle)"; *HE* III.19, pp. 270–1).[139] Yet it is instructive to consider what Bede does *not* say about the sea.

Marine imagery offered ready tropes for stories of Felix's evangelization of East Anglia, as it went on to do for the twelfth-century historian William of Malmesbury, who recounts that the missionary bishop "ingenti studio et uigilanti labore toti regioni Christianam credulitatem infunderet" ("flood[ed] the entire region with the Christian faith thanks to his high endeavour and sleepless industry").[140] Here Felix is imagined not as a cultivator but as a kind of human pump, pouring the new religion everywhere into East Anglia in a benign version of that literal inundation by which the Fens "are never reclaimed, only being reclaimed."[141] Unlike William, Bede missed an opportunity to depict the Christianization of East Anglia in maritime terms; the oversight (as it may seem) is striking, given that "[s]ituated as he was on the banks of the Tyne, and drawn by the powerful spiritual currents of the Irish Sea, Bede's writing was the product of a littoral, as much as literary, environment."[142] Currents, however, have a way of shaping and reshaping landscapes in unexpected ways. As Tim Pestell has commented, "[c]ertainly, the inhabitants of what was to become East Anglia were geographically well-placed to absorb or react to the beliefs and material culture of those passing through or choosing to settle within the local landscape."[143] Perhaps from Bede's perspective Rædwald's court was too well placed in that regard. Although coastal or fen environments are literally the places where Felix, Fursey, and Æthelthryth establish their retreats, only farmland is evoked by Bede as a figural or metaphorical setting for pastoral endeavour, and maritime locales are not exploited for any symbolism that might be apt to figure the work of proselytization.

In fact, as Lawrence Martin has shown, "Bede's favourite metaphor for preaching in his *Ecclesiastical History* is agricultural."[144] With its connotations of stability, abundance, earnest production, and harmony between human enterprise and the natural environment, the image of harvesting aptly enables Bede to characterize the evangelization of East Anglia by its first bishop. During his own, secular reign, Rædwald is shown to have embodied none of those aforementioned virtues; and although Bede does not associate his *imperium* with seaborne ideological flux, he does link the more reassuring imagery of reaping with the settled Christian pastoral work that proceeded after Rædwald's time. According to Peter J. Fowler, the metaphor of prayer as harvest evokes the early Christianization of the Germanic peasantry, who regarded agricultural and religious labour as "really the same thing," for "once you get Christian religion coming in as the latest of religions, it very quickly colonizes the agrarian cycle, which is, if you like, God-given."[145] Like long-persistent prehistoric earthworks, East Anglia's pagan substratum is ploughed under by Felix's zealous cultivation.[146] One recalls that in *Super parabola Salomonis* Bede figures the church as a strong woman planting a vineyard of faith, and that in Luke 11:23 (which we know Bede read) Christ uses the sowing trope to distinguish believers from unbelievers.[147] Finally, the "potius fructum" ("abundant harvest") that Felix reaped in his territory recalls the agricultural turn of phrase deployed by Bede himself in his Preface, in which, ruminating on his own authorial labours, he asks the audience of his "historia ... nostrae nationis" ("history of our nation") to pray together on his behalf: "apud omnes fructum piae intercessionis inueniam" ("let me reap among them all, the harvest of their charitable intercessions"; *HE*, *Praefatio*, pp. 6–7).[148] Shared imagery hints at similarity between two kinds of spiritual reward: that which Bede hopes to gain for himself, and that which East Anglia has secured for itself thanks to Felix's ministry. The harvest-tide trope nicely resolves the early cultural uncertainty of the "Angles" as a whole, who, Bede reported, had deserted their Continental homeland for greener pastures in Britannia. With Felix as their happy reaper, the eastern Angles are shown finally to have accepted a well-regulated, healthy religious life and to have stopped feeding the demons that had hungered for the victims Rædwald is said to have sacrificed to them. The *HE* seeks to reassure its readers that the most restive of the Angles have found their proper niche in the English church and that Felix's labours have fortified East Anglia against heathenism originating elsewhere in England.

Conclusion

Although the danger posed by the Mercian king Penda was a thing of the past, heresy and paganism remained constant perils in Bede's imagination. The expectancy voiced in the active subjunctive *inueniam* present in the Northumbrian scholar's *captatio benevolentiae*, where he asks for his readers' prayers, also suffuses the depiction of Felix.[149] For couched though it may be in the certainty of indicatives – *inuenit*, *perduxit* – the account of his episcopacy nevertheless exudes Bede's earnest hope (more than wishful thinking, less than absolute certitude) that the Christian faith had now become securely planted in East Anglian soil.

Early readers of the *HE* did not necessarily share Bede's dismay at Rædwald's influence. In fol. 43v of the Saint Petersburg Bede,[150] the phrase "ad uictimas daemoniorum" is written in a smaller script than the rest of the text but apparently in the same hand, and appears at the bottom of the second column below what seems to have been intended as that column's last line: "[habe]ret ad sacrificium xrī et arulam." It looks as if the scribe had initially pondered excluding the line about the devils' victims, possibly believing it was unimportant, but then changed his mind in a show of faithfulness to Bede's text. The OE translation of the *HE* adds nothing in the way of astonishment or disdain to Bede's account of the East Anglian king.[151] As Sharon Rowley has demonstrated, however, the fact that the OE version "decenters Roman authority and significantly reduces the voice of Gregory the Great"[152] in comparison to the Latin original suggests that, in comparison to Bede, the translator may have been less tetchy anyway about the ideological implications of Rædwald's two altars.

Oxford, Bodleian Library, MS. Hatton 43 is an early eleventh-century manuscript of the *HE* and contains many corrections and marginal notes; yet the annotator has ignored the passage about Rædwald's dual shrine.[153] On fol. 60v a possibly twelfth-century corrector intervened at the mention of *reduuald* (ninth line) and *ræduuald* (nineteenth line), but merely to add the siglum "·)" above the "d" in the East Anglian king's name to indicate that the Latin nominative ending *-us* should be understood. In and of itself this correction is unexceptional, as it appears also over the names *alduulf* (seventeenth line), *eorpuuald* (line 22), *sigberct* (line 25), and *ælfuuin* and *ædilred* on fol. 124r. To that reader such names stood out not because they activated memories of their bearers' piety or impiety, but rather because their OE forms had not been properly integrated into the Latinity of the surrounding text of the *HE*. Beyond striking the exacting corrector as lexically incomplete, the names had effectively ceased to signify.[154] Bede associated Rædwald's name with syncretism, but his disappointment and his anxieties belong to the eighth century; scribes at work four hundred or so years later could frown over grammatical case endings because they could afford to take for granted so much else. Latinizing Old English names becomes a priority when the question of religious adherence can be laid to rest.

For his part, Bede knew that Britannia comprised many cultural layers, many ideological influences originating elsewhere. Paganism as he understood it still survived, and he feared it as later copyists of the *HE* could not have done, for to him it had been the common ground among otherwise distinct early Insular realms. Writing of the rich inhumation mounds created in eastern England during Bede's lifetime, Martin Carver remarks that "the burials signal a new cultural unity between the kingdoms of the heptarchy, as if, in wishful imagination at least, a unified England already existed."[155] Bede's *imperium*-list also signals unity of a kind, albeit frequently coerced, always temporary, and sometimes wrought by kings who had not been Christian, or not sufficiently Christian for Bede's tastes. It is rather the church that the *HE* proclaims as the sole legitimate basis of unity, and thus the only true foundation of a politically credible East Anglia. For this reason Bede might have reacted to the Sutton Hoo ship-burial in Mound 1 with the same tactical ambivalence he shows with regard to wielders of *imperium*. According to J.M. Wallace-Hadrill, "Sutton Hoo was unknown to Bede; and, had it been known, would have struck him as repellent and irrelevant."[156] Repellent in itself? Perhaps. Irrelevant? Not necessarily, for if the modern consensus is right, the tomb honoured someone – Rædwald, maybe – who had, after all, aspired to pre-eminence as a ruler and who exercised a specifically royal power on which the church depended in order to bring about eventual cohesion in England.

Bede acknowledged the importance of wide-ranging rule; what he opposed was the ideological mutability that he found most egregious in East Anglia's early history but that had characterized the early histories of all the English kingdoms. To show that the English "nation" and church had successfully joined the larger world of Roman Christianity, Bede demonized Rædwald's East Anglia, literally associating it with devils, and then effected its historiographical exorcism lest that realm's influence should have confined all England to the spiritual equivalent of that remote *angulus* to which it was sometimes relegated by medieval Continental writers and mapmakers.[157] Among the English *provinciae* East Anglia occupied a privileged position in the easternmost part of the island world that Bede knew best, for it lay closest to the rising sun and to Christianity's roots "in primis orbis partibus" ("in the first parts of the world").[158] As chapter 2 will show, Bede depicted Æthelthryth – East Anglian princess, sometime Northumbrian queen, and founder of a monastery in the liminal Ely borderland – as a force that had decisively returned East Anglia to the orbit of Christianity and so augmented the "happiness" brought to the kingdom by Bishop Felix.

2
Æthelthryth in a Virgin Wilderness

In likening the East Anglian missionary-bishop Felix to a reaper and his converts to a harvest, Bede, as we saw in chapter 1, conjured up a vision of fields made productive by the plough, an image that would have resonated with those of Bede's eighth-century monastic readers familiar with land transactions recorded in charters and reckoned in acres and furlongs.[1] Such readers would have known that enclosing a field for agricultural use involved demarcation, either the reuse of earlier boundaries or the creation of new ones, as well as occasional "trouble with neighbours and the law" when the property rights of others were infringed upon.[2] But when Bede celebrates Felix's activities in East Anglia, he says nothing about that kingdom's internal divisions; his remark that "fructum in ea multiplicem credentium populorum pius agri spiritalis cultor inuenit" ("the devoted husbandman reaped an abundant harvest of believers in this spiritual field"; *Historia ecclesiastica* [*HE*] II.15, pp. 190–1) neither discloses any boundary disputes arising from the establishment of *Domnoc*[3] nor alludes to any of the toil involved in evangelization. The agricultural conceit succeeds because Bede focuses on the fight against paganism, or rather the fight against the tolerance of paganism that he associates with Rædwald and his queen; out of sight for the time being are unpleasant political realities, especially the pagan Mercian warlord Penda, likely the most unpleasant reality of all for the East Angles of the middle seventh century. Though absent from Bede's vignette of Felix, Penda nevertheless figures prominently in the *HE*'s accounts elsewhere of Mercian aggression against East Anglia. "Trouble with the neighbours" is, then, a recurrent theme of the latter kingdom's early to mid-seventh-century political fortunes and forms the background of Bede's account of Æthelthryth's foundation of a religious house at Ely.

My argument in this chapter is that Bede uses the sainted abbess, her miraculous incorruption, and the fervour and loyalty of her community at Ely to show that the kingdom once cut off from correct Christian worship by Rædwald has been brought out of its idiosyncratic, ideologically ill-defined corner of history to play a central role in the English church, a role all the more noteworthy because of lingering threats posed by Mercia in the latter half of the seventh century despite that kingdom's conversion to Christianity following Penda's death. The *HE* demonstrates the reintegration of part with whole by praising the achievements of Eorpwald, Sigeberht, Felix, Fursey, and especially Æthelthryth, who for Bede was the greatest East Angle of all. Despite the evangelization program spearheaded by the male leaders whom Bede acknowledges (and by St. Botwulf, whom he does not acknowledge), it is Æthelthryth's virginity that confirms East Anglia's spiritual intactness.

Although the abbess is often and correctly regarded by modern scholars as generally English, Bede himself stresses her regional identity; for this reason she should be seen as his personification of East Anglia at its best. He identifies Æthelthryth as "filiam Anna regis Orientalium Anglorum" ("daughter of Anna, king of the East Angles"; *HE* IV.19, pp. 390–1) and explains her decision to establish a religious community at Ely by saying simply that "de prouincia eorundem Orientalium Anglorum ipsa ... carnis originem duxerat" ("she sprang from the race of the East Angles"; *HE* IV.19, pp. 396–7). In thus bookending her *Vita*, such regnal particularization does two things. As Catherine Matthews has pointed out, it "subtly emphasize[s] the earthly status of this saint as a way of indicating the successful spread of Christianity."[4] Yet the technique also invites us to contrast Æthelthryth to Rædwald and to deduce that East Anglia has indeed been transformed from outpost of lingering Germanic heathenism to vanguard of Christian asceticism (the rigid dichotomy between heathenism and Christianity reflecting Bede's own thinking, as pointed out in chapter 1). If Rædwald and his queen's persistent attraction to paganism be understood as spiritual fornication, as suggested persuasively by Stacy Klein,[5] then the *HE*'s pairing of virginity with orthodoxy in the figure of Æthelthryth takes on that much more resonance as Bede's way of announcing the ideological redemption of the East Anglian *gens*: once a land of spiritual "unhappiness," East Anglia has returned to *felicitas*. Along with Sigeberht's royal sponsorship of the missionary endeavours of Felix and Fursey, Æthelthryth's community at Ely signals what, much later and in a very different context, would be called "the effects of good government in the countryside."[6] Within Bede's narrative scheme, this triumph redounds generally to the English church because it heralds the recovery of the formerly troubled and troublesome East Anglia, now incomparably fertile in holiness – as Bede implies – thanks to Æthelthryth.

Like Felix, Ely's virgin abbess is shown to succeed as a cultivator of Christian piety; but it is because of its local importance that her success story belongs at least as much to the conflict-ridden early chorography of East Anglia as to the turbulent wider history of the Christian church in England. Her tireless self-dedication to Christ gains Æthelthryth a reputation for sanctity that becomes associated with her monastic community at Ely and with a spiritually renewed royal genealogy and kingdom. Though self-exiled to the latter's periphery in the Fens, Æthelthryth becomes the main attraction of East Anglia's ecclesiastical culture in the late seventh century, her hagiography a series of performances of holiness that redounds to the credit of *stirps* and *provincia* alike.

Politics and Religion

According to Bede, Felix had established his East Anglian bishopric at *Domnoc* (Walton Castle), and Fursey had founded a hermitage at *Cnobheresburg* (?Burgh Castle); the Parker or "A" manuscript of the Anglo-Saxon Chronicle (ASC) dates the former event to 636.[7] By this time, Rædwald himself was history; but the East Anglian kingdom and church remained threatened as long as Penda could disrupt political stability everywhere south of the Humber,[8] as the three East Anglian kings Sigeberht, Ecgric, and Æthelthryth's own father Anna discovered at the cost of their lives (*HE*, III.18, pp. 268–9). Meanwhile, St. Fursey was forced to leave England for the Continent, founding a monastery at Lagny in Francia (*HE*, III.19, pp. 276–7) and dying there ca. 650. We occasionally need to go beyond the *HE* to unearth Penda's long career as a warlord; that career is hinted at in the brief hagiography of St. Foillán, the *Additamentum Nivialense de Fuilano*, which mentions the expulsion of King Anna and the sacking of Fursey's monastery.[9] The *Liber Eliensis* (*LE*) blames Penda for ravaging a monastery at *Cratendune*, in or near Ely, which is said to have been established by King Æthelberht of Kent as a Canterbury initiative;[10] a precursor to the more illustrious double abbey created by Æthelthryth, it may have been known to her when she was a girl.[11] As an adult, she is more likely to have known that her uncle, Anna's brother Æthelhere, was set up as a puppet king after Penda had killed her father, and that her foundation at Ely replaced the earlier *Cratendune* wiped out by Penda's army surging in from the west.[12] Æthelthryth would have remembered a time when nearby Mercia, not faraway Angeln, threatened a return to paganism.

Remarking on this threat, Norman Scarfe maintains that "Felix's bishopric was no kind of pastoral idyll, more a saga: Penda put East Anglia's new Christianity on the anvil: an enduring link was forged between Christianity and patriotism."[13] Æthelthryth is not typically regarded by scholars as a patriot, nor her religious devotion likened to a sword hammered in the smithy of war; yet when Bede turned her life into hagiography he distinguished perhaps too neatly between Vergil's hero Aeneas and his own saintly protagonist. In his hymn he writes "Bella Marò resonet; nos pacis dona canamus" ("Let Virgil echo wars, let us sing the gifts of peace");[14] but if Æthelthryth knew anything at all about her father Anna's and her kinsman Sigeberht's deaths at Penda's hands, she would have realized that the site of her religious house lay close to enemy territory and that "the gifts of peace" were always on loan. Proximity to an expansionist Mercia could make the Isle of Ely a dangerous place to live, not unworthy of comparison with the hagiographical desert of St. Antony.

When Æthelthryth finally is shown establishing a house for religious women and men at Ely ca. 673, the prospects for monastic survival in East Anglia may have looked brighter; Penda had died eighteen or nineteen years earlier at the battle of the *Winwæd* (*HE* III.24, pp. 290–5), and the Mercians had been converted to Christianity. On Bede's own evidence the Mercians even contributed to the growth of the English church, especially through the good offices of their Christian king Wulfhere,[15] whom, it may be noted, the *LE* identifies as the husband of Eormenhild, daughter of King Eorcenberht of Kent and of Æthelthryth's own sister Seaxburh.[16] Yet the Mercians broke the peace even after adopting the new faith. In 676 their ruler Æthelred invaded Kent, the focal *provincia* of the Gregorian mission, and attacked monasteries in the process, acts that provoked Bede's wrath in *HE* IV.12 (pp. 368–9). Well after Bede's time, in 794, the Christian Mercian king Offa murdered, or commanded to be murdered, the Christian East Anglian king Æthelberht II; this later event warrants mention here only to underscore the point that Mercian aggression never resulted solely from differences of religion. As J.M. Wallace-Hadrill asserted, "Bede's Anglo-Saxons showed no community of political sentiment";[17] at a time when hostilities erupted frequently, Æthelthryth's community at Ely depended on luck or the Fenland for whatever calm could be enjoyed close to the Mercian sphere of influence.

The rise of Ely, then, seems to have been part of a larger trend in which East Anglian religious communities gambled on a climate of relative if uncertain peace. The last half-dozen years or so of the missionary endeavours of St. Botwulf, who made his *minster* at Icanhoe (Iken) in Suffolk ca. 653/4–ca. 680, overlapped with Æthelthryth's tenure at Ely from 673 to about 679. Evidence for Botwulf's life and work is found not in Bede but in the ASC's brief annal for the year 654,[18] in an even briefer reference in the list of saints' resting places known as the *Secgan be þam Godes sanctum þe on Engla lande ærost reston*,[19] and in the post-Conquest *Vita sancti Botolphi* by Folcard of St. Bertin.[20] Though unremarked by the Northumbrian scholar, Botwulf's mission formed one of several important mid-seventh-century efforts by the Christian East Anglian royal court to evangelize the kingdom's far-flung, still-pagan corners. According to Wallace-Hadrill, "conversion of the countryside – and not only of the countryside – was still a living issue in Bede's time,"[21] and Bede states that Fursey "multos et exemplo uirtutis et incitamento sermonis uel incredulos ad Christum conuertit uel iam credentes amplius in fide atque amore Christi confirmauit" ("converted many both by the example of his virtues and the persuasiveness of his teaching, turning unbelievers to Christ and confirming believers in His faith and love"; *HE* III.19, pp. 268–9).[22] Significant populations of what Bede regarded as "pagans" probably lived far from the Wuffings' seat in the Rendlesham–Sutton Hoo area, far too from the aristocratic circles expected to follow the royal lead in conversion.

Bede, when he is aware of them, records that such royally sponsored East Anglian evangelization efforts took place in remote or liminal areas. As we saw in chapter 1, Fursey, for example, is said to have undertaken his missionary work at a site given to him by King Sigeberht that "[e]rat ... siluarum et maris uicinitate amoenum, constructum in castro quodam quod lingua Anglorum Cnobheresburg, id est Vrbs Cnobheri, uocatur" ("was pleasantly situated close to the woods and the sea, in a Roman camp which is called in English *Cnobheresburg*, that is the city of Cnobhere (Burgh Castle)"; *HE* III.19, pp. 270–1). Whether *Cnobheresburg* was modern Burgh Castle, as is often claimed, is less important for present purposes than the text's implication that it lay at some distance from established settlements and made use of a former Roman military outpost.[23] A religious community arising there will have taken advantage of existing walls, associated itself with imperial cultural authority, and impressed upon villagers the antiquity of the church itself.[24] Fursey's famous visions may be said to build upon the physical foundations specified by Bede: on one occasion the missionary was taken out of his own body and raised "in altum" ("up to a great height"), where "iussus est ab angelis, qui eum ducebant, respicere in mundum" ("he was told by the angels who were conducting him to look back at the world"; *HE* III.19, pp. 272–3). When he turned around, he saw four enormous flames threatening the planet, each with its own allegorical meaning. The vision cannot be said to have been influenced by Fursey's perception of the East Anglian countryside, nor need it be thought a commentary on life there;[25] but a commonality nevertheless suggests itself between the fort-turned-hermitage at *Cnobheresburg* and the hermit's out-of-body visionary transports. In each case the physical shell, useful though it may be in itself, proves especially valuable as a foundation for or threshold to the divine, whether the shell be the body of the saint or the *Romanitas* of the structure he appropriates.

Penda's depredations obliged Fursey to flee East Anglia for Francia. Almost a quarter-century later Æthelthryth founded her own community at a site that was now safe enough to support it. Like both Fursey and Rædwald, she was not unique in Insular history; as Bede was well aware, other women had founded religious houses, such as Hild at Whitby (e.g. *HE* III.24, pp. 292–3; IV.23, pp. 404–15) and Æbbe at Coldingham (*HE* IV.19, pp. 392–3, 424–7). Æthelthryth's sister Seaxburh created two abbeys, at Milton Regis and at Minster-in-Sheppey, though Bede knew only that she eventually would serve as abbess of Ely. Likewise, the Mercian noblewoman Kyneburga had been instrumental in co-founding the double house at Medeshamstede (later Peterborough) in the 650s, but for this information we need to turn to Dugdale's *Monasticon*;[26] Bede tells us simply that Kyneburga had been a daughter of Penda and the wife of the (perhaps) Deiran sub-king Alhfrith (*HE* III.21, pp. 278–89, and n. 3). There was also Æthelburh, who received from her brother Eorcenwold, bishop of London, the monastery of Barking that he had founded (*HE* IV.6, pp. 354–61).

Bede praises Æthelburh and Hild warmly but singles out Æthelthryth for special veneration, describing her piety with an intensity that diverts attention away from the militarily sensitive border area in which that piety is shown to take root. This is not to say that Bede makes physical environments wholly irrelevant to his heroine's devotion; on the contrary, he shows her body to be deeply integrated with her spirituality and thus characterizes her very differently from how he portrays Fursey, whose flesh proved such an encumbrance to his transcendental visions that he needed to leave it behind. Furthermore, Bede's portrait of her in *HE* IV.19 (pp. 390–401) attributes to Æthelthryth a somatic self-awareness that is intimately linked to the geographical place in which her community arises.[27] Her *Vita* and later Old English and Anglo-Latin texts deriving from it have shed much light on the roles women were expected to play qua women in the early English church;[28] some scholars have explored the sainted abbess's hagiography as the mother lode of Ely Abbey's institutional power before and after the Norman Conquest.[29] Virginia Blanton's recent monograph has done the most to discern in her cult a catalyst for broader English national identity formation from the early medieval to early modern period.[30] Less has been written, though, about how the saint's textual representation furthered East Anglian regional identities specifically. Jacqueline Stodnick regards Bede's depiction of Æthelthryth as a spur to "local and regional identities" but emphasizes the absorption of those identities into the larger national-ecclesiastical destiny envisaged in the *HE*.[31] Blanton, Mechthild Gretsch, Christine Wille Garrison, Paul Szarmach, and most recently Ian David Styler similarly view the Æthelthryth textual corpus as connecting Ely to England.[32] Of course, Bede himself insists on celebrating the abbess as a paragon of English holiness generally, and I agree with Stodnick, Blanton, and the other scholars named above who demonstrate that her cult bridges the categories of "region" and "nation," even if my own interest is in the ways regional identities responded to, accommodated, or even resisted narratives of wider English unification.

Æthelthryth among Men

Because inter-dynastic unions created at least the hope of concord between kingdoms, Æthelthryth was under considerable pressure to marry. Bede's *HE*, unlike the much later *LE*, provides relatively few details of this pressure, though he shows plainly enough that her future lay in the hands of powerful men. An intriguing alternation between passivity and activity characterizes Bede's Æthelthryth, by turns an East Anglian princess, Northumbrian queen, and finally East Anglian abbess; the alternation recalls Rædwald's own oscillation between passivity and activity earlier in the *HE*. This trait contributes to Bede's representation of East Anglia as a kingdom that, having earlier (in effect) shunned the universal church, came to place itself wholly at the church's service. Bede's *Vita* of and abecedarian hymn to Æthelthryth exalt her sanctity as a transcendent and trans-temporal virtue that redounds to Ely's fame and secures East Anglia's political redemption as a polity fully reformed, even on its liminal Fenland periphery.

In Bede's well-known account, Æthelthryth is a princess of the East Anglian royal house who has been married off twice but eventually exchanges the secular for the cloistered life. Her decision takes her first to Coldingham Abbey ca. 672, a monastery under Northumbrian royal patronage, and thence after one year to Ely.[33] Prior to becoming a nun of the former and abbess of the latter, however, she was beholden to men:

> Accepit autem rex Ecgfrid coniugem nomine Aedilthrydam, filiam Anna regis Orientalium Anglorum, cuius saepius mentionem fecimus, uiri bene religiosi ac per omnia mente et opere egregii; quam et alter ante illum uir habuerat uxorem, princeps uidelicet Australium Gyruiorum uocabulo

> Tondberct. Sed illo post modicum temporis, ex quo eam accepit, defuncto, data est regi praefato. Cuius consortio cum XII annis uteretur, perpetua tamen mansit uirginitatis integritate gloriosa[.]
>
> (King Ecgfrith married a wife named Æthelthryth, the daughter of Anna, king of the East Angles, who has often been referred to, a very religious man and noble both in mind and deed. She had previously been married to an ealdorman of the South Gyrwe, named Tondberht. But he died shortly after the marriage and on his death she was given to King Ecgfrith. Though she lived with him for twelve years she still preserved the glory of perfect virginity. [*HE* IV.19, pp. 390–1])

Unsurprisingly, Bede and later hagiographers present Æthelthryth as a woman ensconced and even objectified in a man's world.[34] Her passivity before male power reveals much about early medieval gender roles, especially as Bede understood and represented them, and is reflected at the level of grammar and syntax, which juxtapose the bride's passivity with the king's agency. The verbal phrase "accepit … coniugem," for example, presents Ecgfrith as wife-taker and Æthelthryth as wife taken, the construction being one of several in the passage that portray the saintly heroine "as a packaged gift, being presented to one husband after another with no voice at all in any of the transactions."[35]

Life on the marital merry-go-round delays Æthelthryth's brilliant career at Ely, but Bede was in no position to blame Ecgfrith, the very king "quo concedente et possessionem terrae largiente ipsum monasterium fecerat" ("who had given permission and granted land for the founding of the monastery") in which Bede himself lived. Without Ecgfrith, there could have been no Wearmouth-Jarrow, because he "uoluisse" ("had desired") that Pope Agatho should give Benedict Biscop "in munimentum libertatis monasterii quod fecerat, epistulam priuilegii" ("a letter of privileges … protecting the liberty of the monastery he had founded"; *HE* IV.18, pp. 388–9).[36] In support of Benedict Biscop's foundation of Wearmouth in 674, Ecgfrith needed to grant land and secure privileges.[37] "The court of Ecgfrith," writes Stephen Harris, "seems to me a metonymy for political and ecclesiastical reform,"[38] and Bede knew that the demands of such reform sometimes obliged individuals to sacrifice personal career preferences. In this context, Æthelthryth was herself a resource, valued as a means to promote the temporal well-being of the Northumbrian kingdom.

Her tendency – as Bede portrays it – to be acted upon more frequently than to act finds parallels in Bede's earlier characterization both of Rædwald and of the dependent state of the East Angles after his death. In the middle of the seventh century, the *gens* was hemmed in by other *gentes* and obliged to pursue strategic alliances for its very survival. Sought by a prince of the South Gyrwe and subsequently by a Northumbrian king, the princess Æthelthryth looks to be the linchpin of stable political relations.[39] Yet her potential to advance peace for the East Angles mattered much less to Bede than her determination to remain a lifelong virgin.[40]

We hear very little to nothing, for example, of the political fallout of Æthelthryth's decision to end her royal marriage to take monastic vows. She must have plunged the Northumbrian court into confusion by leaving Ecgfrith, though it must remain an open question whether her doing so "would have ... rendered him something of a laughing stock within the court," eventually "leaving him with an overwhelming feeling of self-pitying failure."[41] Nor do we know the extent of the problems, if any, she posed for her own family when she sundered the tie between the East Anglian and Northumbrian *gentes*. In saying so little about her political life, Bede has insulated his heroine from the flux of history. The resulting image of the Isle of Ely is of a place of tranquil contemplation, glad asceticism, and (precarious) safety along East Anglia's western border zone during a time of Mercian expansion.[42] Bede's silence about tensions between the two polities allows him to concentrate on the purely spiritualized frontier between life within and life without the cloister.

As students of Æthelthryth's *Vita* have long known, even the portrait of the saint herself accords her very little political volition, aside from simple acknowledgment of the fact of her twelve-year Northumbrian queenship: "Sponsa dicata Deo bis sex regnauerat annis" ("The devoted betrothed of God had reigned for twice six years"; *HE* IV.20, p. 398).[43] Æthelthryth typifies most subjects of hagiography in embodying a paradox: total self-effacement on one hand; formidable self-possession, usually in the face of familial pressures, on the other.[44] The latter is given restricted scope for development. As Lisa M.C. Weston observes, "[h]er marriages are acts of dynastic politics that she accepts (by marrying) even as she denies (by remaining virgin)."[45] In the eighth century we are a far cry from her cult's later and especially post-Conquest developments, in which Ely hagiography revels in the saint's ability to punish from beyond the grave any sceptics who impugn her reputation.[46] Combining agency with passivity, Bede's Æthelthryth looks not forward to the twelfth century but backward to the early seventh, the era of Rædwald, whom the *HE* portrays as both wielder of *imperium* and servant of his queen and court teachers. Although they have little else in common, Bede's Æthelthryth and Rædwald both raise the prestige of their *provincia* by confronting and overcoming external disparagement. The converted king fights against and kills Æthelfrith of

Bernicia; Æthelthryth resists potential calumny by those who would question her virginity. Bede uses reported evidence about her body to validate the foundation story on which the community at Ely rested:

> [S]icut mihimet sciscitanti, cum hoc an ita esset quibusdam uenisset in dubium, beatae memoriae Uilfrid episcopus referebat, dicens se testem integritatis eius esse certissimum, adeo ut Ecgfridus promiserit se ei terras ac pecunias multas esse donaturum, si reginae posset persuadere eius uti conubio, quia sciebat illam nullum uirorum plus illo diligere. Nec diffidendum est nostra etiam aetate fieri potuisse, quod aeuo praecedente aliquoties factum fideles historiae narrant, donante uno eodemque Domino, qui se nobiscum usque in finem saeculi manere pollicetur. Nam etiam signum diuini miraculi, quo eiusdem feminae sepulta caro corrumpi non potuit, indicio est quia a uirili contactu incorrupta durauerit.
>
> (When I asked Bishop Wilfrid of blessed memory whether this was true, because certain people doubted it, he told me that he had the most perfect proof of her virginity; in fact Ecgfrith had promised to give him estates and money if he could persuade the queen to consummate their marriage, because he knew that there was none whom she loved more than Wilfrid himself. Nor need we doubt that this which often happened in days gone by, as we learn from trustworthy accounts, could happen in our time too through the help of the Lord, who has promised to be with us even to the end of the age. And the divine miracle whereby her flesh would not corrupt after she was buried was token and proof that she had remained uncorrupted by contact with any man. [*HE* IV.19, pp. 390–3])

Just as in life Æthelthryth refuses Ecgfrith's sexual advances, so too in death her body resists decay; for Bede, the notion of resistance to corruption applies to both contexts. His passive infinitive construction "corrumpi non potuit" (literally "would not be corrupted") and past-participial adjective phrase "incorrupta durauerit" ("remained uncorrupted") strikingly capture the synthesis of activity and passivity in Æthelthryth's *Vita*. A passive grammatical construction is what one expects when a cadaver is being discussed, since the dead cannot act but only be acted upon; yet even while prone and subject to decomposition, the body composes itself in a show of personal agency that survives corporeal death.

East Anglia itself is shown to have been a damaged body politic whose integrity, once restored, needs to be displayed. Bede's emphasis on the saint's wholeness enhances his portrayal of the efforts made by earlier male missionaries to dissolve Rædwald's baleful legacy and improve East Anglia's reputation. Success in this regard mattered to Bede and probably to his intended readers too, who would have included the Northumbrian king Ceolwulf, like-minded monastic and secular readers or listeners (female as well as male), and evidently "certain people" – perhaps at Wearmouth-Jarrow or at the royal court? – who seem to have persisted in doubting the late queen's marital chastity.[47] An attentive reader of an earlier version of the *HE*, Ceolwulf wished to aid the book's greater diffusion throughout England "ob generalis curam salutis" ("in [his] zeal for the spiritual well-being of us all"; *HE Prefatio*, pp. 2–3).[48] He will have noticed the shadow cast earlier on East Anglia's character by Rædwald's mixed heathen and Christian temple, and will already have known that that king's successor Eorpwald had been baptized a Christian under the supervision of Edwin (*HE* II.15, pp. 188–9),[49] Ceolwulf's illustrious predecessor, who had reversed the roles of Northumbria and East Anglia and had "made sure to set the tune for the East Anglian king to play."[50] Ceolwulf would have had reason to welcome Æthelthryth's sanctity as evidence that Edwin's baptism of Eorpwald had created a lasting foundation for East Anglia's re-Christianization, one that would help rather than hinder the growth of the larger English *ecclesia*.[51]

Vitality at the Edge

In the *HE* Æthelthryth is a paragon of virtue for the English church as a whole, but her accomplishments redound first of all to her own credit, to the prestige of her local community, and to the renown of her *gens*. She is said to have departed from Ecgfrith not precipitously but only after having waited many years for his permission to go; her kingly husband, for his part, is not portrayed in an unflattering light, and Bede reports nothing of his responses to his wife's years of pleading with him. Given his need for tactfulness when recounting this episode, Bede depicts Æthelthryth's behaviour as a mixture of passivity with agency:

> Quae multum diu regem postulans, ut saeculi curas relinquere atque in monasterio tantum uero regi Christo seruire permitteretur, ubi uix aliquando impetrauit, intrauit monasterium Aebbae abbatissae, quae erat amita regis Ecgfridi, positum in loco quem Coludi urbem nominant, accepto uelamine sanctimonialis habitus a praefato antistite Uilfrido. Post annum uero ipsa facta est abbatissa in regione quae uocatur Elge, ubi constructo monasterio uirginum Deo deuotarum perplurium mater uirgo et exemplis uitae caelestis esse coepit et monitis.
>
> (For a long time she had been asking the king to allow her to relinquish the affairs of this world and to serve Christ, the only true King, in a monastery;

when at length and with difficulty she gained his permission, she entered the monastery of the Abbess Æbbe, Ecgfrith's aunt, which is situated in a place called Coldingham, receiving the veil and habit of a nun from Bishop Wilfrid. A year afterwards she was herself appointed abbess in the district called Ely, where she built a monastery and became, by the example of her heavenly life and teaching, the virgin mother of many virgins dedicated to God. [*HE* IV.19, pp. 392–3])

Not despite but rather in keeping with his characteristic portrayal of Æthelthryth as the object of men's desires, Bede explains that the royal abbess resolved "in monasterio tantum uero regi Christo seruire" ("to serve Christ, the only true King, in a monastery"; *HE* IV.19, pp. 392–3). A hagiographical convention, Æthelthryth's synthesis of self-abnegation with self-advancement reaches its fulfilment in her geographical movements, and these culminate in her return to Ely. Of course the move may well have been arranged by her family behind the scenes; it is easy to picture King Ealdwulf and his court mulling over the advantages of bringing Æthelthryth back home now that her marriage had been annulled.[52] If the saintly woman was going to devote the rest of her life to prayer anyway, why not have her do it on behalf of her fellow East Angles in East Anglia?

Bede, however, does not explain the transfer from Coldingham to Ely as the result of such manoeuvrings. Curiously, even the *LE*, which so often fleshes out Bede's accounts with details not found in the *HE*, is just as silent as Bede is on this score, citing no Wuffing fiat as the reason for the move.[53] According to Tim Pestell, "Ely's foundation in the seventh century may be understood as a border outpost and a symbolic statement of presence by the East Anglian royal family."[54] Bede, however, suggests that the former queen's Fenland homecoming is shown to have been willed by Æthelthryth herself, who carves out what Virginia Woolf might have called "an island of one's own" in contrast to her earlier forced emplacement among Tondberht's Gyrwe and, later, Ecgfrith's Northumbrians. To be sure, her separation from her Northumbrian royal spouse will have cost her time and effort; Bede heavily underscores her suppliant's role when he characterizes her as requesting (*postulans*) that she might be permitted (*permitteretur*) to leave behind worldly cares ("saeculi curas relinquere"). The wording stresses the queen's patience and submissiveness even as it indicates her desire to escape from secular affairs.[55] Such agency as she can exercise is hinted at in Bede's verbs *impetravit* and *intravit*. The former, a compound translated by Colgrave as "she gained his permission," normally presupposes "request or entreaty," and even without Bede's *vix aliquando* it connotes exertion on the part of the petitioner rather than unsolicited generosity on the part of the giver.[56] The latter verb, *intravit*, may (but needn't) imply a free choice "to go into, enter (a closed or defined space)";[57] here the only power ascribed to Æthelthryth is simply the renunciation thereof. Bede attends chiefly to her personal choice to grow in spiritual perfection. Whether Æthelthryth deplored Coldingham for its lack of discipline or had simply quarrelled with Ecgfrith's aunt Æbbe, Bede does not say, though her departure invites speculation.[58] His silence on these issues enables him to strengthen her semblance of autonomy.

East Anglia, of course, is shown to have benefited from Northumbria's loss of the pious queen-turned-nun, but Bede plays down the impact of that loss upon his own region. What Sharon Rowley has said about Book IV of the OE translation of the *HE* applies to the same section of Bede's Latin original: "In many ways, Book IV is the success story of the Church in England, with the English saints and miracles far outweighing the problems, like the monastery at Coldingham."[59] Æthelthryth's, and by extension East Anglia's, relationships with others are characterized by collaboration, negotiation, and understated supersession; simply put, by the transition from a good to a better state of affairs rather than by the outright rejection of bad for good. As Bede depicts her, the abbess moves from place to place generating no ill will.[60] Through a narrative approach that exploits or inserts key silences in the record,[61] the East Angles are made to look like more sociable partners within the English church than they had ever been under Rædwald, their reincorporation into it aided by Æthelthryth's relatively smooth passage between communities.

"In Bede's narrative," Harris observes, "Aethelthryth ... moves temporally through a series of sites and stages," specifically from royal milieus "such as we might see in the Books of Kings or Samuel," to "a minster, an apostolic community wed to Christ such as we might see in the Gospels," and then lastly "to sanctity in the universal Church, as we see exhibited in the Epistles."[62] Interestingly, these series take the form of transitions presented in pairs, in which the saint improves upon prior experience of stability. The first pair comprises her two journeys "outward" – from East Anglia to Middle Anglia and, later, to Northumbria, the territories (respectively) of her two husbands; these journeys are essentially transpositions into the secular space and time of the married state.

The second pair of transitions brings Æthelthryth "homeward," as it were, ever closer to sacred space and time in the form of the monastic life she longs for; this trajectory comprises her stint at Coldingham and her extended sojourn at Ely. In each pairing, the first undertaking reads like a pen trial for a later, more sustained, more successful venture: that is, her marriage to Ecgfrith endured longer than her brief relationship with Tondberht, and her seven years at Ely were more fruitful than her single year at Coldingham.

Æthelthryth's career of improvements aptly complements the spiritual progress of the East Anglian *gens*. Although I risk getting ahead of myself by looking ahead to Bede's discussion of the abbess's marble sarcophagus, I find it necessary to cite here Jacqueline Stodnick's analysis of that section of the *HE* because of its influence on my thinking about Æthelthryth as an integral part of the East Anglian chorography adumbrated by Bede:

> As Ely is to Britain, so Æthelthryth is to her new sarcophagus, which exactly replicates the contours of her body[.] ... Bede's attention to the rewrapping and containment of Æthelthryth's body restates the microcosmic relation between Ely and Britain itself, and provides a way to think about her as simultaneously a local and an insular saint. ... Bracketing Æthelthryth's narrative, this chapter [*HE* IV.18, concerning the sojourn at Wearmouth-Jarrow by John the Archcantor] mirrors its concern with a synecdochic notion of regionality that asserts the symbolic value of the part in relation to the whole.[63]

One way the *HE* constructs East Anglia as a place is by showing its progression, greatly spurred by Æthelthryth, from *infelicitas* to *felicitas*. Her story recalls the history of her country's Christianization, begun unsatisfactorily with Rædwald and set to rights by Sigeberht and his missionaries. The reading I propose here does not challenge Stodnick's claim that Bede's *Vita* uses Æthelthryth's coffin at Ely to encapsulate a potential for sanctity that applies broadly to Britain as a whole; instead it simply suggests that before Æthelthryth's holiness could be appropriated for the greater glory of the national church, it needed to be proved fit for purpose at the regional level to show that the East Anglian kingdom had been fully converted.

Chorography between Home and Rome

Bede depicts the founding of the Ely community not as a feat of reclamation and engineering, as the physical rehabilitation of fen or mound,[64] but rather as a social process, one centred on Æthelthryth herself as an example to be imitated, or at least lauded, by Ely's cenobites and by the *HE's* intended readers. After telling us about the abbess in her role as teacher, Bede evaluates her day-to-day routine, noting that Æthelthryth denied herself most luxuries and wore "solum laneis uestimentis" ("only woollen garments"). She rarely bathed except during major liturgical celebrations, and seldom ate "plus quam semel per diem" ("more than once a day"; *HE* IV.19, pp. 392–3). In practising this kind of regimen, she served as a model for her fellow inmates. The social cast of her piety seems to typify women's saints' lives generally;[65] in Bede's account it suffuses Æthelthryth utterly.

As a pattern for the spiritual formation of others (in this case Ely's nuns and monks), the abbess's conduct resembles Æthelburh's devotional life at Barking and its influence on Torhtgyth (*HE* IV.6–9, pp. 354–63) as well as the asceticism of Hild at Whitby (*HE* IV.23, pp. 408–15). Even in her last moments Æthelthryth is shown to be indivisible from her companions, men as well as women: in Bede's phrasing, "[r]apta est autem ad Dominum in medio suorum" ("[s]he was taken to the Lord in the midst of her people"; *HE* IV.19, pp. 392–3), the masculine genitive plural *suorum* standing for both sexes and probably referring to the mixed membership of the Ely community itself, though the meaning "her kinsfolk" cannot be ruled out. Even after her death the abbess was bound indissolubly to a community: "et aeque, ut ipsa iusserat, non alibi quam in medio eorum iuxta ordinem quo transierat ligneo in locello sepulta" ("she was buried by her own command in a wooden coffin, in the ranks of the other nuns, as her turn came"; *HE* IV.19, pp. 392–3).[66] It is striking that her final expression of agency occurred when Æthelthryth ordered that her body should be placed amidst the remains of the monastery's deceased inmates; forsaking the pomp and exceptionalism befitting her status, she instead chose interment in a small casket (*locellus*) made of wood. In Bede's narrative, such perishable material aptly complements the simple ceremony at her entombment; substance and form combine to showcase the humility with which Æthelthryth becomes one with East Anglian soil.

It is in part to confirm that that soil and, by extension, the whole ideological foundation of the East Anglian *provincia* have been sanctified that the abbess's humility must be showcased. Betokening her resistance in life to worldly marriage, her virginal *integritas* unites the saint with East Anglian territory, which becomes more prestigious thanks to her interment in it. Yet again, however, and some sixteen years after the interment, the wishes of Æthelthryth were overturned, not by a man but by her own sister Seaxburh, who had succeeded her as abbess of Ely and had come to believe that her saintly predecessor merited elaborate commemoration in a marble sarcophagus.[67] This, the last example of supersession in Bede's *Vita*, shows that even the disposition of her own body was finally not up to Æthelthryth to decide but depended on the will of others:

> Et cum sedecim annis esset sepulta, placuit eidem abbatissae leuari ossa eius et in locello nouo posita in ecclesiam transferri; iussitque quosdam e fratribus quaerere lapidem, de quo locellum in hoc facere possent. Qui ascensa naui (ipsa enim regio Elge undique est aquis ac paludibus circumdata, neque lapides maiores habet) uenerunt ad ciuitatulam quandam desolatam non procul inde sitam, quae lingua Anglorum Grantacaestir uocatur, et mox inuenerunt iuxta muros ciuitatis locellum de marmore albo pulcherrime factum, operculo quoque similis lapidis aptissime tectum. Vnde intellegentes a Domino suum iter esse prosperatum, gratias agentes rettulerunt ad monasterium.
>
> (After Æthelthryth had been buried for sixteen years, the abbess [Seaxburh] decided that her bones should be raised and placed in the church in a new coffin; she therefore ordered some of the brothers to look for some blocks of stone from which to make a coffin for this purpose. So they got into a boat (for the district of Ely is surrounded on all sides by waters and marshes and has no large stones) and came to a small deserted fortress not far away which is called *Grantacæstir* (Cambridge) in English, and near the walls of the fortress they soon found a coffin beautifully made of white marble, with a close-fitting lid of the same stone. Realizing that the Lord had prospered their journey, they brought it back to the monastery. [*HE* IV.19, pp. 392–5])

So much for a simple burial; Æthelthryth is now an institution unto herself. A new, properly monumental shrine is required and must be built of stone; the challenge lies in finding enough of it. Later texts celebrate Fenland sites like Ely, Peterborough, and Huntingdon as *loci amoeni* blessed with abundance;[68] but Bede makes it clear that workable stone is one commodity for which Seaxburh and her community needed to search afield.

Accordingly, the abbess despatched to the hinterland several "brothers" who seemed to know exactly where to look for the prized material: a disused *civitatula* or small fortified settlement.[69] This is the Romano-British site of the future city of Cambridge; already a known quantity as the toponym *Grantacæstir* in the early English calculus of place-names,[70] it was evidently familiar as a supply point for materials apt for long-term commemoration. In an address to the Cambridge Antiquarian Society in 1933, Helen Cam remarked that "the first recorded archaeological discovery in this county [i.e. Cambridgeshire] was made by the monks who found under its walls the stone coffin that they needed for enshrining the bones of Etheldreda."[71] The find is a form of "harvesting" worthy of comparison with Bishop Felix's pastoral labours and Fursey's renovation of a Roman fort. In Bede, the Ely monks quarry the ancient past, recycling a relic of imperial colonization for better use. Their redeployment of Roman *spolia* is matched by Bede's decontextualization of the site itself; one would like very much to know what the monks had seen at *Grantacæstir*. Christopher Taylor offers an intriguing speculation but adds to the questions raised by the *HE*:

> The old Roman town where they discovered a Roman coffin may have been partly derelict but it is unlikely that the settlement was completely abandoned. In any case the picture of destruction that the monks recorded may well have been only a temporary phase resulting from the savage wars between Mercia and East Anglia earlier in the seventh century.[72]

Bede's claim that the site was *desolata* allows one to surmise that it was partly or nearly *vastata* as well. Was the fort a casualty of old strife between the two neighbouring kingdoms? "The watercourses of Cambridge," Helen Cam wrote, "lead back to the days when 'East Angle and Mercian glared at each other across Magdalene Bridge.'"[73] Hostilities may have subsided enough to allow a quick scavenging operation, but the monks must have been stout-hearted souls anyway to conduct one in such an area.

Assuming (as I do, agreeing with Christopher Taylor) that by Bede's time *Grantacæstir* marked the spot of ancient conflict, and assuming too that it signalled a frontier zone rather than a sharply delineated "border" in our sense of the word, one is still faced with questions about the sarcophagus and the rival histories it encapsulates. Had it served as the final resting place of a Romano-British pagan? If so, would it therefore have been understood by Bede and his audience as a symbol of the old order? Or had it been intended for a Christian Briton, either at the time of its commissioning or at some point after the Edict of Thessolonica of 380, when Christianity became obligatory throughout the empire? The latter scenario is possible, though a comparable Roman sarcophagus in the Church of Saint-Étienne (Déols, dép. Indre) houses the remains of St. Lusor; it was known to Gregory the Great and has been described thus by John Crook: "pagan, adorned with hunting scenes, but this evidently did not worry those who reused it for the saintly burial."[74] Beautifully wrought Roman artefacts seem not to have worried Bede either. As Nicholas Howe has reminded us, the Northumbrian scholar knew very well "that Rome had once been physically part of the island's culture" and that "[its] remains contributed, as architectural spolia, to the making of Christian England."[75] The Christian recycling of antiquity meant appropriation, and it is very probable that Bede regarded the sarcophagus found outside the fort's walls as a remnant of both a bygone culture and an archaic world view.

More important than what it originally signified is the new purpose it acquires at Ely in Bede's narrative. Seaxburh's enhancement of Æthelthryth's shine would be that much more successful if suitable stone could be not only discovered and transported but "converted" as well. In his hymn to Æthelthryth, as we shall see later, the glory of Bede's subject is said to surpass that of Vergil's Aeneas; the account of Seaxburh's effort to enrich her sister's shrine is especially impressive as an instantiation of much the same principle, which Clare Lees and Gillian Overing have identified as one in which "[t]he new triumphs by incorporating the old within its ideology just as Pope Gregory recommended to Augustine (*EH* 1. 30)."[76] A symbol of Insular paganism is recovered by monks and brought into Ely's crypt, but rather than retaining its old identity and being placed on the same level as a Christian artefact (like Rædwald's *arula*, allowed to stand near an *altare*), the sarcophagus is transformed altogether, in service of what Bede would have maintained was the one true faith. Its earlier Roman identity poses no threat to the community but rather adds to the lustre of the shrine and its guardians.[77] Transferred effortlessly from a Romano-British cultural environment to an English one, the casket is not unlike its place of discovery, *Grantacæstir*, which the *HE* shows to have been incorporated into the *lingua Anglorum* – not just "the language of the English" but specifically "the language of the Angles," for, as John Hines has shown, the spelling of the place-name reflects specifically Anglian dialectal features.[78]

The "conversion" of the casket – if the object was pagan originally – furnishes an opportunity for Bede to drive the last nail into the coffin of East Anglia's heathen past, and to do so more decisively than he could do when narrating the account of Rædwald's two altars.[79] Bede's statement that the casket "[m]irum uero in modum ita aptum corpori uirginis sarcofagum inuentum est, ac si ei specialiter praeparatum fuisset" ("was found to fit the virgin's body in a wonderful way, as if it had been specially prepared for her"; *HE* IV.19, pp. 396–7) conforms the vestiges of an earlier culture to the monastic agenda of the *HE*'s carefully curated textual space. Among the bits and pieces of East Anglian history gathered therein, Roman fragments, whether pagan or Christian, reveal enduring cohesive power. This cultural augmentation-via-appropriation technique has been used already: the Ely community's reuse of the coffin parallels Fursey's rehabilitation of *Cnobheresburg*,[80] both salvage operations testifying, in monumental form, to the redemption of East Anglia itself after Rædwald's misguided fusion of Christian and pagan altars.[81] Ely's Roman fragment is no less important than those altars, despite the use of the word *locellus* ("chest, casket, box") to refer to it.[82] The diminutive endings of *locellus* and *civitatula* understate major appropriations. Removed from its original place of burial, the casket has quasi-figural meaning in a hagiographic context because the transfer heralds a synthesis of Christian and pagan that is really the former's supersession of the latter, a sign of cultural maturation on the margins of East Anglia.[83]

Healing the Scarred Body Politic

The more important transfer, however, is that of Æthelthryth's remains from the old to the new coffin. Before the *translatio*, Seaxburh had expected to exhume only her sister's bones; instead the body "ita incorruptum inuentum est, ac si eodem die fuisset defuncta siue humo condita" ("was found to be as uncorrupt as if she had died and been buried that very day": *HE* IV.19, pp. 394–5). In a period when fledgeling religious communities often had to make do with fragments of saints' remains, and in certain cases only with burial cloths that failed to excite universal appreciation,[84] Ely boasts a whole body in addition to the "powerful contact relics"[85] of the saint's clothing; the discovery stands to confer upon the Fenland community a high degree of prestige.

As in the account of Æthelthryth's marital virginity, so too in the discussion of her posthumous pristine state, male expertise is brought in for purposes of verification. The authority of Bishop Wilfrid is cited once more, as is that of a physician, Cynefrith, who recounts how he had lanced a tumour just below the abbess's jaw and, years later during the translation ceremony, discovered "tenuissima ... cicatricis uestigia" ("only the slightest traces of a scar"; *HE* IV.19, pp. 394–5).[86] Bede's narrative treatment of Æthelthryth's scar has been interpreted as a textual "performance" of the female saint's gender; as a reflection of male monastic writers' control over the representation of female purity; and as a locus of clerical anxieties about the challenges of historiography itself.[87] Stodnick diachronically analyses the *Life of Æthelthryth* and the *Life of Edmund* in Ælfric's *Lives of Saints*, and connects the abbess's scar with the king's wound in order to situate Bede's exaltation of the East Anglian princess within a long-term nation-building project on the part of early English writers.[88] Yet even as it adumbrates pan-English sanctity, the image of Æthelthryth's posthumous healing also confirms, via metonymy, that East Anglia has been fully healed of the ideological wound inflicted upon it by Rædwald. Just as an oyster forms a pearl around an irritating grain of sand, so Æthelthryth is shown to envelop her tumour in pious allegory, and the Ely community to enfold the remains of Fenland Roman paganism within a shrine to a paragon of Christian asceticism.

In both cases, sacred identities accrue around points of origin presumed to be profane. As Æthelthryth lay dying, she is said to have confessed to a youthful love of jewellery and to have interpreted the malignant growth on her neck as God's punishment for it:

> "Scio certissime quia merito in collo pondus languoris porto, in quo iuuenculam me memini superuacua moniliorum pondera portare; et credo quod ideo me superna pietas dolore colli uoluit grauari, ut sic absoluar reatu superuacuae leuitatis, dum mihi nunc pro auro et margaretis de collo rubor tumoris ardorque promineat."
>
> ("I know well enough that I deserve to bear the weight of this affliction in my neck, for I remember that when I was a young girl I used to wear an unnecessary weight of necklaces; I believe that God in His goodness would have me endure this pain in my neck in order that I may thus be absolved from the guilt of my needless vanity. So, instead of gold and pearls, a fiery red tumour now stands out upon my neck." *HE* IV.19, pp. 396–7)[89]

Embedded in her self-glossing is a rare detail about Æthelthryth's childhood life as an East Anglian princess. Though raised a Christian, she neither had denied herself, nor had been denied by her parents, the pleasure of jewellery; only in deathbed retrospection does she apply the word *supervacua* both to the necklaces of her girlhood and to the vanity she believes they represented. A further connection is drawn, via the word "weight," between the jewellery and the tumour ("pondus ... pondera"). Her urgent disavowal of the perceived sins of long ago links past to present and also indicates how Æthelthryth wished to be remembered by posterity, or rather how Bede intended her to be remembered. She is depicted longing for eternal salvation, but her self-glossing expresses concern for the kind of posthumous renown she sought within the Ely community. A member of a Christianized social elite who deliberately renounces the trappings of earthly wealth, she is implicitly aligned with post-Rædwaldian kings: as her father Anna and as Sigeberht and Eorpwald did before her, she consolidates her *gens*'s break with the pagan traditions that had followed her ancestors in their migration from the Continent to East Anglia.

Howard Williams has situated individual burials, whether cremation or inhumation, within larger cultural patterns. He sees both kinds of mortuary practice as "relational technologies" that, despite the differences between them, "were employed to define coherent group mnemonic traditions as well as to simultaneously create social and religious distinctions between groups, both within and between burying communities."[90] In the cases of women dressed for burial, "[m]ortuary costume varied between and within cemeteries, suggesting its complex and changing use as a medium for the expression of female identities at multiple levels."[91] According to Williams, the five wealthy female interments at the seventh- to eighth-century cemetery at Harford Farm, Norfolk (near Caistor St. Edmund) are connected by "the social construction of the body and the body's use to mediate the identities of the living and the deceased."[92] By contrast, the trait that Bede attributes to Æthelthryth in her last moments is that of self-spoliation, the choice to renounce not only "gold and pearls" but also the attachment to them, an attachment that would have formed part of her early self-identity but that, in retrospect, she thinks marred her youth. Yet the textual performance of renunciation is itself a kind of "relational technology" because it commemorates Ely's founder and impresses upon early readers of the *HE* the vitality of the English church on the very margins of East Anglia. As a way of mediating regional identities for those readers, Bede's scene of Æthelthryth's deathbed asceticism contrasts with the cultural signalling performed by the dual shrines of Rædwald and his queen.

Æthelthryth's reputation for holiness affects even the way her clothes are regarded posthumously. Rather than being placed in the new coffin to mark her privileged social position, these are kept for the spiritual and physical healing of others: "Contigit autem tactu indumentorum eorundem et daemonia ab obsessis effugata corporibus et infirmitates alias aliquoties esse curatas" ("It happened also that, by the touch of the linen clothes, devils were expelled from the bodies of those who were possessed by them, and other diseases were healed from time to time"; *HE* IV.19, pp. 396–7). This is Bede's testimony, not the physician Cynefrith's, and it adds further depth to a before-and-after tableau vivant that can be imagined juxtaposing Rædwald and his court with Æthelthryth and her cloister. In this pairing, the mere clothes of an East Anglian royal abbess would, in theory, help to vanquish the kind of diabolical power allegedly supplicated by the earlier East Anglian king. Of the Harford Farm mortuary context Williams has observed that "artefacts were displayed and disposed of to create specific mnemonic connections to the dead among the living";[93] in a roughly similar vein, the passage from the *HE* just quoted displays the sainted abbess's clothes strengthening Christian cohesion in the Ely community. In life,

Rædwald is said by Bede to have sacrificed to devils in the East Anglian royal temple itself, presumably at or close to the centre of regnal power; in death, Æthelthryth indirectly exorcises demons from the kingdom's periphery and, in effect, from the East Anglian body politic.

Although the abbess fails to get her way even in the final disposition of her body, one detects neither tension in her characterization by Bede nor discord within the Ely *monasterium*. All is communal endeavour and mutual support, as when Bede has Cynefrith recollect the gender inclusivity of the ceremony at Æthelthryth's *translatio*: "Cumque post tot annos eleuanda essent ossa de sepulchro, et extento desuper papilione omnis congregatio, hinc fratrum inde sororum, psallens circumstaret" ("When, some years later, her bones were to be taken out of the sepulchre, a tent was erected over it and the whole congregation stood round singing, the brothers on one side and the sisters on the other": *HE* IV.19, pp. 394–5).[94] Though divided by gender, "the whole congregation" chants the Psalms as one body. Æthelthryth's cloistered life and commemorative afterlife exemplify conventual fellowship, a show of unity in this corner of East Anglia that compensates for the disunity of cult allowed by Rædwald.

Why Ely?

After Bede expresses wonderment at the perfect fit of the Roman sarcophagus to Æthelthryth's body, especially with regard to the space reserved for the head, he abruptly turns to contemplate the Isle of Ely itself. The scant transition between these two topics serves a purpose. Despite, or perhaps because of, its distance from Wuffing centres of power further to the east, the isle is figured as the spiritual "head" of the East Anglian church and kingdom. At this point in the *HE*, Bede is thinking in spatial terms about the shape of Æthelthryth's body and that of her coffin, and about the relationship between her head and the space seemingly allotted for it in the original making of the artefact. This spatial emphasis invites us to ponder Ely as itself a spiritual headland, mostly detached from the main body of its *provincia* but essential to that body's function, organization, and proper reorientation towards Christian orthodoxy. In his mini-chorography of Ely, one very small portion of the East Anglian kingdom stands for the whole,[95] and one woman's extreme zeal for bodily purity undoes an earlier period of impurity presided over by a misguided syncretistic king.

Bede's *Vita* of Æthelthryth resists linear chronology and intersperses details about her posthumous incorruption and holiness with accounts of her life. Given this oscillation, it is unsurprising that Bede should bring us decidedly away from the miraculous and back to earth by remarking on Ely's geography:

> Est autem Elge in prouincia Orientalium Anglorum regio familiarum circiter sexcentarum, in similitudinem insulae uel paludibus, ut diximus, circumdata uel aquis, unde et a copia anguillarum, quae in eisdem paludibus capiuntur, nomen accepit; ubi monasterium habere desiderauit memorata Christi famula, quoniam de prouincia eorundem Orientalium Anglorum ipsa, ut praefati sumus, carnis originem duxerat.
>
> (Ely is a district of about 600 hides in the kingdom of the East Angles and, as has already been said, resembles an island in that it is surrounded by marshes or by water. It derives its name from the large number of eels which are caught in the marshes. This servant of Christ wished to have her monastery here because, as has also been said, she sprang from the race of the East Angles. *HE* IV.19, pp. 396–7)

There are several points of interest in this paragraph. First of all, Ely is described as a *regio* ("region," "district") belonging to the larger East Anglian *provincia* ("race" or, better, "kingdom"). It is not wholly severed from the world but instead assigned a specific East Anglian political identity that links it to the seventh-century kingdom's administrative core in eastern Suffolk. The linkage seems insouciant, regardless of whether Bede is establishing the connection on his own authority or relying for it on his sources. By so casually including the Isle of Ely in the "prouincia … Orientalium Anglorum," the *HE* glosses over the problem of its distance from the royal court at Rendlesham. It is likely that what eventually became an East Anglian *regio* had once been an independent sociopolitical unit that went on to lose its autonomy during the Wuffings' expansion from south-eastern Suffolk in the sixth and early seventh centuries. The text, however, remains squarely focused on Æthelthryth's desire to return to the land of her people, the East Angles; Ely is implicitly no less "East Anglian" an area than any other part of the *provincia*.

Furthermore, no matter how fluid its environs, the settlement lies firmly within a familiar system of land reckoning, a territory parcelled into *familiae* ("hides," "households"), units of lived territory or "practised place," to borrow Michel de Certeau's phrasing.[96] The so-called *Tribal Hidage* uses "hides" to measure territory and thus "indicates a degree of orderliness, or coherence in the exercise of power."[97] In a similar vein, Bede's Ely is made out to be a known quantity, a landscape ordered by a community. It is also recognizable by its commodities, which are implicitly prized according to this-worldly criteria; the toponym is said to have originated with the eels living at the site. While hardly enough to make Bede's Ely a *locus amoenus* or "pleasant place," the reference to the area's large quantity of autochthonous marine animals recalls the symbolic and real value of "landscape as bounded, as contained by human-defined purposes."[98] As natural resources go, the isle's eels have long been appreciated in the Fens.[99] In the early 1070s, as Richard of Ely reflects in the *Gesta Herwardi* through the speech of the captured Norman knight Duda, Hereward and his men were able to keep William the Conqueror at bay simply with the materials they had to hand in their fastness on the isle;[100] but even five centuries earlier, Ely's eels are said to have helped Æthelthryth and her fellow monks and nuns hold out against the world. Contributing to the wealth of food with which all England is blessed (*HE* I.1, pp. 14–15),[101] they enable Ely to join a larger national economy, the part finding its meaningful place within the whole. That this particular part should be characterized in terms of its marshes (*paludibus*) and its aquatic life implies sparseness of human settlement, another potential reason for the area's strategic value, especially in the seventh-century Wuffing economy. "Remote and marginal locations," Tom Williamson reminds us, "fitted in well with the needs of Dark Age kings, for it was easier to donate the land necessary for a new community in areas of woodland, marsh, and waste, away from the main cores of long-settled tribal land."[102]

The emphasis on abundant marine food also complements the piety to be found in the isle, for the "copia anguillarum" ("large number of eels") befits the "uirginum Deo deuotarum perplurium" ("many virgins dedicated to God"; *HE* IV.19, pp. 392–3) nurtured by Æthelthryth herself. The intensive prefix *per-* in the adjective *perplurium* really suggests not merely "many" virgins but "very many." Ely is a wriggling Eden, but just as there are no snakes, so too are there no sins. The abbess's virtue, a paradoxical combination of virginity and maternity, breeds monks and nuns who are inspired by the example of their foundress to be fruitful and multiply in virginal perfection.[103]

Such abundance hardly arises *ex nihilo* in a wilderness. Rather, Æthelthryth is said to have chosen Ely as the site of her double house because it was the place of her own origins.[104] The *HE* does not reveal whether she was given a specific grant of land by the East Anglian king;[105] although "charters do belong at the heart of the history of the christianisation of England,"[106] Bede apparently saw no need to treat Æthelthryth's choice of the isle as a matter of land grants. It is unlikely that he possessed a copy of the seventh-century Ely equivalent of the

Chelsworth diploma discussed earlier in this book. The new abbey's origin at Ely is explained, evidently to Bede's satisfaction, by the foundress's wish to dwell among her own people; practicalities of land transfer disappear from view. The return to ancestral beginnings enables a sanctified future in situ that transcends a charter's merely archival permanence.

The *HE* likewise suppresses other prosaic ramifications of Æthelthryth's founding of Ely. As Christine Wille Garrison has astutely pointed out, there is a paradox in the princess's stated preference for her native East Anglia as the setting of her new monastery, in that going back to her roots entailed returning to the land whose ruling *gens* had forced the reluctant bride into her two marriages.[107] Moreover, Ely was situated in an area of the kingdom where dynastic influence was at its most tenuous.[108] In general "royal women monastics lived in a liminal context, between court and church";[109] but Æthelthryth's Ely would have been that much more liminal – its natural wealth and its quantifiability in hides notwithstanding – because of its physical situation in the "frontier region" between Mercia and East Anglia,[110] an area marked by the odd relic of tempestuous times.

Bede, however, makes it clear that his protagonist regarded the Isle of Ely as part of her homeland, and that fact was enough to justify the house's establishment therein. He slyly connects the isle's quasi-insular appearance to the abbess's self-identification as an East Angle. Although his parenthetical asides "ut diximus" and "ut praefati sumus" seem merely to indicate awareness of self-repetition, they also serve to link Bede's discussion of the shape of Ely's landscape with his reference to Æthelthryth's roots in that landscape via the East Anglian *gens*. One would have expected Bede to identify the abbess primarily in relation to that *gens* as such, but instead he associates her with a *provincia*. The preference for the territorial over the social term situates his heroine in place. And the construction "de prouincia eorundem Orientalium Anglorum ipsa ... carnis originem duxerat" – literally "she herself drew the origin of her flesh from the kingdom of the selfsame East Angles" – emphasizes corporeal attachment to place that is surprising in a textual culture known for preferring tribal to spatial identification.

There may be a good reason for this emphasis. By stressing the "kingdom" over the dynasty, the *stirps*, Bede forestalls questions about any undue influence the latter might have had in the founding of Ely. In life, Æthelthryth may well have acted freely to colonize her part of the Fens, but the East Anglian royal family from which she "drew the origin of her flesh" will have had its own interests to pursue in the 670s. Barbara Yorke points out that aristocratic convents were guided by political and familial concerns, not merely spiritual and personal motives:

> Entering the religious life was one of the gendered roles allotted to women within the royal family nexus, and the considerable investment of resources in these nunneries implies that they were considered to have a valuable role in sustaining and promoting the interests of the royal kin-group. These roles may have been primarily religious, but some are also likely to have had political connotations, and it may not have been easy, then or now, to draw a clear distinction between them.[111]

King Ealdwulf and his court surely discerned political utility in Æthelthryth's foundation at Ely. Although they apparently preferred her to marry into a powerful foreign *gens*, they will also have benefited from prayers offered on behalf of the East Anglian dynasty in her prestigious double house, which may be regarded as a cloistered extension of that dynasty. The less-than-clear distinction between Ely's religious and political functions must have been blurred further after Æthelthryth's death, when the abbacy was assumed first by her sister Seaxburh, then – if later evidence is reliable – by Seaxburh's daughter Eormenhild, and later still by Eormenhild's daughter Werburh.[112] "If this was indeed the case," Simon Keynes notes, "Ely takes on the appearance of a house serving the particular interests of a royal family, in a way which might not have met entirely with Bede's approval."[113]

But Bede plays down the importance of such familial interests in Æthelthryth's case. To find so much as a hint of a royal retinue we need to turn to an altogether different chapter of the *HE*'s fourth book, in which the historian comments almost in passing that a certain monk named Owine had accompanied the East Anglian princess to Northumbria: "Venerat enim cum regina Aedilthryde de prouincia Orientalium Anglorum, eratque primus ministrorum et princeps domus eius" ("He had come with Queen Æthelthryth from the kingdom of the East Angles, being the chief of her officers and the head of her household"; *HE* IV.3, pp. 338–9). The *HE* also minimizes Æthelthryth's political influence as queen of the Northumbrians, and in this regard differs from Stephen of Ripon's *Vita sancti Wilfridi*.[114] By associating Æthelthryth with the East Angles, naming her as King Anna's daughter, and placing her in a Fenland district reckoned in "hides" and known for its eels, Bede accords her just enough nobility and physical reality to support the allegoresis he will impart to her life in the hymn that conveys his homage to her. Henceforth Bede's East Anglia will be represented not by half-pagan *imperatores* or by slain Christian kings, but by a holy woman who is shown to spurn temporal prestige altogether, in favour of the spiritual glory of religious houses, "islands of repose and springboards to eternity."[115] By exalting Æthelthryth, Bede shores up that corner of the English church occupied by the militarily evanescent East Angles. It is small wonder that the mid-eighth-century East Anglian king Ælfwald should have wanted to build on his dynasty's success at sponsoring saints' cults, even if his own choice, the Crowland hermit Guthlac, had been a Mercian.

Rebuilding the prestige of the East Angles was by no means an eccentric pursuit for the Northumbrian monastic historian. According to J.M. Wallace-Hadrill, "Bede … knew the Western Church for what it was: a confederation of churches, often fissile, divergent, ignorant, and passionately local."[116] He perceived regional peoples in much the same light; Barbara Yorke has shown that Bede regarded the individual *gentes* of his island as more palpable, more real political entities than the *gens Anglorum* itself, which always mattered more to him as an ideal than as an ethnically demonstrable fact.[117] Such particularism, especially of regional churches, needed to be harnessed to the church as a whole. His way of ending the *Vita* of the holy abbess elevates the local and regional precisely as a condition for articulating the national.

Where Bede's prose account of Æthelthryth's life celebrates her local impact, his verse treatment proclaims her universal significance. The hymn is ostensibly *uirginitatis* ("on the subject of virginity"; *HE* IV.20, pp. 396–7) but really about Æthelthryth in particular.[118] Penned "ante annos plurimos … elegiaco metro" ("many years ago in elegiac metre"; *HE* IV.20, pp. 396–7),[119] the text preceded the composition of the *HE* and displays Bede's interest in showing how the present incorporates the past and how wholes embrace many parts. Æthelthryth is shown defeating time itself, her virtue linking her to the great Roman virgin martyrs Agatha, Eulalia, Tecla, Euphemia, Agnes, and Cecilia. Her transcendence exists alongside her fitness as a spiritual heroine for Bede's own time and place: it is precisely her supernatural piety that makes her such an urgently needed model of conduct for the here and now. In what follows, not all the hymn's lines will be considered, partly for reasons of space, but mostly because of the comprehensive philological treatment the text has received in Stephen Harris's 2016 monograph *Bede and Aethelthryth*. Readings of several excerpts, however, will demonstrate that Bede adapted the themes and mode of secular panegyric to Christian hagiography to create a verbal shrine to the sainted abbess, a textual monument that paradoxically, and probably against her wishes, transformed her simplicity and passivity into the stuff of heroism. In so doing, Bede's hymn establishes Æthelthryth's eternal virtue as a defining trait of the East Anglian church that enables it to be accommodated securely within the larger *ecclesia gentis Anglorum*.

Bede's versified elegy is specifically an epanaleptic abecedarian hymn, as scholars of the hymn have pointed out. In its progress through the Latin alphabet, it displays a strict linearity not to be found in the *Vita* itself; yet the epanalepsis, the repetition of words at the end of a clause that have also appeared at the clause's opening, has the effect of making us as readers look backwards even as we know we must move forwards. I defer to Harris's terminologically precise explanation: "Bede constructs his elegiac *Hymn to Aethelthryth* so that in each stanza the clauses run chiastically A1-B1/B2-A2, where A1 is repeated verbatim in A2, and B2 varies a theme from B1."[120] This structure results in a quasi-paradoxical recursive advancement that parallels the historical oscillation that Bede effects between past and present:

Alma Deus Trinitas, qui saecula cuncta gubernas,
  adnue iam coeptis, alma Deus Trinitas.

Bella Maro resonet; nos pacis dona canamus,
  munera nos Christi; bella Maro resonet.

Carmina casta mihi, fedae non raptus Helenae;
  luxus erit lubricis, carmina casta mihi.

Dona superna loquar, miserae non proelia Troiae;
  terra quibus gaudet, dona superna loquar.

(God, nourishing Trinity, you who govern all the ages,
  grant now this undertaking, God, nourishing Trinity.

Let Virgil echo wars, let us sing the gifts of peace;
  let us sing the rewards of Christ, let Virgil echo wars.

Chaste songs for me, not the abduction of shameful Helen;
  sumptuousness suits the inconstant, chaste songs for me.

I will speak of heavenly gifts, not of wretched Troy's battles;
  I will speak of heavenly gifts by which the earth rejoices.)[121]

The beginning of the *carmen* leads us back to the beginning of time and beyond, since from Bede's perspective the everlasting Trinity precedes and frames temporality itself. We move quickly forward, however, to postlapsarian *saecula*, the epochs of the Trojan War and of Vergil's later poetic celebration of it. Storied though they may be, epic battles pale in comparison to Æthelthryth, the greatest of "the gifts of peace," even as the abandoned Roman *civitatula* of *Grantacæstir* must yield pride of place to Ely, adorned with the marble sarcophagus taken away from the ruined fort. Employing the "outdoing" *topos*,[122] Bede exalts the nobility of Æthelthryth's life, and by extension elevates his own Life above the subject matter of Vergil's *Aeneid*. "The themes of grand secular poetry are devalued in contrasts," as Paul Szarmach argues; "[t]he foundation myth of the West cannot equal the celebration of the life of Æðeldreda and the *dona superna* that are the poet's theme."[123] Lofty poetic subjects such as the Troy legend could be invoked even in this context because they inspired admiration, even Bede's; the historian was not trying to disparage the Greco-Roman cultural patrimony. Rather, as Harris points out, "Bede is consciously writing in a 'modern' Christian age, viewing the classical past as ancient and outdated."[124] According to Szarmach, the *HE* is "a collective hagiography or a compendium of early Anglo-Saxon saints, whatever else scholars may wish it to be,"[125] so in this context, and from Bede's viewpoint, the virginal Æthelthryth may be said to have built upon and superseded Aeneas' accomplishments without calling into question the latter's validity as *comparanda*.[126]

As Winthrop Wetherbee has observed, Bede's engagement with Vergil suggests neither hostility nor parody but rather "domestication":

> As in dealing with the intractable elements in the culture of his own day, his approach to the most influential of classical authors is one of clear-sighted tolerance, and enables him to establish a *modus vivendi* in which the potentially disruptive force of Vergil's eloquence is neutralized; ... Bede's appropriation of Vergil ... is one more example of his unique ability to recognize value in the product of an alien culture and make it serve his own sure Christian purpose.[127]

The effect is not unlike that of Ely Abbey's own reuse and reinterpretation of a Roman funerary artefact to honour Æthelthryth herself.[128] *Romanitas* is not limited, however, to Vergil and colonial military outposts; it also includes virgin saints like Agatha, Eulalia, Thecla, Euphemia, Agnes, and Cecilia (*HE* IV.20, pp. 398–9). All were venerated by the medieval church for having endured martyrdom at the hands of pagan

Romans; all are adduced by Bede as champions of self-sacrificing Christian devotion whose glory Æthelthryth matches or outdoes.

With all due respect to the East Anglian abbess and to her Northumbrian hagiographer, it must be said that her escape from Ecgfrith was a good deal less dramatic than Thecla's rescue from being raped, burnt at the stake, and devoured by wild animals; nor can her marriage to him have been as excruciating as the torments and executions of Agnes, Cecilia, Eulalia, and Euphemia. Bede's point, however, is not to prove exact similarity between Æthelthryth and the Roman saints but rather to show that England has produced a paragon of sanctity worthy of being named with them. His English heroine can claim a place on the family tree of illustrious East Angles (King Anna having been her father), but even more impressive to Bede's way of thinking is a lineage that connects her to victims of state-sponsored torture in the days of the empire. At least one member, then, of the Northumbrian historian's "sanctified East Anglian royal family," as Christine Fell has called it,[129] has managed to obtain holiness without having to be killed.

Charters of land "substituted permanence for precariousness,"[130] but in their own way the *Vita* and hymn likewise elevate the abbess of Ely beyond time by figuring her home environment as the foundation of her transcendence, a process that synthesizes the local, national, and spiritual. The effect instantiates on a small scale a pattern that Anthony Smith discerns globally, in which nations create ethnic self-consciousness out of diverse kinds of text that provide pleasure while enhancing the enterprise of nationalism:

> [E]thnic symbols provide satisfying forms, and ethnic myths are conveyed in apt genres, for communication and mobilization. As they emerge from the collective experiences of successive generations, the myths coalesce and are edited into chronicles, epics and ballads, which combine cognitive maps of the community's history and situation with poetic metaphors of its sense of dignity and identity. The fused and elaborated myths provide an overall framework of meaning for the ethnic community, a *mythomoteur*, which "makes sense" of its experiences and defines its "essence."[131]

Collectively, the many spiritual triumphs recorded in the *HE* prove Bede's England to be eminently worthy of admiration within the cosmos of Christendom; this much has become a near-truism of scholarly comment on the book's purpose. If we also bear in mind, though, that *provinciae* such as those of the Northumbrians, Mercians, West Saxons, and East Angles were more politically palpable to Bede than England was, that "the wider concept of the *gens Anglorum*" coexisted with "the political reality of the several *gentes* who inhabited *provinciae* and were ruled by kings,"[132] then of necessity the *mythomoteur* of regional sanctity that Bede constructed in his Life of Æthelthryth would have empowered East Anglia's prestige first and England's second. Either as myths or as mechanical contrivances, motors work well only if all their moving parts are in good repair, and Bede needed to show that the part originally broken by Rædwald had indeed been fixed by Æthelthryth. It is true that, as David Pelteret has pointed out, "the literary virtuosity of Bede's composition serves only to distract us from Æthelthryth's physical presence and her accomplishments by shifting our focus away from her to the abstraction celebrated by the poem, Virginity."[133] Nevertheless, in emphasizing her bodily intactness, Bede established the soundness of the English church in a place where the "true" faith (as he would have understood it) had been undermined to the harm of *Britannia*.

Conclusion: Overlapping Identities

In this chapter I've argued that Bede's Æthelthryth embodies a certain form of East Anglian identity, the assertion of total Christian self-denial in a way that supersedes Rædwald's accommodation of paganism. Yet nothing prevented Æthelthryth from having several social identities; and the caveats in this regard that I offered in the Introduction, with regard to East Anglia as a place, surely apply to the abbess of Ely as a person. As a noblewoman she was deployed to serve dynastic interests, as were her kinswomen; Bede introduces his readers to Æthelthryth in the first place by mentioning her arranged marriages. Such unions multiplied identities in the case of Seaxburh, too; prior to her own abbacy she had been queen of Kent and wife of Eorcenberht.[134] Eormenhild, Seaxburh's daughter and Æthelthryth's niece, had been married to King Wulfhere of Mercia before eventually becoming abbess of Ely in her own right.[135] Monasteries, like dynasties, *gentes*, and individual persons, were not exclusively defined by their immediate regional surroundings, as the influence of Frankish monasteries on religious houses in and out of East Anglia reveals.[136]

Nevertheless, the vicissitudes of aristocratic and religious life in early England manifested themselves differently in different communities. To illuminate the emplaced quality of the peoples described by Bede, Clare Lees and Gillian Overing have recently adapted Alan Thacker's insights on space and sanctity to their own work on saints' cults:

> Getting one's own saint – and thereby becoming a focus and *locus* for holy relics – not only puts a community on the map but also *creates* that map.

> Local saints designate the coordinates of place and region in geographic, political, and spiritual terms. Indeed, the saint, the relic, and/or the shrine carry the power to particularize place, to make a geographic and spiritual purview; these are particularly profound examples of the sacred jurisdiction of place.[137]

These arguments help to shed light on Bede's spiritual chorography of Ely by enabling us to discern Æthelthryth's cult as a living landmark, which completed East Anglia's ecclesiastical and ideological fortification long after the kingdom had lost its military hegemony. Æthelthryth's "virginitatis integritate gloriosa" becomes proof in Bede's history that East Anglia's earlier defining rupture with Canterbury has been healed for good. If, as Christine Fell argues, "Ely probably faded into oblivion after Seaxburh's death" to be resurrected only by Æthelwold in the late tenth century,[138] then Bede will have prized all the more deeply Æthelthryth's personal "power to particularize place" (to borrow Lees and Overing's phrase). On the other hand, if Ely's status as an *Eigenkloster* increased the chances for the outpost's survival, Bede might not have objected too strenuously to such an arrangement; if nothing else, a royally sponsored monastic community would strengthen the enduring link between church and *stirps* on East Anglia's western border.

As Barbara Yorke has observed, aristocratic early English women maintained lifelong and influential familial bonds even in the cloister.[139] Although distaste for Coldingham may well have prompted Æthelthryth to seek a new home, the remark that "she was ... appointed abbess" ("facta est abbatissa") at Ely may be Bede's way of intimating that her relatives in East Anglia were still working on her behalf, over long distances. Her spiritual aspirations may have been fulfilled by dynastic manoeuvrings rather than being thwarted by them.[140] In claiming that she established her own religious house at Ely, though, Bede emphasizes her agency: once installed, Æthelthryth is said to have become, as we have seen already, "the virgin mother of many virgins dedicated to God."[141] In the *HE*, her spiritual relationships are portrayed more lovingly than her familial ties, but the latter are by no means effaced; even an *Eigenkloster* could house lofty transcendent aspirations.

Many places in the *HE* are said to have undergone change through evangelization, the very process whereby Bede shows any kind of change happening for the better.[142] Not all English *provinciae* improved uniformly, and some witnessed spectacular cultural transformation because of the specific leaders who effected it. Æthelthryth's corner of East Anglia in particular proves to be a scene of renovation on a grand and even epic scale, or so Bede implies when he exalts the abbess's glory over that of Aeneas. Her triumph is also her country's, and her earlier marriages to Middle Anglian and Northumbrian leaders fortify rather than dilute East Anglia's distinctness by signalling her own family's efforts to prolong the kingdom's survival via strategic wedlock. Her eventual break from Ecgfrith may have undermined these efforts by jeopardizing the alliance with Northumbria, but that is a political reality evaded by Bede, at whose hands a Fenland *monasterium* more than makes up for the country's diminished secular clout. Although Bede never uses the phrase *mulier fortis* to describe Æthelthryth, his gloss on the trope in his commentary on Proverbs 31 – quoted in the previous chapter – prizes the church-as-woman for cultivating in "missis ubique doctoribus" ("teachers sent everywhere") the virtue of bringing in "audientibus" ("listeners") who become believers in Christ.[143] His Æthelthryth exemplifies the church's mission and inspires a mixed community of men and women to imitate her; they help to compose an East Anglia in which far-reaching pastoral work outlasts political overlordship.

3
Solace for a Client-King: Felix's *Vita sancti Guthlaci*

Felix, an eighth-century monk, is known only for his *Vita sancti Guthlaci* (*VSG*), which he claims to have written for Ælfwald, king of the East Angles (r. ca. 713–49).[1] Thanks to his explicit reference to a named patron identifiable from other sources, it is possible to assign to the *Vita* "a date somewhere between 730 and 740."[2] Understanding why Ælfwald commissioned the text poses a more intriguing challenge. Medieval kings and nobles not infrequently patronized works of hagiography and history (e.g. Bede's *HE*), so the fact that this work was royally sponsored is in itself unsurprising. What is surprising, as D.P. Kirby put it, is that this is "rather strangely an East Anglian piece of hagiography about a Mercian saint."[3] Kirby's puzzlement is shared by others, myself included, despite Bertram Colgrave's influential supposition that

> the favourable picture of King Æthelbald in the Life, and the important place he occupies, suggest that the relationship between Æthelbald and Ælfwald was good at the time Felix was writing. It may well be that Æthelbald had taken refuge in East Anglia during the exile and so, though according to Bede all English provinces were subject to him, yet he had grateful remembrances of kindnesses received during his time of exile.[4]

Colgrave's hypothesis points to collaboration between the two *provinciae* to promote the hermit's cult, a joint enterprise that would have reinforced the Christianization of south-eastern England, not least by showing that Æthelthryth's success in the Fens could be repeated.

The initiative may have been a dynastic family undertaking. Ælfwald had an important monastic connection in the person of Ecgburh, an East Anglian noblewoman whom Felix identifies as an early patron of the Fenland hermit's cult.[5] Abbess of the Mercian house of Repton, where Guthlac had spent two formative years, she was also a daughter of the

East Anglian king Ealdwulf and therefore probably Ælfwald's own sister.[6] "Perhaps," Audrey Meaney speculates, "it was because of his sister's friendship with Guthlac that the East Anglian king [Ælfwald] asked Felix to write the *Life* of a Mid Anglian saint."[7] Penda's aggression in the mid-seventh century would have made it desirable for the East Anglian dynasty in the mid-eighth to contribute to a religious culture shared with its old enemies across the Fenland. The Mercians coalesced gradually and fitfully as a people,[8] often overawing their neighbours in the process; it may thus have been as an act of self-preservation that, as Alan Thacker speculates, Ælfwald "intended the work as a tribute to his overlord."[9] If this was the case, both patron and hagiographer used a saint's life to legitimize Mercian dynastic interests.[10]

The present chapter accepts Colgrave's theory that "the relationship between Æthelbald and Ælfwald was good," but it argues that their relationship was not so good that the latter ruler could have afforded to remain complacent about the former's increasing power or about the East Anglian kingdom's own future. As Thacker suggests, the *VSG* may have been written as a form of "tribute"; nevertheless, the East Anglian royal house had its own dignity, prestige, and independence to safeguard, and it may be supposed that Ælfwald supported Guthlac's cult and *Vita* to compete, not just to cooperate, with the Mercian ruling dynasty. Rivalries of all sorts – between abbeys, kingdoms, individuals – existed in contested spaces, or "spheres of influence" as Tim Pestell terms them in his discussion of relationships between East Anglia and Mercia.[11] The overlap between the "spheres" of these two polities lay in the land of the Middle Angles, a conglomeration of tribes gradually swallowed up by them in the seventh century;[12] their territory included not only Guthlac's Crowland but also the areas around Peterborough and Ramsey. In retrospect Middle Anglia, dominated by the Fens, is easily viewed as a transitional and volatile area;[13] and if the Mercians or *Mierce* were already "the 'Marcher-people' or 'borderers,' that is surely *not* those living adjacent to the border, but rather those living between borders, those in the middle of others' edges,"[14] then the Middle Angles must have been the Marchers' Marchers. Barbara Yorke, however, reminds us that Bede saw the Middle Angles as a *gens* in their own right (*HE* I.15 and III.21) and "believed they should have their own bishopric even though they were not always politically or episcopally independent."[15] A certain fluidity in their status is detectable in the case of Ely, placed in East Anglia by Bede (*HE* IV.19, pp. 396–7) but later absorbed by the Mercians.[16] In the *VSG* Middle Anglia as a whole is an invisible medium, discernible only in a criss-cross of "regnal"[17] initiatives originating from Mercia on one side and East Anglia on the other; it is a charged "borderland," "frontier zone," or transitional area rather than a sharply delineated geopolitical entity. Represented chiefly by Crowland and the inhabitants of its periphery, the district emerges through negotiations between two militarily superior polities as a virtual stage on which those polities' own identities are projected and performed.[18]

One such performance seems to have been executed by Ecgburh, who as abbess of Repton and as an East Anglian princess possesses two attributed social identities in Felix and perhaps harboured dual loyalties as well. Her activities in the cloister potentially served Mercian dynastic purposes; on the other hand, as a noblewoman she may have identified less with her adoptive territory than with her native *provincia*, not unlike Æthelthryth. The fact that Felix refers to her as an East Anglian and not just as an abbess of Repton shows his desire to underscore her ties to Ælfwald's family and that family's strategic interests. In his 2004 book *Landscapes of Monastic Foundation*, in an aside concerning the rivalry between the abbeys of Ramsey and Bury in the promotion of St. Edmund's cult in the late tenth century, Tim Pestell points out that "as a similar principle, few people seem to have taken King Ælfwald commissioning Felix to write his *Life of Saint Guthlac* as evidence for eighth-century East Anglian claims for Mercian territory."[19] Since then, Nicholas Higham has argued that Ælfwald's commissioning of the *VSG* represents deliberate East Anglian poaching on a Mercian saint: "the East Anglian establishment had ambitions regarding the future of this fenland cult site [of Crowland]. Indeed, dynastic ambitions may provide one explanation for the commissioning of Felix's *Life* by the king."[20] These arguments have received serious consideration,[21] and I subscribe to them myself even if I disagree with Higham's accompanying claim that "Æthelbald's stature is ... systematically minimised by Felix" so that East Anglian cultural and political aims may be furthered.[22] Because Felix shows the Mercian nobleman befriending Guthlac and later acting as the cult's chief secular patron, Catherine Cubitt is surely correct to assert that Felix "legitimises the rule of Aethelbald"[23] rather than detracting from it.

So we have, then, a Life of Guthlac that simultaneously bolsters the prestige of the Mercian king Æthelbald and seeks to appropriate a Mercian cult for East Anglian dynastic ends, as implied by the very fact of Ælfwald's commission. The conundrum becomes even more perplexing if we suppose that Felix "could have been a clerk of the East Anglian royal household" and if we also believe that the Mercian orientation of the text, "together with Crowland's location in the Gyrwe and Guthlac's early period at Repton, suggests that Felix was attempting to establish Guthlac's appeal within a pan-Mercian context."[24] This scenario envisions a member of the East Anglian royal court using a hagiographical commission to extend Mercian cultural influence. But why would he have done so? One answer is that Ælfwald always intended the book as homage to his overlord Æthelbald, as has frequently been claimed. Another possible answer is that the *VSG* is a *speculum principis*,[25] and that Felix is indirectly offering spiritual and political advice to Ælfwald, the advice being that Mercia's ascendancy makes it incumbent upon an East Anglian *subregulus* to learn from Guthlac's humility.[26] A weaker king would do better to imitate a hermit's self-effacement than to appropriate a stronger ruler's cult to increase his own "cultural capital."[27] Laying claim to Guthlac would increase Wuffing prestige but at the cost of straining relations with the more formidable Mercians. My argument, then, is that although Felix credits Ælfwald with the *Vita*'s commission, he also tacitly warns him against expropriating a key agent of Mercian sanctity and perhaps even proposes the eremitic life as a legitimate career path for his royal patron.

Overview of the *VSG*

Though often discussed and analysed, Felix's account of Guthlac's life warrants summary. A stylistically complex text, it goes well beyond the laconic entry on Guthlac in the Anglo-Saxon Chronicle (ASC) *s.a.* 714: "Her forþferde Guþlac se halga" ("Here [i.e. in this year] Guthlac the saint passed away").[28] Following the author's dedication to Ælfwald are a conventional but spirited justification for the work, a list of his fifty-three chapters, and then the story proper. We are told that during the reign of the Mercian king Æthelred, styled "inlustris Anglorum re[x]" ("illustrious king of the English"), the aristocratic Penwalh and Tette had a son whom they named Guthlac and whose birth had been heralded with a miraculous sign from heaven. Guthlac proved the perfect child, tractable and affectionate, but as a young man became warlike, butchering his enemies and destroying their lands. Nine years of bloodshed elapsed, after which Guthlac's foes *quieverunt* ("kept the peace," pp. 80–1), even though the hostilities seem to have been initiated by our protagonist. Eventually, at age twenty-four, he underwent a road-to-Damascus conversion that led him to abandon comrades, family, and homeland to take up the religious life at the Mercian monastery of Repton.[29] After two years of study there, he went forth to pursue the hermit's vocation in the forbidding eastern Fenland aided by his supernatural protector St. Bartholomew.

Once settled, Guthlac implements his martial training.[30] Inter alia he vanquishes diabolical, Brittonic-speaking spirits; exorcises a devil from a malevolent visitor named Beccel, who stays on as a fellow hermit; triumphs over yet more demons, disguised as wild animals; masters the area's avian life; reveals to a local abbot the deceitfulness of two of the latter's servants; and cures the visiting Æthelbald's retainers Ecga of "an unclean spirit" (§42, pp. 130–3) and Ofa of a wound caused by a thorn (§45, pp. 138–41). Mercian overtures towards Guthlac continue: Bishop Headda arrives and consecrates him a priest (§47, pp. 144–7), Headda apparently being the same prelate who headed the Mercian see of Lichfield from ca. 690 until his death ca. 716–27.[31]

Significant East Anglian contact is belated, limited to Guthlac's exorcism of the young aristocrat Hwætred, driven insane by an evil spirit (§41, pp. 126–31), and to Ecgburh's gifting of a leaden coffin and linen burial shroud to Guthlac himself.[32] As his benefactor, the abbess is unsubtle in staking her claim to the hermit's posthumous reputation; but in starkly evoking Guthlac's afterlife, her funerary gifts only place in that much higher relief the lack of sustained East Anglian involvement in Guthlac's life. By contrast, the Mercian connections to the hermit remain strong throughout his time at Crowland.

Guthlac lives in eremitic purity for fifteen years until his death; afterwards his holiness manifests itself in miracles. The most important of these occur twelve months after his burial, when his body is found to be incorrupt; his devoted sister Pega then houses it in a shrine and so inaugurates the famous cult. Unlike Æthelthryth's tomb, which was reconstructed and beautified by a religious community with no apparent royal involvement (that Bede was aware of), Guthlac's shrine is said to have been enriched by King Æthelbald himself (*VSG* §51, pp. 162–3), evidently in gratitude for the consolation and hospitality he had received twice from the Crowland hermit while fleeing the anger of Ceolred, then king of the Mercians. The first of those two occasions took place while Guthlac was still alive (§49, pp. 148–51), the second after he had died, when Guthlac's spirit came to Æthelbald to reassure him that he would soon triumph over his foe to become king of the Mercians in his own right by the grace of God (§52, pp. 164–7). The friendship between king and recluse led, or at least was thought to have led, to tangible benefits for the monastic community that eventually arose at Crowland; much later, Orderic Vitalis (1075–1142), as a guest of that community, would report that Æthelbald had granted land and exemptions to Guthlac before the latter's death.[33]

Identifying the King: Felix's Greetings to Ælfwald

As the above summary shows, the *VSG* gives the impression of having been commissioned by a Mercian rather than by an East Anglian king. Its lopsidedness in this regard has been noted often;[34] one imagines

Felix tossed by two competing yet unequal political tides and obliged to yield to the greater pull of Mercia, much as Guthlac's cult itself appears to have been so obliged before, during, and after the posthumous saint's translation.[35] The Prologue, which praises not Æthelbald but Ælfwald, is thus all the more arresting for its concealment of the Mercian preoccupations that permeate the *VSG*:

In Domino dominorum domino meo, mihi prae ceteris regalium primatuum gradibus dilectissimo Ælfwaldo regi, Orientalium Anglorum rite regimina regenti, Felix catholicae congregationis vernaculus, perpetuae prosperitatis in Christo salutem.

(In the name of the Lord of Lords, to my lord King Ælfwald, beloved by me beyond any other of royal rank, who rules by right over the realm of the East Angles, Felix, a servant of the Catholic community, sends greetings and wishes him everlasting happiness in Christ. [Prologue, pp. 60–1])

Conventional though it may be, the dedication is the work of a highly talented author.[36] Felix tactfully honours Ælfwald as a king, as a self-assured ruler fully in command of his own *gens* in south-eastern England, rather than as the mere promoter of a saint's cult. The latter role will go on to eclipse the former in the *VSG*, but at this early juncture the hagiographer employs textual diplomacy in a way that establishes his own corporate monastic identity and – to borrow a term of Umberto Eco's – "actuates" its royal patron both as a culturally literate defender of St. Guthlac's prestige and as the lord of his own people.[37]

In this latter regard the opening sentence anticipates the king's self-styling in a letter to Archbishop Boniface ca. 747–9, the dedication of which reads as follows:

AⳁΩ domino gloriosissimo et cum omni honoris affectu venerantissimo Bonifatio archiepiscopo Aelbuualdus [*sic*] Aestanglorum Deo donante regia potestate fretus simul et tota abbatia cum omni congregationi servorum Dei in nostra provincia altithronum pro ecclesiarum incolomitate die noctuque precibus pulsantem in Deo remuneratori omnium salutem.

(To Archbishop Boniface, illustrious and reverend master, gifted with every honorable quality, Aelbwald [*sic*], ruler by the grace of God over the East Anglians, together with the whole abbey and community of the servants of God in our country, beseeching Him who is enthroned on high with prayers day and night for the welfare of the churches, send greeting in the name of God, the rewarder of all.)[38]

Despite differences of emphasis, both dedications stress that the East Anglian king governs alone. Felix claims that his patron "rules by right" ("rite … regenti"); Ælfwald asserts that his power derives from God ("Deo donante regia potestate").[39] The Letter to Boniface associates the king's authority with a *provincia* rather than with a mere *regio*;[40] in doing so, it implies continuity of royal status between Ælfwald and his predecessors. One assumes the distinction would not have been lost on Boniface, a shrewd stylist in his own right who could adapt the tone of his letters to royal or ecclesiastical correspondents as circumstances required.[41]

Felix's address to his patron in the *VSG* is vaguer than Ælfwald's self-styling in the Letter to Boniface. The former refrains from defining the territory of the East Angles as either a *provincia* or a *regio*, perhaps because the hagiographer wished to avoid committing himself on this score. Nevertheless, in writing for a ruler who knew courtly rhetorical conventions and orbited within the Bonifatian epistolary system, Felix was aware of the need to flatter, so although it avoids the word *provincia*, his phrasing shows him delectating in the language of lordship – "Domino dominorum domino meo," "regi … regimina regenti" – in a way that was surely calculated both to please his addressee and to advertise Felix himself as a scrupulous advisor and *auctor*.

Eighth-century English regional identity derived as much from loyalty to a king as from geographical affinity.[42] Although Felix may have been a Mercian, it is perhaps likelier that he was an East Angle.[43] Then again, he may have been a Middle Angle; if so, and if he was thus obliged to negotiate between Mercian and East Anglian loyalties, then he was in roughly the same position as Barbara Yorke's hypothetical border-dweller, "[s]omeone living in the Peak District" who "may have been both one of the Pecsaete, answerable to a local lord or administrator, and at various points in the seventh century also a Mercian or a Northumbrian depending on the destination of his tribute payments."[44] Felix will have needed to reconcile East Anglian with Mercian political pressures if, Janus-like, he was obliged to look in two different directions to stake out safe Middle Anglian ground.

His tactful dedication to Ælfwald notwithstanding, Felix goes on to acknowledge the earlier Mercian king Æthelred, in whose reign Guthlac had been born, as "inlustris Anglorum re[x]" ("the illustrious king of the English," §1, pp. 72–3). At the end of the *VSG*, as the summary given earlier indicates, he even goes so far as to have Guthlac prophesy that once Æthelbald assumes the throne he will enjoy God's favour and be made "principem populorum" ("chief over the peoples"; §49, pp. 148–9). Furthermore, speaking in his own voice, Felix adds: "Ex illo enim tempore usque in hodiernum diem infulata regni ipsius felicitas per tempora consequentia de die in diem crescebat" ("For from that time until the present day, his happiness as king over his realm has grown in succeeding years from day to day"; §52, pp. 166–7). The phrase "principem populorum" seems to mean "wielder of *imperium*" in Bede's sense, though it coyly omits to add *Anglorum* ("of the English").[45] The reference to Æthelbald's *felicitas* is a bigger understatement, for it was not only the Mercian ruler's "happiness" that had grown but also his *imperium* over all the kingdoms of the southern English. Whether or not Bede disliked Mercian hegemony south of the Humber, he identified it as such; Felix, living far closer than Bede did to both the Mercian and East Anglian heartlands, and writing for an East Anglian king, resorted to circumlocution.[46]

He also drew upon rhetorical tradition, deploying phrases and imagery that allowed him to adopt a corporate monastic scholarly persona, the guise of the early-medieval public intellectual connected to networks of textual authority.[47] For example, Felix claims that he has composed his *Life* of Guthlac "[i]ussionibus tuis obtemperans ... non absque procacitatis inpudentia" ("[i]n obedience to your commands, though not without a bold forwardness"; Prologue, pp. 60–1). Here one detects the trope of the learned person's duty to teach others,[48] a *topos* that allows Felix to proclaim Æthelbald as the true *princeps populorum* however much in accordance with right or rite Ælfwald may have ruled his own *gens*. The latter, as an East Anglian king, may have objected to the often brutal realities of Mercian overlordship, but he could ill afford to ignore them. Literary subtlety allowed Felix to be both honest and politic.

Guthlac and Ælfwald, Mired in the World

Conventional language will have come in handy if any of Felix's readers besides Ælfwald bristled at the *VSG*'s pro-Mercian politics. As Gernot Wieland has persuasively argued, the hagiographer probably had in mind a reading and/or listening public that went beyond the solitary figure of the king.[49] It needn't have been numerically imposing to be influential and may have been similar to the audience Bede had envisaged for the *HE*, a coterie public limited to the Northumbrian ruler and "only ... the nobles immediately associated with him."[50] Felix, anticipating criticism from some in his audience, made this appeal: "pestiferis obtrectantium incantationibus aures obturantes, velut transvadato vasti gurgitis aequore, ad vitam sancti Guthlaci stilum flectendo quasi ad portum vitae pergemus" ("let us stop our ears against the pestiferous incantations of our detractors as though we were traversing the waters of a vast whirlpool and let us steer our pen towards the life of

St. Guthlac as though we were making for the haven of life"; Prologue, pp. 62–3). Inveighing against *obtrectantes* recalls stylized anxiety about public censure and the difficulty of fulfilling a powerful patron's request.[51] By using this rhetorical commonplace, Felix implicitly likens appreciation of his work to salvation, and criticism of his work to an impediment thereto. His wording both figures Guthlac's own "portum vitae" in the Fens as a gateway to heaven and positions Felix as his readers' guide.

Writing has long been compared to sailing through turbulent seas.[52] Felix uses the trope to imply a commonality between his own scholarly labours and his protagonist's toil in the Fens, and additionally to make himself and Guthlac out to be, in effect, Odysseus figures tormented by sirenic adversaries,[53] demons in Guthlac's case, envious textual saboteurs in his own. Going into the Fenland, whether as spiritual abode or as literary subject, entails risks that build character.

The *VSG* famously describes the formidable landscape in a passage that reveals Felix's keen interest in threshold states of being, or liminality (spiritual, psychological, social), especially in the depiction of Guthlac's encounter with supernatural forces. The hermit's struggle against proto-Welsh-speaking demons, I argue later in this chapter, is a red herring that Felix lays in our path to distract us from tensions between the East Angles and the Mercians.[54] More certainly, the setting of Guthlac's supernatural battles dramatizes the heroism of Guthlac himself (as commentators on the *VSG* have often pointed out) even as it establishes a sharp distinction between the Fens and civilization (again, an oft-repeated assertion in scholarship on the text):

> Nec plura, intervenientibus aliquorum dierum cursibus, cum seniorum licita volentia, incoepto aeternae prosperitatis itinere, solitudinem invenire perrexit. Est in meditullaneis Brittanniae partibus inmensae magnitudinis aterrima palus, quae, a Grontae fluminis ripis incipiens, haud procul a castello quem dicunt nomine Gronte, nunc stagnis, nunc flactris, interdum nigris fusi vaporis laticibus, necnon et crebris insularum nemorumque intervenientibus flexuosis rivigarum anfractibus, ab austro in aquilonem mare tenus longissimo tractu protenditur. Igitur cum supradictus vir beatae memoriae Guthlac illius vastissimi heremi inculta loca conperisset, caelestibus auxiliis adiutus, rectissimo callis tramite tenus usque perrexit.
>
> (Briefly, after some days had passed, with the willing consent of the elders, he started out on the path to eternal bliss and proceeded to look for a solitary place. There is in the midland district of Britain a most dismal fen of immense size, which begins at the banks of the river Granta not far

> from the camp which is called Cambridge, and stretches from the south as far north as the sea. It is a very long tract, now consisting of marshes, now of bogs, sometimes of black waters overhung by fog, sometimes studded with wooded islands and traversed by the windings of tortuous streams. So when this same man of blessed memory, Guthlac, had learned about the wild places of this vast desert, he made his way thither with divine assistance by the most direct route. [§24, pp. 86–7])

Liminality characterizes Guthlac's passage from secular to consecrated life but also the Fens themselves, where the natural and supernatural meet in a border zone separating the Mercian and East Anglian kingdoms.[55] Katherine O'Brien O'Keeffe, commenting on the district's ambiguous nature, observes that the *VSG*'s Crowland is both land and sea, "at once contiguous territory and clearly marked as apart," "known and unknown," an adaptation of the desert motif in Evagrius's *Vita sancti Antonii* "to produce the Crowland fen as a particular space of incompatibles."[56] The semi-liquid borderland looks like the virtual antithesis of civilization.[57]

Appropriately, Felix describes the place with the imagery of churning waters. Yet the reference to "intervenientibus flexuosis rivigarum anfractibus" ("the intermittent windings of its [i.e. the Fens'] tortuous streams")[58] parallels passages elsewhere in the text, where it is the everyday world familiar to human beings, not the liminal Fenland, that is characterized as a hostile aquatic environment. Felix has already urged us to guard against his Siren-like critics, as if braving calumny were like crossing the sea of an enormous whirlpool ("transvadato vasti gurgitis aequore"; Prologue, pp. 62–3). He later observes that Guthlac was rescued from secular life as if "de tumido aestuantis saeculi gurgite, de obliquis mortalis aevi anfractibus" ("from the eddying whirlpool of these turbid times, from the tortuous paths of this mortal age"; §27, pp. 92–3). The vortical imagery also recalls Guthlac's conversion, when he "fluctuantes inter saeculi gurgites iactaretur" ("was being storm-tossed … amid the whirling waves of the world"; §18, pp. 80–1). As conventional as all this language may be, it is being used pointedly, to link the Fenland with the world beyond it, and to connect both to the imagined challenges of writing the *VSG*.[59]

Guthlac's much-emphasized renunciations are therefore less total than they look. To be sure, Felix's Crowland is indisputably different from Bede's Ely: while the latter presents no formidable obstacle to Æthelthryth's homecoming, the former drives away most would-be inhabitants, except for Guthlac. The contrast, of course, is down to deliberate and selective literary emphasis. As Jack Ravensdale has observed, "[t]he eremitical tradition could fulfil itself in isolation in small communities: the hagiographer's description of St. Guthlac's settlement at Crowland in the demon-tormented fens could well have been written of any of them."[60] The fact that Felix's Crowland doesn't resemble Bede's Ely says much about the two authors' distinct projects. One of the chief aims of the *VSG* seems to have been to persuade Ælfwald, the work's patron, that Guthlac's corner of the Fenland was simultaneously forbidding and attractive. "In the eighth century," Katherine O'Brien O'Keeffe plausibly surmises, "however cooperatively subordinate East Anglian kings might have been, they must have looked both nervously and hopefully to the fens as a buffer with their Mercian overlords."[61] As both retreat from and source of danger, Felix's dualistic Fenland makes an appropriate subject of contemplation for a mid-eighth-century East Anglian king who was and was not master of his own house, a ruler of his own *gens* who also lived in the growing shadow of a foreign "princ[eps] populorum."

By imagining such an evocative environment and placing Guthlac in it, Felix performs an exquisitely delicate balancing act. He makes the hermit seem, at first, insulated from the world, much as St. Antony, his contemporaries, and his successors in Egypt are made to appear in earlier hagiography, which shows them rejecting altogether the fertile Nile valley "for its awesome antithesis, the neighboring desert."[62] The opposition between Mercia and Crowland seems just as stark. The latter is made out to be worlds apart from the former, whose value in terms of land-related service is reckoned at thirty thousand hides in the *Tribal Hidage*.[63]

The contrast, however, is more apparent than real because Guthlac's passage from civilization to solitude is not absolute, any more than the Fenland itself was utterly removed from the concerns of people dwelling in eastern England.[64] The warrior leaves behind only the secular Mercia, and that gradually, for an ascetic and sacred projection of that kingdom upon the Crowland fastness. His trajectory has him spend two years at Repton Abbey (§§20–4; pp. 84–7), a transitional period in which Guthlac learns monastic discipline without becoming a monk per se. Æthelthryth herself spent a short period of time in an intermediate place, Coldingham Abbey, linked to the Northumbrian dynasty, before leaving to found a religious house of her own on the East Anglian side of the Fens. Bede, we recall, blames no one for her move; although he notes that Coldingham had its shortcomings (*HE* IV.19, pp. 392–3; IV.25, pp. 420–7), he says only, and without explanation, that a year after entering that house Æthelthryth was appointed to lead Ely. Felix too steers clear of fault-finding when recounting Guthlac's stint at Repton and eventual departure for Crowland. Monastery and hermitage are complementary, their relationship supersessive not oppositional. Guthlac is said to surpass his confrères in piety, but not because of any deficiency in the monks, who in any event were won over by his earnestness at the beginning of his novitiate (notwithstanding their initial hostility) and whose own wholesome traits furnished him with models for imitation (§§21–3, pp. 84–7).[65]

In the story of Guthlac's religious life, the stint in a *coenobium* marks an important phase in the hero's spiritual growth.[66] A way station between the throng of the world and the solitude of the hermitage, Repton's communal life is portrayed as an intrinsic good in itself, not least because it provides Guthlac the opportunity to receive the Petrine tonsure, "misticam sancti Petri apostolorum proceris tonsuram accepit" (p. 84). This doubtless helps to distinguish him from those "pseudo-anachoritas diversarum religionum simulatores" ("false hermits and pretenders of various religions") whom Wigfrith, one of Bishop Headda's attendants, claims to have encountered among the Irish ("inter Scottorum ... populos," §46, pp. 142–3).[67] This specific kind of tonsure symbolizes orthodoxy and thus connects Mercia to Rome,[68] the symbolic "capital of Anglo-Saxon England" in Nicholas Howe's provocative phrase.[69] As a synecdoche for the Christianized Eternal City, the Roman tonsure follows Guthlac into the Fenland's depths as a reminder that the world, itself a fusion of the secular and the sacred, is always closer than we think as we read the *VSG*. Even Egypt's fourth-century anchoritic communities had lain close to towns, which provided them with resources and furnished them with the means to conceptualize their very vocation by enabling them to define their solitary existences contrastively. Pachomius, in Peter Brown's formulation, had transformed the Egyptian desert into "a 'counter-world,' a place where an alternative 'city could grow" out of nothing.[70] Felix exaggerates the harshness of the Fenland "desert,"[71] but he also praises the site of Guthlac's hermitage as a place of spiritual transformation where even the most ambitious secular lords can renounce the world without losing all contact with it.

A Desirable Desert

After first hearing of the Fens, Guthlac craves more information about them and so makes enquiries among nearby residents. The mere fact that there are people living thereabouts ("a proximantibus accolis," §25, pp. 88–9) suggests the area's desirability; even demon-infested Crowland must have had something to recommend it because Tatwine, a local, informs Guthlac "quam multi inhabitare temtantes propter incognita heremi monstra et diversarum formarum terrores reprobaverant" ("[in what way] many had attempted to dwell there, but had rejected it on account of the unknown portents of the desert and its terrors of various shapes"; §25, pp. 88–9). Would-be settlers have long been spooked by certain things that Tatwine leaves ill-defined: phantasms, cognitive shocks, multiform creatures that defy taxonomy.

Appropriately enough, the liminal zone of Crowland is located in the larger threshold area of Middle Anglia, a frontier space affected by the coinciding peripheries of Mercian and East Anglian "spheres of influence."[72] A linear border between the two polities need not have existed for the *VSG* to emphasize what Dick Harrison describes as "qualitatively important space" and "invisible cultural and geographical boundaries," as opposed to "the mostly hypothetical boundaries between early medieval *regna* that historians are so fond of trying to pin down on maps."[73] Had Guthlac hoped to gain specific information about Crowland, cartographic or otherwise, he would have been disappointed, *incognita monstra* and *terrores* being difficult landmarks to make sense of; nevertheless, undeterred he avails himself of the navigational skills of Tatwine, who transports him by skiff "per invia lustra inter atrae paludis margines" ("through trackless bogs within the confines of the dismal marsh"). Arriving at Crowland on 25 August, St. Bartholomew's feast day, Guthlac discovers that with the help of that saint and of God he can thrive in the wilderness: "[A]damato illius loci abdito situ velut a Deo sibi donato, omnes dies vitae suae illic degere directa mente devoverat" ("He loved the remoteness of the spot, seeing that God had given it him, and vowed with righteous purpose to spend all the days of his life there"; §25, pp. 88–9). He sees it as a *locus amoenus* even if nobody else does.[74]

Nevertheless, Guthlac is said to have returned to Repton to spend three final months there to take proper leave of his erstwhile companions. Afterwards, he returns to Crowland "quasi ad paternae hereditatis habitaculum" ("as though to a home inherited from his father"; §26, pp. 90–1). Though evoked only by way of simile, the mere suggestion of inheritance is striking,[75] marking the second time Felix has situated Guthlac in relation to his forebears, the first having been his glance at the warrior's ancestry (§§1–2, pp. 72–5).[76] In a saint's Life set in a borderland, it is noteworthy that a descendent of Icel, who "would appear to have been regarded as the founder of the dynasty and of the Mercian people,"[77] should be said to have made himself at home in undisputed territory, as if the site had been bequeathed by his father and, moreover, "granted" or "bestowed" (*donatus*) by God Himself as a divine birthright.

"We must not read too much into this passage, though," Eric John cautions, "since it is evident from the surviving wills that a homestead was sharply separated from 'land' in Anglo-Saxon thinking."[78] Felix, however, deliberately muddies this distinction by stabilizing the impermanent, by representing Guthlac's right to Crowland as de facto ownership of the land itself rather than as mere possession of the legal power to bequeath it or to determine how its goods or concomitant services will be exacted.[79] It is as if Felix were gently reminding Ælfwald that Crowland, though undergoing sanctification, was also a specifically Mercian royal patrimony.

Other Guthlac texts imply different concerns. In discussing the Old English *Guthlac A* in relation to Latin diplomas, Scott T. Smith writes that the poem "shares with those documents a conflation of the tenurial and the sacred within a reward of property for service and loyalty," but adds that the poem's "redemptive conflict" over the *beorg* between Guthlac and Bartholomew on one hand and the demons on the other "importantly occurs within an abstraction of place which frees it [i.e. the conflict] from the pressure of historical forces and context."[80] This analysis is commensurate with other pronouncements on *Guthlac A* that stress or assume its topical non-specificity.[81] Unlike Felix's *VSG*, which articulates a specific sense of place within the context of eighth-century politics, *Guthlac A* displays a more abstract poetics of emplacement, usually explained as the product of the tenth-century English Benedictine Reform movement.[82]

In comparison to the vernacular poem, the Old English prose *Life of Guthlac* is closer in spirit to the *VSG*.[83] Kelley M. Wickham-Crowley has adapted Sam Lucy's research on prehistoric tumuli to her analysis of the prose *Life*'s depiction of Guthlac's barrow:

> Beyond the Christianization of a pagan site ... Guthlac's claiming of a fen island and its burial mound may be an exercise of religious control over more than ghostly echoes: it asserts real power over the land, over the past, and over the imagination. For peoples who immigrated to Britain, staking such a claim links up with the mutable boundaries of water and land to extend their history in them, blending pasts and the present.[84]

Yet even more so than the Old English prose *Guthlac*, the *VSG* treats the Fenland not merely as the sum of its sinewy streams but also as the correlative of the processual ebb and flow of political aspiration.[85] Home to many previous occupants, the Crowland environs is always up for grabs. Only Guthlac, however, can consolidate the fluctuating landscape, for his settlement of it is compared to a lawful inheritance, which itself implies continuity of ownership over time. This implication, in turn, is grist for the mill of Mercian not East Anglian expansionism, for the duration of Guthlac's life and beyond.[86]

Despite settling what looks like forbidden ground, Guthlac comes into his own as a landowner. Within the context of his Life, the Fens are never so hostile or diabolical that ascetic devotion proves unable to tame them.[87] Indeed, Felix would have us believe that, appearances aside, Crowland and its environs are the real earthly paradise, and what lies outside them is a land of torments. Clare Lees and Gillian Overing have written that "places … are the means by which the general becomes local, by which we comprehend a sense of region."[88] Some localities do typify or at least recall their larger "national" cultures; others stand out and are said to be "unique" within them. The *VSG* manipulates readers' expectations of the "general" and the "local" by using – as we have seen – the imagery of whirlpools and serpentine waterways to attribute horrors to a specific Fenland landscape and to everything beyond it: Guthlac, we recall, was rescued from secular life as if "de tumido aestuantis saeculi gurgite, de obliquis mortalis aevi anfractibus" ("from the eddying whirlpool of these turbid times, from the tortuous paths of this mortal age," §27, pp. 92–3). Felix's metaphors project onto the temporal world those "eddying whirlpools" and "tortuous paths" usually thought to characterize the Fens uniquely.

Although the description of Crowland may well owe something to its author's first-hand knowledge of the place, landscape historians and scholars of saints' Lives have warned us that it draws on hagiographic convention.[89] A separate but related observation about the text's imagery, made earlier but worth repeating here, is that it recalls wording used elsewhere in the *VSG* to refer to secular life in general, and to the pressures of writing the *VSG* itself in particular (Prologue, pp. 62–3; §18, pp. 80–1). For Felix, whirlpools and tortuous rivers aptly conjure up this-worldly stresses and strains, perhaps too the burdens of secular rule in a kingdom long past its political prime. The remedy for "turbid times" is to be found in the very "dismal marsh" Guthlac calls home. If a Mercian nobleman can forsake worldly chaos for the hermit's life, so too can an East Anglian king. Although the *Vita* militates against the East Anglian dynasty's unproblematic appropriation of Guthlac's cult, it does hint that Ælfwald might emulate Guthlac's pious renunciation to remain in Æthelbald's good graces.

Cautionary Chorography: Roman *Gronta* and East Anglia's Limits

On one level, the site of Crowland embodies a negation of, even a "reproach" to (in Thomas Merton's sense of the word), the hectic secular life well known to Guthlac as a nobleman and to Ælfwald as a king.[90] The site's rude simplicity drives home the point:

> Erat itaque in praedicta insula tumulus agrestibus glaebis coacervatus, quem olim avari solitudinis frequentatores lucri ergo illic adquirendi defodientes scindebant, in cuius latere velut cisterna inesse videbatur; in qua vir beatae memoriae Guthlac desuper inposito tugurio habitare coepit.
>
> (Now there was in the said island a mound built of clods of earth which greedy comers to the waste had dug open, in the hope of finding treasure there; in the side of this there seemed to be a sort of cistern, and in this Guthlac the man of blessed memory began to dwell, after building a hut over it. [§28, pp. 92–5])

Though nothing like the Devil's Dyke or other earthworks, the tumulus proves adequate fortification for Guthlac by helping him resist diabolical temptations to make him give up Crowland and the hermit's life. St. Bartholomew arrives on the scene, "nec sopor illud erat" ("[n]or was it just a dream"; §29, pp. 96–7), and aids him in his struggle against despair. Subsequently Guthlac fends off two devils who try to persuade him to exceed reason and moderation in fasting (§30, pp. 100–1).[91] Several days later, a horde of grotesque demons attacks his "cellulam," "domum ac castellum" ("tiny cell," "home and castle"; §31, pp. 101–3), drags him through the Fens, and takes him "ad nefandas tartari fauces" ("to the accursed jaws of hell"; pp. 104–5), threatening to toss him in. Again Bartholomew intervenes, rescuing the hermit and cowing the demons into escorting him safely back to Crowland (§§32–3, pp. 106–9).

The text's tumulus or "mound"/"barrow" has attracted much scholarly attention.[92] The supernatural encounters that take place there have local relevance thanks to the adaptability of hagiographical convention to specific circumstances. Guthlac's Fenland barrow has known attacks from "avari solitudinis frequentatores," a phrase rendered by Colgrave as "greedy comers to the waste" but which may also be translated as "greedy frequenters of the wilderness." Either way, the place cannot have been completely forlorn if so many people frequented it, and Jan Peer Hartmann has recently noted that the noun *frequentatores* "perhaps indicat[es] more strongly some sort of ongoing clandestine and illicit behaviour."[93] Tatwine had spoken to Guthlac of would-be settlers who, one assumes, wished to exploit its visible resources; others apparently sought out treasures that lay hidden from view. Repeated visits by scofflaws recall Guthlac's own early predations as a freebooter within Mercian territory, his seizure of Crowland for himself,[94] and, for that matter, Ælfwald's poaching on Æthelbald's cultural property. In the *VSG*, Crowland boasts a many-layered history, with actors from each layer keen to help themselves to other layers.[95]

When, as we have seen already, Felix locates Crowland in that vast stretch of the Fens "a Grontae fluminis ripis incipiens, haud procul a castello quem dicunt nomine Gronte" ("begin[ning] at the banks of the river Granta not far from the camp which is called Cambridge"; §24, pp. 86–7), he adds further local, regnal, and international depth to his Fenland chorography. The localization orientates the text's readers in relation to the same *Grantacæstir* referred to by Bede in his account of Æthelthryth. Although Felix neglects to mention that the royal abbess's marble sarcophagus had come from that very place, Ælfwald cannot have been so "encyclopaedically lacking" as to have heard in the name of *Gronta* a mere *flatus vocis* that needed to be explained to him by Felix.[96] Audrey Meaney thinks that "it is unlikely that he [Ælfwald] would not have heard of Æthelthryth and very probably her sister too."[97] Even if the cult of those abbesses had been abandoned by the mid-eighth century, as Christine Fell has proposed, it is hard to believe that Ælfwald knew nothing of Æthelthryth's shrine at Ely and the strategic significance of *Gronta/Grantacæstir* in enhancing it.[98] Felix himself seems not to have read the *HE*, but he did know and borrow from Bede's prose *Life of St. Cuthbert* and from the anonymous *Life of St. Fursey*.[99] It is at least possible that Æthelthryth's absence from the *VSG* was the result of choice rather than of ignorance on its author's part. If, as Katherine O'Brien O'Keeffe supposes, "the short-lived marriage between Tondberht, a prince of the (Middle Anglian) South Gyrwas and the East Anglian princess, St. Æthelthryth (*c*. 652) suggests a related, perhaps defensive, political interest, given [the Mercian ruler] Penda's record of aggression,"[100] then Felix may have kept quiet about the royal abbess to avoid reminding Ælfwald or Æthelbald of the East Angles' earlier attempt to subject the Fens to monastic colonization. In any event, Æthelthryth's Ely disappears as a precedent to Guthlac's enterprise, and the marshy frontier zone between Mercia and East Anglia reverts to a quasi-"virgin" wilderness.[101]

Despite obvious differences between Bede's Ely and Felix's Crowland, in each setting the abandoned fort serves to recall Roman imperial authority. Occasionally the *caput totius mundi* figures in early English writings as the imagined if distant centre of Insular cultural renewal;[102] as D.P. Kirby observes, "[c]ommunications tended to bring the Anglo-Saxons back again and again to old Roman towns" abandoned by their former, British occupants.[103] Kirby warns that early English settlers valued utility over all else, such as the advantages for travel and commerce created by Roman roads; yet he concedes the prestige of association with Roman civilization itself.[104] Writers like Bede and Felix would have been especially alive to the power of even fragments of *Romanitas* to conjure up Britannia's earlier participation in a great empire; Felix, as discussed earlier, relies on Guthlac's Roman tonsure to place his hero and the Repton community squarely in the mainstream of orthodox Catholic practice. To invoke *Gronta* is to evoke cultural overlap: the old *castellum* might have reminded Ælfwald of his dynasty's claim to descent from Julius Caesar,[105] or of his familial relationship to Æthelthryth. Then again, thoughts of *Gronta* may have stimulated Æthelbald to equate expansion into the Fens with appropriation of East Anglia's vestigial (or purely notional) *Romanitas*. More certainly, Felix's allusion to the ruined fort renders the Fenland environs less forbidding and untamed than the phrase *aterrima palus* ("most dismal fen") suggests; and by linking Roman culture geographically to Guthlac's career, if only as a means of spatial orientation, the allusion also complements Felix's emphasis on Roman tonsuring as proof of Repton's orthodoxy.

Both details ground Guthlac in a cultural tradition that stretches from antiquity to his own day and connects eastern England to Rome. By alerting us in the first place to a barrow that earlier *frequentatores* had come to plunder, Felix invites us to think of the Fenland itself as a place to be mentally probed, its layered identities awaiting selective excavation. The archaeological site that furnished Ely with a marble sarcophagus for Æthelthryth's *translatio* is apparently off-limits, mentioned only briefly and with no indication of its importance to East Anglian cultural prestige in the eastern Fens. Where Bede links *Grantacæstir* to Ely and thus plots it on a textual map of East Anglia, Felix brings *Gronta* into a Mercian frame of reference.

Even as it evoked memories of Roman hegemony, the ruin stood for the ravages wrought by time and by people. Although the old *castrum* probably had been used by Roman forces to pacify restive Britons before the Angles arrived, it would have retained some military value afterwards during what Christopher Taylor describes as "the savage wars between Mercia and East Anglia."[106] Sir Henry Clifford Darby likewise believed that the site "was probably a relic of border warfare."[107] Despite its seeming state of abandonment by Bede's and Felix's time, Cambridge is not therefore inscrutable. It would have reminded eighth-century readers of the *HE* and the *VSG* that the area had been a battleground, and that "[t]he fenland which stretches for many miles to the south and east of Crowland played an important part in early English history, for it prevented the Mercian kings from making East Anglia a Mercian province."[108] Yet even if *Gronta* served to reassure Ælfwald that "the Mercian kings [had] never obtained in East Anglia the unchallenged ascendancy that was theirs in Lindsey,"[109] it also would have recalled Penda's victories in the past and the uncertainty of the border district's future. In the seventh century Ely belonged to the East Angles, but Peterborough and Crowland fell to the Mercians; the latter *gens* had done much to erode Middle Anglian autonomy.[110] Mercia did not win East Anglia outright later in that century, but neither did East Anglia enjoy unlimited freedom.[111] As a point of orientation for Ælfwald and his court, the ancient riverine fortification at *Gronta* stands in the *VSG* as a concrete reminder of the "eddying whirlpool of these turbid times" over which East Anglian political history stood poised.

Demon-Expulsion as Mercian Triumph

Mercian power is further signposted in the account of Guthlac's defeat of Crowland's guardian devils. Felix recounts that during the reign of the Mercian king Coenred, "cum Brittones, infesti hostes Saxonici generis, bellis, praedis, publicisque vastationibus Anglorum gentem deturbarent" ("while the Britons, the implacable enemies of the Saxon race, were troubling the English with their attacks, their pillaging, and their devastations of the people"; §34, pp. 108–9), Guthlac, while praying in his cell, fell asleep and heard a throng of men yelling outside. Realizing that the din was no dream, he sprang up, ventured out of his dwelling, and realized that the men were speaking in a British Celtic language:

> nam ille aliorum temporum praeteritis voluminibus inter illos exulabat, quoadusque eorum strimulentas loquelas intelligere valuit. Nec mora; per palustria tectis subvenire certantes, eodem paene momento omnes domus suas flamma superante ardere conspicit; illum quoque intercipientes acutis hastarum spiculis in auras levare coeperunt. Tum vero vir Dei tandem hostis pellacis millenis artibus millenas formas persentiens, velut prophetico ore sexagesimi septimi psalmi primum versum psallebat: Exsurgat Deus, et reliqua; quo audito, dicto velocius eodem momento omnes daemoniorum turmae velut fumus a facie eius evanuerunt.

> ([he] realized that British hosts were approaching his dwelling: for in years gone by he had been an exile among them, so that he was able to understand their sibilant speech. Straightway they strove to approach his dwelling through the marshes, and at almost the same moment he saw all his buildings burning, the flames mounting upwards: indeed they caught him too and began to lift him into the air on the sharp points of their spears. Then at length the man of God, perceiving the thousand-fold forms of this insidious foe and his thousand-fold tricks, sang the first verse of the sixty-seventh psalm as if prophetically, "Let God arise," etc.: when

they had heard this, at the same moment, quicker than words, all the hosts of demons vanished like smoke from his presence. [§34, pp. 110–11])

At first, what Guthlac the latest Fenland *frequentator* sees are simply devils who manipulate his mind, apparently resurrecting memories of British raiders he had encountered earlier while in exile. Yet if Æthelthryth's Ely was known for its eels, Felix's Crowland could, as I proposed early in this chapter, produce the odd red herring along with the occasional crow.[112] The demons can assume many forms; even without their ethnic and linguistic role-playing, they comprise parts of many species. But like monstrous versions of Umberto Eco's Casaubon, they possess multitudinous surfaces that disguise lack of depth.[113] The mere fact of the *VSG*'s genre makes their defeat a foregone conclusion, no matter how many shapes they take. Whatever existential threat they might pose pales in comparison to the cultural tensions they intimate.

The demons' British guise is meant primarily to recall the hero's literal experiences as a warrior among the Britons, but it is striking that we learn about these experiences only now. Perhaps the information is disclosed abruptly because Felix obtained it only belatedly. The (unexpected) ethnic dimension of the *VSG* has been seen as part of Felix's broader nation-building enterprise; O'Brien O'Keeffe, for example, notes that "[i]n the merging of Britons and demons, Felix produces a node in which religious and political discourses, the material and the spiritual, are folded into one."[114] The node is peculiarly dense, uniting all those belonging to the *Saxonicus genus* and *gens Anglorum* against a similarly homogenized British population.[115] The true enemies of the English are Celts dwelling far from Crowland and beyond the "English" border altogether in present-day Wales.[116] So neatly does the passage dichotomize relations between the "English" and the "Britons" that it distracts us from more pertinent conflicts between Mercians and East Angles in the Fens.

On the basis of Guthlac's vision, historians used to speculate that actual Britons had inhabited the Fenland as late as Guthlac's time, and that position has been revived forcefully by Susan Oosthuizen.[117] Sir Frank Stenton challenged such speculation long ago, thinking it unwarranted; recently Lindy Brady has repeated such doubts and endorsed – laudably, in my view – Colgrave's warning against literal inference of Britons from the above-quoted passage in the *VSG*.[118] Felix's polysemous demons need not betoken an actual British presence in the Fens of Guthlac's day; but their invasion of Crowland speaks to the processual history of that district and of Britannia as a whole, histories that were alike constructed over time by patterns of migration in which Germanic peoples competed for resources with, and on occasion dispossessed, the Romanized British Iceni, Trinovantes, and Catuvellauni.[119] Felix portrays the Fenland in terms of what Richard Morris calls "the wider process of fluctuating coming and going" characteristic of ancient landscapes in general; if "the idea of wilderness as being on culture's edge takes shape about three thousand years ago … the boundary moves back and forth."[120] Early medieval hagiographic texts foreground the mutability of certain landscapes that have already been culturally constructed as places of flux, where "the saints modify the world's spatial organization and redefine the distribution of familiar and alien regions."[121] Felix's narrative centres on land shaped by transitions between ownership and desuetude and back again; Guthlac's dispelling of British-seeming demons re-enacts *in parvo* the Angles' conquest of Britain. The triumph, however, redounds to Mercia, not to East Anglia, notwithstanding Ælfwald's designs on the Crowland hermit's legacy; as Jeffrey Jerome Cohen puts it succinctly, "[a]fter Guthlac removes the demons from their last remaining dwelling, the land belongs to Mercia."[122] Ælfwald, then, would have done well to reflect on his and his *gens*'s diminishing stature in eastern England and to consider, moreover, that Mercian power could deal handily with any encroachment on Guthlac's cult, whether by evil demons or by rival dynasties.

In plumbing the depths of Crowland, Guthlac is not wholly unlike us as we make our way through the *VSG*'s various surprises, dredging the numerous identities and prior claims that compose the locale he settles as his own. Because his arrival involved the expulsion of demons who loudly insisted on their own rights to the land, Felix in effect portrays the Mercian domestication of Crowland as a conflation of homecoming and exorcism. The site of Guthlac's hermitage is not truly "wild" but rather "derelict," "not … a story of desolation" but "a cycle of recurrent reconfiguration"[123] upon a landscape whose history resists erasure. The Fens are places of habitation and visitation; Guthlac's hermitage sees no shortage of guests who need his help.[124] With its record of ancient grave-plunderers and its pilgrims eager for contact with the saint, Felix's Crowland is a culturally stratified site, its heterogeneous history complementing the *VSG*'s mixed patronage. Its often-reused territory could not be seized easily by the East Anglian dynasty even as a form of cultural capital, for the Mercians had the stronger claim.

Conclusion

As John Hines has reminded us, for the early English in general "control and use of land … remained the foundation stones of social position and power," and "there was scope for considerable variation and creativity in the manipulation of the land to achieve these goals."[125] In literary texts, the manipulation in question sometimes takes the form of seemingly solitary heroic resistance in, and even against, the land itself. Jennifer Neville has pointed out that Beowulf, Andreas, and the protagonists of the vernacular *Guthlac A* and *Guthlac B* "are literally 'outstanding,' for they prevail against the natural world without the aid of society – they stand outside."[126] The *VSG* celebrates a similarly "outstanding" character who tames a diabolically protected corner of the Fenland. But Guthlac does not triumph alone: he is one of many "Saxons" and "Angles" – equated by Felix with the Mercians[127] – whom the "Britons" allegedly persecuted and whom the Mercian king Æthelbald potentially benefits through his enhancement of the saint's shrine and his future *imperium* over all the English people. By honouring the potentate as well as the recluse, the *VSG* exalts Mercian prestige and, in effect, signals the limits of East Anglian authority.

The text ends suggestively with a miracle story in which Guthlac's sister Pega, who has laid the cultic foundation later built upon by Æthelbald,[128] pours salt water into the eyes of a blind pilgrim, thus restoring his sight (§53, pp. 166–71). Salt had been an important Fenland commodity since Roman times, and the particular piece of it used by Pega had been "consecrated" (*consecratam*, p. 168) by the hermit before his death. Touched by an autochthonous Crowland resource made holy by Guthlac, the pilgrim undergoes renewal; having regained his sight, he can bring others to spiritual reawakening. Moreover, he is now a leader (*dux*, p. 170) in his own right to those who had led him, "nec sic reversus ut erat, viditque videntes quos prius videre negavit, grates Deo persolvens dignas, quas nullus reddere nescit" ("[nor did he] return as he was before, for he saw those who saw him and whom he once said he could not see. And he returned fitting thanks to God, such as none could fail to give," §53, pp. 170–1).[129] At the outset of the *VSG* Felix urged his readers not to mistake the darkness of ignorance for the light of wisdom (Prologue, pp. 62–3); approaching the end of his text, he depicts a blind man regaining sight, a fitting conclusion to an eye-opening read for Ælfwald, who would have been made keenly aware that East Anglia was losing literal and figurative ground to Mercia. Although it has been said that Felix offers his patron a "Guthlac cast in the mould of East-Anglian culture of the first half of the eighth century,"[130] on closer inspection he champions Mercian *imperium*, repackages East Anglian identity as East Mercian, and implies that the safest way Ælfwald can continue as a *dominus* is to govern happily as Æthelbald's *subregulus*.

The Mercian overlord was himself no saint, as later events in his life suggest;[131] yet despite the impiety for which he was later criticized, and notwithstanding his successor Offa's power to evoke, in retrospect, the image of "a species of Mercian octopus,"[132] Æthelbald himself is no monster in the *VSG*. That role is assigned to Guthlac's enemies, demons who assume the form of Brittonic-speaking warriors. The Mercians in effect superintend God's Country, a land romanticized by Felix; in it, Guthlac's pre-conversion crimes are forgotten while Æthelbald's own enormities are as yet untold. Sacred Mercia produces a saint and so redeems itself, however stealthily and off-stage secular Mercia might be inching its way eastwards. Felix's depiction of the Fenland encourages belief in political harmony between the Mercians and the East Angles, insofar as both *gentes* are implied to be cooperating in the spread of holiness in the Fens. Such an alliance, however, is an "imagined community" of a very high order of wishful thinking.[133] Although the liminal Crowland of the *VSG* is the nexus of East Anglian and Mercian collaboration, it is also the centre of Mercian rather than East Anglian ideological gravity.[134]

Commissioning a *Life* of Guthlac that was ostensibly sympathetic to East Anglian interests would have allowed Ælfwald to further the reputation for sanctity established earlier by Æthelthryth at Ely, Bishop Felix at *Domnoc*, Fursey at Cnobheresburg, and Botwulf at Iken, and perhaps to make further amends for Rædwald's earlier ambivalence towards Christianity. At a time when East Anglian *imperium* in Southumbrian England was a thing of the past, a regnal reputation for sanctity would have been a valuable compensatory resource.[135] Indeed, when they are read together, Felix's *VSG* and Bede's *HE* give the impression that, in the Fenland, the East Anglian ruling dynasty had been deploying holy men and women to tame wildernesses, recycle Roman *spolia*, and establish beachheads of holiness if not of actual military or tactical strength. Yet when its Mercian emphases are considered fully, Felix's homage to Guthlac suggests that in the early to middle eighth century the Wuffingas and the Iclingas were competing in a hagiographical and chorographical space race, using aristocratic or even royal exemplars of eremitic piety to stake claims of ownership in the watery march lying between them.

Perhaps Ælfwald himself could become such an exemplar? It cannot have been so very far-fetched for a royally sponsored hagiographer to propose, in a tactfully roundabout way, that his patron should take up the cloistered life. As Audrey Meaney has observed on the basis of the hermit's depiction in the *VSG*, "Guthlac may have started a trend in royal Mercian retreat into monasteries, for Æthelred abdicated for that purpose in 704, and his nephew and successor Cœnred left for Rome in 709."[136] Clare Stancliffe identifies a half-dozen seventh- and eighth-century "kings who opted out" of royal rule in favour of the monastery, several of whom we have met already: the East Anglian Sigeberht; the West Saxon Centwine; the Mercian Æthelred; the East Saxon Sebbi; Ceolwulf, Bede's own dedicatee in the *HE* who renounced the Northumbrian kingship in 737 (two years after Bede's death) to become a monk at Lindisfarne; and Ceolwulf's successor Eadbert.[137] "The monk-kings of the seventh and eighth centuries," Stancliffe argues, "coincided with a monastic 'craze,' which swept up both kings and their thegns."[138] King Ælfwald took monastic piety seriously: in his letter to Boniface in the late 740s, he declared his readiness to implement the great missionary's advice on celebrating mass and on praying in his kingdom's monasteries.[139] A few years earlier, he might well have struck Felix as the sort of pious monarch who could learn from, and be induced to imitate, an aristocratic warrior's turn to the ascetic life. The historical Guthlac may or may not have wished to influence the decision of later potentates to renounce rule; but the hagiographical Guthlac, reconstructed by Felix as a once-viable royal scion,[140] may have been intended to inspire Ælfwald of the East Angles to contemplate precisely that choice. Indeed, Felix's Guthlac is, in effect, shown to have made virtue of necessity by "opting out" rather than waiting to be booted out; what in reality may have been the political marginalization of "a potential king" (Stancliffe) is thus glorified by Felix as the free choice of the periphery. Far from seeking self-aggrandizement for himself, the Mercian warrior traded worldly power for otherworldly holiness, a hint Felix may have hoped would be taken by his patron.

Epilogue: Æthelberht II

Whatever harmony may have prevailed between East Anglia and Mercia did not survive to the end of the eighth century. Many years after Felix's time, in the 790s, the East Anglian *subregulus* Æthelberht II showed that he had little use for the option of royal abdication and ordered the minting of pennies bearing the inscription of his own name and title, "REX EÐILBERH[T]." His gesture looks no more audacious than Ælfwald's own royal self-styling, but making it appears to have been a dangerously bold thing to do, for Mercia was now even more powerful than it had been in Felix's time. Only a single specimen of the penny coinage exists, having been unearthed in 2014. It is thought that the Mercian over-king Offa approved the issue at first but later became so offended by its implication that an East Anglian sub-king should be ruling as a *rex* in his own right that, in 794, he ordered the decapitation of his would-be rival,[141] thus shattering any illusion of political community or ideological continuity that may have kept the peace since Ælfwald's day. The regicide is accorded scant notice in the ASC, but twelfth-century hagiography romanticizes the story by explaining that Æthelberht had provoked the wrath of Offa by seeking the hand of the latter's daughter.[142]

Regardless of the exact *casus belli*, the mere fact that Æthelberht had to be killed to be neutralized "implies that [Offa's] overlordship in the east did not go unchallenged."[143] If the East Anglian king indeed strove to become something more than Offa's puppet, his coinage reflects a more tangible version of the manoeuvre tried earlier by Ælfwald to assert influence within, and despite the constraints of, Mercian hegemony. Eventually the ambitious Æthelberht would be culted as a martyr; an early twelfth-century *Vita* preserved in Cambridge, Corpus Christi College, MS. 308 even parallels his doomed journey to Mercia in supposed search of a bride to the exodus of Abraham and his kin ("uelut abraham patriarcha de terra et de cognatione sua").[144] Such typological liberties in a post-Conquest codex tell us little about how Æthelberht was regarded just after his death, but they do offer eloquent testimony to how an East Anglian ruler murdered for purely secular reasons eventually became a lightning rod for his realm's devotional energies. In the context of the late eighth century, the regicide was probably just an instance of business as usual, a late round of that "fiercely contested knock-out competition" which Steven Bassett sees as the essence of the formation of eighth-century England.[145] Nevertheless, although ca. 800 East Anglia was weaker than its western neighbour, it refused to go down without a fight. As the next two chapters illustrate, texts of the later ninth and tenth centuries underscore the distinctness of that kingdom within England and signal the potential of the part to destabilize the whole.

4
Made in Wessex: Danish East Anglia and the Alfredian Court

According to Clare Stancliffe, the royal and thegnly "craze" for monasticism waned after the eighth century;[1] at around the turn of the millennium, Ælfric in the *Life of St. Edmund* (*SEKM*) would espouse a "royal pacifism" that envisaged kings imitating Christ Himself.[2] The intervening period saw profound political transformation in East Anglia. When Scandinavian "raiding-armies" or *hergas* killed Edmund in 869, an ancient English kingdom became, in effect, foreign. This was a new development. Previously, East Anglian *imperium* had been eclipsed by the Northumbrians, Mercians, and West Saxons; but with those *gentes* the East Angles had shared a language, a religion, and a migration-myth. Furthermore, East Anglian kings are recorded between the 790s and 850s, a fact that has suggested to modern historians that before 869 the Wuffings had been "able to resist both the reimposition of Mercian overlordship and the establishment of a West Saxon one."[3] The death of Edmund reintroduced the concept of utterly foreign conquest, not recorded in Britain since the mid-fifth century; the vikings from far away succeeded where the East Angles' nearer neighbours had failed.

As scholars have often noted, West Saxon texts responded to this innovation by manufacturing the idea of the *Angelcynn* in contradistinction to the type of the Scandinavian marauder-turned-settler.[4] In terms of the inter-regnal relationship between Wessex and East Anglia, this process of identity-formation reacted to a paradox in which the nominally English (or at least Anglian) *Eastængle* were bound by alien law. To resolve the paradox, Cerdicing rulers redefined Edmund's former domains as a now-hybrid land of Scandinavian East Anglians and indigenous East Angles.

Recent scholarship explores the extent to which Alfred invented the *Angelcynn* on the basis of political and ideological rather than ethnic considerations; always a construct in the first instance, the invented ideal was performed by repeated textual iterations.[5] The process had a regional and territorial dimension as well. The interrelated nature of polity and ethnicity, nation and district can be seen clearly through a recognition of the cultural work performed by texts of the period. Robert Barrett, in his consideration of later, twelfth- to seventeenth-century writings about Cheshire, has shown how those writings "work together to complicate persistent academic binaries of metropole and margin, center and periphery, and nation and region."[6] Texts about East Anglia that date to earlier periods likewise trouble neat dichotomies and jostle modern scholarly fixation on the origins of the *Angelcynn*. Specifically, the present chapter argues that the Anglo-Saxon Chronicle (ASC) and the Alfred-Guthrum Treaty (AGT) represent East Anglia as, in effect, the *condicio sine qua non* of Cerdicing self-aggrandizement; the region became the chief problem to which the unification of the "English" people was urged as the solution. In the eighth century, as shown in previous chapters, Bede's *HE* and Felix's *VSG* depicted East Anglia as a religiously orthodox kingdom, active in the promotion of saints despite its earlier experiment in syncretism (as lamented by Bede) and its encroachment on Mercian cultural capital (as indulged cautiously by Felix). By contrast, the ASC and the AGT, reflecting secular and military priorities, portray Scandinavian East Anglia as an ongoing amorphous and volatile threat to an "England" that West Saxon leaders were imagined to represent and defend.

"Viking" East Anglia

The Scandinavian conquest of East Anglia was heterogeneous rather than monolithic.[7] Cyril Hart identifies "Outer," "Northern," "Southern," and "Eastern" Danelaws,[8] each of whose war-bands or *hergas* likely thought of themselves as possessing distinct identities and loyalties.[9] Danish East Anglia and Danish Northumbria, however, are roughly distinguishable from each other to modern eyes and seem to have been so to contemporary West Saxon observers as well.

In 865, the Danish "Great Army" invaded England, wintered in East Anglia, promised an expensive peace to its unwilling hosts, and then took ship for Northumbria,[10] where they spent the next four years campaigning with their commander Ívarr the Boneless before following him from York back down to East Anglia, which they conquered after killing its ruler Edmund in 869. Later, Ívarr returned to Northumbria to join his brother Ubba but left northern Britain for Dublin in 871. A different contingent of the Great Army, led by another brother of Ívarr named Hálfdan, campaigned in Wessex in 871, aggravating the havoc being wrought on that kingdom by a separate wave of invaders who had arrived the same year. Known as the Great Summer Army, this latter troop may have been led by Guthrum, who warred against Alfred before being defeated by him at the Battle of Edington (Wiltshire) in 878, following which defeat he submitted to baptism as Alfred's godson Æthelstan. The treaty he signed with Alfred in or shortly after 880 acknowledged him as the new ruler of a hybrid Anglo-Danish East Anglia.

From this time onward, the Scandinavian *here* ("raiding-army") in the easternmost part of England raided less frequently and turned to a more settled way of life.[11] How it did so hints at differences between their colonization of East Anglia and their counterparts' takeover of Northumbria. In ca. 876, the year after they captured Repton (Derbyshire), Hálfdan and his forces reached the north, where, according to the "A" recension of the ASC, they took up farming. It was only in 880 that Guthrum began "sharing out" East Anglia with his followers,[12] but he appears to have encouraged or at least enabled a more stable life for them than Hálfdan, who craved dominions in Ireland, had done for his soldiers. As Alfred Smyth puts it, "in spite of the settling of the Danish army in Yorkshire in 876, Hálfdan himself remained a *herkonungr* or warrior-king to the end of his life."[13] Perhaps, as David Rollason has cautioned, it would be better to use the word "king" loosely in his case, for Hálfdan's hunger for gain outstripped his capacity for proper digestion, his ardent claim to the Norse kingdom of Dublin ending not long afterwards with his death at the Battle of Strangford Lough in 877.[14] No immediate successor inherited the state he had carved out for himself in Northumbria, with its centre at York.[15] It is noteworthy that before he died many of his followers had defected, weary after ten years of fighting and eager to exploit their hard-won Northumbrian territories. Such large-scale resentment had no parallel in East Anglia, where Guthrum's decision to settle seems to have appealed to soldiers ready to enjoy the fruits of rich farmland.[16]

Around the time of Guthrum's death in 890, things seem to have changed in both parts of Scandinavian England. A muddled picture of governance obtains for East Anglia, a somewhat clearer picture for Northumbria; in the latter, English kings can be glimpsed ruling from Bamburgh, and Danish leaders can again be seen holding York. Focusing on the early to middle tenth-century West Saxon conquests that had begun earlier under King Edward, Matthew Innes distinguishes between "the divergent histories of Northumbria, with its relatively centralized kingship and its constant influx of 'new' Vikings, and East Anglia and the East Midlands, where small-scale regional units based on the personal obligation of 'Danes' towards their local *here* were easily and quickly swallowed up into the English kingdom."[17] Each of Northumbria's principal parts, Bernicia and Deira, was relatively cohesive and sometimes at war with the other; Scandinavian invaders exploited these conditions to impose their own rule on the territory.[18] By contrast, the scarce evidence of Danish East Anglian kingship following Guthrum's death in 890 may indeed reflect decentralization of authority and diffusion of governance in a series of small semi-urban communities. In theory, an increasingly fissiparous East Anglia would have posed fewer obstacles to West Saxon expansion.

Yet that expansion did not happen quickly. As James Campbell has observed, "[King Edward's] system of fortress building as a means to conquest did not apply there," despite the increased urgency of Edward's campaigning in the east after the rebellion of the West Saxon royal pretender Æthelwold (about whom more later) following Alfred's death in 899. Campbell adduces the apparently uneven nature of Edward's activities in East Anglia to explain Scandinavian peculiarities in that region, peculiarities that persisted up to the late eleventh century. Moreover, indigenous East Anglian influences seem to have been grafted onto those peculiarities. Of Æthelwold's alliance with the East Anglian Danes Pauline Stafford remarks that "Viking settlers were a novel element in relations among the kingdoms of the English, but not a totally transforming one. They acted as Northumbrian and East Anglian armies, identifiable at least to southern observers within older political divisions."[19] Indeed, Campbell suggests that "[w]e ought to consider the possibility that East Anglia between ca. 869 and ca. 920 was less a Scandinavianised conquest than the ongoing Kingdom of East Anglia, not so very different from what it had been before, but with a Danish dynasty which struggled hard to acclimatise itself."[20] Despite King Edward's crucial victory over Danish forces in that kingdom in 917,[21] then, East Anglia remained a hybrid land, having adapted to and then influenced Danish rule, and then later accepting while obstructing West Saxon hegemony. Eric John has suggested that even the English king Æthelstan's reforms of East Anglian coinage and mints may have been intended to check dangerous separatist tendencies.[22]

Differences between the East Anglian and Northumbrian "Danelaws," or at least differences in how they were perceived by the West Saxons, may explain the disparate ways in which Alfred's descendants expanded their power in the two areas. East Anglia's relative closeness to Wessex and its sphere of influence in the south (which facilitated Edward the Elder's recapturing of Essex in 917) may have encouraged the Cerdicing court all along to believe that the erstwhile kingdom of Edmund could be absorbed more readily than Northumbria into the "English" fold.

Pauline Stafford has emphasized that sheer distance alone would have prevented Cerdicing kings from doing in Northumbria what they were able to do in East Anglia and Mercia, where they placed ealdormen (e.g. Æthelstan "Half-King" in East Anglia) in positions of power, slowly built up local loyalties to the descendants of Alfred, and were at least in a position to try to stay regionalist impulses.[23] Shane McLeod suggests that, unlike the Scandinavian army in Northumbria, which had campaigned extensively in Ireland before first coming to northern England, the Scandinavians who seized East Anglia had had extensive previous exposure to Francia. If this was the case, then a degree of Carolingian acculturation among the latter group will have made them seem slightly more familiar to the West Saxon court, especially if that group included some Scandinavians who had been baptized in Francia even before Guthrum's baptism under Alfred.[24]

Sense of distance manifested itself in other ways. West Saxon texts reveal that Cerdicing kings struggled not only to control Northumbria but also to understand its territorial extension, as George Molyneaux gathers from entries in the ASC for the 940s–50s and for 1016.[25] In terms of language, it may be significant that at an early stage in Scandinavian Northumbria's history the Danish word *jarl* entered the English language as "earl," while south of the Humber the English noun *ealdorman* sufficed until Cnut's reign.[26] It has been claimed that "[i]n general, Wessex could relate to the Danelaw as a less civilized version of itself, in the same terms it used for thinking about its own past, with its paganism and its crude, violent heroics."[27] The West Saxon court may have deemed Scandinavian Northumbrian social and political designations more conceptually remote than Scandinavian East Anglian and Mercian ones.[28]

That Northumbria lay farther from Wessex than did East Anglia meant that West Saxon kings would need to expend more time and resources travelling to and managing the north than they needed to do when dealing with the east. In 926, for example, Æthelstan gave his sister Eadgyth in marriage to Sihtric, the viking king of York, and then capitalized on Sihtric's death the following year by invading Northumbria and seizing its late ruler's capital.[29] Yet in and of itself that victory failed to secure Cerdicing hegemony over the "Danish" north. As indicated in several recensions of the ASC, the Northumbrians in the 940s and 950s occasionally defied that hegemony by choosing Scandinavian rulers. Such acts provoked swift and repeated West Saxon military intervention, which only highlights how difficult it was to manage Scandinavian Northumbria from afar.[30] Only in 959 do the Abingdon manuscripts of the ASC claim confidently that "Eadgar ... feng to rice ægðer ge on

Westseaxum ge on Myrcum ge on Norðhymbrum, 7 he wæs þa .xvi. wintre" ("Edgar ... succeeded to the kingdom both in Wessex and in Mercia and in Northumbria; and he was then 16 years old").[31] Even this entry looks suspicious, however, because it implicitly equates the obeisance that Edgar achieved in Wessex and Mercia to the fealty he obtained in Northumbria, as if the compiler's economical phrasing could erase all memory of the trouble Cerdicing kings had had in dislodging viking control of the north.

For its part, East Anglia is omitted entirely in the 959 entry, perhaps because Edgar had failed to consolidate his power in the east, or perhaps because East Anglian submission could be taken for granted. Such complacency, if that is what it was, must have been hard won, as will be considered a bit later in this section; but in retrospect a bit of complacency could have been justified on the historical grounds that the East Anglian vikings had, after all, adopted the Christianity of their erstwhile West Saxon enemies earlier than the Northumbrian vikings had done, Guthrum having been baptized after his defeat by Alfred in 878. By contrast, the Christianization of Scandinavian Northumbria seems to have taken longer. Several years after Hálfdan's death in Ireland in 877, the Dane Guthfrith (or Guthred) succeeded him as king of York. The Roman religion certainly proved influential there to some extent, for the monastic community of St. Cuthbert seems to have effected the conversion of Guthfrith before his death and burial at York in 895, even if some uncertainty continues to surround the exact nature and date of that conversion.[32] Yet his adoption of the new faith (if indeed he ever adopted it) set no irreversible trend: although the aforementioned Sihtric of York married the Christian Eadgyth in 926, "[n]either his new wife nor his new religion was acceptable to the York Vikings, so he repudiated both."[33]

Its earlier conversion likely made East Anglia look less outlandish than Northumbria to West Saxon eyes, and thus more amenable to assimilation to Cerdicing "England." It is true that after Edward the Elder's victory in 917 the eastern region never regained the autonomy it had possessed before Guthrum's arrival; East Anglia became an early English ealdormanry and later an Anglo-Danish earldom.[34] Yet idiosyncrasies persisted. Lucy Marten and other scholars argue compellingly that East Anglia retained its tenacious local identity well after Edward's time, even during the ealdormanry of the West Saxon appointee Æthelstan "Half-King," who from ca. 932 to 956 commanded almost as much power as the West Saxon monarch himself.[35] Viking raids began afresh in the early 980s, a trend that would culminate in Sweyn's capture of the throne in 1013; the subsequent long reign of his son Cnut (1016–35) ushered in a renewed period of volatility in East Anglia that saw the banishment of several earls.[36] A history of unsettled conditions in the region anticipated the more serious, anti-Norman rebellion of Hereward, later called "the Wake," in the early 1070s.

Viking Conquest and the Anglo-Saxon Chronicle

The documentary account of Anglo-Scandinavian East Anglia's tortuous history begins when the ASC records King Edmund's defeat by Scandinavian raiders in 869 (870 according to the text). As in their references to St. Guthlac and King Æthelberht II, here too the West Saxon annals economize on detail:[37]

> Her rad se here ofer Mierce innan Eastengle 7 wintersetl namon æt Þeodforda. 7 þy wintra Eadmund cyning him wiþ feaht, 7 þa Deniscan sige namon 7 þone cyning ofslogon 7 þæt lond all geeodon.[38]

> (Here [i.e. in this year] the raiding-army rode across Mercia into East Anglia, and took winter-quarters at Thetford; and that winter King Edmund fought against them, and the Danish took the victory, and killed the king and conquered all that land.)[39]

Laconic and detached, the entry from the "A" recension presents no obvious point of view despite marking "the first time the *Chronicle* refers explicitly to an Anglo-Saxon kingdom being conquered by the Vikings,"[40] and despite having been worked up at least twenty years after the fact as part of the ASC's so-called "Common Stock," organized possibly in response to renewed Scandinavian raids.[41] What does seem clear is that, unlike Sigeberht much earlier, Edmund "fought against" his kingdom's invaders with a view to winning. Æthelweard's *Chronicon* even claims that Edmund "[a]duersus quos *optauit* bellum" ("*decided* on war against them"; ed. and trans. A. Campbell, pp. 36–7).[42] The annalist neither elaborates nor reflects on the event.

Many Chronicle entries, including the 870 annal, are notoriously terse and presuppose wide background knowledge of the events summarized therein. "That which to us seems a lean and barren sentence, was to them the text for a winter evening's entertainment," Charles Plummer famously observed of the work's early readers.[43] They would have filled in the annalists' silences to reconstruct a coherent order, a textual system.[44] What was Thetford, for example? A village or a sizeable town? Ecclesiastical centre or royal estate?[45] For the annalists and their intended readers, it was surely a known entity, an *apertum verbum* rather than a mere *flatus vocis*.[46] Because the "A" recension stands at some remove from the original annals,[47] one might have expected a copyist somewhere along the line of transmission to add details about the place. No one did, or for that matter took the trouble to link East Anglia's conquest one year to its occupation and divvying-up ten years later, the process that made new East Anglians out of marauders.

As Paul Strohm has reminded medievalists, "[t]he text is found always to exist in intimate dialogue with the external/extratextual world," which "exerts a constant pressure on the text" even when the latter seems reticent about divulging it.[48] Returning to the 870 annal, one gathers that in its dialogue with the world much was said sotto voce. The vikings seem to have occupied Thetford seasonally and only for military purposes, treating it as *wintersetl* ("winter-quarters")[49] before slaying Edmund and taking his realm. For the annalist, then, Thetford was both strategic stopping-point and geographical resource, the assumption being that before it was conquered it had existed as an English settlement, specifically as a "public" or "tribal ford," or "ford of the people/nation" (*þeōde* + *ford*).[50] Archaeological evidence hints at a fuller story, a "pressure on the text" the annalist counters with taciturnity. The Danes appear to have improved what they seized, eventually turning Thetford into a large, prosperous, and ecclesiastically important town.[51] As Barbara Crawford points out, the "process of settlement and assimilation … was hugely important in turning the Viking raiders into neighbours," who in that capacity would have been "settled, provided with land, and obliged to live according to a political code rather than a military one."[52] Janet Nelson similarly cautions that "[i]n the historic ninth century, there were indeed Northmen who threatened and damaged the people they encountered in England and on the Continent. But there were also Northmen that opted in."[53] Nelson's reference to "the *historic* ninth century" implies a distinction from the *textual* ninth century, the period as it was written about; indeed, texts composed from a West Saxon point of view hint at Anglo-Scandinavian assimilation in East Anglia but rarely dwell on the complexities arising from it.

One of the most striking examples of such unremarked fusion appears in the entry for the year 1004 in the "C" recension, in which a prominent local named Ulfcytel is said to have fought against newly arrived plunderers who had targeted Thetford, among other places. The annal has Ulfcytel's Scandinavian foes acknowledge the singular prowess of their English adversary: "hi sylfe sædon þæt hi næfre wyrsan handplegan on Angelcynne ne gemitton þonne Ulfcytel him to brohte" ("they themselves admitted that they had never met with harder hand-play in England than Ulfcytel gave them").[54] This was the

Ulfkell Snillingr, Ulfcytel the Bold, of Old Norse saga;[55] the 1004 entry implies (but only implies, as scholars have noted) that he was the East Anglians' ealdorman. To attentive early eleventh-century readers of the ASC he was certainly living proof that East Anglia had long been bathed by cultural influences washing over it repeatedly from across the North Sea. "[F]or Anglo-Saxons who had not yet identified geography as a separate subject," writes Nicole Guenther Discenza, "inhabitants could define a place."[56] In the 1004 annal, Ulfcytel, by virtue of his very name, defines East Anglia as an Anglo-Scandinavian land that had been produced by cultural assimilation but was not therefore open to any and all forms of further Scandinavian influence.

As Dawn Hadley has observed, towns in northern and eastern England that had changed hands in the late ninth century grew substantially in the tenth, their growth owing much to the complex interaction of local English, Scandinavian, West Saxon, and Continental cultural influences.[57] Mentioned in two very terse Chronicle entries, the place of Thetford is allowed to stand for a comparatively simplified process of change: hostile takeover by foreigners in 869, stalwart defence against more foreigners in 1004. What would the site have meant to the foreigners themselves? Having traversed East Anglia in 865 on their way to York, the *here* of 869 had already learnt something about the local landscape and the importance of its towns. They could have contented themselves with a merely symbolic victory, capturing any small village in eastern Cambridgeshire close to the old Mercian frontier; instead they penetrated deeply into the kingdom to make their base at Thetford. If the county names "Suffolk" and "Norfolk" reflect longstanding settlement by two distinct peoples, a probability Dorothy Whitelock adduced to explain Archbishop Theodore's division of the East Anglian see into two bishoprics in 672,[58] then siting "winter-quarters" at Thetford, roughly at the modern boundary between the two shires, would have made it easier for the vikings to repel defending levies advancing from either of the kingdom's principal *regiones*. Even if the divisions "Suffolk" and "Norfolk" originated only in Cnut's reign, as suggested by Lucy Marten, the invaders' choice of Thetford still would have been astute for the same reason the site would later appeal to Cnut at *Assendun* in 1016: "The existing communication network of the 'Peddars Way' and cross routes made Thetford a nodal point from which troops could be deployed across East Anglia."[59]

If, as Strohm claims, "[t]he meaning of a particular text exists somewhere in the range between broad tradition and unique articulation,"[60] then the ASC's 870 annal may be said to signify on several planes. It traces the undoing of a whole English kingdom back to the takeover of a single settlement, yet simultaneously – by its very nature as an annal – confines catastrophe at Thetford to a single year, and marks the year itself as but one moment in an orderly temporal process supervised by God, the source of time itself.[61] It also allows, or at least implies a basis, for future elaboration of the Edmund story, effected spectacularly in the 980s in Abbo's *Passio*. In that text Thetford is simply an unnamed *ciuitatem* ("city"),[62] but even the use of that single Latin word is enough to suggest a deep cultural opposition between "civilized" (i.e. Roman-derived and Christian) East Angles and "uncivilized" Scandinavians.

These inferences amount to only a few ways to discern meaning in a breviloquent annal. Recent scholarship offers other ways, which read across entries diachronically so as to obtain a full range of meanings for any one of them.[63] Building upon heterogeneous work by Dominick La Capra, Hayden White, and Cecily Clark, Jacqueline Stodnick finds that "these entries are shaped and, moreover, that their 'simplicity' is part of this shaping,"[64] and demonstrates that even their limited set vocabulary can be deceptively rich in its effects. For example, Stodnick identifies the phrase *sige namon* ("they took the victory"), used in the 870 annal and elsewhere, as one of several rhetorical formulae peculiar to ninth-century Chronicle entries about Anglo-Danish skirmishes. Though seemingly unrevealing in isolation, together they served an overall strategy to "enforce and mark differences between the English and their Scandinavian opponents."[65] What looks to be only a brief note about what the vikings did in East Anglia is actually one feature of a larger quasi-gazetteer of conquest, an inventory of geographical dispossession whose vocabulary was developed for the purpose.[66]

Lordship and Land: The Annalist's Knowing Silences

Even terseness could serve the West Saxon annals' function as "propaganda."[67] Alfred Smyth has claimed plausibly that the 870 annalist refrained from elaborating on Edmund's murder because he wished to avoid making the slain king look like a rival to King Alfred in prestige.[68] In what follows, I concur with Smyth by arguing that the Chronicle does indeed play down the impact of Edmund's death, allowing West Saxon historiography to absorb rather than be distorted by East Anglian particularism. Where I depart from Smyth is in suggesting that this absorption was facilitated by the very choice to accord Edmund his full status as an erstwhile king. West Saxon texts and Anglo-Scandinavian coins honouring Edmund imply distinct rationales for celebrating the royal saint, yet East Anglia's character as both threat and stimulus to Cerdicing security emerges from the intersection of those rationales.

Even something as seemingly trivial as the 870 annal's use of the word *cyning* came charged with enough meaning to serve West Saxon interests. Acknowledgment of kingship would have been a matter of course in a work centred on kings.[69] Although it conferred less honour upon Edmund than, say, attribution of sanctity would have done (by contrast, the Danish coins styled him both "king" and "saint," as we shall see later), the nod to royal status sufficed to measure the value of the territorial prize that "England" had lost and that Alfred and his successors might one day gain. More than a princeling or client ruler, more than a mere ealdorman, Edmund had wielded royal power in his own right; his *lond* was a kingdom, not some mere district within another polity that it had been when Offa had had Æthelberht killed. Had East Anglia always been but a *regio* governed by a *princeps* or *subregulus*,[70] its loss could have been endured as a temporary setback to be overcome once a sufficiently large English army or *fyrd* drawn from surrounding *regiones* had been organized to expel the intruders.

But East Anglia was a *provincia* in the Bedan sense of that word. Its foreign capture meant the disappearance from the mental map of the *Angelcynn* of the independent "Eastengla cyning 7 … þeod" ("king and … nation of the East Angles"), as the ASC's "A" recension styles them for the year 823.[71] Early readers of that recension would have registered the full meaning of the word *cyning*; and when moving on to the entry for 827, they would have seen, in a vernacular version of Bede's *imperium*-list, a reminder that the East Angles had even produced a *bretwalda*.[72] Despite Æthelberht's murder in 794, East Anglia by Edmund's time had been a resurgent "nation" or "people," still maintaining its own royal genealogy and court customs and enjoying a measure of its old prestige. When the 870 annal uses the word *cyning* in regard to Edmund, it attributes regnal cohesion to the East Anglian *þēod* and turns the monarch's death into a focal point for larger-scale West Saxon political thinking by hinting at the stakes involved. "Nothing," Susan Reynolds observes, "could be more misleading than the textbook idea that a king of the 'feudal age' was merely *primus inter pares*, dependent on 'feudal bonds' for what little authority he had. Only kings were crowned: only kings could draw on the fund of prestige which came from the church and from the kings of the Old Testament."[73] With a single word designating royal power, the annalist posthumously grants to the defeated lord of the East Angles access to that same "fund of prestige," and suggests to West Saxon readers the quality of the cultural capital on which Cerdicing expansion might one day draw.

The same noun is, of course, used to refer to invading warlords like Guthrum, but the effect is different. Unlike the 870 annal's association of the *cyning* Edmund with the *lond* of the East Angles, the entry for the year 875 – like the AGT, as we shall see later – uses the title to indicate a mere leader of "raiding-armies." Such so-called kings have no history of living in English territory, no status as heads of *gentes*, let alone dynastic ties to regional saints. According to the annal for 875, "for Godrum 7 Oscytel 7 Anwynd, þa .iii. cyningas, of Hreopedune to Grantebrycge mid micle here 7 sæton þær an gear" ("Guthrum and Oscytel and Anund, the 3 kings, went from Repton to Cambridge with a great raiding-army, and settled there for a year").[74] All three leaders are *cyningas* because of the Chronicle's already-mentioned royal interests; but they are kings of nothing except the "great raiding-army" that has separated itself from Hálfdan, who went on to lead his own men from Repton to Northumbria.[75] And even the word *here* ("raiding-army") implies more unity than may have existed among "various individual bands that occasionally operated together but often pursued their own interests."[76] Lordship alone, the word *cyning* alone, would not have raised Guthrum or any other Danish chieftain to equality with their English counterparts. On the basis of Æthelweard's *Chronicon* and entries in the vernacular annals beginning with the one for 871, Smyth asserts that the West Saxon court distinguished among the several *hergas* roving over England.[77] Despite this awareness, however, the ASC homogenizes the armies, in part by leaving their discrete objectives unexplained, in part by suggesting the lower status of their leaders' command of their followers. The 875 annal does not say, for example, why the two contingents went their separate ways, or why the one that stayed in the south went on to march from Repton to Cambridge. And by naming kings without kingdoms, the 875 entry characterizes the Danish leaders as but roving collectors of allegiance, unless we see the reference to *cyningas* as a prolepsis reflecting their later dominion over eastern England.

The precise naming of Repton and Cambridge at least identifies sites as points where the so-called kings and their armies stopped, if not as parts of future realms actually governed. Nevertheless, although Smyth is right to claim that the annalist for 875 "had good reason to observe the movements of the southern division of this army very closely,"[78] the annal itself discloses very little observation. Instead, as Alice Sheppard remarks of the entries for 872–5,

> [T]he annalist does not allow the reader to see exactly how much of Anglo-Saxon England is under Danish occupation. With one exception (Mercia in 874), the annalist just names the places that the Danes occupy, the places to which the army moves, and the places in which the Danes encounter Anglo-Saxon resistance. He strives to keep each town as a separate entity, represented only by a place-name, and refuses to draw for his

> readers the kind of verbal map that would point out Alfred's vulnerability. Instead, by naming only the towns, the annalist suggests that the landscape across which the army moves is merely terrain.[79]

We are, then, in danger of missing the forest for the trees because Repton and Cambridge have become toponyms divorced from English governance. At moments like this, the ASC suspends the histories of places that surely continued to have histories, albeit ones no longer determined by native English people. Just as repeated silences in annals would not have diminished the annalists' perception of divinely ordained "fullness and continuity ... in the sequence of the years" themselves,[80] and just as formulaic phrases connect Chronicle episodes and generate a piecemeal ethnography of us-versus-them, so too can the mere unadorned mention of toponyms suggest a fleeting chorography, a landscape punctured by gaps and robbed of its ancient attachments to English kingships. The mere presence of these names hints at some kind of spatial framework, an underlying "conception of England as a territorial totality,"[81] yet one predicated on a disrupted history.

How we interpret East Anglia's changing regional identities from the late ninth century onward, especially in the often less-than-voluble ASC, hinges on the old question whether rulers were thought to govern peoples (*gentes, populi*) or places (e.g. *regiones, provinciae, regna*). This issue has been touched upon already, in this book's Introduction, and must be considered further here. Alice Sheppard has offered pertinent insights on the Chronicle's economical presentation of place-names: "In times of political uncertainty when the borders of the land are disputed and collective identity stressed, the annalists put aside land-based notions of kingdom and identity" in favour of stressing how "the people are at once created and defined by their acceptance of the king's lordship."[82] On her analysis, towns mentioned in the annals as having been captured by the vikings become "uninterpreted" places, thanks to a documentary practice that "disguises ... territorial losses" and consequently evokes "Alfred's kingdom ... in the intangible relationship of man and lord" rather than in terms of geographical sites that can be won or lost at a time of profound political instability.[83] In the annals, when place recedes into the background, the people who live in it or occupy it enter the foreground. The "uninterpreted" Thetford of the 870 annal, then, is where the initial stage of the momentous redefinition of East Anglian lordship begins. Sheppard's approach illuminates other passages in the ASC where regional histories disappear altogether from view; certain annals resort to a "strategy of obfuscation [in] not explaining the significance of the towns the army occupies."[84] By considering this "strategy of obfuscation" vis-à-vis its spatial sensibilities, we can better understand the ideological mapping done by the West Saxon annalists.

In part, Sheppard's argument reformulates the notion that early medieval writers regarded kings as rulers of peoples rather than of territories.[85] Yet her analysis also obliquely illuminates the importance of the latter, for it discloses the Chronicle's occasional tendency to use barebones references to leadership to overwrite and even silence regional histories. When the entry for 875 names Cambridge, for example, it discloses nothing about the town's importance in orientating readers of the hagiography of Æthelthryth and Guthlac.[86] Once a *castellum* and even a *civitatula* known for its Roman antiquity and quarriable stone, *Grantebrycg* loses its storied regnal associations as its new masters go winter-settling their way through the landscape. Again, much remains unsaid. Like Thetford, Cambridge went on to see urban renovation of a sort, a new *burh* being constructed by the Danes to replace the one built earlier by Offa.[87] Readers would not know this from an annal that figures the newcomers as transients pursuing wider submission and Cambridge as but a means to that end ("it was from this sure base at Cambridge that Guthrum launched his war against the West Saxons in 876").[88] The once-abandoned fort reprises its older, Bedan role as the collateral damage of warfare but also takes on a new (if laconically articulated) military identity as a landmark on a Scandinavian trajectory of conquest.

From Cambridge to Edington and Back to East Anglia

The invaders retained control of both Cambridge and Thetford despite seeing their grander ambitions thwarted when, in the spring of 878, Alfred of Wessex defeated the viking leader Guthrum at the Battle of *Ethandun* (Edington, Wiltshire). According to the ASC, earlier in that same year Guthrum and his army "geridon Wesseaxna lond" ("over-rode and occupied the land of Wessex"),[89] vanquishing all opponents except for the West Saxon ruler, who eventually prevailed. As victor, Alfred stood sponsor to Guthrum at the latter's baptism, a two-part ceremony in Somerset that began at Aller and concluded a week later at Wedmore.[90] Only in 880 (*recte* 879) are Guthrum and his followers reported by the Chronicle to have settled permanently in East Anglia after having sojourned a year at Cirencester; and even then, and in retrospect, the annalist cannot fully convince himself that the newcomers have been incorporated into their new surroundings: "Her for se here of Cirenceastre on Eastengle 7 gesæt þæt lond 7 gedęlde" ("Here the raiding-army went from Cirencester into East Anglia, and settled that land, and divided it up").[91] Baptized and allotted an adoptive homeland, the Danes are still "the raiding-army." This habit of thus referring to the Danes affects the ASC's characterization of East Anglia as a region, in part because, as Sheppard maintains, it is indeed lordship that the annals place in the foreground: the East Anglians (that is, the Danish army in East Anglia) are shown simply to be following the leader. As the annals represent them, Guthrum and his men will not stay settled for long, and even when appearing to do so they are always primed to mobilize for an offensive against Alfred's England.

Yet the ASC's concern with lordship does not preclude sensitivity to geography.[92] Its frequent references to settlement and land-parcelling show that, as Simon Keynes observes, "[t]he Alfredian chronicler was able in retrospect to distinguish between the year in which the Danes 'conquered' a kingdom and the year in which they 'shared out' the land."[93] Territory was coveted at least as often as obedience was sought. In the ASC "sharing out" land is simply what Scandinavian armies do after winning battles.[94] The phrase is a formula, of a piece with locutions like "to take the victory," which Stodnick has found to typify "ninth-century annals concerned with battles against Viking invaders."[95] East Anglia has become the place of the raiding-army that divvies up territorial spoils, captured land formerly owned by English East Angles who now must obey new masters.

The Alfred-Guthrum Treaty: Unequal Kingships

A substantial effort to contain the danger posed by Scandinavian East Anglians newly provided with local resources was made by Alfred in the form of his peace treaty with Guthrum. The agreement between the two leaders merits extended discussion here because, in tandem with certain entries in the Chronicle, it indicates how the West Saxons perceived East Anglia after it was conquered and how they defined their own territory and ambitions in relation to it. The AGT was certainly written at some point after the 878 Battle of *Ethandun*;[96] it was originally thought to be later than 886, when Alfred was believed to have captured London. But Mark Blackburn's redating to the late 870s of coins minted there in Alfred's name suggests that the Scandinavians could not have controlled the city between 878 and 886, as was formerly thought, and that therefore the treaty could conceivably have been written quite early in that period. Jeremy Haslam has suggested a very early date indeed, in the second half of 879, but Paul Kershaw's loose dating of the text to the 880s will suffice for present purposes. And as Kershaw indicates, such a dating still supports Patrick Wormald's supposition that the document may predate Alfred's law code or *Domboc*,[97] thus making it "the earliest legislative statement we have from Alfred"[98] and one that legislates a new East Anglia into existence.

The AGT survives in three forms. Two Old English versions, one short, the other shorter, are extant in Cambridge, Corpus Christi College, MS. 383, itself datable to the late eleventh or early twelfth century.[99] A Latin translation exists as well, one of many items preserved in the twelfth-century legal compilation known as the *Quadripartitus*. The treaty sketches a very rough boundary between the territories controlled by the West Saxons and by the East Anglian Danes; stipulates compensation for certain crimes; sets terms by which accused persons from either side may clear themselves; and prescribes conditions of interaction between the two sides and of relocation from one side to the other. According to Jeremy Haslam, through the AGT King Alfred "contained the Viking threat by giving them a 'homeland,'" and "[b]y sparing [Guthrum] and facilitating the formation of the sovereign state of East Anglia, Alfred gave himself an enhanced status as king of the Anglo-Saxons."[100] I mostly agree with Haslam's observation but would add that Alfred never intended that this "homeland" should remain in Scandinavian hands; although he treated with his defeated adversary nominally as if they had both been on equal terms, he would not have recognized East Anglia as a "sovereign state." Alfred himself was Guthrum's overlord and, as Haslam himself points out, negotiated from a position of marked strength vis-à-vis his Scandinavian counterpart.[101] What follows is an analysis first of key aspects of the AGT's Prologue and boundary-clause, then of the document's unspoken ideology, which was related to Alfred's wider cultural program and to the image of East Anglia that was predicated on this program.

The beginning of the treaty sets out the terms that ostensibly define the two powers and their spheres of influence:

> Ðis is ðæt frið, ðæt Ælfred cyninc 7 Gyðrum cyning 7 ealles Angelcynnes witan 7 eal seo ðeod ðe on Eastænglum beoð ealle gecweden habbað 7 mid aðum gefeostnod for hy sylfe 7 for heora gingran, ge for geborene ge for ungeborene, ðe Godes miltse reccen oððe ure.
>
> 1. Ærest ymb ure landgemæra: up on Temese, 7 ðonne up on Ligan, 7 andlang Ligan oð hire æwylm, ðonne on gerihte to Bedanforda, ðonne up on Usan oð Wætlingastræt.[102]

> (*Prologue*. This is the peace which King Alfred and King Guthrum and the councillors of all the English race and all the people who are in East Anglia have all agreed on and confirmed with oaths, for themselves and for their

subjects, both for the living and for the unborn, who care to have God's favour or ours.

§1. First concerning our boundaries: up the Thames, and then up the Lea, and along the Lea to its source, then in a straight line to Bedford, then up the Ouse to Watling Street.)[103]

It's important to note that the text refers to both Alfred and Guthrum as kings, one ruling the *Angelcynn*, the other the *Eastængle*. Both leaders are accorded the same degree of prestige associated with the royal title specifically.[104] Smyth believes that "[t]he Christian tone of the text is noticeable as is the fact that it is a treaty between equals – in no way indicative of a relationship between a conqueror and the vanquished."[105] This ostensible equality is an illusion, however, and it will be necessary to return quickly to the Chronicle to see why.

The annals, not surprisingly, do not treat West Saxon and Scandinavian kingship alike. In the "A" recension, Alfred's royal status is emphasized so strongly that it is announced early on in the elaborate West Saxon regnal list that prefaces the whole work.[106] Bede, we recall, used partial genealogies to confirm the stature of Rædwald and Æthelthryth, and Felix did likewise with Guthlac. The genealogical preface at the beginning of the ASC's "A" version associates historiography itself with the royal house of Wessex and signals the role of Alfred in that association, whether or not he himself commissioned the annals. In its own way, the 878 entry also proclaims the West Saxon king's exalted position; but it does so by exposing differences between Alfred and Guthrum, first by stating the former's victory over the latter at Edington, second by implying that the Danish leader, quite unlike his English counterpart, had been sidelined by his own soldiers.

After being defeated by Alfred, "salde se here him foregislas 7 micle aþas, þæt hie of his rice uuoldon 7 him eac geheton þæt hiera kyning fulwihte onfon wolde, 7 hie þæt gelæston swa" ("the raiding-army granted him hostages and great oaths that they would leave his kingdom, and also promised him that their king would receive baptism; and they fulfilled it").[107] Thomas Charles-Edwards spots a striking incongruence here: "The initial transactions are between the [Danish] army on the one side and Alfred on the other. Guthrum, at the beginning, and the West Saxon people, throughout, occupy far less prominent positions: Guthrum's baptism is the fulfilment of an undertaking by the Danish army not by Guthrum."[108] In his capacity as leader, the man identified by the treaty as a *cyning* is seemingly displaced in the 878 annal by the men under him. How to account for this? Viking armies in England may well have been only loosely organized anyway, as Ben Raffield demonstrates,[109] so perhaps the annalist is simply being accurate in crediting the Scandinavian leader with limited authority. Or perhaps the annalist meant that the raiding-army had spoken *for* Guthrum once they had been directed by him to convey his promises to Alfred. Yet by foregrounding the *here*'s power to speak and to act, the annal implies that the duty to honour a vow had been fulfilled not by the commander but by his subordinates. The *kyning* who went on to "share out" land in East Anglia looks oddly diminished in this context; like the "kings" of raiding bands in the 875 annal, Guthrum seems a king in name rather than in substance.

If we return to the treaty and ask of what or of whom it makes Guthrum king, we find that the seemingly obvious answer, "eal seo ðeod ðe on Eastænglum beoð" ("all the people who are in East Anglia"), is more ambiguous than it looks at first sight. The key signifier has been detached from its signified; the AGT has had to break with tradition by using a form of the word "Angles" or "Anglians" to refer to a *gens* that effectively had ceased to be Anglian. On lexical grounds alone, the *frið* looks to be a dubious agreement between two rather ill-defined groups. On one side, there are Alfred's *Angelcynn*, the demonym purporting to represent all the "English people" (whether or not the Cerdicing monarch seriously intended to conquer them eventually),[110] but perhaps indicating more importantly the authentic "Angles," whoever Alfred might have thought them to be. On the other side, there are the "East Angles" or "East Anglians," who are neither properly Anglian nor led by an Anglian ruler. Nor are they even associated exclusively with the historical *provincia* of that people, for the AGT assigns to Guthrum Essex and eastern Mercia.[111] Add to this confused state of affairs the dual meaning of the noun *Eastængle* itself (the treaty's *Eastænglum* being the dative plural form), which can mean either the East Anglian territory or the East Anglian people,[112] and it becomes unclear whether "eal seo ðeod ðe on Eastænglum beoð" with whom Alfred is entering into a pact should be taken to mean "all the (Danish) people who are among the (English) East Angles" or "all the (Danish) people who are in East Anglia."[113] The AGT presupposes that the *ðēod* is distinct from the *Eastænglum* (whether people or place), and the presupposition opens a loophole in Alfred's favour. The upshot is that the text obliged Guthrum and his "people" to respect the boundary stretching from the Thames to Watling Street, that is, to acknowledge that the West Saxon king held sway over all his own subjects living to the west and south of it. Alfred, for his part, was to heed the boundary-clause's implicit injunction forbidding him to encroach on land belonging to the Danish *ðēod*. Evidently the treaty did not necessarily prohibit him from entering lands occupied by all the people *on Eastænglum* who lived under Scandinavian overlordship; the text applied only to the Danish *ðēod* living *in* East Anglia or *among* the indigenous East Angles, not to the indigenous East Angles themselves.

The treaty formalizes an East Anglia at once outlandish and familiar, governed by foreigners yet situated in Britannia. It seeks to isolate a raiding-army whose very nature, the ASC implies, is to remain mobile and defy containment. To this end, the AGT's boundary-clause, while hardly a model of topographical precision,[114] forged a frontier of sorts out of known landscape features. In conceptualizing even an inexact frontier, Alfred may have been influenced by changes in border-thinking underway across the Channel. Hans-Werner Goetz has surveyed developing Continental notions of realms and their boundaries between the fifth and ninth centuries, and concludes that "Carolingian authors ... perceived kingdoms ... as geographical units with clear border-lines," and that "the Carolingian border was not an undefined 'march' or border-land (at least not in theory), but a very concrete frontier, thus documenting a clear notion of realms notably distinct from each other."[115] More recently, Shane McLeod has suggested that Guthrum and his retinue themselves may have brought these Carolingian attitudes with them to England after having been exposed to them on the Continent.[116] As a literate king and as the victor at Edington, however, Alfred would have been in a better position than Guthrum to dictate the treaty's terms and exploit the textual effects of written *landgemæra* ("borders").

The Alfred-Guthrum Treaty: The Performance of Welcoming

With its seemingly equal treatment of Alfred and Guthrum and its ostensibly objective delineation of the frontier, the AGT looks like a serious effort at constructive policy, its very status as a document calculated to convince the Danish *here* that East Anglia was to be theirs indefinitely. So impressive is the performance that one might reckon the *frið* to "have been a genuine offer of welcome into the religio-ethnic family of Christendom"[117] and to have "present[ed] Guthrum as a Christian king, and as a legislator in the Christian, western European tradition."[118] This was the very impression the treaty sought to convey. Yet Alfred knew how unruly the international Christian family could be; the English branch alone offered many examples, and Guthrum, despite being christened Æthelstan, was not English.[119] Neither was the polity he led. Paul Kershaw has noticed that the treaty juxtaposes a precisely termed English *witan* with a less clearly described Danish *ðēod*; he suggests that the latter noun "covered a mixed population of settlers and pre-existing inhabitants" and "may also have denoted a general vagueness on the part of the English as to the political organization of the Scandinavian settlers."[120] Though acknowledged as human beings rather than as mere pirates or as the hagiographer's "satellites of the devil," Guthrum's subjects are still the *here* and the *ðēod*.[121] It is the English who are defined politically as a council, as if Guthrum and his retinue were imagined contrastively to live in a primitive, pre-political state; perhaps the difference between the two terms opened up another loophole that Alfred might some day exploit.

Even if it did not, the treaty's terminology still suggests a hierarchy of value. A *witan* will have possessed a certain degree of structural development along a continuum leading to what Simon Keynes has called "procedures of royal government in the tenth and eleventh centuries … which historians are pleased to describe as 'sophisticated.'"[122] The term *ðēod* may imply something similar in certain contexts, but not, it seems, in the AGT. What it does imply instead is social and territorial unity, another illusion. George Molyneaux has noted the fissiparity of the several eastern English *hergas* as they appear in early tenth-century Chronicle annals; he reads that heterogeneity back into the viking armies of the 880s and questions the AGT's ability to reflect or impart organization on the Danish side of the *landgemæra*. Similar cautions against "exaggerat[ing] the political coherence of the Scandinavian regions" in England have been raised by Lesley Abrams.[123]

Vagueness about the frontier may be related to the frequency with which it was violated. R.H.C. Davis and Cyril Hart claim that the boundary persisted only until the year 911;[124] Simon Keynes and Michael Lapidge are less optimistic, adducing the Chronicle's reference to an ealdorman of Essex who served Alfred from 893 to 895 as evidence that the boundary had changed at some point in that period and that Alfred had changed it.[125] Perhaps it would be more accurate to say that he had changed it back; even before *Ethandun* the West Saxon king would have known that Essex had been under Cerdicing control in the 820s.[126] Alfred's willingness to cede it to Guthrum in the 880s amounts to short-term generosity to make his counterpart feel anchored in the east, far from the West Saxon heartland. Guthrum, for his part, seems to have been bound to the letter rather than to the spirit of the frontier, for in 885 the *Eastængle* endangered Wessex indirectly by doing nothing to stop a band of newly arrived vikings at Rochester. Æthelweard, in his *Chronicon*, states explicitly that these latter raided across the Thames and that the Scandinavian East Anglians, "plebs immunda" ("[t]he foul people"), actively aided them.[127] Provoked, Alfred sent a fleet into East Anglia. This counter-offensive had mixed results, and the chronicler dwelt on the district's treachery by way of concluding the year's heterogeneous entry: "7 þy ilcan geare se here on Eastenglum bręc friþ wiþ Ęlfred cyning" ("And the same year the raiding-army in East Anglia broke the peace with King Alfred").[128] Alfred and Guthrum's *frið* proved no more fixed than the East Anglians themselves.

The foregoing discussion confirms Chris Rumford's insight that "[h]ow we experience borders and how we think about borders depends very much on our personal circumstances: what constitutes a border to some is a gateway to others."[129] Hastings Donnan and Thomas Wilson point out that

> [i]t is something of a truism to claim that borders unite as well as divide, and that their existence as barriers to movement can simultaneously create reasons to cross them. Though the rigour with which different borders are policed can make them more or less difficult to cross, the imbalance between the opportunities which may exist on either side can create compelling reasons to try.[130]

Borders in early England were similarly regarded as spaces that opened as well as closed windows of opportunity. "Space," writes Andrew Scheil, "is characterized by the implementation of boundaries and by intermittent (and essential) transgression across those boundaries."[131] Elaine Treharne argues that "[f]or the Anglo-Saxons, the fluidity of borders is discernible in their desire to fix them and make the space between them known, even if left unmapped"; the resulting border space "is often better defined as a center not a margin, an expanse of the in-between, rather than abutting the boundary."[132] The act, or threat, of traversing a frontier area can shape a society's sense of identity, of how it understands its own "side."

On the basis of the above formulations, I suggest that the AGT's border between "England" and "East Anglia" instantiated a *mythomoteur* (to borrow again Anthony Smith's term) of West Saxon identity-formation predicated on East Anglian difference. In so doing, the border functioned simultaneously as a "clearly demarcated line," which helped to stabilize identities either side of it, and as a "frontier area," "frontier zone," or "transition zone." Such a zone would have created opportunities for Alfred, not necessarily to devise shared cross-border legal categories to meet the possibly unique needs of border-dwellers, but rather to stimulate planning for eventual West Saxon expansion and to develop an ideological basis for it.[133] The engine of imaginary nation-building was fuelled by the nearby presence of a rival kingdom that occasionally crossed the line and would need to be subdued. As

Kershaw has pointed out, the text did not, after all, envisage lasting and unproblematic harmony between the two peoples concerned:

> Alfred and Guthrum's peace settlement was tempered with realism. It did not seek to stop all violence *per se* between English and Danish communities, but rather sought to foster the peaceful resolution of disputes through the due process of law. This was, then, a peace within which there was an acceptable level of violence, and acceptability turned on the possibility of its ready resolution.[134]

The treaty and its terms arose in the transition between war and peace and indeed compose that transition.[135] They advance the chorography of East Anglia by contributing to the choreography of "quick dance-steps of attraction and repulsion, conflict and curiosity" performed by the early English and the Anglo-Scandinavians alike in the late ninth and early tenth centuries.[136] More specifically, in assuming that individual persons from either territory would try to cross over to the other, as well as commit crimes, Alfred did not regard the "raiding-army" problem as settled. For the time being, though wary of the existing Scandinavian presence, he nevertheless may have feared the arrival of "future Guthrums," as Richard Abels has persuasively surmised; for that reason he may have sought to use the present Guthrum's *Eastængle* as "a buffer zone" against subsequent Scandinavian attack.[137] As shown above in the discussion of the "A" recension's 885 annal, the strategy had little long-term success; but the attempt is interesting not least because it signals the role the West Saxon court may have been devising for East Anglia. As a Cerdicing projection of Alfred's concern to safeguard his own kingdom, it had already in a sense been co-opted into the West Saxon portfolio of geopolitical assets.

As Thomas Charles-Edwards observes in comparing ninth-century Anglo-Danish and Franco-Danish treaties, "the making of a treaty, and sometimes also the initial negotiations, occurred on the frontier, *in marca*." Although the AGT itself "does not claim to be a treaty drawn up on the boundary," it is nevertheless alive to the challenges and opportunities arising in that volatile space.[138] A potentially restive though settled enemy was the challenge, its usefulness in discouraging further invasions the opportunity. In addition to exploiting East Anglia as a vast rampart against new seaborne incursions, Alfred may have intended the treaty to stabilize a land he expected eventually to conquer.

To be sure, the AGT does acknowledge the importance of the West Saxon *witan* in deliberations and thus suggests a concern for wider social representation than just the figure of the king.[139] Alfred might have felt duty-bound to honour the traditional advisory role of the political community.[140] The nod to the *witan*, however, amounts to little more than a courtesy. Jenny Benham has reminded us that "for the medieval period it was primarily the individual, usually but not always the ruler, who entered into agreements. ... [T]reaties were essentially agreements between rulers, and 'international,' in the absence of nation states, should be taken to mean 'inter-ruler.'"[141] To focus on the AGT's interpersonal aspect is, then, to confront territory itself as royal projection,[142] East Anglia as the creation of Alfredian diplomacy despite being ceded to Guthrum. Negotiated into existence by Alfred as Guthrum's bailiwick, the new East Anglia symbolizes the clash between competing imperatives: on one hand, the Scandinavians' desire to rule and to settle; on the other hand, the West Saxons' concern to limit disruption to their day-to-day economic, political, and ecclesiastical affairs and to promote long-term cultural improvement, conceived by Alfred in specifically Christian and literate terms. These terms are crucial to an understanding of Cerdicing designs on East Anglia.

The Alfred-Guthrum Treaty: Ideological Boundaries

As his biographer Asser took pains to show, Alfred as a young man had not been content simply to hear texts read aloud to him. He had wanted to learn to read on his own, and as king he famously included reading in his regimen of daily activities, thus providing ample justification for David Pratt's analysis of "the force and status of Alfred's texts in relation to contemporary structures of kingship and political authority," and of "the effects of Alfred's learning as a tool of kingship."[143] Asser, for one, was greatly impressed with "devotam erga studium divinae sapientiae voluntatem eius" ("his devout enthusiasm for the pursuit of divine wisdom"),[144] and Alfred's *Pastoral Care* advocates a cultural program centred on literacy as the key to England's political and spiritual revival. Even Malcolm Godden, who has raised serious doubts about the authorship of several texts usually ascribed to the king, claims that the *Pastoral Care* with its polemical prefaces *could* have been written by Alfred, probably was not, but in any event "was almost certainly circulated in Alfred's reign and with his approval."[145] In the "Prose Preface," Alfred, or whoever it was who wrote in his name and with his consent, maintains that illiteracy among the clergy had resulted from the destruction of monasteries and libraries by Scandinavian invaders and from the carelessness of the English clergy themselves. This period of cultural loss had marked the nadir of English history, a lamentable trend that Alfred wished to be seen as reversing.[146] "For

Alfred learning and the wisdom that could be acquired as a result of it were essential to the spiritual as well as to the economic health of his kingdom: loss of wisdom, he believed, brought with it calamity."[147] Between Alfred's and Guthrum's territories, then, there lay not only a political border zone but also the boundary between the Christian, bookish enlightenment spearheaded by Alfred and the very recent religious conversion undertaken by a coerced Guthrum, thanks to whose compatriots "eall forhergod wære & forbærned" ("everything was ransacked and burned") in the England that the West Saxon king wished to re-educate.[148] If Alfred's "Prose Preface" is any guide, the future the West Saxon king longed for in its most idealized form was one in which book-learning enjoyed royal favour. This desideratum certainly would be pursued by Alfred, less certainly by Guthrum; for although the former could read, the latter could not, and that distinction affects the representation of East Anglia during the period of Scandinavian occupation beginning ca. 880.

As it has come down to us, possibly as a revised version of an early draft,[149] the treaty envisions readers, and exclusively English ones at that. Pierre Chaplais groups the document with three other extant pre-Conquest diplomatic texts that, as he puts it, "read like records drawn up unilaterally on the English side for domestic use rather than copies of treaties actually delivered by one side to the other."[150] Both sides will have known and accepted the treaty's substance because both sides formed – to borrow Brian Stock's and Martin Irvine's terminologies – a "textual community," one whose participants, "literate, semiliterate, and illiterate," were "expected to participate in textual culture, having the necessary texts, and their interpretation, read to them."[151]

If Chaplais is right, though, Alfred and his court would have believed themselves superior to their unlettered Danish adversaries regardless of whatever knowledge the latter might have acquired during their Frankish campaigns.[152] As Kathleen Davis has said of the "Prose Preface," "Alfred's literary project emerges as both conforming to universal Christian tradition and as distinguishing England within that tradition as a national, homogeneous unit with its own language and a single political, as well as spiritual, identity."[153] To these cultural aspects of the king's agenda should be added a military component. The "Prose Preface," as Scott Thompson Smith has shown, reveals Alfred's deep admiration for past English kings who not only heeded God's laws and maintained order domestically but also widened the scope of their rule and "ut hiora eðel gerymdon" ("expanded their homeland outwards").[154] Bookishness and bellicosity complemented each other in the West Saxon king's world view.[155]

When the ASC figures the Danes primarily as restless conquerors of English places, it creates a role for Alfred and his successors as stabilizers of a too-liquid landscape. The notion of expanding one's homeland, it should be said, verges on the paradoxical, for the word *ēðel* ("a person's native country," "fatherland")[156] possesses a temporal as well as territorial meaning. Strictly speaking, the land of one's birth cannot be enlarged, because it is a remembered place defined in part by a tradition of agreed borders.[157] To aggrandize it is necessarily to change the very idea of the homeland by encroaching on someone else's time-honoured boundaries. Viewed in light of this Alfredian ideal of *ēðel*-enlargement, the AGT sets out the terms of a provisional peace that countenances "an acceptable level of violence" (Kershaw) in the short term, even as it undertakes reconnaissance work in potentially hostile territory in the long term. The treaty probes ideological frontiers even as it establishes territorial confines; it assumes, rather than declares, that literacy betokens intellectual progress. By this measure of cultural achievement, a land ruled by an illiterate *subregulus* who had become Christian only through forced baptism risked lapsing into ignorance.

The AGT would have meant more to Alfred and his court than to its Danish hearers, but uneven agendas seem to have been normal in early pact-making. According to Sarah Foot, typical land charters, for example, "were designed ... to ensure that of all the plural memories and recollections available, only this one story was, and could be, told. Charters were not written down in case memory should fail, but rather to prevent the wrong memory from triumphing."[158] Michael Clanchy puts the matter even more bluntly when discussing Domesday Book and other post-Conquest texts: "Making records is initially a product of distrust rather than social progress."[159] For sheer reasons of diplomacy, of course, the arrangements between the two rival polities needed to look fair, needed to convey the impression of reining in potentially lawless behaviour among Alfred's own subjects no less than Guthrum's.[160] The agreed frontier, however, speaks to West Saxon political ambition; the treaty "projected control: Alfred had made the peace,"[161] and it was primarily Scandinavian behaviour that was to be controlled, appearances of equal treatment notwithstanding.

Theorists of border spaces, literal as well as ideological, have taught us that such spaces test the limits of centralizing power and serve as the arenas for that power's implementation. In response to Homi Bhabha, Robert Young, and Marjorie Perloff, Daniel Boyarin has acknowledged that borders can indeed serve as "sites where identities are performed and contested," but he issues this stern caveat: "Borders, I might add, are also places where people are strip-searched, detained, imprisoned, and sometimes shot. Borders themselves are not given but constructed by power to mask hybridity, to occlude and disown it."[162] When read in conjunction with the emphases on book-learning found in Asser's *Life of King Alfred* and in the "Prose Preface" *to Pastoral Care*, the treaty strengthens one's impression that the geographical reconfiguration of England had not been decided in isolation from considerations of cultural and ideological differentiation, in short from strategies for the exercise of power.

To borrow Kathy Lavezzo's phrasing from a different context, "[n]ational fantasies … can have historical agency."[163] The AGT was willed by the same mind that conceived the foundational narrative of the *Angelcynn*. Kershaw persuasively argues that "[b]y the 880s both kings were ruling over territories in which their authority was new: Alfred in 'English' western Mercia and Guthrum in East Anglia. Both seized the opportunity afforded by the treaty to follow strategies of image-building and legitimation within those territories."[164] Alfred's strategizing, I suggest, knew no bounds. Precisely because the *frið* permits the Danish East Anglians to come into view "in familiar terms" to West Saxon commentators and to Cerdicing political interests,[165] it also puts them in Alfred's crosshairs despite its ostensible affirmations of peace. George Molyneaux believes that neither Alfred nor Edward seriously planned to expel Guthrum and other Scandinavian leaders from England,[166] but Bede and Felix had shown that past overlords could make or break client-kings.[167] Guthrum was already, in effect, a West Saxon sub-ruler of the East Angles; Cerdicing *imperium* over East Anglia, a process that would begin militarily in the early tenth century, was probably a fantasy with agency in the late ninth. According to David Dumville, "[u]nification of the English was an essential aspect of policy, leading to Alfred's promotion of his '(over)kingdom of the Anglo-Saxons.'"[168] The AGT and the ASC suggest the aspirations of a West Saxon governing class content to play the long game in East Anglia.

The 890 Annal: The Exception That Proves the Rule

A momentous event worth recording in itself, Guthrum's death gave the writer of the ASC annal for 890 a chance to express West Saxon attitudes about what the Danish East Anglian ruler was and what he was not: "Godrum se norþerna cyning forþferde, þæs fulluhtnama wæs Ęþelstan, se wæs Ęlfredes cyninges godsunu, 7 he bude on Eastenglum 7 þæt lond ærest gesæt" ("Guthrum, the northern king, whose baptismal name was Athelstan, passed away; he was King Alfred's godson, and he lived in East Anglia, and was the first to settle that land").[169]

Although the text stops short of heralding the now-vacant East Anglian throne as an opportunity for Cerdicing expansion, it indicates Alfred's role in domesticating that throne's recently deceased occupant. Baptized and transformed into a settler, Guthrum in the early 880s had had to settle for less than what he had originally sought, which had been "submission rather than loot."[170] Although the annal's obituary of Guthrum leaves out these details, its use of Alfred's influence to supplement the foreign king's stature makes East Anglia seem a land of unfinished business.

To his credit, the 890 annalist refrains from dismissing the deceased as a mere leader of pirates, instead characterizing him as "the northern king," a seemingly neutral description. It has been said that, on the whole, the notice conveys "a solemnity that reveals nothing but respect for an adversary who had kept his word and his new religious faith."[171] In describing his royal status, however, the entry characterizes Guthrum as being northern, not East Anglian; and when his realm is eventually mentioned, it is identified as the land he had inhabited rather than the kingdom he had ruled. It is *þæt lond*, i.e. "that land" which Guthrum had been the first to settle, but also *that* land, that peculiar bit of England which, though literally settled, remains figuratively unsettled and unsettling, neither English nor Scandinavian but somehow both. Its late ruler is recognized as "se norþerna cyning" but not *se Eastengla cyning*, the status implicitly conferred on Edmund by the ASC entry for 870 and insisted upon by Abbo of Fleury and Ælfric of Eynsham more than a century later.

The annalist's recollection that Guthrum "þæt lond ærest gesæt" could be as much complaint as compliment, perhaps a wistful recollection of the time when Guthrum's raiding-army had been the only one in eastern England. So laconic is the claim that, if taken literally, it would anticipate Sellar and Yeatman's tongue-in-cheek textbook lesson that "the Danes invented a law called the Danelaw, which easily proved that since there was nobody else alive there, all the right-hand part of England belonged to them."[172] Of course, the annalist simply meant that Guthrum had been the first of the Scandinavian invaders to live in a formerly Anglian area of eastern England.[173] The annalist's past participle *gesæt* derives from *gesittan*; along with "settle" and a host of other possible Modern English translations, the renderings "occupy" and "take possession of" are permissible, and even preferable.[174] As Tim Ingold might put it, the 890 annal represents Guthrum as "neither placeless nor place-bound but place-*making*,"[175] though it presupposes the reader's knowledge that the late ruler, who was neither the heir of King Edmund nor demonstrably the recipient of divine favour (as Guthlac was said to have been), had necessarily depended on Alfred's blessing to obtain his pre-eminent place in the east.

Early readers of the 890 entry would have known not only about Guthrum's desire for all of Wessex (this from the 878 annal),[176] but also about his people's succour of the new Scandinavian army arriving at Rochester in 885 mentioned earlier. Although the 890 entry partly incorporates the Scandinavian leader into his East Anglian surroundings, then, it does not fully concede the legitimacy of his kingship, which still has something of the "northern" or alien to it.[177] Indeed, in the decade after Guthrum died, his East Anglian heirs and subjects still eluded West Saxon control.[178] Coins and annals of the period reveal local leaders striving for legitimacy at home and assailing West Saxon power abroad. When read in tandem with subsequent Chronicle entries, the 890 entry represents Guthrum not as the exception to the rule of typically Scandinavian aggression in England, but rather as the exception that proves the rule.

Buying Legitimacy: Danish East Anglia in the 890s

A foray into ninth-century numismatics must precede the plunge back into the Chronicle's wars. To appropriate King Edmund's authority, East Anglia's new rulers availed themselves of non-military as well as military means; this much is suggested by the roughly 1,800 unearthed pennies and halfpennies (mostly the former) bearing the legend "S[an] c[t]e Eadmund Rex" ("O St. Edmund, King!" or "O Holy King Edmund!"). Minted between ca. 895 and ca. 917/18 in Danish-controlled areas,[179] the coins indicate the complexity of Scandinavian East Anglian cultural politics. Seemingly situated on the opposite end of the behavioural spectrum to raiding and plundering, their minting formed part of a broad strategy of regional self-determination that included force, much as the minting of coins harmonized with the arts of war in Alfred the Great's own policymaking.[180]

There are different explanations for the coinage. Mark Blackburn and Hugh Pagan have suggested that "by the mid 890s the cult [of St. Edmund] had built up such a head of steam across the region generally that it was politically astute for the local Danish king to associate his regime with it by putting the saint's name on his coins."[181] Susan Ridyard earlier identified more specific reasons for the Danes to be politically astute: one was "to perform an act of expiation and political reconciliation," the other "to draw the sting from a cult of rebels," i.e. from whoever had remained of the old East Anglian aristocracy following Edmund's death.[182] Anna Chapman instead sees "Alfred and his successors" behind the coinage: "Instead of acknowledging whoever had succeeded Guthrum to the kingship, they chose to honour Edmund as the only king; undermining Viking claims to legitimacy by removing them from the list of East Anglian rulers altogether."[183] Chapman argues that such West Saxon intervention, if this is what it was, allowed the Cerdicings to connect their own lineage to that of Edmund so as to promote themselves as East Anglia's rightful kings.

For Gareth Williams, however, the coinage implies "a conscious resurgence of East Anglian identity, and perhaps a corresponding *rejection* of West Saxon influence."[184] Rebecca Pinner does not adjudicate between the different positions but instead argues that "this ambiguity is precisely what led to Edmund's popularity"; that is, "the ambiguity which so frustrated generations of modern scholars was actually one of the greatest strengths of Edmund's cult, as, in the absence of fact, Edmund was a blank canvas onto which could be written the ideologies and aspirations of generations of devotees."[185] As a diachronic evaluation of the cult's social and political utility through the ages, Pinner's analysis is compelling; but it need not invalidate the assumption, shared by all the scholars named above, including Pinner herself, that those who commissioned the coins had unambiguous motives for doing so.

The Scandinavian East Anglian elite were in a better position than Alfred's court to turn motive into action. The former had wielded power in East Anglia since 869, and there is no record of a local insurrection against their (possibly distant) overlordship over the following decade. Nor does there seem to have been any rebellion against their direct control of the district between 879 (880 according to the ASC's "A" recension), when the Danes first began to "share out" the land, and ca. 895, when the commemorative coins were struck. Guthrum's earlier "Æthelstan" coinage of the 880s, so-called because it bears his baptismal name, deliberately imitated Alfredian models; but that coinage was Guthrum's own issue and reflects his own power to mint.[186] According to Shane McLeod, the use of the name "Æthelstan" on those coins may have been intended to "highlight a fictional continuity between his rule and that of his Anglo-Saxon predecessors."[187] Because no evidence points to broken Danish control of East Anglia after Guthrum's death in 890, the Edmund memorial pennies and halfpennies of the following decade seem best interpreted as evidence that such "fictional continuity" was ongoing, that a Scandinavian ruler or rulers were directing the local East Anglian economy and manipulating Edmund's cult to augment their mastery of the land.

The vocative ending of the word *sancte* on the coins implies an appeal to Edmund for forgiveness, or a request for his protection, or both;

it voices the Scandinavians' desire to draw on the "fund of prestige" (to return to Susan Reynolds's term) associated with the saint-king to enhance their own political standing in East Anglia.[188] As Blackburn and Pagan have pointed out, the Edmund coins circulated chiefly among the Scandinavians in their territories, and "have rarely been found in areas under Anglo-Saxon control or in Francia, but that is as one would expect since their monetary systems operated on different weight standards and would have required the St. Edmund coins to be reminted."[189] Furthermore, Stewart Lyon's study of early tenth-century coinage explains the differences between Edward the Elder's issues and Danish imitations, and shows why West Saxon control of the Danelaw mints of Thetford, Cambridge, Norwich, and Lincoln was unlikely even well after Alfred's death.[190] The St. Edmund memorial issue would seem to be the East Anglian Danes' economic, ideological, perhaps even apotropaic supplement to their raiding activities in the middle to late 890s and beyond. For his part, Alfred will have had to confront the *Eastængle* both as a future goal for eventual English unification and as a present threat of catastrophe, a military foe now appropriating Edmund himself as its spiritual protector.[191]

The Chronicle entry for 894 (*recte* 893), for example, shows that, far from losing their grip on East Anglia, the Scandinavians there were able – with the Northumbrian army's help – to put the squeeze on Wessex itself.[192] The annals for 895–7 (*recte* 894–6) suggest likewise, despite occasional victories by Alfred's forces.[193] Two entries record that women among the Danish raiders were placed in East Anglia for their own safety;[194] clearly the Scandinavian forces regarded the entire ex-kingdom, not just Thetford or Cambridge, as their own stronghold. Alfred had little leisure to challenge that assumption in the short term. Threats to Cerdicing territory were frequent and severe, coming both from established and from newly arrived *hergas*; in this period battles erupted from Devon to Essex. Alfred could hardly have had the time or means to usurp East Anglian minting in the mid-890s when he was fighting for his own kingdom's life. The ASC's annal for 897 (896) claims that natural causes proved more devastating to the English in that year than the *here* had done: "Næfde se here, Godes þonces, Angelcyn ealles forswiðe gebrocod, ac hie wæron micle swiþor gebrocede on þæm þrim gearum mid ceapes cwilde 7 monna, ealles swiþost mid þæm þæt manige þara selestena cynges þena þe þær on londe wæron forðferdon on þæm þrim gearum" ("The raiding-army, by the grace of God, had not altogether utterly crushed the English race; but they [i.e. the English] were a great deal more crushed in those three years with pestilence among cattle and men, most of all by the fact that many of the best of the king's thegns there were in the land passed away in those three years").[195] Nevertheless, the sense of general chaos is clear enough, and insofar as the vikings were blamed for part of it, they were blamed implicitly as enemies to the adopted religion of Guthrum-Æthelstan. In the same year, a sea battle was fought somewhere off the Devon or Dorset coast; although the West Saxons lost fewer lives (62 casualties along with 11 Frisian mercenaries slain, versus 120 Scandinavian dead), the fight was revealingly understood by the annalist to have a religious aspect, for only the West Saxon force is described as *cristnan* ("Christians").[196]

The Chronicle's entries for the middle 890s suggest that the Scandinavian East Anglians, notwithstanding their defeats and losses, were secure in the mastery of their own house and keen to weaken Alfred's hold on his. However "timeless" the English landscape may seem to be as a result of the annals' use of geographical detail, however convincingly the ASC uses "accepted and traditional forms" of spatial description to "produce place as stable and as a totality,"[197] these effects are phantasmic, designed to conjure up stability where none existed. Guthrum was the exception that proved the Chronicle's rule of viking untrustworthiness; East Anglia was the proximate threat that created England as a country. In her analysis of the copying of the ASC in Northumbria between the mid-tenth and mid-eleventh centuries, Pauline Stafford urges us simultaneously to see the chronicles as "multiple and fluid" and to bear in mind the "core narrative" of Englishness they all share. "Are plural chronicles texts for an age of devolution?" she asks. "Not if we are searching for separatist tales, or local stories. These chronicles are neither, though reading one of them provoked an expression of northern pride if not resistance in Northumbrian scribes."[198] Entries between the 880s and, as we shall see below, the early 900s likewise contain no "separatist tales, or local stories"; but this is because they busily suppress such accounts, preventing them from being told in ways that would unravel the core of the textual narrative that Stafford rightly discerns binding together the ASC's multifarious iterations. My regional emphases, both here in this chapter and throughout this book, complement more familiar ethnic or political analyses that credit Scandinavian incomers with spurring the West Saxons to fashion England as a cohesive entity. The East Anglia of the 880s and 890s challenged the Alfredian program of a totalized *Angelcynn*; as the next section shows, the region's influence was contagious, infecting even a nephew of King Alfred himself; and the various versions of the ASC responded to the threat by grounding, in different ways, a "separatist tale" before it could really take off: the story of an unholy if short-lived West Saxon-East Anglian alliance against the House of Cerdic.

East Anglia's Secret Weapon? Æthelwold *Ætheling*

A neat geopolitical dichotomy is found in the "A" recension's entry for the year 900 (*recte* 899), which styles the recently deceased Alfred as "cyning ofer eall Ongelcyn butan ðæm dæle þe under Dena onwalde wæs" ("king over all the English people except that part which was under Danish control").[199] Although it concedes Scandinavian *onwald* of certain parts of England, it trumpets the West Saxon monarch's pre-eminence everywhere else. Alice Sheppard claims that the term *Ongelcyn* presupposes not just ethnic Englishness but also, and more importantly, "acceptance of Alfred's lordship."[200] The meaning of the entry is thus more complex than it looks. The alliterative echo of *Ongelcyn* in the word *onwald* invites readers to contemplate each noun in relation to the other, and to reflect that at the turn of the tenth century there were English people living under non-English rule, as well as historically English territories that had no kings of their own, let alone "overlords" or *bretwaldan*, as the "A" Chronicle's entry for 827 translates the Bedan concept of rulers who exercised *imperium*.[201] In the 900 annal Scott Thompson Smith detects the wish to underscore "quietly but emphatically" the shrunken boundaries of England during Alfred's reign;[202] a good *dǣl* of Insular territory had been taken away by Scandinavian invaders who, in Northumbria as well as in East Anglia, subsequently *gedǣled* it out amongst themselves. "It would fall to Alfred's descendants to realize the political ideal of both achieving domestic security and extending dynastic lands."[203] Because the *Eastængle* proved especially eager and able to thwart these aims, they appear to be depicted virtually as the "other" in the ASC. Yet the seemingly straightforward "us-versus-them" dichotomy so often noted by scholars of the annals is also more complex than it looks, because English West Saxons as well as Scandinavian East Anglians trespassed across the boundary fixed by the AGT. Lines of cultural demarcation were tested from both sides.

The West Saxon *ætheling* (or royal heir) Æthelwold is a case in point.[204] He was a son of Alfred's predecessor Æthelred I and his queen Wulfthryth; as Alfred's nephew, he had a good claim to the throne of Wessex and pressed it. Sensing trouble in advance, Alfred had sought to bolster the position of his own son Edward (r. 899–924) by trying to satisfy his nephew with lands in remote Sussex and Surrey. According to Ryan Lavelle, "a marginalization of Æthelwold seems to be shown in the distance of these bequeathed lands from the heart of power – indeed … from Æthelwold's own support base."[205] Shunted aside, the *ætheling* had reason to resent Edward's eventual coronation. Among the various narratives of his rise and fall, the entry in the "A" text of the Chronicle stands out because of its singularly strenuous effort to diminish the rebellion's importance. According to Hart, the "B" recension contains "[t]he oldest and more authoritative" account of the story, while "the official version in the 'A' text is clearly a late revision, intended to justify King Edward's position and to reinforce his authority."[206] The "A" recension's propaganda, however, erases neither the rebel's importance nor East Anglia's destabilizing potential.

As "A" has it, the disappointed thegn first seized the royal estate at Wimborne in Dorset but then sneaked away after nightfall, avoiding Edward's forces and escaping to Northumbria in hopes of finding allies among its Scandinavian elite (perhaps because he initially expected to find greater anti-Wessex hostility in Northumbria than in the more nearby East Anglia?). The text neglects to clarify whether Æthelwold enjoyed much luck in the north – other versions admit he did, as we shall see below – but it does make plain that he met with great success when he extended his recruitment drive to East Anglia. According to the entry for 905 (904),

> Her aspon Æðelwald þone here on Eastenglum to unfriðe, þæt hie hergodon ofer Mercna land oð hie comon to Creccagelade 7 foron þær ofer Temese 7 namon ægðer ge on Brædene ge ðær ymbutan eall þæt hie gehentan mehton 7 wendan ða eft hamweard. Þa for Eadweard cyning æfter, swa he raðost mehte his fird gegadrian, 7 oferhergade eall hira land betwuh dicum 7 Wusan, eall oð ða fennas norð. … 7 þær wæs on gehwæðre hond micel wæl geslægen, 7 þara Deniscena þær wearð ma ofslægen, þeh hie wælstowe gewald ahton.[207]

> (Here [i.e. in this year] Æthelwold enticed the raiding-army in East Anglia into hostility, so that they raided across the land of Mercia until they came to Cricklade [Wiltshire] and there went over the Thames, and took all that they could grab, both in Braydon [Wiltshire] and round about there, and then turned back homewards. Then King Edward went after them as quickly as he could gather his army, and raided across all their territory between the Dykes and the Wissey, all as far north as the Fens. … [A]nd on either hand there was great slaughter made, and there were more of the Danish killed there although they had possession of the place of slaughter.)[208]

The annal does not disclose, let alone justify, a Cerdicing thegn's motives for pursuing a seemingly unholy alliance with the enemy. Nor does it concede that there had been a precedent for this sort of thing: in 878 disaffected West Saxon thegns had similarly aligned themselves with vikings, even with Guthrum at Edington, because seven years earlier Alfred had assumed the throne by sidelining the sons of his predecessor and brother King Æthelred.[209] Instead, the annalist seeks to sustain the ASC's standard bifurcation of geopolitical realities into tidy English and East Anglian categories.

Rather than delving into details and adducing precedents, the 905 entry foregrounds the treachery of Æthelwold and the battle that followed. The *wælstowe* is explicitly identified in the "C" recension as Holme, probably the Fenland Holme located in Huntingdonshire (itself now within Cambridgeshire);[210] but the "A" annalist seems to have thought it sufficient to leave the general region unspecified and to rely on the reference to the *here*'s home territory "on Eastenglum" to provide geographical contextualization. Peter Sawyer has rightly reminded us that "[s]ettlement did not mean that these invaders abandoned their warlike ways," and that "for the Chronicler there was perhaps little to choose between a *here* of raiders without permanent homes and one that had."[211] That is, regardless of whether they were mobile or settled, the *Eastengle* were still dangerous in West Saxon eyes, and their territory continued to signify the potential for destabilization. The annal's "on Eastenglum" and "eall hira land" imply a sense of geography just sufficient to allow West Saxon readers to imagine the fray taking place in an enemy territory that, while liable to ravaging by Edward, was still capable of exacting a high price from his forces.

Indeed, a Kentish contingent is said to have ignored Edward's order to withdraw from the area and stayed behind while the rest of the "English" army departed; thus isolated, the men of Kent came under attack from the East Anglians. Among the casualties on both sides was one Eohric, the region's Scandinavian king, and Æthelwold himself, "ðe hine to þæm unfriðe gespon" ("who had incited him to that hostility").[212] The annal explicitly blames the West Saxon pretender for violating the peace, as if the East Anglians had been guilty only of being "incited" to violence. Twice in this context the annalist uses the verb *aspanan*, "to incite, provoke" (present also in the form *gespon*);[213] the effect is to slight the quality of Æthelwold's leadership but also to figure "þone here on Eastenglum" as a readily unleashed force, to be harnessed against Wessex. The *frið* between Alfred and Guthrum proved unable to prevent a later generation of Scandinavian East Anglians from being stirred *tō unfriðe*. Tacitly the 905 annal judges the vikings according to the terms by which they had entered the larger Insular political order, even as it plays down their active role in helping a Cerdicing nobleman wage war against other Cerdicings.

Ryan Lavelle has plausibly surmised that the annal conceals "a level of tragedy of legendary proportions that has been lost to us: an English *Chanson de Roland*, perhaps?"[214] James Campbell argues that "[h]ad Æthelwold won the battle … England could, we may fairly guess, have been united in a different manner, involving much less warfare than ultimately proved to be the case."[215] Such pronouncements speak to the enormous threat posed to West Saxon security by East Anglian armies, the less-than-total ideological cohesion among the Cerdicings themselves, and the selectivity with which the ASC records the past. A telltale hint of the magnitude of the danger is betrayed by the "A" annalist's concession that "hie wælstowe gewald ahton" ("they had possession of the place of slaughter"), another phrase from that "Common Stock" vocabulary of warfare-related formulae that serves "to enforce and mark differences between the English and their Scandinavian opponents."[216] Even after Guthrum's time, and despite the 890 annal's reassurance that Guthrum had been baptized a Christian, the ASC has not altogether put aside its tendency to demonize the East Anglians. They remain the *here* or "raiding-army," capable of creating a *wælstowe* in 905 on the sociopolitical map of England into which they are supposed to have been ostensibly incorporated by King Alfred about a quarter-century earlier.

Yet the ASC's ethnographic demarcation seeks to disguise the extent of Æthelwold's own blurring of borders between friend and foe. According to Stodnick, the 905 annal uses the *wælstowe*-formula to portray Æthelwold's rebellion ostensibly "as one between insiders and outsiders, when in fact it arises from a dynastic struggle that is being mapped onto complex, mutable, and internal categories of difference both regional and ethnic."[217] Scandinavian East Anglians endangered the English West Saxons, but at least one of the latter was willing to align himself and his followers with the former. The 905 entry would have its readers believe that the new East Anglians were always poised to revert to their old viking habits, but clearly in this case it took a rogue Cerdicing to trigger their relapse. The alienness of the *Eastængle* was partly intrinsic to them, partly "incited," as it were, by West Saxons themselves.

One sees why the revisions in the "A" recension, as Cyril Hart has shown, "play down the whole affair, and understate Æthelwold's authority as a leader" in comparison to "B," which concedes the rebel's stature as an *ætheling* and admits that the Northumbrians "hine underfengon heom to cinge 7 him to bugan" ("accepted him as king and [undertook] to bow down to him").[218] The *Annals of St. Neots* expose the inconvenient truth even further, styling the rebel "king of the Danes" ("rex Danorum") and "king of the pagans" ("rex paganorum").[219] Sir Frank Stenton doubted such assertions and supposed that the claim by "B," "C," and "D" that the Northumbrians had made Æthelwold their king was "improbable in itself" and unlikely in the face of the "A" recension's "silence" on this score.[220] But "A" is just as silent on the matter of Æthelwold's elite status; I defer again to Hart's insight (adumbrated above) that "the A text compiler embarked on a systematic revision, with the objective of eliminating any suggestion that the *ætheling* Æthelwold might have received legitimate recognition in his bid for the English crown."[221] It would seem that the pretender evidently had done more to unify the various "raiding-armies" – Northumbrians as well as East Anglians – than they had managed to do on their own. Moreover, the "A" compiler refused to admit that the rebel, rather than having merely "enticed" the East Anglians to attack, had virtually become an East Anglian himself. In observing that Æthelwold and his Scandinavian allies "foron … ofer Temese," the "A" recension recalls the river's status as a frontier but glosses over its nature as the site of an unspeakable enormity, a double-cross no less than a double-crossing, a betrayal signalled by a Cerdicing's dual traversal of early tenth-century England's Rubicon: the first time as a West Saxon, the second time as a de facto East Anglian.

If the AGT incorporated the Anglo-Scandinavian East Anglians into a known cultural and political order, as scholars have claimed, such textual domestication did not necessarily make for cosier affinity. Stenton asserted that, over time and thanks to the *frið*, the Danes had been "making Englishmen familiar with their language and customs," and that for this reason Æthelwold was able to betray his own house and people "without placing himself outside the pale of civilization."[222] This last statement, however, is debatable. The "A" recension denies Æthelwold lordship of the East Anglians, dismissing his influence over them as mere enticement; such characterization detracts from the princeling's stature by denying him his role as a leader. The strategy is consonant with the AGT's reference to Guthrum's followers as but a *ðēod*, a word whose power to evoke "civilization" falls short of that possessed by the word *witan*, the treaty's term for Alfred's counsellors. Even more resistant to Stenton's claim is the *St. Neots Chronicle*'s identification of the rebel's supporters as but "pagans." Both sets of annals, then, complicate the thesis that by ca. 900 Scandinavian East Anglia had been integrated into a wider European system of political legitimacy.

The facts may well warrant a more optimistic view of that integration than the one I offer here. Lavelle proposes "that the Vikings only discredited Æthelwold's cause *after* his defeat"; before his defeat, he argues, they could have provided credible support for a disinherited but victorious West Saxon *ætheling*. This was so because, Lavelle adds, "the Vikings of late ninth-century England were part of the political 'establishment' in a way that the roving bands of Vikings in ninth-century West Francia or Magyar armies in tenth-century Ottonian Germany could not be for Frankish or Saxon rebels. Perhaps, ultimately, Æthelwold had chosen well."[223] But did Æthelwold really seek out the aid of the Anglo-Scandinavians because he valued their legitimacy? He certainly valued their military prowess; but by recruiting viking aid against his own relatives, he overturned the familiar political order, a gesture not easy to reconcile with a deep concern for optics. If his allies in northern and eastern England seem more respectable than their counterparts on the Continent, it is at least in part because they were more settled. Yet the mere fact that the East Anglians were not "roving bands" would not have sufficed to make them part of the "establishment" in any meaningful sense of the term. It is rather because they continued to be regarded as simultaneously volatile and settled "pagans" that their treachery ripples through the pages of the annals and resists modern efforts to smooth it into the surrounding normative cultural context. To King Edward, the conquest of East Anglia must never have looked more urgent than after Scandinavian *hergas* had helped a West Saxon magnate betray his own house and after that same magnate had coaxed the viking East Anglians to disavow the legitimacy outwardly conferred upon them earlier by Alfred.

The princeling's rebellion hints at the psychological no less than geopolitical impact of Scandinavian East Anglia as a place that both threatens West Saxon stability and excites Cerdicing disloyalty. Twice the *ætheling* is said to have "enticed" (*aspon, gespon*) the East Anglians to join him, but more disquieting is what remains unsaid: the enemy had succeeded in enticing a West Saxon thegn away from his own kin and country. According to Lavelle, the subsequent peace that Edward secured in 905 with the East Anglians and the Northumbrians at Tiddingford (Bucks) marked a stepping-up of his efforts to intervene in Scandinavian England.[224] The danger to Wessex posed by the vikings, especially those in *þæt lond* of East Anglia, had been far greater than Alfred's premature speaking for all the *Angelcynn* might suggest.[225] Although the conversion of Rædwald's successors had assuaged Bede's fears in the 730s, the christening of Guthrum in the late 870s failed to dispel the threat of East Anglia, a land that could induce a Cerdicing scion to behave like a "king of the pagans."

Wishful Thinking: West Saxon East Anglia

If entries in the Chronicle's "A" recension for the period 912–21 are to be believed, Edward offset the disaster at Holme in 905 by siphoning large numbers of East Anglians from their Anglo-Scandinavian lords. The annals scrupulously avoid using the verb *aspanan* or *gespanan* to describe Edward's success, the implication being that the king's lordship was legitimate from the outset and that his enemies had been itching to acknowledge it as such. No explanation is given for their surrender, and early tenth-century readers probably knew enough about the background not to need one; yet if taken on their own terms, the relevant entries create an impression of instant and thorough East Anglian allegiance to Edward. Until recently, this illusion of sudden willingness to embrace West Saxon overlordship did much to convince modern historians that Alfred's descendants had "reconquered" East Anglia rather than using it as an object of wishful thinking.

In 912, claims the Chronicle, Edward and his forces were constructing a stronghold or *burh* at Witham in northern Essex, close to the present border with Suffolk and thus to East Anglia proper. Suddenly, "him beag god dæl þæs folces to þe ær under deniscra manna anwalde wæron" ("a good part of the people who were earlier under the control of Danish men submitted to him").[226] We are not told *which* "dæl þæs folces" surrendered at Witham or why. Perhaps they were "English" men and women, or Anglo-Scandinavians like that Ulfcytel the Bold who almost a century later would defend East Anglia against a fresh wave of Danish attackers. In the years before his success in Essex King Edward had encouraged his subjects to buy property in Danish-held territory, as two charters from Æthelstan's reign strongly suggest;[227] the seemingly sudden switch of local East Anglian allegiance at Witham may thus have been simply the culmination of a gradual process whereby West Saxons had already begun to make themselves at home in East Anglia. Rather than being inextricably linked to East Anglian territory and allegiance, as it is in the annal for 900 (899) that records Alfred's death, Danish *anwald* a dozen years later is shown loosening dramatically. The East Anglians come to Edward; he has no need to go to them. The 912 entry thus neatly counterpoints, and cleverly compensates for, the 905 annal, which shows Æthelwold travelling throughout Danish England to "entice" allies to join him.

Supposed East Anglian willingness to accept West Saxon lordship is made yet more explicit in the entry for the year 917. Here the propaganda is more pointed because it has the East Anglian Danes, not the English population, offering submission. While the king was at Colchester repairing its damaged fortifications,

> him cirde micel folc to ægþer ge on Eastenglum ge on Eastseaxum þe ær under Dena anwalde wæs, 7 eal se here on Eastenglum him swor annesse þæt hie eal þæt wolden þæt he wolde, 7 eall þæt friþian woldan þæt se cyng friþian wolde, ægþer ge on sæ ge on lande; 7 se here þe to Grantanbrycge hierde hine geces synderlice him to hlaforde 7 to mundboran 7 þæt fæstnodon mid aþum swa swa he hit þa ared.[228]

> (a great tribe, both in East Anglia and in Essex, that was earlier under the control of the Danes, turned to him; and all the raiding-army in East Anglia swore union with him: that they wanted all that he wanted, and would keep peace with all with whom the king wanted to keep peace, both on sea and on land. And the raiding-army that belonged to Cambridge individually chose him as their lord and protector, and confirmed that with oaths just as he determined.)[229]

To contemporary readers of the ASC the year 917 must have seemed an *annus mirabilis* in the history of West Saxon-East Anglian hostilities. Edward yet again receives spontaneous submission from people who have not obviously been coerced into offering it or been threatened with destruction if they withhold it.[230] The text's repetitive diction, emphasizing unity both of desire and of the will to make peace ("hie eal þæt *wolden* þæt he *wolde*, 7 eall þæt *friþian woldan* þæt se cyng *friþian wolde*"), suggests that the annalist was thinking of the rhetoric of treaties in general, or perhaps of a specific, actual agreement; indeed, Lucy Marten has argued that "[t]he use of lyrical repetition in the phrasing of this Chronicle extract certainly suggests that it originated in a genuine oath."[231] The echo effect – the enemy's sudden adoption of the victor's rhetorical and military terms – conjures up perfect ideological sameness between the Scandinavian East Anglians and the English under West Saxon leadership. Where the AGT sought to impose mutual cultural intelligibility through the letter of the law, the 917 annal imagines uniformity of spirit, depriving the East Anglians of a voice and figuring Edward as a conqueror who can compel both the formal undertaking and the earnest desire of a *frið*.

This supposed outbreak of like-mindedness between West Saxon king and East Anglian population contrasts sharply to the strong likelihood, discussed by Dawn Hadley, that West Saxon soldiers arriving in Danish-held lands were not universally embraced as liberators; in reality, the prospect of imminent invasion may have led English and Scandinavian East Anglians to defend their common home.[232] Furthermore, by suggesting East Anglian desire for West Saxon lordship, the "A" Chronicle entry for 917 suppresses the region's general reputation for volatility and opportunism as well as the specific fact that, as Stenton put it, "for all its recent defeats, the army of East Anglia was still formidable" and that, even at the oath-swearing, it was "still an organized army."[233] In attributing military cohesion to the East Anglian *here*, the Chronicler can plausibly claim that it displayed further volitional concord rather than a tendency to make decisions on the basis of random circumstances or mere whim.[234] It is upon this imagined (though not necessarily fictitious) foundation of unity that the annalist constructs the region's commitment to obeying Cerdicing political will.

The ASC's entries portray the relationship between West Saxon England and Scandinavian East Anglia in terms of conflict and its resolution, by violent or non-violent means. During the early tenth century, visitors to the land of Guthrum and his successors, or to any other part of what was later called the Danelaw, would have beheld more complex realities. These could be seen daily, in hybrid metalworking designs for strap-ends used on clothing;[235] in farmsteads with new Anglo-Scandinavian rather than strictly foreign features;[236] in the choices made by Scandinavians to live and work in West Saxon territory; in the decisions taken by West Saxons to throw in their lot with the "enemy" (Æthelwold being only the most illustrious example);[237] in pennies that showed St. Edmund's influence on a foreign elite's public image;[238] in linguistic comprehension between native and newcomer even when each spoke only his or her own language.[239] In short, our hypothetical visitors might have grasped the essential truth of Dawn Hadley's insight that "ethnic identities were mutable, that they were especially liable to be transformed in the face of contact with new peoples, as social circumstances changed and the political tide turned, and that they were not invariably expressed through a standard set of characteristics."[240] The AGT and the annals instead prefer simplified identities, predicated on persistent mutual antagonism.

Such antagonism was only gradually resolved, *pace* the ASC's entry for 917. The annals' later tenth-century readers would have had to admit that the Cerdicing takeover of East Anglia had remained incomplete even in their own day. Lucy Marten concedes that two extant tenth-century charters show West Saxon kings granting land in East Anglia: one dated 945 (from King Edmund I to Bury Abbey), the other dated 962 (from King Edgar to Æthelflæd of Damerham; the Chelsworth diploma discussed in the Introduction, above). But both transactions,

Marten argues, were made possible by the agency of "women with East Anglian connections," respectively Edmund I's queen Æthelflæd and Edgar's queen Ælfthryth.[241] The likelihood that the Chelsworth estate had been destined eventually to pass to Bury St. Edmunds points to a nascent relationship between the West Saxon court and the East Anglian ecclesiastical establishment, or at least to the former's interest in cultivating one.[242] It bears repeating that the local West Saxon ealdorman Æthelstan had wielded so much autonomy in East Anglia before his death in 956 that he was styled "Half-King" and "for a while during Eadred's reign [946–55] … was practically a regent of all England."[243] Surveying all these West Saxon encroachments upon the land once held by Guthrum and his *ðēod*, Marten acknowledges that "the tenth century in East Anglia was a period of developing and strengthening ties between the region and the successors to Edward the Elder"; but she alerts us to "one fundamental development of Edgar's reign [959–75] that was noticeably absent from East Anglia: the symbolic mix of royal politics and religion known as the 'tenth-century monastic reform movement.'" Marten explains this phenomenon by suggesting that Edgar's lack of land in the region prevented him from acting often as a monastic benefactor.[244]

Military setbacks too, as Simon Keynes acknowledges, slowed the transformation of ideas of Englishness in the late ninth and tenth centuries through their various "West Saxon," "Anglo-Saxon," and finally "English" stages. Generally that development can be traced from Alfred to Edward (aided by the Mercian ealdorman Æthelred and by Æthelflæd, Lady of the Mercians) and then to Æthelstan.[245] In this scenario, "events are driven by far-sighted design towards their eventual outcome"; but Keynes warns "that the Alfredian vision of a new political order was not embraced by all, and that the new order was not necessarily exclusive of other, more traditional, perceptions of its component parts."[246] East Anglia's self-perception comes foremost to mind. Detecting it in texts is a bit like identifying a black hole; one discerns it by observing its effects on nearby matter. Late ninth- and early tenth-century East Anglian identities come into view because they affected Cerdicing plans, either "far-sighted" schemes for eventual national unification (if we prefer the teleological model) or piecemeal management of troublesome Scandinavian raids on an ad hoc basis.

The chorographic product that emerges was, in any event, intended for West Saxon consumption. As Hadley remarks, "the kings of Wessex manipulated the concept of Englishness for political purposes, but it cannot be claimed that this was meaningful to the majority of the population; indeed, the main audience for such propaganda may have been

Wessex itself rather than the whole of England."[247] The result is that the West Saxon claim to speak for all the *Angelcynn* left little room for East Anglia to be regarded as anything other than a shifting, unpredictable land in need of stabilization. It was the very slipperiness of the concept of the *Eastængle* that threatened to make the notion of Englishness less complete or settled than Alfred and his royal successors would have wished.

Conclusion

The AGT and several key entries from the ASC represent East Anglia as a menace to be defeated or at least contained, or as a prize waiting to offer itself to West Saxon hegemony. As Richard Abels points out, "[t]hough Alfred's dealings with his viking godson had at times been stormy, overall he could take satisfaction in having achieved the transformation of a heathen viking raider into what could pass for a Christian king."[248] But the qualification "what could pass for" gives pause for thought; *mutatis mutandis* George Bernard Shaw's Henry Higgins could have used the same phrase to describe his linguistic makeover of Eliza Doolittle. Like Eliza, Guthrum enjoyed the practical benefits of cultural "improvement," but it was for his own benefit that he staged the performance of Christian kingship. Neither for him nor for Shaw's protagonist would self-possession be sacrificed to an enforced decorum. New Scandinavian raiders in the mid-880s sought the help of Guthrum;[249] his collaboration with them, and his successors' minting of the Edmund coins in the 890s, show that the new East Anglians refused to remain mere West Saxon subjects.

"Conquest and crisis," observes Pauline Stafford, "remained the major stimuli to the writing of historical narratives in tenth- and eleventh-century England."[250] Chroniclers and hagiographers who were thus stimulated helped to construct East Anglia as both threat and invitation to West Saxon *imperium*. The oscillation between these poles of perception is akin but not identical to the factitious ethnic dichotomy between "vikings" and "English" that Catherine E. Karkov has so admirably identified as the source of further misleading dichotomies:

> The "Vikings," as they were labeled, were a transnational imaginary constructed by the peoples with whom diverse groups from the countries that are now Denmark, Norway, and Sweden came into contact. … The Viking invasions allowed King Alfred and his successors to forge a strong sense of English identity, both literate and Christian, around which the country could rally, and through which Bede's *gens Anglorum* could be transformed into the Anglo-Saxons and eventually the English. And that

> process allowed for the creation of a set of cultural binaries that carried over into modern scholarship: Christian vs. pagan, literate vs. illiterate, civilized vs. barbaric, peaceful vs. violent.[251]

Such binaries, like the foundational vikings-vs.-English pairing itself, distort the heterogeneity that existed within so-called Danish communities as well as the instances of overlap or accommodation between "Danes" and "English."[252] As R.I. Page notes of the long-held dichotomy between "Christian" West Saxons and "pagan" Scandinavians, "[t]he distinction ... is too stark for historical truth. It is a rhetorical one, designed to stress the virtue of the English and the vice of the Vikings."[253] Judith Jesch demurs from Karkov's analysis, maintaining instead that Scandinavian settlers were capable of defining their own identities apart from medieval or modern (mis)representations of them.[254] The difference between the two positions is one of emphasis: Jesch's is on extra-textual reality whereas Karkov's, like mine, is on textual characterization. Both aspects of "viking" history are important and correspond roughly to the processes of identity-attribution I have been concerned with all along: those originating with the locals and those imposed by outsiders.

The West Saxon-vs.-East Anglian binary is another pairing that invites discussion in terms of attributions of identity; such a discussion was attempted earlier in this chapter with the juxtaposition of English texts with Anglo-Scandinavian coins. The regional dichotomy, however, is distinct from the ethnic one, because whereas the latter made use of labels that were clearly intended to differentiate "us" from "them" ("Danish," "northern," "viking," "pirate," even "the raiding-army"), the former employed a term, "East Anglian," that preserved a lexical reminder of sameness, of common – if always to a certain point factitious – Anglian origins. That is, ethnic likeness to Alfred's *Angelcynn* is embedded within the very word *Eastængle*; the name of the place and its people threw down an explicit challenge to the West Saxon rhetoric of differentiation, rhetoric that was more successful when it branded the adversary as the *hergas*, the *Deniscan*, or the *norþerna cyning*.

By contrast to the term *Eastængle*, the word *Norþhymbra* ("Northumbria," "the Northumbrians") would have implied to late ninth- and early tenth-century West Saxons a greater degree of cultural as well as geographical distance, the Northumbrian Bede's own impeccable "Englishness" notwithstanding. The residual familiarity connoted by the "Anglian" root of the name *Eastængle* instead likely served as a "minor stimulus" (to adapt Pauline Stafford's phrasing, above) to West Saxon efforts to conceptualize and to realize a united

England. The *ēþel* or "homeland" could be legitimately expanded once it had been articulated comprehensively, whether or not the process of articulation was itself legitimate in the view of those living outside of Wessex. The Chronicle's 905 entry shows Edward coming close to beating the Anglo-Scandinavian East Anglians at their own game: he "oferhergade eall hira land" ("raided across all their territory"), the verb *oferhergade* hinting at the West Saxons' ability to overtake and even out-*here* the *here* despite failing to secure the battlefield. As if to make up for the disappointment at Holme in 905, Edward is shown to have succeeded at Witham in 912 and at Colchester in 917 in detaching the East Anglians from, respectively, "deniscra manna anwalde" ("the control of Danish men") and "Dena anwalde" ("control of the Danes"). Those two annals' sense of a foregone outcome implies a deceptively easy dissolution of that bond between Scandinavians and East Anglians to which Alfred had originally given his temporary blessing.

The later hagiography of St. Edmund capitalizes on a century of retrospection during which Cerdicing rulers sought to consolidate their claims to East Anglia, claims that further separated the *Eastængle* from Scandinavian *anweald*. Late in the tenth century, however, new viking raids threatened to reverse those gains, and Edmund became the embodiment and epiphenomenon of a struggle for East Anglia's complex identities. Although those identities also encompassed strategic territorial resources (e.g. the region's fertility, rivers, and fortified towns), hagiography came once more to play a major role in defining East Anglia's character. In the eighth century, Bede and Felix had employed that genre to project their own visions of the *provincia*'s relationship to the rest of England. Towards the end of the tenth, Abbo of Fleury and Ælfric of Eynsham wrote *vitae* of Edmund that likewise sought to articulate a place for the East Anglian region within an English nation. That nation was tested by the return of "Danish men" despite being increasingly united by Cerdicing kings allied with Benedictine reformers.

5
Edmund, East Anglia, and England

East Anglia was absorbed by the West Saxon political elite only gradually, despite the suggestion in the Anglo-Saxon Chronicle (ASC) that Edward extracted oaths of firm allegiance from its populace. During renewed Scandinavian raids in the late tenth century, Benedictine hagiography allowed the Cerdicings to redouble their effort at absorption by seizing upon St. Edmund and his territory as vital features of an England that was increasingly falling under their sway. Even in the late tenth century, however, East Anglian regionalism proved an idiosyncratic and tenacious reality not easily reconcilable with the West Saxon program of national unification. Much has been written about Edmund's role in the medieval identities of Bury Abbey, Bury St. Edmunds, Suffolk, East Anglia, and England itself.[1] To avoid reinventing too many wheels, the present chapter restricts its focus to Abbo's *Passio sancti Eadmundi* (*LSE*), Ælfric's *Life of St. Edmund, King and Martyr* (*SEKM*), and the debate over East Anglia's uniqueness – as proposed by Abbo and challenged by Ælfric – that the relationship between the two texts implies.[2]

Abbo (b. ca. 945–50; d. 1004) was a French monk who resided for a time at the recently founded Ramsey Abbey, located in the Mercian fens just west of East Anglia proper and close to the Mercian sphere of influence.[3] The English Benedictine Ælfric (ca. 950–ca. 1010) lived at Cerne (Cerne Abbas) in Dorset before becoming abbot of Eynsham in 1005.[4] Both authors were agents of the Benedictine Reform that was spearheaded by West Saxon kings and archbishops; both would have been aware that the Reform had struggled to establish itself in Edmund's ancient *provincia*. Moreover, both would have known that "[c]ults were powerful centres of local gravity," to borrow Patrick Wormald's insight.[5] Hagiography often made its subjects the foci of territorial identities, regional *mythomoteurs*, as Anthony Smith might call them. In East

Anglia, the cult of Edmund, slain by "pagans," eventually outshone the combined cults of Fursey, Botwulf, Æthelthryth, Guthlac (who had never been fully "East-Anglianized" to begin with), and Æthelberht. So successful were Abbo and Ælfric in this regard that William of Malmesbury later asserted that Edmund was "patriae compatriotarum sanctorum primus" ("the first of the saints of his country").[6]

Nevertheless, and despite their common Benedictine formation, the two authors reveal distinct geopolitical concerns and ecclesiastical priorities. Abbo exalted East Anglia as a land whose holiness, thanks to Edmund, had set it apart from the rest of England. Rebecca Pinner has drawn attention to "[t]he overwhelming sense of regional identity with which Abbo imbued his Passio";[7] and Mark Taylor has observed that "Abbo himself established a symbiotic link between Edmund and the East Anglian landscape; as a holy but vulnerable kingdom, it shared the characteristics of the king as perceived by Abbo, and vice versa."[8] Singularly blessed, the realm is shown to have been threatened neither by dodgy amalgamation of pagan and Christian altars, nor by attacks involving fellow Angles hostile to conversion, nor even by Brittonic-speaking demons evoking memories of ancient Anglo-British strife. Instead, as the *Passio* conjures it up, East Anglia's halcyon perfection is menaced by an indomitable peril: the invading Danes, whose eventual settlement as Christians in East Anglia over a century earlier Abbo conveniently suppresses so that he can essentialize them as evil incarnate, sprung from the septentrional abode of Satan himself.[9] As Julia Barrow observes, "the story of an English king killed by Vikings had added relevance in the 980s, since from 980 onwards England was once more threatened by Scandinavian raids."[10] Although Abbo ostensibly concerned himself with the events of 869, he was also sensitive to contemporary dangers – new viking assaults for one; encroachment on abbeys by powerful, home-grown lay magnates for another.[11] This dual perspective, embracing past and present simultaneously, was common among early medieval historical writers, who often imposed their own topical concerns upon their versions of the past.[12] The protagonists of saints' Lives in particular were raised beyond their own local and temporal contexts. For hagiographers, "[t]he saints were distinguished – if at all – by the glory of their martyrdoms (a visible token of their acceptance to God) and by their efficacy in dealing with various human suffering."[13] Unencumbered by the modern historian's need to recover the "true" circumstances of Edmund's death, "Abbo was effectively recounting a myth-making process,"[14] using hagiographical topoi that would edify his immediate readers. Those topoi make his East Anglia stand out from its neighbours.

Ælfric of Eynsham took a different route to commemorate the East Anglian king. It is, of course, a testament to the adaptability of Edmund's cult and of the complexity of hagiography as a genre that Ælfric should have used the very same saint to articulate an alternative moralized geography. But his efforts seek to fit the region within a broader national church by playing down East Anglia's uniqueness and asserting instead the widespread diffusion of holiness throughout English territory. Like his Latin *auctor*, the monk of Eynsham wrote about the past from a "presentist" perspective, envisaging broad English unity by evoking a recurrent external threat. The year 993 had seen fresh marauding campaigns;[15] and if a version of the Anglo-Saxon Chronicle was indeed kept up at Winchester,[16] where Ælfric had studied, he might well have known the conventional annalistic practice of equating Scandinavians with land-based *hergas* and ship-born plunderers. Conventional West Saxon wisdom held that Danish violence was the rule rather than the exception, and Ælfric would have been no stranger to such preconceptions, or to the realization that East Anglia lay especially prone to viking violence and might act more quickly than other districts to come to terms with new invaders, as Guthrum had done in 885.

Yet when Ælfric mentions the invasions of the 860s, he says only this: "[h]it gelamp ða æt nextan þæt þa Deniscan leode ferdon mid sciphere hergiende and sleande wide geond land *swa swa heora gewuna is*" (Ælfric, *SEKM*, pp. 44–5; "[t]hen eventually it happened that the Danish people came with a pirate force, harrying and slaying widely throughout the land, *as their custom is*"; Ælfric, *PSE*, p. 98).[17] In comparison to Abbo's invective, Ælfric's remarks about the invaders are quite restrained. Are all the "Danish people" barbaric, or just those who make up the "pirate force"? It is suggestive that although Hinguar and Hubba, the *sciphere*'s leaders, are said to have been "geanlæhte þurh deofol" (Ælfric, *SEKM*, p. 45; "united by the Devil": Ælfric, *PSE*, p. 98), the Scandinavians as a people are not denigrated as the spawn of Satan.[18] Unlike Abbo, Ælfric lived permanently in England; he would have paused at the implications of disparaging a group of people whose members included the ancestors of powerful Englishmen like Oswald, archbishop of York. Instead Ælfric would have his readers believe that the abiding enemies were the Jews. His OE Life of St. Edmund concludes with a bizarre, gratuitous foray into antisemitism, a radical departure from Abbo that was evidently the Grammarian's way of reinforcing Edmund's exemplarity and of implementing West Saxon Benedictine efforts to unify England. By taking aim at an easy because perennial target of Christian persecution, Ælfric, I argue, suppresses the challenge presented by East Anglian particularism. The Jews serve him as a means to distract his readers from regional identities that in fact had thwarted visionary programs of national synthesis since Bede's time.

Sainted Edmund and Sanctified Kingdom

Abbo's hagiographical promotion of Edmund exalted the East Angles over their neighbours by crediting them with a kind of spiritual *imperium*, which, in its impact on early English hagiography, went well beyond the short-lived political overlordship enjoyed by Rædwald two and a half centuries earlier. Moreover, the *Passio* surpassed the hagiography of Sigeberht, Æthelthryth, Guthlac, and Æthelberht by depicting its protagonist as a martyr whose self-sacrifice in Christ's name infused his country with unrivalled holiness.[19] Before idealizing the kingdom and its king, however, the scholar from Fleury needed first to create the right context.

Abbo composed the *LSE* during a two-year sojourn in England at Ramsey Abbey ca. 985–7;[20] his pupil Byrhtferth would recall later that an account of Edmund's martyrdom fulfilled a request by the Ramsey monks for instruction in advanced Latin grammar.[21] Indeed, as the author of a treatise entitled *Quaestiones grammaticales*, Abbo will have sensed no sharp divide between grammar and history, and in all likelihood would have thought hagiography as apt a genre for his pedagogical needs as any other.[22] The resulting textual monument to the life, death, and miracles of the murdered king is extant in three manuscripts from the eleventh century and over a dozen from the twelfth and thirteenth, including abridgements.[23] The *LSE* also laid a sturdy foundation for many subsequent stories. Some of these may derive from anecdotes not recorded by Abbo; others reveal decidedly creative, "romancing" minds at work.[24] In his Prologue Abbo claims to have derived his information about the Danes' killing of Edmund from first-hand reportage by Archbishop Dunstan, the work's dedicatee,[25] who in turn had heard it as a boy from an elderly sword-bearer of Edmund's who had lived to tell the tale to King Æthelstan.[26] Scholars continue to debate the soundness of this chain of oral testimony;[27] but the chain matters not least because it links the story of a regional ruler to a larger national context, an England that Abbo believed to have been unified by a king and an archbishop.

This emplacement of a regional saint's life within national power structures exemplifies what Jacqueline Stodnick has called, in relation to Bede's portrait of Æthelthryth, a "synecdochic notion of regionality that asserts the symbolic value of the part in relation to the whole," a notion that enables the very discourse of nationhood itself from the time of Bede's *HE* to the anonymous fourteenth-century *Life of St. Erkenwald*. According to Stodnick, "[e]ven though their immediate energies may be being harnessed by their authors in the service of local identity formation, these texts bear a fascinating relation to Englishness precisely because they promote and develop the type of thinking necessary to uphold such a concept."[28] That Abbo himself had such a broad "national" perspective is amply confirmed when he repeats the hallowed "migration myth" so dear to Bede.[29] In his hands, however, the *adventus Saxonum* serves to highlight the distinctness of East Anglia at the expense of that of England.

At the outset, the usual (Bedan) folk-units of Saxons, Jutes, and Angles are named as the first Germanic arrivals in Britain to be summoned by the indigenes to defend their land against enemy attack. As in Bede so too in Abbo the newcomers seize much of the island for themselves once they perceive its owners' weakness. They

> se et suos defensarent fortiter, illi uero ignauiae operam dantes quasi prolaetarii ad solam uoluptatem domi residerent, fisi de inuicta fortitudine stipendianorum militum quos conduxerant, ipsos miseros indigenas domo patriaque pellere deliberant: factumque est. Et exclusis Britonibus statuunt inter se diuidere uictores alienigenae insulam, bonis omnibus fecundissimam, indignum iudicantes eam ignauorum dominio detineri, quae ad defensionem suam idoneis posset prebere sufficientem alimoniam et optimis uiris.
>
> (defended themselves and their clients with courage; but as the latter were given over to sloth, and stayed at home, as might be expected of a proletariat, absorbed in pleasure alone, trusting to the unconquered bravery of the hireling soldiery whom they had retained, the protectors took counsel for the expulsion from home and country of the wretched natives. And so it was done; the Britons were turned out, and the alien conquerors set to work to parcel out among themselves the island, replete, as it was, with wealth of every kind, on the ground that it was a shame that it should be retained under the rule of a lazy populace, when it might afford a competent livelihood to men of mettle who were fit to defend themselves. [*LSE*, pp. 68–9; *Passion*, pp. 11–13])

This outsized historical backdrop has been said to amount to mere rhetorical "padding" and to be "somewhat irrelevant" to the life of an otherwise obscure regional English leader.[30] Yet it seems likely that both Abbo and the Ramsey novices would have discerned in this padding some relevance to their own historical situation. Might not the pre-viking East Angles of the ninth century, and for that matter the East Anglians or West Saxons of the late tenth, warrant comparison to those fifth-century Britons condemned as slothful sybarites? Hundreds of years earlier, "alien conquerors" had seized much of the island for themselves; the process had happened again when, in 869, a Danish *here* in East Anglia had "gesæt þæt lond, 7 gedælde," as we saw in chapter 4. After 980, new Scandinavian raids might have portended, to some, yet another *translatio imperii*.[31]

For his part, Abbo seems not to have encouraged such speculation, even if later embroiderers of Edmund's life did.[32] The *adventus Saxonum* could be a disabling or enabling cultural myth; Nicholas Howe has shown that "its central motif for ordering experience is that of migration," and that therefore "[b]y its very nature, this motif is dynamic rather than static."[33] Writers thus responded to it, as they did to stories of diaspora in general, with appropriate flexibility, deriving this inference or driving home that moral as needed. Although Bede in the eighth century had been drawn to God's covenant with the ancient Israelites, he did not necessarily think that his own ancestors, let alone his contemporaries, deserved to suffer hardships of biblical proportions.[34] Between the late ninth and early tenth century, the OE translator of Bede's *HE* exercised similar independence of thought, departing from some of his contemporaries by sharply distancing the *adventus Saxonum* motif from recent viking irruptions, as Sharon Rowley has demonstrated.[35] From a different perspective, as George Molyneaux has emphasized, ninth-century evocations of the migration myth suppressed any notion of divine favour that might have been read into Bede's Latin *Historia*.[36] To be sure, the myth is predicated on unworthiness, the belief in justifiable "transference of dominion" having animated Bede's account of slothful British natives losing Britannia to vigorous Germanic settlers.[37] But in certain contexts, it could be used simply to express patriotic fervour, as in the Old English poem *The Battle of Brunanburh*, inserted in several manuscripts of the ASC *s.a.* 937 to mark King Æthelstan's victory over an alliance of Dublin vikings, Scots, and Strathclyde Britons.[38] In that text, the *adventus Saxonum* heightens the importance of the English king's triumph with terms of comparison from the distant past.

Abbo too counted on the adaptability of England's origin story. Although he follows precedent in blaming the slothful Britons for having lost Britannia to Germanic settlers, he departs from tradition by using the migration myth's grandeur to frame a narrative about a region not a nation. In retrospect, the successful culmination of the *adventus* is not England but East Anglia; it is the latter that is shown to enjoy divine favour. Thus does the *LSE* supply East Anglia with its very own *origo gentis* narrative; the only element missing from it is a dynastic genealogy, notwithstanding that genre's possible overtones of Germanic paganism.[39]

Narrowing his focus from England to its easternmost corner, Abbo anticipates Malcolm Bradbury in describing Edmund's land as a kind of quasi-island, cut off only partly from the rest of England and bathed by the waters of the North Sea (*oceanus*) and the Fens (*immensae paludes*). By the late tenth century a sure way to evoke the holiness of East Anglia was to bring up the Fenland, despite the latter's location at the region's westernmost fringe:

> At predicta orientalis pars cum aliis tum eo nobilis habetur quod aquis pene undique alluitur, quoniam a subsolano et euro cingitur oceano, ab aquilone uero immensarum paludum uligine, quae exorientes propter aequalitatem terrae a meditullio ferme totius Brittanniae per centum et eo amplius milia cum maximis fluminibus descendunt in mare. (*LSE*, p. 69)
>
> (But the aforementioned eastern part is held to be distinct on account of this as well as other [reasons]: that is, it is washed almost on all sides by waters, for on the east and south-east it is girded by the ocean [i.e. the North Sea], [and] on the north [i.e. north-west] by the dampness of truly immense swamps. These rise up almost from the centre of Britain, and because of the levelness of the land make their way downward towards the sea, together with many rivers, for more than a hundred miles.)[40]

Abbo adduces the region's quasi-insular topography both to explain why the area is distinct or celebrated (*nobilis*) and to provide the proper, "noble" element for his protagonist. East Anglia would have resembled those parts of Essex lying just south of the River Stour as well as the easternmost fringe of the Mercian fens;[41] nevertheless, his wording suggests that Abbo knew the local landscape well enough to imply that, with its beauty and its lack of pronounced defensive features, it made an apt and even singular environment for a saintly king willing to die for his faith. Edmund's personal nobility looms large in the *Passio* not only as the result of rhetorical embellishment but also as a kind of hagiographical counterpart to East Anglia's geomorphic exposure. John of Worcester's later assertion – repeated by the *Annals of St. Neots* and by Geoffrey of Wells – that Edmund was crowned at the *villa regia* or "royal vill" of Bures makes the king address the problem of his land's vulnerability in a dramatic way. The town, which today comprises Bures St. Mary in Suffolk and Bures Hamlet in Essex, straddles the River

Stour, the ancient frontier between the East Angles and the East Saxons. If John of Worcester is correct, Edmund may have chosen this spot in which to assert his authority because he sought to firm up a border zone that, like border zones in general, all but invited transgression.[42]

Where John depicts Edmund displaying secular majesty in a specific liminal area in the kingdom's south-east, Abbo attends to the problem of East Anglia's over-accessible topography by focusing on the south-west. In delineating its borders, as he goes on to do, he seems to be aware that all land is merely on loan to its users,[43] but especially so when it presents an easy target for invaders. To its west the East Anglian district (*prouincia*)[44] is said to be bounded by land and therefore vulnerable and traversable (*peruia*), necessitating defence through human intervention: "sed ne crebra irruptione hostium incursetur aggere ad instar altioris muri fossa humo praemunitur" (*LSE*, pp. 69–70; "but so that it is not chronically molested by the irruption of armies, a ditch in the earth is fortified by means of a rampart resembling a substantially high wall"; translation mine).[45] The *fossa* is the Devil's Dyke, "one of several dykes in Cambridgeshire which were apparently intended to control the main route into East Anglia from the south-west."[46] In a saint's life that pits English against Danes as polarized enemies, the dyke epitomizes the proverbial line in the sand; its mention at this juncture in the text serves to prepare readers for the cultural bifurcation on which Abbo's whole narrative turns.

Although the *LSE* deploys the dyke to foreshadow the eventual clash between "us" and "them," specifically between late ninth-century East Anglia's insiders and outsiders, it neglects to mention that the earthworks had formed part of a system "which had been thrown up, arguably by the East Anglians against the Mercians in the early eighth century," as pointed out by Cyril Hart.[47] Ryan Lavelle notes that "[e]ven in the ninth century it had been more usual for the Anglo-Saxon kingdoms to fight with each other than with external enemies."[48] James W. Earl uses Ælfric's *SEKM* as a launch-point for a psychoanalytic study that concludes that "[t]he tendency to orientalize the Vikings as a barbaric Other is really a way of deflecting attention away from Anglo-Saxon violence."[49] Abbo's treatment of the Devil's Dyke has a similar if smaller-scale deflective purpose in the text: as innuendo, it presages the author's eventual account of East Anglia's Scandinavian invaders, the *LSE*'s inevitable villains; yet it suppresses any reference to the kingdom's older battles with Mercia and its more recent tensions with Wessex, just as Felix's Brittonic-speaking phantoms in the *VSG* served to sublimate trans-Fenland tensions in the middle of the eighth century.[50]

"Landscape," writes Yi-Fu Tuan, "is personal and tribal history made visible."[51] In the case of tenth-century East Anglia, Abbo uses writing to render this connection that much more visible by depicting the kingdom's vulnerability in geographical terms. Describing a frontier as *peruia* makes a statement about territory but also hints at the diminished strength of local governance; by contrast, Bede ventured no such hint about East Anglia's frontier when describing Rædwald. In the *LSE*, Edmund becomes his own country's spiritual bulwark in part because his realm's literal defences chronically give way. Credit has to be given to the dyke's original architects for trying to defend a stubbornly flat landscape; but in the end, as Bill Bryson waggishly observes, "it didn't take a whole lot of tactical genius to realize that all an invading army had to do was go around it, which is what all of them did, and within no time at all the Devil's Dyke had ceased to have any use at all except to show people in the fen country what it felt like to be sixty feet high."[52] Yet if East Anglia's earthworks, fens, and rivers proved no bar to invasion, they did help writers impart form to the landscape and map the ebb and flow of regnal power. It was by reference to the dykes and the River Wissey (or Ouse) that the annalist of the "A" version of the Chronicle *s.a.* 905 (904) had measured the havoc wrought by Edward the Elder on the Fenland.[53]

Having considered its strategic weaknesses, Abbo then defines the kingdom's territory by considering its natural beauties. To East Anglia's doubtful ability to repel is added an undoubted power to attract; both traits are connected through Abbo's use of landscape commentary as an element of political analysis. By conjuring up a *locus amoenus* he answers the unasked question why an army should have wanted to invade this country in the first place:

> Interius ubere glebae satis admodum loeta, ortorum nemorumque amoenitatae gratissima, ferarum uenatione insignis, pascuis pecorum et iumentorum non mediocriter fertilis. De piscosis fluminibus reticemus, cum hinc eam, ut dictum est, lingua maris allambit, inde paludibus dilatatis stagnorum ad duo uel tria milia spatiosorum innumerabilis multitudo preterfluit. Quae paludes prebent pluribus monachorum gregibus optatos solitariae conuersationis sinus, quibus inclusi non indigeant solitudine heremi; ex quibus sunt sancti monachorum patris Benedicti caelibes coenobitae in loco celebri hac tempestate. (*LSE*, p. 70)

> (In the interior the fortunate [province] is quite sufficiently fertile of soil, and exceedingly pleasant thanks to the charms of its gardens and groves. It is distinguished for the hunting of wild animals, nor is it indifferently

> fruitful in pasturage for sheep or beasts of burden. We remain silent about the rivers filled with fish, since, as has been said already, on one side a tongue of the sea licks it [i.e. the province], and on the other side an innumerable multitude of wide marshes flows past it, in fens spreading out for two or three miles. These fens provide hollows[54] desired by many flocks of monks for the solitary monastic life, through which [fens] may the enclosed hermits never want for the solitude of the desert. Among these [monks] are celibate brothers of the monastic order of the holy father Benedict, in a place now famous.) [Trans. mine, but see too Hervey's trans. in Abbo, *Passion*, p. 15.]

The Devil's Dyke, then, is so necessary because East Anglia is so desirable – especially to monks and hermits, for example those living "in loco celebri hac tempestate" ("in a place now famous"), about which we shall hear more soon. As much as any other part of the *LSE*, this descriptive vignette of local topography is a literary exercise, yet its chorographic potential is in no way diminished by the pedagogical concerns that prompted Abbo to write it.

In distinguishing between agrarian interior and watery edge, the French hagiographer provides what has been called a "remarkably accurate" and "precise" topography of the region.[55] His is topography with an agenda, however, for it seeks to illustrate how the district's natural resources serve people, how they fit into humanly devised economies of animal husbandry or spiritual salvation. Even when it conforms to the *locus amoenus* tradition,[56] Abbo's East Anglia evinces a concern with practical ends; fen, river, and pasturage were all serviceable commodities, made by God for people. The *LSE* and other texts "envision not a universe where men and women struggle to impose meaning on vast emptiness, but a cosmos already full of meaning for humanity to interpret," as Nicole Guenther Discenza has remarked of early English perceptions of space.[57] This is quite a different world view from that implied in Julian Tennyson's modern recollections of East Anglia; aided, or perhaps burdened, by the influence of landscape painting on regional writing, Tennyson laboured in his famous *Suffolk Scene* to define the region's *je ne sais quoi*,[58] believing, for example, that "[t]he marsh has a character and an atmosphere, a mystery and a rarity that cannot be transcribed."[59] His Fens transcend human purposes and thus elude language; their "meaning" (if any) resists our capacity to interpret it. Not so for Abbo, or for Bede and Felix before him, or for Hugh Candidus and Richard of Ely after him, all of whom believed that landscapes rewarded or tested human endeavour, fashioned as they were by a deity who envisioned them as human habitats.[60]

The "Pleasant Place" and Reformed Monasticism

Although Abbo's East Anglian chorography is influenced by concerns for utilitarian value, it embraces other aspects of place as well. There is a spiritual quality to his *locus amoenus* characterized not by a transcendence that eludes language but by the idiosyncrasies of monastic reform. As Catherine Clarke observes with regard to Exeter Book poems like *The Phoenix, Guthlac A*, and *Genesis A*, "[t]he *locus amoenus* plays a central role within the reforming rhetoric and ideology of revival, renewal and Englishness" during the tenth-century Benedictine movement on the island.[61] Abbo perceived no incommensurability between praising East Anglia's beauty and affirming England's cohesion from Æthelstan's reign down to Dunstan's archiepiscopate. His own vocation and his ties to the archbishop of Canterbury suggest a personal stake in upholding at least some aspects of Benedictine reform, and his image of East Anglian particularism was doubtless intended to encompass those larger, overarching aspects. Before proceeding with an analysis of Abbo's use of the *locus amoenus* to celebrate East Anglia, we need first to acknowledge the multifaceted nature of the Benedictine Reform itself and to situate Abbo's royal politics in relation to it, the better to elucidate the "national" as well as royalist agendas that the *LSE*'s chorography of East Anglia eclipses even as it depends on them. These agendas will later be restored to full prominence by Ælfric of Eynsham in his OE life of St. Edmund.

What has long been called the tenth-century Benedictine Reform movement in England is increasingly coming to be understood as a collection of diverse emphases and affiliations.[62] Basic commonalities among them, as well as heterogeneity within the movement, have been ably explored by Christopher A. Jones:[63] "'Reform' from its beginnings was a complex and pliable notion, and even its three great proponents, Dunstan, Æthelwold, and Oswald, appear to have fostered their own individual standards."[64] Abbo, for his part, cites Dunstan as the ultimate source of his material, as we have seen, and in so doing transmits his *LSE* through the most important channel of ecclesiastical authority in the England of the 980s. As scholarship on his text has often noted, Abbo sought to narrate a story rather than merely list events; he went far beyond both the 870 annal in the ASC and the courtly and secular horizons of that composite work as a whole. Abbo celebrated Edmund as a martyr who had refused to take up arms against his would-be killers and had instead chosen death at their hands in imitation of Christ's example of voluntary self-sacrifice.[65] This portrayal of royal transition from majesty to martyrdom required little effort, since Abbo believed, as Marco Mostert has shown, that kingship by its very nature conferred quasi-divine status on its wielder.[66] Focusing in particular on the eighth chapter of the *LSE*, which has Edmund boast to the vikings of his peculiarly tenth-century Christian approach to governance, Mostert argues that "Abbo showed himself to stand firmly in the Carolingian tradition which had made kings part of a 'corpus mysticum' which consisted of kings, martyrs, priests and prophets."[67] Infusing Edmund with holiness even before his death, Abbo preferred a theologically influenced model of royal characterization to contemporary political reality.[68]

The Frankish scholar agrees with the 870 ASC reference to Edmund as a king in his own right but avails himself of more recent Continental political thought to portray him as a royal martyr. Likewise, he has him fulfil the more general early medieval Christian requirement that royal sanctity should be achieved rather than assumed, conferred by the church after the king's death rather than being taken for granted as a natural concomitant of rule.[69] With these emphases the hagiographer suppresses the kingly prerogative of war even in a kingdom's defence, and instead stresses exemplary Christ-like self-sacrifice. This tack perhaps defers to local legends about Edmund; more likely it shows Abbo developing ideas about kingship that would benefit contemporary monasteries in their dealings with royal patrons, who had the power to confirm existing privileges.[70] His interest in mystical kingship reflects tensions between monasteries and local bishops that would increasingly occupy his attention after returning to Fleury ca. 987. Even in the *LSE* he touches on the subject of monastic exceptionalism in a way that suggests continuity with his later, more explicit defences of religious houses against episcopal meddling.[71] If a king has a moral obligation to protect monasteries and ensure the diffusion of Christianity, he should behave accordingly in war. Abbo sacralizes the official image of Edmund and in consequence promotes East Anglia itself both as a bastion of monastically sanctioned privilege and as a spiritual fortress against renewed Scandinavian paganism.

Within the text of the *LSE*, the trope of the "pleasant place" thus brings out the splendours of a timeless landscape while fashioning a new identity for the old *provincia* as a hub around which the rest of the English church might revolve. It was suggested in chapter 1 that, for Bede, Rædwald's Christian *altare* conjoined with a pagan *arula* contaminated all of East Anglia and threatened the unity of the whole ecclesiastical enterprise. A related understanding of the link between a king's religious adherence and the resulting prosperity of the realm informs Abbo's view of East Anglia's charmed landscape. Even grace can be commodified in the royal presence; though different from the potential yield of garden, grove, or river, the blessings conveyed through Edmund's body and shrine similarly nourish the surrounding polity. As Abbo tells us in his penultimate chapter – to which we shall return later – East Anglia warrants special admiration because it produces more wonders (*uirtutes*) than does any other part of England.[72] This chorographical singularity owes much to the mystical power of Edmund, whose spiritual exceptionalism sets him apart from the common run of humanity, much as East Anglia's aqueous surroundings (nearly) divide the kingdom from its Insular neighbours.

"Ramsey St. Edmunds"? Abbo's Monastic Mediations

In the topographical passage considered earlier in this chapter, Abbo writes that hermits and monks are drawn to make their homes in the East Anglian fens, especially "in loco celebri hac tempestate" ("in a place now famous") where religious devotion is, one may assume, held to be especially commendable. Antonia Gransden understands this allusion to an unnamed but renowned establishment as "an oblique reference to Ramsey,"[73] its inclusion in the *LSE* an unobtrusive gesture of thanks to the cloister that had hosted Abbo for two years and fed him the strange food and beer he would later blame for his obesity.[74] One of the great Fenland Benedictine houses, Ramsey was situated on an island surrounded by just the sort of watery terrain evoked by Abbo in his topographical passage. According to his student Byrhtferth, the natural bounty of the environs had struck the house's founder St. Oswald (bishop of Worcester before becoming archbishop of York) as "congruam monachis ad habitaculum" ("suitable for housing monks"); Byrhtferth's description of the local landscape chimes with Abbo's verbal portrait of the Fenland as a whole.[75] Abbo's choice of the adjective *celeber* to describe Ramsey is no hyperbole: at the death in 992 of its patron, ealdorman Æthelwine "Dei Amicus," the house was "a powerhouse of the monastic reform movement."[76] No meagre contribution to its legacy had been made by Abbo himself, whose scholarship and the books he had brought with him from Fleury "immediately put the new foundation on the intellectual map of Anglo-Saxon England. His visit was perhaps the most significant event in Ramsey's early history."[77] If Abbo did indeed have Ramsey on his mind when he wrote the description of the Fens in the *LSE*, then associating it with the cult of Edmund, even by means of the most subtle and passing aside, can have only redounded to the abbey's prestige – likely his patrons' objective all along.

It is noteworthy, though, that Abbo refrains from naming the house; doing so would have added that much more lustre to Ramsey's reputation, but perhaps he wished to avoid implying a contrast between the timeless beauty and abundance he attributes to East Anglia proper and the newness of Ramsey Abbey, founded only in 966.[78] Perhaps too he wanted to avoid stoking undue pride in his pupils, though this lesson (if such it was meant to be) seems to have been lost on one of them. As Michael Lapidge has noted, "Byrhtferth was inordinately proud of his learning, and took every possible opportunity to display it,"[79] having no qualms about inserting in his *Life of St. Oswald* Abbo's own learned and highly flattering fourteen-line poem on Ramsey, "*O Ramesiga cohors*." An example of *encomium urbis*, the work praises Ramsey to the stars, indeed almost literally, for it localizes the abbey in relation to the three constellations Hercules, Boötes, and Cynosura,[80] as if the orientation of the cosmos itself somehow depended on the monastery's prestige. Such explicit adulation has no parallel in the *LSE*, in which Abbo appears to rein in his prose just at the moment when he might have been expected to acknowledge Ramsey by name before returning abruptly to the matter of Edmund. I linger over that abrupt transition because it seems that Abbo wanted neither to dwell on it himself nor to invite his original readers to do so. Had they paused in that textual space between the absent presence of Ramsey and the explicit presence of Edmund, they might have connected the unnamed location to the person. They surely would have done so had Abbo named the place of his "exile," praised it as he does in "*O Ramesiga cohors*," and then woven in an explicit transition to the life of Edmund.

Abbo, however, connects Edmund's life neither to Ramsey nor to the house's Mercian fenland site, some thirty-seven miles from Bury St. Edmunds as the crow flies. Ramsey is sometimes said to have "colonized" Bury in the later tenth century by introducing the Benedictine rule there. Tim Pestell, however, has expressed doubts about this theory and infers from surviving evidence that it was only Cnut's patronage in ca. 1020, coupled with colonization from St. Benet's Abbey, Hulme (near Horning in Norfolk), that brought the Benedictines to Edmund's cult; this arrangement will have confirmed "Bury's situation in an East Anglian rather than Fenland/Mercian sphere."[81] Bury's slow adoption of the rule has led Pestell to surmise, very plausibly, "that the people of East Anglia may have retained a distinctive regional identity. Within this, Edmund could be employed as a totem to highlight their unity and independence."[82] This analysis has received support recently from Lucy Marten, who, as was discussed in chapter 4, also finds scant evidence of Bury's Benedictinism before Cnut's time and, just as important, a dearth of royal Cerdicing grants in East Anglia generally. According to Marten, these factors militate against Ramsey's influence, bespeak East Anglian resistance to West Saxon–sponsored Benedictine reform efforts, and thus indicate tenacious regionalism persisting beyond the conventionally agreed period of homogenization under King Edgar.[83] By keeping the *locus celeber* anonymous, indeed by making only fleeting mention of it at all, Abbo prevented his hosts in the western part of the Fenland from exaggerating their association with the Edmund story, despite their apparent interest in doing precisely that.

Played down though it may be, Ramsey's role in sponsoring the Life of a royal martyr culted at Bury nevertheless suggests "a bid by the Benedictine order to manage and control the memory of East Anglia's greatest saint."[84] It also hints at competition between Ramsey and Bury[85] reminiscent of the East Anglian king Ælfwald's attempt to infringe on the cult of the Mercian hermit Guthlac. In this case the rivalry, if such it was, seems to have arisen not between kingdoms but between Fenland religious communities, an understandable development when one recalls how thick the general area was with religious houses, each of which depended on land and on the good will of its lay benefactor, who was not necessarily above hostility towards a rival monastery.[86] The *Passio* testifies to the various and complex pressures that moulded eastern English regional identities in the late tenth century. The mere fact that Abbo should have treated the *locus celeber* as part of East Anglia is itself intriguing: the association plays down ideological divergence between Edmund's realm (and by extension the secular priests guarding his shrine, about whom more later) and the Benedictine Reform that had been implemented at Ramsey. If at this time the area around Bury was nicknamed *sǣlig Sūþfolc* or "holy Suffolk" (a phrase heard even today, though often garbled as "silly Suffolk"),[87] that reputation would be strengthened by subtle linkage to properly regulated monasticism, while *arriviste* Ramsey, for its part, would see its own "cultural capital" enriched by connection with East Anglia's heartland and royal core.

Then again, the monks of Ramsey, and for that matter Abbo too, may have thought they were living in East Anglia proper. By the 980s the district had changed much since Alfred's or Edmund's time, let alone Rædwald's; once a kingdom, it was now an ealdordom within an increasingly united England. It had also grown, having vaulted over the Fens that had long separated it (more or less) from Mercia; under Æthelwine (r. 962–92), the East Anglian ealdordom comprised the ancient Norfolk-Suffolk core, Cambridgeshire, Huntingdonshire, "and perhaps also parts of Hertfordshire, Buckinghamshire, Lincolnshire and Northamptonshire."[88] Naturally Ramsey was included, so if (as Young suggests) "the monks of Ramsey viewed Edmund as a saint for all East Anglians – for all English people, even,"[89] and if Abbo himself regarded Ramsey as an East Anglian foundation, then the enlarged ealdordom of the *LSE* simply reflects the administrative reality created by Æthelstan "Half King" and maintained by his son Æthelwine.

Turf sensitivities and hard-won privileges, however, made each monastic house in eastern England, in the traditional Mercian as well as East Anglian lands, acutely aware of its own identity, its own territorial extension, and the boundaries it shared with its competitors. Jealousies between abbeys sharpened the notional outlines of jurisdictions, which persisted in the enlarged late-tenth-century East Anglian ealdordom. Furthermore, by invoking the *adventus Saxonum* legend and by citing the Fens and the Devil's Dyke as regnal boundaries, Abbo reveals that his East Anglian geography derives at least as much from centuries-old tradition as from the relatively recent Cerdicing apportionment of East Anglia. Book lore no less than landscape determined his sense of the kingdom's extent. If his Ramsey pupils were paying attention when Abbo traced the watery boundaries of East Anglia, explaining that the ancient kingdom "nobilis habetur" ("is held to be distinct") precisely because "aquis pene undique alluitur" ("it is washed almost on all sides by waters"), they would have had to concede that their own house lay outside those boundaries. Historically the area around Ramsey had belonged to Mercia, and Abbo was being asked by a geographically Mercian and politically West Saxon monastery to poach on the turf of an East Anglian and as yet "un-Benedictinized" house. Mediating between Ramsey's patronage and Bury's cult, he was conscripted to assist in a hagiographical raid on Bury from across the Fens, an elegantly textualized smash-and-grab that could be justified, from Ramsey's perspective, as a victimless crime insofar as it sought to honour the unbowed fortitude and Christ-like piety of Edmund.

To sum up: Abbo wrote the *LSE* at the instancing of the Benedictine house of Ramsey – as Pinner puts it, "[i]t ... seems most likely that the *Passio* was written for, if not at, Ramsey"[90] – and abetted an act of textual appropriation of Edmund's cult orchestrated by that house. Though new, the Fenland abbey held several estates in East Anglia;[91] it was extending its territorial reach into the ancient kingdom of the Wuffings even though it lay "in a fundamentally Mercian sphere of influence," along with Crowland, Peterborough, St. Albans, and Thorney.[92] The monks of Ramsey in the late tenth century, like Ælfwald, king of the East Angles roughly two hundred and fifty years earlier, hoped to adopt an out-of-town saint's cult and thus enhance the prestige of their own community, even though it lay outside the place where the cult had actually arisen. By exalting the sanctity of East Anglia and its murdered ruler, Abbo enriched the chorography of the ancient *provincia* while simultaneously bolstering the prestige of the Mercian house that underwrote his propaganda campaign.

The *LSE* reaffirms the distinctly East Anglian character and territory of Edmund's spiritual reach, promoting Bury as a model for Ramsey's emulation but also permitting Ramsey to partake somewhat of Bury's glory. Antonia Gransden has surmised that Abbo's aim "to add another illustrious name to the catalogue of East Anglian saints … would have appealed to the Ramsey monks";[93] indeed, the appeal would have been that much stronger for any inmates who knew that their house occupied land in what had once been Middle Anglia, that ancient battlefield between Mercian and East Anglian interests. Some of those monks may even have been amused to reflect that "the catalogue of East Anglian saints" was about to be increased by the efforts of a house that could boast neither an illustrious history nor traditional ties to the ancient East Anglian kingdom itself.

A King "for" East Anglia

His loving delineation of the kingdom's identities would not be complete if Abbo neglected to attend closely to the virtues of the king. Edmund is said to have been "atauis regibus aeditus" (*LSE*, p. 70) or "begotten by royal ancestors,"[94] and to have been compelled by the East Angles to rule over them: "omnium comprouincialium unanimi fauore non tantum eligitur ex generis successione quantum rapitur ut eis praeesset sceptrigera potestate" (*LSE*, p. 70; "he was, by the unanimous choice of all his fellow-provincials, not so much elected in due course of succession, as forced to rule over them with the authority of the sceptre": *Passion*, p. 15). According to the *LSE*, the East Anglian *gens* in the mid-ninth century sought a benevolent rather than an ambitious ruler. If the *witan* had been hoping to revive their country's early seventh-century *imperium*, they would have crowned a king more like Rædwald than like Sigeberht; Abbo's verb *rapitur* describes a man who virtually had to be dragged to the throne.

Inexplicably, the great and the good of East Anglia had seen martial potential in Edmund; even his looks told them that "erat ei species digna imperio" (*LSE*, p. 70; "He had an appearance that was worthy of overlordship": my translation, though Hervey appealingly translates *imperio* as "for sovereignty" in Abbo, *Passion*, p. 15). Either Abbo is letting his rhetoric get the better of him, or he is using irony to foreshadow Edmund's later and utter disregard for overlordship. Then again, the power of which Edmund's bearing is said to have been worthy may not, from the hagiographer's point of view, have been strictly secular. The use of the noun *imperium* in this context warrants a closer look; Abbo may have understood it to signify mere "rule" over the East Anglian *gens*, but his knowledge of Bede's *HE* makes it likely that he sought to exploit more far-reaching connotations.[95] These need not have been purely secular in nature. Marco Mostert writes that

> When Abbo addressed Hugues [Capet] and Robert [II, the Pious], or when he talked about Edmund of East Anglia, or about some other king or emperor, he chose his allocutions from the common stock provided by Scripture and the traditions of the Roman empire. Both of these sets characterized kings invariably by some aspect deriving from their majesty, their sovereignty, or from one of the royal virtues or functions.[96]

Imagining Edmund's authority required a retrospective approach, however; Abbo was not addressing a living monarch but commemorating a dead one who had been killed by non-Christian invaders. His subject embodies what Mostert terms "'majestas' … [which] derived from God's majesty," for "the characteristics of the theocratic ruler were borrowed from the source of his authority."[97] Abbo's use of the word *imperium* in relation to Edmund anticipates the *LSE*'s later emphasis on the vertical rather than horizontal dimension of that king's authority, not military dominion over other peoples but supremacy over them in holiness.

Imperium as spiritual *potestas* ("power") would be feasible for a ruler who wanted to die like Christ at the hands of violent persecutors. Although his rationale for thus defending his kingdom is open to serious challenge on the grounds of strategy and common sense, Edmund nevertheless is said to have believed that eternal salvation in heaven mattered more to him than short-term earthly safety. Such pious quietism, as we shall see, is more than just the result of the hagiographer Abbo's having to making virtue of necessity (which in part, of course, it is) when narrating the death of a king who refused to fight. When one of his chief episcopal counsellors advises Edmund to flee or face torture and death at viking hands, Edmund rejects the option of outliving his own people and consequently being derided as a coward; instead he affirms "honestum michi esset pro patria mori" (*LSE*, p. 75; "it would be honourable for me to die for my country": translation mine). Adducing the three principal signs of his authority, i.e. the robes of healing, his confirmation by the bishop, and popular as well as clerical acclaim,[98] Edmund declares: "Anglorum reipublicae decreui plus prodesse quam praeesse, aspernando subdere colla iugo nisi diuino seruitio" (*LSE*, p. 76; "I have determined to be the benefactor rather than the ruler of the English Commonwealth, in scorning to bow my neck to any yoke but that of the service of God": *Passion*, p. 29). The point goes undeveloped, but Abbo clearly wishes to show that Edmund's stance is not tantamount to self-centredness. Adapting the famous Horatian sentiment "dulce et decorum est pro patria mori" ("it is sweet and fitting to die for one's country"; *Odes* 3.2.13),[99] Abbo characterizes Edmund's impending death not as a matter of subjective sweetness or of vague fittingness, but as an objective marker of the ruler's noble origins and rigorous ethics. These traits, however contingent, are grounded in shared social custom rather than in mere individual judgment. Edmund's behaviour implicitly reflects the East Anglian *gens*'s conviction, and Abbo's own, that good kings give up their lives to imitate Christ.

At this point Bede's ambivalence towards Sigeberht's suicidal piety – discussed in chapter 1 – may come to mind, along with the persuasive analyses of that ambivalence by Susan Ridyard, Sarah Foot, and others. It seems that Abbo's Edmund is pursuing his own spiritual welfare over his subjects' physical safety when he treats Inguar's Danish messenger to a long speech that defends dying in Christ's name as a guarantee of "perpetuam ... libertatem" ("perpetual liberty," i.e. eternal salvation). In retrospect, Æthelthryth's life had lent itself more easily than Edmund's to hagiography because, never having been queen of East Anglia, the Ely abbess never obliged later writers to explain how such royal renunciation as hers might benefit a country under attack. Neither her *Vita* nor St. Æthelwold's tenth-century refounding of her community forced Wulfstan to strain for the purely metaphorical meaning of the concept of "perpetual liberty." For Wulfstan, the "aeternae libertatis priuilegio" ("privilege of eternal liberty") meant only the legal protection Æthelwold had procured for Ely from King Edgar.[100]

By contrast, Abbo's memorialization of Edmund beggars belief, for it has him reject not only the king's prerogative to increase the *ēðel* or "homeland" but also his minimal duty to defend what he currently governs. According to Laura Ashe, such renunciation exemplified a larger millennial trend in English writing whose "effect was to offer the severest practical challenge yet to the ideological identity of secular, English culture, at the very time when clerical theorizing withdrew all support from the culture's secular ideals."[101] Abbo's form of this challenge has chorographic implications, for it risks leading readers to assume that Edmund's ascetic passivity characterizes East Anglia itself.

As Mark Taylor and Rebecca Pinner have pointed out, Abbo's East Anglia aptly complements its king insofar as both are preternaturally beautiful yet vulnerable to attack.[102] If late tenth-century readers at Ramsey took the hint of complementarity between king and kingdom to its logical conclusion, they would have wondered if the Anglo-Scandinavian East Anglia of the 980s should or would turn the other cheek to viking invaders or, with the right kind of pressure, willingly embrace Cerdicing influence along with the same West Saxon Benedictinization that had underwritten Ramsey's own founding. By commissioning a Life of St. Edmund, Ramsey appears to have wanted to exercise control of the slain king's cult, possibly to facilitate Wessex's eventual total mastery of East Anglia.

If I understand him correctly, Francis Young maintains the opposite view, that Abbo and the Ramsey community together aimed not to undermine but to validate East Anglian distinctness: "Abbo's emphasis on the role of the people in Edmund's story may have been his way, and Ramsey Abbey's way, of channelling East Anglian anxieties about being ruled by the House of Wessex and being incorporated into a larger English kingdom."[103] That is, Abbo, in concert with Ramsey, wished to create the impression that the East Angles retained agency. Their integrity as a ruling *gens* would be symbolized by their initial discernment of *imperium* (whether secular or spiritual) in Edmund and by their later success in recovering and reassembling the slain king's body and inaugurating his cult.

The Ramsey monks, however, were poaching on Bury's cult and thus infringing on its independence; for this reason it seems unlikely that they were "channelling East Anglian anxieties" about losing their autonomy. It may be that Abbo's patrons wanted to present themselves, via their commissioning of the *LSE*, as protectors of both Edmund's cult and the clerical community who tended it at Bury; but as protectors against whom? The Benedictines at Ramsey surely would have had no reason to oppose either the Benedictinization of Bury or the West Saxon leadership that would have sponsored it. It seems rather the case that it was Abbo's, not Ramsey's, choice to emphasize "the role of the people in Edmund's story" discerned by Young, and that Abbo supported the independence of the cult and the East Anglian people despite Ramsey's commissioning of the *LSE*. The general absence of tenth-century East Anglian charters issued by West Saxon kings, excepting Sawyer 507 (Bury, 945) and Sawyer 703 (Chelsworth, 962), hints at a degree of regional freedom only decades before Abbo composed the *Passio*.[104] Young is right to note Abbo's attentiveness to the East Angles' agency in fostering Edmund's cult; but this emphasis, especially when read alongside the earlier passages describing the *locus amoenus* and the kingdom's vulnerable borders, raises the possibility that Abbo was critical rather than supportive of his patrons' attempt to co-opt Edmund's shrine and cult on behalf of Mercian-West Saxon Benedictinism. Boundaries, the *LSE* implies, should be respected, whether they be political or monastic. In conjuring up a land resolved on maintaining its integrity even in the face of invasion, Abbo invests East Anglia with a familiar capacity to synthesize passivity with activity, a trait we have already seen in Bede's vignettes of Rædwald, his queen, and Æthelthryth; in the ambivalence suggested in Felix's *VSG* towards its patron Ælfwald; and in the AGT's and ASC's representations of Guthrum and his fellow East Anglian Danes.

In Abbo this oscillating quality centres on Edmund himself. The hagiographer praises Edmund's pacifism as a saintly virtue; as Catherine Matthews observes,

> in accepting that his choice will likely result in his death, Edmund moves the battlefield from the land itself to his own body. Arguably, this moment is one where the king's body becomes identified with something greater than just his identity as Edmund. He is offering himself in place of East Anglia and is willing to suffer for the land and its people.[105]

Edmund's strategy hints at an unconventional form of agency, very different of course from the use of the Devil's Dyke as a means of straightforward physical defence, but nevertheless indicative of a deliberate royal policy, a considered choice. On the basis of this (admittedly suicidal) choice, East Anglian self-defence becomes a spiritual rather than military objective.[106] In the 980s, in the face of renewed viking attacks on a land that was already partly Scandinavian and had, in Guthrum's day, given aid to enemy fleets, Abbo projected onto the past a symbolic victory of Christian piety over pagan aggression. Moreover, the theological currents of his own time allowed him to depict Edmund's form of heroism as a legitimate kind of anti-Scandinavian resolve and as a characteristically East Anglian form of service to the rest of Britannia. The quality of being *integer* ("whole"), later said to characterize Edmund's body (*LSE*, p. 82; *Passion*, p. 45), becomes an ideological virtue, more important than a somatic trait like Æthelthryth's virginity (though Abbo credits Edmund with virginity too, as we shall see), and more resonant than a merely political triumph like the victories won for East Anglia by Rædwald at the expense of the Kentish Æthelberht and the Bernician Æthelfrith. By demonstrating his intact Christian faith, Abbo's Edmund continued to *be for* the East Angles, to be of use to them (*prodesse*, from *prosum*), as opposed to merely being before them or ruling over them (*praeesse*, from *praesum*).[107] To be martyred is to enable a realm's spiritual cohesion amidst dynastic dissolution.[108]

Wounds and Wholeness

Even the localization of the king's remains served to strengthen the bond between *rex* and *regnum*. The vikings are said to have decapitated their victim and thrown his severed head into the wood at *Hæglesdun*.[109] A mysterious wolf is shown to guard the head until help can arrive (*LSE*, pp. 79–81; *Passion*, pp. 36–43), and subsequently the body is given proper burial at the presumably nearby *Bedricesgueord* (i.e. *Bedricesweorth*, Bury St. Edmunds). Years later an inspection reveals that the head has been reunited with the body, with only "una tenuissima riga in modum fili coccinei" (*LSE*, p. 82; "an extremely thin red crease, like a scarlet thread": *Passion*, pp. 45–7) on the neck to indicate the place of the wound. Just as Æthelthryth's own healed neck reinforced the sense of monastic community at Ely, Edmund's reattached head speaks to an enduring connection between the saint-king and Bury specifically, as well as East Anglia generally, despite his abdication of the royal duty to defend the *patria*. Perhaps that bond was symbolically reinforced, in Abbo's eyes, by the guardianship of the wolf, with its relevance to the East Anglian *gens*'s perception of itself as being descended from Wuffa and from Rome. One suspects, though, that if Abbo had wanted to play up East Anglia's *Romanitas*, he would have referred to the dynasty's traditional self-derivation from Julius Caesar.[110]

This issue invites curiosity about whether all the important details of the *LSE* were in fact authored by Abbo. Antonia Gransden has speculated that several well-known episodes, including the one explaining the translation of Edmund's body to Bury, were not actually written by the Frankish scholar himself but were inserted at Bury during the time of Abbot Baldwin, ever keen to marshal documentation proving his house's exemption from episcopal interference.[111] In Gransden's view, the addition of a passage specifying *Bedricesgueord* as a royal vill (*villa regia*) would have suited Baldwin's purpose by suggesting to meddlesome bishops that Bury St. Edmunds had enjoyed kingly protection since the time East Anglia itself was a kingdom.[112]

Several considerations, however, support the view that the passage in question was instead original to Abbo. Firstly, adding a bit of local detail in the form of a place-name, presented first in Old English, then in its Latin equivalent, is just the sort of thing the Fleury hagiographer would have done to flesh out his narrative, given his penchant for elaboration and embellishment and his awareness that he was writing for an East Midlands monastery whose inmates would have been generally familiar with East Anglian geography and thus would have appreciated the reference. Secondly, the fact that Ælfric of Eynsham makes no mention of Bury in his Old English translation of the *LSE* need not imply that the manuscript of Abbo's text that lay before him lacked the passage referring to it.[113] As a translator, Ælfric frequently condensed and rearranged his source material and could easily have dispensed with a toponym if he had deemed it irrelevant to his purpose or to his audience.

Lastly, if Baldwin inserted, or caused to be inserted, an overt reference in the *LSE* to *Bedricesgueord* for the purpose of underscoring Bury's royal establishment and exemption from episcopal taxation, then why did he not also delete, or order to be deleted, the text's potentially damaging concluding lines? In them Abbo refers to the saint's *famulantes* at Bury (*LSE*, p. 87; literally "servants" but translated by Hervey as "those who render to him the ministry of human reverence" in *Passion*, p. 57), implies they are not in celibate orders (for he hopes they may be mindful of "virgineo flore pudicitiae" / "the flower of virgin modesty"), and prays for their eternal salvation (*LSE*, p. 87; *Passion*, pp. 57, 59). If the *famulantes* were not Black Monks, they must have been secular or diocesan priests; acknowledging their guardianship of Edmund's relics would have bolstered a post-Conquest bishop's argument that the saint's shrine properly belonged under episcopal control. For all the above reasons, the *LSE*'s specific reference to Edmund's burial and veneration at *Bedricesgueord* looks to be Abbo's own work. It links the piety of the East Angles' last native ruler to the territory he governed, and in effect makes of that territory both a *locus amoenus* and a *locus sanctus*.

The recomposition and veneration of important bodies mattered to the East Anglian sense of place in specific local communities. To the examples of Edmund and Æthelthryth should be added Byrhtnoth, ealdorman of Essex and hero of the OE poem *The Battle of Maldon*.[114] A benefactor of Ely Abbey, he was himself killed and decapitated by vikings in 991 and his headless body brought back to Ely Abbey for inhumation. The *Liber Eliensis* (*LE*, II.62) explains that before his burial a ball of wax had had to be placed in his coffin to substitute for his unrecovered head, which had been taken by the attackers.[115] In Byrhtnoth's case the virtual reheading of the acephalous patron honours a man who had lived and died for the community.[116]

All three cases, though quite different from one another, speak to a common, deeply felt desire for closure. Unassailable virginity needed to be proved, as Blanton and others point out with regard to Æthelthryth; historiographical truth or finality needed to be achieved, as Stodnick suggests, also with regard to the Ely abbess; and finally, intact individual bodies needed to be shown to be capable of signalling the wholeness of place, the seamless union in East Anglia of religious houses with the royal or noble figures who lead the people with "integrity" (in both its literal and metaphorical senses).[117] It is for this reason that the *LE* compiler cherishes Byrhtnoth's substitute head as a *signum* or "sign": "quo signo diu postea in temporibus nostris recognitus honorifice inter alios est locatus" ("Long afterwards, in [our own] times, he was recognized by this sign, and was honourably entombed among the others").[118] Just as St. Æthelthryth was said by Bede to have been "in medio eorum ... sepulta" ("buried ... in the midst of them," i.e. Ely's monks and nuns)[119] following her death of a neck tumour, so too is the ealdorman of Essex united with a community of fellow benefactors to signal Ely's corporate wholeness in the wake of a corporeal wound.[120] Pagan decapitation sought to ensure that the victim stayed dead.[121] Christian reheading, in the contexts cited above, instead testifies to the desire for unity of religious institutions with their defenders, their patrons, and their territories.

In the *LSE*, the saint's posthumous miracles continue the fight against fragmentation that has already been won by the proof of Edmund's bodily intactness. Abbo tells of an arrogant layman, Leofstan, who insisted on viewing the saint's body; for his arrogance he was blinded by Edmund's supernatural power and subsequently ejected from his house by his own father (*LSE*, pp. 85–6; *Passion*, pp. 52–3). Abbo likens Edmund in his role of vengeful punisher to St. Lawrence, who had killed eight people who were likewise too eager to exhume his corpse; he then apostrophizes the East Anglian king and the site of his veneration: "O quanta reuerentia locus ille dignus existit qui sub specie dormientis tantum Christi testem continet, et in quo tantae uirtutes fiunt et factae esse referuntur, quantas hac tempestate apud Anglos nusquam alibi audiuimus!" (*LSE*, p. 86; "Oh! what deep reverence was due to that place, which contains in the guise of one asleep so august a witness to Christ, and in which such wondrous works are said to have occurred, and do occur, as in these times we have heard of in no other part of England!": *Passion*, p. 55). Further on, Abbo makes a passionate case for virginity and associates this trait too with Edmund.[122] Like Bede's Æthelthryth, Abbo's Edmund showcases East Anglia as a land where wounded bodies are miraculously made whole and corporate territorial identities prove indissoluble.

Such praise was especially apt for the ruler of a part of England poised to revert to paganism. Written a century after the AGT and Alfred's "Prose Preface" to Gregory the Great's *Pastoral Care*, the *LSE* amounts to a hagiographical second front in post-Alfredian efforts to steel English resolve in the face of renewed invasion. As mentioned in chapter 4, Scott Thompson Smith has emphasized that in the "Prose Preface" Alfred expressed deep admiration for past English kings who not only heeded God's laws and maintained order in their own domains but also "ut hiora eðel gerymdon" ("extended their homeland outward"),[123] i.e. widened their rule by conquest. Although Abbo could not rewrite history to make Edmund defeat the Danes and so extend the East Anglian homeland outwards, he did adopt a strategy of symbolic appropriation when decisive military victory proved elusive. Within the conventions of the saint's Life, Abbo has his hero prevail spiritually over his enemies and lay the ideological foundation of the Bury community as both extension of the Christian *ēðel* and as spiritual capital of East Anglia. By supposedly renouncing literal warfare, Edmund is shown to score a decisive victory for Christianity even as his kingdom is taken over by then-pagan Scandinavians.

Although that victory is represented by Abbo in binary ethnic terms, it eventually brought together English East Angles and Scandinavian East Anglians. Writing of the role of Edmund's cult in unifying late ninth-century East Anglia, Michel Sot observes that "[i]l s'agissait de réconcilier autour de lui les Angles, plus anciennement chrétiens, et les Vikings, nouvellement convertis, qui formaient désormais la population de l'East-Anglia" ("around it [i.e. the body of Edmund] it was necessary to reconcile the more anciently Christian Angles and the newly converted Vikings, who formed henceforth the population of East Anglia").[124] This need recurred in the late tenth century, long after the Scandinavian population had been converted to Christianity but during a period of renewed invasions on Æthelred II's watch. As depicted by Abbo, however, Edmund's self-sacrifice neatly divides the East Anglia of 869 into foreign pagans and native Christians.

To Abbo's way of thinking, Edmund's sanctity had indeed transcended the confines of his body to hallow the territory where his cult went on to flourish. Far from being a liability, the king's supposed virginity elevated him beyond the normal ranks of royal men and women; according to Louis-Marie Gantier, Abbo associated virginity with contemplation and regarded spiritualized bodily wholeness as a *desideratum* not just for monks but for all members of the church.[125] That blessed trait appears to be linked in the text to East Anglia's beauty and fecundity; the pristineness of virginal ruler and realm depends on the viking threat to both, a threat made to seem all the more enduring by Abbo's silence on the intermingling of Angles and Scandinavians in the century since 869. As Antonia Gransden surmises, Abbo "tailored his narrative, with the approval of the Ramsey monks, primarily to please [Archbishop] Dunstan"; he may well have remembered that "Dunstan wanted to encourage the growth of St. Edmund's cult at *Beadericesworth* [Bury] in order to increase the prestige and prosperity of the community serving his shrine."[126] The ethnic and ideological (pagan-vs.-Christian) dichotomies of the *LSE* seem thus to have been intended to enhance the text's appeal to a wide social range of religious readers. The dichotomies affect the characterization of East Anglia as a whole, not just Bury: the whole *provincia* is that much more exalted than the rest of England because it witnessed the local triumph of Christianity over adversity. Abbo surely meant no offence to Archbishop Dunstan, but his *Passio* enshrines East Anglia's uniqueness apparently in an effort to prevent interference from outside forces, whether archiepiscopal or abbatial.

Ælfric of Eynsham and Monastic Reform

When in the 990s Ælfric of Eynsham set himself the task of translating the *LSE* into Old English for inclusion in his *Lives of Saints*, he had his own pedagogical and moralizing concerns. These, like Abbo's, have been oft noted.[127] His vernacular rendering is much condensed and largely devoid of rhetorical ornament, and it has been said that Ælfric approached Abbo "in an adapted and simplified way that shows he knew how much a half-lettered and not very learned audience could take."[128] That audience, however, was more heterogeneous than this remark allows, and certainly included the layman Æthelweard, author of a Latin translation of the ASC, as well as his son Æthelmær.[129] This fact and the concerns evident in the OE rendering suggest that however simplified the translation may be in comparison to the *Passio*, it was by no means simplistic. In his reworking of Abbo's text, Ælfric engages with the Frankish scholar's sanctification of East Anglia and attends closely to the relationship between region and nation. As we shall see, where Abbo implied that only East Anglia could boast such sanctity as Edmund's, Ælfric reminds his readers of the wealth of saints to be found throughout the country, a point that enables him to play down the potential of Edmund's martyrdom to stimulate East Anglian regionalism. England was still a political work in progress, "a single *regnum*, albeit one only recently and perhaps rather insecurely united," as Sarah Foot reminds us;[130] it could be undone by domestic rivalries no less than by foreign aggression. Ælfric was alive to roughly the same danger that Benedetto Croce tried to combat in the first decade of the twentieth century, a trend whereby – as Croce saw it – an inability to think beyond strictly regional terms prevented certain Italian critics from evaluating works of Italian literature as such, as the cultural building blocks of a recently unified kingdom.[131]

By emphasizing holy plenitude throughout England, Ælfric contributed to the creation of a centuries-long national commonplace according to which, as Kathy Lavezzo expounds it, "apparent territorial deficiency is paired with remarkable fecundity" so that "notwithstanding its marginalization, medieval England is superlatively abundant."[132] In bringing this strategy to bear on Edmund and East Anglia, however, Ælfric found in Abbo's *LSE* a similar technique of regional description that seemingly elevated the region over the nation. In the Latin text, Edmund's holiness compensates for East Anglia's territorial featurelessness, anticipating the modern observer's praise of the district's huge skies to mitigate the absence of stunning mountain vistas.[133] Ælfric was more focused than Abbo on constructing an early "national" identity, and his *SEKM* seeks to minimize regional particularism and interregional competition so as to enhance England's prestige.

This priority reflects Ælfric's approach to the Benedictine Reform movement, one that overlapped with but was not identical to Abbo's. Ælfric's choice of the vernacular, as well as his own pedagogical and political agendas, resulted in a translation distinct from its Latin source. Elaine Treharne writes that "beyond doubt, his corpus of religious and instructional texts – the homilies and saints' Lives, the *Grammar* and *Colloquy* – consolidated the growing status of English as a prestigious medium of writing," so that "[i]n promoting his own work, Ælfric promote[d] the ideology of the Benedictine Reform, though in a way that is often quite idiosyncratic and doctrinaire."[134] Ælfric had close contacts with subsequent archbishops of Canterbury but, as Joyce Hill has observed, "of the three leading reformers, Ælfric makes no reference at all to Oswald, and only limited reference to Dunstan: his declared allegiance is always, and repeatedly, to Æthelwold, whose period as bishop of Winchester covered all but the last three years of Ælfric's time there."[135]

His allegiances, however, knew limits, especially with regard to the promotion of royal authority in the monastic sphere.[136] Ælfric's view of kings as patrons of the church and of religious houses was tempered by his disappointment in Æthelred II, whose expropriation of monastic lands affected even Ælfric's former house, the Old Minster, Winchester. During his reign, local nobles reversed the trend of royal control of monastic property favoured by Edgar and sought "to assert the priority of regional identity over royalist attempts to consolidate a centralized national government."[137] As Christopher Jones observes, "[w]hen, in the late 980s, Scandinavian raids followed close upon this early souring of the royal-monastic partnership, the king's critics within the church did not hesitate to view the events as cause and effect. When Ælfric himself implicitly rebukes Æthelred for failing to ward off the attacks, his criticism is, tellingly, couched in nostalgic praise of Edgar."[138] For good reason, then, Ælfric's attitude towards the figure of the king and the kind of influence he could wield over monasteries differed from Abbo's; where the scholar of Fleury promoted regal authority nearly to the point of apotheosizing it, the English "Grammarian" was more measured and occasionally critical in assessing its actual implementation.[139]

Ælfric objected, for example, to Æthelred's misuse of royal authority to seize monastic estates;[140] though subtle, his criticism signals a departure from the mysticism with which Abbo suffused kingly power. The author of *SEKM* could hardly attack kingship itself, of course, especially when he was writing for a lay nobleman like Æthelweard, who was conscious of being "directly descended from Æthel[red] I (865–71), elder brother of King Alfred the Great."[141] In Ælfric's view, an English king could and should lead his nation's spiritual reform, which might move God to show mercy in a time of renewed Scandinavian oppression. Precisely because of the stakes involved, however, it would have been pointless to attribute to a king a mystical holiness to which his actions conceivably could give the lie. Successful reform required the king to work with his magnates and prelates on a national rather than merely regional level. According to Mechthild Gretsch, such is the viewpoint on offer in the Prayer of Moses that Ælfric included as the thirteenth item in the *Lives of Saints*: "a cruel enemy can be overcome only by a concerted programme of prayer offered by all groups of society."[142] A program of this sort could be realized more readily if the whole of England boasted supreme achievements in holiness.

As Gretsch has shown, however, the limited influence enjoyed by Edmund made that king an unlikely choice of saint to fill such a niche; in the eyes of Æthelwold and his pupil Ælfric, the leading candidate for that role had to be Cuthbert. "The newly forged 'Kingdom of the English' needed pan-English saints to form what in modern jargon would be called 'a corporate identity,' and Cuthbert, not having been actively involved in contemporary politics, had a better potential to be developed into a such a truly pan-English saint than (say) kings Oswald of Northumbria or Edmund of East Anglia, both of whom were firmly rooted in the history of their respective peoples."[143] The latter's cult nevertheless invited appropriation on a grand scale; Edmund had been killed by invaders, then remade into a martyr by a Continental scholar with his own ties to the Benedictine Reform via the former archbishop Dunstan. With such credentials as these, Edmund's cult demanded attention; especially during a reign as problem ridden as Æthelred's, the example of a king supposed to have given his life in imitation of Christ could not be dismissed as a merely regional figure.

In translating the *LSE* into English, then, Ælfric outdid Abbo's already considerable effort to draw Edmund out of his East Anglian corner into national prominence. Indeed, Young argues that among all the changes introduced to the Old English version of Abbo's text, "[m]ost significantly of all, Ælfric's *Passion* explicitly portrays Edmund as an English rather than an East Anglian saint," and that "Ælfric seems to have been more comfortable than Abbo with the idea of Edmund as a universal saint for England."[144] Gretsch's and Young's divergent perspectives both have much to commend them, though in my view the former underestimates Ælfric's efforts to salvage even Edmund as a "pan-English saint," while the latter plays down the discomfort Ælfric apparently felt with Edmund's regional pre-eminence. The OE Life suppresses Abbo's emphasis on East Anglia's distinctness by implying that the slain monarch was a first among equals rather than England's sole exemplar of royal holiness. East Anglia itself, no longer singled out for divine favour, becomes a part restored to its uniformly blessed whole. Adorning but not outshining the rest of England, the region produces a Christ-like king to edify all the *Angelcynn*.

Ælfric, *auctoritas*, Englishness

Ælfric's *SEKM* is one of twenty-seven hagiographical works in the *Lives of Saints*. Although it by no means denies the royalty of its protagonist, it refers to him first as a saint – "Sancte Eadmunde" (*SEKM*, p. 43) – and reserves the regal title initially for kings of all England. Despite his misgivings about Æthelred, Ælfric uses that monarch's reign to ground the narrative about Edmund in an English macro-history that subtends the micro-history of East Anglia. His first sentence states that Abbo had come from overseas "on Æþelredes cyningces dæge to Dunstane ærcebisceope þrim gearum ær þam þe he forðferde" (Ælfric, *SEKM*, p. 43; "[i]n the time of King Æthelred … to Archbishop Dunstan, three years before he died": Ælfric, *PSE*, p. 97); Abbo had heard from Dunstan the story of Edmund's death just as the old sword-bearer had in turn told it in King Æthelstan's presence. Readers enter the Old English translation much as they would have entered the Latin *Passio*, proceeding past the names and titles of dignitaries both royal and archiepiscopal who had wielded far-ranging rather than merely local or regional power. According to Hugh Magennis, it is because Ælfric, like Abbo, "is promoting a saint not universally acknowledged" that he "feels obliged to provide more by way of authenticating detail than is normally the case with hagiographical texts," "trac[ing] the line of transmission … back, via several unimpeachable intermediaries, to the testimony of an eye-witness who was close to Edmund himself."[145] To be sure, the extra authentication builds upon what Ælfric already found in Abbo, who also cited Archbishop Dunstan as dedicatee and King Æthelstan as a vital link in the chain of oral testimony to Edmund's death. The use of authoritative figures to frame hagiographic narrative is a venerable tack, deployed for example by Wulfstan of Winchester, who in the twenty-seventh chapter of his *Vita sancti Æthelwoldi* celebrates the recent spate of monastic foundation by invoking King Edgar, Archbishop Dunstan, and Bishop Æthelwold as the triune force driving it.[146] Large-scale monastic reform included inter alia the writing or rewriting of saints' Lives; institutional renovation and hagiographical production alike promoted spiritual endeavour in an explicitly English cultural context. Naming royal and religious leaders confirms the integrity of the achievements being touted.

Having laid the ideological foundation of his narrative, Ælfric credits the scholarly authority of his Latin *auctor* in a way that implies the different cultural environments he and his predecessor inhabit. He acknowledges that Abbo first wrote Edmund's *Passio*; that he, Ælfric himself, has translated it into English; and that "[s]e munuc þa, Abbo, binnan twam gearum gewende ham to his mynstre and wearð sona to abbode geset on þam ylcan mynstre" (Ælfric, *SEKM*, p. 43; "within two years the monk Abbo returned home to his monastery and was straightway appointed abbot in that very monastery": Ælfric, *PSE*, p. 98). Ælfric thus contextualizes his Life by referring to distinct spheres of influence: the English king governs the island; the foreign scholar, his duties discharged, returns to France as abbot of his own house. Abbo's newly acquired authority seems to fulfil the promise of his very name (Abbo/*abbode*) and signals a degree of personal merit that might rub off on Ælfric too by association.[147] A subtext in the Old English rendering, however, is that meritorious accomplishments should be improved upon, not merely acknowledged as such. Just as Æthelred might benefit from reading about an earlier king who had put Christ's kingdom before his own, so too would Abbo's *LSE* spread Edmund's glory all the more widely if it could be rendered into English and condensed.[148] Furthermore, by stating that Abbo returned home to his Frankish cloister, Ælfric tactfully nudges his foreign *auctor* out of the picture, removing a Continental competitor from the field of English writerly activity.

The Grammarian's immediate audience, as mentioned above, comprised two powerful secular West Saxon patrons, Æthelweard and his son Æthelmær. Yet the former, in his eponymous *Chronicon*, had written that in 870 "[a]duersus quos optauit bellum rex Eadmundus, breui spatio a quibus et interimitur ibi" ("King Eadmund decided on war against them [i.e. the Danes], and after a brief interval he was killed by them there [at Thetford]." Although Æthelweard decried the invaders as *barbari* ("barbarians"),[149] he did not depict Edmund as a martyr for the faith; surely he would have noticed that Ælfric's hagiographical Life was taking liberties with the received account of the event, especially because Æthelweard himself had been involved in peace negotiations with viking invaders in 994.[150] Ælfric, however, seems not to have worried that his translation from Abbo might have struck his patron as inaccurate; he was, after all, trying to bring a merely regional king into line with broader political and ecclesiastical concerns, such as nostalgia for the religious reforms undertaken during Edgar's reign. Within the agenda of Ælfric's *SEKM*, those concerns meant that East Anglia needed to look less distinct than in it did in Abbo's original.

The vernacular historian knew, for example, that Edmund had not been the only early English king to succumb to attack by "pagans." In the seventh century, the insatiable Penda had killed and mutilated the Northumbrian king Oswald, who went on to become the subject of a formidable hagiography in his own right, Bede "developing a 'mirror of princes'" out of stories of his pious life and posthumous miracles.[151] Ælfric praised both the Northumbrian and East Anglian royal "martyrs," but not, as Gretsch points out, as fulsomely as he did Cuthbert and Æthelthryth, whose cloistered lives shielded them from the regional politics that made Edmund and Oswald more problematic cases.[152]

Edmund, having died more recently than Oswald and having been killed by vikings, posed special difficulties for Ælfric. The East Anglian king could inspire local resistance to foreign influence, a possibility acceptable if the foreigners were Scandinavians, but less so if they were Cerdicings accompanied by Benedictines. According to John Hines, its proximity to the North Sea enabled East Anglia to negotiate its own alliances with incoming Scandinavian invaders, alliances that the Anglo-Saxon Chronicle admits threatened West Saxon security; for this reason "it ... mattered to the tenth-century West Saxon monarchy to write East Anglian kingship out of the script of continuing history with the hagiographical legend of a model Benedictine end for Eadmund, last king of East Anglia, virgin martyr, and saint."[153] Susan Ridyard has similarly observed that Abbo of Fleury had used Æthelstan's name in the *Passio* to shore up West Saxon efforts at "claiming and proclaiming a right of legitimate succession to [Edmund's] kingdom" at the expense of any local heir to the East Anglian crown.[154] Slipping in Æthelstan's name would have reminded Abbo's audience that, over the course of the tenth century, England had achieved such cohesion as it possessed thanks to Cerdicing leadership. To survive new viking attacks, it would need all the unity it could muster. That unity would not have been served by Abbo's claim that "orientalem ipsius insulae partem, quae usque hodie lingua Anglorum Eastengle uocatur, sortito nomine Saxones sunt adepti" (*LSE*, p. 69; "the eastern part of the island, which, even to this day, is called 'Eastengle' in the speech of the Angles, fell to the lot of the Saxons": *Passion*, p. 13). That East Anglia's first settlers are here being identified as *Saxones* rather than *Angli* has been noted previously, as has Abbo's claim that Edmund himself was descended from the Saxons.[155] Francis Young claims that "by ascribing a Saxon identity to Edmund he made him a kinsman of the kings of Wessex/England" and "thereby legitimated West Saxon rule over East Anglia";[156] but if by doing so Abbo augmented the prestige of the *Saxones* as a group and of the Cerdicings as a *stirps*, he also highlighted the tenacity of the people living in East Anglia by suggesting that after the *adventus Saxonum* they, the Angles, had taken eastern England for themselves, despite the Saxons' alleged prior linguistic claim to it. This awkwardness, with its potential to legitimate East Anglian exceptionalism or at least remind readers that the various "English" *regna* did not always have commensurate political agendas, is made to disappear in Ælfric's OE Life.

Within the context of East Anglia's evolving chorography, Ælfric's most significant changes to Abbo's Latin come at the expense of East Anglian particularism and appear at the very end of the text, after the discussion of Edmund's miracles.[157] The *Passio*, following its own enumeration of those miracles, claimed that the spot where Edmund was buried merited great reverence and had witnessed more miracles than any other place in England.[158] Ælfric neither doubts Edmund's achievement nor contests Abbo's praise of it as such but departs from his source to correct its apparent underestimation of England's treasury of holiness:

> Nis Angelcynn bedæled Drihtnes halgena, þonne on Engla landa licgað swilce halgan swylce þæs halga cyning, and Cuþberht se eadiga, and Æþeldryð on Elig, and eac hire swustor, ansunde on lichaman, geleafan to trymminge. Synd eac fela oðre on Angelcynne halgan þe fela wundra wyrcað – swa swa hit wide is cuð – þam Ælmihtigan to lofe, þe hi on gelyfdon. (Ælfric, *SEKM*, p. 58.)

> (The English nation is not deprived of the Lord's saints, since in England lie such saints as this saintly king, and the blessed Cuthbert, and in Ely Æthelthryth, and her sister also, incorrupt in body, for the confirmation of the faith. There are also many other saints among the English who work

many miracles – as is widely known – to the praise of the Almighty, in whom they believed. [Ælfric, *PSE*, p. 102.])

It is not enough for Ælfric to say that England abounds in saints; he insists that England has not been *bedæled* ("deprived") of them, his choice of verb recalling the term used to characterize the vikings' partitioning of East Anglia in the ASC entry for 870. Nothing – neither Scandinavian raiders nor Frankish hagiographers – will rob the *Angelcynn* of their justly won hoard of holy men and women. The use of the OE word for "deprived" has a further function. Litotes or understatement, common in OE literature, is used here so that Ælfric can avoid the unseemly act of bragging in a work that honours a king's supreme self-effacement. Having drawn from Abbo the inference that saints are few and far between in England, he replies with a turn-of-the-first-millennium form of "one-downmanship," that "subtle, indirect boasting – the showing-off disguised as deprecation" that Kate Fox sees in Ælfric's modern compatriots.[159]

As the passage clearly indicates, however, the translator is earnest in his claim. "The English dimension of Ælfric's hagiography," Hugh Magennis points out, "is ... apparent, and may be viewed as an aspect of his larger commitment to the idea of a national English church." Surveying the *Lives of Saints* as a whole, Magennis observes that "[i]t is ... interesting that Ælfric's English saints happen to represent different parts of the country."[160] As Catherine Cubitt has shown, Ælfric represented a tenth-century Reformist tendency to diffuse English holiness widely, to broaden what had been the merely local culting of saints: "The tenth-century reformers drew upon this latent pool of sanctity for their own ideological aims, asserting the moral continuity of their reforming programme with the church of Cuthbert and Bede."[161] Imagined cohesion between past and present would not have been strengthened by admissions of regional distinctiveness, and Abbo's East Anglia presented a potential source of fissiparity within Ælfric's *Angelcynn*. As Cubitt, Magennis, Young, and other scholars have underscored, Ælfric's insistence on the abundance of saints in England speaks to his promotion of a "national" church. The Grammarian's case is weakened, however, by the East Anglian origins of three of the four saints he adduces.[162] Perhaps he sought to appropriate them as honorary West Saxons, but his list of holies leaves the impression that the Reform movement ostensibly sponsored by the descendants of Alfred is dominated by East Anglian contributions.[163]

For reasons discussed earlier, especially his anachronistic endorsement of royal overlordship,[164] Abbo in the middle to late 980s would have had no natural inclination to stir up interregional strife by exalting East Anglia over the rest of England; to do so might have seemed tantamount to undermining King Æthelred's sovereignty. Yet in praising East Anglia as he did, he created a suitable landscape for a ruler wielding a peculiarly tenth-century Frankish type of *imperium* whose spiritual majesty compensated for its diminished territorial reach. Even if it be dismissed as just one more rhetorical exercise in the *Passio*, Abbo's spiritualized chorography of East Anglia inadvertently elevates region over nation, in effect "depriving" England of her other saints. When Ælfric approached Abbo's Latin text with a view to translating it into the vernacular, he sought to prevent the chief written repository of information about St. Edmund from dimming the glory of other paragons of English holiness. No doubt he intended Æthelthryth and her unnamed sister Seaxburh, notwithstanding their East Anglian links, to represent the common cultural patrimony of the English church; indeed, Mechthild Gretsch argues that Ælfric had precisely this aim in the *Life of Æthelthryth*, which he included in the *Lives of Saints*.[165] If, as Rebecca Pinner suggests, Abbo's emphasis on Edmund's healed body (following the king's decapitation) provided Bury St. Edmunds with a means of scoring off its rival Ely, whose patron saint had not died a violent death,[166] Ælfric insists that the saints and shrines of England should be seen as a homogeneous and harmonious ensemble.

James Campbell has discerned in the evolution of Edmund's cult the apparent derailing of "East Anglian particularism" in favour of royal and national agendas:

> One might have supposed that Edmund, a king of East Anglia martyred by the Danes, would have been an ideal focus of East Anglian particularism, should there have been such a thing. Nothing of the kind happened. … The cults of the saints are nodes and links in a network which connected royal power to local piety over most of England.[167]

By showcasing a treasury of saints who, as Magennis remarks, had hailed from all over the country, Ælfric refrained from bestowing honour upon individual *provinciae*; highlighting the "nodes and links" pinpointed by Campbell was simply his way of weaving a textual tapestry representative of England as a whole. In part this strategy may have been an attempt to resist the renewed danger of cultural fragmentation posed by a reprisal of viking attacks, which had been launched only a few years before Abbo's Ramsey sojourn and would increase in ferocity in the 990s.[168] Pauline Stafford has gone so far as to say that notwithstanding these attacks, the tenth-century Benedictine Reform succeeded so thoroughly that "England was experiencing a minor renaissance, in which Ælfric and Wulfstan are only the most famous names."[169] Abbo's *LSE* did not seek to promote "East Anglian particularism" as a foundation for political separatism; Ælfric's translation seems designed to ensure that the vernacular *SEKM* will have no such consequences, intended or otherwise. By insisting that English sanctity was not confined to Edmund's kingdom, however, the English translator nearly legitimates the regional exceptionalism he is trying to suppress, thanks to his association of Æthelthryth and her (unnamed) sister Seaxburh with Ely.

The Jewish Other: Blessing in Disguise

A perhaps more promising way to distract readers from East Anglia's pre-eminence in holiness and to reduce any strain on English unity that it might create would be to fashion an enemy, the Jews, against which all the various Insular *provinciae* and *gentes* might unite. By spewing antisemitism at the end of the *Life*, Ælfric descends gratuitously and contemptibly into ethnic hatred:

> Crist geswutelað mannum þurh his mæran halgan þæt he is Ælmihtig God þe macað swilce wundra, þeah þe þa earman Iudei hine eallunga wiðsocen, for þan þe hi synd awyrgede, swa swa hi wiscton him sylfum. Ne beoð nane wundra geworhte æt heora byrgenum, for ðan þe hi ne gelyfað on þone lifigendan Crist; ac Crist geswutelað mannum hwær se soða geleafa is, þonne he swylce wundra wyrcð þurh his halgan wide geond þas eorðan. Þæs him sy wuldor a mid his heofonlican Fæder and þam Halgan Gaste. Amen. (Ælfric, *SEKM*, pp. 58–9)
>
> (Through his glorious saints Christ makes clear to men that he who performs such miracles is Almighty God, even though the wretched Jews completely rejected him; wherefore they are damned, just as they wished for themselves. There are no miracles performed at their graves, for they do not believe in the living Christ; but Christ makes clear to men where the true faith is, inasmuch as he performs such miracles through his saints widely throughout this earth. Wherefore to him, with his heavenly Father and the Holy Spirit, be glory for ever. Amen. [Ælfric, *PSE*, pp. 102–3])

Virulent though it is, this display of antisemitism participates in *SEKM*'s moralistic and pedagogical program. As an expression of belief in the reality and efficacy of miracles performed by God through Christian saints, the aside is consistent with what Ælfric displays in his homily on the Catholic faith, as Malcolm Godden has shown.[170] Furthermore, as Carl Phelpstead explains, "[i]n comparing Edmund's enemies to the Jews Ælfric constructs a clear parallel between the king and his model, strengthening the identification of Edmund with Christ by identifying his enemies with the supposed enemies of Christ."[171] This interpretation is convincing; but it is just as plausible to argue that, by scapegoating in this manner, Ælfric is resorting to a red-herring tactic similar to what may be present in Felix's *VSG*. Specifically, he is attempting to minimize any East Anglian exceptionalism that might be centred on the *locus sanctus* of Edmund's enshrined body.

Both Felix and Ælfric target marginalized groups as threats to "normative," i.e. Christian English, societies. Whether or not Guthlac's spectral Britons recalled seventh- and eighth-century proto-Welsh raids into Mercia, or perhaps even vestiges of an actual British population in the Fenland, they also would have distracted Ælfwald from the more irksome aspects of Mercian overlordship while rallying East Anglian support around the Mercian royal house's unassailable sponsorship of Guthlac's cult. It is significant that, in comparison to its Latin source, *Guthlac A* is much less specific as to setting; perhaps its author, not unlike Ælfric, believed that playing down regional particularism (and thus avoiding local political issues) would better serve a Benedictine Reform agenda.[172] The Jews of *SEKM* bespeak an agenda roughly similar to Felix's insofar as they, like the British-speaking demons, are used to catalyse English cultural unity; distraction caused by a foreign common enemy (likely absent in real life)[173] serves to allay any misgivings about old rifts among "English" people. Ælfric conjures up that unity while excising Abbo's praise of East Anglia's unusual virtues; the tack resembles in a general way *Guthlac A*'s strategy of replacing regional consciousness with a cosmic perspective.

In suggesting that the Jews in *SEKM* function more or less like the demons in Felix's *VSG*, that is, as red herrings, I do not mean to practise the "interpretive supersession" that Elisa Narin van Court has detected in some scholarly readings of the fourteenth-century *Siege of Jerusalem* and the Croxton *Play of the Sacrament*. In her view, this form of interpretation errs by treating the Jews in those texts as surrogates for other groups, such as Lollards.[174] In the case of *SEKM*, Ælfric clearly intended the Jews to represent themselves, or rather to represent themselves as he perceived them, as the collective embodiment of what he thought Jewish culture might signify and offer to his readers: the basis for a unity that was otherwise fragile. By effacing or distorting Jewish identities, he indulges in hagiographical triumphalism, the depiction of an entire people in terms of their alleged rejection of Christ. He then harnesses that factitious ethnic attribution to his Reform-inflected project of literary nation-building. Demonized as spiritual foes yet constructed as proofs of Christian holiness on a national scale, the Jews enter *SEKM* as England's blessing in disguise.

This exploitative ethnography has been ably illuminated by Andrew Scheil in his analysis of other Ælfrician texts:

> Honoured yet derided, repudiated yet ever-present, external yet internal, the Jews embody a rhetorical effect of Christian identity. By repudiating Judaism, defining it as lack, Christianity inexorably yokes itself into a tormented relationship with its sibling. This ambivalence gives the Jews a curious ideological mobility, a capacity to be deployed as sheer rhetoric in the flux of everyday life. The anti-Judaism of Ælfric's homily *Maccabees* in the *Lives of Saints* exemplifies this capacity for the Christian understanding of the Jews to function as a mobile, all-purpose political signifier in specific historical circumstances.[175]

Ælfric's contribution to fashioning the Jews as the "rhetorical effect of Christian identity" is paralleled by comments in his sermon on the Assumption that in effect, according to Adrienne Williams Boyarin, reduce a living people to the dead language of the Hebrew Bible.[176] *SEKM* goes further by ignoring any self-expressed cultural identity for the Jews, substituting for it an identity attributed by Ælfric: wilful self-damnation, a supposed defining trait being derived from Matthew 27:25.[177] Erased in life, the Jews are silenced even in death, their tombs made out to be antithetical to miracles.[178] In order, then, to underscore the plenitude of English *Christian* holiness – or rather, the extent to which England has not been "bedæled Drihtnes halgena" – Ælfric deprives the Jews of any "miracles" even as he accuses them of having deprived themselves of all hope of salvation. With this distraction technique East Anglia's uniqueness is forgotten; suppressed too is the region's potential to remind tenth- and early eleventh-century English readers of the nation's sometimes conflicting internal identities.

No Jews had barged in on Ælfric from the pages of Abbo's *Passio*. That they should have been thought to pose any threat at all to the "imagined community" of Christian England is the fiction maintained by the OE Life of St. Edmund, and this fiction obscures abiding dangers to that community presented by its constituent English regions. By fabricating a Jewish enemy whose essence is "lack" (as Scheil points out) because their holy places are judged unable to compete with Christian shrines in the generation of sacred power, Ælfric skirted the perennial problem posed by bellicose yet Christian Danes, particularly those settled in East Anglia who might offer assistance to new waves of Scandinavian invaders making the south-east their first port of call.[179]

The fissiparity of "England" into numerous *partes* was, after all, only gradually being arrested and reversed in the late tenth century. In the Old English translation of Bede's *HE*, for example, their particular identities are so much more prevalent than in Bede's Latin original that Sharon Rowley has argued that "the *OEHE* is much more likely to atomize than generalize when it comes to naming political or tribal affiliations."[180] Insofar as the *Angelcynn* assumes singular cohesion in *SEKM*, it is because Ælfric hopes that the Jewish outliers to the "true" faith will inspire uniform censure in East Anglian, Mercian, and West Saxon alike. According to Scheil, for Ælfric and his tenth-century contemporaries "the Jews became not only a surpassed people supplanted by the 'New Israel' [i.e. the English themselves] and a dark repository of Christian anxieties, but also a rhetorical cipher, a political tool used to promote the visions of the Benedictine reform."[181] As a feature of *SEKM*, antisemitism is used further to unite "England" against the regional particularism that Ælfric found in Abbo.

Conclusion

The *Passio sancti Eadmundi* shows its Frankish author cleaving to his animosity towards Scandinavians as if hostilities had persisted unbroken since 869, and as if the trauma of foreign conquest had remained as fresh in the minds of Abbo and his audience as it had been for Edmund's sword-bearer. Nothing in the *LSE* reminds readers that a *frið* (however short lived and insincere it may have been) had stabilized, if only temporarily, relations between Alfred's English subjects and Guthrum's Danes; that "[t]he kingdom of St. Edmund had passed into Danish but not into heathen hands";[182] or that subsequent assimilation had gone some way towards bridging the cultural divide imagined by some annalists at the West Saxon court to be unbridgeable.[183] The text's vitriol responds to contemporary realities, specifically to the "second wave" of Scandinavian attacks that had begun only a few years before Abbo arrived at Ramsey. By associating East Anglia with Edmund's attributed holiness, the *LSE* prepares the region for new spiritual battles it soon would need to fight if the viking armies that had ravaged Southampton, Thanet, Cheshire, and the Devon and Welsh coasts in 980–1 should turn eastward.[184] Ælfric, born and raised in England and equipped with his own contacts within the Benedictine Reform movement, plays down the Scandinavian menace because he knows better than Abbo that, by the late tenth century, a fine line separated "Dane" from "English."[185] For the *Grammaticus* the real spiritual war that needed to be fought was one against Jews, a war that, from his perspective, was already being won by Christians.

Although Cerdicing power had made inroads into East Anglia by the early tenth century, the district's persistent idiosyncrasies and long-standing Anglo-Scandinavian amalgamation made the region seem just outré enough to aggravate existing dread of new attacks from across the North Sea. Politically, as Lucy Marten has shown, East Anglia remained distinct until at least Cnut's reign;[186] though more a duchy than a kingdom, it occupied a conceptual middle ground between such polities, having grown during the ealdormanries of the powerful Æthelstan "Half-King" and his son Æthelwine. Abbo does not term this virtual half-kingdom a *media provincia*; for him it is a *provincia*, and although both he and Ælfric may have understood that word to signify nothing more than "province," Ælfric followed his Latin *auctor* in acknowledging that Edmund had been a ruler in his own right, an *Eastengla cynincg* (Ælfric, *SEKM*, p. 43; "King of East Anglia": Ælfric, *PSE*, p. 98). To be sure, the monk of Eynsham maintained that the "true home [of the English was] heaven" rather than England itself,[187] yet he also affirmed a broadly English foundation for Edmund's sanctification as a way of demonstrating the value of local cults to the universal church. To establish that foundation more firmly, he resorted to demonization – as Bede, Felix, Abbo, and the annalists of the Anglo-Saxon Chronicle had done before him – as a way of curbing East Anglia's potential to disrupt cohesion within the wider imagined kingdom of England.

Conclusion

In his recent fine book, Francis Young proposes St. Edmund as a "foundation on which an English national identity can be rebuilt" following Britain's departure from the European Union.[1] His study proves the ongoing vitality of Edmund's legacy and the amenability of the king's cult to a dazzling array of cultural and political needs.[2] Young convincingly demonstrates the Englishness of Edmund and of East Anglia, and if on occasion his partisanship makes the region stand in for the nation in a way reminiscent of what Richard Morris describes as nineteenth-century English historiography's "tendency to expect local history to be national history in microcosm,"[3] it also confirms that no region is an island: to explore any discrete area is by definition to ponder the bridges, literal or symbolic, connecting it to its surroundings. Moreover, far from being peculiar to the modern period, this necessarily dual perspective of chorography, which glances at part and whole together, informs Abbo of Fleury's *Passio sancti Eadmundi* (*LSE*) and Ælfric of Eynsham's *Life of St. Edmund, King and Martyr* (*SEKM*). In their divergent ways, those hagiographical works make the local answerable to a programmatic concept of the national and vice versa.

The present book, insofar as it seeks to reconstruct certain aspects of early English geographical thought, is liable to the charge of what Emily Thornbury identifies as the historian's "imaginative sympathy."[4] I have tried to address this risk by not treating early East Anglia as essentially a mini-England but instead approaching it as a self-contained construct whose textual identities, though (in part) defined by writers from elsewhere, were not therefore reduced wholly to local particularizations of "Englishness." It has sometimes been challenging to distinguish between "East Anglian" and "English" as these two concepts emerge from the writings of the period. In his classic study *Space and Place*, Yi-Fu Tuan touches on this general problem, though in a different context, when he remarks on one hand that "[t]he part may be essential to the functioning of the whole, but the part is not the whole in miniature and in essence," yet on the other hand, and in his very next sentence, concedes that "[i]n mythical thought the part can symbolize the whole and have its full potency."[5] As represented in early texts, the "part" of the East Anglian *provincia* oscillated between perfecting and threatening the English "whole."

As was pointed out in the Introduction, Roy Rainbird Clarke believed that East Anglia had long had more in common with the Continent than with the rest of England; nevertheless, the Mercians, West Saxons, and Northumbrians lived close enough to the East Angles (and, later, to the Anglo-Scandinavian East Anglians) to tap into the region's cultural capital at strategically opportune moments. The East Angles sometimes reciprocated, as Ælfwald's interest in the Mercian Guthlac shows. Regional and supraregional identities co-existed. Bede famously claimed individual *provinciae* as parts of a common *gens Anglorum* despite their regnal differences and their occasional mutual animosities. Illustrious East Anglian personages were likewise appropriated within larger geopolitical causes once the English nation or church had been asserted to exist and had subsequently demanded ideological uniformity. The accounts in the *Historia ecclesiastica* (*HE*) of Rædwald and his queen, of Æthelthryth, of Bishop Felix, and of Fursey were diverse in origin but were given their final shape within Bede's agenda. His attribution of identities was made possible by a dialogue of sorts between local information and external synthesis, though in the last analysis the dialogue was moderated by Bede himself as the agent of the latter. *Pervia* ("accessible"), we recall, is the word Abbo of Fleury later used to describe the Fenland portion of Edmund's realm;[6] the adjective implies simultaneously the presence of a barrier tangible enough to be passed through and the reality of the barrier as a thing separating travellers from some ulterior destination. The word speaks to the broader identities that East Anglia has long possessed, for at least as long as people have been writing about it and certainly longer than the period in which kings governed it. To return to Yi-Fu Tuan: "landscape is personal and tribal history made visible."[7] Although Tuan has in mind the relationship between Indigenous societies and their territories, the texts surveyed in the present book likewise testify to, and shaped in their own times, a dynamic bond between peoples, texts, and land.

The impulse to claim regional identities for wide English consumption persisted long after the ages of Rædwald, Æthelthryth, Guthlac, Æthelberht, and Edmund. Late eleventh- and twelfth-century hagiography takes us beyond this book's temporal limits, but a glance at it is necessary to disclose ongoing efforts to incorporate East Anglian and Middle Anglian saints' cults into a pan-English church. As Edmund is the royal personage most often associated with the region's history, the following short foray beyond the period covered in this book will restrict itself to him.

The much-studied post-Conquest boom in the slain king's hagiography is only one indication that Ælfric had not had the last word about East Anglia's place within England. Many scholars have explored the ways in which Herman the Archdeacon in the 1090s depicted Edmund's power to defend Bury Abbey's privileges against powerful post-Conquest East Anglian landowners and bishops.[8] Describing such attributed power required, as always, selective emphasis; to this end Herman seems to have laid greater stress on Edmund's sanctity than on his royalty, perhaps because the saint had proved unable or unwilling to protect his kingdom consistently from foreign aggression.[9] In gathering stories of Edmund's miracles, Herman contributed to the ongoing process of defining the place of East Anglia, as in the following passage:

> Qui regioni Est Engle cui fuerat quasi eptarcha, patrocinator permanens cum Dei gratia, suffragari non destitit circum circa, apud omnipotentem promerens ut credimus, nullum post se preter Deum successorem in illis partibus. Partiebatur enim Anglia tunc temporis regum plurium regimine, sed acciderat in Westsexe maioritas regiminis cuidam Edered nomine[.]
>
> (Remaining, by God's grace, the defender of East Anglia (to which he had been a sort of heptarch), Edmund provided unceasing support all over that region. For we believe he merited this privilege from the Almighty: that none other than God should succeed him in those parts. For England at that time was divided under the rule of many kings, the lion's share having fallen to one called Æthelred in Wessex.)[10]

Herman's creative use of royal titles suggests a desire both to multiply Edmund's roles within East Anglia and to obfuscate the kind of governance those roles might connote. The passage implies not so much a rejection as a diminishment of Edmund's "regnal" regality, a restriction of it to what is now being referred to as a *regio*. From a post-Conquest perspective, even the word *provincia*, which had already dwindled in connotative reach when Abbo used it in the late tenth century, no longer seems appropriate to East Anglia's status. Nevertheless, Herman accords his protagonist a new title, *eptarcha*, which Tom Licence identifies as "a neologism" and as "the earliest known reference to the Heptarchy, as it was later called: the sevenfold division of English kingdoms."[11]

Herman's praise is effusive, especially his assertion that after his death Edmund had no successor and therefore no *patrocinator* except God, as if the client-kings after 869, Guthrum after 880, and subsequent Anglo-Scandinavian rulers of East Anglia had never existed.

Yet as exceptional as Edmund is made to look in this passage, his kingship seems paradoxically devalued by the historical connotation and almost archival "feel" of the word *eptarcha*, despite its newness on the linguistic scene. Such impressions are strengthened by Herman's aside that in Edmund's day, i.e. in the late ninth century, there had been "many kings," the implication being that kingship itself in the distant past had been understood to mean something different from what it meant in Herman's England; in bygone days royal status had been far more commonplace. Though not seriously depleted by the hagiographer's aside, the "fund of prestige" that Susan Reynolds discerns as a unique attribute of royal status[12] loses some of its value because of it. Unlike God's regality, which inhered uniformly "in illis partibus" ("in those parts"), Edmund's own power is both circumscribed by the fact of royal surplus and dispersed by the proliferation of alternative titles such as *eptarcha* and *patrocinator*.

Even as Herman's *Miracula* downgrades Edmund's "national" stature, it bolsters the bond between the disembodied martyr-king and his land, especially Bury Abbey. When the Scandinavian King Sweyn (r. 1013–14) was persecuting the Bury sacrist Aelwine, Edmund is said to have offered succour to the latter while he was sleeping: "martyr adest pretiosus procurator eius ac dictator uie ipsius, alleuians eum ponderis mestitia" ("the martyr appears, his precious guide who directs his footsteps, and relieves his heavy heart").[13] The wording attributes a tenderness to Edmund that underscores his ongoing if posthumous agency within his domains; striking is the note of personal intimacy in his bond with the Bury sacrist. Tom Licence sees titles such as *eptarcha, patrocinator, procurator,* and *dictator* as evidence that "[l]ike no hagiographer in England before him, Herman presented his saint as the heir and patron of a region," "a sort of regional, heavenly heptarch."[14] I agree with this view, despite the titles' cumulative effect of rendering ambiguous the idea of the *regio* as an administrative entity.

This ambiguity is reflected in the different emphases that scholars perceive in Herman's *Miracula,* though the underlying consensus is that some kind of region-vs.-nation tension between East Anglia and England persisted into the post-Conquest era despite having undergone major changes since Bede's time, when the *gens Anglorum* was a by-product of the Northumbrian scholar's vision of a unified English church. Susan Ridyard and Rebecca Pinner have shown that Herman and his fellow Bury monks downplayed Edmund's regional importance in favour of his Englishness and his links to subsequent English rulers.[15] Simon Yarrow instead discerns the continued usefulness of regional identities to Bury Abbey even in the late eleventh century: "When taken up by Hermann in the *De miraculis*, the subsequent history of the saint's cult sustains the idea of St. Edmund as inhabiting a pivotal position between East Anglia as a discrete political entity and those outsiders seeking to consolidate their authority over it."[16] It can be difficult to define what that "pivotal position" was as Herman characterized it near the end of the eleventh century. Ridyard points out that although his posthumous revenge against the intrusive King Sweyn was meant to stress "the political dominance and consequent inviolability within East Anglia of the abbey of Bury St. Edmunds," nevertheless "[t]he Bury monks ... did not press the point too far. A regional protector was always useful, but a separatist saint might be self-defeating."[17] Yet the separatism that may have been "self-defeating" from Herman's perspective had contributed earlier to a *provincia*-wide process of self-promotion and even self-defence when Guthrum's successor in the 890s minted the St. Edmund memorial pennies and halfpennies. A century later Ælfric may have perceived the afterlife of that separatism in Abbo's *LSE* and, deeming it dangerous, eliminated all trace of it in his vernacular translation. For the *Eastængle* and the West Saxons between the late ninth and late tenth centuries, a "separatist saint" could serve as a banner heralding very real regional identities.

This is not the place to settle the debate over whether, a century beyond Ælfric's time, Herman the Archdeacon simply revived the regional or merely asserted the national identity of Edmund's cult. It must suffice here to say that, several decades after the Norman Conquest, writers were still tapping into Edmund's "delayed legacy"[18] and, in the process, trying to achieve chorographic equilibrium for East Anglia, a process that entailed using local *mythomoteurs* to empower the region without threatening its vital conceptual and political bond with the nation.[19] England would become more cohesive (though far from happily so) on the eve of the twelfth century than it had been at the turn of the tenth or even the eleventh; it is undeniable that the East Anglian part eventually came to be fitted within that increasingly unified English whole. Nevertheless, what Sir Henry Clifford Darby wrote in 1934, with regard to the region in the seventh and eighth centuries, applies to East Anglia in the later pre-Conquest centuries as well and could practically stand as an epigram for this entire book: "The old ties of its people," he observed, "were replaced by wider allegiances. Yet still it retained a certain measure of its old life."[20] *Angles on a Kingdom* has attempted to understand the extent to which writers from Bede to Ælfric responded to, represented, and repurposed that "old life" to make it amenable to "wider allegiances," in the negotiations of which East Anglia sometimes but not always participated willingly.[21]

In the thirteen years or so that I have spent planning, researching, writing, and at times cursing this book, I have been haunted periodically by an image more tangible than any dispossessed demon from Crowland or even the redoubtable Black Shuck.[22] The image is that of Helen Cam urbanely disembowelling the American historian Carl Stephenson's Pirenne-esque hypothesis on the origins of the city of Cambridge.[23] It is not so much the specific details of her critique that have given me pause as her critique's general *moralitas*, quite simply that "scholars from another country are at a special disadvantage."[24] Although the present book is a study of other books and not of place as such, and although its writing has been facilitated by technological aids undreamt of in the 1930s, it is still an outsider's study. Moreover, and perhaps more problematically, it is an attempt at interdisciplinarity by a person trained in one discipline only, the study of literature. These facts have doubtless contributed to shortcomings in the book that will become clear to me only in retrospect.[25] For now, by way of apologia I can only repeat that I have sought to capture, synthesize, and make sense of ancient perceptions of a region rather than looking to make momentous discoveries about the region itself, a task best left to others. I have taken heart from the chorographic transports of W.G. Hoskins, who described thus his meditations on the one-inch Ordnance Survey maps of the Wash coasts of Lincolnshire and Norfolk: "One dissects such a map mentally, piece by piece, and in doing so learns a good deal of local history, whether or not one knows the country itself."[26] My own project has taught me much about East Anglia itself, especially about its mediation through texts that refract space and place in highly creative ways.

Even as a study of perceptions, however, the present book cannot pretend to offer a complete picture of its subject. Selectivity having guided my perambulations, the sense of the whole is likely to have suffered distortion. British expatriate novelist Tim Parks, who has written unforgettably about Italy's Veneto region, reflects on this risk in his autobiographical narrative *Italian Neighbours*; in his preface he likens his book to "the gesture ... of a busy but inexpert fellow dashing about the narrow confines of his territory waving a net at the end of a long stick," more specifically "a will-o'-the-wisp net," whose contents never yield quite as much as what the chase itself promised.[27]

Given the fenny and marshy character of some parts of East Anglia, the *ignis fatuus* analogy befits the subject of the present monograph, for the pinpoints of regional awareness briefly flickering across the pages of the authors surveyed here have lured me in many different directions: Bede's *HE* with its accounts of a king's religious syncretism, his successors' widespread missionary labours, and a Fenland abbess's self-abasing spirituality; Felix's *Vita sancti Guthlaci* (*VSG*) with its tantalizing hints of regnal rivalry between the East Angles and the Mercians; the Alfred-Guthrum Treaty (AGT) and the various recensions of the Anglo-Saxon Chronicle (ASC) with their suggestions of alternating viking and West Saxon efforts to control the *Eastængle*; and finally Abbo of Fleury's and Ælfric of Eynsham's hagiographies of Edmund with their compatible but competing reflections on that king's holiness and its implications for the region's place within the English church.

In making sense of the contents of my own "will-o'-the-wisp net," I have tried to resist the temptation to mount East Anglia's early literary identities within a too-rigid framework that ignores distinct authorial purposes and audience expectations. Nevertheless, I have hazarded to suggest that various texts responded variously to the region's cultural ambiguities and did so from the vantage points of would-be architects of order – kings or monks, historians or hagiographers – who sought to contain and correct East Anglia's destabilizing potential. In his recent wide-ranging book *The English and Their History*, Robert Tombs has said that, between the age of Bede and the period of the Scandinavian invasions, England's wider self-perception crystallized under the pressure of perils introduced from without: "If English identity began as a religious concept, it took political form in response to a deadly external threat, which overturned the political structures of the island and the near Continent: the Vikings."[28] Sometimes, however, the threat was an internal one emanating from East Anglia. Rædwald's perceived syncretism threatened Bede's vision of English Christian orthodoxy as no other *imperium*-wielder had done. Ælfwald's commissioning of a *Vita* of St. Guthlac risked upsetting political stability in the Fens by encroaching on a cult protected by the Mercian king Æthelbald, whom Felix suggestively styles "principem populorum" ("chief over the peoples"; ed. Colgrave, §49, pp. 148–9]. Scandinavian *hergas* ("armies") may have been regarded in Wessex as strange and intractable, but after 869 they dwelled within the confines of Britannia. Even the West Saxon nobleman Æthelwold was regarded as a "king of the pagans" by the St. Neot's Chronicler because he had joined forces with them.

In its relationships with the rest of England, early East Anglia gave rise to textual representations that sometimes proffer binaristic ethnographies, at other times begrudge continuities. Like the vikings as a whole in James Earl's analysis,[29] the *Eastængle* known to Alfred and his successors defied neat categorization; for although the Scandinavian East Anglian elite originally embodied a "deadly external threat" to Wessex (to borrow Tombs's phrase), after Guthrum's baptism they made a show – as many scholars have noted – of embracing the same Christian religion and the same cult of King Edmund that were honoured by the West Saxons, even while keeping their options open when dealing with newly arriving Scandinavian attackers. Commentators on East Anglian identities had increasingly to reckon with complex admixtures of ethnicities, political allegiances, and monastic loyalties that blurred boundaries between "us" and "them."

East Anglia, then, emerges from this book as a region simultaneously distinct and fissiparous, characterized by discrete attributions of piety or impiety, holiness or strangeness, yet also prone to invasion from without as well as dissolution from within. In speaking meaningfully of an East Anglia whose early character could comprise seemingly opposed tendencies, specifically Romano-Frankish and Scandinavian influences, Tom Williamson has shrewdly refused to align the region's identities with one cultural pole or the other but rather insists that the whole should be regarded as distinct in its way of amalgamating these influences.[30] In an early phase of its existence the *gens Orientalium Anglorum* may have formed by overcoming hostilities amongst its constituent folk-groups in what are now Norfolk, Suffolk, and eastern Cambridgeshire; such political cohesion as there was arose either by force or by diplomacy. It may well be that East Anglia's crowning trait throughout and beyond the early English period was its knack for survival and adaptation, its ability to persist through internal contradictions and foreign confrontations to maintain hybrid identities. Texts from the mid-eighth to the very late tenth century show the region's resistance to that utter absorption by other powers which, in retrospect, sometimes looks to have been an all but inevitable feature of that "fiercely contested knock-out competition" among early polities that has been so evocatively described by Steven Bassett.[31] Although none of the writers discussed in this book are likely to have believed in the existence of a literal *genius loci*, their various chorographies at least tacitly credit the spirited resilience of East Anglia. The kingdom had typically lain at some remove from the various centres of early English political authority that had sprung up between the age of Æthelberht of Kent and the time of Æthelred "*Unræd*"; yet the ancient *provincia* remained indispensable to that authority's claims to wield control over "England," itself a construct always in need of elaboration. Given the region's strategic importance, writers from Bede to at least Ælfric found it imperative to fashion a place for East Anglia, in the process defining it as both bane and boon, with the potential either to make or to unmake the *Angelcynn*.

Notes

Introduction

1 One thinks of Amanda Prynne's line "Very flat, Norfolk" in Coward's *Private Lives*, act I, p. 30; but see Dutt, *Highways*, pp. 2–3; Tennyson, *Suffolk Scene*, passim; Seymour, *Companion Guide*, p. 9; Muir, "Landscapes," p. 36; Whiteman and Talbot, *East Anglia*, pp. 10–11; Dymond, *Norfolk Landscape*, pp. 24–5; Christopher Taylor, *Cambridgeshire Landscape*, pp. 21–2; Parker, *Men*; Barkham, "This Sinking Isle." The demands of village life are illustrated in Blythe, *Akenfield*; Chamberlain, *Fenwomen*; and Craig Taylor, *Return*. J. Page lyrically surveys a large body of writings about the region in "Is There an East Anglian Literature?"

2 Bradbury, "Loving Norfolk," p. 124; compare Young, *Edmund*, p. 19; Pestell, "Kingdom" (on East Anglia as "an almost island-like territory itself on England's east coast").

3 The Norfolk-Suffolk distinction is explored fully by Williamson, "East Anglia's Character," pp. 47–8, 57–62, and will be revisited later.

4 Blythe, *Akenfield*, p. 111.

5 "Even in the nineteenth century, 'The Shires' beyond were often regarded with suspicion by the folk of Norfolk and Suffolk": Ravensdale and Muir, *East Anglian Landscapes*, p. 14.

6 See e.g. Williamson, *Sutton Hoo*, esp. pp. 132–41, and the various contributions to Bates and Liddiard, *East Anglia*.

7 The phrase "Anglo-Saxon" continues to be used by institutions aiming at wide audiences, for example by the British Library during its major exhibit "Anglo-Saxon Kingdoms: Art, Word, War" (19 October 2018–19 February 2019). Yet when the International Society of Anglo-Saxonists decided in November 2019 to change its name to the International Society for the Study of Early Medieval England, it did so amidst far-reaching and well-substantiated scholarly discussion. Important interventions

include Remein, "ISAS"; Miyashiro, "Decolonizing"; Rambaran-Olm, "Anglo-Saxon Studies"; Karkov, "Post 'Anglo-Saxon' Melancholia"; Dockray-Miller, "Massachusetts Medievalist"; Wilton, "What Do We Mean…?" I am grateful to an anonymous reader for recommending these contributions, to which should be added Ellard's *Anglo-Saxon(ist) Pasts*. Also relevant are Townsend's adoption of the word *Englisc* ("Cultural Difference," esp. p. 71, n. 12); Harland's interrogation of the term "Germanic" ("Memories," p. 966; see below, n. 95); and now Karkov's analysis, in *Imagining*, of the proto-imperialistic, utopian self-imaging embedded in Alfredian and later ideas of the "Anglo-Saxon" people.

8 Geoffrey of Wells, *De infantia*, ed. and trans. Hervey, pp. 136–7. The issue of the antiquity of Norfolk and Suffolk is considered below and in n. 126.

9 M. Taylor, *Edmund*, p. 94, includes Essex in East Anglia, but Hart, *Danelaw*, p. 562, trenchantly excludes it. Wareham, *Lords*, p. 6, groups Essex, Cambridgeshire, and Huntingdonshire with Norfolk and Suffolk but omits Lincolnshire. For nuanced pronouncements, see Yorke, *Kings*, p. 65; Carver, "Sutton Hoo," pp. 497–8; Williamson, "East Anglia's Character," pp. 60–1; Ravensdale and Muir, *East Anglian Landscapes*, p. 9. Liddiard acknowledges the broader definition but cautions that the medieval region was limited chiefly to Norfolk and Suffolk: "Introduction," p. 8. On Bede's inclusion of Ely, see below, chap. 2, especially the section "Why Ely?", and Pestell, "Kingdom," p. 193. When referring to the Fens/Fenland, I generally capitalize the initial letter *F*, as do R.R. Clarke (*East Anglia*) and Rackham (*History*).

10 E.g., Ravensdale and Muir, *East Anglian Landscapes*, p. 9; Liddiard, "Introduction," p. 8; Hines, "Origins," p. 16; Williamson, "East Anglia's Character," p. 44; Heslop and Thøfner, "Introduction," pp. 1–4; Carver, "Sutton Hoo," p. 499; M. Taylor, *Edmund*, pp. 93–4.

11 I derive the will-o'-the-wisp analogy from Parks's *Italian Neighbours* ("Author's Note") and return to it in the Conclusion.

12 I use "viking" rather than "Viking," following Hadley, "Cockle," p. 111, n. 2; Abels, "Alfred," p. 195, n. 1; McLeod, *Beginning*, pp. 7–9 (who prefers "Scandinavian"); and Downham, "Viking Ethnicities," p. 1.

13 Chapter 4, below, differentiates between textual representations of Scandinavian East Anglia and of Scandinavian Northumbria in the late ninth and early tenth centuries. I have not been able to consult Capper's unpublished master's thesis "Insights," but her summary reflections on it in her "Practical Implications" align some of its findings with those of Pestell, *Landscapes*, and indicate that "[her] project investigated how aspects of regional written and material culture, for example material artefacts, economic ties and religious cults, reflect multiple identities, and how they

were used in accommodation to negotiate the acceptance or resistance of outside identities at a regional level" ("Practical Implications," p. 13).

14 *Life of St. Æthelwold*, ed. Lapidge and Winterbottom, pp. 38–9. For the date 996, see Lapidge and Winterbottom's introduction, p. xvi.

15 Hines, "Becoming," p. 49, emphasis in original. Gillingham (*English*, pp. 139–40) considers "not only self-identification but also identification by others" in references to English crusaders in the *Annales Sancti Disibodi*. See too Bassett, "In Search," p. 22. For Härke ("Ethnogenesis," p. 4), "ethnicity is not a given, but a flexible and situational concept; ethnicity is 'in the heart,' not 'in the blood.'" For the reference to Härke's paper I am indebted to Hartmann, "Monument Reuse," p. 260, n. 85.

16 Wood, *Merovingian North Sea*, p. 4.

17 Strohm, *Theory*, p. 216, n. 12, engaging with the thought of Fredric Jameson and Robert Young. I have also been guided by compatible pronouncements in Le Goff, *Medieval Imagination*, pp. 107–31; Stock, *Implications*, e.g. p. 89; Stock, *Listening*, p. 29; and N.Z. Davis, *Fiction*, pp. 3–5.

18 Hiatt, "*Beowulf*," pp. 18–19 (who also discusses the word's etymology); Rohl, "Chorographic Tradition," pp. 1–2. See too Helgerson, *Forms*, pp. 107–47 and passim. Rohl cites Helgerson and many other scholars who have revived the term. The related term "chorology" is "the study of the areal or habitat differentiation of the earth" (Sauer, "Morphology," p. 316).

19 Hiatt, "*Beowulf*"; Howe, "Angle" and *Writing*; Michelet, *Creation*; Lavezzo, *Angels*, esp. pp. 27–45; Discenza, *Inhabited Spaces*. See too Harvey, *Maps*. The title of the present book was inspired by the titles of Howe's "Angle" and Lavezzo's *Angels*.

20 With regard to the phrase "social map": "especially if a broad definition of 'map' is allowed, including purely verbal maps[,] it is undeniable that from the 'age of Bede,' and certainly by the tenth and eleventh centuries, a culture existed in which both global and local mapping practices were known within educated circles": Hiatt, "*Beowulf*," p. 21.

21 K. Davis, "National Writing," p. 618. Davis uses this phrase to characterize Patrick Wormald's tracing of English self-consciousness to Bedan and papal notions of a *gens Anglorum* ("English people"); Davis agrees with and furthers Wormald's argument that King Alfred's invocation of *Angelcynn* as a unified place and people was at odds with the actual heterogeneity of the various English kingdoms. See also Karkov, *Imagining*, pp. 1–49, 56.

22 S. Reynolds prefers "regnal" to "national" to emphasize the elite social classes that often confront historians of early medieval "national identity" (*Kingdoms*, p. 254). For spirited defences of the term "nation" as a means of underscoring continuities – often to the detriment of subjugated

peoples – between the early medieval period and the postcolonialist present, see K. Davis, "National Writing"; Mehan and Townsend, "Nation."

23 H.M. Thomas, *English*, p. 270; see too Foot, "Making," pp. 48–9; Higham and Ryan, *Anglo-Saxon World*, pp. 8–10. As McLeod argues of the period 865–900, "the Anglo-Saxon populace were more likely to have a sense of allegiance to whichever kingdom they were living in, and to even smaller regional identities, than to 'England' and the 'English'": *Beginning*, p. 3. Compare Abrams's remarks about tenth-century parallels between the West Saxons' "creation of a new allegiance to the kingdom of England" and "the operation of regional identities – shaped, in the Danelaw, by the Scandinavian heritage" ("King Edgar," p. 181).

24 Turville-Petre, *England*, p. 142.

25 Here and throughout I use the terms "Danes" and "Scandinavians" for convenience only. In early English sources, labels like "Danes" and "Northmen" were by no means static in their connotations; see Roffey and Lavelle, "West Saxons," esp. pp. 10–11, 15. (I owe the reference to Roffey and Lavelle's chapter to Konshuh, "Constructing," p. 158, n. 16.) On the heterogeneity of the peoples who settled in England from 865 onwards, see McLeod, *Beginning*, pp. 7–9.

26 Sheppard, *Families*, p. 189. Goscelin of Saint-Bertin, in his *Lectiones in festiuitate Sanctae Sexburge*, strengthens that association in his celebratory account of the marriage between Seaxburh, sister of Æthelthryth, and King Eorcenberht of Kent, as shown by Blanton, "Kentish Queen," pp. 195, 202–12.

27 See the studies cited in nn. 19–23 and 31, as well as Wormald, "Anglo-Saxons" and "*Engla Lond*," and Dumville, "Origins," esp. pp. 86–108. On the fluid state of eastern England ca. 600, see Yorke, "Anglo-Saxon *Gentes*," pp. 389–90, and studies cited therein. Wood, *Merovingian North Sea*, p. 4, explores the gradual development (vs. ethnic continuity) of early medieval European peoples in general. Dumville, "Origins," agrees with the anti-teleological view of early English history but nevertheless argues that "[w]hatever previous perceptions there may have been, England (*Englaland*) and the kingdom of the English certainly now existed" after Æthelstan's conquest of Scandinavian Northumbria in 927 ("Origins," p. 73, and passim). In light of East Anglia's resistance to West Saxon expansion (as noted by Marten and Pestell; see below, chap. 5, pp. 184–5), what certainly existed after 927 is the West Saxons' increased *confidence* in dominating the rest of England.

28 Rollason, *Northumbria*; Stodnick, "Emergent Englishness"; Brown and Farr, *Mercia*; Barrett, *Against All England*; Blanton, *Signs*; Pinner, *Cult*. Many other studies could be cited, and the reader is referred to this book's individual chapters.

29 Kirby, *Earliest English Kings*, p. 21, considers Canterbury's influence on "East," "West," and "Middle" designations.

30 Söderbaum, "Introduction," p. 7, paraphrasing and then quoting Hettne, "New Regionalism," p. 27. An especially poignant analysis in this regard is Harris, *Race*, p. 12.

31 Bassett, "In Search"; Hines, "Becoming"; Yorke, "Political and Ethnic Identity"; Frazer, "Introduction"; Moreland, "Ethnicity" and "Land"; Harris, *Race*; Foot, "Making"; Dumville, "Origins." See too Discenza, *Inhabited Spaces*, pp. 5–9 and passim.

32 D. Newman, "Borders"; Rumford, "Introduction" (citing sea changes in political and sociological thinking beginning in the 1990s); Anzaldúa, *Borderlands*; Mignolo, *Local Histories*; King, "Borders"; Boyarin, *Border Lines*; Rollason, *Northumbria*; Ingold, *Lines*; Pohl, "Ethnic Names"; Treharne, "Borders" (citing Anzaldúa on p. 10); Brady, *Writing*, citing (on pp. 8–10, 21–2 for notes) Anzaldúa as well as recent scholarship on historical frontiers and frontier societies, e.g. Abulafia and Berend, *Medieval Frontiers*; Curta, *Borders*; Bartlett and MacKay, *Medieval Frontier Societies*. See too Wickham-Crowley, "Fens," esp. pp. 75–6. On the heterogeneity as well as mutability of Carolingian frontier areas, see J.M.H. Smith, "*Fines*," pp. 171, 176–7.

33 Bede, *HE*, ed. and trans. Colgrave and Mynors, IV.19, pp. 396–7; Felix, *VSG*, ed. and trans. Colgrave, §24, pp. 86–7; Abbo, *LSE*, ed. Winterbottom, p. 70; Abbo, *Passion*, trans. Hervey, p. 15. Unless otherwise noted, subsequent references to the *HE*, *VSG*, *LSE*, and *Passion* are to these editions and translations.

34 Discenza, *Inhabited Spaces*, p. 100. Yi-Fu Tuan, on whom Discenza draws, makes the related, general point that "space is humanly construed space" (*Space*, 35). One of his examples, the ancient Greek tyrants who "promoted the identity of their capital cities" (p. 176), illustrates the power of elite figures to "construe" space to maximal effect.

35 Such thinking can be traced at least as far back as the Hebrew Scriptures. As Matthews points out in her analysis of Ælfric's *Life of St. Æthelthryth*, the biblical Book of Kings "focuses on the influence that a king's behavior has on his kingdom: good kings, simply put, are those who honor God and do his will, earning God's blessing for their kingdoms; bad kings bring down God's judgment upon their kingdoms" ("Token," pp. 53–4). Loyalty bonds also shaped early English notions of social space, as detailed in Sheppard, *Families*.

36 A. Williams addresses the relative dearth of information about "the lowest groups in society" in pre- and post-Conquest texts: *The English*, pp. 2–3.

37 London, British Library, Harley Charter 43 C 3 (S 703 in the *Electronic Sawyer*); text and translation in Hart and Syme, "Earliest Suffolk Charter,"

repr. in Hart, *Danelaw*, pp. 467–85; for discussion, see their study and Wareham, *Lords*, p. 55. See too PASE, s.v. "Æthelflæd 14."

38 I am indebted in what follows to Hooke, *Anglo-Saxon Landscape*, pp. 50–71; M. Reed, "Anglo-Saxon Charter Boundaries," esp. 285–7 and 297–8 (cited by Howe, *Writing*, p. 39 and p. 239, n. 30); Rackham, *History*, p. 10; Howe, "Angle," pp. 17–21; Howe, "Landscape," pp. 98–102; Howe, *Writing*, pp. 29–46; Lowe, "Development," pp. 63–5; S.T. Smith, *Land*, esp. pp. 155–7.

39 Lowe, "Development," p. 65.

40 Howe, *Writing*, p. 43. See also Ellard, *Anglo-Saxon(ist) Pasts*, pp. 183–4.

41 Manna is identified as "the landowner of Kettlebaston" (Hart, *Danelaw*, pp. 482–3). Asa and Oswyth were women; "women often possessed property in their own right" (pp. 484–5). Hart also provides mini-biographies of the charter's witnesses (pp. 475–8) and adduces a 1632 Chelsworth survey that refers to Culfen Meadow (p. 484). One suspects, though, that "Meadow" was added late in the place-name's history after the original meaning of *Culfen* had been forgotten. Ekwall, *Concise Oxford Dictionary*, p. 135, suggestively derives "Culford" in Suffolk from "Cūla's ford." The names "Manna," "Culla," "Eadwold/Eadwald," and "Oswyth" have entries in PASE, but not for the persons named in this charter.

42 Hart, *Danelaw*, pp. 472, 475; pp. 476, 478 on Abingdon as the likely milieu.

43 Ekwall, *Concise Oxford Dictionary*, pp. 99 (Chelsworth) and 535 (*worþ*); *DOE*, s.v. *ceorl*, I.B.1, I.B.1.a.i, I.C, respectively. At I.B.1 the *DOE* cautions that the noun "carried different legal meanings in different periods and in different areas of England"; section I.F lists 16 Old English place-names that contain the element, including the one under discussion here. According to Hudson, "in a broad sense it covered all free men below the status of thegn, that is[,] all the men of 200s. wergeld. It would therefore cover men elsewhere referred to as, for example, *geburs* or cottars": *History*, p. 208.

44 Hart, *Danelaw*, pp. 479, 480, citing a study by H.P.R. Finberg. On ninth- and tenth-century East Anglia, especially with regard to its occupation by Danish forces, see below, chaps. 4 and 5.

45 This concept is explored in the East Anglian context by G.E. Evans, *Pattern*, pp. 256–7.

46 Howe, "Angle," p. 19, with regard to the charters' bilingualism.

47 See *DMLBS*, fasc. 14, p. 2874, s.v. *ruricola* 1*a*, "one who tills the land, husbandman."

48 Tennyson, *Suffolk Scene*, p. 5.

49 My use of "Cerdicing" to refer to Alfred and the other descendants of the house of Cerdic follows Molyneaux, *Formation*, p. 16.

50 Marten, "Shiring," p. 7 and her important footnote 29, which identifies the wills (in the *Electronic Sawyer*) of Æthelflæd, her father, and her sister,

and localizes in Suffolk the lands mentioned in those wills (on which lands, see too Lowe, "Nature," pp. 41–4; Lowe, "Linguistic Geography," pp. 154–5). Marten adds that Chelsworth "was probably always intended to revert to Bury" (p. 7), a point made also by Hart, *Danelaw*, p. 468.

51 Pestell, *Landscapes*, p. 12. Williamson, in *Environment*, argues trenchantly for the role of landscapes in determining social and political formations throughout early medieval England.

52 R.R. Clarke, *East Anglia*, p. 13. For more nuanced formulations, see Williamson, "East Anglia's Character," pp. 48–50; Pestell, "Kingdom," p. 193.

53 Carver, "Kingship," p. 148, citing, with implicit approval, Böhme, "Das Ende," esp. pp. 558–9. For finely grained interpretation of the relevant archaeological evidence, see T.F. Martin, *Cruciform Brooch*, pp. 174–5. Also important for the question of dating is Härke, "Ethnogenesis," pp. 9–10. Rainbird Clarke placed the beginning of the Germanic migrations to Britain in the late fourth century (*East Anglia*, p. 130), but most scholars have favoured a date in the early to middle fifth (e.g. J. Campbell, "Lost Centuries," pp. 31, 34; Salway, *Roman Britain*, p. 310).

54 McLeod, *Beginning*, p. 58, and noting (on the same page) additional, specifically Swedish connections with Sutton Hoo archaeological finds as discerned by Marzinzik, *Sutton Hoo Helmet*, pp. 34–5, and Bruce-Mitford, *Sutton Hoo Ship-Burial*, vol. 2, pp. 91–9, 205–25. See also Brookes, "Boat-Rivets," p. 2.

55 Higham, "Sources," p. 115; compare A. Reynolds, *Later Anglo-Saxon England*, pp. 43–4.

56 H. Williams, "Engendered Bodies," pp. 30–1. On the many cultures reflected in the burial rites at e.g. Snape (Suffolk), see Filmer-Sankey, "Discussion," p. 264; on the cosmopolitan trade evidenced at Rendlesham (on which site, see below), see Scull, Minter, and Plouviez, "Social," pp. 1603–4; Scull and Williamson, "New Light." Wickham claims that East Anglia was precocious in developing "large-scale exchange relationships … in the eighth century," and therefore relationships between landowners and peasants (*Framing*, pp. 811–14, quotation at p. 812); but Moreland sees a wider eastern context for such developments (see the citation in Wickham, *Framing*, p. 813, n. 206, as well as Moreland, "Land," pp. 185–8). Other important studies of distinct East Anglian agricultural organization and tenurial arrangements include Douglas, *Social Structure*; Marten, "Shiring"; Blackburn, "Expansion," esp. p. 138; Molyneaux, *Formation*, pp. 27–8 (citing inter alia Marten's essay); Williamson, *Environment*, pp. 135, 139 (and source cited in n. 42), 234, 238–40, and passim (but see too pp. 143–5 for cautions). In his study of coinage reforms throughout mid-eighth-century England, Naismith maintains that "minting survived longest and on the largest scale in East Anglia" ("Kings," p. 296).

57 Ravensdale and Muir, *East Anglian Landscapes*, p. 9.
58 Scarfe, *Suffolk Landscape*, p. 36. Compare Carver's observations on East Anglia in general: "It is an unaccentuated landscape, without obvious topographic boundaries (apart from rivers), in which to set a geographically determined agenda" ("Sutton Hoo," p. 497).
59 Rackham, *History*, p. 1.
60 Pestell, *Landscapes*, p. 128. Rivers could be effective (Williamson, "East Anglia's Character," p. 62), and charters demarcated territory on a small scale (see above, and also Pestell, *Landscapes*, pp. 9, 128–39; Rackham, *History*, pp. 9–12, 19). Pestell argues that major frontiers were fairly vague in early medieval Europe, but this vagueness may have decreased by the Carolingian period (Goetz, "Concepts"). J.M.H. Smith points out that the terms *marca, limites, confinia, termini,* and *fines* all refer to boundaries in Carolingian texts, and "[a]ll could refer to either a particular line or a swathe of land at the margin of the empire" ("*Fines*," p. 176).
61 My thinking here is indebted to similar but more nuanced assessments of the rise of early English identities by K. Davis, "National Writing," esp. pp. 617–27, and by several of the studies she cites: Wormald, "Bede, the *Bretwaldas*," "*Engla Lond*," and "Making"; Foot, "Making"; and Howe, *Migration*, pp. 4–7. See also Discenza, *Inhabited Spaces*, pp. 5–9, and Higham's general point that "Dark Age territoriality" was "socially constructed, and both multi-layered and dynamic," and characterized by "accumulation and sub-division [that] will have occurred contemporaneously, in bewildering patterns and often at great speed": "From Sub-Roman Britain," p. 8.
62 Barrett, *Against All England*, p. 27.
63 Exemplary in this regard are Hines's *Voices* and Morris's *Time's Anvil*.
64 Abbo, *LSE*, p. 69. Hervey, *Passion*, p. 13, translates *pervia* as "accessible."
65 Carver, "Sutton Hoo," p. 499. Carver elsewhere argues that East Anglian kingship had a territorial basis from the late sixth century onward: "At this point the concept of 'kingship' could be promoted through genealogies and regalia; such a role would have to be supported by the reimposition of territorially based tribute, that is, tax as opposed to rent" ("Conclusion," p. 198).
66 I have in mind Judith Butler's work on the performative nature of gender (e.g. *Gender Trouble*). In a different context, Yorke, "Anglo-Saxon Origin Legends," p. 24, observes that "[b]urial under mounds ... helped create a visual focus for a new dynasty that tied it to the land it claimed to rule, but also evoked the memory of those who may have ruled it in the past." In support of her claim, Yorke cites (p. 24, n. 51) H. Williams, "Ancient Landscapes," p. 25; and Carver, "Reflections," esp. p. 133, on the self-consciousness of the "new leaders and their heirs" who, at Sutton

Hoo, sought to display their rising power conspicuously and defiantly, "to oppose the imperialism of the Christian Franks" (see too Carver, "Reflections," p. 140). For even more nuanced views of Sutton Hoo's performative qualities, see Pitt, "Enigmatic," and Brookes, "Boat-Rivets."

67 For brief summary of the grave goods, see Carver, "Ship-Burials," pp. 186–91. For fuller treatment in three volumes, see Bruce-Mitford, *Sutton Hoo Ship-Burial*.

68 *HE*, II.15, pp. 188–91. On the Vespasian manuscript witness of the so-called "Anglian Collection," see Newton, *Origins*, pp. 57–8, citing Dumville, "Anglian Collection," pp. 24–5. The genealogy of the *Eost engla* is printed in Dumville, "Anglian Collection," p. 31.

69 Tyler, "Offa's Dyke," p. 160.

70 Bourdieu's concept of "cultural capital" includes "*all* the goods, material and symbolic, without distinction, that present themselves as *rare* and worthy of being sought after in a particular social formation": *Outline*, p. 178 (emphasis in original).

71 See e.g. Hines, *Scandinavian Character*; Higham, "From Sub-Roman Britain," p. 7 and sources cited in his n. 45; and Pestell's caveats about the use of archaeological evidence in "Kingdom," p. 199.

72 Hines, "Origins," p. 17.

73 Lawson, "Lyre Remains," p. 223 and map on p. 222.

74 Newton, *Origins*. Thoughts supportive of Newton's view are offered in Filmer-Sankey, "Discussion," p. 266; Williamson, *Environment*, p. 79; and more conjecturally but nevertheless strikingly by Neidorf, "*Beowulf*," pp. 862–3, 868–9.

75 For Discenza, the scope of that self-perception is broadly English: "*Beowulf* never names England because it never needs to do so. England remains at the heart of its audiences' lived experiences" (*Inhabited Spaces*, p. 124). Neidorf instead claims that the sensibilities of *Beowulf*'s original audiences would have been regional and pan-Germanic rather than national and English ("*Beowulf*," esp. pp. 860–9).

76 North, *Origins*; Neidorf, "Germanic Legend"; Newton, *Origins*, p. 143.

77 Klaeber, "Notes," p. 122, in reference to *Beowulf*, lines 32–52.

78 Fenwick, "Insula," p. 37, citing relevant studies. See too S. West, *Corpus*, p. 273; R.R. Clarke, *East Anglia*, pp. 139, 149; Filmer-Sankey, "Grave 1," p. 194; Filmer-Sankey, "Discussion," p. 265 (citing Ipswich's Buttermarket cemetery); Fulk, Bjork, and Niles, "Commentary," p. 114 (updating Klaeber, "Notes," p. 122); Newton, *Origins*, pp. 136, 138; Pitt, "Enigmatic," pp. 1–2; Brookes, "Boat-Rivets," pp. 1–2.

79 Newton is aware that *Beowulf* occasionally intimates a dark future for the Geatish people (e.g. *Origins*, p. 48, 95–100), but unless I have overlooked it, he does not draw a connection between that aspect of the poem and

East Anglia's own political precariousness in the eighth century. Newton accepts Colgrave's view that East Anglia and Mercia were on good terms when Felix wrote the *VSG* for King Ælfwald, and suggests that "[p]erhaps the cult of St. Guthlac helped to provide a unifying focus for the continuity of goodwill between East Anglia and Mercia, at least during the second quarter of the eighth century" (*Origins*, p. 81). See chap. 3, below. Neidorf observes that "details surrounding Ælfwald suggest how [*Beowulf*'s] patron might have fashioned himself" ("*Beowulf*," p. 868) and stops just short of proposing that king as the poem's actual patron or intended reader.

80 On the question of Snape's visibility, see Williamson, *Sutton Hoo*, p. 108. For Sutton Hoo and the Deben, see Pitt, "Enigmatic," pp. 15 (citing inter alia Williamson, *Sutton Hoo*, p. 102), 19, 28–9. Brookes ("Boat-Rivets," p. 15) discusses the ideological implications of the conspicuousness of Sutton Hoo and of several possible precursor "pseudo-boat burial" sites in Kent.

81 H. Williams, *Death*, p. 161.

82 Williamson, *Sutton Hoo*, pp. 101–6.

83 Williamson, *Sutton Hoo*, p. 106; Pitt, "Enigmatic," p. 16 (citing H. Williams and Williamson). Pitt also points out that "Roman age barrows on the opposite bank of the River Deben ... would have been visible from the Sutton Hoo burial mounds at the time they were constructed" ("Enigmatic," p. 19, citing a study by Roberta Frank). The Deben's visibility from Rendlesham as well (on which site, see below) has been noted by Scull, Minter, and Plouviez, "Social," pp. 1597–8, 1602.

84 Williamson, *Sutton Hoo*, p. 108.

85 A wide geographical and chronological overview of England's bond with the sea is offered in the essays in Sobecki, *Sea*.

86 H. Williams, *Death*; see too H. Williams, "Mortuary Practices," esp. p. 258. With regard to Sutton Hoo's strategic position, H. Williams writes that "the scale of the exclusive burial plot chosen on the prominent ridge above the Deben took mound-building and the elaboration of mortuary theatre to new heights": *Death*, p. 158. Influential on my wording above is Carver's statement that "the burial mound, ostensibly for the celebration of the dead, was also the principle instrument for mobilising the living" ("Burial Mounds"). Pitt has recently built upon these insights in "Enigmatic," esp. pp. 9–15, 26–9. See also, now, Ellard's rich discussion in *Anglo-Saxon(ist) Pasts*, pp. 108–15.

87 Williamson, *Sutton Hoo*, cites numerous examples in Norfolk and Suffolk (p. 106) while conceding that the East Angles, "[i]n identifying in some way with their local river … were not entirely unique" (p. 112).

88 Carver, "Anglo-Saxon Cemetery," p. 350; compare Carver, "What Were They Thinking?," p. 926; Pitt, "Enigmatic," p. 28.

89 P.H. Blair, *Introduction*, p. 32, favouring a scenario involving attacking Germanic peoples defending themselves via these earthworks against counter-attacking Britons. For more cautious views, see Higham and Ryan, *Anglo-Saxon World*, pp. 52–4. See too Oosthuizen, *Anglo-Saxon Fenland*, p. 73; M. Taylor, *Edmund*, pp. 80–5.

90 On Iron Age and Roman East Anglia, see Collingwood and Myres, *Roman Britain*, pp. 59, 81, 87–104 and passim; R.R. Clarke, *East Anglia*, pp. 91–131; Dymond, *Norfolk Landscape*, pp. 37–68; Warner, *Origins*, pp. 20–66; Williamson, *Origins*, pp. 20–58; Williamson, *Sutton Hoo*, pp. 124–7; Ravensdale, "Themes," pp. 24–9. See too D.N. Briggs, "Sacred Image" (on the Iceni in Norfolk); Mattingly, *Imperial Possession*, pp. 49 (map), 100–1 (on the Iceni), 106–8 (Iceni and Trinovantes).

91 See"Hoxne Hoard," Google Arts and Culture, https://www.google.com/culturalinstitute/beta/entity/m0cls08, and Hobbs, *Mildenhall Treasure*.

92 See Salway, *History*, p. 189, for discussion and dating of the *Notitia* and for the customary translation of what he regards as "a thoroughly unsatisfactory but completely entrenched term." The name "Saxon Shore" seems to derive from the threat of "Saxon" invasion on the coast, not from any large-scale Teutonic settlement already in place: P.H. Blair, *Introduction*, p. 4, n. 1.

93 On the possibility that *foederati* had established themselves at such an early date in Britain, see J. Campbell, "End," p. 18; Scarfe, *Suffolk Landscape*, pp. 72–4, 82–3. Difficulties with this hypothesis have been pointed out by Salway, *History*, pp. 287–9, 300–1, 310, and by Härke, "Ethnogenesis," pp. 19–20. Mattingly (*Imperial Possession*, p. 536) favours a date after 409 but does not rule out the use of Germanic mercenaries earlier.

94 Hines, *Scandinavian Character*, pp. 109, 198, 286 (cited by J.F. Kershaw, *Viking Identities*, p. 213), and pp. 270–85, 300 (as cited by McLeod, *Beginning*, pp. 56–7). See too Hines, "Origins," pp. 19–43; Young, *Edmund*, p. 21, citing (n. 7) Plunkett, *Suffolk*, pp. 33–5; and Bede, *HE* V.9, pp. 476–7 (discussed below). Furthermore, Härke concedes that "there clearly was some *foederati* presence in [East Anglia], particularly around Norwich," specifically at Caistor-by-Norwich ("Ethnogenesis," p. 11).

95 Goffart argues that ethnic heterogeneity was so great that the label "Germanic" should be discarded altogether (*Barbarian Tides*); see too the compelling archaeological critique of the term in Harland, "Memories" (esp. pp. 961, 965–6). I share Harland's misgivings about the term but cannot easily do without it, because my primary focus is textual rather than ethno-historical. Bede, for example, spoke of Saxons, Angles, and Jutes as "tribūs Germaniae populis" (*HE* I.15, pp. 50–1); and a "pan-Germanic perspective" is, as Neidorf convincingly argues, central to *Beowulf*'s implicit anti-Celtic xenophobia as well as to its explicit, "not

merely pre-national, but perhaps even anti-nationalist" political outlook ("*Beowulf*," pp. 860–1, 869).

96 *HE* I.15, pp. 50–1; V.9, pp. 476–7. For further discussion of this list, see below, chap. 1. On the problem of simplification, see e.g. P.H. Blair, *Introduction*, pp. 10–11; Hines, "Becoming," pp. 50–2.

97 Wood, "Before and After," p. 44. See too Filmer-Sankey, "Discussion," p. 264. Wood underscores cultural heterogeneity but adds that "within this overall diversity there will have been some very close-knit groups" (p. 45).

98 On Angeln, see Young, *Edmund*, pp. 20–1. More generally, "[m]odern Y-chromosome DNA points to Anglo-Saxon origins in Dutch Frisia, northern Germany and Denmark": Härke, "Ethnogenesis," p. 5.

99 P.H. Blair claims that "there are many grounds for thinking that [Bede's] threefold division reflects the orderliness of his own mind rather than the realities of the settlements" (*Introduction*, pp. 10–11), but Blair emphasizes ethnic similarities among the settlers rather than differences. Higham cautions that, *pace* Bede, "neither term [i.e. neither 'Anglian' nor 'Saxon'] need have any bearing on contemporary perceptions of nomenclature and group identity in the fifth century" ("From Sub-Roman Britain," p. 7).

100 Collingwood and Myres long ago rightly insisted upon "a continuous process extending over a considerable period": *Roman Britain*, p. 352; compare Härke's argument for "a process rather than an event, with implications for variations of the process over time" ("Ethnogenesis," p. 10). The vast bibliography on the so-called *adventus Saxonum* also includes Wormald, "*Engla Lond*"; Howe, *Migration*; Howe, *Writing*, pp. 50–1, 141–3; P.H. Blair, *Introduction*, pp. 13–34; Sims-Williams, "Settlement," esp. pp. 19–41; Hines, "Becoming"; Wood, "Before and After"; Moreland, "Ethnicity"; Harris, *Race*, pp. 60–72; N. Brooks, "English Identity"; Michelet, *Creation*, pp. 198–269; Mattingly, *Imperial Possession*, pp. 535–7; Yorke, "Anglo-Saxon Origin Legends"; Scully, "Bede, Orosius"; Brugmann, "Migration"; Hedges, "Anglo-Saxon Migration"; Konshuh, "Constructing," esp. pp. 164–70 (on the *adventus* as represented in the ASC).

101 *MS A*, ed. Bately, p. 17; *ASC*, p. 12.

102 Gildas, *Ruin*, trans. Winterbottom, pp. 25–9 (English), pp. 96–9 (Latin); Nennius (attrib.), *Historia*, pp. 44–7, 54–65 (Latin on even-numbered pages, English on odd-numbered).

103 Hooke, *Landscape*, pp. 39–47; Hooke, "Anglo-Saxons," pp. 66–7, and her discussion with John Hines on pp. 89–90. See, however, Powlesland, "Early Anglo-Saxon Settlements," esp. p. 102. Also pertinent is Frazer's postcolonial response to Moreland's "Ethnicity" in "Introduction," p. 8.

104 Hooke (on the West Midlands, Kent, and Essex), *Anglo-Saxon Landscape*, pp. 17–18; Hooke, *Landscape*, p. 46. For East Anglia, see Williamson,

Sutton Hoo, pp. 124–7; Warner, *Origins*, pp. 66–7. Powlesland concedes the tenacity of major estate boundaries during the transition period; see his discussion of Hooke's "Anglo-Saxons," p. 91.

105 Oosthuizen, "Culture." See too her recent *Anglo-Saxon Fenland*. I am grateful to Stephanie Lahey for this reference.

106 Oosthuizen, *Anglo-Saxon Fenland*, p. 137.

107 Wood, "Before and After," p. 46; compare Dumville, "Origins," pp. 75–80; Higham, "From Sub-Roman Britain," p. 6; and Wickham-Crowley's response in "Fens," p. 70, to certain of Oosthuizen's claims. See also the sources cited above in nn. 103–4. Young (*Edmund*, pp. 21–2) cites genetic and place-name evidence to prove Continental absorption rather than destruction of indigenous British culture; Scull, Minter, and Plouviez ("Social," pp. 1600–1) show continuity between the "late Roman element" and the "culturally Germanic presence" at Rendlesham in Suffolk (see below); Härke ("Ethnogenesis," p. 17) adduces DNA, archaeological, and linguistic evidence to point generally to "a one-way process" of assimilation that "was essentially Anglo-Saxon, not mixed or hybrid Anglo-British." Dumville's claim of "cultural genocide" ("Origins," p. 75) seems to apply to some geographical areas more than to others.

108 For convenient summary of these issues, see Young, *Edmund*, pp. 23, 28–31, synthesizing important studies by Newton, Plunkett, A.C. Evans, and Pinner. See also Klaniczay, *Holy Rulers*, p. 90 and his n. 91, citing a study by Erich Hoffman. On the Vespasian regnal genealogies, see below, n. 122.

109 Young, *Edmund*, pp. 30, 31; see also below, chap. 1, n. 130 (Ridyard replying to Górski on the use of saints' cults to compensate for lost political pre-eminence).

110 Young, *Edmund*, p. 31.

111 Sauer, "Morphology," p. 325, building on an insight by Oswald Spengler.

112 Pestell, *Landscapes*, p. 12.

113 Rollason, *Northumbria*; Brown and Farr, eds., *Mercia*; Dumville, "Origins," pp. 90–100 (on sub-kingdoms and other small folk-units within the East Saxon, South Saxon, West Saxon, and Mercian polities). See too Capper, "Practical Implications," p. 13, summarizing the argument of her "Contested Loyalties," on the transformation of peoples and polities once they had been absorbed into Mercia.

114 Carver and Williamson have reaffirmed (though the latter tentatively) the traditional connection between the ship-burial and the East Angles put forward by Bruce-Mitford: Carver, "Sutton Hoo," pp. 496–8; Williamson, *Sutton Hoo*, pp. 20–1. See also Bruce-Mitford, *Sutton Hoo Ship-Burial*, vol. 1, pp. 690–1, and most recently Pitt, "Enigmatic." The Essex position is set forth in Pearson et al., "Three Men," and emphatically dismissed in

Filmer-Sankey, "Discussion," pp. 265–6. Williamson, *Sutton Hoo*, pp. 119–26, summarizes their arguments and challenges them less emphatically, conceding the territorial divisions within Suffolk and within the ancient Wuffing kingdom that their arguments raise to the fore.

115 Bruce-Mitford, *Sutton Hoo Ship-Burial*, vol. 1, pp. 715–17. For discussion, see e.g. Keynes, "Rædwald"; J. Campbell, "Impact"; Kirby, *Earliest English Kings*, p. 66; Plunkett, *Suffolk*, pp. 70–96; Marzinzik, *Sutton Hoo Helmet*, pp. 54–5; Hines, "Origins," p. 17; Pitt, "Enigmatic," 7–10. None of the arguments advanced in the present study depend on proving that Sutton Hoo's Mound 1 is the grave of Rædwald.

116 See Bede, *HE*, III.22, pp. 284–5. McClure and Collins (trans., *Ecclesiastical History*, "Explanatory Notes," p. 395) warn against assuming a relationship between Sutton Hoo and Rendlesham; but J. Newman's article "Late Roman and Anglo-Saxon Settlement Pattern," which they cite in implicit support of their caution, actually argues quite confidently for "yet another link" between the two (p. 38). The link is also supported by Davies and Vierck, "Contexts," p. 274; by Williamson, *Sutton Hoo*, p. 18; and by Pitt, "Enigmatic," pp. 7–8, 20–1.

117 On which, see Filmer-Sankey and Pestell, *Snape*.

118 Williamson, *Sutton Hoo*, p. 20, citing Filmer-Sankey, "Snape," pp. 50–1. On Snape's idiosyncrasies, including its complex social character and resemblances to Sutton Hoo as well as to Mucking II cemetery in Essex, see Filmer-Sankey, "Discussion," pp. 262–5. Carver notes differences between Snape and Sutton Hoo in "Sutton Hoo," p. 497.

119 Filmer-Sankey, "Discussion," pp. 265–6. Filmer-Sankey retreats somewhat from this view in "Snape," but in my opinion without providing as cogent an explanation as the one supporting his earlier position.

120 Williamson, *Sutton Hoo*, pp. 20, 109, citing Warner, *Origins*, pp. 120–1 (see too Warner's p. 157). See also Williamson, *Environment*, pp. 83–4.

121 On Blythburgh as Anna's burial place, see *LE*, I.7, ed. Blake, p. 16 (trans. Fairweather, p. 22), noted too by Newton, *Origins*, p. 135, n. 8. Blythburgh may have been chosen simply because Anna had died in the immediate vicinity, or because it was already an important royal vill, as Haslam argues ("*Dommoc*," pp. 43–4). An early monastery or *minster* has been inferred from the discovery there of an eighth-century whalebone writing tablet (Newton, *Origins*; Pestell, *Landscapes*, p. 92; Warner, *Origins*, pp. 120–1), but I do not know whether this supposed community existed prior to 654 or was founded to commemorate the slain king.

122 "Eni Tyttling, Tyttla Wuffing," quoted and discussed in F. Stenton, "East Anglian Kings," reconstructing the genealogy from the Vespasian MS. and from Bede. See too PASE, s.vv. "Anna 1" and "Eni 1"; Newton's genealogies in *Origins* (p. xiii), *Reckoning* (p. 44), and "Forgotten";

Kilpatrick, "Place-Names," p. 42; and Yorke, *Kings*, pp. 67–8 and pp. 58–71 on the early kingdom and on difficulties associated with the genealogy. See also below, chap. 1, n. 116.

123 See Anderson, *Imagined Communities*, esp. pp. 5–7.

124 Williamson, *Sutton Hoo*, p. 14. On differences between northern and southern East Anglia, see Williamson, "East Anglia's Character," pp. 58–60. A compelling case for the early medieval kingdom's identity as a synthesis of different cultural influences from Scandinavia, the Continent, and northern as well as central England is made by Hines, "Origins," esp. pp. 42–3.

125 From his Suffolk perspective, Jocelin of Brakelond thought Abbot Samson's Norfolk dialect different enough to warrant mention: *Chronica*, ed. Rokewode, p. 30; *Chronicle*, trans. Greenway and Sayers, p. 37. See too Lowe, "Linguistic Geography," pp. 156–7.

126 Yorke, *Kings*, p. 69, for this quotation and for general discussion of the kingdom's internal division and two bishoprics. See too Whitelock, "Pre-Viking Age Church," pp. 1, 8 and n. 5; Scull, "Before Sutton Hoo," p. 5; Bassett, "In Search," p. 26. The single diocese of East Anglia was established only ca. 1095, at Norwich (Whitelock, "Pre-Viking Age Church," p. 1). On *Domnoc* as Walton Castle, see below, chap. 1, p. 64.

127 Marten, "Shiring."

128 A point made by Kirby, *Earliest English Kings*, p. 64, regarding East Anglia and Northumbria. Rush's unpublished "Cultural Transition" (which I have not seen) argues that Romanized Britons contributed to the heterogeneity of early medieval East Anglia.

129 On the *Tribal Hidage*: Dumville, "Tribal Hidage," pp. 228–9; Davies and Vierck, "Contexts"; Bassett, "In Search," pp. 26; Pestell, *Landscapes*, pp. 128–9; Oosthuizen, "Culture," pp. 10–14; Wickham-Crowley, "Fens," pp. 74–6 (citing David Roffe). On the first, eleventh-century appearances of the words "Norfolk" and "Suffolk," see Scarfe, *Suffolk Landscape*, p. 42.

130 Kirby, *Making*, p. 55, identifying the prehistoric Icknield Way as the likely route of military expansion.

131 "The absence of any rival centres visible in the archaeology of the late sixth and early seventh centuries suggests that this family [i.e. the East Anglian kings and their kin] networked effectively and reconciled potential rivals from an early date": Higham and Ryan, *Anglo-Saxon World*, p. 141, noting the clutch of important sites (Rendlesham, Snape, Sutton Hoo) in south-eastern Suffolk.

132 E.g. Tennyson, *Suffolk Scene*, pp. 40–2; Scarfe, *Suffolk Landscape*, pp. 36–43. According to Plunkett, "Suffolk's western cultural area" extended, "[i]n archaeological terms," well into the Fens, into Cambridgeshire and even Lincolnshire: *Suffolk*, pp. 34, 47–8; see too Williamson, *Sutton Hoo*,

p. 126. The area would thus include Ixworth, near Bury St. Edmunds; on the seventh- to eighth-century treasures unearthed there in the 1850s, see M.F. Reed, "Sculpture."

133 Williamson, "East Anglia's Character," pp. 58–62; Williamson, *Sutton Hoo*, pp. 123–6. See too the discussion in Filmer-Sankey, "Discussion," p. 265. The Scandinavian features of East Anglian material culture have been set out by Bruce-Mitford, *Sutton Hoo Ship-Burial*, vol. 1, p. 693; Hines, *Scandinavian Character* (confirming Bruce-Mitford); Hines, "Origins." See too Carver, "Kingship," passim and p. 149 (agreeing with Hines and thus with Bruce-Mitford). Yorke, noting the likely English provenance of goods formerly thought to have been made in Sweden, speaks of "contacts between the East Anglian and Scandinavian courts": *Kings*, p. 61, citing (in n. 27) A.C. Evans, *Sutton Hoo Ship Burial*, pp. 114–16. On the Frankish influences: Wood, "Franks"; Wood, *Merovingian North Sea*, pp. 12–17 and *Merovingian Kingdoms*, pp. 177–8, 314; Wood,, "Before and After," p. 49; J. Campbell, "Impact"; Wickham, *Framing*, pp. 810–18 (discussing, inter alia, Frankish influences on East Anglia and on Kent).

134 Williamson, "East Anglia's Character," p. 60.

135 Ravensdale and Muir, *East Anglian Landscapes*, pp. 13–14. Their co-authored book has been a major influence on my own thinking about East Anglia.

136 Williamson, "East Anglia's Character," p. 62; emphasis in original.

137 See e.g. Hamerow, Hinton, and Crawford, eds., *Oxford Handbook*, especially but by no means exclusively the essays by Hills, Brugmann, Richards, D. Griffiths, Hedges, and Owen-Crocker. Literary and material intersections are explored with characteristic richness by Hines, "Literary Sources." Other relevant studies include Pohl, "Ethnic Names"; Harris, "Overview"; Harris, *Race* (esp. p. 43); Frazer, "Introduction"; Moreland, "Ethnicity." In the East Anglian context, Capper, "Insights" (cited in Capper, "Dialogue," p. 13), and Rush, "Cultural Transition," are also important.

138 See pertinent cautions by Hills, "Overview," pp. 3–11; Harris, *Race*, p. 4; Frazer, "Introduction," p. 3.

139 Yorke, "Anglo-Saxon *Gentes*," p. 390; Sims-Williams, "Settlement," p. 24; Moreland, "Ethnicity," p. 46. According to A.D. Smith, however, Bedan and other early medieval evocations of *regna* suggest "broader popular loyalties and rationales": *Ethnic Origins*, p. 72.

140 On the terminology, see J. Campbell, *Essays*, pp. 85–98, 132 (quotation at p. 86); J. Campbell, "Secular and Political Contexts," p. 27 and studies cited on p. 39, n. 5; Loyn, "Kings," pp. 75–6; Foot, "Historiography," p. 130 (for *regnum*, *imperium*, and *provincia* in Bede, and citing J. Campbell); Yorke, "Political and Ethnic Identity," pp. 73–6, 82;

F. Stenton, *Anglo-Saxon England*, p. 305; Dumville, "Origins," p. 91 (on Isidore as source of Bede's use of *provincia*).

141 Sturdy, *Alfred*, p. 4. Commensurate insights can be found in Wood, *Merovingian North Sea*, p. 4; Yorke, "Anglo-Saxon *Gentes*," pp. 389–90.

142 The formidable power of the ealdormen in the middle to late tenth century is ably illustrated by John, *Reassessing*, pp. 10–16 and passim; by Higham, *Death*, pp. 4–14, 22–5 and passim; and by Hart, *Danelaw*, pp. 569–604.

143 F. Stenton, *Anglo-Saxon England*, p. 450; Hart, *Danelaw*, p. 471; Wareham, *Lords*, pp. 14, 23–8; PASE, s.v. "Æthelwine 2."

144 See e.g. Stafford, *Unification*, p. 37; Sheppard, *Families*, pp. 4, 10–11, 39–40 and passim; Higham, "From Tribal Chieftains," p. 140; Wood, "Monasteries," pp. 11–12; P.H. Blair, *Introduction*, p. 12; Scull, "Before Sutton Hoo," p. 6 (citing Davies and Vierck, "Contexts," pp. 228–9); Hiatt, "*Beowulf*," p. 32; Neidorf, "*Beowulf*," pp. 855–60.

145 Higham and Ryan, *Anglo-Saxon World*, p. 8; compare P.H. Blair, *Introduction*, pp. 11–12; Foot, "Making," and "Historiography," pp. 129–32; Sheppard, *Families*, esp. pp. 16–19 and 48–9 (citing Foot); Discenza, *Inhabited Spaces*, pp. 8, 60; Molyneaux, *Formation*, pp. 201–6; Dumville, "Origins," p. 81. Molyneaux's challenges to Foot and Wormald are not immediately germane to the present discussion.

146 K. Davis, "National Writing," pp. 619–21; Nelson, "Presidential Address," p. 27; S.T. Smith, *Land*, p. 153; Lavelle, "Geographies." S. Reynolds, *Kingdoms*, pp. 219–49, explores the sometimes fluid interrelation between "private lordship" and "public province." I return to this topic below, in chap. 4.

147 Oosthuizen, *Anglo-Saxon Fenland*, pp. 53, 57–60, 66, 87.

148 P.H. Blair, *Roman Britain*, p. 169.

149 *MS A*, ed. Bately, p. 41; *ASC*, p. 60 (*s.a.* 823 for 825). Italics mine.

150 *MS A*, ed. Bately, p. 47; *ASC*, p. 70.

151 The treaty may date to the early 880s; see below, chap. 4. Kathleen Davis discerns a similar fluidity in the Alfredian noun *Angelcynn*, which can refer to a people or a place: "National Writing," pp. 619–21.

152 Attenborough, *Laws*, p. 98; Keynes and Lapidge, *Alfred*, p. 171.

153 With regard to the phrase "eal seo ðeod ðe on Eastænglum beoð," Hadley suggests that it "probably indicates both settlers and pre-existing inhabitants of East Anglia": *Vikings*, p. 32. Roffey and Lavelle ("West Saxons," p. 8) similarly view the AGT as "implying that provision [for the Angelcynn] was being made for the *Engliscne* inside Danish-held territory" ("West Saxons," p. 8). But would the original "English" inhabitants of East Anglia have been involved in the peace-making between Alfred and his *witan* on one side and Guthrum and his followers on the other?

154 Howe, "Angle," p. 18, n. 41 (citing Dorothy Whitelock and Eric John); Hadley, *Vikings*, p. 56 and n. 125 (citing an early work of Frank Stenton's); John, *Reassessing*, p. 91.

155 Rowley, *Old English Version*, p. 2.

156 This view is based on Rowley's argument that the OE Bede was neither produced by the Alfredian court nor associated with its ideological program: *Old English Version*, esp. pp. 57–70. (One should also note Waite's argument ["Preface"] that the Preface to the OE Bede and the body of that text were not written by the same person.) Furthermore, Molyneaux, by way of critiquing Wormald, argues that neither Bede nor his OE translator was appropriated by that program: "*Old English Bede*," pp. 1289–90 and passim. See also Molyneaux's "Did the English Really Think" and *Formation*, pp. 199–206 and passim.

157 *Old English Version*, ed. and trans. T. Miller, I.14, pp. 56–7. I depart slightly from Miller's translation, but my use of ModE *kingdom* for OE *rīce* echoes Miller's.

158 *Old English Version*, ed. and trans. T. Miller, III.18, pp. 208–9. For the phrase *fore beon* "to rule over," see *DOE*, s.v. *fore*, A.3.a.i.

159 *Old English Version*, ed. and trans. T. Miller, III.19, pp. 216–17. Compare III.19, pp. 210–11.

160 Bede consistently uses *provincia* not *regio* to refer to the East Anglian kingdom. On the word *regio*, see Dumville, "Origins," p. 96; J. Campbell, *Essays*, pp. 86–7. For *mægð* and the definitions I have provided in parentheses, see Bosworth-Toller, s.v. *mægð*, senses IVa, IVb, IVc. It should be noted, though, that one of the examples given in Bosworth-Toller's definition "province, country" (sense IVc) is taken from the OE Bede and treats *mægþ* as the equivalent of Bede's Latin word *provincia*.

161 *Old English Version*, ed. and trans. T. Miller, II.5, pp. 108–9. I am grateful to an anonymous reader for pointing out to me that Miller's translation "temporal" is based on the emendation of MS. *willendlecan* to *hwilendlican*. On the latter word and its variants, see *DOE* s.v. *hwīlwendlic, hwīlendlic*.

162 Michelet, *Creation*, p. 26.

163 Saints' cults were of course widespread in early England; see e.g. Thacker, "Dynastic Monasteries," with special emphasis on Wessex.

164 See the works of these authors cited below in chaps. 2, 3, and 5.

165 See Hart, *Danelaw*, pp. 37–41, and Plunkett, *Suffolk*, pp. 155–213, for post-749 regnal histories that supplement F. Stenton, "East Anglian Kings." Their reconstructed genealogies may be paraphrased thus: Beonna (749–ca. 760; on whom see also Naismith, "Kings," pp. 295, 307–11), perhaps reigning with the co-rulers Hun and Alberht (Æthelberht I); Æthelred I (ca. 760–79); Æthelberht II (779–94); Eadwald (794–ca. 821); Æthelstan I (ca. 821–ca. 845); Æthelweard (ca. 845–54); and Edmund

(854–69). See the respective entries in PASE. For the post-869 period, Hart notes numismatic studies of coins bearing the names of another Æthelred and a certain Oswald (*Danelaw*, p. 41). Blackburn cites and builds upon Michael Dolley's placement of those two kings between 869 and 879–80 and writes that they "ruled briefly in East Anglia immediately after Edmund's demise, before Scandinavian control was fully established" ("Expansion," p. 127; see too Capper, "Practical Implications," p. 17, citing Blackburn, and Capper, "Insights" and "Contested Loyalties"). Hadley plausibly surmises that the two kings were Danish-nominated puppets (*Vikings*, p. 11–12), as do McLeod, *Beginning*, pp. 181 and passim, and Young, *Edmund*, p. 70; but G. Williams is less certain ("Coins," p. 23).

166 The term "Danelaw" is traceable only as far back as the early eleventh-century so-called Laws of Edward and Guthrum but is often used to refer to that enormous swath of eastern, central, and northern England that fell to the vikings in the late ninth. On the word's problematic nature, see John, "Age," p. 161; Holman, "Defining"; McLeod, *Beginning*, p. 9.

Chapter 1

1 An earlier, shorter version of this essay appeared in *New Medieval Literatures* 15 (2013): 97–122. I thank Brepols Publishing for permission to include this revised and expanded iteration here. Monographs and essay collections on Bede include A.H. Thompson, *Bede*; Bonner, *Famulus*; C.W. Jones, *Bede*; G.H. Brown, *Bede* and *Companion*; Houwen and MacDonald, *Beda*; Lebecq, Perrin, and Szerwiniack, *Bède*; Gunn, *Bede's* Historiae; DeGregorio, *Cambridge Companion* and *Innovation*; Darby and Wallis, *Bede*. Also important are Brown and Biggs's *Bede: Part 1* and *Bede: Part 2*, in the Sources of Anglo-Saxon Literary Culture series.

2 My thinking here owes much to Thacker's insight that Bede "sought to chart how the English became part of the universal Church and to establish their particular role in the economy of salvation" ("Bede and History," p. 172); to G.H. Brown's observation that "the main aim of the whole work [i.e. the *HE*] is to expound the development of God's plan for the English as a chosen people and the development of one unified Church in a violent and feuding land" (*Companion*, p. 106; cf. Brown, *Bede*, p. 89); and to Goffart's pronouncement that the *HE* is "a tale of origins framed dynamically as the Providence-guided advance of a people from heathendom to Christianity" (*Narrators*, p. 235).

3 Merrills, *History*, p. 235 (and similar pronouncements passim), citing Tugène, "L'Histoire," pp. 140–2. Merrills's chapter on Bede (pp. 229–309) masterfully explores the intersections among the Northumbrian scholar's historical, geographical, computistical, and exegetical concerns.

4 On this dual use of *gens*, see Thacker, "Bede and History," p. 176; Thacker, "Bede's Idea," p. 4.
5 Merrills, *History*, p. 233.
6 Howe, *Writing*, pp. 5–8. On the early medieval "relationship between God and the material world, set out graphically and symbolically" in mapping practices, see Harvey, *Maps*, p. 10.
7 Tugène, *L'idée*, p. 333. Translation mine.
8 Lozovsky, *"Earth,"* p. 92.
9 When I use words like "paganism," "Christianity," "backsliding," "apostasy," and "syncretism," I intend no moral judgment but rather seek to reconstruct Bede's own attitudes and to gauge their effect on his representations of place. On the questionable value of such labels within early English cultural contexts, see below, nn. 17, 47, 70, 71, and 95.
10 Bede's limited scope and Northumbrian bias are well known: Thacker, "Bede and History," pp. 184–5; Thacker, "Bede's Idea," pp. 7–9; Goffart, *Narrators*, p. 240 and passim; Sims-Williams, "Settlement," pp. 25–6; Yorke, *Conversion*, pp. 21–2; Merrills, *History*, p. 234. Merrills does, however, emphasize Bede's concern for the "wider context," as does Tugène in *L'idée*.
11 *HE*, Preface, pp. 2–7. See Whitelock, "Pre-Viking Age Church," pp. 2–3; Yorke, *Kings*, pp. 3, 25, 32, 58. The Northumbrian royal family was also a likely source, as proposed by Whitelock and seconded by Wallace-Hadrill, *Historical Commentary*, p. 76.
12 Ian Wood has argued that Bede and other eighth-century ecclesiastical writers, especially Northumbrian historians, "rarely purveyed information without moulding it in one way or another. They played an active part both in the development of the Northumbrian kingdom and in the process of its memorialisation": Wood, "Monasteries," pp. 12–13, citing Geary, *Phantoms*, p. 7 and passim.
13 A.D. Smith, *Chosen Peoples*, p. 137.
14 Only a very terse reference to Rædwald appears in the Anonymous Monk of Whitby's *Earliest Life of Gregory the Great*, ed. and trans. Colgrave, pp. 98–9. His regnal dates are uncertain. "(?–616/627)": J. Campbell, "First Christian Kings," p. 53 (compare PASE, s.v. "Rædwald 1"); "(*ante* AD 600–ca. 625)": Hoggett, *Archaeology*, p. 28. See too Newton, *Reckoning*, pp. 40, 44 (suggesting a date of death as "c. 625"); Hines, "Origins," pp. 16–17; Bruce-Mitford, *Sutton Hoo Ship-Burial*, vol. 1, p. 698. On the difficulty of precise dating, see Bruce-Mitford, *Sutton Hoo Ship-Burial*, vol. 1, pp. 696–8; Wood, "Franks," pp. 3–4.
15 On Bede's understanding of pagan worship (e.g. its use of idols), see Church, "Paganism," p. 170 (cited in Barrow, "How Coifi Pierced," p. 694, n. 6); Petts, *Pagan*, pp. 73–96; Reilly, "Islands"; Wilson, *Anglo-Saxon Paganism*, pp. 29–32. Tyler, "Reluctant Kings," discusses Bede's disregard

both for the utility of paganism and for the strategic reasons kings sometimes had for resisting Christianity.

16 My use of "scapegoat" is indebted in a general way to Northrop Frye's "*pharmakos*, or scapegoat," the "sacrificial victim, who has to be killed to strengthen the others," "the human symbol that concentrates our fears and hates": *Anatomy*, pp. 41, 148, 45.

17 As shown e.g. by Barrow, "How Coifi Pierced"; O'Brien, "Quotation," pp. 185–6; Del Giacco, "Exegesis," esp. pp. 26 and 28; Wetherbee, "Some Implications," p. 26; Tyler, "Reluctant Kings," pp. 153–4.

18 Studies of the importance of the list genre in early medieval England include Sisam, "Anglo-Saxon Royal Genealogies"; Dumville, "Kingship"; Howe, *Catalogue Poems*; Stodnick, "Old Names" (citing and building upon Sisam and Howe); Yorke, "*Bretwaldas*," pp. 85–6.

19 Scholarly commentary is extensive, but see e.g. Wormald, "Bede, the *Bretwaldas*"; J. Campbell, *Anglo-Saxon State*, pp. 43–6 (responding to Wormald); Yorke, "*Bretwaldas*"; Fanning, "Bede," pp. 24–5; Keynes, "Rædwald"; and further bibliography in Grossi, "Place," pp. 97 and 99, nn. 10 and 16 respectively. See now Dumville, "Origins," pp. 99–101. On *bretwalda* as the ASC's term for a king who wielded *imperium*, see below, chapter 4, n. 201.

20 Keynes, "Rædwald," p. 115.

21 Pohl, "Ethnic Names," pp. 13–14. See too Wood's thoughts on genealogies in "Before and After," pp. 49–51, as well as Hines's important remarks on Bede's "authentic information in a distorted form": "Becoming," pp. 50–1.

22 Hines, "Becoming," p. 50 (emphasis in original). Concerning the list in Book V Morris remarks: "This is more like it – yet we cannot be sure that even this list is complete, or that its definitions were stable either in Bede's day or two centuries before" (*Time's Anvil*, p. 233). Härke adduces archaeological evidence to add Franks, "at least one Goth," Norwegians, and Alemanni to Bede's second list: "Ethnogenesis," p. 11.

23 Howe, *Migration*, p. 60. See too Yorke, "Anglo-Saxon Origin Legends." Critiques of the inaccuracy of that myth abound; Ellard cites a cluster of them in *Anglo-Saxon(ist) Pasts*, p. 176, n. 2 (specifically, Magennis, *Cambridge Introduction*, pp. 34–5; Pohl, "Ethnic Names," p. 25; and Higham and Ryan, *Anglo-Saxon World*, pp. 7–10).

24 See e.g. Wormald, "*Engla Lond*"; Howe, *Migration*; Howe, *Writing*, pp. 50–1, 141–3; Dumville, "Origins," p. 74 (citing *HE*, I.22).

25 Harris, *Race*, p. 15; Merrills, *History*, pp. 271–4, 290–308; Tugène, *L'idée*, p. 336; and especially Molyneaux, "Did the English Really Think" and "*Old English Bede*."

26 As, according to Fairweather, it connoted to readers of the twelfth-century *Liber Eliensis* (*LE*): "'angle,' 'corner,' 'nook,' 'a retired, unfrequented place': roughly, then … the 'Outback'": *LE*, trans. Fairweather, p. 12, n. 38.

27 As pointed out by Howe, *Migration*, pp. 51–2. In a reading of Bede, Felix, and several OE texts, Neidorf compellingly suggests that "pan-Germanic identity did not travel to Britain with the Germanic migrants, but was rather generated there in the context of ethnic hostility with the indigenous Celtic peoples" ("*Beowulf*," p. 865).

28 I use "wasteland" in the merely idiomatic sense; for the technical meaning, see Rackham, "Medieval Countryside," p. 15, cited by Discenza, *Inhabited Spaces*, p. 142, n. 6, in her rich discussion of literary representations of wasteland in *Beowulf*, *Guthlac A*, and *Andreas*.

29 In this quotation I have slightly modified Colgrave and Mynors's punctuation of the Latin and have replaced their translation of Bede's remarks on Rædwald with the translation proposed by Wormald and Charles-Edwards in Addenda, p. 222.

30 It is possible but unlikely that subject *gentes* consented to foreign rulers' *imperium*; see Wallace-Hadrill, *Historical Commentary*, pp. 59–60; Wormald, "Bede, the *Bretwaldas*," pp. 132–3, nn. 2, 3.

31 The debate is summarized in Grossi, "Place," pp. 100–1.

32 As emphasized by Higham, *Convert*, pp. 102–3.

33 Tugène, *L'idée*, p. 249.

34 *DMLBS*, fasc. 4, pp. 1002–3, s.v. *fractus* 1, 13, 13*b*; *DMLBS*, fasc. 2, p. 502, s.v. *corrumpere* and sense *b*.

35 On the likelihood that Rædwald controlled eastern Mercia, see Dumville, "Essex," p. 132, cited approvingly by Kirby, *Early English Kings*, p. 66 and p. 74, n. 29. Newton thinks Rædwald's control of Lindsey "possible"; "[i]f not, the military power of Rædwald might have been just too large for the king of Lindsey to challenge": *Reckoning*, p. 33.

36 *Pace* Higham, *English Empire*, p. 198; but see Higham, *Convert*, p. 152.

37 Kirby, *Earliest English Kings*, pp. 19–20.

38 R. Hill, "Bede," p. 100. Compare Newton, *Reckoning*, p. 30; Scarfe, *Suffolk*, pp. 30–5 (on the queen's strength of will, her commitment to her religious beliefs, and, perhaps, her role in depositing the famous coin hoard at Sutton Hoo); Mayr-Harting, *Coming*, pp. 21, 65–6; J. Stevenson, "Christianity," p. 180; Carver, *Sutton Hoo*, p. 34; and especially Klein, *Ruling Women*, p. 35. Tyler stresses the influence queens had over their husbands: "Reluctant Kings," pp. 155–7, discussing, among others, Rædwald's spouse.

39 Bede, *Letter to Ecgbert*, ed. and trans. Grocock and Wood, esp. pp. 135–49.

40 Ravensdale and Muir, *East Anglian Landscapes*, pp. 13–14, quoted and discussed above in the Introduction, p. 26.

41 Young, *Edmund*, p. 27.

42 Edwin later died in battle against Penda of the Mercians at Hatfield Chase; Bede praises him in a manner reminiscent of hagiography (*HE* II.20, pp. 202–5), and Lutterkort characterizes the account as a "miracle story": "Beda," pp. 94–9. See too Higham, *Convert*, pp. 166–7.

43 Wallace-Hadrill, *Historical Commentary*, p. 75; Kirby, *Earliest English Kings*, pp. 78, 79; Tugène, *L'idée*, pp. 132–3; Plunkett, *Suffolk*, p. 97; Higham, *Convert*, pp. 181–3; PASE, s.vv. "Eorpwald 1," "Edwin 2"; Pitt, "Enigmatic," pp. 8–9.
44 Uncertainty about Christianity remained his crowning trait long after he became king of Northumbria, as stressed by Lutterkort, "Beda," p. 95; see too Kirby, *Earliest English Kings*, p. 62 (though on p. 79 Kirby stresses how unusual Edwin's baptism was in the first place, as royal conversion outside of Kent was rare in the 620s); Higham, *Convert*, pp. 166–7. Tyler discusses Edwin's strategic hesitation in "Reluctant Kings," pp. 147–8. According to Tugène, however, Bede defends Edwin's protracted deliberation on the grounds that it reveals the Northumbrian king's desire to learn the new faith thoroughly, a motive quite different from that of the pagan priest Coifi: *L'idée*, pp. 204–9. See too Gunn, *Bede's* Historiae, pp. 160–1.
45 Thacker, "Bede's Ideal," pp. 146, 152; Foot, "Bede's Kings," p. 43, drawing a parallel between Bede and Isidore and citing a study of Michael Wallace-Hadrill's.
46 Higham, *English Empire*, p. 305; in the same study Higham writes that Rædwald was "the champion of religious conservatism [i.e. paganism] and political orthodoxy in an England already touched by the new Christian monotheism" (p. 183). See too Wallace-Hadrill, *Historical Commentary*, p. 76; Newton, *Reckoning*, pp. 6, 14–15; and Kilbride's perspicacious defence of Rædwald's agency in "Why" (pp. 5–8), cited in Hoggett, *Archaeology*, p. 29, n. 50.
47 See e.g. Diesner, "Inkarnationsjahre," p. 22, building on work by Karl Hauck. (Diesner's study is cited in Wallace-Hadrill, *Historical Commentary*, p. 76.) Carver's caution in this regard should be noted: see "Agency," p. 7. Compare Kilbride, "Why," p. 8.
48 Undoubtedly Rædwald underwent conversion to "advance his own personal prestige" (Young, *Edmund*, p. 26, citing Hoggett, *Archaeology*, p. 29). That prestige, however, depended for its meaning on an aristocratic East Anglian social context that Bede disregards because it predated Christianity's arrival among the Wuffings.
49 Carver, "Agency," p. 3. For related insights, see Newton, *Reckoning*, p. 14, citing (n. 23) Chaney, *Cult*, pp. 25–8; Higham, *Convert*, p. 36. Women in pagan Germanic societies were valued for their political counsel and religious authority: Klein, *Ruling Women*, pp. 11, 35. See too Tyler, "Reluctant Kings," pp. 155–7 for examples of influential conversion-age queens.
50 It is also significant that, on the basis of grave goods, East Anglia may be said to be "one of the first regions in which women living in Britain are giving their allegiance to the Germanic cultural idea": Carver, "Sutton Hoo," p. 498.
51 Bede shows Boniface quoting 1 Cor. 7:14 (noted by Colgrave and Mynors, p. 175, n. 1).

52 On Bertha, see Wood, *Merovingian Kingdoms*, pp. 121, 176–8; Wood, *Missionary Life*, pp. 9–10; Rowley, *Old English Version*, passim, but esp. pp. 101–2, 117–18 (summarizing recent scholarship). Dunn explores the complexities of Bertha's involvement in the Christian mission in Kent in *Christianization*, pp. 48–56, 101–5.

53 E.g. McClure, "Bede's Old Testament Kings"; Thacker, "Bede's Ideal"; Tugène, *L'idée*, esp. pp. 13–19, 207–8; DeGregorio, "Old Testament"; Holder, "New Testament." For related suggestive remarks, see Cowdrey, "Bede," pp. 517–19, 23. I owe the reference to Cowdrey's article to Molyneaux's "*Old English Bede*," p. 1289, n. 3.

54 In the *HE* Bede includes his commentary on Proverbs among works he had completed earlier, "a major group of mature commentaries" begun with the commentary on 1 Samuel, "dedicated to Acca and written around 716" (Thacker, "Ordering," p. 54).

55 Here and elsewhere, I quote scriptural passages from *Vulgate Bible*, ed. Edgar and Kinney. Bede's Commentary on Proverbs further idealizes Bede's notion of the early church as a "strong woman": "Mulier autem vineam plantavit, cum ecclesia primitiva latius per orbem missis praedicatoribus fidei semina dispersit. Consideravit namque agrum, cum orbem universum vitiorum spinetis horrentem, cultore spirituali opus habere perspexit. Emit vero eum, cum, missis ubique doctoribus, talentum verbi audientibus contulit, ut eos credentes felicissimo Christi mancipatui subderet" ("The woman, moreover, *planted the vineyard*, because the primitive church scattered seeds of faith more widely by means of preachers sent throughout the world. And because she *considered* the entire world a *field* bristling with thorn-groves of vices, she perceived [it] to have a need for a spiritual cultivator. Truly she *bought it*, when by means of teachers sent everywhere she exchanged the talent of speech for listeners, in order that, by means of a most felicitous purchase, she might add them as believers in Christ"). For the Latin text, see Bede's *Super parabola Salomonis*, ed. Giles, pp. 175–6. Translation and emphases mine.

56 Tyler, "Reluctant Kings," p. 155. My analysis follows and builds on North's.

57 Thacker, "Ordering," pp. 55–6, and pp. 56–7 on Bede's excoriation of the British Christians as heretics and as modern equivalents to the Jews.

58 North, *Heathen Gods*, p. 322.

59 On Bede's belief that Christianity was linked to prosperity, see Rollason, *Northumbria*, pp. 201–2; Foot, "Bede's Kings," p. 33.

60 Kirby, *Earliest English Kings*, p. 41; *HE* II.6. See too N. Brooks, *Early History*, p. 64; compare Higham, *English Empire*, pp. 202–4; Wilson, *Anglo-Saxon Paganism*, p. 174.

61 Compare *HE* II.5 (Eadbald) and II.15 (Rædwald). Penda, it should be admitted, comes in for perhaps the harshest censure of all, largely because of his hostility to Northumbria; see Thacker, "Bede's Idea," pp. 11–12.

62 J. Blair, "Anglo-Saxon Period," p. 77. Compare Kirby, *Earliest English Kings*, p. 62; Wilson, *Anglo-Saxon Paganism*, p. 174. On certain kings' refusal to baptize their sons, and the "intra-dynastic competition" the practice implies, see Tyler, "Reluctant Kings," pp. 157–60 (discussing e.g. Eadbald and the sons of Sæberht).

63 Diesner ("Inkarnationsjahre," p. 22) notes that in general Bede "das ständige Hin und Her zwischen Christentum und Heidentum in den angelsächsischen Staaten des 7. Jahrhunderts bewußt war" ("was aware of the constant back-and-forth between Christianity and paganism in the Anglo-Saxon states of the seventh century"; translation mine).

64 Wood suspects that, *pace* Bede's own chronology of events, Æthelberht may have been baptized two years before St. Augustine's arrival: *Merovingian North Sea*, p. 15. This possibility would not affect my reading of the implicit contrast between Æthelberht's conversion and Rædwald's as Bede viewed it.

65 Klein, *Ruling Women*, pp. 39–45 (pp. 39, 42). According to North, "there is neither reaction nor apostasy in this tale" because "Rædwald's wife and friends did not expel the Christian cult": *Heathen Gods*, p. 322. The corrective, however, raises Bede's demonization of Rædwald to that much higher relief. Compare Wallace-Hadrill: "[Rædwald] was not hostile to Christianity and not unique in his decision to keep his options open. … It is clear that East Anglian paganism was strong enough to resist conversion and possible that the dual-purpose temple was the brave effort of a defeated Christian at a serious form of religious syncretism; but Bede does not give Redwald the benefit of the doubt" (*Historical Commentary*, p. 76). See too Higham, *Convert*, p. 138.

66 On baptism's performative and even "exorcistic character," see Dumitrescu, "Bede's Liberation Philology," p. 49 (and sources cited therein); Dunn, *Christianization*, p. 142; Foxhall Forbes, *Heaven*, pp. 99–100.

67 North, *Heathen Gods*, p. 322. Eric John claims that the advising role of the *witan* or "wise men" was normally a mere formality and that kings took decisions unilaterally: "When there appears to be evidence of genuine debate it is unwise to make too much of it" (*Reassessing*, p. 17). On the other hand, "Redwald, returning home [from Kent, where he had undergone conversion to Christianity], found his wife and some of his senior *witan* opposed, so he sought a compromise" (p. 29).

68 Noticing sexual connotations in Bede's critique, Klein claims that, both in this passage and in his account of the impiety of Eadbald of Kent, Bede concurs with "the pervasive formulation within biblical and patristic writings of apostasy as spiritual fornication": *Ruling Women*, p. 41 (and sources cited on p. 215, n. 57). The biblical Jezebel was an antitype of queenship in early English thought; see Matthews, "Token," pp. 53–5, citing Klein's discussion in *Ruling Women*, e.g. pp. 126, 128, 133–4. Biblical

associations between harlotry and worldliness in general are discussed in MacCarron, "Æthelthryth," and "Adornment," pp. 143–4.

69 See the salutary critiques of historicist enterprises in Cramp, "Not Why," and Capper, "Practical Implications."

70 Against such over-simplification, see Carver, "Agency," pp. 14 and 8, respectively; Kilbride, "Why"; Pestell, "Paganism"; Yorke, *Conversion*, pp. 98–109; Petts, *Pagan*, pp. 73–96; Pluskowski, "Archaeology" (who, like Petts, cites Kilbride); Hines, "Religion," p. 377; Wormald, "Bede, *Beowulf*," pp. 66–7; Higham, *Convert*, p. 136.

71 Dunn, *Christianization*, p. 164, citing (p. 239, n. 165) Carver, *Sutton Hoo*, p. 503. See too Wood, "Franks," p. 2. Pitt suggests that Sutton Hoo's ideological orientation needn't amount to proof of pagan religious belief as such but instead displays what Judith Jesch calls "cultural paganism" ("Enigmatic," p. 23, citing, in her n. 154, Jesch, "Scandinavian," pp. 58, 67–8), though it should be noted that Jesch primarily discusses survivals in the otherwise explicitly Christian England of the age of Cnut and Wulfstan.

72 "Saulos" may be merely an incompetent rendering of "Paulos"; see Bruce-Mitford, who plausibly suggests that, regardless of the engraver's intention, "[t]he 'uneducated copy' could still have been read as *Saulos* … and the antithesis with *Paulos* could still have been intended by those who arranged the burial": *Sutton Hoo Ship-Burial*, vol. 1, pp. 707–9.

73 See above, Introduction, p. 26, as well as Pestell, "Kingdom," pp. 217–18; Oosthuizen, "Culture," p. 8.

74 Harris, *Race*, p. 64. On the relationship between *rex* and *gens* in Bede's thinking, see also Tugène, *L'idée*, pp. 49–90.

75 Howe, *Migration*, p. 52.

76 O'Brien, *Bede's Temple*, p. 140 and sources in his notes 79 and 80. DeGregorio notes that Bede understood true *doctores* and *praedicatores* as members of his intended audience, "namely people in positions of spiritual leadership anywhere whose charge it was to oversee the salvation and moral edification of the faithful": "Old Testament," p. 130. On the role of *doctores* in combatting heresy as expounded in Bede's commentary on the Book of Samuel, see Thacker, "Britons," p. 143. S. Coates, "Ceolfrid," p. 84, shows that in the same commentary Bede condemned clerical laxity as a compromise with paganism.

77 Examples include *HE* IV.11, pp. 368–9 (regarding the pious East Saxon king Sebbi's burial in "ecclesia beati doctoris gentium" ["the church of the blessed doctor of the Gentiles"]); *HE* III.7, pp. 232–3 (Bishop Birinus' promise to Pope Honorius that "se … in intimis ultra Anglorum partibus, quo nullus doctor praecessisset, sanctae fidei semina esse sparsurum" ["he would scatter the seeds of the holy faith in the remotest regions of

England, where no teacher had been before"]; and *HE* III.22, pp. 282–3 (the East Saxon king Sigeberht's request that the Northumbrian king Oswiu send *doctores* to his realm "qui gentem suam ad fidem Christi conuerterent ac fonte salutari abluerent" ["to convert his people to the faith of Christ and wash them in the fountain of salvation"]).

78 Thacker, "Ordering," p. 55, discussing the *Super parabola Salomonis* and other exegetical works written ca. 716. Compare Thacker, "Bede's Ideal," pp. 132–4.

79 For discussion of *HE* V in this regard, see Wood, *Missionary Life*, pp. 42–5, and Wood, *Merovingian North Sea*, p. 7, on "[t]he strength of continuing paganism in the region [of Frisia] into the eighth century."

80 Thacker, "Why Did Heresy Matter?," p. 47; "[f]or Bede, 'heresy' was code for a whole spectrum of contemporary problems," p. 66. See too Thacker, "Britons," pp. 142–4; Wallace-Hadrill, *Historical Commentary*, p. xxiii; Laistner, *Thought*, pp. 124–5. Bede may even have believed that Monothelitism, tackled by the Council of Constantinople (680–1), might survive and spread to Britain: see *HE* IV.17–18 and V.19, discussed by MacCarron, "Christology," p. 171.

81 Dunn intriguingly supposes that the dual temple "enabled Rædwald to keep up two alliances, the pagan one probably to another emergent ruling family represented by his wife": *Christianization*, p. 103.

82 Indeed, "polluted" would not be too strong a word for this context, as Bede held that each of the two baptized kings Eanfrith (a Bernician) and Osric (a Deiran) had returned to paganism "polluendum perdendumque" ("thereby to be polluted and destroyed"): see *HE*, III.1, pp. 212–13 and Dunn's discussion in *Christianization*, pp. 107–8.

83 Whitelock, "Pre-Viking Age Church," p. 3. Whitelock ventured the remark as an aside only.

84 Wallace-Hadrill, *Historical Commentary*, p. 76. According to *DMLBS* (fasc. 1, pp. 70 and 135, respectively), in the context of *HE* II.15 *altare* means simply "altar (Christian)" and *arula* "little altar."

85 Newton, *Reckoning*, p. 16, citing Plummer, *Venerabilis Baedae Historiam*, vol. 2, p. 60.

86 Dunn, *Christianization*, p. 68.

87 *VSG*, ed. and trans. Colgrave, §31, pp. 101–2.

88 *VSG*, §28, pp. 92–5.

89 I thank an anonymous reader for suggesting a possible link among these three *–ulas*.

90 Wilson, *Anglo-Saxon Paganism*, p. 36, discusses the relevant passage in Bede's *Life of St. Cuthbert*. This instance of apostasy in rural Northumbria is not associated with royal sponsorship and thus differs from Rædwald's official tolerance of paganism in East Anglia.

91 Pagan English sacrificial *victimae* probably were animals, not human beings: Wilson, *Anglo-Saxon Paganism*, pp. 33–4, 37, 99 (citing Bede's quotation from Gregory's letter to Mellitus in *HE* I.30, pp. 106–9). See too Dunn, *Christianization*, p. 74.

92 Like Bede, Gregory of Tours understood the ideological nature of spatial borders: see Goetz, "Concepts," p. 77.

93 I am grateful to an anonymous reader for referring me to this passage from Acts.

94 For discussion of this contrast as it informs Bede's thinking in *De templo*, see O'Reilly's introduction to Bede, *On the Temple*, ed. Connolly, pp. xlvi–vii.

95 Hines, "Religion," p. 389; J. Blair, "Anglo-Saxon Pagan Shrines," p. 22; Pluskowski, "Archaeology," p. 772 (citing Blair).

96 Boyarin, *Border Lines*, p. 72 for the quotation, and p. 6 for the discussion of Lieu's insights. The story of Jesus's cleansing of the Temple appears in Mt. 21:12–17, Mk. 11:15–19, Lk. 19:45–8, and John 2:13–16.

97 Molyneaux discusses the omission of this passage in the Old English translation of the *HE*: see his "*Old English Bede*," p. 1303. I retain Colgrave's translation but prefer Molyneaux's substitution of the untranslated Latin word *gens* for Colgrave's "race."

98 Church, building on work by Barbara Yorke, speculates that Rædwald's influence retarded the conversion of Essex, Kent, and Northumbria: "Paganism," pp. 177–8 and n. 78. See too Higham, *Convert*, pp. 136, 141–2.

99 Thacker, "Bede and History," p. 185.

100 On Rendlesham's importance, see Williamson, *Sutton Hoo*, esp. pp. 96–101; Scull and Williamson, "New Light"; Bruce-Mitford, *Sutton Hoo Ship-Burial*, vol. 1, pp. 30–2; R.R. Clarke, *East Anglia*, p. 138; Newton, *Reckoning*, pp. 18–24 (and sources cited therein); Newton, *Origins*, pp. 127, 139; Ravensdale, "Themes," p. 30; Scull, Minter, and Plouviez, "Social." Scarfe, *Suffolk*, p. 30, cites Martin Carver's suggestion that Kingston may have been meant, and Wood ("Franks," p. 13) also defends Kingston; but archaeological finds in 2008–14 support the traditional view of Rendlesham's significance: see Scull, Minter, and Plouviez, "Social." On Rendlesham's connection to the important East Anglian port of Ipswich, see Wickham, *Framing*, p. 809; though Scull, Minter, and Plouviez ("Social," pp. 1606–7) provide a more nuanced interpretation.

101 Klein, *Ruling Women*, p. 43.

102 On the topic of the queen's influence in matters of royal conversion, see Tyler, "Reluctant Kings," pp. 156–7.

103 Colgrave and Mynors note the quotation from Luke 11:26 (*HE*, p. 190, n. 1).

104 See e.g. Higham, *English Empire*, p. 188; North, *Heathen Gods*, p. 322.

105 North, *Heathen Gods*, p. 322.

106 As Newton points out on the basis of II Kings 17:41, the Samaritans long worshipped the Hebrews' God along with their own gods, so it is fair to ask with Newton "Is it thus an exact analogy to the situation of Rædwald?" (*Reckoning*, p. 15). To be sure, Bede was selective in the way he applied scriptural allusions and quotations to English history.

107 See above, n. 66.

108 As discussed below, Bede credits St. Felix for bringing the East Angles "a longa iniquitate atque infelicitate" ("from long-lasting evil and unhappiness"; *HE* II.15, pp. 190–1). Bede's rigid dichotomy between Rædwald's long-lived *iniquitas* and its later eradication by Felix recalls Jesus's stern admonition in Luke 11:23: "Qui non est mecum adversum me est, et qui non colligit mecum dispergit" ("He that is not with me is against me, and he that gathereth not with me scattereth").

109 On the dating, see *HE*, ed. and trans. Colgrave and Mynors, p. 385, n. 3. The Synod is sometimes dated 680, and the beginning of Ealdwulf's reign to 663 or 664.

110 Plunkett puts the first year of Ealdwulf's kingship at 664 and speculates that "Ealdwulf ... was perhaps about 35" at the time: *Suffolk*, p. 120.

111 On the date, see above, n. 14. The speculation that the *fanum* persisted well after Rædwald's death finds some support in J. Stevenson, "Christianity," p. 182; Scarfe, *Suffolk*, pp. 30–1, 36; Newton, *Reckoning*, pp. 15, 17; Hoggett, *Archaeology*, p. 29.

112 Respectively, Wilson, *Anglo-Saxon Paganism*, p. 17; Bruce-Mitford, *Sutton Hoo Ship-Burial*, vol. 1, p. 705. Compare F. Stenton, "East Anglian Kings," in *Preparatory*, p. 399.

113 Wormald, "Bede, *Beowulf*," pp. 60–1, discusses Bede's fear of pagan resurgence.

114 See above, p. 45.

115 According to Carver, Penda's wars against the East Angles "should be seen in the light of interfactional struggles within East Anglia": "Kingship," p. 155, quoted by Kirby, *Earliest English Kings*, p. 110, n. 58. Did Penda's influence lie behind the pagan Ricberht's murder of Eorpwald as well? Pitt observes that Ricberht, like any other claimant, would have needed to enjoy "the support of (most of) the East Anglian elites," and that therefore "it is tempting to infer that Ricberht's pagan beliefs made him a palatable alternative to the Christian Sigeberht" ("Enigmatic," p. 9). See too Higham's analysis in *Convert*, pp. 182–3.

116 Wood, "Franks," p. 4, noting the tangled picture of the East Anglian dynastic succession in *HE*. For reconstructions and studies of the East Anglian royal genealogy, see above, Introduction, nn. 122 and 165.

117 *HE*, II.15, pp. 190–1; III.18, pp. 166–9; Colgrave and Mynors's notes, pp. 266, 268. See now Pitt's conjectural reconstruction of the power

dynamics involving Eorpwald, Sigeberht, and Ricberht ("Enigmatic," pp. 8–10).

118 Kirby, *Earliest English Kings*, p. 81.

119 Yorke, *Kings*, pp. 69–70. Scull, "Before Sutton Hoo," p. 6, surmises that the two kings, as well as the origins of Norfolk and Suffolk, can be explained by earlier "administrative subdivisions, or … smaller constituent groupings under East Anglian hegemony." See too Bassett, "In Search," pp. 23, 26. Norfolk is often secondary in discussions of the early East Anglian kingdom, but see Williamson, *Origins*, pp. 76–7. In 2016, sumptuous grave goods, including coins dated to ca. 650–75, were unearthed in Winfarthing, Norfolk; they belonged to a woman "who probably had aristocratic or royal connections" (Kennedy, "Detectorists").

120 Howe, *Writing*, p. 130.

121 Higham, *English Empire*, p. 189. Newton seems to interpret Bede's remark about ignobility to refer not to Rædwald himself but to his deeds, "because he had been badly advised by his wife and others": *Reckoning*, p. 16.

122 Pohl, "Ethnic Names," p. 9.

123 My argument here is inspired by Stodnick's analysis of the form and function of royal genealogies in "Old Names." On Bede's occasional statements in the *HE* that this or that person's "nobility of birth was matched by nobility in virtue," see Yorke, *Conversion*, pp. 246–7, discussing Bede's passages on St. Æthelthryth. Yorke claims that "Bede's personal respect for Æthelthryth may have been underpinned by the deference he would naturally have felt as a member of the Northumbrian nobility for a princess of the East Angles who had been a queen of Northumbria" (p. 247). Such "personal respect" clearly did not extend to Rædwald, despite the vital aid he had given to the Northumbrian Edwin.

124 Newton, *Origins*, pp. 60–1, building upon Dumville, "Kingship," p. 83. On the propagandistic function of early English, especially West Saxon, genealogies more generally, see Yorke, "Political and Ethnic Identity" (esp. p. 78), and sources cited above in n. 18.

125 Tugène, *L'idée*, p. 95 (translation mine); see too his general discussion on pp. 94–6, in which Tugène proposes the view that it was this attitude towards genealogies that induced Bede to exclude them from his accounts of Northumbrian kings. Wormald takes a different view of regnal lists in "Bede, Beowulf," p. 57.

126 Wallace-Hadrill, *Historical Commentary*, p. 111. Bede mentions but does not dwell on the death of the (perhaps) pagan Ecgric; his terseness in this regard keeps the reader's attention fixed on Sigeberht's piety. See PASE, s.vv. "Sigeberht 3," "Fursa 1," "Ecgric 1."

127 Ridyard, *Royal Saints*, p. 92. See too Hare, "Heroes"; Hill, "*Non nisi.*"

128 Thacker, "Bede's Ideal," p. 146; compare McClure, "Bede's Old Testament Kings," pp. 87–92.

129 Foot, "Bede's Kings," pp. 48–9.

130 Ridyard, *Royal Saints*, p. 5, and reference to Górski's work in her n. 5. For a comparable suggestion on the East Anglian *stirps*'s use of the Roman wolf symbol to compensate for their political weakness after Rædwald's time, see Young, *Edmund*, pp. 30, 31 (see above, Introduction, n. 109).

131 On pagan "sacral" and Christian "sacred" kingship, see Chaney, *Cult*, p. 48; Nelson, "Royal Saints"; Ridyard, *Royal Saints*, pp. 76–8; Rollason, *Northumbria*, pp. 198–200; Cubitt, "Sites"; Klaniczay, *Holy Rulers*, pp. 78–94; Phelpstead, "King," pp. 33–4 (also citing most of these studies). Hare, "Heroes," discusses Bede's varied portrayals of the Christian rulers Æthelberht of Kent, Edwin of Northumbria, and Oswald.

132 It should be conceded, however, that devotion to royal saints had popular as well as political origins; see e.g. Cubitt, "Sites."

133 *MS A*, ed. Bately, p. 28; *ASC*, p. 26, though I have substituted "East Angles" for "East Anglians."

134 Plunkett, *Suffolk*, p. 102; "647x648" according to PASE, s.v. "Felix 2."

135 Ridyard, *Royal Saints*, pp. 75–6.

136 Ridyard, *Royal Saints*, p. 75, identifies this quality along with the *pax* and *prosperitas* associated with kings' "attainment of national *felicitas*."

137 Merrills, *History*, p. 247. See too McClure, "Bede's Old Testament Kings," pp. 83–5, 94–5.

138 Breeze, "Bede's *Civitas Domnoc*," building upon R. Coates, "*Domnoc/Dommoc*" and confirming Rigold's hypothesis in "Supposed See" and "Further Evidence." Other contributions to the debate include Wallace-Hadrill, *Historical Commentary*, p. 78; Wormald and Charles-Edwards, Addenda, p. 224; Scarfe, *Suffolk*, p. 41; Haslam, "*Dommoc*"; Hoggett, *Archaeology*, pp. 36–9; J. Campbell, *Anglo-Saxon State*, pp. 108–10. I am grateful to Dr. Breeze for referring me to his own and Coates's articles.

139 Bede's "siluarum et maris uicinitate amoenum, constructum in castro quodam" follows the wording of his source, the *Vita sancti Fursei*, but with changed word order; see *Vita virtutesque Fursei*, ed. Krusch, p. 437, §7. On the question whether Cnobheresburg was indeed Burgh Castle in Norfolk (but part of Suffolk until 1974), see below, chap. 2 and n. 23.

140 *Gesta Pontificum Anglorum*, II.74, ed. and trans. Winterbottom, vol. 1, pp. 234–5.

141 Swift, *Waterland*, p. 8.

142 Merrills, *History*, p. 252.

143 Pestell, "Paganism," p. 66.

144 L.T. Martin, "Bede," p. 159, quoting Bede on Felix's mission to East Anglia and citing further examples in the *HE*.

145 Fowler, "Discussion,'" p. 403. See too Fowler's analysis of the converted farmers' point of view: "And, you know, it doesn't take a great deal of

energy to say a prayer: it's a good thing to do and it's not much effort. It seems to me that the Christian religion very quickly moved in and took over in the thought processes that go along with the physical activity of farming" (p. 403).

146 My argument here is informed by Frantzen, *Desire*, pp. 141–6 (and need not conflict with Dumitrescu's claim in "Bede's Liberation Philology" that the Cædmon story, despite its Latinity, exalts the English language).

147 See above, n. 108. On Luke's parable of the sower as Bede's inspiration, see L.T. Martin, "Bede and Preaching," p. 159.

148 In what Mynors calls the *c* (earlier) version of *HE*, and in copies descended from it, this prayer concludes the entirety of the work; in the *m* (later) type, the prayer appears at the end of the Preface ("Textual Introduction," pp. xl–xli; see too Waite, "Preface," p. 85).

149 In what follows, my thinking about Bede's subjunctive is influenced by Hines's discussion of the Old English *Seafarer*'s appeal to its readers to contemplate how they might discover and reach their true spiritual home: "The sentiment, and in particular the variability implied by those two subjunctives ["hwær wē hām āgen" and "hū wē þider cumen" in lines 117b and 118b], were indeed deeply embedded in the Anglo-Saxon experience": "No Place," p. 39.

150 Formerly the Leningrad Bede; here and in what follows I refer to the facsimile edition by Arngart.

151 *Old English Version*, ed. and trans. T. Miller, vol. 1, pp. 140–3.

152 Rowley, *Old English Version*, p. 56. Rowley, and Molyneaux in "Old English Bede," both explore the ideological shift between the *HE* and its later OE translation and question the latter's influence on King Alfred's reform program.

153 A very late, elegantly written manuscript of the *HE*, Glasgow, Hunterian Library, MS. Hunter 86 (ca. 1515) lacks marginalia altogether.

154 In London, British Library, MS. Royal 13.C.v (an eleventh-century manuscript of the *HE*), an annotator has added, on fol. 56r, a superscript *9* (for the Latin noun termination *-us*) to the end of each of the names *ræduuald, aeduin, osuuald*, and *osuiu*, but not to *aelle, celin, ceaulin*, or *æðilberht*. On similar corrections to London, British Library, MS Royal 13.A.xv, a tenth-century manuscript of Felix's *VSG*, see Voth, "Three," p. 128.

155 Carver, "Sutton Hoo," p. 499.

156 Wallace-Hadrill, *Historical Commentary*, p. 77.

157 On Bede's manipulation of the tropes of Rome as centre and Britain as periphery, see Howe, "Angle," esp. pp. 9–12; Howe, *Writing*, pp. 104–11; Lavezzo, *Angels*, pp. 7, 30 (also citing Howe); Scully, "Bede," pp. 37–42; O'Reilly, "Islands." Discenza ("Map") traces the flexibility of this dichotomy in the Alfredian era. My use of Thietmar of Merseburg's word

angulus to describe Britain is indebted to Howe's discussion in "Angle," esp. p. 12. Compare Michelet, *Creation*, pp. 142–60. Pohl comments on Widukind's reference in the *Rerum gestarum Saxonicarum* (ed. Hirsch and Lohmann) to Britain's location "in angulo … maris": "Ethnic Names," p. 17.

158 The quotation is from Bede's preface to *In cantica canticorum* as quoted in turn and translated by Merrills, *History*, p. 237. See too Merrills' astute insight on pp. 238–9 into Bede's belief that England lay "[s]ituated simultaneously at the end of Christian time and at the fringes of the Christian world" (and compare p. 273).

Chapter 2

1 Hooke, *Anglo-Saxon Landscape*, pp. 192–3, on land transactions. For discussion of the Bedan passage in question, see chap. 1 above, pp. 63–4.

2 Rackham, *History*, p. 155.

3 On *Domnoc* as modern Walton Castle, Suffolk, see above, chap. 1, n. 138.

4 Matthews, "Token," p. 39.

5 Klein, *Ruling Women*, p. 41; see discussion above, chap. 1, p. 49 and n. 68.

6 I have in mind Ambrogio Lorenzetti's painting *Effetti del buon governo in campagna* (Siena, Palazzo Pubblico, 1338–9).

7 Respectively, *HE* II.15, pp. 190–1; *HE* III.19, pp. 270–1; *MS A*, ed. Bately, p. 28; *ASC*, p. 26.

8 Though see Hart, "Kingdom," p. 53, on the use of earthworks by neighbouring kingdoms to hinder Mercian aggression.

9 *Additamentum*, ed. Krusch, p. 449, and translation in Fouracre and Gerberding, *Late Merovingian France*, p. 327. For discussion of the *Additamentum*, see Whitelock, "Pre-Viking Age Church," p. 6 (cited in Hoggett, *Archaeology*, p. 45), and Luckhardt, "Gender," pp. 46–50. I owe the reference to Fouracre and Gerberding's book to Luckhardt's article (p. 46, n. 55).

10 *LE*, ed. Blake, pp. 3–4; trans. Fairweather, pp. 4–6.

11 This is highly conjectural. Æthelthryth would have been in her teens when she married the Middle Anglian nobleman Tondberht "before 654" (Blanton, *Signs*, p. 6), her father King Anna having been killed by Penda either in that year or in 655, according to Kirby, *Earliest English Kings*, p. 51, on the basis of *HE* III.7. The Mercian king may have destroyed *Cratendune* at roughly this time. See PASE, s.vv. "Æthelthryth 2," "Tondberht 1," "Penda 1."

12 Penda had secured Æthelhere's aid in the Battle of the *Winwæd* in 654/5, in which both men died (*HE*, III.24). *LE* I.7 (trans. Fairweather, p. 22) makes explicit what is only implicit in Bede, that Æthelhere was Penda's client-king rather than an independent ruler. See Kirby, *Earliest English Kings*, p. 93; PASE s.v. "Æthelhere 1"; Prestwich, "King Æthelhere," p. 90

(citing Plummer's study of the *LE*), referenced by McClure and Collins in the "Explanatory Notes" to their edition of Bede's *Ecclesiastical History*, p. 396.

13 Scarfe, *Suffolk*, p. 42.

14 *HE* IV.20, p. 398 for the Latin text; for the translation, I turn to the word-for-word rendering in Harris, *Bede and Aethelthryth*, p. 158, but without Harris's use of small capitals to correspond to initial words in Bede's strophes.

15 E.g. *HE* III.24; III.30; IV.3; IV.13; V.13; V.19. Wulfhere reigned 659–75; see PASE, s.v. "Wulfhere 1."

16 *LE*, I.7, ed. Blake, p. 19; trans. Fairweather, p. 23.

17 Wallace-Hadrill, *Historical Commentary*, pp. xviii–xix, commenting on the accuracy of Charles Plummer's insight about the lack of cohesion among the early English *gentes* as represented by Bede.

18 See e.g. the "A" recension's notice for 654 that "Her Onna [i.e. King Anna] cyning wearþ ofslægen, 7 Botulf ongon mynster timbran æt Icanho": *MS A*, ed. Bately, p. 29. "Here [i.e. in this year] King Anna was killed; and Botwulf began to build a minster at Icanho": *ASC*, p. 28. On Botwulf and the identification of Icanho with Iken in Suffolk, see Swanton's note 7 on p. 28, citing F.S. Stevenson, "St. Botolph"; West, Scarfe, and Cramp, "Iken." See too Scarfe, *Suffolk*, 44–51; Hoggett, *Archaeology*, pp. 47–51; Pestell, *Landscapes*, pp. 25, 97; PASE, s.v. "Botwulf 1"; and Newton, "Forgotten History."

19 Where Botwulf's body is said to lie at Thorney Abbey (*on Þornige*) along with the remains of saints Athulf, Huna, Thancred, Torhtred, Hereferth, Cissa, Benedict, and Tova: see Liebermann, *Heiligen Englands*, p. 15. On the *Secgan*, see Rollason, "Lists," esp. p. 66 (noting that Botwulf's body was translated to Thorney only during King Edgar's reign), and Blanton, *Signs*, pp. 126–7 (citing Rollason's article).

20 On which, see Love, "Folcard"; Love, "Anglo-Saxon Saints"; Newton, "Forgotten History," p. 5. The year 654 is given by John of Worcester for Botwulf's foundation at Icanhoe and Penda's killing of Anna: *Chronicle*, ed. Darlington and McGurk, trans. Bray and McGurk, vol. 2, p. 105, and n. 7 referring to various recensions of the ASC.

21 Wallace-Hadrill, *Historical Commentary*, p. xxii.

22 For discussion in relation to Irish missionary activity, see Wormald, "Venerable Bede," p. 16, contrasting Bede's account of Fursey to Bede's source, the Merovingian *Vita virtutesque Fursei* (ed. Krusch; Fursey's visions, however, are edited separately in Ciccarese, "Le visioni," cited in Thacker, "Guthlac and His Life," p. 13, n. 67). According to Gunn, Bede presents Fursey's hermitage favourably because, though Irish in foundation, it was not in Northumbria and therefore could not compete

with Wearmouth-Jarrow for Northumbrian royal patronage (*Bede's* Historiae, pp. 76–8).

23 On Bede's borrowing from the *Vita sancti Fursei*, see above, chap. 1 and n. 139. For discussion of the problem of the site's identification, see Wallace-Hadrill, *Historical Commentary*, p. 113; J. Campbell, *Essays*, p. 101; Pestell, *Landscapes*, pp. 56–7; Pestell, "Kingdom," p. 197, n. 5; Hoggett, *Archaeology*, pp. 56–60; Williamson, *Sutton Hoo*, p. 19. For Wallace-Hadrill, "[a]t least it is certain that Fursa's site was a royal gift, and thereafter an object of royal bounty; and this interests Bede" (*Historical Commentary*, p. 113).

24 On monastic re-use of Roman sites, see Pestell, *Landscapes*, pp. 48, 56–62; Hoggett's full discussion in *Archaeology*, pp. 53–67; Young, *Edmund*, p. 32.

25 Because the account is not explicitly connected to Fursey's physical environment or indeed to any particular historical context, it is not surprising that it survives in excerpted form in manuscripts that do not contain the *HE*; see Colgrave and Mynors's note, p. 270, n. 3.

26 Dugdale, *Monasticon*, ed. Caley, Ellis, and Bandinel, vol. 1, p. 344.

27 Bede's focus on Æthelthryth's body-centred piety at Ely (e.g. her fasting and infrequent bathing) is noted by Blanton, *Signs*, p. 39. See too Matthews, "Token," pp. 33–58; Elliott, "Sex," chap. 4. For a seminal study of the relationship among bodily, cognitive, and spiritual states in early English writing generally, see Lockett, *Anglo-Saxon Psychologies*.

28 Blanton, *Signs*; Garrison, "Lives" (cited in Blanton, *Signs*, p. 31, n. 29); Black, "*Nutrix pia*"; Karkov, "Body"; Elliott, "Sex"; Pulsiano, "Blessed Bodies"; Pelteret, "Bede's Women"; G. Griffiths, "Reading"; Waterhouse, "Discourse"; Foot, *Veiled Women*, vol. 1, p. 22; Gulley, *Displacement*, pp. 11–12, 115–18; Lees and Overing, *Double Agents*, pp. 20–9 and 65–9; Hollis, *Anglo-Saxon Women*, pp. 12–13; Meyer, "Queens"; Szarmach, "Æðeldreda"; and Watt, "Earliest Women's Writing?" I thank my students Claire Hutchinson and Danielle Criddle for alerting me to Watt's article.

29 See e.g. Higham, *(Re-)reading*, p. 119; Blanton, *Signs*; Blanton, "Presenting"; Love, *Goscelin*; Rabin, "Holy Bodies," pp. 234–43, 259–65.

30 Blanton, *Signs*. See also Styler's recent doctoral thesis "Story."

31 Stodnick, "Emergent Englishness," p. 501.

32 Blanton, *Signs*, p. 63; Gretsch, *Ælfric*, p. 225; Garrison, "Lives," pp. 3, 7, 35, 42 and 46; Szarmach, "Æðeldreda," pp. 145, 149; Styler, "Story." Originating in the *HE*, the Ely-England connection is drawn too in e.g. the *Miracvla Sancte Ætheldrethe*'s claim that Ely was created by Æthelthryth, "this bright lamp of the English and brilliant gem of paradise" ("hec Anglorum lampas perspicua gemmaque paradisi clarissima"): Love, *Goscelin*, pp. 104–5.

33 On the date of ca. 672, see Blanton, *Signs*, p. 32; Hoggett, *Archaeology*, p. 33. The *LE* claims that Æthelthryth had retired to Ely after Tondberht's

death and was subsequently forced by her kinsfolk to leave in order to marry Ecgfrith: *LE*, I.8, ed. Blake, p. 20; trans. Fairweather, pp. 24–5.

34 See especially the studies cited above in notes 27 and 28, and Gunn, *Bede's* Historiae, p. 155–6, on Merovingian influences upon Bede's depiction of Æthelthryth's relationship with Ecgfrith.

35 Garrison, "Lives," p. 40.

36 See too Bede's *History of the Abbots*, ed. and trans. Grocock and Wood, pp. 22–3 and 36–7. On Ecgfrith's endowment, see Gunn, *Bede's* Historiae, pp. 45–50; Wickham-Crowley, "Fens," p. 80. Wood suggests that Wearmouth may have been founded on land expropriated from Benedict Biscop's family: "Foundation," pp. 87–9. Levison situated Pope Agatho's granting of privileges to Wearmouth within the context of enduring early English awareness of Rome's place in the English church (*England*, pp. 15–26).

37 As an aside, it should be noted that Bede transposes the order of events; Ecgfrith's endowment of Wearmouth followed his separation from Æthelthryth by two years.

38 Harris, *Bede and Aethelthryth*, p. 134. Compare p. 136.

39 See P.A. Thompson, "St. Æthelthryth," p. 484; Weston, "Saintly Lives," p. 403; Garrison, "Lives," pp. 9–13; Bullimore, "Unpicking," e.g. pp. 838 and 849.

40 Relevant is the concept of *freoðuwebbe*, "peace-weaver" (see e.g. *Beowulf*, line 1942a, in *Klaeber's Beowulf*, p. 66), but Cavell, in "Formulaic *Friþuwebban*," has shown that the word was not uniquely applied to women. I thank an anonymous reviewer for this reference. Bede may have been sceptical of the efficacy of "peace-weavers" anyway (Hollis, *Anglo-Saxon Women*, p. 230), though in Æthelthryth's case he may have discerned a queen's special ability to make or break international peace (Bullimore, "Unpicking," p. 849).

41 Sneesby, *Etheldreda*, p. 74. The possibility is strong. By depriving Ecgfrith of offspring, Æthelthryth "prevented him from fulfilling his proper duty of fathering princes to rule after him," as observed by Foot ("Bede's Kings," p. 38). As Matthews puts it, "an obdurately celibate queen would have been a political crisis" ("Token," p. 34, building upon insights by Ridyard). See too Bullimore's analysis of the alliance networks that Æthelthryth's separation from Ecgfrith will have disrupted ("Unpicking").

42 For a different view, however, see Oosthuizen, *Anglo-Saxon Fenland*, p. 74.

43 See Harris, *Bede and Aethelthryth*, p. 159. On Bede's general suppression of Æthelthryth's "political and social activities as an East Anglian princess," see Blanton, *Signs*, p. 27; for full discussion of the mentality behind that suppression, see Ridyard, *Royal Saints*, pp. 82–9.

44 Female sainthood is discussed in the context of familial and sexual obligations by Heffernan, *Sacred Biography*, pp. 188–9; and P. Brown, *Body*, pp. lvi–lvii, 343–5, 356, and 363. On women's agency in certain hagiographical contexts, see Pelteret, "Bede's Women," pp. 39–46; Pulsiano, "Blessed Bodies," p. 41; Meyer, "Queens," pp. 91 and 108–9; Higham, "Bede's Agenda," p. 490; Hollis, *Anglo-Saxon Women*, pp. 73 and 136 (but cf. pp. 12–13); Garrison, "Lives," pp. 24–8 and 41–6 and studies cited therein; Matthews, "Token," pp. 44–5 (on Bede's and Ælfric's portrayal of Æthelthryth). Szarmach, "Æðeldreda," pp. 146–9, is trenchant in his defence of the abbess's agency ("[t]he powerful Æðeldreda cannot be denied"; p. 147). Harris explains her monastic vows as "not a diminishment of her will, but an exercise of will to reform her appetites in the service of right order" (*Bede and Aethelthryth*, p. 137).

45 Weston, "Saintly Lives," p. 403. Compare the "ambiguously passive and active" sexuality attributed to the saint by the *LE* as discussed by Otter, "Temptation," p. 141.

46 See *Miracvla Sancte Ætheldrethe*, in Love, *Goscelin*, pp. 95–131, at pp. 104–11 and 122–31; *LE*, II.131–4 and III.92, ed. Blake, pp. 210–17 and 338–41; *LE*, trans. Fairweather, pp. 250–60 and 415–19. Commentary includes Blanton, *Signs*, pp. 161–71; Otter, "Temptation"; Ridyard, *Royal Saints*, pp. 192–3 and 208–10; P.A. Thompson, "St. Æthelthryth," p. 485; Thompson and Stevens, "Gregory of Ely's Verse Life," pp. 345–7; Rollason, *Saints*, p. 223; Garrison, "Lives," pp. 158–60; Lundgren, "Hereward," pp. 73–4 (citing Ridyard, "*Condigna*," pp. 184, 185); Black, "*Nutrix pia*," pp. 178–80 (on Ælfhelm's tenth-century accounts of Æthelthryth's posthumous violence later added to *LE* Book I). See also Styler's subtle analyses in "Story," p. 6, 16, 122–4, 139, 141, 149–62.

47 Bede's audience may have numbered not only male clerics such as "the Northumbrian religious hierarchy" (Styler, "Story," p. 55, paraphrasing Higham, *(Re-)reading*, p. 41) but also "high-status female readers or listeners" (Yorke, "Weight," p. 108). On Bede's expectation of a monastic but "no 'popular' audience for *HE*," see Wallace-Hadrill, *Historical Commentary*, p. 113; compare Gunn, *Bede's* Historiae, pp. 36–7, 186.

48 On this passage see Thacker, "Bede's Ideal," p. 146. Gunn questions Ceolwulf's Latin literacy (*Bede's* Historiae, pp. 31–3), but it surely matters that Bede's wording indicates expectation of the king's support of thoroughgoing Christianization, regardless of how much Latin Ceolwulf could actually read.

49 See above, chap. 1, p. 45.

50 Mayr-Harting, *Coming*, p. 67.

51 Concerning the debate over Bede's "reform agenda," Higham remarks on "the assumption that runs across Books IV and V of the *History* that

everything that was wrong in the present was the consequence of a long-running failure of royal leadership, even alongside churchmen who had retained their excellence throughout": "Bede's Agenda," p. 483. Whether or not early readers of *HE* IV.19 blamed Ecgfrith for Æthelthryth's departure from Northumbria, they would have been justified in crediting Edwin for the conversion process that had nurtured Æthelthryth's piety. Styler ("Story," p. 34) argues that Bede "used elements of Æthelthryth's story and character as examples to the Northumbrian church of how it could peacefully co-exist, under the umbrella of Christianity, with the other kingdoms of Britain."

52 The *LE* identifies Ealdwulf as Æthelthryth's brother (trans. Fairweather, pp. 14, 44, 68). For the view that she was his cousin, see J. Stevenson, "Brothers and Sisters," p. 20.

53 See *LE*, I.13–16, ed. Blake, pp. 29–35; trans. Fairweather, pp. 38–46. The text claims that Æthelthryth's move to Ely was spurred by Ecgfrith's persecution of her; that she had received Ely from her first husband Tondberht; that King Ealdwulf (identified, as mentioned above, as her brother) merely helped her in the building works she had commenced at Ely rather than arranging for her transfer there in the first place; and that Wilfrid, bishop of York, consecrated her abbess of Ely in situ. This last claim has no basis in Bede, as noted by Fairweather, *LE*, p. 45, citing *LE*, ed. Blake, p. 34, n. 2: "This may be a local tradition or more probably – and without justification – inferred from Bede[.]"

54 *Landscapes*, p. 129. Blanton, *Signs*, p. 49, and Ridyard, *Royal Saints*, pp. 178–9 also explore Ely's links to the East Anglian royal dynasty.

55 Unlike the *HE*, the Middle English *Vita* of Æthelthryth in London, British Library, MS. Egerton 1993 portrays Ecgfrith as passive and his queen as determined: "Þe king wel longe hit wiþsede and loþ him was þerto./ Ate laste he graunted hit, þo he ne miȝte non oþer do" (fol. 163r–v, quoted by Pulsiano, "Blessed Bodies," p. 36).

56 *DMLBS*, fasc. 5, p. 1254, s.v. *impetrare* 1: "to obtain by request, demand, or sim." I am grateful to an anonymous reader of an earlier version of this chapter for asking me to inspect Bede's verb forms closely.

57 *DMLBS*, fasc. 5, p. 1452, s.v. *intrare* 1.

58 Bede identifies Coldingham as lying in Ecgfrith's domains and the abbess Æbbe as Ecgfrith's aunt: *HE* IV.19, pp. 392–3. Blanton notes the atypicality of Æthelthryth's move: *Signs*, p. 39, n. 51. On lax standards at Coldingham, see *HE* IV.25, pp. 420–7, and commentary by Blanton, *Signs*, p. 39; Fell, "Saint Æðelþryð," p. 22; Plunkett, *Suffolk*, p. 122; Foot, *Veiled Women*, vol. 1, p. 22. Coughlan, "Notes," sees Æthelthryth's house as a foil to Æbbe's.

59 Rowley, *Old English Version*, p. 147. Compare DeGregorio, "Monasticism," cited by Harris, *Bede and Aethelthryth*, p. 126.

60 The *HE*'s preference for mere transition over strife is evident in Æthelthryth's unlikeness to Roman virgin martyrs, a difference that, as Hollis observes, "suggests that the conversion of England was not marked by domestic conflict between parents and the monastic aspirations of their daughters" and thus differs profoundly from the subject's treatment in Norman hagiography (*Anglo-Saxon Women*, p. 71).

61 A point forcefully made by Kirby, "Bede's Native Sources," pp. 361, 363, and 370–1.

62 *Bede and Aethelthryth*, p. 136.

63 Stodnick, "Emergent Englishness," pp. 500, 501. Similarly, Blanton observes that "the multiple enclosures of [Æthelthryth's] body are symbols for the institution's boundaries, both architectural and geographical": *Signs*, p. 136. Compare Otter, "Temptation," p. 147, citing Otter, *Inventiones*, pp. 31–3.

64 More detailed in this regard are the accounts in *LE*, I.8 and I.15 (ed. Blake, pp. 20, 33; trans. Fairweather, pp. 24, 43), which admit the hardships involved. On the Crowland fens as a landscape to be subdued, see *VSG*, ed. Colgrave, pp. 86–7, and discussion below in chap. 3.

65 On differences between men's and women's *Vitae*, see Pulsiano, "Blessed Bodies," pp. 11–42; Bynum, *Fragmentation*, pp. 27–51.

66 Although Colgrave and Mynors translate "in medio eorum" as "in the ranks of the other nuns," the masculine genitive plural *eorum* refers to Æthelthryth's already-mentioned "people" (genitive plural *suorum*), who included men; Bede normally stresses different roles for nuns and monks but here emphasizes community between them. Bede's "non alibi quam in medio eorum … sepulta" is more persuasively translated by J.E. King as "buried … in none other place than in the midst of them," Bede's "in medio suorum" being rendered by him as "in the midst of her company": see Bede, *Ecclesiastical History*, IV.19, trans. J.E. King, p. 107.

67 Matthews, "Token," p. 52, analyses the difference between Æthelthryth's "simultaneous expression of humility and authority" and Seaxburh's more forceful display of authority in Ælfric's *Life of St. Æthelthryth*.

68 *Chronicle of Hugh Candidus*, ed. Mellows, p. 5; *Peterborough Chronicle of Hugh Candidus*, trans. Mellows and Mellows, p. 2; Henry, Archdeacon of Huntingdon, *Historia Anglorum*, VI.6, ed. and trans. Greenway, pp. 348–9; *De Gestis Herwardi*, ed. and trans. Meneghetti, chap. 23, pp. 136, 138; *Deeds of Hereward*, trans. Swanton, pp. 72–3. Darby discusses other examples of twelfth- and thirteenth-century praise of Fenland monasteries (e.g. Crowland, Ramsey, Thorney) in *Medieval Fenland*, pp. 52–4.

69 Or, possibly, "a small city," "a small *civitas*," according to Luscombe, "City," p. 45, in reference to Cambridge.

70 On *Granta/Gronte*, "a Celtic name interpreted as 'muddy or fen river,'" see Oosthuizen, *Anglo-Saxon Fenland*, p. 40, and sources cited in her note.

71 Cam, *Liberties*, p. 4.

72 Christopher Taylor, *Cambridgeshire Landscape*, p. 259. Charles-Edwards, weighing Bede's story of Æthelthryth's sarcophagus as well as accounts (in the *Anonymous Life of St. Cuthbert* and in Bede's own prose *Life* of the saint) of the Northumbrians' taking of the Romano-British city of Carlisle, suggests that "[e]arlier Englishmen may sometimes have deliberately avoided Roman sites, regarding them as foreign to their way of life, although this was certainly not a consistent attitude": *Early Christian Ireland*, p. 324.

73 Cam, *Liberties*, p. ix, quoting Collingwood and Myres, *Roman Britain*, p. 393; see too Cam, "City," p. 2. Cam cites, with apparent approval, the arguments put forth by Gray (*Dual Origin*; "Ford"), whose findings are also used by Leader, *History*, p. 9. For a not altogether convincing challenge to Gray's thesis, see Lobel, *Cambridge*, p. 3, n. 20.

74 Crook, *English Medieval Shrines*, p. 31. Crook describes other surviving examples and also discusses, on pp. 31–2 and 60, Æthelthryth's shrine, though without saying whether he thinks it specifically pagan in origin. Higham refers to "[t]he Roman practice of coffin-use" in "From Sub-Roman Britain," p. 13.

75 Howe, "Angle," p. 11 and n. 18 (citing Hooke, *Anglo-Saxon Landscape*, pp. 190 and 249); Howe, *Writing*, pp. 83–5; Hunter, "Germanic and Roman Antiquity," pp. 35–6 (e.g. "Roman remains were used as a quarry for current needs," regarding Bede on Æthelthryth's coffin); Brady, "Echoes," p. 671 and n. 11, citing Howe and Hunter.

76 Lees and Overing, *Double Agents*, p. 20, in an analysis of Bede's treatment of Cædmon's "Hymn."

77 On the Christian equation of *Romanitas* with cultural *auctoritas*, see de Lachenal, *Spolia*, pp. 133–4, and her discussion of the ninth-century Milanese bishop Angilbert's reuse of an ancient sarcophagus to unite the bones of saints Gervasius, Protasius, and Ambrose.

78 Hines, "Becoming," p. 51, and source cited therein.

79 In similar fashion, early Christians reused Roman building materials to effect both cultural continuity with the pagan past and a "quasi-exorcistic" ("quasi esorcistico") conquest of that past: Lugli, *Naturalia*, pp. 14–15.

80 On which, see Rowley, *Old English Version*, pp. 140–3; and nn. 22–3 above. Also pertinent is Pestell's discussion of "the influence of *romanitas*" in *Landscapes*, pp. 56–8, 62.

81 Compare Guthlac's appropriation of a prehistoric *tumulus* or barrow in *VSG*, pp. 92–5 (discussed below, chap. 3); see J. Blair, *Church*, p. 184; Hines, *Voices*, pp. 62–3. For pertinent reflections on the ways in which the reuse of Roman stonework "allows … for the creation of a monumental palimpsest that maps the transitions and negotiations between cultures," see Karkov, "Postcolonial," p. 155.

82 *DMLBS*, fasc. 5, p. 1630, s.v. *locellus* 2*a* (derived from the primary meaning of "small place, space"; *DMLBS*, s.v. *locellus* 1).

83 My analysis here is influenced by Auerbach, *Scenes*, pp. 70–1.

84 Thacker, "*Loca*," pp. 18–19. On the efficacy of Æthelthryth's clothes and even of her original wooden coffin, see Rollason, *Saints*, p. 35.

85 Crook, *English Medieval Shrines*, p. 61, for the use of this phrase in discussing Æthelthryth's translation as recounted by Bede.

86 On Bede's use of the authority of the physician Cynefrith, see Blanton, *Signs*, pp. 42–3; Matthews, "Token," pp. 36–8.

87 For discussion of the first two points, see Blanton, *Signs*, pp. 13, 41–56; on all three points, see Stodnick, "Emergent Englishness," pp. 501–2.

88 Stodnick, "Emergent Englishness," pp. 502–3. In Styler's commensurate analysis, Cynefrith's expertise serves as a foundation on which Bede could build the national reputation of a regional saint: "Story," pp. 56–60.

89 MacCarron, "Adornment," provides an especially full analysis. See too Matthews, "Token," pp. 49–52, on the equivalent passage in Ælfric's *Life* of the saint.

90 H. Williams, "Mortuary Practices," p. 242.

91 H. Williams, "Mortuary Practices," p. 249.

92 H. Williams, "Engendered Bodies," pp. 33–4.

93 H. Williams, "Engendered Bodies," p. 33.

94 Æthelthryth's biological sister Seaxburh would have presided over the ceremony. The role of siblings in saints' cults is explored by Schulenburg, *Forgetful*, pp. 270–305, with discussion of Æthelthryth and Seaxburh on pp. 302–3. See too Blanton, "Kentish Queen," esp. p. 199 (Bede's depiction of Seaxburh's role in Æthelthryth's translation). On the strong East Anglian familial ties at Ely, see Schulenburg, *Forgetful*, p. 278; Blanton, "Kentish Queen"; Rollason, *Saints*, p. 125; Ridyard, *Royal Saints*, pp. 176–80 (cited too by Rollason); Gretsch, *Ælfric*, p. 205; J. Stevenson, "Brothers and Sisters," p. 20.

95 Ely and its environs seem to have been a third territorial division within the East Anglian kingdom alongside Suffolk and Norfolk; see Oosthuizen, *Anglo-Saxon Fenland*, pp. 69–89. The general district of the Isle of Ely may have been originally under the control of the South Gyrwe and acquired by the East Angles only during and after the time

of Æthelthryth's foundation of a religious house there; see Yorke, *Kings*, pp. 69–70, thus interpreting *HE* IV.19.

96 de Certeau, *Practice*, p. 117. Donnan and Wilson make what is, for me, an even more cogent distinction between space as "conceptualisation of the imagined physical relationships which give meaning to society" and place as "the distinct space where people live ... encompass[ing] both the idea and the actuality of where things are" (*Borders*, p. 9, citing work in cultural anthropology). See too Discenza, *Inhabited Spaces*.

97 J. Campbell, "First Christian Kings," p. 61. On "hides" as "units of service, not area," see John, *Reassessing*, p. 15; compare Keynes, "England," pp. 21–5; Davies and Vierck, "Contexts," p. 229. On Bede's use of the hide (*familia*) in observations about English geography in the *HE*, see Merrills, *History*, pp. 246–7, discussing previous scholarship and cautioning that "no two regions are described in precisely the same way by the historian."

98 Howe, discussing early English charters in *Writing*, p. 39 (reprinting Howe, "Landscape," p. 102), quoted by S.T. Smith, *Land*, p. 157.

99 On the resources of wetlands, see Hooke, *Landscape*, pp. 170–95; Oosthuizen, *Anglo-Saxon Fenland*; J. Blair, *Church*, pp. 193–4.

100 *De Gestis Herwardi*, ed. and trans. Meneghetti, ch. 23, p. 136; *Deeds of Hereward*, trans. Swanton, pp. 72–3. The case for Richard of Ely's authorship of the *Gesta* is cogently put forward by van Houts, "Hereward and Flanders," pp. 202–3.

101 On this passage, see Howe, *Writing*, p. 141.

102 Williamson, *Origins*, p. 146. See too Muir, "Landscapes," pp. 179, 186. For a recent, full discussion of early English literary treatments of wasteland, see Discenza, *Inhabited Spaces*, pp. 140–78, building upon work by Rackham and Hooke inter alios.

103 On the ideal – nurtured by saints Jerome, Marcella, Paula, and Melania – of "virginal fertility, through spiritual guidance and scholarship," see P. Brown, *Body*, p. 369. Black, in exploring Æthelthryth's evolving role from the eighth to the tenth century, detects a "shift from the narrow emphasis on corporeal virginity to the more inclusive notion of chastity/steadfastness and resultant fruitfulness": "*Nutrix pia*," p. 169. For Black, this shift is gradual and is anticipated by Bede himself, both in the *HE* and in the earlier *Chronica maiora* included in *De temporum ratione* ("*Nutrix pia*," pp. 172–5, building upon Blanton's insights in her *Signs*, pp. 245 and 246).

104 *LE* I.3 (ed. Blake, p. 13; trans. Fairweather, p. 15) identifies the saint's birthplace as Exning, in the far west of Suffolk and only about a dozen miles from Ely. For further discussion, see Oosthuizen, *Anglo-Saxon Fenland*, p. 71.

105 Oosthuizen writes that Bede "explain[ed] that [Ely] had formed the endowment with which Æthelthryth, the daughter of King Anna of East Anglia, had founded her monastic house in about 673" (*Anglo-Saxon Fenland*, p. 69). This is a plausible inference from the *HE*, though Bede does not actually refer to Ely as an endowment by a donor to a recipient.

106 Wood, "Monasteries," p. 13, commending Patrick Wormald's choice of title in "Bede and the Conversion." Wood's article is cited in his, "Foundation," p. 96, n. 23.

107 Garrison, "Lives," p. 40.

108 See above, p. 80 and n. 54. The first chapter of Sneesby's *Etheldreda*, "The Outpost," is aptly titled. In the late tenth century the monastery would be absorbed into the Mercian diocese of Dorchester (Pestell, *Landscapes*, pp. 129 and 103); later still it would become part of the diocese of Lincoln (*LE*, II.65, trans. Fairweather, p. 164).

109 de Vegvar, "Saints," p. 75.

110 Colgrave, "Introduction," p. 2. For discussion of "frontiers" and "borderlands," see above, p. 10 and n. 32; and below, pp. 147, 151–2, and 267, n. 18. On the Fenland's "liminality," see Pestell, *Landscapes*, pp. 52–6; O'Brien O'Keeffe, "Guthlac's Crossings," pp. 1 and 12. On places "hidden, inaccessible, and liminal – enclosed within surrounding curtains of hills, or by marsh, water, or sea," see Semple, "Sacred Spaces," pp. 756–7.

111 Yorke, *Nunneries*, p. 9.

112 See PASE, s.vv. "Seaxburg 1," "Eormenhild 1," "Wærburg 4." For evidence of these last two abbesses we must turn yet again to the *LE*, specifically I.36–7, pp. 51–2, cited and discussed by Keynes, "Ely Abbey," p. 13 and n. 56, drawing attention to differences between the *Liber*'s account and that provided by Goscelin's *Vita sancte Werburge*.

113 Keynes, "Ely Abbey," p. 13. On Ely as a probable *Eigenkloster*, see too Gretsch, *Ælfric*, p. 205 (remarking on the hereditary nature of the abbacy); Ridyard, *Royal Saints*, p. 178; Blanton, "Presenting"; Klaniczay, *Holy Rulers*, p. 88.

114 *Eddius' Life of Wilfrid*, ed. Colgrave, pp. 40–1, 44–7; *Life of Wilfrid*, trans. Webb and Farmer, pp. 125–6, 128. See discussion in Blanton, *Signs*, pp. 32–3; Black, "*Nutrix pia*," pp. 170–1; and esp. Bullimore, "Unpicking." As Gunn observes, though, Bede does not omit all evidence of Æthelthryth's royal authority (*Bede's* Historiae, p. 154).

115 The phrasing is that of Rouche, "Early Middle Ages," p. 433. Szerwiniack argues that by idealizing the monastic life, especially in seventh-century England, Bede was criticizing corruption and urging a return to Britain's purported original state of Eden-like moral purity: "L'Histoire ecclésiastique," esp. pp. 169–70 (which includes an analysis of the *HE*'s praises of Æthelthryth).

116 Wallace-Hadrill, *Historical Commentary*, p. xxiii.
117 Yorke, "Political and Ethnic Identity," pp. 73–4.
118 For Harris, "Bede's lexical doublets signal that the poem does double duty, in praise of virginity generally and in praise of Aethelthryth specifically": *Bede and Aethelthryth*, p. 129.
119 Perhaps ca. 709, the year Wilfrid left England for good (Thornbury, *Becoming*, pp. 187–8). On the debts to Venantius Fortunatus evident in Bede's hymn, see Gretsch, *Ælfric*, p. 213, n. 204 (with regard to the *De virginitate*); Gunn, *Bede's* Historiae, pp. 152–3 (*De virginitate* and *Life of St. Radegund*). The influence of Sedulius and Aldhelm is traced in Thornbury, *Becoming*, pp. 187–9.
120 Harris, *Bede and Aethelthryth*, pp. 124–5. See too Thornbury, *Becoming*, p. 188.
121 *HE* IV.20, p. 398; Harris, *Bede and Aethelthryth*, p. 158 (slightly modified). As indicated above in n. 14, quotation from the hymn will be based on Colgrave and Mynors's Latin text and on Harris's translation.
122 On which see Curtius, *European Literature*, pp. 162–5.
123 Szarmach, "Æðeldreda," p. 134.
124 Harris, *Bede and Aethelthryth*, p. 98.
125 Szarmach, "Æðeldreda," p. 132, referring to and agreeing with Whatley's inclusion of the OE translation of Bede's *HE* among "major Old English prose works that are hagiographic in content but collective in form" (Whatley, "Introduction," p. 3).
126 I thank an anonymous reader for pointing out that Bede is not so much comparing Æthelthryth and Aeneas literally as preferring her sacred achievements to his secular triumphs. I also have in mind Szarmach's analysis of the ways in which Bede uses Æthelthryth to exalt virginal over Vergilian heroism ("Æðeldreda," p. 134).
127 Wetherbee, "Some Implications," p. 28.
128 On this aspect of the hymn, as well as on Bede's departure from Roman hagiographical convention, see e.g. Fell, "Saint Æðelþryð," pp. 21–2; P.A. Thompson, "St. Æthelthryth," p. 477; Yorke, *Nunneries*, pp. 34–5 (citing Fell's article); Blanton, *Signs*, p. 22; Hollis, *Anglo-Saxon Women*, pp. 71–2.
129 Fell, "Saint Æðelþryð," p. 27. In context Fell's tone is actually rather snarky but is justified by her analysis of the "power politics that family played," a fact of Æthelthryth's life that Bede largely ignores.
130 J. Campbell, "Secular and Political Contexts," p. 31. See too S.T. Smith, *Land*, passim, but esp. pp. 9–13 and 28–30; Howe, *Writing*, pp. 43–6.
131 A.D. Smith, *Ethnic Origins*, p. 24, citing (on *mythomoteurs*) earlier studies by John Armstrong (who in turn derived the word from the Catalan medievalist Ramon d'Abadal i de Vinyals) and Henry Tudor. Smith clearly understands the word "essence" as a social construction rather than a real thing (hence his scare quotes), as does Frazer, "Introduction," p. 3. Similar to the

idea of the *mythomoteur* is Frazer's recognition that "stories of social life, to some extent, steer action" (p. 4). Compare Pohl, "Ethnic Names," p. 9.

132 Yorke, "Political and Ethnic Identity," p. 74.

133 Pelteret, "Bede's Women," p. 38. Watt, "Earliest Women's Writing?," pp. 541–2 (building upon Love, *Goscelin*, p. xiv, and Blanton, *Devotion*, p. 62), persuasively argues that Bede's narrative strategy also distracts us from the role played by Seaxburh and other women at Ely in promoting Æthelthryth's cult.

134 Blanton, "Kentish Queen," attending especially to Seaxburh's representation in Goscelin's *Lectiones in festiuitate Sanctae Sexburge*.

135 PASE, s.v. "Eormenhild 1." See discussion in Fell, "Saint Æðelþryð," pp. 33–4 (doubting the historicity of Eormenhild and her daughter Wærburh as abbesses of Ely). According to Blanton, Goscelin of Saint-Bertin used his lections on Seaxburh and Eormenhild and his *Vitae* of Wærburh and Wihtburh (the latter a supposed fifth daughter of King Anna) to represent "the community at Ely … [as] the locus of Christian England, the place from whence royal daughters go out to evangelize" ("Kentish Queen," p. 212). Because intermarriage multiplies identities, Goffart regards Æthelthryth as one of two "Northumbrian saints [whose bodies were elevated] outside Northumbria," the second being Oswald (*Narrators*, pp. 259–60).

136 Yorke, *Nunneries*, pp. 24–7, 35–6, 51; Hollis, *Anglo-Saxon Women*, p. 93 and n. 96; Thacker, "*Loca*," pp. 39, 42; Crook, "Enshrinement," pp. 206–8; Rosser, "Æthelthryth"; Styler, "Story," pp. 47–51.

137 Lees and Overing, "Anglo-Saxon Horizons," p. 21 (on Thacker, "*Loca*").

138 Fell, "Saint Æðelþryð," p. 34. Blanton, *Signs*, p. 39, n. 49, cites Fell's hypothesis with apparent approval. There are more cautious formulations in E. Miller, *Abbey*, pp. 1–15; Ridyard, *Royal Saints*, pp. 184–5; Gretsch, *Ælfric*, pp. 162, 167–9, 197–204; and Oosthuizen, *Anglo-Saxon Fenland*, pp. 76–7, 128. (The continuity of Ely's and Æthelthryth's fame is a different matter; see Keynes, "Ely Abbey," p. 15.) The twelfth-century *Libellus Æthelwoldi* says nothing about conditions in the early to middle eighth century: see *LE*, ed. Blake, Appendix A, p. 396, sec. 19; Fairweather, trans., *LE*, Appendix A, p. 487, sec. 1. I thank Catherine Clarke for recommending the *Libellus* to me and for alerting me to Simon Keynes and Alan Kennedy's forthcoming edition and English translation.

139 Yorke, *Nunneries*, pp. 7–8; compare Schulenburg, *Forgetful*, p. 80.

140 A wide evangelization program may have underlain the appointment of Æthelthryth at Ely; the years 672 and 673 saw both this event and the splitting of the East Anglian diocese. On the latter: R.R. Clarke, *East Anglia*, p. 148; F. Stenton, *Anglo-Saxon England*, p. 134; Whitelock, "Pre-Viking Age Church," p. 8.

141 These "virgins" included men as well as women; see above, n. 66. On Bede's appropriation of the maternal role to serve clerical ideological purposes, see Lees and Overing, *Double Agents*, pp. 22–9 (discussing Bede's treatment of Hild).

142 As Howe reminds us in *Writing*, pp. 129–30.

143 For the Latin text, see Bede's *Super parabola Salomonis*, pp. 175–6. Translation mine. See also chap. 1 above, p. 47.

Chapter 3

1 Ælfwald's dates of reign are so given in Newton, *Reckoning*, p. 44; see too PASE, s.vv. "Ælfwald 6," "Felix 3," "Guthlac 2" (whose lifespan is given as "c. 674–716"). In the present chapter I occasionally refer to other texts in the Guthlac corpus, such as the Old English poem *Guthlac A* and the Old English prose *Life of Guthlac*, but my focus is largely on the *VSG* because of the contextualization made possible by its naming of historical personages.

2 Colgrave, "Introduction," p. 19. Schütt followed C.W. Jones in suggesting the 720s or 730s ("Vom heiligen Antonius," p. 88 and n. 56, citing Jones, *Saints' Lives*, p. 219, n. 12); see too Leeser, "On the Edge," p. 154. On background and sources, see Colgrave's "Introduction," pp. 1–25; Kurtz, "From St. Antony"; the studies by Jones and by Schütt (pp. 88–91); Lapidge, *Anglo-Latin Literature*, pp. 1–91; Liebermann, "Über ostenglische Geschichtsquellen," pp. 245–6; Berschin, *Biographie*, part 2, §9.10, pp. 301–5 (cited in Lapidge, *Anglo-Latin Literature*, p. 10, n. 45); Love, "Sources"; Downey, "Intertextuality," pp. 25–66; Thacker, "Guthlac." Invaluable too is Roberts, "Inventory." T. Hall provides bibliography in "Handlist," pp. 5–6.

3 Kirby, "Bede's Native Sources," p. 370. For roughly similar reactions, see Roberts, *Guthlac*, p. 5 ("Despite the dedication of the life to an East Anglian king, its centre of interest is Mercia"); Roberts, "Seals," pp. 113–14; Thacker, "Bede's Idea," p. 17; Cheong, "Felix's Life"; Hartmann, "Monument Reuse," p. 259, n. 59.

4 Colgrave, "Introduction," p. 16, citing (n. 1) *HE* V.23; compare Colgrave, "Earliest," p. 55; Newton, *Origins*, pp. 80–1 (agreeing with Colgrave); Leeser, "On the Edge," pp. 153–4 (with caveats on pp. 154–5); Bacola, "*Vacuas*," p. 77. See too PASE, s.v. "Æthelbald 4." "There can be little doubt that both kings and kingdoms were manoeuvring around the cult, and Felix probably wished to ensure the satisfaction and benevolence of both": Cavill, "Naming," p. 38 (though Cavill adds that Felix sought "to promote the cult of Guthlac ... as independent" of either king's authority; "it was worthy of royal respect and enrichment, but [was] not to be

subject to undue royal control," p. 44). On Mercian hegemony: Kirby, *Making*, p. 63; Hart, "Kingdom," p. 43; Keynes, "England" (refining Sir Frank Stenton's famous "Mercian supremacy" thesis).

5 On Ecgburh, see *VSG* §48, pp. 146–9; Colgrave, "Notes," p. 191; Roberts, "Seals," pp. 113–14; PASE, s.v. "Ecgburg 1"; Bacola, "*Vacuas*," p. 77; Leeser, "On the Edge," p. 155. See too *LE*, I.7, ed. Blake, p. 19 ("Ædburga"); trans. Fairweather, p. 23 ("Eadburh"). On the genealogy of the East Anglian kings, see the studies cited above, pp. 232–3, n. 122.

6 Roberts, "Seals," pp. 113–14; Kilpatrick, "Place-Names," p. 44. Repton's royal Mercian associations were confirmed with the burial of King Æthelbald (after the time of the *VSG*'s composition), though it may have had them earlier: see J. Blair, *Church*, pp. 128, 229, 293–4; Biddle and Kjølbye-Biddle, "Repton"; Rollason, *Saints*, pp. 117–18; Yorke, "Burial," pp. 251–3; Kilpatrick, "Place-Names," 14–15.

7 Meaney, "History …?," p. 75. Roberts goes further: "Ecgburh … may have been involved in the commissioning of the life" (*Guthlac*, p. 5); compare Kilpatrick, "Place-Names," pp. 16–18, 46–7. Roberts elsewhere discusses Ecgburh's career at Repton, a Mercian house, and suggests that "despite the dedication of the *vita* to an East Anglian king, the impetus for the writing of the life of Guthlac probably came from Repton" ("Hagiography," p. 70). See too Roberts and Thacker, "Introduction," p. xxiv. On the possibility that Felix actually wrote the *Vita* at Repton, see Wragg, "Early Texts," p. 255, citing (n. 20) Cohen, *Machines*, p. 118, and Roberts, *Guthlac*, p. 6.

8 As often mentioned in scholarship on their kingdom and on the *VSG*, e.g. Hart, "Kingdom," p. 47; N. Brooks, "Formation," pp. 160–1; Keynes, "England," p. 27; Yorke, "Origins," pp. 13–22; Thacker, "Kings," p. 14; Siewers, "Landscapes," p. 8; Cohen, *Machines*, p. 121; Noetzel, "Monster," pp. 129–30, building upon Siewers and Cohen; Brady, "Colonial Desire" (responding to Siewers and Cohen); Brady, *Writing*, pp. 67–70; Wragg, "Vernacular Literature," pp. 46–9. I am grateful to Ken Streutker for bringing my attention to Noetzel's article.

9 Thacker, "Social," p. 325, citing (for the claim about Mercia) D.M. Stenton, *Preparatory*, pp. 48–58. In a similar vein, Colgrave plausibly argued that "Ælfwald was a subject king" under Æthelbald and adduced as evidence Felix's higher regard for the latter than for the former ("Earliest," p. 52); compare Colgrave, "Notes," p. 176, citing Whitelock, *English Historical Documents*, p. 453. See too Leeser, "On the Edge," p. 154 (cautioning, however, that Ælfwald needn't have been a "subject king" if the *VSG* was written as early as the 720s). Keynes acknowledges the plausibility of Colgrave's supposition and of Kirby's view that "this alliance with the East Angles was in fact 'the cornerstone of Æthelbald's ascendancy'": "Kingdom," p. 8, quoting Kirby, *Earliest English Kings*, pp. 131–2.

10 Thus Wragg argues that "Felix's Latin *vita*, though composed for an East Anglian king, reflects Mercian perspectives during its developing hegemony" ("Vernacular Literature," p. 46); compare Wragg, "Early Texts," pp. 256–7, and "*Guthlac A*," pp. 216–17, 224–5, 228. Yet Leeser argues powerfully for shared East Anglian and Mercian interests in promoting Guthlac's cult: "On the Edge," esp. pp. 151–6. On Guthlac's cult as a means to "stimulate [Mercian] contacts with East Anglia," see Thacker, "Kings," p. 17.

11 Pestell prefers "spheres of interest" to "territories": *Landscapes*, p. 103, n. 9. Wragg situates Ecgburh's Repton within the Mercian dynasty's own "sphere of influence" ("Vernacular Literature," pp. 51, 54–5), as does Kilpatrick in her full discussion in "Place-Names," pp. 11–18.

12 Bede distinguishes between the East and Middle Angles in *HE* I.15. *Tribal Hidage* individuates further but within Middle rather than East Anglia, specifying *Suþ gyrpa, Norþ gyrpa, Spalda, Wigesta*, etc.: see Dumville, "Tribal Hidage," pp. 228–9, Oosthuizen, *Anglo-Saxon Fenland*, pp. 53–68; Leeser, "On the Edge," pp. 138–41. For further discussion of the Middle Angles, see F. Stenton, *Anglo-Saxon England*, pp. 42–3; Dumville, "Essex," pp. 130–4; Bassett, "In Search," p. 26; Courtney, "Early Saxon Fenland"; Pestell, *Landscapes*, pp. 128–9; Kilpatrick, "Places," pp. 100–4; and sources cited below in n. 15. Hines, "Origins," p. 17, remarks that "[b]y the mid-seventh century … the historical records imply that at best East Anglia could continue to exercise some power or influence within the Middle Anglian zone [between it and Mercia]."

13 H.C. Darby, "Fenland Frontier," p. 190; O'Brien O'Keeffe, "Guthlac's Crossings," p. 7. Oosthuizen, *Anglo-Saxon Fenland* (pp. 23–8, 35, 50–68, 96, 135 and passim), argues for continuous and ample settlement in the Fenland between the Roman and early English periods (though for a more cautious view, see Kilpatrick, "Places," pp. 110–11). Whether conditions remained peaceful is another matter.

14 Treharne, "Borders," p. 14, citing Yorke, "Origins," pp. 19–20 (who pinpoints known sites of Mercian power – Repton, Tamworth, Lichfield – but from the *Tribal Hidage* infers Mercia's overlap with adjacent tribal areas). See too Sims-Williams, *Religion*, pp. 16–17; N. Brooks, "Formation," p. 162; Charles-Edwards, "Wales," p. 91; D. Hill, "Mercians." Yorke and Charles-Edwards both cite Brooks's study.

15 Yorke, "Political and Ethnic Identity," p. 74 and n. 33. For the view that the Middle Angles never were an autonomous kingdom, see Davies and Vierck, "Contexts," p. 237; for more guarded scepticism, see P.H. Blair, *Roman Britain*, pp. 178, 183. Their existence as a people is attested by archaeological finds dating back to the sixth century: Hines, "Origins," p. 38. Bede, in *HE* III.21, recounts that Penda created Middle Anglia for

his son Peada: see discussion in Roberts, "Hagiography," p. 73 (citing F. Stenton, *Anglo-Saxon England*, p. 120); Dumville, "Origins," pp. 94–5, 97–8; Kilpatrick, "Place-Names," p. 9 (citing, in her n. 36, Wallace-Hadrill, *Historical Commentary*, pp. 116–18).

16 Pestell, *Landscapes*, p. 129, notes that by 970 Ely had been absorbed into the Mercian diocese of Dorchester. See also the rich discussion of Ely and the Isle in Oosthuizen, *Anglo-Saxon Fenland*, pp. 69–89.

17 I borrow again S. Reynolds's term (*Kingdoms*, p. 254), as in the Introduction, p. 8, and p. 221, n. 22.

18 Relevant studies of in-between "borderland" spaces include Treharne, "Borders," pp. 9, 17, 19–20; Rumford, "Introduction," pp. 161–2; D. Newman, "Borders," pp. 173, 179–81; Donnan and Wilson, *Borders*, pp. 2, 15–16, 45–53; Wickham-Crowley, "Fens," esp. pp. 75–6. See too Capper, "St. Guthlac," p. 182, on the *VSG's* conceptualization of "Guthlac's cult as having a mediating role in relations among Middle Anglian groups," wedged between Æthelbald's Mercia and Ælfwald's East Anglia.

19 Pestell, *Landscapes*, p. 110, n. 39.

20 Higham, "Guthlac's *Vita*," p. 86; "Felix reflects a sense of competition between Mercian and East Anglian establishments in his treatment of Bishop Headda and abbess Ecgburh" (p. 87). Compare Noetzel, "Monster," p. 117, citing Colgrave's "Introduction," p. 16.

21 Like Kirby (above, n. 3), Cheong finds it "intriguing … that Guthlac, a Mercian saint, was … chronicled after his death by an East Anglian scribe for an East Anglian king. This raises questions of political machinations at work in the attempt by one Anglo-Saxon kingdom to claim a popular saint from another": "Felix's Life." See also Grossi, "Barrow Exegesis" and "Felix"; Hartmann, "Monument Reuse," p. 259, n. 59 (citing Higham).

22 "Guthlac's *Vita*," p. 86. Leeser disagrees with the general drift of Higham's argument but does treat the *VSG* as an expression of the East Anglian royal house's ongoing desire to shape ecclesiastical life in its larger sphere of influence ("On the Edge," pp. 152, 154–5).

23 Cubitt, "Memory," p. 56; cited by Higham (who disagrees), "Guthlac's *Vita*," p. 86.

24 Cubitt, "Memory," pp. 56 and 57. Colgrave writes that "Felix was either an East Angle or at least living in East Anglia when this was written" ("Introduction," p. 16). Noetzel both claims that "Felix does mention Guthlac's Mercian origins, but he spends much more time and places greater importance on the saint's settlement in the local Fens, thereby writing him into the East Anglian cultural narrative," and believes that "Guthlac represents a (specifically Mercian) Anglo-Saxon notion of national unity and identity": "Monster," pp. 117, 129.

25 The *speculum principis* is usually reckoned a somewhat later medieval genre, but G.H. Brown sees the "mirror for princes" function adumbrated in Bede's dedication to Ceolwulf in the *HE* ("Royal," p. 20). Mattéoni, "Mirrors," detects *Fürstenspiegel* qualities in Augustine's *Civitas Dei*, V.24, but sees the distinct genre itself emerging only in Jonas of Orléans's *De institutione regia* and Hincmar of Reims's *De regis persona et regio ministerio.*

26 On Ælfwald as "a subject king" under Mercian sovereignty, see above, n. 9. See too Foot, "Bede's Kings," p. 33, citing *HE* V.23 in her n. 37; and Dumville, "Origins," pp. 90–1 on *subreguli*. Bacola argues that, on a general level, "Felix's narrative defines the process by which his audience may likewise reform their own lives" and notes that "Felix wrote his *Vita* for Ælfwald" ("*Vacuas*," p. 76).

27 On Bourdieu's phrase "cultural capital," see above, Introduction, n. 70. As Higham observes, "[i]ncreased East Anglian influence over the cult might offer enhanced status for East Anglian kings, much as the Mercian embrace of St. Oswald had brought Æthelred success" ("Guthlac's *Vita*," p. 88).

28 *MS A*, ed. Bately, p. 33; *ASC*, p. 42. The difference is also noted by Downey, "Intertextuality," p. 165, who goes on to discuss the divergent kinds of interest in Guthlac taken by chroniclers and more self-consciously literary writers.

29 Schütt explores Felix's thinking on predestination and grace with regard to Guthlac's conversion ("Vom heiligen Antonius," pp. 89–90).

30 Felix does not fault his warrior past but rather puts it to good hagiographical use; see Bolton, "Background," pp. 597–600; Iamartino, "San Guthlac," pp. 785–96; Damon, *Soldier Saints*, p. 74 and passim; Appleton, "Psalter," pp. 63, 82–3; Bacola, "*Vacuas*," 74–5. (Iamartino's chapter is cited by Thacker, "Guthlac," p. 12, n. 62.) For a different view, see A. Hall, "Constructing." Guthlac's activities at Crowland are described in military metaphors (§27, pp. 90–1); on the use of such language in *VSG* and in the OE *Guthlac A*, see Olsen, *Guthlac*, esp. pp. 25–67; Lundgren, "Hereward," pp. 31–4, 73–4. On "the Christian Latin tradition of using military language in religious contexts," see Neville, *Representations*, p. 124, and source cited in her n. 155.

31 Keynes, "Appendix II," p. 556.

32 Nevertheless, Bacola is right to observe that "[t]hese few references to East Anglia suggest that Ælfwald was the impetus for a *Vita* in which he found material favourable to him" ("*Vacuas*," p. 77). It should be noted that Felix confusingly claims that the shroud was gifted by the abbess Ecgburh (§50, pp. 154–7) and by an anchorite Ecgberht (§51, pp. 162–3). "Perhaps the names have been confused; and yet there is no MS. evidence of such confusion, so that such confusion, if confusion there be,

goes back to a very early stage in the history of the transmission of the Life" (Colgrave, "Notes," p. 194). This possibility hardly seems far-fetched. Sims-Williams discusses different misspellings of "Ecgburh" in two relatively late manuscripts of the *VSG* and in the *LE* (*Religion*, p. 223).

33 Vitalis, *Ecclesiastical History*, IV, pp. 338–9. For the Pseudo-Ingulph's account of the friendship between Guthlac and Æthelbald as contained in the late medieval *Historia Croylandensis*, and for the early Croyland Abbey charters ostensibly preserved in the *Historia*, see Pseudo-Ingulph, *Chronicle*, ed. Riley, pp. 3–11. Partly derived from Orderic's own language, the charters are spurious but nevertheless shed fascinating light on Croyland's self-understanding. See Liebermann, "Über ostenglische Geschichtsquellen," p. 247; Chibnall, "Introduction," vol. 2, pp. xx-viii; and especially Brady, "Crowland Abbey." I am thankful to Henry Ansgar Kelly for bringing the Pseudo-Ingulph to my attention.

34 E.g. by Thacker, "Social," pp. 324–6; C.A.M. Clarke, *Writing*, p. 32; Bacola, "*Vacuas*," p. 76; Orchard, "*Lege*," pp. 26–7; Wragg, "*Guthlac A*," p. 215; Wragg, "Vernacular Literature," pp. 43–61; Wragg, "Early Texts," p. 255 ("textual clues indicate that the *vita* was primarily intended to promote the cult of Guthlac as a Mercian saint, and perhaps to extend the political and ecclesiastical claims and prestige of Repton into East Anglia"). "Even the dating of incidents in the *Life* is by Mercian regnal years": Thacker, "Social," p. 325.

35 J. Blair observes that Guthlac's and other "very opulent and well-publicized translations were in reaction to special pressures from politics or inter-monastic competition, and the practice did not become general": *Church*, p. 145.

36 Whose numerous talents have been noted by Kurtz, "From St. Antony"; C.W. Jones, *Saints' Lives*, pp. 85–7; Schütt, "Vom heiligen Antonius," esp. p. 91 (concurring with Kurtz and Jones); Thacker, "Social," p. 324; Downey, "Intertextuality," pp. 25, 67–106, and passim; and contributors to the 2014 conference "Guthlac of Crowland: Celebrating 1300 Years," organized by Jane Roberts and Alan Thacker. See now Roberts and Thacker's co-edited *Guthlac: Crowland's Saint.* On the question whether Felix was an Englishman named Eadwald, see Orchard, "*Lege*," pp. 52–4, citing (p. 52, n. 63) Lapidge, "Felix."

37 According to Eco, "a text is emitted for someone who actualizes it – even if the concrete and empirical existence of this someone is not hoped for (or wanted)" ("un testo viene emesso per qualcuno che lo attualizzi – anche se non si spera (o non si vuole) che questo qualcuno concretamente o empiricamente esista"): *Lector*, p. 53.

38 Ælfwald, Letter to Boniface, in *Sancti Bonifatii et Lulli epistolae*, ed. Tangl, p. 181; *Letters*, trans. Emerton, p. 128. For comment see Pestell, *Landscapes*,

p. 21; Plunkett, *Suffolk*, pp. 153–4; Hoggett, *Archaeology*, pp. 34–5 (citing Pestell, Plunkett, and others).

39 Felix's declaration that Ælfwald "rules by right" signifies more than ceremony and "may be an implicit reference to his lord's royal pedigree": Newton, *Origins*, p. 78. On Felix's use of alliteration in this passage (to which I return briefly in the following paragraph) and elsewhere in the *Vita*, see Downey, "Intertextuality," pp. 77–82.

40 At least for Bede, "the primary unit … was the individual kingdom, for which his normal term was *provincia*, whose inhabitants could also be designated as a *gens*": Yorke, "Political and Ethnic Identity," citing approvingly J. Campbell, "Bede's *Reges*" (in J. Campbell, *Essays*, pp. 85–98). Yorke also discusses "*regiones* as subdivisions of kingdoms" (pp. 82–6, quotation at p. 82).

41 Herren, "Boniface's Epistolary Prose Style," pp. 23, 25. On Boniface's circle, see Thornbury, *Becoming*, pp. 200–8.

42 On geography and loyalty as determinants of Mercian cultural identity, see Yorke, "Origins," pp. 20–1. Harris acknowledges the malleability of tribal identity as stressed by Patrick Geary, but he is especially interested (as I am) in "how an author (or group of authors) imagined a collective, and the categories by which those images came into physical being in narrative": *Race*, p. 9. See also above, Introduction, p. 28.

43 Roberts favours a Mercian identity (*Guthlac*, p. 5), while East Anglian origins are proposed by Cubitt ("Memory," pp. 56) and especially persuasively by Leeser, who envisions an East Anglian milieu for the writing of the *VSG* ("On the Edge," p. 152).

44 Yorke, "Origins," pp. 20–1. For his part, Felix is not as explicit in his ethnograpy as one might wish. He tells us that Guthlac's father Penwalh was "de egregia stirpe Merciorum … cuius mansio in Mediterraneorum Anglorum partibus" ("of distinguished Mercian stock … whose dwelling … was in the district of the Middle Angles"; *VSG* §1, pp. 72–3), but he neglects to localize that "stock" within Mercia or to specify which Middle Angles Penwalh lived among (for examples, see the following note). I thank Jane Roberts for drawing my attention to this passage (email message to author, 14 March 2018).

45 Unless the various "peoples" in question are simply folk-groups subject to Mercian lordship (the North Gyrwe, South Gyrwe, Spalda, etc.).

46 On Bede's acknowledgement of Æthelbald's Southumbrian hegemony, see *HE* V.23, cited by Colgrave, "Introduction" to his edition of the *VSG*, p. 7 and n. 1. Leeser, sensing a backhanded compliment in Felix's remark about Æthelbald's *felicitas*, suggests that the *VSG*'s composition in the 720s might explain why the remark "seems to damn him with faint praise" ("On the Edge," p. 153–4). Yet *felicitas* was reckoned a sign

of politically and spiritually sound kingship; see Ridyard, *Royal Saints*, pp. 75–6 (cited in chap. 1, above, nn. 135–6).

47 According to Antonio Gramsci, the individual "intellectual" can operate not only alone but also within groups, and more broadly within "'the ensemble of the system of relations' within which knowledge is produced": Crehan, *Gramsci*, p. 133. See too Weston, "Guthlac Betwixt," pp. 5–7 (on Felix's use of "intertextuality" to signal his scholarly authority); B. Brooks, "Felix's Construction"; Bacola, "*Vacuas*"; Orchard, "*Lege*"; Appleton, "Psalter"; Grossi, "Barrow Exegesis"; and especially Downey, "Intertextuality."

48 See Curtius's overview of the classical and biblical commonplace that "[t]he possession of knowledge makes it a duty to impart it": *European Literature*, p. 87, and the discussion of hagiographical convention in Townsend, "Hagiography," pp. 618–20.

49 Wieland, "*Aures*," p. 176. Wragg believes that "[t]hough the work was dedicated to Ælfwald, Guthlac's cult was predominantly Mercian. It seems likely, then, that the vita's implied audience was also Mercian" ("Early Texts," p. 256). Like Leeser (in "On the Edge"), I believe that the audience comprised Mercian and East Anglian readers and that the process of defining the political orientation of the cult was still in flux when Felix wrote.

50 Rollason, *Saints*, p. 87. Thacker posits a mixed audience embracing both "a clerical community of some kind" and an "elite secular culture": "Guthlac," p. 4.

51 On these various "modesty topoi," see Curtius, *European Literature*, pp. 83–5.

52 Curtius, *European Literature*, pp. 128–30, cited by Keynes and Lapidge, *Alfred*, p. 239, n. 45, adducing (in addition to Asser) Aldhelm, Alcuin, and Æthelweard. See too Smyth, *King Alfred*, p. 297, referring to Byrhtferth of Ramsey and Æthelweard, as well as Asser (or Pseudo-Asser, as Smyth controversially styles him).

53 I thank Gernot Wieland for stressing the Homeric connection in this regard.

54 Brady (*Writing*, p. 57), similarly describes this passage as "a critical red herring" but because, in her view, it has been misinterpreted to suggest that the Anglo-Welsh marches were places of constant conflict between two opposed peoples. "In fact … this passage actually indicates the opposite: that the Welsh borderlands during Guthlac's life were a site of mixed Anglo-Welsh culture, not strife" (p. 58).

55 A few of the many commentators on various kinds of border or threshold space in the *Vita*, the OE *Guthlac A*, and/or the OE prose *Life of St. Guthlac* include Wentersdorf, "Battle," p. 140; O'Brien O'Keeffe, "Guthlac's

Crossings," passim, esp. pp. 7, 11, 22; Sharma, "Reconsideration," pp. 199, 200; Siewers, "Landscapes," p. 24 (and citing Wentersdorf's article in n. 105); Cohen, *Machines*, pp. 137–9, 141–3; Symonds, "Territories," p. 36; Hines, *Voices*, pp. 62–70; Wickham-Crowley, "Living," pp. 96–105; Wickham-Crowley, "Fens"; C.A.M. Clarke, *Literary Landscapes*, pp. 45–58; Brady, "Echoes," p. 674 (also citing Sharma's article); Brady, *Writing*, pp. 53–81; Weston, "Saintly Lives," p. 391; Weston, "Guthlac Betwixt"; Noetzel, "Monster"; Wragg, "Vernacular Literature," pp. 59–60; Estes, *Landscapes*, pp. 92–4, 98–116; Frenze, "Holy Heights"; Hartmann, "Monument Reuse."

56 O'Brien O'Keeffe, "Guthlac's Crossings," p. 11; compare p. 22. See too Pinner, "Thinking Wetly," p. 7. Pertinent too is Eliade, *Myth*, pp. 9–10, on the ritual taming of wild places.

57 For comparable remarks on *Guthlac A*, see Discenza, *Inhabited Spaces*, pp. 177–9, and Sharma, "Reconsideration," p. 200 ("[i]n their imagination, Old English poets seemed to assume a natural relation between evil, especially of the supernatural sort, and border-space").

58 The rare word *rivigarum* is translated by Colgrave as "of … streams," and this is the sense adduced in *DMLBS*, fasc. 14, p. 2843, s.v. *riviga*, "stream, river." For the meaning "[of] the banks of a river, or lake," see Maseres, *Historiae anglicanae*, p. 330, note *c*, citing du Cange's *Glossarium* and the passage from *VSG* as reproduced by Orderic Vitalis. See also *DMLBS*, fasc. 14, p. 2843, s.v. *rivagium* senses 1 and 1*b*, "shore, bank of a river, land beside river," "landing-place." Then again, Felix's noun may simply be "a misreading of the Vulgate, Isaiah xix. 6" (Colgrave, "Notes," p. 180).

59 The foregoing analysis has, in part, been anticipated by Noetzel, "Monster," pp. 120–1 (adapting Mircea Eliade), who sees the imagery as linking the Fens and "humanity's corporeal existence on Earth"; and by Downey, who notes Felix's use of the word *gurgites* to characterize both "worldly turmoil" and Guthlac's "spiritual change" ("Intertextuality," pp. 18–19).

60 Ravensdale, *Liable*, p. 5, discussing principally the former monastic sites of Elmeney, Waterbeach, and Denney, roughly half-way between Cambridge and Ely and near the confluence of the rivers Great Ouse and Cam. Some heterogeneity of landscape is, however, documented in H.C. Darby, *Medieval Fenland*, and in Oosthuizen, *Anglo-Saxon Fenland*.

61 "Guthlac's Crossings," p. 7; see too Hartmann, "Monument Reuse," p. 239 (also citing O'Brien O'Keeffe). H.C. Darby, seemingly less attentive than O'Brien O'Keeffe is to the unequal power of East Anglia and Mercia, observes simply that "[k]ingdoms, finding their limits here, partitioned the marshy wastes between them, and the barrier of the Fens became a permanent feature in the political geography of the Anglo-Saxon Heptarchy" ("Fenland Frontier"), p. 185.

62 P. Brown, *Body*, p. 215, with specific reference to the protagonists of Palladius of Galatia's *Historia Lausiaca* (419–20 CE).

63 On the thirty thousand hides of the "Myrcna landes," see Featherstone, "Tribal Hidage," p. 24; Yorke, "Origins," p. 20. Difficulties of interpreting the document are discussed in Featherstone's and Yorke's essays; Dumville, "Tribal Hidage"; Keynes, "England," pp. 21–5; Keynes, "Kingdom," p. 11. John notes that the "hides" of the *Tribal Hidage* refer to "units of service, not area": *Reassessing*, p. 15.

64 Kilpatrick makes this point in "Place-Names." On the literary situation of religious houses in seemingly liminal places, J. Blair observes that "the tension between the ideal of the wilderness and the reality of embeddedness in secular life required an element of make-believe": *Church*, p. 194. In arguing that "the evidence of place-names and archaeology indicates a region full of people," Oosthuizen goes furthest in disputing the Fens' reputation for otherworldly terrors (*Anglo-Saxon Fenland*, p. 50).

65 At this point in the *Vita* Felix is drawing upon two sources, the *Lives* of St. Antony and St. Fursey; see Colgrave's marginal notes in *VSG*, pp. 84–7; Mayr-Harting, *Coming*, p. 230; Rollason, *Saints*, p. 84; Downey, "Intertextuality," p. 56 (on echoes of the *Vita sancti Fursei*).

66 Constable helpfully distinguishes between *coenobium* and *monasterium* in *Reformation*, p. 9. See too C.A. Jones's analysis of the different approaches to the cenobitic life in the *VSG* and *Guthlac A* ("Envisioning"). I speak of Guthlac's period of monastic training as intermediate between his warrior and eremitic lives, but within "[a]n ascetic's optimum career-path," as reconstructed by J. Blair, it marks but the first step: *Church*, p. 218.

67 On Felix's indirect asides on Irish monasticism, see Colgrave, "Introduction," p. 16 and n. 2. The tonsure also distinguishes Guthlac from the wayward *gyrovagi* condemned by Benedict: *Rule of Saint Benedict*, ed. Fry et al., I.10–11. As C.A. Jones demonstrates ("Envisioning"), *Guthlac A* suppresses the protagonist's two years at Repton and instead characterizes Guthlac's eremitic life as containing the core elements of communal *conversatio*.

68 Repton's Roman associations, perhaps deliberately cultivated, are discussed by Yorke, "Burial," pp. 252–3.

69 Howe, "Rome"; Howe, *Writing*, pp. 101–24. See Discenza's refinement upon Howe's thesis in "Map," p. 84. On Bede's exaltation of "papal and not imperial Rome," see Scully, "Bede," p. 37. According to Hoenicke Moore, Bede was devoted to the ecclesiastical universalism that Rome represented, a virtue that could be transferred to Wearmouth-Jarrow's library ("Bede's Devotion"). On the reduced emphasis on papal Rome in the OE translation of Bede, see Rowley, *Old English Version*, pp. 4, 12, 98–113.

70 P. Brown, *Body*, p. 217.

71 On the exaggeration, see Rackham, *History*, pp. 374–5; Oosthuizen, *Anglo-Saxon Fenland*, p. 50. The Fens' natural resources are discussed by Rackham, *History*, pp. 381–2, 387; Barley, *Lincolnshire*, pp. 123–6; H.C. Darby, *Medieval Fenland*, p. 21 (quoting Hugh Candidus); Morris, *Time's Anvil*, pp. 110–11. (Darby's *Medieval Fenland* is cited in its first edition by Colgrave, "Introduction," p. 2, n. 4.) Some scholars instead emphasize Felix's descriptive accuracy, e.g. B. Brooks, "Felix's Construction," pp. 55, 65–70, and studies cited therein.

72 On Pestell's term, see above, n. 11. On spaces influenced by the presence of borders, see D. Newman, "Borders," and above, p. 266 and n. 14, as well as n. 15 on the situation of Middle Anglia.

73 Harrison, "Invisible Boundaries," p. 91 (Harrison's article is cited in Michelet, *Creation*, p. 5, n. 15).

74 On the *locus amoenus* in early English literature, see C.A.M. Clarke, *Literary Landscapes*, esp. pp. 7–66, and pp. 31–4 for discussion of the trope as used in the *VSG*. The OE *Guthlac A* explicitly shows Crowland becoming transformed into a "pleasurable place."

75 Four centuries later, the *Gesta Herwardi* will describe the root cause of Hereward's rebellion against William the Conqueror as precisely the desire to reclaim a paternal inheritance.

76 For rich discussions of Guthlac's name and Felix's understanding of its origins, see Cavill, "Naming," and Bolton, "Background." On political and propagandistic uses of genealogy, see Sisam, "Anglo-Saxon Royal Genealogies"; Dumville, "Kingship"; Yorke, "Origins," pp. 16–17 (referring e.g. to Felix's *Vita* and citing Dumville's work); Stodnick, "Old Names" (and citing Sisam and Dumville). Meaney writes that "it sometimes appears that royal ancestry is, if not a prerequisite, certainly a useful contributory factor in the attribution of Anglo-Saxon sanctity" ("Hagiography," p. 31).

77 Yorke, "Origins," p. 15. On Icel's importance within the *VSG* see too Thacker, "Kings," p. 5; Newton, *Origins*, p. 62; Roberts, "Seals," p. 119, n. 38. Thacker nevertheless cautions that Felix may have thought Icel was simply "the founder of a dynasty of Mercian origin which included famous kings" (email message to author, 21 February 2017).

78 John, *Land Tenure*, p. 62.

79 The use of the land being referred to in laws and charters as *facultas*, "the right to dispose of property, and not … the landed property itself": John, *Land Tenure*, p. 13. In greater depth than I can attempt here, S. Clark explores this term and its relevance to *Guthlac A* in "More Permanent Homeland," p. 81, n. 26, citing John and Wormald.

80 S.T. Smith, *Land*, pp. 212, 213.

81 E.g. Neville, *Representations*, p. 127; Black, "Tradition," §9; S. Clark, "More Permanent Homeland," p. 83; S. Clark, "*Guthlac A*," p. 52; Brady,

"Colonial Desire" (esp. p. 74, on the connection between the "fluid landscape" of *Guthlac A* and Mercia's unstable boundaries during Guthlac's lifetime); Discenza, *Inhabited Spaces*, pp. 153–7, 162–3; Wragg, "Vernacular Literature," pp. 65–6; Weston, "Guthlac Betwixt," p. 19.

82 Downey et al., "Books Tell Us," esp. pp. 156–7, furthering arguments by Patrick Conner and Christopher A. Jones. For an ecocritical analysis of the poem's engagement with the Benedictine Reform, see Bovaird-Abbo, "Redeeming."

83 Analyzing the stylistic relationship between the prose *Life* and the *VSG*, Downey concludes that the former "appears to be the work of a consistent and careful translator or redactor(s); its composition shows both respect for the source text and a willingness to adapt when necessary" ("Intertextuality," pp. 144–5).

84 Wickham-Crowley, "Living," p. 99. On Guthlac's barrow, see below, n. 92.

85 Again Wickham-Crowley's insights warrant quotation: "Boundaries distinguish differences on either side, yet have identities and characters of their own. Introducing water into landscape considerations gives us a variable that suggests permeable, dynamic boundaries; in some circumstances, such as the siting of religious foundations, their inherent uncertainty and ambiguity may be cultivated": "Living," p. 105.

86 It is not a contradiction to argue that the *VSG*'s depiction of Guthlac's tumulus "inheritance" both serves specifically Mercian political interests and encourages pious longing for eternal salvation, beyond time and place. For the latter argument as it pertains to *Guthlac A*, see S. Clark, "More Permanent Homeland," p. 76.

87 In this Felix may be typifying the representation practice found in OE poetry: see Neville, *Representations*, pp. 44 (referring to the *Guthlac A*).

88 Lees and Overing, "Anglo-Saxon Horizons," p. 6.

89 The debate is ongoing; see above, n. 71 and n. 2.

90 Manhattan's Cloisters Museum, notwithstanding its "[s]ynthetic" amalgamation of elements from five medieval French and Spanish monasteries, represented to Merton "a reproach to everything else around it, except the trees and the Palisades": *Seven Storey Mountain*, p. 7.

91 For a full analysis, see Downey, "Too Much."

92 Discussions of the mound in the *VSG* and corresponding *beorg* in *Guthlac A* are many and varied; see e.g. Colgrave, "Earliest," p. 54; Colgrave, "Notes," pp. 182–4; Shook, "Burial Mound"; Reichardt, "*Guthlac A*"; Wentersdorf, "Battle"; Roberts, *Guthlac Poems*, p. 132; Sharma, "Reconsideration," pp. 194–8; Kilpatrick, "Place-Names," 24–5, 31–3; B. Brooks, "Felix's Construction," pp. 70–1; S. Clark, "*Guthlac A*"; Michelet, *Creation*, pp. 173–89 passim; Foxhall Forbes, *Heaven*, pp. 93–4; Brady, "Colonial Desire," and, *Writing*, pp. 60–7. On the multiple identities of ancient burial mounds, see

e.g. J. Blair, *Church*, pp. 53–4 (and sources in n. 170); Morris, *Time's Anvil*, pp. 43–4 and 206; Semple, "Fear," pp. 112–13 (cited by Weston, "Guthlac Betwixt," p. 24, n. 2); Estes, *Landscapes*, pp. 111–15; Frenze, "Holy Heights"; Hartmann, "Monument Reuse"; Ellard, *Anglo-Saxon Past(s)*, pp. 107–29 (with particular reference to the barrow in *Beowulf*).

93 Hartmann, "Monument Reuse," p. 236. Hines shows that Guthlac's revolutionary Fenland colonization is belied by evidence of widespread settlement: *Voices*, p. 67; see also Oosthuizen, *Anglo-Saxon Fenland*, p. 50 (as cited above in n. 64). For a more guarded view, see Kilpatrick, "Place-Names," pp. 33–6. By contrast, Pestell asserts that "[t]he archaeological evidence for the site is equivocal … and that the whole island of Crowland was one of very low intensity occupation, and probably only properly settled with the establishment of the Benedictine monastery [in the tenth century]": *Landscapes*, p. 133. The issue is explored sensitively by Hartmann, "Monument Reuse," pp. 239–40, 243–5.

94 This last point is made by Wickham-Crowley, "Living," p. 97.

95 Wickham-Crowley's remarks about the corresponding passage from the OE prose *Life of Guthlac* are relevant here: "Are these [demons] the spirits of the ancient burial mound? Or are they more recent battle victims, those killed in battle with the Mercian English? While modern archaeology might choose one over the other, the text leaves that identity open, allowing ancient and recent pasts to merge in the fens": "Living," p. 98. See also Brady, "Echoes," p. 679. As Lees and Overing have evocatively observed, "[p]laces, like their inhabitants, are redolent with contradiction and with the multivalence of the past": "Anglo-Saxon Horizons," p. 16 (with reference to Bede's account of England's fitful Christianization).

96 Here I borrow Scholastic terminology from Eco, *Lector*, p. 55.

97 Meaney, "Hagiography," p. 44.

98 Fell, "Saint Æðelþryð," p. 34 (see discussion above, chap. 2). Kilpatrick plausibly surmises that "[i]f the place-name [*Gronta*] was not integral to Guthlac's biography, it was perhaps significant to the patron of the text or his relations": "Places," p. 108; see too her long n. 61 (same page) on Æthelthryth's translation in *HE* IV.19.

99 So much so that Cubitt observes that "Bede's *Life of St. Cuthbert* forms the essential backdrop to the *Life of St. Guthlac* which attempts to show Guthlac's superiority over Cuthbert" ("Memory," pp. 53–4, building upon Alan Thacker's insights). Higham goes further, describing Guthlac as but "a clone of Cuthbert": "Guthlac's *Vita*," p. 85. See also Downey, "Intertextuality," pp. 55–65, on Felix's borrowings from the *Vitae* of Fursey and Cuthbert.

100 O'Brien O'Keeffe, "Guthlac's Crossings," p. 6. If Higham ("Guthlac's *Vita*") is right to sense "competition" between Mercia and East Anglia in the promotion of Fenland saints, then the presence of Æthelthryth and

Guthlac in the territory of the Gyrwe may itself have been a sensitive issue. As noted by Colgrave ("Introduction," p. 2, n. 7), the document known as the *Secgan* (*Resting Places of the English Saints*) places Crowland in the territory of the Gyrwe: "Đonne resteð sancte Guðlac on þare stowe, þe is genemnod Cruland, þæt mynster is on middan Girwan fænne" (text in Liebermann, *Die Heiligen Englands*, pp. 9–20, at p. 11, §10).

101 Relevant here is Elliott's term "revirginization" to describe the holy women of Aldhelm's *De virginitate*, the OE *Elene*, and Ælfric's Homily on Judith and *Lives of Saints* (especially the *Life of Æthelthryth*): Elliott, "Sex," pp. 16–81. Kilpatrick, "Place-Names," persuasively conjectures that Felix's silence about other Fenland monasteries may have been a means "to portray Guthlac either as a trendsetter or to claim him as the first hermit of the fens" (p. 37); compare Kilpatrick, "Places," pp. 111–15.

102 See the references to Howe's "Rome" and *Writing*, above, n. 69.

103 Kirby, *Making*, p. 249. For a probing theoretical analysis of Roman and other ruins in the early English context, see Estes, *Landscapes*, pp. 61–87.

104 Kirby, *Making*, pp. 249–50.

105 On the early East Angles' singular interest in claiming an ancestral Roman identity for themselves, seen in e.g. their alignment of the she-wolf motif with their own lupine dynastic imagery, see above, Introduction, p. 23 and notes 108 and 109.

106 Christopher Taylor, *Cambridgeshire Landscape*, p. 259. Taylor believes the ruins found by the Ely monks near the end of the seventh century represented a period of conflict "earlier" in that century.

107 H.C. Darby, "Fenland Frontier," p. 196.

108 F. Stenton, *Anglo-Saxon England*, p. 50. This theme recurs in H.C. Darby, "Fenland Frontier," whose findings are supported in Davies and Vierck, "Contexts," pp. 251–2.

109 F. Stenton, *Anglo-Saxon England*, p. 50. Compare P.H. Blair, *Roman Britain*, pp. 182–3. The Fenland was not as impenetrable as formerly thought, however; see Oosthuizen's analysis of its varied topography in *Anglo-Saxon Fenland*, pp. 13–30, and discussion by Hartmann, "Monument Reuse," pp. 243–5.

110 H.C. Darby, "Fenland Frontier," p. 194, assigning Thorney and Whittlesmere to Middle Anglia and thus to Mercia; yet "[t]he division was not without fluctuation" (p. 194, cited in Colgrave, "Introduction," p. 2).

111 For a similar view, though one emphasizing East Anglian expansion rather than freedom, and Mercia's inability to conquer its eastern neighbour, see Yorke, *Kings*, p. 65. My own formulation merely reverses the emphases in Yorke's analysis.

112 "As sure as there are holy crows in Crowland," swears Martin Lightfoot in Kingsley's *Hereward* (p. 64); but Ekwall, *Concise Dictionary*, p. 133, s.v. "Crowland," surmises that *crow-* here derives from "an otherwise

unknown word *crūw* (*crūg*)," which may have "meant 'a bend'" in what is now the River Welland. Ekwall is cited by Colgrave, "Notes," p. 181; Kilpatrick, "Place-Names," p. 22 (in a rich analysis); and Kilpatrick, "Places," p. 106. See too Noetzel, "Monster," p. 105. The riverine landscape itself throws a kink into this theory, however; see Chisholm, "Crowland," pp. 319–25.

113 Lia describes Casaubon as follows: "You sometimes seem profound, but it's only because you piece a lot of surfaces together to create the impression of depth, solidity. That solidity would collapse if you tried to stand it up": Eco, *Foucault's Pendulum*, p. 50. Nevertheless, the *VSG*'s British phantoms and other terrors are solid enough in Guthlac's mind to warrant interpretation as evidence of psychological trauma (Lee, "Healing Words"), as obstacles to be overcome on the way to psychological recovery (Anlezark, "Stand Firm"), or even as hallucinations caused by the eating of a certain kind of fungus that grows on barley bread (Foxhall Forbes, *Heaven*, p. 92, and source cited in her n. 143).

114 O'Brien O'Keeffe, "Guthlac's Crossings," p. 21.

115 On the text's pitting of a cohesive English people against the Britons tout court, see (in addition to O'Brien O'Keeffe's article) Cohen, *Machines*, pp. 117, 142–4; Siewers, "Landscapes," pp. 10–14, 25 (with regard to *Guthlac A*); J. Davies, "Literary Languages," p. 265; Brady, "Echoes," esp. pp. 676–82; Brady, *Writing*, pp. 57–9; Harris, *Race*, p. 37 (cited by Brady, "Echoes," p. 677); Capper, "St. Guthlac" in toto; Estes, *Landscapes*, pp. 107–11; Hartmann, "Monument Reuse," pp. 243–51; Neidorf, "*Beowulf*," pp. 865–7. According to Higham, "What Felix was seeking to do by reference to Britons was to contrast Guthlac's reputed victory over 'British' devils with the failure of Coenred's protection of the English nation against actual British attacks. He did this in a context that would not have offended the current Mercian establishment, dominated as that was by Aethelbald" ("Guthlac's *Vita*," p. 88).

116 Scholars who adduce a western context for Guthlac's British-speaking demonic foes include Colgrave, "Introduction," p. 3; Colgrave, "Notes," p. 185; Kirby, "Welsh Bards," p. 38; Cohen, *Machines*, pp. 143–4; Yorke, "Origins," p. 19; Brady, *Writing*, pp. 53–81; and Capper, "St. Guthlac," esp. p. 211. Colgrave ("Notes," p. 176) and Sims-Williams (*Religion*, p. 26) caution against assuming Guthlac's own possible British origins (implied by the name of his father, Penwalh); but see Siewers, "Landscapes," p. 11 (citing sources), and especially Brady, *Writing*, pp. 54–5, and Hartmann, "Monument Reuse," pp. 243, 250–1, who suggest that Felix may have wished to promote a Mercian (or English?) policy of inclusiveness that embraced ethnic Britons or at least envisaged ethnic British acceptance of Mercian sovereignty. Härke ("Ethnogenesis," pp. 18–19) argues for

early English supersession, not just continuation, of British culture in the "increasing inclusion of Britons into Anglo-Saxon society." In response, Hartmann claims that "Guthlac's burial next to a pre-Anglo-Saxon barrow can be read as an act of transforming, rather than erasing, past meaning" ("Monument Reuse," p. 248), but the tone of *VSG* §34 persuades me that Härke's argument better explains what Felix is up to.

117 Oosthuizen, *Anglo-Saxon Fenland*, pp. 38–42, 136, relying in part on what strikes me as a too-literal reading of the above-quoted passage from Felix. A similar concern is registered in Hartmann, "Monument Reuse," p. 243. The question of continuous British occupation of the Fens is also explored in Higham, "Guthlac's *Vita*," p. 88; Siewers, "Landscapes," pp. 11–12 and sources cited therein; Capper, "St. Guthlac," pp. 188–94; Brady, "Echoes," pp. 676–81; Estes, *Landscapes*, p. 103; and Hartmann, "Monument Reuse," who is, like me, interested in the Fens primarily as the *VSG* represents them (pp. 244–5).

118 Brady, *Writing*, p. 58; see too Colgrave, ed., *VSG*, pp. 185–6; Colgrave, "Earliest," pp. 53–4; F. Stenton, in D.M. Stenton, *Preparatory*, p. 362; Roberts, *Guthlac*, p. 17. This is not to deny that, in real life, Britons may have co-existed (albeit on unequal terms) with the Germanic newcomers and their descendants, in and out of the Fens; surveying a wide range of evidence in late fifth- to late seventh-century cemeteries, Härke concludes that "Britons made up as much as half of the male population of the communities we identify as 'Anglo-Saxon' on the basis of their material culture": "Ethnogenesis," p. 13. See too Härke's reference ("Ethnogenesis," p. 15 and n. 90, and p. 16) to a 1985 study by Christopher Scull of a sixth-century British cultural presence in the south-eastern Fens.

119 On these tribes, see above, Introduction, pp. 20–1 and sources cited in n. 90, to which may be added the following brief references to the Catuvellauni: Collingwood and Myres, *Roman Britain*, pp. 46–7, 54–7 and passim; Salway, *History*, pp. 29–31, 38–9, 47, and passim. A similar point concerning multiple cultural layers is made by Cohen, *Machines*, pp. 142–3.

120 Morris, *Time's Anvil*, pp. 156–7.

121 Michelet, *Creation*, p. 166.

122 Cohen, *Machines*, p. 144. Wragg too situates the *VSG* firmly in a Mercian context ("Vernacular Literature"; "*Guthlac A*"). On Guthlac's lineage as but one branch of the Mercian royal dynasty, see Leeser, "On the Edge," pp. 143–6; Wragg, "Vernacular Literature," pp. 48–9, 57–8, 78; Roberts and Thacker, "Introduction," p. xxiii. For the opinion that the Mercians' "original connections were with the Wash and East Anglia," see Stafford, *East Midlands*, pp. 96 and 202, n. 5 (citing *VSG*); W. Davies, "Annals," pp. 20–4. Against this view, see N. Brooks, "Formation," p. 162, and Yorke, "Origins," p. 15.

123 On these distinctions, see Morris, *Time's Anvil*, pp. 156–9 and p. 111, referring, respectively, to Snowdonia and the Fenland. Estes notes that both the *VSG* and the OE prose *Guthlac* "refer quite clearly to several layers of pre-existing occupancy" (*Landscapes*, p. 102). J. Blair situates Guthlac's takeover of Crowland in the context of Christian appropriation of pagan sites: *Church*, p. 184; and Hartmann's brilliant "Monument Reuse" touches on these and a host of other aspects of the *VSG*.

124 C.A.M. Clarke emphasizes Guthlac's enduring links to society: *Writing*, pp. 20–1. Compare Wickham-Crowley, "Living," p. 97; Wickham-Crowley, "Fens," p. 84; Kilpatrick, "Place-Names," pp. 35–8, and "Places," pp. 111–13 (noting, in both studies, Felix's likely exaggeration of Crowland's desolation); Weston, "Saintly Lives," pp. 394–5, and "Guthlac Betwixt," pp. 10–12. Cohen instead stresses Guthlac's isolation and relates it to the flux of eighth-century Mercia: *Machines*, pp. 116–53.

125 Hines, *Voices*, p. 54.

126 Neville, *Representations*, p. 124. See also Michelet, *Creation*, p. 171.

127 *VSG* §34, pp. 108–9. Brady instead argues that neither Felix's references to *Saxonici* and *Anglorum* nor his recollections of British hostilities against those peoples pertain to the Mercians; "the separate identities of the Anglo-Saxon kingdoms should not be elided" (*Writing*, p. 58). Although I agree with this principle as she formulates it, I also believe that Felix himself deliberately resorts to ethnographic elision in *VSG* §34 and blurs Anglian, Saxon, and Mercian identities in order to justify Æthelbald's eventual authority over all the English. See Thacker, "Bede's Idea," p. 17, suggesting the influence on Felix of Boniface's conflation of Mercians with Angles.

128 On Pega, see *VSG* §50–1, pp. 154–63; §53, pp. 167–71; Colgrave, "Introduction," pp. 6 and passim; Colgrave, "Notes," pp. 192–3; Leeser, "On the Edge," pp. 142–3; Lumley Prior, "*Pegeland* Revisited," esp. pp. 326–9.

129 Translation slightly emended from Colgrave's "but he did not return as he was before[.]" Felix's last words in describing the cured man's gratitude echo Vergil's *Aeneid*, as noted in Colgrave's edition (p. 170). Perhaps the allusion is meant to persuade Felix's readers that even praising God and spreading word of Guthlac's miracles are heroic acts that can substitute for lost military might? Guthlac's similarities to Aeneas are noted in C.A.M. Clarke, *Literary Landscapes*, p. 32; Bacola, "*Vacuas*," pp. 78–82; Orchard, "*Lege*," pp. 26–7. Other accounts of Felix's borrowings from Vergil include Thacker, "Guthlac," pp. 16–18; Appleton and Robinson, "Further Echoes"; Anlezark, "Stand Firm." B. Brooks, in "Felix's Construction," cautions against over-interpretation of such echoes, and

Downey's remarks in "Intertextuality," pp. 64–5, also warrant mentioning in this context.

130 Mayr-Harting, *Coming*, pp. 230, 231. He continues: "That does not mean that the *Life* is far removed from the real Guthlac, who was himself part of that culture and indeed helped to fashion it" (p. 231). Elsewhere in his book, however, Mayr-Harting refers to Felix's saintly protagonist as "the Mercian prince Guthlac" (p. 20).

131 Colgrave, "Introduction," p. 7.

132 Keynes thus memorably describes Offa (r. 757–96) in "Kingdom," p. 14.

133 I refer of course to Anderson's *Imagined Communities*.

134 I am influenced by Michelet's remark that *Guthlac A*, *Andreas*, and Cynewulf's *Elene* "redefine centrality and periphery … and they transform the border-lands – non-places – into religious centres": *Creation*, p. 197. On the ambiguity of medieval representations of border spaces, see too Treharne, "Borders"; Brady, "Echoes." Applicable to Felix's Crowland is Howe's remark, regarding boundary clauses in charters, that "the periphery is … more central than what fills the center" (Howe, *Writing*, p. 39).

135 See above, Introduction, p. 23, n. 109; and chap. 1, p. 62, n. 130.

136 Meaney, "History …?" p. 77; compare Stancliffe, "Kings," p. 157 and especially p. 171 ("[t]he phenomenon of kings adopting the religious life gathers momentum only in the latter part of the seventh century, peaking in the years 685–710 when no fewer than six kings took this decision"). Was Felix gently prodding his patron to join this trend?

137 Stancliffe, "Kings," pp. 154–5.

138 Stancliffe, "Kings," p. 172.

139 For text and discussion of the Letter to Boniface, see the references above in n. 38.

140 Stancliffe observes that "Guthlac was never a king; but he was a potential king, a man of royal blood who gathered a warband about him and lived by pillage, much as Caedwalla had done before he seized power in Wessex": "Kings," p. 167. Compare Stafford, *East Midlands*, pp. 96, 107; Charles-Edwards, "Early Medieval Kingships," p. 37.

141 "'Unique' Anglo-Saxon Coin"; Naismith, "New Type."

142 Bately, ed., *MS A*, *s.a.* 792 [*recte* 794]; James, "Two Lives"; Plunkett, *Suffolk*, pp. 171–5; Yorke, *Kings*, pp. 59; Rollason, *Saints*, pp. 122, 128; Ridyard, *Royal Saints*, p. 244, citing James in n. 20; Wright, *Cultivation*, pp. 94–106 and the appendices on pp. 259–65 (cited, as is the article by James, in Garmonsway, *Anglo-Saxon Chronicle*, p. 55, n. 3); Thacker, "Kings," pp. 16–18; Cubitt, "Sites," pp. 75–7 (who also cites, inter alia, Thacker's article on p. 54, n. 1). The studies by James and Thacker are also cited by Yorke, *Kings*, p. 185, n. 9.

143 Keynes, "Kingdom," p. 10.
144 James, "Two Lives," p. 238.
145 Bassett, "In Search," pp. 26–7. Williamson, however, believes "Anglian" leaders achieved domination only over fellow "Anglians" with whom they had "certain aspects of a common culture" (*Sutton Hoo*, pp. 138–41).

Chapter 4

1 Stancliffe, "Kings," p. 172.
2 Earl, "Violence," p. 135, extending an insight by Eric John. For a more polemical perspective on Ælfric and other late tenth- and early eleventh-century writers in this regard, see Ashe, *Conquest*, pp. 14–20 and passim.
3 Ryan, "Anglo-Saxons," p. 240; cf. Wormald, "*Engla Lond*," p. 5. See the Introduction above, n. 165, for kings' reigns in the period 794–854; Pestell, "Kingdom," pp. 212–13, for the coinage of King Æthelstan I from the 820s to the 840s. Keynes envisions East Anglia during this period "minding its own business in typical obscurity" ("Power," p. 186).
4 E.g. Wormald, "Anglo-Saxons," esp. the trenchant point made on p. 26; Wormald, "*Engla Lond*," esp. p. 6; Foot, "Making"; Foot, "Historiography," p. 129; K. Davis, "National Writing," pp. 617–27 (inter alia critiquing Foot, as does Stodnick, "What (and Where)," p. 89; but see the reply to Davis by Discenza, "Map," p. 85, n. 6); P.J.E. Kershaw, "Alfred-Guthrum Treaty," p. 59; J. Campbell, "What Is Not Known," p. 22; Keynes, "Edward," pp. 57–62; N. Brooks, "English Identity," pp. 46–8; Higham and Ryan, *Anglo-Saxon World*, p. 9; Molyneaux, *Formation*, p. 9; Konshuh, "Constructing," pp. 157–60; Karkov, *Imagining*, pp. 9–11, 14–19, 26–49. Molyneaux's critique (*Formation*, pp. 201–11) of Wormald and Foot will be considered later.
5 See especially Wormald, "*Engla Lond*"; Foot, "Making"; K. Davis, "National Writing"; Chapman, "King Alfred," pp. 40–1; Pratt, *Political Thought*, pp. 106–7; Discenza, *Inhabited Spaces*, p. 111; Dumville, "Origins," p. 109–10.
6 Barrett, *Against All England*, p. 1.
7 E.g. Abrams, "Edward the Elder's Danelaw," pp. 132–3 (and sources cited therein); McLeod, *Beginning*. See too notes 10, 11, and 17 below.
8 Hart, *Danelaw*, pp. 8–19.
9 Abels, "Alfred."
10 In what follows I am indebted to Smyth, *Scandinavian Kings*, pp. 22–3, 178–83, 201–4, 240–66; Hadley, *Vikings*, pp. 10–11; Molyneaux, *Formation*, pp. 21–5; and Abels, "Alfred," pp. 265–6. See too McLeod, *Beginning*, pp. 6–7; Richards and Haldenby, "Scale," esp. pp. 327–8.
11 Though not germane to my discussion, the question whether the Danes arrived in sufficient numbers to replace or merely to command the native

English peasantry has been raised often. See Abrams, "Edward the Elder's Danelaw," p. 134; Hadley, *Vikings*, pp. 1–27 (who argues for "a diversity of forms of Anglo-Scandinavian interaction"; pp. 20–1); Raffield, "Bands" and sources cited therein. McLeod favours an estimate in the low thousands rather than in the hundreds (*Beginning*, pp. 12–13, citing Else Roesdahl's work). Richards and Haldenby argue convincingly that, in Northumbria, "the sharing out of the land by Halfdan left little room for co-existence with the indigenous Northumbrians," and that "[s]uch extensive dislocation argues against the minimalist position adopted by Sawyer [in *Vikings*] and reinforces the scale of the Great Army, and its impact": "Scale," p. 345.

12 *MS A*, ed. Bately, pp. 50 and 51, *s.a.* 876 and 880, respectively. See Molyneaux, *Formation*, p. 21.

13 Smyth, *Scandinavian Kings*, p. 259. Hadley plausibly reasons that Hálfdan's "humbler warriors and other followers, and doubtless also the pre-existing tenants of these [seized English] estates" would have done the actual work of farming: *Vikings*, p. 85, quoted in Richards and Haldenby, "Scale," p. 344.

14 Smyth, *Scandinavian Kings*, pp. 265–6.

15 Rollason, *Northumbria*, pp. 215–16.

16 Smyth, *Scandinavian Kings*, p. 266.

17 Innes, "Danelaw Identities," p. 80.

18 Rollason, *Northumbria*, p. 235. See too Dumville, "Origins," p. 118.

19 Stafford, *Unification*, p. 24; compare Stafford, p. 27: "Here too [in East Anglia] Viking rule can be seen as reasserting previous independence." Compare Lavelle's remark about Æthelwold's success in Northumbria: "the rivalries of the so-called Heptarchy were surprisingly alive at the beginning of the tenth century" ("Politics," p. 74). Richards and Haldenby's "Scale" nevertheless offers sobering evidence for massive transformation of Northumbrian non-elite town and rural life.

20 J. Campbell, "What Is Not Known," p. 22 (the source too of Campbell's discussion of Edward's fortress-building), and the study by R.H.C. Davis cited therein.

21 On the battle, see e.g. *MS A*, ed. Bately, pp. 67–8, *s.a.* 917.

22 John, *Reassessing*, p. 109. This is not to challenge the claims for Æthelstan's achievements as a "king of the English" advanced by e.g. Foot, *Æthelstan*, and Dumville, "Origins."

23 Stafford, *Unification*, p. 34; pp. 37–9 on Æthelstan "Half-King" as ealdorman of East Anglia and the West Saxon management of regional separatist feeling. On the uncertain character of King Edgar's lordship in Scandinavian territories, "especially in northern England," see Abrams, "King Edgar," p. 172.

24 On these and other connections between Scandinavian Francia (including the northernmost part of Frisia) and East Anglia, see McLeod, *Beginning*,

pp. 132–58, 229, 266–7, 279–80; on the Irish background of Hálfdan's army, see pp. 162–5. Ryan explores Carolingian parallels to aspects of the rebellion of Æthelwold (about whom more later); see *Places*, pp. 114, 165, 169–76, 291–2.

25 Molyneaux, *Formation*, pp. 2–4, 24–5.

26 John, *Reassessing*, p. 105.

27 Earl, "Violence," p. 142, part of his fine psychoanalytical analysis of the "awkward, intimate antagonism" between Scandinavian and non-Scandinavian England in the tenth century (p. 142).

28 The parcelling of land presents specific complexities. Douglas points out that, in the East Anglian Domesday survey, land in Norfolk and Suffolk is divided into "carucates," but these differ from carucates found elsewhere in the Danelaw; furthermore, East Anglia's "hundreds" are unlike both the "wapentakes" of the northern shires and the hundreds found in shires of the South and the East Midlands (*Social Structure*, p. 4).

29 Foot, *Æthelstan*, p. 18; John, *Reassessing*, p. 92.

30 *MS D*, ed. Cubbin, *s.a.* 941, 943, 946, 948, 954, pp. 43–5; *MS A*, ed. Bately, *s.a.* 946, p. 74; *MS E*, ed. Irvine, *s.a.* 944, 954, pp. 55, 56; *ASC*, pp. 111–13.

31 *MS B*, ed. S. Taylor, p. 54; compare *MS C*, ed. O'Brien O'Keeffe, p. 80; *ASC*, p. 113.

32 On Guthfrith, see F. Stenton, *Anglo-Saxon England*, pp. 262, 433; Hadley, *Vikings*, pp. 37–41; McLeod, *Beginning*, pp. 217–18, 246, 275.

33 John, *Reassessing*, p. 92.

34 These evolving territorial terms reflect the tenth- to twelfth-century developments traced by S. Reynolds, *Kingdoms*, pp. 224–27. On the early origins of the title of ealdorman, see F. Stenton, *Anglo-Saxon England*, p. 305; John, "Age," p. 172.

35 Hart, *Danelaw*, pp. 569, 574–84. On the resurgence of regionalism following the death of King Edgar in 975, see Rabin, "Holy Bodies," p. 229, and discussion below in chap. 5, p. 197 and n. 137.

36 These were Thorkill "the Tall" (*MS D*, ed. Cubbin, *s.a.* 1021, p. 63); Osgot or Osgod *Clapa* "the Staller" (Chronicle accounts vary, but see e.g. *MS C*, ed. O'Brien O'Keeffe, *s.a.* 1046, p. 109); Harold Godwineson (*MS C*, ed. O'Brien O'Keeffe, *s.a.* 1051, p. 112; *MS F*, ed. Baker, *s.a.* 1051, p. 124, for a fuller account); and Ælfgar Leofricson (*MS D*, ed. Cubbin, *s.a.* 1058, p. 76).

37 The contrast between the annalistic and hagiographic portrayal of Edmund has been noted by Smyth, *Scandinavian Kings*, p. 206, and many others. Chapter 5 returns to this topic.

38 *MS A*, ed. Bately, p. 47.

39 *ASC*, p. 70.

40 Ryan, "Anglo-Saxons," p. 260.

41 On the term "Common Stock," and on the dating of key interventions to the early 890s, followed by revisions of ca. the 920s and 950s, see Bredehoft, *Textual Histories*, p. 4 and p. 171, n. 2; Keynes, "Alfred," pp. 15, 34–5; S. Irvine, "Anglo-Saxon Chronicle," esp. pp. 344, 350–2, 362–6; Ryan, "Sources," pp. 271–6; Konshuh, "Constructing," p. 154.

42 Emphasis mine. Even from the ASC's terse wording Young plausibly infers that "Edmund, not the Danes, was the aggressor" (*Edmund*, p. 48), and quotes (p. 48) Asser's claim in the *Life of Alfred*, as trans. by Keynes and Lapidge, that Edmund had "fought fiercely against that army" (*Alfred*, p. 78). Damon argues that Æthelweard's claim, by portraying Edmund as a warrior-king who had lost in battle, would have validated West Saxon expansion into the Danelaw "as the righting of old wrongs" (*Soldier Saints*, pp. 173–4).

43 Plummer and Earle, eds., *Two of the Saxon Chronicles*, vol. 2, p. xxi, cited by Stodnick, "Sentence," p. 91. For relevant insights into the terseness (and sometimes blankness) of the *Annals of St. Gall* (*Annales Alamannici*), see White, *Content*, esp. p. 11, and discussion in Stodnick, "What (and Where)."

44 In saying this, I have been anticipated by Stodnick, "What (and Where)," pp. 99–104, though my sense of the order imagined by the annals differs from her claim that the "ordered and systematic whole" (p. 100) generated by the Chronicle is related to a process whereby the "annals begin to write a map of the landscape and produce a sense of relations between places that is visible and timeless" (p. 104).

45 It was probably not a royal vill, unlike Rendlesham, where according to Bede the East Saxon king Swithhelm had been baptized, evidently under East Anglian influence ("in uico regio qui dicitur Rendlaesham, id est mansio Rendili" ["in the royal village called Rendlesham, that is, the residence of Rendil"; *HE* III.22, pp. 284–5]).

46 Eco discusses the "open word" and "empty word" in the context of the rapport between authors and their audiences, and the "encyclopaedias" that the former require of the latter: *Lector*, p. 55. See too M. Irvine, "Medieval Textuality," p. 209.

47 S. Irvine, "Anglo-Saxon Chronicle," p. 350 and n. 28, citing studies by Bately, e.g. "Introduction" to *MS A*, pp. lxxiii–lxxxix.

48 Strohm, *Theory*, p. xv.

49 The distinction is stressed by Charles-Edwards, "Alliances," p. 56, n. 50.

50 With the first element of the compound in the genitive singular. On Thetford as "public ford," see Cameron, *English Place-Names*, p. 170. On the element *þeōd* "a nation, people," see Bosworth-Toller, s.v. *þeōd*, I.

51 On Scandinavian contributions to English towns in general, see Jesch, *Viking Diaspora*, p. 27. With regard to Thetford, see Dymond, *Norfolk*

Landscape, p. 90; Hadley, *Vikings*, 174–6 (expressing reservations); Haslam, "King Alfred," p. 125; Rogerson, "Vikings" (cited by Haslam, "King Alfred," p. 148, n. 15); Hart, *Danelaw*, pp. 47–53; Marten, "Shiring," pp. 3, 17–18; Poole (cited by Marten), "Skaldic Verse," p. 279 (and sources cited in his nn. 77–8). On the Danes' expansion of Ixworth in Suffolk, see M.F. Reed, "Sculpture," pp. 39–40.

52 Crawford, "Vikings," p. 61. See too Pratt, *Political Thought*, p. 93.

53 Nelson, "Presidential Address," p. 28. Hadley remarks that Insular ethnic identities "were mutable … especially liable to be transformed in the face of contact with new peoples, as social circumstances changed and the political tide turned" (*Vikings*, p. 9).

54 *MS C*, ed. O'Brien O'Keeffe, pp. 90–1; *ASC*, p. 136, n. 1, noting the presence of the statement in the "C" recension (the second of two Abingdon compilations) and the "D" (Worcester) manuscript.

55 F. Stenton, *Anglo-Saxon England*, pp. 380–2 and n. 1. Freeman, *History*, vol. 1, p. 433, surveys the Scandinavian sources mentioning Ulfcytel. See too Hart, *Danelaw*, pp. 52, 195, 525–6 and passim; Marten, "Shiring," pp. 14–18. See too PASE, s.v. "Ulfcytel 3."

56 Discenza, *Inhabited Spaces*, p. 100.

57 Hadley, *Vikings*, chap. 4 and esp. p. 182. See too Cam, *Liberties*, pp. 2, 10.

58 Whitelock, "Pre-Viking Age Church," p. 8, n. 5. As noted above in the Introduction, Whitelock's view is echoed by Yorke, *Kings*, p. 69.

59 Marten, "Shiring," p. 17, citing (n. 82) Poole, "Skaldic Verse," p. 279. Smyth also explains Thetford's suitability in *King Alfred*, pp. 28–9. For Marten's suggestion about Cnut's creation of Norfolk and Suffolk, see p. 17.

60 Strohm, *Theory*, p. xvi.

61 This analysis is partly indebted to White, *Content*, pp. 8–9, on the *Annals of St. Gall*. But see now Ashe, *Conquest*, pp. 46–52, on the crisis of historiography and epistemology evident in some of the Chronicle's entries ca. 1000.

62 Abbo, *LSE*, p. 72.

63 Relevant here is Wallace's succinct defence of diachronic literary analysis in the *Cambridge History*: "General Preface," pp. xxii–iii.

64 Stodnick, "Sentence," p. 94.

65 Stodnick, "Sentence," p. 105.

66 The word *here*, used by the ASC rather than *fyrd* or *folc*, is a further example of West Saxon distinctions between Scandinavian and English military forces, as shown by Abels, "Alfred," pp. 267–8.

67 Ashe, *Conquest*, p. 35, adduces Æthelweard's Latin chronicle as evidence for the vernacular annals' propagandistic nature. See too Ryan, "Sources," pp. 272–3; Smyth, *King Alfred*, pp. 71, 73, 89–98, 510, and especially 514–26; M. Irvine, "Medieval Textuality," p. 207 (on the "A" or Parker MS as "a monument to the Alfredian dynasty"); Sheppard's

Families; and Konshuh, "Constructing." For caveats, see Keynes, "Power," p. 180; Dumville, "Origins," p. 110; Stafford, "Making," p. 83.

68 Smyth, *King Alfred*, p. 29.

69 As stressed by N. Brooks, "Why…?"

70 On these terms, see Bassett, "In Search," pp. 17–18; J. Campbell, *Essays*, pp. 85–98, 132; Yorke, "Political and Ethnic Identity," pp. 73–6 (citing Campbell); Harris, "Overview," pp. 748–9. See also above, Introduction, n. 140, and chapter 3, n. 26.

71 *MS A*, ed. Bately, p. 41; *ASC*, p. 60, *s.a.* 823 for 825.

72 *MS A*, ed. Bately, p. 42; *ASC*, p. 60, *s.a.* 827 for 829.

73 S. Reynolds, *Kingdoms*, p. 259.

74 *MS A*, ed. Bately, p. 49; *ASC*, p. 74, *s.a.* 875 (874).

75 *MS A*, ed. Bately, p. 49; *ASC*, pp. 72, 74, *s.a.* 875 (874). On Guthrum as leader of the "Great Summer Army," see Smyth, *Scandinavian Kings*, p. 243. Abels argues that the involvement of Guthrum, Oscytel, and Anund in the summer 871 invasion of England "is sheer speculation" ("Alfred," p. 276). Smyth argues that the split between the two cohorts at Repton "would seem to derive from the distinct character of the two separate armies (which never again reunited) and from a definite plan of action arrived at by the leaders at Repton in 875" (*Scandinavian Kings*, p. 243). Elsewhere Smyth hypothesizes that the division of the army in two reflects a generation gap between older warriors keen to settle land in Northumbria and younger ones "who were still hopeful of yet further conquests in the south": *King Alfred*, p. 67.

76 Abels, "Alfred," p. 265. See too Raffield, "Bands," pp. 310–12, 324–6 (and passim), building upon Abels's remarks; and McLeod (*Beginning*, pp. 70, 101, 107, and passim), who argues for kin groupings within an otherwise heterogeneous Great Army.

77 Smyth, *Scandinavian Kings*, pp. 241–3.

78 Smyth, *King Alfred*, p. 66.

79 Sheppard, *Families*, pp. 38–9, adapting the spatial theory of Michel de Certeau.

80 White, *Content*, p. 9.

81 Stodnick, "What (and Where)," p. 96, regarding the annals for 892–96.

82 Sheppard, *Families*, p. 4; compare pp. 10–11. This view dovetails with N. Brooks's argument about the kingly emphasis of the Chronicle ("Why…?"), as well as with Harris's observation that, following the Scandinavian migrations of the late ninth century, "ethnic identity was not necessarily of interest *per se*: the various identities on offer were chiefly markers of legal obligation": "Overview," p. 750.

83 Sheppard, *Families*, pp. 39 and 40. Influenced by de Certeau, Lefebvre, and Bhabha, Sheppard's analysis is full of compelling insights such as the following: "In this picture of Alfred's kingdom [drawn by the entry

for 871], the West Saxons continue to lose physical territory, but retain the metaphorical moral high ground in their practice of lordship" (p. 42).

84 Sheppard, *Families*, p. 39. Also, "though some contemporary readers of the *Chronicle* would have known whether the towns and battlefields mentioned had any political or cultural significance, this knowledge is never brought to bear on the text by the annalist himself" (p. 39).

85 E.g. Stafford's observation that "political identities were manipulable," and their "raw material was loyalty and identification"; "[p]olitical geography," she concludes, "may have been shaped in the mind as well as on the ground and the battlefield": "Kings," p. 16. See also the discussion above (in the Introduction) as well as Oosthuizen, *Anglo-Saxon Fenland*, which discerns land use as a basis for folk-identities in the Fens.

86 Guthlac's cult was also associated with Repton in Derbyshire, as noted in chap. 3. For two different opinions about the viking impact on that royal estate, see Biddle and Kjølbye-Biddle, "Repton and the 'Great Heathen Army'" (compare Raffield, "Bands"); and Hadley, *Vikings*, pp. 12–15.

87 Haslam, "Development."

88 Smyth, *Scandinavian Kings*, p. 244. Compare R.H.C. Davis, "East Anglia," p. 31.

89 *MS A*, ed. Bately, p. 50; *ASC*, p. 74.

90 *MS A*, ed. Bately, p. 51; *ASC*, p. 76. See too PASE, s.vv. "Alfred 8" and "Guthrum 1." A helpful summary account is Keynes and Lapidge, *Alfred*, pp. 20–3. "'Civilizing' entailed not only the creation of stable political units, but the Christianization of the native populace, to provide a common cultural ground upon which to deal": Abels, *Alfred*, p. 167.

91 *MS A*, ed. Bately, p. 51; *ASC*, p. 77. Swanton's "Here" means "in this year."

92 The former is not incommensurate with the latter; see e.g. Lavelle, "Geographies," pp. 200–2 (acknowledging Sheppard's argument); S.T. Smith, *Land*, p. 153; Nelson, "Presidential Address," p. 27. H.C. Darby notes the "bond between the soil and the state": "Fenland Frontier," p. 188.

93 Keynes, "Alfred," p. 22.

94 In the wake of dispossession, some English persons may have been retained as administrators; Smyth, *Scandinavian Kings*, adduces the precedent in Northumbria and Mercia to argue that "[t]his Danish practice of carving up or 'sharing out' (*dividere*) an English kingdom into a Danish and an English region, with the latter ruled by a tributary English king, seems likely to have been Ívarr [the Boneless]'s original plan for East Anglia" (p. 207, citing R.H.C. Davis, "East Anglia," pp. 26–7). See too McLeod, *Beginning*, p. 214.

95 Stodnick, "Sentence," p. 104. See also above, n. 65, and below, n. 216.

96 In what follows, I am indebted to P.J.E. Kershaw, "Alfred-Guthrum Treaty," pp. 46–8; Blackburn, "London Mint," pp. 122–3 (cited by Kershaw); Pratt, *Political Thought*, pp. 105–6; Hadley, *Vikings*, pp. 30–3; Keynes and Lapidge, *Alfred*, p. 311; Keynes, "King Alfred and the Mercians," pp. 29–34; Keynes, "Alfred," p. 23; Haslam, "King Alfred"; Attenborough, *Laws*, pp. 96–7. On the treaty's codicological circumstances, see Gobbitt, "Manuscript Contexts."

97 Wormald, *Making*, I, p. 286, cited by P.J.E. Kershaw, "Alfred-Guthrum Treaty," p. 47.

98 P.J.E. Kershaw, "Alfred-Guthrum Treaty," p. 47, building upon Wormald. However much legislative or military confidence Alfred might have felt in the 880s, Dumville reminds us that in the first half of 878, as the Chronicle recounts, the West Saxon kingdom looked to have been all but lost: "Origins," pp. 111–12.

99 "From the material evidence incorporated in the manuscript page, version 2 [the fuller one] seems primarily to have served as a reference text to correct and otherwise expand and clarify the information incorporated in the more functional version 1": Gobbitt, "Manuscript Contexts," p. 51.

100 Haslam, "King Alfred," p. 125. Compare Lambert's aside that "the text's presentation of Alfred as acting on behalf of all the English ... is most naturally interpreted as ideological self-aggrandisement": "Frontier Law," p. 22, n. 6. See too Konshuh, "Constructing," pp. 159–60.

101 Haslam, "King Alfred," p. 127. Compare Olsson, "Peace Agreements," pp. 270–4 (noting Alfred's advantageous position but also pointing out concessions to Guthrum).

102 Attenborough, *Laws*, p. 98.

103 Keynes and Lapidge, *Alfred*, p. 171.

104 See S. Reynolds's formulation, above, p. 137 and n. 73.

105 Smyth, *King Alfred*, p. 92.

106 *MS A*, ed. Bately, pp. 1–2; *ASC*, pp. 2, 4.

107 *MS A*, ed. Bately, p. 51; *ASC*, p. 77.

108 Charles-Edwards, "Alliances," p. 47.

109 Raffield, "Bands."

110 I take Molyneaux's point (*Formation*, pp. 203–4, by way of reply to Foot and Wormald) that the term *Angelcynn* need not encode an aspiration to subjugate all the English peoples, given that in the OE translation of Bede's *Historia* the noun lacks the ideological sense of nation-building found in Alfred's works. Nevertheless, the fact that the *Old English Bede* employs the word neutrally would not have prevented Alfred from imbuing it with his own meaning and his own aspirations. See Keynes, "Edward," pp. 57–62.

111 Lapidge, Blair, Keynes, and Scragg, eds., *Wiley Blackwell Encyclopedia*, map 11, p. 571; Keynes, "King Alfred and the Mercians," fig. 1, p. 32; McLeod, *Beginning*, pp. 233, 241. Dumville (*Wessex*, pp. 1–27) thought the treaty's boundary had been misunderstood, that in reality it had given to Guthrum some lands west of the Lea and to Alfred certain territories to the east of it; but his argument has been challenged persuasively by Abels, *Alfred*, p. 163, n. 100; by Keynes, "King Alfred and the Mercians," p. 33; by Molyneaux, *Formation*, p. 22, n. 26; and especially by Haslam, "King Alfred," pp. 123–4.

112 See, e.g. Dumville, *Wessex*, p. 8. In the *Passio sancti Eadmundi*, Abbo refers to "orientalem ipsius insulae partem, quae usque hodie lingua Anglorum Eastengle uocatur" ("the eastern part of the same island, which to this day is called *Eastengle* in the language of the English"): *LSE*, ed. Winterbottom, p. 69. Translation mine.

113 *Angelcynn* too can refer to either the English people or the place of England: Stodnick, "What (and Where)," p. 104, n. 60; Karkov, *Imagining*, pp. 33–4 and sources cited therein. On the word as "a term of distinction from non-English-speaking peoples" even before the vikings' arrival, as well as its capacity to signify "a reality of anti-Danish lordship" afterwards, see Pratt, *Political Thought*, p. 107.

114 As noted by P.J.E. Kershaw, "Alfred-Guthrum Treaty," pp. 45–6.

115 Goetz, "Concepts," pp. 81–2. Whether frontiers were actually so cut and dried is another matter: see especially Curta's polemical "Introduction," and J.M.H. Smith, "*Fines*." Goetz's insights inform my own because they attend to perceptions conveyed in texts, as do those of Pohl, "Frontiers," and Berend, "Hungary," pp. 201–3 (though criticized by Curta, "Introduction," pp. 3–4, n. 9). See too Lambert, who argues that the AGT, the *Ordinance concerning the Dunsæte*, and the peace treaty *II Æthelred* "treat frontiers not as zones but as clearly demarcated lines" ("Frontier Law," p. 39). For the more abstract purpose of identity-formation (as opposed to legal formulation), however, "zones" and "clearly demarcated lines" need not be sharply distinguished from each other; see below and n. 133. I owe the references to Curta's, Pohl's, and Berend's studies to Brady, *Writing*, pp. 9–10. For cautionary remarks against a totalized "Carolingian" mindset, however, see Pratt, *Political Thought*, pp. 4–5.

116 McLeod, *Beginning*, pp. 209–13. McLeod is careful to concede that Alfred's court would have been familiar with treaties and boundary clauses from their own experiences.

117 Harris, "Alfredian *World History*," p. 508; compare Harris, *Race*, p. 104. For similar insights about the political acculturation of Guthrum's Danes, effected either by the treaty or by Guthrum's baptism, see P.J.E. Kershaw, "Alfred-Guthrum Treaty," pp. 45–6, 56, 58–9; Charles-Edwards,

"Alliances," p. 49; Abels, *Alfred*, p. 165; Hadley, *Vikings*, pp. 32–3 (concurring with Kershaw).

118 Hadley, *Vikings*, p. 33. Compare McLeod, *Beginning*, pp. 210, 241; Abels, "King Alfred's Peace-Making," pp. 30–2.

119 As Abels pointedly puts it, "Alfred had succeeded in bringing the Viking chieftains into the Anglo-Saxon political structure, but this made them no more safe or reliable than their Anglo-Saxon counterparts" ("King Alfred's Peace-Making," p. 34).

120 P.J.E. Kershaw, "Alfred-Guthrum Treaty," p. 57, and sources cited therein. This view is cited approvingly by Hadley (*Vikings*, p. 32 and n. 21). McLeod infers from the treaty's prologue that Guthrum "ruled by some form of consensus" (*Beginning*, pp. 210, 225).

121 "7 ealle we cwædon … þæt ne ðeowe ne freo ne moton in ðone *here* faran butan leafe" ("And we all agreed … that no slaves or freemen might go over to the *army* without permission"): Attenborough, *Laws*, p. 100; Keynes and Lapidge, *Alfred*, p. 172. Emphases mine.

122 Keynes, "Edward," p. 60.

123 Abrams, "Edward the Elder's Danelaw," p. 132; Abrams, "King Edgar," p. 172. Compare Molyneaux, *Formation*, p. 22 ("it is unlikely that the territory on its north-eastern side formed a coherent unit"). Doubts about the unity of the viking armies qua armies have been raised by the scholars cited above, p. 287 and n. 76.

124 R.H.C. Davis, "Alfred and Guthrum's Frontier," pp. 804–6; Hart, *Danelaw*, p. 7. Also commenting on the treaty's short life are Abrams, "Edward the Elder's Danelaw," p. 132 (citing both Davis and Dumville), and Lambert, "Frontier Law," p. 22.

125 Keynes and Lapidge, *Alfred*, p. 289, n. 29; p. 311, n. 1 (citing R.H.C. Davis and their own note on p. 289); see too Hadley, *Vikings*, pp. 34–5. When the Scandinavians changed the frontier is, for my purposes, less important than the West Saxons' belief that they had broken the peace after the treaty, as conceded by Dumville, *Wessex*, e.g. at pp. 8 and 10, and by Hart, *Danelaw*, p. 28, n. 5, on incursions from 885 to 920.

126 On the West Saxons' conquest of Kent, Surrey, Sussex, and Essex, see *MS A*, ed. Bately, *s.a.* 823, p. 41; *ASC*, *s.a.* 823 (825), p. 60; Hadley, *Vikings*, p. 34; Keynes, "Power," p. 186.

127 See *MS A*, ed. Bately, p. 52, *s.a.* 885; *ASC*, p. 78; *Chronicon Æthelweardi*, ed. and trans. A. Campbell, p. 44–5. Swanton, *ASC*, p. 78, n. 6, and D.M. Stenton, *Preparatory*, p. 112 (cited by Swanton) helpfully yoke together these sources to produce a coherent picture of events, one in which the raiders' incursion across the Thames explains Alfred's dispatching a fleet to East Anglia in his own violation of the AGT.

128 *MS A*, ed. Bately, p. 53; *ASC*, p. 80.

129 Rumford, "Introduction," p. 159, and pp. 163–6 on the limits of borderlessness.

130 Donnan and Wilson, *Borders*, p. 87.

131 Scheil, "Space," p. 198.

132 Treharne, "Borders," p. 20. If strategies of negotiation and compromise can be described as "central" to ninth-century Continental political ideologies, one can readily understand why for the Carolingians "shifting alliances of Christian with non-Christian were a normal part of frontier politics": J.M.H. Smith, "*Fines*," p. 176.

133 Others have had a similar hunch about Alfred's long-term plans; see Konshuh, "Constructing," pp. 160, 177, 179; Roffey and Lavelle, "West Saxons" (cited by Konshuh, p. 158, n. 16); and Wormald, *Making*, pp. 285–6 (cited in turn by Roffey and Lavelle, p. 27, n. 16). My own thinking draws on the language and/or thinking of Lambert, "Frontier Law," p. 39; Donnan and Wilson, *Borders*, p. 87; Treharne, "Borders," p. 20; and Rackham, *History*, p. 1 (see above, Introduction, n. 59). Also suggestive in this context are Karkov's remarks on Alfred's "Prose Preface" in *Imagining*, pp. 33, 56 (amplifying an insight by Davis, "National Writing," p. 621). My understanding of a "border area" or "transition zone" nevertheless differs from that of Lambert, who regards it as the space inhabited by "a cohesive frontier community straddling a border, united by a distinctive legal culture" ("Frontier Law," p. 39). Lambert persuasively claims that the AGT never envisaged such a space or such a "distinctive legal culture," though he does believe, as I do, that the text's seemingly sharp boundary served "to bolster the internal cohesion of each side" (p. 39). He also suggests, quite plausibly, that the treaty would have given rise to a geopolitical area with its own unique social and psychological realities, one where "the pressures of frontier politics" may, "[f]rom the perspective of the heartlands," have made inhabitants of that zone "appear unsettlingly anarchic and uncivilised" (p. 40).

134 P.J.E. Kershaw, "Alfred-Guthrum Treaty," p. 54; see too Lambert, "Frontier Law," pp. 22–3 (agreeing, in his n. 6, with Dumville, *Wessex*, p. 22), 28, 38.

135 In his book *Peaceful Kings* (pp. 243, 252–61), P.J.E. Kershaw demonstrates that Alfred, though seriously committed to peace-making, entertained a "vision of peace as the product of strong rule" (p. 260).

136 Frank, "Terminally Hip," p. 23.

137 Abels, "Reflections," p. 55; compare Abels, "Alfred," pp. 277–8. For Frankish *comparanda* see J.M.H. Smith, "*Fines*," pp. 171, 172, 175; Dunbabin, "West Francia," p. 378 (on Dudo of Saint-Quentin's account of Rollo of Normandy).

138 Charles-Edwards, "Alliances," pp. 55, 56.

139 On the communal imaginary of the Prologue, see Wormald, *Making*, p. 286, and P.J.E. Kershaw, "Alfred-Guthrum Treaty," p. 47, building upon Wormald. Smyth, *King Alfred*, p. 92, is trenchant on the point of the *witan*'s representation.

140 S. Reynolds, "Idea," p. 57.

141 Benham, "Law," p. 488. I am thankful to an anonymous reader for insisting that I bear in mind this aspect of medieval treaty-making.

142 "Many ... borders are imposed, top-down, upon a public who are not always aware of the immediate implications and significance of this form of societal compartmentalization": D. Newman, "Borders," p. 175.

143 Pratt, *Political Thought*, p. 7, as well as his pp. 130–4, discussing the distinctive authorizing features of Alfredian texts. Also, see now Ellard, *Anglo-Saxon(ist) Pasts*, pp. 192–208, on authorizing representations of sovereignty in Asser's *Life of King Alfred*; and Karkov, *Imagining*, pp. 27–52 (also citing Pratt), 59–62.

144 Asser, *Life of King Alfred*, ed. Stevenson, p. 73; *Life of King Alfred*, in Keynes and Lapidge, *Alfred*, p. 99. See too Howe, "Cultural Construction," pp. 15–17. In his *Life of King Alfred* (pp. 99–100), Asser makes much of Alfred's acquisition of Latin literacy in 887, but his references to the king's longstanding knowledge of English (pp. 75, 91) lead Keynes and Lapidge to surmise that Alfred had learnt to read texts in that language ca. 860: Keynes and Lapidge, *Alfred*, p. 239. On Asser's use of Latinity as a means of articulating cultural and ethnic difference in England despite indulging Alfred's wish to have himself styled *rex Angulsaxonum*, see Townsend, "Cultural Difference."

145 Godden, "Did King Alfred," p. 15 (and p. 18 for his conclusions).

146 See Alfred's "Prose Preface" to his translation of Gregory the Great's *Regula pastoralis*, in Keynes and Lapidge, *Alfred*, pp. 124–6. For an analysis of the expansionist, anti-viking aspirations and anxieties underlying Alfred's ostensibly cultural and educational concerns in that text, see now Karkov, *Imagining*, pp. 11, 14–19, 26–59. Especially relevant to this discussion is Discenza's astute observation about the political and linguistic authority that Alfred claims for himself in both his verse and prose prefaces to *Pastoral Care*: "His assertion of this authority also helps justify extratextual interventions, such as the acquisition of church lands during the Viking wars" ("Alfred's Verse Preface," p. 631, cited in Karkov, *Imagining*, p. 49 and n. 58). See also the studies cited above, n. 133.

147 Nelson and Bately, "Alfred," p. 28. P.J.E. Kershaw observes that both "reorganiz[ing] Wessex's defences" and "reviv[ing] Southumbrian learning ... served peace, or at least that was how Alfred, and some others, saw it" (*Peaceful Kings*, p. 253); Kershaw goes on to discuss a missive by

Fulk of Rheims to the West Saxon king as well as several texts associated with the latter and his court.

148 Alfred, *West-Saxon Version*, ed. Sweet, p. 5 (Oxford, Bodleian Library, MS Hatton 20); "Prose Preface," in Keynes and Lapidge, *Alfred*, p. 125. Hadley reminds us that Guthrum converted for practical reasons ("Cockles," pp. 125, 133–4) and that there may have been a "distinction between private conversion and public Christianization" (p. 130; see too M. Taylor, *Edmund*, p. 57). Abels raises a similar point in *Alfred*, p. 166, but emphasizes Guthrum's agency in representing himself as a Christian king.

149 As Lavelle plausibly surmises in *Alfred's Wars*, p. 328.

150 Chaplais, *English Diplomatic Practice*, p. 36.

151 M. Irvine, "Medieval Textuality," p. 185. Irvine differentiates (p. 184) between his concept of "textual communities" and the more famous formulation by Stock, but the latter's admission of oral recitation in *Listening* is just as pertinent here. See too Howe's engagement with Stock's work ("Cultural Construction," esp. pp. 11–18). "As the use of the written word backed by religious sanction was a major political element of the Christian world into which Guthrum was allowed in 878, it did not matter whether he could actually understand the words themselves, but it did matter that the written word was invoked": Lavelle, *Alfred's Wars*, p. 328.

152 See above, pp. 131 and 145 and nn. 24 and 116. Alfred himself knew something about political culture across the Channel, perhaps too the Carolingian principle that in theory and in most cases "rulers of peripheral kingdoms, pagan or Christian, were expected to defer to Carolingian superiority and recognise Frankish overlordship" (J.M.H. Smith, "*Fines*," p. 176).

153 K. Davis, "National Writing," p. 615. Furthermore, "the dominance of English square minuscule from the late ninth through the tenth century ... coincides with the military events contributing to unification under the West Saxon dynasty, with the beginning of the Benedictine Reform movement" and other cultural developments (p. 628).

154 S.T. Smith, "Marking Boundaries," p. 167; S.T. Smith, *Land*, p. 150, citing Alfred's recollection of bygone days in *King Alfred's West-Saxon Version*, ed. Sweet, I, 3. The translation is Smith's. Relevant here too is K. Davis's argument ("National Writing," pp. 620–1) that in the "Prose Preface" to *Pastoral Care* Alfred's insistence upon translation, and his refusal to name East Anglia, Mercia, and other regional kingdoms, obscure political heterogeneity within late ninth-century England. See too Karkov, *Imagining*, p. 35.

155 Although, as Keynes observes, a dating of the Treaty to ca. 878–80 "place[s] it some time before the Alfredian revival got under way," "Alfred's use of the written word depended on a *revival* of literacy in the late 880s" that included making use of "practices which were deep

rooted in Wessex, if largely unseen." Drawing upon these practices, even amidst the distractions of governance and warfare, was not "a king with a series of different identities: the soldier, the law-maker, the statesman, the educator, and the scholar," "not Alfred the Great, but the integrated Alfred, for whom all these things were inseparable aspects of his determination to discharge the responsibilities of his high office for the good of his subjects and in the service of God": "Power," pp. 192, 197 (emphasis in original).

156 Bosworth-Toller, s.v. *ēþel*, I.1. S.T. Smith, citing the *DOE*, glosses the word to mean "homeland" and "hereditary land or ancestral domain" (*Land*, p. 150). Note the temporal aspect of these translations.

157 "In the same way that boundaries are associated with the restriction of mobility, they are also structured by movement within territories which avoids them. It is as much the absence of movement across them, as the activity contained within them, which contributes to the association people have with a particular territory, and the recognition of boundaries as definitive liminal spaces between social groups": Symonds, "Territories," p. 28. On Alfred's fabrication of a shared English memory as a way of conjuring up England as a nation, see K. Davis, "National Writing," pp. 621–4, and the studies cited above in n. 4.

158 Foot, "Reading," p. 63.

159 Clanchy, *From Memory*, p. 6.

160 On the scope for West Saxon malfeasance, see Lavelle, *Alfred's Wars*, p. 96.

161 Lavelle, *Alfred's Wars*, p. 325, and source cited in his n. 51. Abels too emphasizes Alfred's superior position: "King Alfred's Peace-Making," p. 30, as does Konshuh, "Constructing," pp. 160, 177 (characterizing Guthrum as "a sub-king under Alfred"). That Alfred took for granted that the English nation (as he imagined it) should grow both spiritually and militarily, i.e. at other peoples' expense, is shown by K. Davis, "National Writing," pp. 623–5.

162 Boyarin, *Border Lines*, p. 15.

163 Lavezzo, *Angels*, p. 9. Her insights are more nuanced than my selective quoting reveals. For commensurate remarks, see A.D. Smith, *Chosen Peoples*, p. 137.

164 P.J.E. Kershaw, "Alfred-Guthrum Treaty," p. 59. Compare Wormald, "Anglo-Saxons"; Haslam, "King Alfred," p. 125; Lambert, "Frontier Law," p. 39 (who approvingly cites, in his n. 58, the chapter by Kershaw).

165 P.J.E. Kershaw, "Alfred-Guthrum Treaty," p. 56; yet Kershaw also suggests that Alfred "seems to have sought to understand [the Scandinavians in England] on their own terms" too (p. 56).

166 Molyneaux, *Formation*, pp. 45–6. But see Davis, "National Writing," p. 21, and now Karkov's remarks on Alfred's "Prose Preface" in *Imagining*,

pp. 33, 56 (agreeing with and building upon Davis), 67–8. Also important is Konshuh's argument that even those of the ASC's entries concerning the *adventus* and its aftermath plant the "seeds" of eventual Cerdicing incursions into Scandinavian East Anglia and Northumbria by "creat[ing] a unified English and Christian identity" ("Constructing," p. 179; compare her pp. 159–60 and 177).

167 Much the same point is made by Abrams, "Edward the Elder's Danelaw," p. 134. Furthermore, with regard to Carolingian relationships with pagan sub-kings, "[b]aptism and benefices, separately or together, completed the ritual expressions of overlordship" (J.M.H. Smith, "*Fines*," p. 183).

168 Dumville, "Origins," pp. 114–15. See also now Konshuh's persuasive argument that the ASC's construction of a coherent English identity, one based on West Saxon authority, would eventually bolster "the narrative of liberation and subsequent rule [of viking-held East Anglia] by Wessex" under Edward the Elder: "Constructing," p. 177.

169 *MS A*, ed. Bately, p. 54; *ASC*, p. 82.

170 Abels, *Alfred*, p. 152. Haslam explains the settlement of East Anglia as the sacrifice of Guthrum's Mercian gains: "King Alfred," p. 126.

171 Smyth, *King Alfred*, p. 97. "It has been pointed out that the language of Asser's account of Alfred's sponsorship of Guthrum, following that of the Chronicle, glorifies Guthrum and the Danes as well as Alfred, while simultaneously establishing a political hierarchy in which Alfred indisputably occupies the most powerful position": Karkov, *Ruler-Portraits*, p. 27, citing Charles-Edwards, "Alliances," and Dumville, *Wessex*, chap. 1.

172 Sellar and Yeatman, *1066 and All That*, p. 8.

173 As pointed out by commentators; e.g. Swanton, *ASC*, p. 82, n. 8; Keynes and Lapidge, *Alfred*, p. 282, n. 7.

174 Bosworth-Toller, s.v. *ge-sittan*, III.b.α, "to settle," "of permanent occupation, to settle, live in a country"; III.1, "to occupy, take possession of," "to possess territory."

175 Ingold, *Lines*, p. 101, on the active quality of wayfaring.

176 On the different compilers of the annals of the 870s and of the 880s, see Keynes and Lapidge, *Alfred*, p. 278.

177 Written long after the "Viking Age," the Latin *Annals of St. Neots*, produced at Bury St. Edmunds ca. 1100–50, admitted Guthrum into the local regnal culture by noting his burial at Hadleigh (Suffolk), referred to as a "uilla regia" (*Annals of St. Neots*, ed. Dumville and Lapidge, *s.a.* 890, p. 95), as if the viking with his "royal vill" had been another Wuffing.

178 Marten, "Shiring," esp. pp. 6, 10, 13–14. Guthrum's immediate successor may have been Eohric, who perished in battle against a Kentish contingent under the command of King Edward the Elder; see below, n. 212.

179 Smyth, *King Alfred*, p. 29. See too Blunt, "St. Edmund Memorial Coinage"; Blackburn and Pagan, "St. Edmund Coinage"; Grierson and Blackburn, *Medieval European Coinage*, vol. 1, pp. 319–20; Lyon, "Coinage," pp. 73–4; Damon, *Soldier Saints*, p. 172 (citing Ridyard, *Royal Saints*; Rollason, *Saints*, p. 157, n. 89; and Blunt's article as well, esp. pp. 242 and 252–3), and Blackburn, "Expansion," on the number of coins and the date range.
180 J. Campbell, "Placing."
181 Blackburn and Pagan, "St. Edmund Coinage," p. 2. Compare Abels, "King Alfred's Peace-Making," p. 32; McLeod, *Beginning*, p. 275 (citing a study by Lesley Abrams), and Young, *Edmund*, p. 73. Mostert associates the coinage with the Anglo-Scandinavian East Anglians' "need for a reconciliation between [their] recently accepted Christian attitudes and [their] own Scandinavian traditions" (*Political Theology*, p. 41).
182 Ridyard, *Royal Saints*, p. 216; Pinner quotes this passage in *Cult*, p. 6. For more on the Edmund coinage in its Anglo-Danish context, see Abrams, "Conversion," p. 147; Innes, "Danelaw Identities," p. 79; Blackburn, "Expansion," pp. 127, 134; Pestell, *Landscapes*, pp. 76–9; Abels, *Alfred*, pp. 166–7.
183 Chapman, "King Alfred," p. 43, also quoted by Pinner, *Cult*, p. 6. See too Smyth, *King Alfred*, pp. 29 30. Chapman's analysis seems, to me, more convincing when applied to the later hagiography of Edmund penned by Abbo and translated by Ælfric than when applied to the coinage. See Hines, "Origins," p. 42 (quoted below, chap. 5, p. 201).
184 G. Williams, "Coins," p. 22; emphasis mine.
185 Pinner, *Cult*, pp. 6, 9.
186 The "Æthelstan" coinage is thought to herald Guthrum's involvement in English political culture (Chapman, "King Alfred," p. 39; Harris, "Alfredian *World History*," p. 508; Harris, *Race*, p. 104; Abels, *Alfred*, p. 167). Blackburn instead sees only "a Christian or perhaps Anglo-Saxon approach to coin design" ("Expansion," p. 136). For Hadley, the coinage reflects Alfred's influence but also "local East Anglian demands" (*Vikings*, pp. 29–37, quotation at p. 34). Guthrum-Æthelstan's coins may indicate sincere Christian belief but more certainly shows strategic alignment of the royal persona with Romanized Canterbury.
187 McLeod, *Beginning*, p. 229.
188 See above, n. 73. Regarding the coinage, Abels reminds us that there is a connection between "integration … into an Anglo-Saxon Christian culture" and the fact that viking leaders in England "aspired to possess the power and authority of Anglo-Saxon rulers": *Alfred*, p. 167.
189 Blackburn and Pagan, "St. Edmund Coinage," p. 10. See too Blunt, "St. Edmund Memorial Coinage," pp. 239, 252–3 and studies cited

therein; and McLeod, *Beginning*, pp. 230–1 on Scandinavian East Anglia's dual economy, based on bullion and on coin.

190 Lyon, "Coinage," pp. 73–7.

191 My analysis has been partly anticipated by Young, who discerns the West Saxons' own appropriation of Edmund in the following: Edward the Elder's naming of one of his sons (on which, see also Damon, *Soldier Saints*, p. 174; and Moilanen, "Writing," p. 65 and citing in her n. 66 Klaniczay, *Holy Rulers*, p. 89); King Æthelstan's involvement in Edmund's cult (hinted at in Abbo's *Passio*); and Æthelstan's self-styling as *rex Anglorum*. According to Young, Edmund "was in danger, before 917, of becoming as much a Danish as an English saint, and a determined effort had to be made to recover him for the English" (*Edmund*, p. 77). Marten and Pestell, however, suggest (see below, p. 167 and n. 244) that Cerdicing domination of East Anglia was incomplete even in Edgar's reign (959–75). Moreover, this was no "English reconquest" (*pace* Young, *Edmund*, p. 77) but a new West Saxon conquest (see e.g. Wormald, "*Engla Lond*," p. 6; Dumville, "Origins," p. 115).

192 Scores of their ships reached Devon and Exeter; Chester was attacked later that year (*MS A*, ed. Bately, pp. 56, 58; *ASC*, pp. 86, 88). It should be noted that the entries for 893–96 continue the "Common Stock" of annals but are regarded as distinct from it (see Keynes and Lapidge, *Alfred*, p. 279).

193 *MS A*, ed. Bately, pp. 58–61; *ASC*, pp. 88–91.

194 *MS A*, ed. Bately, pp. 58, 59, *s.aa.* 894 and 896; *ASC*, pp. 88 and 89 (*s.aa.* 894 [893], 896 [895]).

195 *MS A*, ed. Bately, pp. 59–60 (*s.a.* 896); *ASC*, pp. 89–90 (*s.a.* 897 [896]).

196 *MS A*, ed. Bately, p. 61; *ASC*, p. 91.

197 Stodnick, "What (and Where)," p. 104.

198 Stafford, "Making," p. 85.

199 *MS A*, ed. Bately, p. 61; *ASC*, p. 91 (*s.a.* 901 [899]), though I have substituted "people" for Swanton's "race."

200 Sheppard, *Families*, p. 49. Sheppard sees a distinction between the concepts of *bretwalda* and "cyning ofer eall Ongelcyn" in her discussion of the 900 annal.

201 *MS A*, ed. Bately, p. 42; *ASC*, p. 60 (*s.a.* 827 for 829); see also *ASC*, p. 61, n. 10. On *anweald* in the context of the Chronicle, see S.T. Smith, *Land*, pp. 150–3, 158–66.

202 S.T. Smith, *Land*, p. 151.

203 S.T. Smith, *Land*, p. 151.

204 In what follows I depend on Lavelle, "Politics," esp. pp. 55–9; Lavelle, *Places*, pp. 30–31, 161–76, 288–98; Hart, "B Text," pp. 252–3; Hart, *Danelaw*, pp. 511–15; S.T. Smith, *Land*, pp. 158–60, 162–3; Dumville, "Ætheling,"

pp. 4, 22, 33; F. Stenton, *Anglo-Saxon England*, pp. 321–2; J. Campbell, "What Is Not Known." See also PASE, s.v. "Æthelwald 35." Dumville's and Stenton's studies are also cited by Smith, and I owe the reference to Campbell's study to Lavelle, "Politics," p. 54, n. 11.

205 Lavelle, "Politics," p. 59, and *Places*, p. 168.

206 Hart, *Danelaw*, p. 512.

207 *MS A*, ed. Bately, pp. 62–3.

208 *ASC*, pp. 92, 94, *s.a.* 905 (904). Swanton identifies the Wusan as the River Wissey but "possibly the Ouse": *ASC*, p. 94, citing a study by P.H. Reaney. Hart, *Danelaw*, acknowledges that Charles Plummer identified the Wusan as the Ouse but adds that "the River Nene was also called the *Wusan*" (pp. 513–14).

209 As expounded by Nelson, "Alfred's Carolingian Contemporaries," pp. 299–300.

210 *MS C*, ed. O'Brien O'Keeffe, *s.a.* 902, p. 75 ("æt þam Holme"); *ASC*, p. 93 ("at the Holm"). Hart places this Holme in Huntingdonshire: *Danelaw*, p. 515, cited by Lavelle, "Politics," p. 54, n. 11. Swanton's supposition "[p]resumably in Kent, but not certainly identified" (*ASC*, p. 93, n. 11) is less convincing, as an East Anglian location would have made it easier for the Danes to retain control of the battlefield despite losing more men than the West Saxons did.

211 Sawyer, *Age*, p. 150. Compare Innes, "Danelaw Identities," p. 81.

212 *MS A*, ed. Bately, p. 63; *ASC*, p. 94. On Eohric's identification as "[k]ing of East Anglia," see Swanton, *ASC*, p. 94, n. 4; PASE, s.v. "Eohric 1."

213 *DOE*, s.v. *ā-spanan*, 2, citing the "A" manuscript entry for 904. "'B' tells us that Æthelwold induced ('A' says 'seduced') the army in East Anglia to break the peace": Hart, *Danelaw*, p. 513. Compare "A's" verb *aspon*, "enticed," with "B's" *gelædde*, "led," "induced": *MS A*, ed. Bately, p. 62; *MS B*, ed. S. Taylor, p. 46. Bately characterizes the verb *gelædde* as "emotively neutral" ("Introduction," p. cxi), but the verb connotes leadership, not only incitement. See Stodnick, "Sentence," pp. 106–8.

214 Lavelle, "Politics," p. 79; see too Lavelle, *Places*, pp. 297–8.

215 J. Campbell, "What Is Not Known," p. 22.

216 Stodnick, "Sentence," p. 105; see above, nn. 65 and 95.

217 Stodnick, "Sentence," pp. 105, 107. Æthelwold's status as an English "insider" is discussed by Bredehoft, who argues that the 900 annal essentially uses the famous story of Cynewulf and Cyneheard *s.a.* 755 as a template: "the composition of post-Alfredian annals (as here) can extend the Common Stock's narrative precisely by interpreting more recent events in terms of the *Chronicle*'s own historical record" (*Textual Histories*, p. 62). For earlier, Carolingian parallels and contrasts to Æthelwold, see J.M.H. Smith, *"Fines,"* pp. 180–1.

218 *MS B*, ed. S. Taylor, p. 46. Translation mine. See discussion in Hart, "B Text," pp. 252–3; Hart, *Danelaw*, pp. 511–15. S.T. Smith similarly points out discrepancies between the two Chronicle accounts: *Land*, pp. 159–60.

219 Hart, "B Text," p. 253; see now Lavelle, *Places*, p. 292, on the St. Neots annalist's "notable acknowledgement of Æthelwold's position in eastern England"; "[t]his verdict on Æthelwold may have been inherently hostile, but it reflects the manner in which Æthelwold had moved on to an altogether larger political stage." For the appellations, see *Annals of St. Neots*, ed. Dumville and Lapidge, *s.aa.* 903 and 904, pp. 104–5. As Hart points out, Æthelwold was "king long enough for coins bearing his name to be struck at York" (*Danelaw*, p. 513, citing studies by C.E. Blunt).

220 F. Stenton, *Anglo-Saxon England*, p. 322, n. 2.

221 Hart, "B Text," pp. 252–3.

222 F. Stenton, *Anglo-Saxon England*, p. 322.

223 Lavelle, "Politics," p. 77. Emphasis in original. See too Lavelle, *Places*, p. 297, as well as his consideration of the possibility that "Vikings may not have helped his cause in retrospect in terms of legitimacy" (p. 291).

224 Lavelle, "Politics," pp. 78–80.

225 "Practically the whole of the Danelaw was … represented, and this shows the true measure of Æthelwold's rebellion, the threat of which has been underestimated by modern historians": Hart, *Danelaw*, p. 514. Compare Lavelle, "Politics," esp. pp. 53–4, 74–7; Lavelle, *Places*, pp. 297–8; J. Campbell, "What Is Not Known," pp. 21–3; and Yorke, "Edward," pp. 29–37.

226 *MS A*, ed. Bately, p. 64; *ASC*, p. 96, *s.a.* 913 (912). S.T. Smith (*Land*, pp. 158–66) discusses this annal in relation to other ASC entries in the period 912–20 that track Cerdicing expansion by reference to strongholds or "burhs" (OE *byrig*).

227 Sawyer 396 and 397; information and texts at the *Electronic Sawyer*. For references and discussion, see Abrams, "Edward the Elder's Danelaw," p. 136; Keynes, "Edward," p. 56. Again there are Carolingian precedents: J.M.H. Smith, "*Fines*," p. 186.

228 *MS A*, ed. Bately, p. 68, *s.a.* 917 as emended by Bately.

229 *ASC*, p. 103, *s.a.* 921 (920).

230 F. Stenton reconstructs the surrender's context in *Anglo-Saxon History*, pp. 327–9.

231 Marten, "Shiring," pp. 4–5.

232 Hadley, "Cockles," p. 121. Compare Abrams, "King Edgar," p. 174 and n. 14, citing revealing remarks by William of Malmesbury concerning widespread opposition to Edward the Elder.

233 F. Stenton, *Anglo-Saxon England*, p. 329.

234 On the general viking willingness to switch allegiance depending on circumstances, see Hadley, "Cockles," p. 120.

235 G. Thomas, "Anglo-Scandinavian Metalwork," pp. 242–52. McLeod discusses "hybrid" as well as "distinctly Scandinavian" artefacts (*Beginning*, pp. 66–9 and passim), as does J.F. Kershaw, *Viking Identities*, p. 213, cited approvingly by Richards and Haldenby, "Scale," p. 324.

236 Richards, "Identifying," esp. pp. 302–3, 306.

237 P.J.E. Kershaw, "Alfred-Guthrum Treaty," p. 53.

238 On the Edmund coinage, see above, and Abrams, "Conversion," p. 147; Innes, "Danelaw Identities," p. 79; Blackburn, "Expansion," pp. 127, 134; Chapman, "King Alfred"; Ridyard, *Royal Saints*, pp. 216–17; Pestell, *Landscapes*, pp. 76–9.

239 Townend, "Viking Age England," p. 90. See now his *Language*, esp. pp. 181–3 for conclusions.

240 Hadley, *Vikings*, p. 9. See too Richards, "Anglo-Scandinavian Identity," p. 48 (citing Hadley, *Vikings*, pp. 28–71); Frank's brilliant "Terminally Hip"; Halstad McGuire, "Sailing" (on ship-burials in the Orkneys and in Iceland); and Roffey and Lavelle, "West Saxons," p. 9 ("an early medieval perception of ethnicity could include both its attribution to a geographical area and … the activities undertaken by a group").

241 Marten, "Shiring," pp. 7–8. The charters are 507 and 703 in the *Electronic Sawyer*. The former's authenticity has been doubted, but Marten reports that Sarah Foot and Kathryn Lowe believe the charter to be genuine ("Shiring," p. 7, n. 30), while Hart maintains that at least the boundary clause is (*Danelaw*, p. 59).

242 Marten, "Shiring," p. 7.

243 Dumville, "Ætheling," p. 31.

244 Marten, "Shiring," pp. 9–10. See too Whitelock, "Wulfstan," p. 19; Pestell, *Landscapes*, pp. 149–51; Abrams, "Edward the Elder's Danelaw," pp. 136–9.

245 Keynes, "Edward," p. 61.

246 Keynes, "Edward," pp. 61, 62. On King Edgar's apparent recognition of a degree of Scandinavian regional autonomy in legal matters, see Abrams, "King Edgar," with special reference to the ASC's entry for 959 ("D" recension) and the laws known as IV Edgar. Also pertinent here are Stafford's insights in "Making," p. 85 (see above and n. 198).

247 Hadley, "Cockles," p. 121.

248 Abels, *Alfred*, p. 176.

249 See above, p. 146 and n. 127.

250 Stafford, *Unification*, p. 6.

251 Karkov, "Postcolonial," p. 153. See too Nelson, "Presidential Address"; R.I. Page, "Most Vile People"; Chapman, "King Alfred," pp. 40–1.

252 R.I. Page, "Most Vile People," pp. 8–9; Poole, "Anglo-Scandinavian Language," pp. 579–80, citing Hadley, *Vikings*, pp. 83–4. Also relevant in

this context are Hadley, "Cockles" and "Hamlet"; Stodnick, "Sentence," pp. 107–10; McLeod, *Beginning*.

253 R.I. Page, "Anglo-Saxon Aptitudes," p. 13.

254 Jesch, *Viking Diaspora*, p. 3.

Chapter 5

1 McKeehan, "St. Edmund"; Loomis, "Growth"; Whitelock, "Fact"; C. Clark, "Ælfric"; J.I. Miller, "Literature"; McDougall, "Serious Entertainments"; Gransden, "Legends"; Gransden, "Abbo of Fleury's *Passio*"; Mostert, "King Edmund" (which I have been unable to consult in its entirety); Ridyard, *Royal Saints*, pp. 61–73, 211–33; V.B. Jordan, "Monastic Hagiography," passim; Cownie, "Cult"; Cavill, "Analogy"; Cavill, "Fun"; Chapman, "King Alfred"; Frantzen, *Bloody Good*, pp. 53–72; Yarrow, *Saints*, pp. 24–62; the essays gathered in Bale, *Saint Edmund* (and review by Allen); Faulkner, "Like a Virgin"; Liddiard, "Introduction," pp. 8–10 (citing Yarrow); M. Taylor, *Edmund*; Licence, "Cult"; Pinner, *Cult*; Young, "St. Edmund" (on the saint's late-medieval to modern afterlife); Young, *Edmund*. See too T. Hall, "Handlist," p. 10 (for bibliography). I have been unable to consult Lesley Allen's 2008 Ph.D. dissertation (University of Illinois at Urbana-Champaign) "Inventing the Sacred Nation: Saint Edmund of East Anglia and English Identity in Medieval Text and Image."

2 See PASE, s.vv. "Edmund 6," "Abbo 1," "Ælfric 94." In this chapter, reference will be made parenthetically to Abbo's *Passio*, ed. Winterbottom, as "Abbo, *LSE*"; to Hervey's 1907 English translation as "Abbo, *Passion*"; to Ælfric's *St. Edmund, King and Martyr* (in *Lives*, ed. Needham, pp. 43–59) as "Ælfric, *SEKM*"; and to Swanton's translation (in *Anglo-Saxon Prose*, ed. and trans. Swanton, pp. 97–103) as "Ælfric, *PSE*." Occasionally, however, the need for more literal translation obliges me to provide my own rendering.

3 On Abbo's life and career, see Mostert, "Abbo" and *Political Theology*; Damon, *Soldier Saints*, pp. 167–9; Riché, *Abbon*; Dufour and Labory, eds., *Abbon*; Dachowski, *First*.

4 Studies of Ælfric include Skeat, "Preface"; Clemoes, "Chronology," "Ælfric"; Pope, "Introduction"; Hurt, *Ælfric*; Gneuss, *Ælfric*; Godden, "Ælfric," "Ælfric's Saints' Lives," "Introduction"; Clayton, "Ælfric"; Magennis and Swan, *Companion*; Gretsch, *Ælfric*; C.A. Jones, *Ælfric's Letter* and "Ælfric and the Limits"; Magennis, "Warrior Saints"; Wilcox, "Ælfric in Dorset"; Stanton, *Culture*, pp. 144–71; Damon, *Soldier Saints*, pp. 192–246, 264–74 and passim; Phelpstead, "King"; Faulkner, "Ælfric"; Halbrooks, "*Maccabees*"; Arthur, "Giving" (citing several of the above studies); Gulley, *Displacement*.

5 Wormald, "*Engla Lond*," p. 13, adding, however, that "Anglo-Saxon saints were more than focuses of local sentiment. They were a heritage all '*Angelcynn*' shared."

6 *Gesta Pontificum Anglorum*, II.74.20, ed. and trans. Winterbottom, pp. 242–3. I owe the reference to Bates, "Abbey," p. 5.

7 Pinner, *Cult*, p. 65. Pinner contrasts this feature of Abbo's narrative to the illustrations in New York, Pierpont Morgan Library, MS M.736, which contains the *LSE* and Herman's *Miracula* ("[i]nstead, the artist locates the events of Edmund's life and death in a national context"; p. 65). The aim of the present chapter is to show that the regional and national contexts are both distinct from each other and mutually reinforcing.

8 M. Taylor, *Edmund*, p. 29. A similar point is made by Pinner, *Cult*, p. 43. See below, pp. 189–90 and n. 102.

9 Abbo explains that the cruelty of the Danes should not be wondered at, "cum uenerint indurati frigore suae malitiae ab illo terrae uertice quo sedem suam posuit qui per elationem Altissimo similis esse concupiuit" (*LSE*, p. 71; "seeing that they came hardened with the stiff frost of their own wickedness from that roof of the world where he [i.e. Satan] had fixed his abode who in his mad ambition sought to make himself equal to the Most High": *Passion*, pp. 18–19).

10 Barrow, "Danish Ferocity," p. 84. Compare Young, *Edmund*, p. 3.

11 On the prevailing sense of crisis, see Ashe, *Conquest*, p. 13. On anti-monastic reaction after Edgar's death in 975, see C.A. Jones, "Ælfric and the Limits," p. 70; Hart, *Danelaw*, p. 594; Clayton, "Ælfric," pp. 67–8, 74; Pestell, *Landscapes*, pp. 103, 128; Lapidge, *Byrhtferth of Ramsey: Lives*, p. 122, n. 101; Rabin, "Holy Bodies"; and sources cited by these authors.

12 Burke, *Renaissance Sense*, pp. 1–20, is still valuable, but for more nuanced insights on historiographical self-consciousness (esp. concerning Richerus of Reims's *Historiarum libri quatuor* of the mid- to late 990s), see White, *Content*, pp. 17–22.

13 Lapidge, "Saintly Life," p. 269.

14 M. Taylor, *Edmund*, p. 25; compare Cavill, "Analogy" and "Armour-Bearer."

15 *MS A*, ed. Bately, p. 79; *ASC*, p. 126.

16 On the controversy, see Bately, "Introduction," pp. xiv, xxxiii. Ælfric himself had been schooled at Winchester before being transferred to Cerne Abbas.

17 Emphasis mine in each case.

18 Mitchell and Robinson (*Guide*, p. 97, §187, i[b]) show that, in this passage, the past participle *geanlæhte* is plural in number, agreeing with the compound predicative nominal "Hinguar and Hubba" rather than with the dative-singular noun in the phrase "[o]n þam flotan" (Ælfric, *SEKM*,

p. 45; "[i]n that fleet": Ælfric, *PSE*, p. 98). In this narrow context Ælfric is not even demonizing all Scandinavian fleets, let alone all Scandinavians. Earl, "Violence," offers additional reasons for Ælfric's reticence in this regard; see below, n. 50.

19 Edmund's supersession of Æthelberht was particularly dramatic. After the turn of the twelfth century, a church dedicated to the latter at Hoxne was rededicated to Edmund thanks to the machinations of Herbert de Losinga, bishop of Norwich (Scarfe, *Suffolk Landscape*, p. 155).

20 Which he would have considered "a hardship equivalent to exile," a "sacrifice": Dachowski, *First*, p. 64, and pp. 66–9 for the reasons. For the dates of Abbo's stay at Ramsey, see Lapidge, "Saintly Life," p. 254; Dachowski, *First*, p. 69. For the background to Abbo's stint there, see Riché, *Abbon*, pp. 30–5; Dachowski, *First*, pp. 57–64. Riché discusses the *Passio* on pp. 40–6. See too Lapidge, *Anglo-Saxon Library*, pp. 242–3. Licence cautions that "[i]t is far from certain that Abbo did write the *Passio* at Ramsey" ("Origins," p. 57, n. 60, citing Dumville, *English Caroline Script*, p. 36).

21 "Abbo ... inhabitans in eodem loco [i.e. Ramsey] atque doctrinam grammatice artis affluenter suos erudiens discipulos" ("Abbo ... living in that same place and instructing his disciples copiously in the art of grammar"): Byrhtferth of Ramsey, *Vita s. Oswaldi*, ed. and trans. Lapidge, III.18, pp. 91–2. On Abbo's teaching mission at Ramsey, see e.g. V.B. Jordan, "Monastic Hagiography," pp. 52–3; Dachowski, *First*, p. 72. Though commissioned by a specific monastic milieu, "[t]he *Passio* is an extravagant work, aiming at an international audience" (Stanton, *Culture*, p. 163).

22 On Abbo's historiography, interest in language, and conceptual accommodation between history and hagiography, see Sot, "Pratique," esp. pp. 205–6.

23 On the many MSS of Abbo's *Passio*, see Winterbottom, *Three Lives*, pp. 8–10.

24 For studies, see above, n. 1.

25 On Dunstan's role in the gestation of the *Passio*, see John, "Return," p. 206; Pinner, *Cult*, p. 38. Faulkner suggests that "Oswald, along with Dunstan, encouraged Abbo to write" because Oswald had spearheaded the founding of Ramsey Abbey: "Like a Virgin," p. 51.

26 *LSE*, p. 67; *Passion*, p. 9. The story's transmission has been discussed often. See e.g. McKeehan, "St. Edmund"; Loomis, "Growth"; Whitelock, "Fact"; Smyth, *Scandinavian Kings*, p. 205; Gransden, "Abbo of Fleury's '*Passio*"; Ridyard, *Royal Saints*, pp. 63–5; Damon, *Soldier Saints*, pp. 169–70; Pinner, *Cult*, pp. 35–8; Cavill, "Analogy," "Fun," and "Armour-Bearer."

27 Pinner, *Cult*, pp. 35–8, questions the faith in Abbo's story placed by Whitelock ("Fact," p. 221), Ridyard (*Royal Saints*, pp. 63–4, 67), and

Gransden ("Abbo of Fleury's *Passio*," p. 57). Earl admits the unlikeliness of the transmission but argues that it "accords with independent Viking traditions about the episode" ("Violence," p. 129). Cavill has done much to illuminate the account's derivativeness; see his "Analogy," "Fun," and "Armour-Bearer." V.B. Jordan, "Monastic Hagiography," pp. 46–51, considers Abbo's rhetorical strategies, as does Young, *Edmund*, pp. 51–8, accepting in Abbo's account a core of veracity but nevertheless identifying numerous incongruities.

28 Stodnick, "Emergent Englishness," pp. 501, 509.

29 Among the relevant studies cited above in the Introduction, special mention should be made of Howe, *Migration*, and Michelet, *Creation*. Among Abbo's many known sources was Bede's geography of Britain in *HE* I.1, as noted by Gransden, "Abbo of Fleury's '*Passio*,'" p. 31 (citing, in her n. 56, Whitelock, "Fact," p. 219), and by Winterbottom, *Passio*, p. 68, and his note to chap. 1, line 1. Lapidge's survey of the roughly one hundred books known to have been owned by Ramsey Abbey during Abbo's two-year stint there suggests that no version of the ASC is likely to have existed in its library (*Anglo-Saxon Library*, pp. 122–7, 242–3); but see Hart's "Anglo-Saxon Chronicle" and "B Text."

30 McKeehan, in her wide-ranging "St. Edmund," p. 15. V.B. Jordan identifies the historical background as a rhetorical exordium and discusses its purposes in the *LSE*, e.g. its contextualization of Edmund and its evocation of biblical parallels to early England: "Monastic Hagiography," pp. 58–9.

31 Resemblances between those chronologically far-flung invasions have not been lost on modern scholars. Commenting on Continental Saxon "pirates, who had taken advantage of the collapse of the Saxon shore defences to plunder both sides of the Channel and the Atlantic coast of Gaul," Wood observes that "[i]n a sense, despite the vast development of maritime technology between 450 and 800, this was a first Viking age" (*Merovingian North Sea*, p. 5).

32 As Curtius famously explains it, *translatio imperii* "implies that the transference of dominion from one empire to another is the result of the sinful misuse of that dominion" (*European Literature*, p. 29, tracing the notion back to Ecclesiasticus 10:8 [p. 27]). The twelfth-century illustrator of the Pierpont Morgan Library manuscript of Abbo's *Passio* and Herman's *Miracula* exploited such parallels: Pinner, *Cult*, pp. 65–7. Keynes shows that Wulfstan earlier had done likewise ("Abbot," pp. 207–8) and that Ælfric had blamed the invasions of the 990s and afterwards on his fellow English rather than on the Scandinavian invaders themselves ("Abbot," p. 170). Ælfric's thinking on the subject evolved over time, however, as shown by Godden, "Apocalypse," pp. 131–42.

33 Howe, *Migration*, p. 6; compare pp. 63–5, 70–1. See too Wormald, "*Engla Lond*," p. 14 (on Bede's ideological use of the phrase); Harris, *Race*, pp. 60–72 (on the relationship between the *adventus* and Bede's concept of a *gens Anglorum*).

34 On Bede's interest in the biblical Israelites as offering models for interpreting early English history, see e.g. Harris, "Anglo-Saxons," p. 37; Foot, "Bede's Kings," p. 39; Zacher, *Rewriting*, pp. 26–8 and 103–4 (as cited by Foot); Dumville, "Origins," p. 74. See also Wormald, inter alia his "*Engla Lond*," as well as the summary and response in Molyneaux, "*Old English Bede*," p. 1289. Molyneaux does not wholly refute Wormald's argument but challenges its comprehensiveness: "Old English Bede," p. 1302, and "Did the English."

35 Rowley, *Old English Version*, pp. 51–3, 75–6. Elsewhere, Rowley points out that "[t]he main translator … never compares the recent (or perhaps ongoing) Scandinavian invasions with the Germanic ones, and refrains from interpreting the invasions as punishment" (*Old English Version*, p. 92). Similarly, *The Battle of Maldon* rejects the notion that the vikings embodied divine wrath directed at English unworthiness, as Trilling shows in *Aesthetics*, pp. 129–33, 159–74.

36 Molyneaux, "*Old English Bede*."

37 Howe, *Migration*, pp. 51, 53, 58–9, 69; Wormald, "*Engla Lond*," p. 14; Michelet, *Creation*, pp. 247–51, 257–8.

38 *MS A*, ed. Bately, pp. 70–2; *ASC*, pp. 106, 108–10. See too Neidorf, "*Beowulf*," p. 850. I thank an anonymous reader for suggesting the appropriateness of *Brunanburh* in this context.

39 Tugène, *L'idée*, pp. 94–6 on the pagan associations of regnal lists. Wormald, however, plausibly claims that those genealogies satisfied a persistent "need for a heroic past … even in educated, and thus presumably clerical, circles" ("Bede, *Beowulf*," p. 57).

40 The rendering is mine, but I have also consulted Hervey's translation, which for stylistic elegance is much to be preferred.

41 On this point, see the Introduction. Young, *Edmund*, p. 19, emphasizes the isolation of Norfolk and Suffolk from their neighbours though not their topographical distinctness from them.

42 Whitelock ("Fact," pp. 224, 225) notes that the story of Edmund's Bures coronation appears in "Florence [i.e. John] of Worcester" and the *Annals of St. Neots*. For the passage in Geoffrey of Wells on Bures as "uilla corone antiquitus regie certus limes exassye et sudfulchie sita super staram fluuium cursu rapidissimum" ("of old a town belonging to the Crown, and … the boundary mark between Essex and Suffolk, being situated on the Stour, a river which … flows with extreme rapidity"), see *De infantia*, ed. and trans. Hervey, pp. 154–5. See also John of Worcester, *Chronicle*, ed.

Darlington and McGurk, trans. Bray and McGurk, vol. 2, p. 630; *Annals of St. Neots*, ed. Dumville and Lapidge, *s.a.* 856, p. 51.

43 On this concept in vernacular OE texts, see Fell, "Perceptions," pp. 181–3; S.T. Smith, *Land*, pp. 8–15; P.J.E. Kershaw, *Peaceful Kings*, p. 256.

44 Here used to mean simply "district," "region," or "province," rather than "kingdom" in Bedan usage. See above, Introduction, for discussion of political terminology.

45 Pinner astutely points out that "Abbo's assertion that the eastern province is vulnerable on account of its western land border with the rest of the island is … disingenuous, as it is its wateriness which proves its undoing in this instance. Water was therefore both a means of defence and East Anglia's greatest vulnerability" ("Thinking Wetly," p. 5).

46 J. Campbell, "First Christian Kings," p. 67, caption to illustration 67. Campbell continues: "It may well be Dark Age, and is about 5 miles long, 40 yards across and 30 feet from ditch bottom to bank top." See too Christopher Taylor, *Cambridgeshire Landscape*, pp. 48–9 and passim; M. Taylor, *Edmund*, pp. 80–1; Oosthuizen, *Anglo-Saxon Fenland*, pp. 73, 122. For Winterbottom, the *aggere* is "probably the Devil's Dyke": *LSE*, p. 69, n. to 2.9.

47 Hart, *Danelaw*, p. 26. On the same page Hart suggests that the various dykes may have been recycled, perhaps dug in the Iron Age, "refurbished by the East Anglians," and subsequently used by the Danish East Anglians against Edward the Elder. On reuse of dykes generally, see Higham, "Britain In and Out," pp. 52–4. See too Hoggett's remarks on the "fluctuating western boundary to the [East Anglian] kingdom" as indicated by a "series of Anglo-Saxon linear earthworks … the most famous of which is the Devil's Dyke": *Archaeology*, p. 2, citing, inter alios (in n. 11), Pestell, *Landscapes*, pp. 11–12.

48 Lavelle, *Alfred's Wars*, p. 45, and sources cited therein.

49 Earl, "Violence," p. 127.

50 Earl, in "Violence," argues that *SEKM* refrains from demonizing the Danes in part because of "the dogmatic non-violence of Ælfric's monastic ideology" and because of "the deep historical relationship between the Anglo-Saxons and the Danes: the enemy was too uncannily familiar to be reduced to the merely Other, but mirror-like instead he seemed to expose the Anglo-Saxons' own moral weaknesses" (p. 143). T.R.W. Jordan observes that Ælfric, by showing restraint in characterizing the Scandinavian invaders, "diminish[es] Edmund as an extreme example of otherworldly holiness" and instead "leaves the emphasis on him as the good king to his people – something Æthelred had not been" ("Holiness," p. 11). As discussed later in the present chapter, however, Ælfric does invite a violent response towards the Jews, who become new "scapegoats"

(Frantzen, *Bloody Good*, p. 63) as well as a distraction from the problem of East Anglian particularism.

51 Tuan, *Space*, p. 157, on the territorial sensibilities of Indigenous peoples in the United States and in Australia.

52 Bryson, *Notes*, p. 157.

53 *MS A*, ed. Bately, p. 62; *ASC*, pp. 92, 94 (*s.a.* 905 [904]). See also the discussion of this annal above in chap. 4.

54 There is a possible play on words here, since the fourth-declension nominative plural noun *sinūs* can mean "hollows," "bays," or "bosoms." Also, although I use "marsh" as a near-synonym for "fen" simply to avoid repeating the latter word unduly, the two forms of wetland differ from each other: see Rackham, *History*, pp. 376–9.

55 Gransden, "Abbo of Fleury's '*Passio*,'" pp. 24 and 31. See also the discussion of the practical usefulness of Fenland resources in Pinner, "Thinking Wetly," analysing not only the *LSE* but also Felix's *VSG*, Hugh Candidus's *Peterborough Chronicle* (see below, n. 60), the *Liber Eliensis* (*LE*), and other sources.

56 For a rich and chronologically ambitious study of this tradition as it was deployed and problematized by English writers, see C.A.M. Clarke, *Literary Landscapes*, esp. pp. 7–66.

57 Discenza, *Inhabited Spaces*, p. 30.

58 "I carry in my head many … true and perfect pictures of marshes, both inland and by the sea; and yet I cannot reproduce them here, for I feel that in print all their charm and colour would be lost in the same way": Tennyson, *Suffolk Scene*, pp. 220, 221.

59 Tennyson, *Suffolk Scene*, p. 221. Compare Turner, *Rivers*: "Marshes and flat lands have some subtle charm which it is not easy to put into words" (p. 3); and Whiteman, *East Anglia*, pp. 10–11.

60 For twelfth-century descriptions of the Fens from the perspectives of Peterborough and Ely, see, respectively, *Chronicle of Hugh Candidus*, ed. Mellows, p. 6 (and *Peterborough Chronicle of Hugh Candidus*, trans. Mellows and Mellows, p. 3); *De Gestis Herwardi*, chap. 21, ed. Meneghetti, p. 128 (and *Deeds of Hereward*, trans. Swanton, p. 68).

61 C.A.M. Clarke, *Literary Landscapes*, p. 41; compare p. 61. See too Downey et al.'s arguments on lexomic grounds for the dating of *Guthlac A* to the period of the tenth-century Reform ("Books Tell Us").

62 For good summaries of the Reform, especially as background to a discussion of the works of Ælfric and Wulfstan, see Hurt, *Ælfric*, pp. 15–22; Gatch, *Preaching*, pp. 8–11. See too Cubitt, "Review Article"; Barrow, "Ideology"; C.A. Jones, "Ælfric and the Limits"; and the following note.

63 The similarities include "a uniform observance of the Benedictine *Rule* in all English monasteries; the professed cultivation of royal over local

aristocratic patronage; a harsh polemic against secular clerks and their expulsion from some cathedral chapters and minsters; the 'restoration' of a monastic episcopacy as witnessed by Bede in the 'golden age' of the Anglo-Saxon church; and, fuelled by that nostalgia, a pride in the 'native' element in Anglo-Saxon monasticism relative to continental trends of revival and liturgical embellishment" (C.A. Jones, *Ælfric's Letter*, pp. 42–3, citing [in n. 103] Wormald, "Æthelwold," and Gransden, "Traditionalism"). Compare Faulkner, "Like a Virgin," p. 51. Summarizing and building on the work of Gransden, Wormald, and Jones, Klein observes that "the reforms were characterized by a rather complicated sense of nostalgia, a desire to return to two different pasts: a faraway Anglo-Saxon golden age, with its firmly entrenched monastic episcopacy; and the more immediate past of Edgar's reign, in which monasteries flourished, Danish invasions were minimal, and the monastic orders were able to depend on wholesale support from the royal family": *Ruling Women*, p. 175.

64 C.A. Jones, *Ælfric's Letter*, p. 42. The heterogeneity of the reforms is masterfully illuminated in Jones's chapter "Ælfric and the Limits." See too Rabin, "Holy Bodies," pp. 224–5 (citing Jones inter alios); and R. Stephenson, *Politics*, pp. 31–6 (on Ælfric and Byrhtferth of Ramsey).

65 See e.g. Pinner, *Cult*, pp. 40–1.

66 Mostert, *Political Theology*, p. 157. Mostert illuminates the creative tension – between traditional Christian theological influences on one hand and tenth-century political considerations on the other – that informs Abbo's portrayal of Edmund, and shows how the former outweigh the latter. Damon builds upon Mostert in his own full analysis of Abbo's portrayal of Edmund's holy kingship: *Soldier Saints*, esp. pp. 176–91.

67 Mostert, *Political Theology*, p. 153, citing (in n. 89) Wolpers, *Die englische Heiligenlegende*, p. 145. Abbo's highly idealized political philosophy required a strong king to limit episcopal power and thus benefit monasteries: Dachowski, *First*, pp. 138–9 (quoting and building upon Mostert, *Political Theology*, p. 155). Dachowski distinguishes between English and Frankish reform movements on pp. 70–1, where she identifies "strong royal power and a generation of monastic bishops" as key English traits.

68 See too Pinner, *Cult*, p. 42, citing (n. 48) Gransden, "Abbo of Fleury's *Passio*," pp. 48–50. Abbo promoted Capetian imperial pretensions even amidst general tenth-century decline in royal economic and political clout; see Dunbabin, "West Francia," pp. 394–7.

69 Ridyard, *Royal Saints*, pp. 76–8. Her discussion of Edmund in particular (pp. 211–35) traces that king's achievement of sanctity and the posthumous recognition of it as such. M. Taylor, however, sees in Edmund's hagiography a confluence of pagan ideas about kingly sacrality and Christian notions of royal sanctity: *Edmund*, esp. pp. 29–30.

70 Mostert, *Political Theology*, p. 157.
71 This continuity is discerned by Head, *Hagiography*, p. 241.
72 *LSE*, p. 86; *Passion*, p. 54.
73 Gransden, "Abbo of Fleury's '*Passio*,'" p. 24.
74 Aimo of Fleury recalls Abbo's complaint in *De vita et martyrio sancti Abbonis*, chap. 11; for the reference and commentary see Wormald, "Æthelwold," p. 23. Dachowski suspects that normal middle-age weight gain, rather than English cookery per se, may have been the culprit: *First*, p. 69.
75 "Intrans denique in illam et cernens sollicitis optutibus ipsam esse congruam monachis ad habitaculum, mirabiliter est letus effectus. Videbat ibi pratum, siluam, stagna aquarum, piscium multa genera, auium multitudinem" ("As he entered and saw with careful inspection that it was suitable for housing monks, he was wondrously overjoyed. He saw there a meadow, woodlands, fish pools, many kinds of fish, and a multitude of birds"): *Vita s. Oswaldi*, 3.16, ed. and trans. Lapidge, pp. 88–9. On Ramsey's early history, see Lapidge, "Introduction" to Byrhtferth's *Lives*, pp. xvi–xxix; for the topography, see too his note 161 to the *Vita*, 3.16, pp. 88–9, as well as Byrhtferth's own chorography of the site, which blends etymologizing with first-hand knowledge of the environs (3.19, pp. 92–5). C.A.M. Clarke, *Literary Landscapes*, chap. 3, discusses Ramsey as a *locus amoenus*; see too C.A. Jones, "Ælfric and the Limits," p. 100 and notes 118 and 119.
76 Pestell, *Landscapes*, p. 110. On Æthelwine "Dei Amicus" and his father, ealdorman Æthelstan "Half-King," see Hart, *Danelaw*, pp. 569–604; Wareham, *Lords*, pp. 13–28 (citing Hart, among others).
77 Lapidge, "Introduction," p. xxv.
78 On this date, see Lapidge, "Introduction," p. xviii. Young, *Edmund*, p. 83, places the foundation in 969. For background on the abbey and its role in the larger social landscape of tenth-century England, see Wareham, *Lords*, pp. 14–28 and passim; F. Stenton, *Anglo-Saxon England*, pp. 450–1.
79 Lapidge, *Anglo-Saxon Library*, p. 122.
80 *Vita s. Oswaldi*, ed. and trans. Lapidge, III.19, pp. 90–3, and Lapidge's comments in notes 176–80. See too C.A.M. Clarke, "Panegyric," which inter alia plumbs the depths of Abbo's "deliberate intellectual puzzle or game" (p. 295), situates the poem within the *locus amoenus* tradition, and shows how the text connects Ramsey Abbey in its Fenland setting to the constellation Hercules, the demigod who slew the Hydra.
81 Pestell, *Landscapes*, p. 118, and pp. 100–18 for the argument leading to this conclusion. In plumping for "the fundamentally East Anglian nature of Bury St. Edmunds and the improbability that Ramsey was involved in its Benedictinisation" (p. 116), Pestell challenges the Ramsey thesis advocated by Gransden, "Legends," p. 101, and by Dumville, *English Caroline*

Script, p. 36 (and also by Hart, *Danelaw*, pp. 471–2). Licence, "Origins," advances his own sustained argument for St. Benet's role in colonizing Bury.

82 Pestell, *Landscapes*, p. 149. Pestell goes on to aver that "Benedictinism was readily associated with West Saxon political influence" (p. 149). Pestell's discussion on pp. 150–1 importantly associates the late tenth- and early eleventh-century Reform with efforts to found houses in East Anglia and the Fens in "isolated locations" that were also "close to old administrative and power centres" (p. 151).

83 Marten, "Shiring," esp. pp. 6, 10, 13–14; see too Pestell, *Landscapes*, pp. 127–31.

84 Young, *Edmund*, p. 83.

85 Pestell, *Landscapes*, p. 110, building upon Gransden, "Legends," pp. 100–1.

86 As the ealdorman Æthelwine, founder of Ramsey, was towards the community at Ely: see *LE*, II, ed. Blake, p. 126 (trans. Fairweather, p. 152), as discussed in J. Paxton, "Lords," p. 234. On rivalry between Bury and Ely in and after the eleventh century, see Pinner, "Thinking Wetly," pp. 14–15 and 19–20, furthering the argument in her *Cult*, pp. 141–4.

87 I have not been able to trace this phrase back to an actual OE source, but for discussion of the thinking behind it see M. Taylor, *Edmund*, pp. 93, 95.

88 Wareham, *Lords*, pp. xvii (map 1) and 16. See too Hadley, *Vikings*, p. 65.

89 Young, *Edmund*, p. 83.

90 Pinner, *Cult*, p. 38.

91 Pestell, *Landscapes*, p. 110, and fig. 24 on p. 111.

92 Pestell, *Landscapes*, p. 103; compare p. 107.

93 Gransden, "Legends," p. 4.

94 My translation. Hervey translates as "[d]escended from a line of kings" (Abbo, *Passion*, p. 15).

95 On Abbo's knowledge of Bede, see n. 29 above.

96 Mostert, *Political Theology*, p. 160.

97 Mostert, *Political Theology*, p. 155, citing a study by Walter Ullmann. On differences between English and Byzantine ideas of *imperium*, see Charles-Edwards, "Alliances," pp. 61–2.

98 As discussed by Mostert, *Political Theology*, pp. 152–3; see *LSE*, p. 76; *Passion*, p. 29.

99 As noted by Winterbottom in *Three Lives*, p. 75, note to *Passio*, 8.26–7. For Horace's ode and the translation, see *Odes and Epodes*, ed. and trans. Rudd, pp. 144–5. On Abbo's use of Horace's *Odes*, see Mostert, *Political Theology*, p. 66, n. 5; Thornbury, *Becoming*, pp. 78–81.

100 For quotation and discussion of Wulfstan's *Vita sancti Æthelwoldi*, see Blanton, *Signs*, pp. 69–71, and in toto her second chapter on Ely's fortunes during the heyday of the Benedictine Reform movement in the last three decades of the tenth century (pp. 65–129).

101 Ashe, *Conquest*, p. 32, preceded by analysis of, among other texts, Abbo's *LSE* and Ælfric's *SEKM*, which she claims urge royal self-sacrifice as the only basis of kingly sanctification (pp. 28–9; but see Sklar, "Constructing," pp. 137–40, for a different reading of *SEKM*'s advice on kingship). Other acknowledgements of the problems caused by Edmund's renunciation are Earl, "Violence," pp. 132–47; Matthews, "Token," pp. 68 and 73; Phelpstead, "King," pp. 36–7; and Damon, *Soldier Saints*, pp. 216–18 (both cited by Matthews). Ælfric nevertheless urged kings to defend their countries ably: Clayton, "Ælfric," pp. 80–8 (citing e.g. Godden, "Apocalypse," pp. 131–2, and C.A. Jones, *Ælfric's Letter*, p. 49).

102 See above, p. 172 and n. 8. Damon neatly sums up the active-passive Edmund represented by Abbo and Ælfric: "Resistance to the Vikings is just, but the saint follows God's chosen path for him, the route of non-violent resistance" (*Soldier Saints*, p. 216 and n. 72 on hagiographic pacifism).

103 Young, *Edmund*, p. 84. Although Young speculates that the *LSE* encourages identification of Edmund with West Saxon interests, e.g. by referring to Edmund as a descendent of Continental Saxons (as opposed to Angles), he also suggests that the acclamation of Edmund by "the people" of his own realm is such that "the *Passion* plays the role of a political assertion of East Anglian rights and privileges within the larger England of the tenth century" (p. 84).

104 See above, pp. 184–5, nn. 82 and 83 (arguments by Pestell and Marten), and chap. 4, p. 167, n. 241, on the two charters.

105 Matthews, "Token," p. 72, referring to Ælfric's *SEKM* but in terms applicable to Abbo's *LSE* as well. Compare Godden, who in a parenthesis notes that, with East Anglia's defences wiped out anyway by the Scandinavian invaders of 869, "we are perhaps invited to suppose that Edmund's sacrifice more effectively defends his people by diverting the Viking assault upon himself": "Ælfric's Saints' Lives," p. 303. See too Frantzen, *Bloody Good*, pp. 58–64. Damon also sees Abbo's reworking of Edmund's royal role as a transformation of defeat into triumph: *Soldier Saints*, p. 172.

106 Noticing this emphasis, a later medieval interpolator of London, British Library, MS. Cotton Tiberius B.ii, fol. 9r, has inserted *fide et* ("for faith and") above and between the words *pro* and *patria* of Edmund's assertion "honestum michi esset pro patria mori" (see above, p. 188), as Winterbottom remarks in his edition of the *Passio* (p. 92, note to chap. 8, line 27; see p. 9 on the interpolator).

107 Klaniczay traces this linguistic opposition back to Isidore of Seville and subsequent Carolingian thought: *Holy Rulers*, p. 92 and sources cited in his n. 95.

108 Scholars debate whether Edmund's self-sacrifice for his kingdom reflects Christian values, residual pagan notions, or a combination thereof; see

M. Taylor, *Edmund*, pp. 30–8 (and passim); F.S. Paxton, "*Abbas*," p. 209; Phelpstead, "King," p. 34, n. 30 (and source cited therein).

109 S.E. West identified the site as Hellesdon Wood (or Ley), belonging to Bradfield St. Clare near Bury St. Edmunds: "New Site ...?," cited by Ridyard, *Royal Saints*, pp. 218–19 and n. 34, and by Pestell, *Landscapes*, p. 80. For an objection, see K. Briggs, "Was *Hægelisdun* ...?," cited by Burgess, "Hidden East Anglia." Young, *Edmund*, pp. 15, 61–6, persuasively reaffirms Hellesdon Wood and adds new evidence to West's.

110 See Introduction, p. 23, and nn. 108 and 109. For Matthews, the wolf's "protective posture toward Edmund, the sacrificial lamb, could be seen as a counterbalance to the ineffectiveness and insufficiency of the bishop as 'shepherd'": "Token," p. 78. Earl argues that the wolf symbolizes the taming and rehabilitation of the vikings (usually likened to wolves) by suggesting a parallel to the domesticated and baptized Guthrum ("Violence," pp. 139–41). T.R.W. Jordan contrasts Abbo's and Ælfric's uses of the wolf motif in "Holiness," pp. 11–12, 18–19.

111 See Gransden, "Baldwin," pp. 72, 73; but note her second thoughts in Gransden, "Abbo of Fleury's '*Passio*,'" p. 41. See too Licence, "Introduction," p. xviii.

112 Abbo does not say which early East Anglian king had made the future Bury St. Edmunds a *villa regia*. An interlineal note in the earliest manuscript of the *Liber Eliensis* identifies *Betricheswyrde* (modern Bury) as the monastery that Sigeberht founded in the 630s: see Whitelock, "Pre-Viking Age Church," p. 4, n. 4, citing *LE*, ed. Blake, p. 11; see too Hoggett, *Archaeology*, p. 32, n. 76 (citing Whitelock, the *Liber*, and a study of his own, but questioning the reliability of the interlineal note); M. Taylor, *Edmund*, p. 66; Young, *Edmund*, pp. 33–4, 66, 79.

113 According to Cavill, "[i]t is more likely that Ælfric wished to diminish the significance of locality, and point out that the saints were not bound by time and place, but were omnipresent and powerful in the fight against the evil that was encroaching in his time in the form of new Viking attacks" ("Analogy," p. 43).

114 *Battle of Maldon*, ed. van Kirk Dobbie, pp. 7–16; trans. Crossley-Holland, *Anglo-Saxon World*, pp. 11–19.

115 *LE*, ed. Blake, p. 136; *LE*, trans. Fairweather, pp. 162–3.

116 For an especially rich reading of the poem's historical, ethnic, and typological implications for an early eleventh-century understanding of the English (not East Anglian) people, see Harris, *Race*, pp. 157–85.

117 In his study of Ælfric's *SEKM*, Earl analyses the reuniting of Edmund's head and body in terms of the idea of the king as *Christus domini* ("the anointed of the Lord") who is returned to his people.

118 *LE*, ed. Blake, p. 136; *LE*, trans. Fairweather, pp. 163. The bracketed insertion is by Fairweather, who also points out that the phrase "inter alios"

refers to "the other six benefactors commemorated in the source-text" (p. 163, n. 305).

119 *HE* IV.19, trans. J.E. King. See above, chap. 2, p. 83 and n. 66, for discussion of this substitution of King's translation for that of Colgrave and Mynors.

120 It is pertinent that the *LE* honours Byrthnoth as a champion of late tenth-century reformed monasteries against their detractors (II.62); see *LE*, ed. Blake, p. 134; trans. Fairweather, p. 160; and discussion in Faulkner, "Like a Virgin," p. 51.

121 Wilson, *Anglo-Saxon Paganism*, pp. 92–5, 98. Wilson is cautious about attributing ritual significance to all cases of early English beheading. He also cites decapitated bodies whose missing heads were replaced at burial with stones, a shield boss, and urns.

122 On the issue of Abbo's attribution of virginity to Edmund, see Ridyard, *Royal Saints*, p. 226; Phelpstead, "King," p. 43 (citing Ridyard); Faulkner, "Like a Virgin," p. 47; Frantzen, *Bloody Good*, pp. 56–61.

123 S.T. Smith, "Marking Boundaries," p. 167, citing Alfred's evocation of bygone days.

124 Sot, "Pratique," p. 212 (translation mine); see too Mostert, *Political Theology*, p. 41, cited and tentatively endorsed by Moilanen, "Writing," p. 65.

125 "La virginité n'est pas l'apanage de l'ordre monastique, ni une condition nécessaire pour y accéder, mais elle y acquiert son expression ecclésiale éminente par son alliance avec la contemplation": Gantier, "L'ecclésiologie," p. 301. Compare Mostert, *Political Theology*, p. 44 (adducing *LSE* chap. 17, lines 9–11, p. 87), p. 99 (analysing Abbo's exhortation to virginity and its relationship to his understanding of relics of the saints, and inferring from *LSE* chap. 17 that Abbo was "[a]dmonishing" the caretakers of Edmund's shrine), and p. 169 ("[i]t is as if the virtues of clerics and laymen, whether kings or simple subjects, could be derived from those of the monks, the group which occupied the highest rank in Abbo's social and moral thought").

126 Gransden, "Abbo of Fleury's '*Passio*,'" pp. 41–2. Pinner argues persuasively that Dunstan would have wanted to revive Bury's fortunes after the viking attacks, though she refrains from endorsing Dumville's theory that Abbo wrote the *LSE* in honour of Bury's supposed refoundation as a Benedictine house in the 980s (*English Caroline Script*, pp. 77–8), and she rejects outright Gransden's hypothesis that Dunstan intended the *LSE* to bolster Bury's prestige as a prospective second episcopal see in East Anglia ("Abbo of Fleury's '*Passio*,'" pp. 41–5). See Pinner, *Cult*, p. 38. I agree with Pinner that Dunstan could have envisaged strengthening the Bury community without necessarily having brought about its regularization himself, let alone having turned it into a bishopric.

127 Studies of Ælfric's teaching priorities (whether for clergy or for laypeople) include Clemoes, "Chronology," pp. 42, 52–3, 57–8 and passim; Gatch, *Preaching*, esp. pp. 47–56, 72–101; Grundy, *Books*; Blanton, *Signs*, pp. 104–22; Upchurch, "Big Dog"; Matthews, "Token," esp. p. 41, 82–8; T.R.W. Jordan, "Holiness"; R. Stephenson, *Politics*, pp. 138–87, 191–4. A conspectus of Ælfric's ideals appears at the end of his *Life of St. Swithun*, ed. Needham, pp. 60–81, at p. 80; see discussion in C.A. Jones, *Ælfric's Letter*, p. 47 and nn. 117 and 118.

128 John, "Return," p. 206.

129 On the mixed nature of Ælfric's audience, see esp. Clayton, "Homiliaries," pp. 175–89; Stanton, *Culture*, p. 162 (citing Clayton); Godden, "Ælfric's Saints' Lives," pp. 299–301; Godden, "Introduction," pp. xxii–xxvii; Cubitt, "Ælfric's Lay Patrons"; Gneuss, "*Ælfric*," pp. 27–9; Phelpstead, "King," p. 29; T. R.W. Jordan, "Holiness," pp. 8–9; Moilanen, "Writing," p. 60. Æthelweard's translation has been edited by A. Campbell as *Chronicon Æthelweardi*.

130 Foot, "Historiography," p. 132. Compare A.D. Smith, *Ethnic Origins*, p. 109; Dumville, "Origins," passim.

131 Croce, "Regionalismo." A.D. Smith sees Italian regionalism as "a grave impediment to national cohesion, if not national consciousness" (*Ethnic Origins*, p. 73).

132 Lavezzo, *Angels*, p. 8.

133 "There may be no spectacular lines of mountains, rushing torrents and high waterfalls ... [But] what need is there then for high hills, when the clouds can create mountains higher and grander than the Himalayas?" (Whiteman and Talbot, *East Anglia*, pp. 10–11).

134 Treharne, "Authority," p. 565.

135 J. Hill, "Ælfric," p. 41.

136 In what follows I incur debts to C.A. Jones, *Ælfric's Letter*, pp. 43–9; Rabin, "Holy Bodies," pp. 224–9; and Klein, *Ruling Women*, p. 173 and p. 252, n. 30 (citing Jones). Concerning Ælfric's departure from Æthelwold in embracing stylistic clarity, see Lapidge, "Æthelwold," pp. 107–8.

137 Rabin, "Holy Bodies," p. 229. On Æthelred's move against the religious houses following Æthelwold's death as a way of placating the anti-monastic nobles, see Yorke, "Æthelwold," pp. 85–6, and Rabin, "Holy Bodies," p. 230, both of whom cite Keynes's *Diplomas*, p. 177.

138 C.A. Jones, *Ælfric's Letter*, p. 47. Jones goes on to discuss (p. 47 and nn. 117 and 118) the aforementioned ending of Ælfric's *Life of St. Swithun* (see above, n. 127) and the *De oratione Moysi*, lines 147–55. See too Rabin, "Holy Bodies," pp. 230–1, and Sklar's discussion of the *SEKM* and contemporary entries in the ASC in the context of what she calls the "terminal trickle-down incompetence" afflicting England at this time ("Constructing," p. 131).

139 C.A. Jones, *Ælfric's Letter*, pp. 43–9, cited in Klein, *Ruling Women*, p. 173 and p. 252, n. 30. Skeat's judgment that Ælfric was "one born to be a teacher" and "a true patriot" ("Preface," p. liii) was informed by his awareness that Ælfric was displeased by Æthelred's failings.

140 Klein, *Ruling Women*, pp. 152–5. As Clayton has argued, even after Æthelred had changed his ways and, beginning ca. 993, selected counsellors who were sympathetic to the Benedictine Reform, monks had reason to distrust him, and Ælfric was especially if tacitly censorious: "Ælfric," pp. 69, 71–3, 80–8.

141 Cubitt, "Ælfric's Lay Patrons," p. 167. With regard to Æthelweard's Latin version of the Chronicle, Cubitt writes that "[h]is preface to this text makes clear his own investment in his royal kinship and in the history of his own people: King and country were central to Æthelweard's identity" (p. 167). Ælfric's defence of unitary kingship appears in the *Preface* to his *Lives of Saints*, where he justifies departing from his Latin sources by pointing out that "gens nostra uni regi subditur, et usitata est de uno rege non de duobus loqui" ("our nation is subject to one king and is accustomed to speak of one king, not of two"): *Ælfric's Lives of Saints*, ed. and trans. Skeat, vol. 1, pp. 3–4; *Ælfric's Prefaces*, ed. and trans. Wilcox, p. 131, both quoted in K. Davis, "Boredom," p. 327 and n. 21.

142 Gretsch, *Ælfric*, p. 57. See too Cubitt, "Ælfric's Lay Patrons," p. 179; C.A. Jones, "Ælfric and the Limits," pp. 74–5.

143 Gretsch, *Ælfric*, p. 96, and pp. 99–100 on Ælfric's special interest in Cuthbert. On Bede's championing of the seventh-century Oswald as the ideal English saint-king, see Foot, "Bede's Kings," pp. 28, 32, 44–5.

144 Young, *Edmund*, p. 85.

145 Magennis, *Cambridge Introduction*, pp. 127–8. With regard to Ælfric's possible doubts about Edmund's universality as discussed by Magennis, Pope held that the *Sermo de memoria sanctorum* was intended "to stand at the head of his set of saints' lives and serve as a general introduction to them" precisely because "[i]n this piece the saints are placed within a universal framework" (Pope, "Ælfric," p. 205).

146 "Sicque factum est, consentiente rege, ut partim Dunstani consilio et actione, partim Æthelwoldi sedula cooperatione, monasteria ubique in gente Anglorum, quaedam monachis, quaedam sanctimonialibus, constituerentur sub abbatibus et abbatissis regulariter uiuentibus" ("And so it came about, with the king's agreement, that thanks both to Dunstan's counsel and activity and to Æthelwold's unremitting aid, monasteries were established everywhere in England, some for monks, some for nuns, governed by abbots and abbesses who lived according to the Rule"): Wulfstan of Winchester, *Life of St. Æthelwold*, ed. and trans. Lapidge and Winterbottom, pp. 42–3.

147 Ælfric's *Lives of Saints* predates Abbo's murder in 1004, so at the time the English translator started working he could not have known Abbo's fate. On Ælfric's use (though in a different context) of "correspondences of sound – for instance, the repetition of the same root in different word-forms … [to] bring out the relationship between ideas that are complementary," see Clemoes, "Ælfric," p. 177.

148 On the widespread promulgation of Ælfric's *Catholic Homilies*, for example, see Wilcox, "Ælfric in Dorset," p. 62, quoted with measured support by Lockett, *Anglo-Saxon Psychologies*, p. 419. On the "cultural recuperation" by which Ælfric reaffirms the Englishness of Edmund and of his own translation of Abbo, see Sklar, "Constructing," esp. pp. 133–5.

149 For both quotations, see *Chronicon Æthelweardi*, ed. and trans. A. Campbell, p. 36.

150 Phelpstead, "King," p. 37; Sheppard, *Families*, p. 100. Æthelweard was, as Godden elucidates, "a man of considerable piety and a staunch supporter of monasticism, but also an ealdorman responsible for the defence of the south-west against the Vikings" ("Ælfric's Saints' Lives," p. 303).

151 Rollason, *Northumbria*, p. 201, noting Bede's reference to Oswald as *rex Christianissimus*.

152 Gretsch, *Ælfric*, p. 96.

153 Hines, "Origins," p. 42.

154 Ridyard, *Royal Saints*, p. 226. Pestell notices that Edmund's lack of offspring was convenient for Anglo-Scandinavian as well as West Saxon rulers: *Landscapes*, p. 78.

155 E.g. by McKeehan, "St. Edmund," p. 28; Whitelock, "Fact," p. 219; Weiss, "East Anglia," p. 104; Pinner, *Cult*, pp. 39–40, 66–7; Young, *Edmund*, p. 42.

156 Young, *Edmund*, pp. 42 and 84, citing (p. 162, n. 82) Newton, *Origins*, p. 140, who in turn builds upon Hervey, *Corolla*, p. xxxvi. The passage in question in Abbo identifies Edmund as "ex antiquorum Saxonum nobili prosapia oriundus" (*LSE*, p. 70) or "sprung from the noble stock of the Old Saxons" (*Passion*, p. 15). Young notes additional signs of West Saxon appropriation of the slain king's cult in *Edmund*, pp. 15–16, 89–92.

157 On Ælfric's changes to his source, see McKeehan, "St. Edmund," p. 22; Whitelock, "Fact," p. 222; Bethurum, "Form" (general observations, though not on the *Edmund*); C. Clark, "Ælfric"; Pope, "Introduction," p. 150 (general observations on the *Catholic Homilies* and *Lives of Saints*; see also Pope, "Ælfric," e.g. pp. 187, 204–5); Hurt, *Ælfric*, pp. 80–2, 131–5; Benskin, "Literary Structure," pp. 9–10 (with "structural synopsis" on p. 9), 21–4; Godden, "Ælfric's Saints' Lives," pp. 288–9, 293; Earl, "Violence"; Stanton, *Culture*, pp. 163–6; Cavill, "Analogy" and "Armour-Bearer"; Frantzen, *Bloody Good*, pp. 61–3; Damon, *Soldier Saints*, p. 218; Gretsch, *Ælfric*, p. 226; Magennis, "Warrior Saints," p. 44; Phelpstead, "King";

Matthews, "Token," pp. 66–75; Arthur, "Giving" (citing Magennis's article on p. 331, n. 27, and Gretsch's book on p. 330, n. 18); T. R.W. Jordan, "Holiness"; Moilanen, "Writing," pp. 68–9, 73–81, 89–94, 104–6.

158 See above, p. 194.

159 Fox, *Watching*, pp. 363–4, where Fox says that this trait "is not the result of careful thought," because "[t]his kind of indirectness just comes naturally to us" (p. 364).

160 Magennis, *Cambridge Introduction*, p. 127.

161 Cubitt, "Universal and Local Saints," p. 450. Along similar lines, Cubitt elsewhere observes that "[t]he new Benedictine houses … were intrusions and included great monasteries such as Abingdon, Ely and Ramsey, established by figures like St. Æthelwold and St. Oswald in alliance with the king and great aristocrats: they advertised their monopoly on sacrality by promoting the new ethos of religious virginity which must have cut across the old ties of family and locality, and by appropriating the relics of local saints": "Ælfric's Lay Patrons," p. 185, citing *LE*, II, ed. Blake, pp. 40 and 53.

162 The East Anglian influence on Ælfric's translation of the *Passio* may have gone beyond these named saints. According to Faulkner, Ælfric chose to write a Life of Edmund in the first place because St. Edwold, a presumed brother of Edmund's, was patron saint of Cerne Abbey (Dorset), Ælfric's home from roughly 987 to 1005 and a house founded by his patron Æthelmær (Faulkner, "Ælfric"). On Ælfric's tenure at Cerne, see e.g. Hurt, *Ælfric*, pp. 31–7; Godden, "Introduction," p. xxi, xxix–xxxi; Upchurch, "Big Dog," p. 522, n. 78; R. Stephenson, *Politics*, pp. 136–7 (citing, in her n. 6, C.A. Jones, *Ælfric's Letter*, p. 7, n. 23); Keynes, "Abbot," p. 160.

163 There may have been a seventh-century precedent for this. Young speaks of incorrupt saints as a "trend in the East Anglian royal family" begun by Æthelburh (d. 664), "a (possibly illegitimate) daughter of Sigeberht's cousin and successor, Anna" (*Edmund*, p. 36). On Æthelburh and the "trend," Young cites Ridyard, *Royal Saints*, pp. 60–1.

164 "Abbo of Fleury, writing for [the Capetian kings] Hugh and Robert, exploited classical and Carolingian sources to exalt what he took to be an unchanged and unchanging monarchy"; "[t]he equation of kingship with empire proved popular among west Frankish churchmen; Abbo of Fleury defended it enthusiastically": Dunbabin, "West Francia," pp. 396 and 396–7, citing Mostert, *Political Theology*, pp. 137–8 and 131, respectively. My remarks that follow are indebted to Dunbabin's incorporation of Mostert's insights.

165 Gretsch, *Ælfric*, pp. 225–31. On Bishop Æthelwold of Winchester's cultivation of Ely within a wide program of English ecclesiastical reform, see Gretsch, *Ælfric*, pp. 195–205; Blanton, *Signs*, pp. 65–129; Otter, "Temptation,"

p. 142 (citing e.g. Ridyard, *Royal Saints*, pp. 181–5); all cited by Stodnick, "Emergent Englishness," pp. 508–9. If the Old English version of Edgar's confirmation of Ely's privileges (*Electronic Sawyer* 779, Latin text dated 970) is really Ælfric's and was composed ca. 1006, as Pope argued, it offers further evidence of the Grammarian's commitment to the universalizing scope of the Benedictine Reform and may be read as "a piece of propaganda, not only for the monks of Ely but for the monasteries in general" (Pope, "Ælfric," p. 112, and endorsing on p. 111 Angus McIntosh's dating of the translation). For Moilanen, Ælfric's emphasis on "[r]eligious assimilation was important not because it implied a connection between the king and his heavenly counterpart, but because it implied the similarity – but not identicalness – of all saints and the universal authority of God": "Writing," p. 106.

166 Pinner, *Cult*, p. 118.

167 J. Campbell, *Anglo-Saxon State*, pp. 41–2. For similar views on the national deployment of local saints' lives in England, see Ridyard, *Royal Saints*; Rollason, *Saints*, esp. pp. 155–7, concerning Edmund as both a local and a West Saxon saint; Stodnick, "Emergent Englishness."

168 Earl, "Violence," explores the connections latent in Ælfric's *SEKM* between late tenth-century monastic reform and the viking invasions. On the difference in impact between the Scandinavian raids of the 980s and those beginning in the following decade, Keynes has pointed out that "[f]rom 991 to 1005, the English suffered the worst and most sustained viking onslaught in over a hundred years" ("Abbot," p. 153).

169 Stafford, "Church," p. 11. I take her point about the inaccuracy of the terms "reform" and "revival" in this context (pp. 11–12). Consonant with her remarks on Ælfric's influence is Wilcox's claim that "[t]he voice of pastoral care in late Anglo-Saxon England is, to a very great extent, the voice of one single writer: Ælfric": "Ælfric in Dorset," p. 52.

170 Godden, "Ælfric's Saints' Lives," pp. 288–90. (Godden's study is cited in Matthews, "Token," p. 94, and Keynes, "Abbot," p. 162, n. 55.) See too Grundy, *Books*, pp. 271–2.

171 Phelpstead, "King," p. 38; see too Frantzen, *Bloody Good*, pp. 62–3, and Sklar's remarks on the Jews of *SEKM* as "a conveniently pre-demonized population" ("Constructing," p. 136). Phelpstead also ably explores (pp. 39–44) the tensions in Ælfric's characterization of Edmund's idiosyncratic approach to kingship. In addition to the Grammarian's hostility towards the Jews, "[t]he common theme running through all the legends [i.e. the *Lives of Saints*] is clear, the triumph of ascetic Christianity over paganism" (Bethurum, "Form," p. 533).

172 On *Guthlac A*'s place in tenth-century monastic reform in England, see C.A. Jones, "Envisioning"; Downey et al., "Books Tell Us." My supposition is commensurate with Brady's argument in "Colonial Desire."

173 On the absence or near-absence of Jews in pre-Conquest England, see Scheil, "Anti-Judaism," p. 65; Harris, "Anglo-Saxons," p. 28; Younge, "New Heathens," p. 124 and studies cited in his n. 5. On the question whether a native British population remained in the Fenland in Felix's time, see above, chap. 3.

174 van Court, "*Siege*." The critical approach she identifies "elides the very real issue of Jewish presence in Christendom that continues to concern the Christian community even in the absence of Jews" (p. 166).

175 Scheil, "Anti-Judaism," p. 73. Scheil's formulation may suggest a legitimate response to van Court's cogent criticism, cited in the previous note. In dialogue with Scheil's work, Younge observes that "[i]n contrast to the immediacy of [viking] paganism in pre-Conquest society, the Anglo-Saxon idea of the Jew was remote and theoretical, mediated entirely through textual traditions," specifically through "the Bible, Late Antique historical works, and patristic commentaries": Younge, "New Heathens," pp. 128, 124, citing Scheil's *Footsteps*. See too the reference to Williams Boyarin's *Miracles* in the following note.

176 Williams Boyarin, *Miracles*, p. 49. See too Lavezzo's theorization of what she terms the "sepulchral Jew" as constructed by Bede and Cynewulf: *Accommodated Jew*, pp. 27–63. Ælfric's exploitation of the Jews is also related to his tendency in the *Catholic Homilies* to dichotomize race by contrasting the whiteness of Anglian slave-boys to the blackness of the devil: see Lavezzo, *Angels*, pp. 38–44 (but also Magennis, "Geography"). For a comparative survey of early English treatments of whiteness, see Harris, *Race*, p. 53.

177 As identified by Needham in Ælfric, *SEKM*, p. 59, note to line 223; and by Swanton in Ælfric, *PSE*, p. 102, n. 5.

178 "The sterility of Jewish sacred places (whatever those might be in Ælfric's imagination) is a strong contrast to the overflowing divine presence at the tombs of Swithun and Edmund, and thus bolsters the English claims by deflecting any doubts onto the Jews": Scheil, "Anti-Judaism," p. 71.

179 Earl points out the more general problem that "[t]he Vikings were too much a part of Anglo-Saxon culture to be conveniently demonized, since the earlier invasion had resulted in a large Danish immigration" ("Violence," pp. 141–2). See too the sources cited above in n. 171.

180 Rowley, *Old English Version*, p. 69.

181 Scheil, *Footsteps*, p. 20, and pp. 295–330 for penetrating readings of Ælfric's *De populo Israhel* and *Maccabees*.

182 Loyn, *Vikings*, p. 43.

183 For examples of this assimilation, see above, chap. 4, p. 166.

184 As recorded in the "C" manuscript of the ASC, *s.a.* 980–1. See *MS C*, ed. O'Brien O'Keeffe, p. 84; *ASC*, p. 124.

185 Earl, "Violence," pp. 141–2. Abbo's anti-Danish sentiment may amount to a mere exercise in rhetoric for his students' benefit, but Abbo must have known that St. Oswald, one of the greatest of the tenth-century reformers as well as the founder of Ramsey, had himself been of Danish extraction; see Wareham, "St. Oswald's Family."

186 Marten, "Shiring"; see too Molyneaux, "Why Were Some …?" Marten's essay is cited by Molyneaux, and Molyneaux's article in turn is referenced in Baker and Brookes, *Beyond the Burghal Hidage*, pp. 22–3. "England, in a political sense, would be the creation of Alfred's grandsons and great-grandsons": Ryan, "Anglo-Saxons," p. 262.

187 Discenza, *Inhabited Spaces*, p. 135, commenting on the *Catholic Homilies*; elsewhere, Discenza observes that even "Alfredian texts, even while they make Anglo-Saxon England a place of importance, deny the importance of place. As *Angelcynn* claims its place in the tradition of learning, the texts present places that signify symbolically" (p. 126).

Conclusion

1 Young, *Edmund*, p. 18.

2 On this adaptability, see Pinner, *Cult* (e.g. pp. 6 and 9), and the studies by Ridyard, Mostert, Cownie, Bale, Licence, Yarrow, and M. Taylor cited in chap. 5 above, n. 1. Kingsnorth, *Real England*, pp. 89–96, recounts a recent appropriation of St. Edmund by citizens of Bury opposed to the homogenizing effects of corporate capitalism.

3 Morris, *Time's Anvil*, p. 187, citing (in n. 27) Hoskins, *Local History*, p. 30, where Hoskins resists "the treatment of local history as only national history writ small."

4 "Imaginative sympathy is so dangerous precisely because it prevents us from seeing the extent to which we have created the past in our own image. And yet without imaginative sympathy, our capacity for discovering anything new in the past is foreclosed": Thornbury, *Becoming*, pp. 2–3.

5 Tuan, *Space*, pp. 99–100.

6 *LSE*, p. 69; *Passion*, p. 13. See above, Introduction, p. 16.

7 Tuan, *Space*, p. 157, also cited above in chap. 5, p. 178 and n. 51.

8 Gransden, "Legends," pp. 8–10, 23; Ridyard, *Royal Saints*, pp. 228–31 (inter alia comparing Bury's struggles with those of Ely); Cownie, "Cult"; Yarrow, *Saints*, esp. pp. 39, 42, 47–52, 61; Pinner, *Cult*, pp. 52–4 (also citing parallel contemporary developments in the cult of Æthelthryth as studied by Blanton, *Signs*, pp. 131–41, 166–71; see too the studies cited in chap. 2 above, nn. 28–32); Licence, "Cult," 113–30 (detailing the hostility towards Herman evident in Goscelin of Saint-Bertin's miracles of Edmund); Young, *Edmund*, p. 97.

9 Yarrow, *Saints*, pp. 35–6.

10 Herman, *Miracles*, ed. and trans. Licence, pp. 6–7. Licence points out (p. 6, n. 27) that the reference to Æthelred is to "King Æthelred of the West Saxons (865–71)," the brother of King Alfred.

11 Herman, *Miracles*, ed. and trans. Licence, p. 6, note 25.

12 S. Reynolds, *Kingdoms*, p. 259.

13 Herman, *Miracles*, ed. and trans. Licence, pp. 22–3.

14 Licence, "Cult," pp. 113–14.

15 Ridyard, *Royal Saints*, p. 230; Pinner, *Cult*, e.g. pp. 57–8 (quoting Ridyard) and p. 67: "Eliding the distinction between the regional and the national locates Edmund within a broader historical context and suggests that his martyrdom, and presumably also his cult, are universally significant" (referring to the cultural work performed by the illustrator of New York, Pierpont Morgan Library, MS. M.736). See too Pinner's discussion in *Cult*, pp. 63–75.

16 *Saints*, p. 34. Yarrow's book is cited passim by Pinner, *Cult*.

17 Ridyard, *Royal Saints*, p. 230; quoted too by *Pinner, Cult*, p. 57.

18 I thank John Black of Moravian College for this felicitous phrase.

19 On the term *mythomoteur* as used by Anthony Smith, John Armstrong, Ramon d'Abadal i de Vinyals, and Henry Tudor, see above, chap. 2, n. 131.

20 H.C. Darby, "Fenland Frontier," p. 197.

21 In this light, it is intriguing that in the late twelfth or early thirteenth century Laȝamon should have claimed that a Romano-British king Gratian had been killed by two peasants from *Æst Ængle* named Eðelbald and Ælfwald (*Brut*, lines 6111–50, ed. Brook and Leslie, vol. 1, pp. 318–20), the two personal names recalling the Mercian and East Anglian royal promoters of Guthlac's cult and *vita*. By repurposing those names, was Laȝamon simply indulging his antiquarianism? Or was he trying to project onto late fifth- or sixth-century history a hint of the complex and sometimes turbulent "wider allegiances" that would arise later in eastern England? I am grateful to Jane Roberts for this reference.

22 On the linguistic relationship between the name of the demonic, dog-like Black Shuck of the Fens and the Old English word *scucca* (see *Beowulf*, line 939a), see Newton, "Forgotten History," pp. 10–11, and sources cited in his notes 86–8 and 92. On *scucca* in some English toponyms, see Foxhall Forbes, *Heaven*, p. 92.

23 Cam, *Liberties*, pp. 1–18, discussing C. Stephenson, *Borough*. My levity aside, Cam does concede the virtue of Stephenson's use of topography in his analysis.

24 Cam, *Liberties*, p. 1.

25 The pitfalls awaiting the monodisciplinary student who attempts interdisciplinarity are explained by Woolf, "Dialogue," p. 6; and especially by Capper, "Practical Implications," pp. 11–12, 18–19. I regret having

discovered these two articles only very belatedly, after the manuscript of this book had undergone its final external review.

26 Hoskins, *Making*, p. 95.

27 Parks, *Italian Neighbours*, "Author's Note."

28 Tombs, *The English*, p. 27.

29 Earl, "Violence," pp. 141–2.

30 Williamson, "East Anglia's Character," p. 62.

31 Bassett, "In Search," pp. 26–7.

Bibliography

Primary Sources

Abbo of Fleury. *Life of St. Edmund*. In *Three Lives of English Saints*, edited by Michael Winterbottom, 65–87. Toronto: Pontifical Institute of Mediaeval Studies, 1972.

– *The Passion of Saint Eadmund*. In Hervey, *Corolla Sancti Eadmundi*, 7–59.

Additamentum Nivialense de Fuilano. In *Passiones vitaque sanctorum aevi Merovingici*, edited by Bruno Krusch, 449–51. MGH, SS rer. Mero. 4. Hannover and Leipzig: Hann, 1902. https://www.dmgh.de/mgh_ss_rer_merov_4/index.htm#page/449/mode/1up.

Additamentum Nivialense de Fuilano. In *Late Merovingian France: History and Hagiography 640–720*, edited and translated by Paul Fouracre and Richard A. Gerberding, 327–9. Manchester: Manchester University Press, 1996.

Ælfric of Eynsham. *Ælfric's Catholic Homilies: Introduction, Commentary and Glossary*, edited by Malcolm Godden, xxi–lxii. EETS S.S. 18. Oxford: Oxford University Press, 2000.

– *Ælfric's Prefaces*. Edited and translated by Jonathan Wilcox. Durham: Department of English Studies, University of Durham, 1994.

– *Life of St. Swithun*. In Ælfric, *Lives*, ed. Needham, 60–81.

– *Lives of Three English Saints*. Edited by G.I. Needham. Exeter: University of Exeter Press, 1976. Reprint, 1992.

– *The Passion of St. Edmund, King and Martyr*. In *Anglo-Saxon Prose*, edited and translated by Michael Swanton, 97–103. London: Dent, 1975.

– *Preface* to the *Lives of Saints*. In *Ælfric's Lives of Saints*, edited and translated by Walter W. Skeat. Vol. 1. EETS O.S. 76, 82, 94, and 114. London, 1881–1900. Reprint, London: Oxford University Press, 1966.

– *St. Edmund, King and Martyr*. In Ælfric, *Lives*, ed. Needham, 43–59.

Ælfwald, King of East Anglia. Letter to Boniface. In *The Letters of Saint Boniface*, translated by Ephraim Emerton, with a new introduction and bibliography by Thomas F.X. Noble, 127–8. New York: Columbia University Press, 2000.

– Letter to Boniface. In *Sancti Bonifatii et Lulli epistolae*, edited by M. Tangl, 181–2. MGH. *Epistolae selectae*. Vol. 1. Berlin: Weidmann, 1916.

Æthelweard. *Chronicon Æthelweardi: The Chronicle of Æthelweard*. Edited and translated by A. Campbell. London: Nelson, 1962.

Aimo of Fleury. *De vita et martyrio sancti Abbonis abbatis Floriaci coenobii*. In *Patrologia Latina, series latina*, vol. 139, cols. 387-414. Paris, 1880.

Alfred, King of Wessex. "The Treaty of Alfred and Guthrum." In Attenborough, *Laws of Earliest English Kings*, 98–101.

– "The Treaty between Alfred and Guthrum." In Keynes and Lapidge, *Alfred the Great*, 171–2.

– *King Alfred's West-Saxon Version of Gregory's Pastoral Care*. Edited by Henry Sweet. EETS, O.S., 45, and 50. London, 1871–72.

– "Prose Preface" [to the Old English translation of Gregory the Great's *Regula pastoralis*]. In Keynes and Lapidge, *Alfred the Great*, 124–6.

The Annals of St. Neots with Vita Prima Sancti Neoti. Vol. 17 of *The Anglo-Saxon Chronicle: A Collaborative Edition*. Edited by David Dumville and Michael Lapidge. Cambridge: Brewer, 1984.

Anonymous Monk of Whitby. *The Earliest Life of Gregory the Great*. Edited and translated by Bertram Colgrave. Cambridge: Cambridge University Press, 1985.

Arngart, O.S. *The Leningrad Bede: An Eighth-Century Manuscript of the Venerable Bede's* Historia ecclesiastica gentis Anglorum *in the Public Library, Leningrad*. Copenhagen: Rosenkilde and Bagger, 1952.

Asser. *Asser's Life of King Alfred Together with the Annals of Saint Neots*. Edited by William Henry Stevenson. Oxford: Clarendon, 1904.

– *Life of King Alfred*. In Keynes and Lapidge, *Alfred the Great*, 65–110.

Attenborough, F.L., ed. and trans. *The Laws of the Earliest English Kings*. Cambridge: Cambridge University Press, 1922.

Baker, Peter S., ed. *MS F*. Vol. 8 of *The Anglo-Saxon Chronicle: A Collaborative Edition*. Cambridge: Brewer, 2000.

Bately, Janet M., ed. *MS A*. Vol. 3 of *The Anglo-Saxon Chronicle: A Collaborative Edition*. Cambridge: Brewer, 1986.

The Battle of Maldon. In *The Anglo-Saxon Minor Poems*, edited by Elliott van Kirk Dobbie, 7–16. New York: Columbia University Press, 1942.

The Battle of Maldon. In *The Anglo-Saxon World: An Anthology*, translated by Kevin Crossley-Holland, 11–19. Oxford: Oxford University Press.

Bede. *Ecclesiastical History of the English Nation, Books IV-V*. In *Bede: Historical Works*, edited and translated by J.E. King. Vol. 2, 1-389. Loeb Classical Library. Cambridge, MA: Harvard University Press, 1930.

– *Ecclesiastical History of the English People*. Edited and translated by Bertram Colgrave and R.A.B. Mynors. Oxford: Clarendon, 1969.

– *Historiam Ecclesiasticam Gentis Anglorum*. Edited by Charles Plummer. Vol. 2. Oxford, 1896.

– *History of the Abbots of Wearmouth and Jarrow*. In Grocock and Wood, *Abbots of Wearmouth and Jarrow*, 22–76.

– *Letter to Ecgbert, Bishop of York*. In Grocock and Wood, *Abbots of Wearmouth and Jarrow*, 123–61.

– *On the Temple*. Translated by Seán Connolly, with introduction and notes by Jennifer O'Reilly. Liverpool: Liverpool University Press, 1995.

– *Super parabola Salomonis* [i.e. *In proverbia Salomonis*]. In *The Complete Works of the Venerable Bede*, edited by J.A. Giles. Vol. 9: *Commentaries on the Scriptures*. Vol. [i.e. Part] 3: *Commentaries on the Old Testament*, 53–185. London, 1844.

Benedict of Nursia. *RB 1980: The Rule of Saint Benedict, in Latin and English with Notes*. Edited by Timothy Fry, Imogene Baker, Timothy Horner, Augusta Raabe, and Mark Sheridan. Collegeville: Liturgical Press, 1981.

Beowulf. In *Klaeber's Beowulf and the Fight at Finnsburg*, edited by Frederick Klaeber, R.D. Fulk, Robert E. Bjork, and John D. Niles. 4th ed. Toronto: University of Toronto Press, 2008.

Blake, E.O., ed. *Liber Eliensis*. Camden Third Series, vol. 92. London: Royal Historical Society, 1962.

Bosworth, Joseph. *Anglo-Saxon Dictionary Online*. With supplement by Thomas Northcote Toller. Maintained by Ondrej Tichy and Martin Rocek. Centre for the Study of the Middle Ages and Faculty of Arts, Charles University, Prague. 2019. https://bosworthtoller.com/

Byrthferth of Ramsey. *The Lives of St. Oswald and St. Ecgwine*, edited and translated by Michael Lapidge. Oxford: Clarendon, 2009.

– *Vita s. Oswaldi: The Life of St. Oswald*. In Byrhtferth of Ramsey, *Lives of St. Oswald and St. Ecgwine*, edited and translated by Michael Lapidge, 1–204.

Ciccarese, Maria Pia. "Le visioni di S. Fursa." *Romanobarbarica* 8 (1984–5): 231–303.

Cubbin, G.P., ed. *MS D*. Vol. 6 of *The Anglo-Saxon Chronicle: A Collaborative Edition*. Cambridge: Brewer, 1996.

Dictionary of Medieval Latin from British Sources. Edited by R.E. Latham, David R. Howlett et al. London: Oxford University Press for the British Library, 1975–2013.

Dictionary of Old English: A to I Online. Edited by Angus Cameron, Ashley Crandell Amos, Antonette diPaolo Healey et al. Toronto: Dictionary of Old English Project, 2007. https://tapor.library.utoronto.ca/doe/.

Dugdale, William. *Monasticon Anglicanum: A New Edition*. Edited by Thomas Caley, Henry Ellis, and Bulkeley Bandinel. Vol. 1. London, 1846.

Eddius Stephanus. *Eddius' Life of Wilfrid*. Edited by Bertram Colgrave. Cambridge: Cambridge University Press, 1927.

– *Life of Wilfrid*. In *The Age of Bede*, translated by J.F. Webb and D.H. Farmer, 105–82. London: Penguin, 1988.

Fairweather, Janet, trans. *Liber Eliensis: A History of the Isle of Ely from the Seventh Century to the Twelfth*. Woodbridge: Boydell, 2005.

Felix. *Life of Saint Guthlac*. Edited and translated by Bertram Colgrave. Cambridge: Cambridge University Press, 1956. Reprint, 1985.

Garmonsway, G.N., trans. *The Anglo-Saxon Chronicle*. London: Dent, 1992 [1953].

Geoffrey of Wells. [*De infantia sancti Eadmundi*.] In Hervey, *Corolla Sancti Eadmundi*, 134–61.

Gildas. *The Ruin of Britain and Other Works*. Edited and translated by Michael Winterbottom. London: Phillimore, 1978.

Goscelin of Saint-Bertin. *Miracvla Sancte Ætheldrethe*. In Love, *Goscelin of Saint-Bertin*, 95–131.

Grocock, Christopher, and I.N. Wood, eds. and trans. *Abbots of Wearmouth and Jarrow*. Oxford: Oxford University Press, 2013.

Henry, Archdeacon of Huntingdon. *Historia Anglorum: The History of the English People*. Edited and translated by Diana Greenway. Oxford: Oxford University Press, 1996.

Herman the Archdeacon. *Miracles of St. Edmund*. In Herman the Archdeacon and Goscelin of Saint-Bertain, *Miracles of St. Edmund*, edited and translated by Tom Licence, with the assistance of Lynda Lockyer, 1–126. Oxford: Clarendon Press, 2014.

Hervey, Francis, ed. and trans. *Corolla Sancti Eadmundi: The Garland of Saint Edmund, King and Martyr*. London: John Murray, 1907. Reprint, La Vergne: Kessinger, 2009.

Horace, *Odes and Epodes*. Edited and translated by Niall Rudd. Cambridge, MA: Harvard University Press, 2004.

Hugh Candidus. *The Chronicle of Hugh Candidus, a Monk of Peterborough*. Edited by W.T. Mellows. With *La geste de Burch*, edited by Alexander Bell. Oxford: Oxford University Press, 1949.

– *The Peterborough Chronicle of Hugh Candidus*. Translated by Charles Mellows and William Thomas Mellows. Rev. ed. Peterborough: Peterborough Museum Society, 1966.

Irvine, Susan, ed. *MS E*. Vol. 7 of *The Anglo-Saxon Chronicle: A Collaborative Edition*. Cambridge: Brewer, 2004.

James, M.R. "Two Lives of St. Ethelbert, King and Martyr." *EHR* 32 (1917): 214–44.

Jocelin of Brakelond. *Chronica Jocelini de Brakelonda, de rebus gestis Samsonis abbatis monasterii sancti Edmundi*. Edited by John Gage Rokewode. Camden Society, first series, 13. London, 1840.

– *Chronicle of the Abbey of Bury St. Edmunds*. Translated with notes and introduction by Diana Greenway and Jane Sayers. Oxford: Oxford University Press, 1989.

John of Worcester. *The Chronicle of John of Worcester*. Edited by R.R. Darlington and P. McGurk. Translated by Jennifer Bray and P. McGurk. Vol. 2. Oxford: Clarendon, 1995.

Keynes, Simon, and Michael Lapidge, eds. and trans. *Alfred the Great: Asser's Life of King Alfred and Other Contemporary Sources*. London: Penguin, 1983.

Laȝamon. *Brut*. Edited by G.L. Brook and R.F. Leslie. 2 vols. EETS, O.S., 250 and 277. Oxford: Oxford University Press, 1978 [1963].

Love, Rosalind, ed. and trans. *Goscelin of Saint-Bertin: The Hagiography of the Female Saints of Ely*. Oxford: Clarendon, 2004.

Miller, Thomas, ed. and trans. *The Old English Version of Bede's* Ecclesiastical History of the English People. EETS O.S., 95, 96, 110, 111. London, 1890–8. Reprint, London: Oxford University Press, 1959–63.

Nennius [attrib.]. *Historia Britonum: The History of the Britons, Attributed to Nennius*. Edited and translated by Richard Rowley. Lampeter: Llanerch, 2005.

O'Brien O'Keeffe, Katharine, ed. *MS C*. Vol. 5 of *The Anglo-Saxon Chronicle: A Collaborative Edition*. Cambridge: Brewer, 2001.

Plummer, Charles, ed., *Venerabilis Baedae Historiam Ecclesiasticam Gentis Anglorum*. 2 vols. Oxford, 1896.

Plummer, Charles, and John Earle, ed. *Two of the Saxon Chronicles Parallel*. 2 vols. Oxford, 1892.

Pseudo-Ingulph. *Ingulph's Chronicle of the Abbey of Croyland, with the Continuation by Peter of Blois and Anonymous Writers*. Edited by Henry T. Riley. London, 1854. Reprint, New York: AMS Press, 1968.

Richard of Ely. *The Deeds of Hereward*. Translated by Michael Swanton. In *Medieval Outlaws: Twelve Tales in Modern English Translation*, edited by Thomas H. Ohlgren, 28–99. Rev. ed. West Lafayette, IN: Parlor, 2005.

– *De Gestis Herwardi: Le gesta di Ervardo*. Edited by Alberto Meneghetti. Pisa: ETS, 2013.

Roberts, Jane, ed. *The Guthlac Poems of the Exeter Book*. Oxford: Clarendon, 1979.

Swanton, M.J., trans. *The Anglo-Saxon Chronicle*. London: Dent, 1996.

Taylor, Simon, ed. *MS B*. Vol. 4 of *The Anglo-Saxon Chronicle: A Collaborative Edition*. Cambridge: Brewer, 1983.

Thietmar of Merseburg. *Thietmari Merseburgensis episcopi Chronicon*. Edited by Johann Martin Lappenberg and Friedrich Kurze. MGH, SS rer. Germ. 54. VIII (VI).xxxvi (xxvi). Hannover, 1889.

Vitalis, Orderic. *The Ecclesiastical History of Orderic Vitalis*. Edited and translated by Marjorie Chibnall. 6 vols. Oxford: Oxford University Press, 1969–80.

Vita virtutesque Fursei abbatis Latiniacensis. In *Passiones vitaque sanctorum aevi Merovingici*. Edited by Bruno Krusch. MGH, SS rer. Mero. 4, 423–49. Hannover and Leipzig: Hann, 1902. https://www.dmgh.de/mgh_ss_rer_merov_4/index.htm#page/(III)/mode/1up.

The Vulgate Bible: Douay-Reims Translation. Edited by Swift Edgar with Angela M. Kinney. 6 vols. Cambridge, MA: Harvard University Press, 2010.

Widukind of Corvey. *Rerum gestarum Saxonicarum libri tres*. In *Die Sachsengeschichte des Widukind von Korvei*, edited by Paul Hirsch and Hans-Eberhard Lohmann. MGH, SS rer. Germ. 60. 5th ed. Hannover, 1935. Digitized by Brian Smith for Bibliotheca Augustana. https://www.hs-augsburg.de/~harsch/Chronologia/Lspost10/Widukind/wid_sax0.html

William of Malmesbury. *Gesta Pontificum Anglorum: The History of the English Bishops*, vol. 1: *Text and Translation*. Edited and translated by Michael Winterbottom, with the assistance of R.M. Thomson. Oxford: Oxford University Press, 2007.

Wulfstan of Winchester. *The Life of St. Æthelwold*. Edited by Michael Lapidge and Michael Winterbottom. Oxford: Clarendon, 1991.

Secondary Sources

Abels, Richard. "Alfred the Great, the *micel hæðen here*, and the Viking Threat." In Reuter, ed., *Alfred the Great*, 265–79.

– *Alfred the Great: War, Kingship and Culture in Anglo-Saxon England*. London: Taylor and Francis, 1998. Reprint, Abingdon: Routledge, 2013.

– "King Alfred's Peace-Making Strategies with the Danes." *Haskins Society Journal* 3 (1991): 23–34.

– "Reflections on Alfred the Great as a Military Leader." In *The Medieval Way of War: Studies in Medieval Military History in Honor of Bernard S. Bachrach*, edited by Gregory I. Halfond, 47–63. Farnham: Ashgate, 2015.

Abrams, Lesley. "Conversion and Assimilation." In Hadley and Richards, *Cultures in Contact*, 135–53.

– "Edward the Elder's Danelaw." In Higham and Hill, *Edward the Elder*, 128–43.

– "King Edgar and the Men of the Danelaw." In *Edgar, King of the English 959–975: New Interpretations*, edited by Donald Scragg, 171–91. Woodbridge: Boydell, 2008.

Abulafia, David, and Nora Berend, eds. *Medieval Frontiers: Concepts and Practices*. Aldershot: Ashgate, 2002.

Allen, Lesley. Review of Bale, *Saint Edmund, King and Martyr*. *JEGP* 110.2 (2011): 247-50.

Anderson, Benedict. *Imagined Communities: Reflections on the Origin and Spread of Nationalism*. 2d ed. London: Verso, 1991.

Anlezark, Daniel. "'Stand Firm': The Descent to Hell in Felix's *Life of Saint Guthlac*." In *Darkness, Depression, and Descent in Anglo-Saxon England*, edited by Ruth Wehlau, 255–76. Kalamazoo: Medieval Institute Publications/Berlin: Walter de Gruyter, 2019.

Anzaldúa, Gloria. *Borderlands/La Frontera*. San Francisco: Spinsters/Aunt Lute, 1987.

Appleton, Helen. "The Psalter in the Prose Lives of St. Guthlac." In *Germano-Celtica: A Festschrift for Brian Taylor*, edited by Anders Ahlqvist and Pamela O'Neill, 61–86. Sydney Series in Celtic Studies 16. Sydney: University of Sydney, Celtic Studies Foundation, 2017.

Appleton, Helen, and Matthew Robinson. "Further Echoes of Vergil's *Aeneid* in Felix's *Vita sancti Guthlaci*." *Notes and Queries* 64.3 (2017): 353–5.

Arthur, Ciaran. "Giving the Head's Up in Ælfric's *Passio Sancti Eadmundi:* Postural Representations of the Old English Saint." *Philological Quarterly* 93.3 (2013): 315–33.

Ashe, Laura. *Conquest and Transformation: The Oxford English Literary History*, vol. 1: *1000–1350*. Oxford: Oxford University Press, 2017.

Auerbach, Erich. *Scenes from the Drama of European Literature*. Translated by Ralph Manheim. New York: Meridian, 1959.

Bacola, Meredith. "*Vacuas in auras recessit?* Reconsidering the Relevance of Embedded Heroic Material in the Guthlac Narrative." In Roberts and Thacker, *Guthlac*, 72–85.

Baker, John, and Stuart Brookes. *Beyond the Burghal Hidage: Anglo-Saxon Civil Defence in the Viking Age*. History of Warfare Series no. 84. Leiden: Brill, 2013.

Bale, Anthony, ed. *Saint Edmund, King and Martyr: Changing Images of a Medieval Saint*. York and Woodbridge: York Medieval Press/Boydell, 2009.

Barkham, Patrick. "This Sinking Isle: The Homeowners Battling Coastal Erosion." *Guardian*, 2 April 2015, http://www.theguardian.com/news/2015/apr/02/sinking-isle-coastal-erosion-east-anglia-environment.

Barley, M.W. *Lincolnshire and the Fens*. London: B.T. Batsford, 1952. Reprint, East Ardsley, Yorks.: E.P. Publishing, 1972.

Barrett, Robert J. Jr. *Against All England: Regional Identity and Cheshire Writing, 1195–1656*. Notre Dame: University of Notre Dame Press, 2009.

Barrow, Julia. "Danish Ferocity and Abandoned Monasteries: The Twelfth-Century View." In Brett and Woodman, *The Long Twelfth-Century View*, 77–93.

– "How Coifi Pierced Christ's Side: A Re-Examination of Bede's *Ecclesiastical History*, II, Chapter 13." *Journal of Ecclesiastical History* 62.4 (2011): 693–706.

– "The Ideology of the Tenth-Century English Benedictine 'Reform.'" In Skinner, *Challenging the Boundaries*, 141–54.

Bartlett, Robert, and Angus MacKay, eds. *Medieval Frontier Societies*. Oxford: Clarendon, 1989.

Bassett, Steven. "In Search of the Origins of Anglo-Saxon Kingdoms." In Bassett, *Origins of Anglo-Saxon Kingdoms*, 3–27.

–, ed. *The Origins of Anglo-Saxon Kingdoms*. London: Leicester University Press, 1989.

Bately, Janet M. "Introduction." *MS A*. Vol. 3 of *The Anglo-Saxon Chronicle: A Collaborative Edition*, xiii–clxxvii. Cambridge: Brewer, 1986.

Bates, David. "The Abbey and the Norman Conquest: An Unusual Case?" In Licence, *Bury St. Edmunds and the Norman Conquest*, 5–21.

Bates, David, and Robert Liddiard, eds. *East Anglia and Its North Sea World in the Middle Ages*. Woodbridge: Boydell, 2013.

Baxter, Stephen, Catherine E. Karkov, Janet L. Nelson, and David Pelteret, eds. *Early Medieval Studies in Memory of Patrick Wormald*. Farnham, Surrey: Ashgate, 2009.

Benham, Jenny. "Law or Treaty? Defining the Edge of Legal Studies in the Early and High Medieval Periods." *Historical Research* 86 (2013): 487–97.

Benskin, Michael. "The Literary Structure of Ælfric's *Life of King Edmund*." In *Loyal Letters: Studies on Mediaeval Alliterative Poetry and Prose*, edited by L.A.J.R. Houwen and A.A. MacDonald, 1–27. Mediaevalia Groningana series. Groningen: Forsten, 1994.

Berend, Nora. "Hungary, 'the Gate of Christendom.'" In Abulafia and Berend, *Medieval Frontiers*, 195–215.

Berkhofer, Robert F. III, Alan Cooper, and Adam J. Kosto, eds. *The Experience of Power in Medieval Europe, 950–1350*. Aldershot: Ashgate, 2005.

Berschin, Walter. *Biographie und Epochenstil im lateinischen Mittelalter*: Quellen und Untersuchungen zur lateinischen Philologie des Mittelalters, 9. Stuttgart: Anton Hiersemann, 1988.

Bethurum, Dorothy. "The Form of Ælfric's *Lives of Saints*." *Studies in Philology* 29.4 (1932): 515–33.

Biddle, Martin, and Birthe Kjølbye-Biddle. "Repton." In Lapidge, Blair, Keynes, and Scragg, *Wiley Blackwell Encyclopedia*, 401–3.

– "Repton and the 'Great Heathen Army,' 873–74." In Graham-Campbell et al., *Vikings and the Danelaw*, 45–96.

Black, John R. "'*Nutrix pia*': The Flowering of the Cult of St. Æthelthryth in Anglo-Saxon England." In Szarmach, *Writing Women Saints*, 167–90.

– "Tradition and Transformation in the Cult of St. Guthlac in Early Medieval England." *The Heroic Age* 10 (May 2007). https://www.heroicage.org/issues/10/black.html

Blackburn, Mark A.S. "Expansion and Control: Aspects of Anglo-Scandinavian Minting South of the Humber." In Graham-Campbell et al., *Vikings and the Danelaw*, 125–42.

– "The London Mint in the Reign of King Alfred." In Blackburn and Dumville, *Kings, Currency, and Alliances*, 105–23.

Blackburn, Mark A.S., and David N. Dumville, eds. *Kings, Currency, and Alliances: History and Coinage of Southern England in the Ninth Century*. Woodbridge: Boydell, 1998.

Blackburn, Mark A.S., and Hugh Pagan. "St. Edmund Coinage in the Light of a Parcel from a Hoard of St. Edmund Pennies." *British Numismatic Journal* 72 (2002): 1–14.

Blair, John. "Anglo-Saxon Pagan Shrines and Their Prototypes." *ASSAH* 8 (1995): 1–28.

– "The Anglo-Saxon Period (*c.* 440–1066)." *The Oxford History of Britain*, edited by Kenneth O. Morgan, 60–119. Oxford: Oxford University Press, 1984.

– *The Church in Anglo-Saxon Society*. Oxford: Oxford University Press, 2005.

Blair, Peter Hunter. *An Introduction to Anglo-Saxon England*. 3d ed. New introduction by Simon Keynes. Cambridge: Cambridge University Press, 2003.

– *Roman Britain and Early England 55 B.C.–A.D. 871*. Edinburgh: Nelson, 1963.

Blanton, Virginia. "The Kentish Queen as *Omnium Mater*: Goscelin of Saint-Bertin's Lections and the Emergence of the Cult of Saint Seaxburh." In Szarmach, *Writing Women Saints*, 191–213.

– "Presenting the Sister Saints of Ely, or Using Kinship to Increase a Monastery's Status as a Cult Center." *Literature Compass* 5/4 (2008): 755–71.

– *Signs of Devotion: The Cult of St. Æthelthryth in Medieval England, 695–1615*. University Park: Pennsylvania State University Press, 2007.

Blunt, C.E. "The St. Edmund Memorial Coinage." *Proceedings of the Suffolk Institute of Archaeology* 31 (1967–9): 234–55.

Blythe, Ronald. *Akenfield: Portrait of an English Village*. London: Allen Lane/Penguin, 1969.

Böhme, Horst-Wolfgang. "Das Ende der Römerherrschaft in Britannien und die angelsächsische Besiedlung Englands im 5. Jahrhundert." *Jahrbuch des Römisch-Germanischen Zentralmuseums Mainz* 33 (1986): 466–574.

Bolton, W.F. "The Background and Meaning of 'Guthlac.'" *JEGP* 61.3 (1962): 595–603.

Bonner, Gerald, ed. *Famulus Christi: Essays in Commemoration of the Thirteenth Centenary of the Birth of the Venerable Bede*. London: S.P.C.K. [Society for Promoting Christian Knowledge], 1976.

Bourdieu, Pierre. *Outline of a Theory of Practice*. Translated by Richard Nice. Cambridge: Cambridge University Press, 1977.

Bovaird-Abbo, Kristin. "Redeeming Wastelands, Building Communities in the Old English *Guthlac A*." *ISLE: Interdisciplinary Studies in Literature and Environment* 24.2 (2017): 196–223.

Boyarin, Daniel. *Border Lines: The Partition of Judaeo-Christianity*. Philadelphia: University of Pennsylvania Press, 2004.

Bradbury, Malcolm. "Loving Norfolk." In *Liar's Landscape: Collected Writings from a Storyteller's Life*, edited by Dominic Bradbury, with an afterword by David Lodge, 123–8. London: Picador/Pan Macmillan, 2006.

Brady, Lindy. "Colonial Desire or Political Disengagement? The Contested Landscape of *Guthlac A*." *JEGP* 115.1 (2016): 61–78.

– "Crowland Abbey as Anglo-Saxon Sanctuary in the Pseudo-Ingulf Chronicle." *Traditio* 73 (2018): 19–42.

– "Echoes of Britons on a Fenland Frontier in the Old English *Andreas*." *Review of English Studies* 61 (2010): 669–89.

– *Writing the Welsh Borderlands in Anglo-Saxon England*. Manchester: Manchester University Press, 2017.

Bredehoft, Thomas A. *Textual Histories: Readings in the* Anglo-Saxon Chronicle. Toronto: University of Toronto Press, 2001.

Breeze, Andrew. "Bede's *Civitas Domnoc* and Dunwich, Suffolk." *Leeds Studies in English* N.S. 3 (2005): 1–4.

Brett, Martin, and David A. Woodman, eds. *The Long Twelfth-Century View of the Anglo-Saxon Past*. Farnham, Surrey: Ashgate, 2015.

Briggs, Daphne Nash. "Sacred Image and Regional Identity in Late-Prehistoric Norfolk." In Heslop, Mellings, and Thøfner, *Art, Faith and Place*, 30–49.

Briggs, Keith. "Was *Hægelisdun* in Essex?: A New Site for the Martyrdom of Edmund." *Proceedings of the Suffolk Institute for Archaeology and History* 42.3 (2011): 277–91.

Brookes, Stuart. "Boat-Rivets in Graves in Pre-Viking Kent: Reassessing Anglo-Saxon Boat- Burial Traditions." *Medieval Archaeology* 51.1 (2007): 1–18.

Brooks, Britton. "Felix's Construction of the English Fenlands: Landscape, Authorizing Allusion, and Lexical Echo." In Roberts and Thacker, *Guthlac*, 55–71.

Brooks, Nicholas. *The Early History of the Church of Canterbury: Christ Church from 597 to 1066*. Leicester: Leicester University Press, 1984.

– "English Identity from Bede to the Millennium." *Haskins Society Journal* 14 (2003): 33–51.

– "The Formation of the Mercian Kingdom." In Bassett, *Origins of Anglo-Saxon Kingdoms*, 159–70.

– "Why Is the Anglo-Saxon Chronicle about Kings?" *ASE* 39 (2010): 43–70.

Brown, George Hardin. *Bede, the Venerable*. Boston: Twayne, 1987.

– *A Companion to Bede*. Woodbridge: Boydell, 2009.

– "Royal and Ecclesiastical Rivalries in Bede's *History*." *Renascence* 52.1 (1999): 19–33.

Brown, George Hardin, and Frederick M. Biggs, eds. *Bede: Part 1, Fascicles 1–4*. Sources of Anglo-Saxon Literary Culture. Amsterdam: Amsterdam University Press, 2017.

–, eds. *Bede: Part 2, Fascicles 1–4*. Sources of Anglo-Saxon Literary Culture. Amsterdam: Amsterdam University Press, 2018.

Brown, Michelle P., and Carol A. Farr, eds. *Mercia: An Anglo-Saxon Kingdom in Europe*. London: Leicester University Press, 2001.

Brown, Peter. *The Body and Society: Men, Women, and Sexual Renunciation in Early Christianity*. 20th anniversary ed. New York: Columbia University Press, 2008.

Bruce-Mitford, Rupert L.S. *The Sutton Hoo Ship-Burial*. With contributions by Paul Ashbee, Angela Care Evans, and others. 3 vols. London: British Museum, 1975–83.

– "The Sutton Hoo Ship-Burial: Some Foreign Connections." In *Angli e Sassoni al di qua e al di là del mare*, Settimane di studio del Centro italiano di studi sull'alto medioevo, 32, Part 1, 143–210. Spoleto: CISAM, 1986.

Brugmann, Birte. "Migration and Endogenous Change." In Hamerow, Hinton, and Crawford, *Oxford Handbook of Anglo-Saxon Archaeology*, 30–45.

Bryson, Bill. *Notes from a Small Island*. New York: HarperCollins Perennial, 1995.

Bullimore, Katherine. "Unpicking the Web: The Divorce of Ecgfrith and Æthelthryth." *European Review of History – Revue européenne d'histoire* 16.6 (2009): 835–54.

Burgess, Mike. "Hidden East Anglia: Landscape Legends of Eastern England." Part 5: "Edmund of East Anglia: The Last Mystery: Where Did Edmund Die?" Accessed 13 November 2020. https://www.hiddenea.com/edmund5.htm,

Burke, Peter. *The Renaissance Sense of the Past*. New York: St. Martin's, 1970.

Butler, Judith. *Gender Trouble: Feminism and the Subversion of Identity*. 2d ed. London: Routledge, 1990.

Bynum, Caroline Walker. *Fragmentation and Redemption: Essays on Gender and the Human Body in Medieval Religion*. New York: Zone, 1992.

Cam, Helen M. "The City of Cambridge." In *A History of the County of Cambridge and the Isle of Ely*, edited by J.P.C. Roach. Vol. 3, 1–149. Victoria County History. London: University of London Institute of Historical Research, 1959. Reprint, 1967.

– *Liberties and Communities in Medieval England*. Cambridge: Cambridge University Press, 1944.

Cameron, Kenneth. *English Place-Names*. London: Methuen, 1969 [1961].

Campbell, James. *The Anglo-Saxon State*. London: Hambledon and London, 2000.

– "The End of Roman Britain." In Campbell, John, and Wormald, *The Anglo-Saxons*, 8–19.

– *Essays in Anglo-Saxon History*. London: Hambledon, 1986.

– "The First Christian Kings." In Campbell, John, and Wormald, *The Anglo-Saxons*, 45–69.

– "The Impact of the Sutton Hoo Discovery on the Study of Anglo-Saxon History." In Kendall and Wells, *Voyage to the Other World*, 70–101.

– "The Lost Centuries: 400–600." In Campbell, John, and Wormald, *The Anglo-Saxons*, 20–44.

– "Placing King Alfred." In Reuter, *Alfred the Great*, 3–23.

– "Secular and Political Contexts." In DeGregorio, *Cambridge Companion*, 25–39.

– "What Is Not Known about the Reign of Edward the Elder." In Higham and Hill, *Edward the Elder*, 12–24.

Campbell, James, Eric John, and Patrick Wormald. *The Anglo-Saxons*. London: Penguin, 1991.

Capper, Morn. "Contested Loyalties, Regional and National Identities in the Midland Kingdoms of Anglo-Saxon England, c.700–c.900." Ph.D. diss., University of Sheffield, 2008.

– "Insights from Obscurity: The Anglo-Saxon Kingdom of East Anglia (c. 700–950)." master's thesis, University of Sheffield, 2003.

– "The Practical Implications of Interdisciplinary Approaches: Research in Anglo-Saxon East Anglia." In Devlin and Holas-Clark, *Approaching Interdisciplinarity*, 10–23.

– "St. Guthlac and the 'Britons': A Mercian Context." In Roberts and Thacker, *Guthlac*, 180–213.

Carver, Martin. "Agency, Intellect and the Archaeological Agenda." In *Signals of Belief in Early England: Anglo-Saxon Paganism Revisited*, edited by Martin Carver, Alex Sanmark, and Sarah Semple, 1–20. Oxford: Oxbow, 2010.

– (M.O.H. Carver), ed. *The Age of Sutton Hoo: The Seventh Century in North-Western Europe*. Woodbridge: Boydell, 1992.

– "The Anglo-Saxon Cemetery at Sutton Hoo: An Interim Report." In Carver, *Age of Sutton Hoo*, 343–71.

– "Burial Mounds and State Formation: Description of a Dialogue." Public lecture, Academy of Science, Moscow, 30 October 2012. http://scibook.net/vsemirnaya-istoriya_775/martin-carver-york-burial-mounds-and-state-53927.html.

– "Conclusion: The Future of Sutton Hoo." In Kendall and Wells, *Voyage to the Other World*, 183–200.

– "Kingship and Material Culture in Early Anglo-Saxon East Anglia." In Bassett, *Origins of Anglo-Saxon Kingdoms*, 141–58.

– "Reflections on the Meanings of Monumental Barrows in Anglo-Saxon England." In *Burial in Early Medieval England and Wales*, edited by Sam Lucy and Andrew Reynolds, 132–43. London: Society for Medieval Archaeology, 2002.

– "Ship-Burials: Mound 2, with a Reconsideration of Mound 1." In Carver, Evans et al., *Sutton Hoo*, 153–99.

– *Sutton Hoo: Burial Ground of Kings?* Philadelphia: University of Pennsylvania Press, 1998.

– "Sutton Hoo in Context." In Carver, Evans et al., *Sutton Hoo*, 489–503.

– "What Were They Thinking? Intellectual Territories in Anglo-Saxon England." In Hamerow, Hinton, and Crawford, *Oxford Handbook of Anglo-Saxon Archaeology*, 914–47.

Carver, Martin, Angela Evans, Christopher Fern, Madeleine Hummler, Frances Lee, and John Newman. *Sutton Hoo: A Seventh-Century Princely Burial Ground and Its Context*. London: British Museum Press, 2005.

Cavell, Megan. "Formulaic *Friþuwebban*: Reexamining Peace-Weaving in the Light of Old English Poetics." *JEGP* 114.3 (2015): 355–72.

Cavill, Paul. "Analogy and Genre in the Legend of St. Edmund." *Nottingham Medieval Studies* 47 (2003): 21–45.

– "The Armour-Bearer in Abbo's *Passio sancti Eadmundi* and Anglo-Saxon England." *Leeds Studies in England*, N.S. 36 (2005): 47–61.

– "Fun and Games: Viking Atrocity in the *Passio Sancti Eadmundi*." *Notes and Queries* 52.3 (2005): 284–6.

– "The Naming of Guthlac." *Nottingham Medieval Studies* 59 (2015): 25–47.

Chamberlain, Mary. *Fenwomen: A Portrait of Women in a Fenland Village*. Gislea: Virago, 1975.

Chaney, William A. *The Cult of Kingship in Anglo-Saxon England: The Transition from Paganism to Christianity*. Manchester: Manchester University Press, 1970.

Chaplais, Pierre. *English Diplomatic Practice in the Middle Ages*. London: Hambledon and London, 2003.

Chapman, Anna. "King Alfred and the Cult of St. Edmund." *History Today* 53.7 (2003): 37–43.

Charles-Edwards, Thomas. "Alliances, Godfathers, Treaties and Boundaries." In Blackburn and Dumville, *Kings, Currency, and Alliances*, 47–62.

– (T.M. Charles-Edwards) *Early Christian Ireland*. Cambridge: Cambridge University Press, 2004.

– "Early Medieval Kingships in the British Isles." In Bassett, *Origins of Anglo Saxon Kingdoms*, 28–39.

– "Wales and Mercia, 613–918." In M. Brown and Farr, *Mercia*, 89–105.

Cheong, Michael. "Felix's Life of Guthlac." *The Eastern Anglo-Saxonist* (blog). 9 May 2013. http://easternanglosaxonist.wordpress.com/2013/05/09/felixs-life-of-guthlac/.

Chibnall, Marjorie. "Introduction." In Orderic Vitalis, *The Ecclesiastical History of Orderic Vitalis*, edited and translated by Marjorie Chibnall, xiii–xliii. Vol. 2. Oxford: Oxford University Press, 1969.

Chisholm, Michael. "Crowland in St. Guthlac's Time." In Roberts and Thacker, *Guthlac*, 316–25.

Church, S.D. "Paganism in Conversion-Age Anglo-Saxon England: The Evidence of Bede's *Ecclesiastical History* Reconsidered." *History* 93 (2008): 162–80.

Clanchy, M.T. *From Memory to Written Record: England 1066–1307*. 2d ed. Oxford: Blackwell, 1993.

Clark, Cecily. "Ælfric and Abbo." *English Studies* 49 (1968): 30–8.

Clark, Stephanie. "*Guthlac A* and the Temptation of the Barrow." *Studia Neophilologica* 87.1 (2015): 48–72.

– "A More Permanent Homeland: Land Tenure in *Guthlac A*." *Anglo-Saxon England* 40 (2011): 75–102.

Clarke, Catherine A.M. *Literary Landscapes and the Idea of England, 700–1400*. Woodbridge: Brewer, 2006.

– "Panegyric and Reflection in a Poem by Abbo of Fleury to Ramsey Abbey." In Sauer and Story, *Anglo-Saxon England and the Continent*, 293–302.

– *Writing Power in Anglo-Saxon England: Texts, Hierarchies, Economies*. Cambridge: Brewer, 2012.

Clarke, Roy Rainbird. *East Anglia*. New ed. with introduction by James Wentworth Day. East Ardsley, W. Yorks: E.P. Publishing, 1971.

Clayton, Mary. "Ælfric and Æthelred." In *Essays on Anglo-Saxon and Related Themes in Memory of Lynne Grundy*, edited by Jane Roberts and Janet L. Nelson, 65–88. London: King's College London, 2000.

– "Homiliaries and Preaching in Anglo-Saxon England." *Peritia* 4 (1985): 207–42. Reprinted in Szarmach and Oosterhouse, *Old English Prose*, 151–98.

Clemoes, Peter A.M. "Ælfric." In *Continuations and Beginnings: Studies in Old English Literature*, edited by E.G. Stanley, 176–209. London: Thomas Nelson and Sons, 1966.

"The Chronology of Ælfric's Works." In *The Anglo-Saxons: Studies in Some Aspects of Their History and Culture Presented to Bruce Dickins*, edited by Peter A.M. Clemoes, 212–47. London: Bowes and Bowes, 1959. Reprinted in Szarmach and Oosterhouse, *Old English Prose*, 29–72.

Coates, Richard. "*Domnoc/Dommoc*, Dunwich and Felixstowe." In *Celtic Voices, English Places: Studies of the Celtic Impact on Place-Names in England*, edited by Richard Coates and Andrew Breeze, with a contribution by David Horovitz, 234–40. Stamford: Shaun Tyas, 2000.

Coates, Simon. "Ceolfrid: History, Hagiography and Memory in Seventh- and Eighth-Century Wearmouth-Jarrow." *Journal of Medieval History* 25.2 (1999): 69–86.

Cohen, Jeffrey Jerome. *Medieval Identity Machines*. Minneapolis: University of Minnesota Press, 2003.

Colgrave, Bertram. "The Earliest Saints' Lives Written in England." Sir Israel Gollancz Memorial Lecture. *Proceedings of the British Academy* 44 (1959): 35–60.

– "Historical Introduction." In Bede, *Ecclesiastical History*, xvii–xxxviii.

– "Introduction." In Felix, *Life of Saint Guthlac*, ed. Colgrave, 1–25.

– "Notes." In Felix, *Life of Saint Guthlac*, ed. Colgrave, 174–95.

Collingwood, R.G., and J.N.L. Myres. *Roman Britain and the English Settlements*. 2d ed. Oxford History of England, vol. 1. Oxford: Clarendon, 1937.

Constable, Giles. *The Reformation of the Twelfth Century*. Cambridge: Cambridge University Press, 1996.

Coughlan, Jenny. "Notes on a Scandal: Bede and Gregory of Tours on Women in the Religious Life at Coldingham and Poitiers." Paper presented at the 20th International Medieval Congress, University of Leeds, 1–4 July 2013.

Courtney, Paul. "The Early Saxon Fenland: A Reconsideration." *ASSAH*, vol. 2, edited by David Brown, James Campbell, and Sonia Chadwick Hawkes, 91–102. BAR British Series, 92. 1981.

Coward, Noël. *Private Lives*. London: Methuen, 2000 [1930].
Cowdrey, H.E.J. "Bede and the 'English People.'" *Journal of Religious History* 11 (1981): 501–23.
Cownie, Emma. "The Cult of St. Edmund in the Eleventh and Twelfth Centuries: The Language and Communication of a Medieval Saint's Cult." *Neuphilologische Mitteilungen* 99.2 (1998): 177–97.
Cramp, Rosemary. "Not Why But How: The Contribution of Archaeological Evidence to the Understanding of Anglo-Saxon England." In *The Preservation and Transmission of Anglo- Saxon Culture*, edited by Paul E. Szarmach and Joel T. Rosenthal, 271–84. Kalamazoo: Medieval Institute Publications, 1997.
Crawford, Barbara. "The Vikings." In W. Davies, *From the Vikings to the Normans*, 41–72.
Crehan, Kate. *Gramsci, Culture and Anthropology*. Berkeley: University of California Press, 2002.
Croce, Benedetto. "Regionalismo." 1908. In *Cultura e vita morale: Intermezzi polemici*, 2d ed., vol. 2 of *Scritti vari*, 139–42. Bari: Laterza, 1926.
Crook, John. *English Medieval Shrines*. Woodbridge: Boydell, 2011.
– "The Enshrinement of Local Saints in Francia and England." In Thacker and Sharpe, *Local Saints and Local Churches*, 189–224.
Cubitt, Catherine. "Ælfric's Lay Patrons." In Magennis and Swan, *A Companion to Ælfric*, 165–92.
– "Memory and Narrative in the Cult of Early Anglo-Saxon Saints." In *The Uses of the Past in the Early Middle Ages*, edited by Yitzhak Hen and Matthew Innes, 29–66. Cambridge: Cambridge University Press, 2000.
– "Review Article: The Tenth-Century Benedictine Reform in England." *Early Medieval Europe* 6.1 (1997): 77–94.
– "Sites and Sanctity: Revisiting the Cult of Murdered and Martyred Anglo-Saxon Royal Saints." *Early Medieval Europe* 9.1 (2000): 53–83.
– "Universal and Local Saints in Anglo-Saxon England." In Thacker and Sharpe, *Local Saints and Local Churches*, 423–53.
Curta, Florin, ed. *Borders, Barriers, and Ethnogenesis: Frontiers in Late Antiquity and the Middle Ages*. Turnhout: Brepols, 2005.
– "Introduction." In Curta, *Borders, Barriers, and Ethnogenesis*, 1–9.
Curtius, Ernst Robert. *European Literature and the Latin Middle Ages*. Translated by Willard R. Trask. New York: Harper and Row, 1963.
Dachowski, Elizabeth. *First among Abbots: The Career of Abbo of Fleury*. Washington, DC: Catholic University of America Press, 2008.
Damon, John Edward. *Soldier Saints and Holy Warriors: Warfare and Sanctity in the Literature of Early England*. Aldershot: Ashgate, 2003.
Darby, H[enry] C[lifford]. "The Fenland Frontier in Anglo-Saxon England." *Antiquity* 8 (1934): 185–201.

– *The Medieval Fenland*. 2d ed. Newton Abbot, Devon: David and Charles, 1973.

Darby, Peter, and Faith Wallis, eds. *Bede and the Future*. London: Ashgate, 2014. Reprint, Abingdon: Routledge, 2016.

Davies, Joshua. "The Literary Languages of Old English." In Lees, *Cambridge History*, 257–77.

Davies, Wendy. "Annals and the Origins of Mercia." In Dornier, *Mercian Studies*, 17–29.

–, ed. *From the Vikings to the Normans*. Oxford: Oxford University Press, 2003.

Davies, Wendy, and Hayo Vierck. "The Contexts of Tribal Hidage: Social Aggregates and Settlement Patterns." *Frühmittelalterliche Studien* 8 (1974): 223–302.

Davis, Kathleen. "Boredom, Brevity and Last Things: Ælfric's Style and the Politics of Time." In Magennis and Swan, *A Companion to Ælfric*, 321–44.

– "National Writing in the Ninth Century: A Reminder for Postcolonial Thinking about the Nation." *Journal of Medieval and Early Modern Studies* 28.3 (1998): 611–37.

Davis, Natalie Zemon. *Fiction in the Archives: Pardon Tales and Their Tellers in Sixteenth- Century France*. Stanford: Stanford University Press, 1987.

Davis, R.H.C. "Alfred and Guthrum's Frontier." *EHR* 97.1 (1982): 803–10.

– "East Anglia and the Danelaw." *TRHS*, 5th ser., 5 (1955): 23–39.

de Certeau, Michel. *The Practice of Everyday Life*. Translated by Steven Rendall. Berkeley: University of California Press, 1984.

DeGregorio, Scott. "Bede and the Old Testament." In DeGregorio, *Cambridge Companion*, 127–41.

–, ed. *The Cambridge Companion to Bede*. Cambridge: Cambridge University Press, 2010.

–, ed. *Innovation and Tradition in the Writings of the Venerable Bede*. Morgantown: West Virginia University Press, 2006.

– "Monasticism and Reform in Book IV of Bede's 'Ecclesiastical History of the English People.'" *Journal of Ecclesiastical History* 61.4 (2010): 673–87.

de Lachenal, Lucilla. *Spolia: Uso e reimpiego dell'antico dal III al XIV secolo*. Milan: Longanesi, 1995.

Del Giacco, Eric Jay. "Exegesis and Sermon: A Comparison of Bede's Commentary and Homilies on Luke." *Medieval Sermon Studies* 50 (2006): 9–29.

de Vegvar, Carol Neuman. "Saints and Companions to Saints: Anglo-Saxon Royal Women Monastics in Context." In Szarmach, *Holy Men and Holy Women*, 51–93.

Devlin, Zoë L., and Caroline N.J. Holas-Clark, eds. *Approaching Interdisciplinarity: Archaeology, History and the Study of Early Medieval Britain, c. 400–1100*. BAR British Series 486. Oxford: Archaeopress, 2009.

Diesner, Hans-Joachim. "Inkarnationsjahre, 'Militia Christi' und anglische Königsporträts bei Beda Venerabilis." *Mittellateinisches Jahrbuch* 16 (1981): 17–34.

Discenza, Nicole Guenther. "Alfred's Verse Preface to the *Pastoral Care* and the Chain of Authority." *Neophilologus* 85 (2001): 625–33.

– *Inhabited Spaces: Anglo-Saxon Constructions of Place*. Toronto: University of Toronto Press, 2017.

– "A Map of the Universe: Geography and Cosmology in the Program of Alfred the Great." In Karkov and Howe, *Conversion and Colonization*, 83–108.

Discenza, Nicole Guenther, and Paul E. Szarmach, eds. *A Companion to Alfred the Great*. Leiden: Brill, 2014.

Dockray-Miller, Mary. "The Massachusetts Medievalist Thinks about the Power Dynamics of 'Anglo-Saxon.'" *The Massachusetts Medievalist*, 17 December 2019. mdockraymiller.hcommons.org/2019/12/17/the-massachusetts-medievalist-thinks-about-the-power-dynamics-of-anglo-saxon/.

Donnan, Hastings, and Thomas M. Wilson. *Borders: Frontiers of Identity, Nation and State*. Oxford: Berg, 1999.

Dornier, Ann, ed. *Mercian Studies*. Leicester: Leicester University Press, 1977.

Douglas, David C. *The Social Structure of Medieval East Anglia*. Oxford: Clarendon, 1927. Reprint, New York: Octagon Books, 1974.

Downey, Sarah. "Intertextuality in the Lives of St. Guthlac." Ph.D. diss., University of Toronto, 2004.

– "Too Much of Too Little: Guthlac and the Temptation of Excessive Fasting." *Traditio* 63 (2008): 89–127.

Downey, Sarah, Michael D.C. Drout, Michael J. Kahn, and Mark D. LeBlanc. "'Books Tell Us': Lexomic and Traditional Evidence for the Sources of *Guthlac A*." *Modern Philology* 110.2 (2012): 153–81.

Downham, Clare. "Viking Ethnicities: A Historiographic Overview." *History Compass* 10.1 (2012): 1–12.

Dufour, Annie, and Gillett Labory, eds. *Abbon, un abbé de l'an mil*. Turnhout: Brepols, 2008.

Dumitrescu, Irina A. "Bede's Liberation Philology: Releasing the English Tongue." *PMLA* 128.1 (2013): 40–56.

Dumville, David N. "The Anglian Collection of Royal Genealogies and Regnal Lists." *Anglo-Saxon England* 5 (1976): 23–50.

– "The Ætheling: A Study in Anglo-Saxon Constitutional History." *ASE* 8 (1979): 1–33.

– *English Caroline Script and Monastic History: Studies in Benedictinism, A.D. 950–1030*. Woodbridge: Boydell, 1993.

– "Essex, Middle Anglia and the Expansion of Mercia in the South-East Midlands." In Bassett, *Origins of Anglo-Saxon Kingdoms*, 123–40.

– "Kingship, Genealogies, and Regnal Lists." In *Early Medieval Kingship*, edited by Peter H. Sawyer and Ian N. Wood, 72–104. Leeds: University of Leeds Press, 1977.

– "Origins of the Kingdom of the English." In Naismith and Woodman, *Writing, Kingship and Power*, 71–121.

– "The Tribal Hidage: An Introduction to Its Texts and Their History." In Bassett, *Origins of Anglo-Saxon Kingdoms*, 225–30.

– *Wessex and England from Alfred to Edgar*. Woodbridge: Boydell, 1992.

Dunbabin, Jean. "West Francia: The Kingdom." In *The New Cambridge Medieval History*, vol. 3: *c. 900–c. 1024*, edited by Timothy Reuter, 372–97. Cambridge: Cambridge University Press, 2000.

Dunn, Marilyn. *The Christianization of the Anglo-Saxons, c. 597–c. 700: Discourses of Life, Death and Afterlife*. London: Continuum, 2009.

Dutt, William A., with illustrations by Joseph Pennell. *Highways and Byways in East Anglia*. London: Macmillan, 1901.

Dymond, David. *The Norfolk Landscape*. 2d ed. Bury St. Edmunds: Alastair, 1990.

Earl, James W. "Violence and Non-Violence in Anglo-Saxon England: Ælfric's 'Passion of St. Edmund.'" *Philological Quarterly* 78.1 (1999): 125–49.

Eco, Umberto. *Foucault's Pendulum*. Translated by William Weaver. San Diego: Harcourt Brace Jovanovich, 1989.

– *Lector in fabula: La cooperazione interpretativa nei testi narrativi*. Milan: Fabbri, Bompiani, Sonzogno, Etas, 1979. Reprint, 1991.

Ekwall, Eilert. *The Concise Oxford Dictionary of English Place-Names*. 4th ed. Oxford: Clarendon, 1960.

Eliade, Mircea. *The Myth of the Eternal Return: Or, Cosmos and History*. Translated by Willard R. Trask. Princeton: Princeton University Press, 1971.

Ellard, Donna Beth. *Anglo-Saxon(ist) Pasts, postSaxon Futures*. S.l.: punctum books, 2019.

Elliott, Winter Suzanne. "Sex and the Single Saint: Physicality in Anglo-Saxon Female Saints' Lives." Ph.D. diss., University of Georgia, 2004.

Estes, Heide. *Anglo-Saxon Literary Landscapes: Ecotheory and the Environmental Imagination*. Amsterdam: Amsterdam University Press, 2017.

Evans, Angela Care. *The Sutton Hoo Ship Burial*. London: British Museum, 1986.

Evans, George Ewart. *The Pattern Under the Plough: Aspects of the Folk-Life of East Anglia*. Illustrations by David Gentleman. London: Faber and Faber, 1966.

Fanning, Steven. "Bede, *Imperium*, and the Bretwaldas." *Speculum* 66.1 (1991): 1–26.

Faulkner, Mark. "Ælfric, St. Edmund, and St. Edwold of Cerne." *Medium Ævum* 77.1 (2008): 1–9.

– "'Like a Virgin': The Reheading of St. Edmund and Monastic Reform in Late Tenth-Century England." In *Heads Will Roll: Decapitation in the Medieval and Early Modern Imagination*, edited by Larissa Tracy and Jeff Massey, 39–52. Leiden: Brill, 2012.

Featherstone, Peter. "The Tribal Hidage and the Ealdormen of Mercia." In M. Brown and Farr, *Mercia*, 23–34.

Fell, Christine. "Perceptions of Transience." In Godden and Lapidge, *Cambridge Companion*, 180–97.

– "Saint Æðelþryð: A Historical-Hagiographical Dichotomy Revisited." *Nottingham Medieval Studies* 38 (1994): 18–34.

Fenwick, Valerie. "Insula de Burgh: Excavations at Burrow Hill, Butley, Suffolk, 1978–81." *ASSAH* 3 (1984): 35–54.

Filmer-Sankey, William. "Discussion." In Filmer-Sankey and Pestell, *Snape Anglo-Saxon Cemetery*, 262–6.

– "Grave 1 (the 1862 Ship Burial): Analysis and Interpretation." In Filmer-Sankey and Pestell, *Snape Anglo-Saxon Cemetery*, 193–8.

– "Snape Anglo-Saxon Cemetery: The Current State of Knowledge." In Carver, *Age of Sutton Hoo*, 39–51.

Filmer-Sankey, William, and Tim Pestell, with contributions from many others. *Snape Anglo-Saxon Cemetery: Excavations and Surveys 1824–1992*. East Anglian Archaeology Report no. 25. Ipswich: Suffolk County Council, 2001.

Foot, Sarah. *Æthelstan: The First King of England*. New Haven: Yale University Press, 2011.

– "Bede's Kings." In Naismith and Woodman, *Writing, Kingship and Power*, 25–51.

– "The Historiography of the Anglo-Saxon 'Nation-State.'" In Scales and Zimmer, *Power and the Nation*, 125–42.

– "The Making of *Angelcynn*: English Identity before the Norman Conquest." *Transactions of the Royal Historical Society*, 6th ser., 6 (1995): 25–49.

– "Reading Anglo-Saxon Charters: Memory, Record, or Story?" In *Narrative and History in the Early Medieval West*, edited by Elizabeth M. Tyler and Ross Balzaretti, 39–65. Turnhout: Brepols, 2006.

– *Veiled Women: The Disappearance of Nuns from Anglo-Saxon England*. 2 vols. Aldershot: Ashgate, 2000.

Fowler, Peter J. "Discussion of John Hines's 'Religion: The Limits of Knowledge." In Hines, *The Anglo-Saxons*, 401–10.

Fox, Kate. *Watching the English: The Hidden Rules of English Behaviour*. London: Hodder and Stoughton, 2004.

Foxhall Forbes, Helen. *Heaven and Earth in Anglo-Saxon England: Theology and Society in an Age of Faith*. Farnham: Ashgate, 2013. Reprint, Abingdon: Routledge, 2016.

Frank, Roberta. "Terminally Hip and Incredibly Cool: Carol, Vikings, and Anglo-Scandinavian England." *Representations* 100.1 (2007): 23–33.

Frantzen, Allen J. *Bloody Good: Chivalry, Sacrifice, and the Great War*. Chicago: University of Chicago Press, 2004.

– *Desire for Origins: New Language, Old English, and Teaching the Tradition*. New Brunswick: Rutgers University Press, 1990.

Frazer, William O. "Introduction: Identities in Early Medieval Britain." In Frazer and Tyrrell, *Social Identity*, 1–22.

Frazer, William O., and Andrew Tyrrell, eds. *Social Identity in Early Medieval Britain*. London: Leicester University Press, 2000.

Freeman, Edward Augustus. *The History of the Norman Conquest of England, Its Causes and Its Results*. Vol. 1. Revised American ed. New York, 1873.

Frenze, Maj-Britt. "Holy Heights in the Anglo-Saxon Imagination: Guthlac's *Beorg* and Sacred Death." *JEGP* 117.3 (2018): 315–42.

Frye, Northrop. *Anatomy of Criticism: Four Essays*. Princeton: Princeton University Press, 1957.

Fulk, R.D., Robert E. Bjork, and John D. Niles. "Commentary [on *Beowulf*]." In *Klaeber's Beowulf and the Fight at Finnsburg*, 4th ed., edited by Fulk, Bjork, and Niles, foreword by Helen Damico, 110–272. Toronto: University of Toronto Press, 2008.

Gantier, Louis-Marie. "L'ecclésiologie bénédictine d'Abbon de Fleury et la basilique de Saint-Benôit-sur-Loire." In Dufour and Labory, *Abbon, un abbé de l'an mil*, 273–310.

Garrison, Christine Wille. "The Lives of St. Ætheldreda: Representation of Female Sanctity from 700 to 1300." Ph.D. diss., University of Rochester, 1990.

Gatch, Milton McC. *Preaching and Theology in Anglo-Saxon England: Ælfric and Wulfstan*. Toronto: University of Toronto Press, 1977.

Geary, Patrick. *Phantoms of Remembrance: Memory and Oblivion at the End of the First Millennium*. Princeton: Princeton University Press, 1994.

Gillingham, John. *The English in the Twelfth Century: Imperialism, National Identity and Political Values*. Woodbridge: Boydell, 2000.

Gneuss, Helmut. *Ælfric of Eynsham: His Life, Times, and Writings*. Translated by Michael Lapidge. *Old English Newsletter* Subsidia 34. Kalamazoo: Medieval Institute Publications, 2009.

Gobbitt, Thomas. "The Manuscript Contexts of the Old English *Frið* of Ælfred and Guðrum." *Manuscripta* 57.1 (2013): 29–56.

Godden, Malcolm. "Ælfric of Eynsham." In Lapidge, Blair, Keynes, and Scragg, *Wiley Blackwell Encyclopedia*, 10–11.

– "Ælfric's Saints' Lives and the Problem of Miracles." *Leeds Studies in English* N.S. 16 (1985): 83–100. Reprinted in Szarmach and Oosterhouse, *Old English Prose*, 287–309.

– "Apocalypse and Invasion in Late Anglo-Saxon England." In *From Anglo-Saxon to Early Middle English: Studies Presented to E.G. Stanley*, edited by Malcolm Godden, Douglas Gray, and Terry Hoad, 130–62. Oxford: Clarendon, 1994.

– "Did King Alfred Write Anything?" *Medium Ævum* 76.1 (2007): 1–23.
– "Introduction." In Ælfric of Eynsham, *Ælfric's Catholic Homilies*, xxi–lxii.
Godden, Malcolm, and Michael Lapidge, eds. *The Cambridge Companion to Old English Literature*. 2d ed. Cambridge: Cambridge University Press, 2013.
Goetz, Hans-Werner. "Concepts of Realm and Frontiers from Late Antiquity to the Early Middle Ages: Some Preliminary Remarks." In Pohl, Wood, and Reimitz, *Transformation of Frontiers*, 73–82.
Goffart, Walter. *Barbarian Tides: The Migration Age and the Later Roman Empire*. Philadelphia: University of Pennsylvania Press, 2006.
– *The Narrators of Barbarian History (A.D. 500–800): Jordanes, Gregory of Tours, Bede, and Paul the Deacon*. Princeton: Princeton University Press, 1988.
Graham-Campbell, James, Richard Hall, Judith Jesch, and David N. Parsons, eds. *Vikings and the Danelaw*. Oxford: Oxbow, 2001.
Gransden, Antonia. "Abbo of Fleury's '*Passio sancti Eadmundi*.'" *Revue Bénédictine* 105 (1995): 20–78.
– "Baldwin, Abbot of Bury St. Edmunds, 1065–1097." *Proceedings of the Battle Conference on Anglo-Norman Studies* 4 (1981): 65–76, 187–95.
– "The Legends and Traditions Concerning the Origins of the Abbey of Bury St. Edmunds." *EHR* 100 (1985): 1–25.
– "Traditionalism and Continuity during the Last Century of Anglo-Saxon Monasticism." *Journal of Ecclesiastical History* 40 (1989): 159–207. Reprinted in *Legends, Traditions and History in Medieval England*, edited by Gransden, 31–79. London: Hambledon, 1992.
Gray, Arthur. *The Dual Origin of the Town of Cambridge*. Cambridge: Cambridge Antiquarian Society, 1908.
– "The Ford and Bridge of Cambridge." *Proceedings of the Cambridge Antiquarian Society* 14, N.S. 8 (1910): 126–39.
Gretsch, Mechthild. *Ælfric and the Cult of Saints in Late Anglo-Saxon England*. Cambridge: Cambridge University Press, 2005.
Grierson, Philip, and Mark Blackburn. *Medieval European Coinage, with a Catalogue of Coins in the Fitzwilliam Museum, Cambridge*. 1: *The Early Middle Ages (5th to 10th Centuries)*. Cambridge: Cambridge University Press, 1986.
Griffiths, David. "The Ending of Anglo-Saxon England: Identity, Allegiance, and Nationality." In Hamerow, Hinton, and Crawford, *Oxford Handbook of Anglo-Saxon Archaeology*, 62–78.
Griffiths, Gwen. "Reading Ælfric's Saint Æthelthryth as a Woman." *Parergon* 10.2 (1992): 35–49.
Grossi, Joseph. "Barrow Exegesis: Quotation, Chorography and Felix's *Life of St. Guthlac*." *Florilegium* 30 (2015 for 2013): 143–65.
– "Felix and His Kings." In Roberts and Thacker, *Guthlac*, 157–79.
– "A Place of 'Long-Lasting Evil and Unhappiness': Rædwald's East Anglia in Bede's *Ecclesiastical History*." *New Medieval Literatures* 15 (2013): 97–120.

Grundy, Lynne. *Books and Grace: Ælfric's Theology*. London: King's College London Centre for Late Antique and Medieval Studies, 1991.

Gulley, Alison. *The Displacement of the Body in Ælfric's Virgin Martyr Lives*. Farnham: Ashgate, 2014.

Gunn, Vicky. *Bede's* Historiae*: Genre, Rhetoric, and the Construction of Anglo-Saxon Church History*. Woodbridge: Boydell, 2009.

Hadley, Dawn M. "'Cockles amongst the Wheat': The Scandinavian Settlement of England." In Frazer and Tyrrell, *Social Identity*, 111–35.

– "'Hamlet and the Princes of Denmark': Lordship in the Danelaw." In Hadley and Richards, *Cultures in Contact*, 107–32.

– *The Vikings in England: Settlement, Society and Culture*. Manchester: Manchester University Press, 2006.

Hadley, Dawn M., and Julian D. Richards, eds. *Cultures in Contact: Scandinavian Settlement in England in the Ninth and Tenth Centuries*. Turnhout: Brepols, 2000.

Halbrooks, John. "Ælfric, the *Maccabees*, and the Problem of Christian Heroism." *Studies in Philology* 106.3 (2009): 263–84.

Hall, Alaric. "Constructing Anglo-Saxon Sanctity: Tradition, Innovation and Saint Guthlac." In *Images of Medieval Sanctity: Essays in Honour of Gary Dickson*, edited by Debra Higgs Strickland, 207–35. Leiden: Brill, 2007.

Hall, Thomas. "A Handlist of Anglo-Latin Hagiography through the Early Twelfth Century (from Theodore of Tarsus to William of Malmesbury)." *Old English Newsletter* 45.1 (2014): 1–23.

Halstad McGuire, Erin. "Sailing Home: Boat-Graves, Migrant Identities and Funerary Practices on the Viking Frontier." In *Memory, Mourning, Landscape*, edited by Elizabeth Anderson, Avril Maddrell, Kate McLoughlin, and Alana Vincent, 165–87. Amsterdam: Rodopi, 2010.

Hamerow, Helena, David A. Hinton, and Sally Crawford, eds. *The Oxford Handbook of Anglo-Saxon Archaeology*. Oxford: Oxford University Press, 2011.

Hare, Kent G. "Heroes, Saints, and Martyrs: Holy Kingship from Bede to Aelfric." *The Heroic Age* 9 (2006). http://www.heroicage.org/issues/9/hare.html.

Härke, Heinrich. "Anglo-Saxon Immigration and Ethnogenesis." *Medieval Archaeology* 55.1 (2011): 1–28.

Harland, James M. "Memories of Migration? The 'Anglo-Saxon' Burial Costume of the Fifth Century AD." *Antiquity* 93 (2019): 954–69.

Harris, Stephen J. "The Alfredian *World History* and Anglo-Saxon Identity." *JEGP* 100.4 (2001): 482–510.

– "Anglo-Saxons, Israelites, Hebrews, and Jews." In *Imagining the Jew in Anglo-Saxon Literature and Culture*, edited by Samantha Zacher, 27–39. Toronto: University of Toronto Press, 2016.

– *Bede and Aethelthryth: An Introduction to Christian Latin Poetics*. Morgantown: West Virginia University Press, 2016.

– "An Overview of Race and Ethnicity in Pre-Norman England." *Literature Compass* 5.4 (2008): 740–54.

– *Race and Ethnicity in Anglo-Saxon Literature*. New York: Routledge, 2003.

Harrison, Dick. "Invisible Boundaries and Places of Power: Notions of Liminality and Centrality in the Early Middle Ages." In Pohl, Wood and Reimitz, *Transformation of Frontiers*, 83–93.

Hart, Cyril R. "The Anglo-Saxon Chronicle at Ramsey." In *Alfred the Wise: Studies in Honour of Janet Bately on the Occasion of Her Sixty-Fifth Birthday*, edited by Jane Roberts, Janet L. Nelson, and Malcolm Godden, 65–88. Cambridge: Brewer, 1997.

– "The B Text of the *Anglo-Saxon Chronicle*." *Journal of Medieval History* 8.3 (1982): 241–99.

– *The Danelaw*. London: Hambledon, 1992.

– "The Kingdom of Mercia." In Dornier, *Mercian Studies*, 43–61.

Hart, Cyril R., and Anthony Syme. "The Earliest Suffolk Charter." *Proceedings of the Suffolk Institute of Archaeology and History* 36 (1985–8): 165–81.

Hartmann, Jan Peer. "Monument Reuse in Felix's *Vita Sancti Guthlaci*." *Medium Ævum* 88.2 (2019): 230–64.

Harvey, P.D.A. *Maps in the Age of Bede*. Jarrow, UK: St. Paul's Parish Church Council, 2006.

Haslam, Jeremy. "The Development and Topography of Saxon Cambridge." *Proceedings of the Cambridge Antiquarian Society* 72 (1984): 13–29. https://jeremyhaslam.files.wordpress.com/2010/11/haslam-development-and-topography-of-anglo-saxon-cambridge.pdf

– "*Dommoc* and Dunwich: A Reappraisal." *ASSAH* 5 (1992): 41–6.

– "King Alfred and the Vikings: Strategies and Tactics 876–886 AD." *ASSAH* 13 (2005): 122–54.

Head, Thomas. *Hagiography and the Cult of Saints: The Diocese of Orléans, 800–1200*. Cambridge: Cambridge University Press, 1990.

Hedges, Robert. "Anglo-Saxon Migration and the Molecular Evidence." In Hamerow, Hinton, and Crawford, *Oxford Handbook of Anglo-Saxon Archaeology*, 79–89.

Heffernan, Thomas J. *Sacred Biography: Saints and Their Biographers in the Middle Ages*. New York: Oxford University Press, 1988.

Helgerson, Richard. *Forms of Nationhood: The Elizabethan Writing of England*. Chicago: University of Chicago Press, 1992.

Herren, Michael. "Boniface's Epistolary Prose Style: The Letters to the English." In *Latinity and Identity in Anglo-Saxon Literature*, edited by Rebecca Stephenson and Emily V. Thornbury, 18–37. Toronto: University of Toronto Press, 2016.

Heslop, Sandy (T.A.), and Margit Thøfner. "Introduction: On Faith, Objects and Locality." In Heslop, Mellings, and Thøfner, *Art, Faith and Place*, 1–18.

Heslop, T.A., Elizabeth Mellings, and Margit Thøfner, eds. *Art, Faith and Place in East Anglia*. Woodbridge: Boydell Press, 2012.

Hettne, Björn. "The New Regionalism Revisited." In Söderbaum and Shaw, *Theories of New Regionalism*, 22–42.

Hiatt, Alfred. "*Beowulf* Off the Map." *Anglo-Saxon Literature* 38 (2009): 11–40.

Higham, Nicholas J. "Bede's Agenda in Book IV of the 'Ecclesiastical History of the English People': A Tricky Matter of Advising the King." *Journal of Ecclesiastical History* 64.3 (2013): 476–93.

– "Britain In and Out of the Roman Empire." In Higham and Ryan, *The Anglo-Saxon World*, 20–69.

– *The Convert Kings: Power and Religious Affiliation in Early Anglo-Saxon England*. Manchester: Manchester University Press, 1997.

– *The Death of Anglo-Saxon England*. Stroud: Sutton, 1997.

– *An English Empire: Bede and the Early Anglo-Saxon Kings*. Manchester: Manchester University Press, 1995.

– "From Sub-Roman Britain to Anglo-Saxon England: Debating the Insular Dark Ages." *History Compass* 2 (2004): 1–29.

– "From Tribal Chieftains to Christian Kings." In Higham and Ryan, *The Anglo-Saxon World*, 126–78.

– "Guthlac's *Vita*, Mercia and East Anglia in the First Half of the Eighth Century." In Hill and Worthington, *Æthelbald and Offa*, 85–90.

– *(Re-)reading Bede: The* Ecclesiastical History *in Context*. Abingdon, Oxon: Routledge, 2006.

– "Sources and Issues 2A: The Anglo-Saxon Cemetery at Spong Hill." In Higham and Ryan, *The Anglo-Saxon World*, 112–19.

Higham, Nicholas J., and D.H. Hill, eds. *Edward the Elder 899–924*. London: Routledge, 2001.

Higham, Nicholas J., and Martin J. Ryan. *The Anglo-Saxon World*. New Haven: Yale University Press, 2013.

Hill, David. "Mercians: The Dwellers on the Boundary." In M. Brown and Farr, *Mercia*, 173–82.

Hill, David, and Margaret Worthington, eds. *Æthelbald and Offa: Two Eighth-Century Kings of Mercia*. BAR British Series, 383. Oxford: Archaeopress, 2005.

Hill, Joyce. "Ælfric: His Life and Works." In Magennis and Swan, *A Companion to Ælfric*, 35–65.

Hill, Rosalind. "Bede and the Boors." In Bonner, *Famulus Christi*, 93–105.

Hill, Thomas D. "'*Non nisi uirgam tantum ... in manu*': Sigeberht's Mosaic Aspirations (Bede, *Historia ecclesiastica* III, 18)." *Notes and Queries* 53.4 (2006): 391–5.

Hills, Catherine. "Overview: Anglo-Saxon Identity." In Hamerow, Hinton, and Crawford, *Oxford Handbook of Anglo-Saxon Archaeology*, 3–12.

Hines, John, ed. *The Anglo-Saxons from the Migration Period to the Eighth Century: An Ethnographic Perspective*. Woodbridge: Boydell and Brewer, 1997.

– "The Becoming of the English: Identity, Material Culture and Language in Early Anglo-Saxon England." *ASSAH* 7 (1994): 49–59.
– "Literary Sources and Archaeology." In Hamerow, Hinton, and Crawford, *Oxford Handbook of Anglo-Saxon Archaeology*, 968–85.
– "No Place Like Home? The Anglo-Saxon Social Landscape from Within and Without." In Sauer and Story, *Anglo-Saxon England and the Continent*, 21–40.
– "The Origins of East Anglia in a North Sea Zone." In Bates and Liddiard, *East Anglia and Its North Sea World*, 16–43.
– "Religion: The Limits of Knowledge." In Hines, *The Anglo-Saxons*, 375–401.
– *The Scandinavian Character of Anglian England in the Pre-Viking Period*. BAR British Series, 124. Oxford: BAR, 1984.
– *Voices in the Past: English Literature and Archaeology*. Woodbridge: Brewer, 2004.
Hobbs, Richard. *The Mildenhall Treasure*. British Museum Objects in Focus series. London: British Museum Press, 2012.
Hoenicke Moore, Michael E. "Bede's Devotion to Rome: The Periphery Defining the Centre." In Lebecq, Perrin, and Szerwiniack, *Bède le Vénérable*, 199–208.
Hoggett, Richard. *The Archaeology of the East Anglian Conversion*. Anglo-Saxon Studies, 15. Woodbridge: Boydell, 2010.
Holder, Arthur G. "Bede and the New Testament." In DeGregorio, *Cambridge Companion*, 142–55.
Hollis, Stephanie. *Anglo-Saxon Women and the Church: Sharing a Common Fate*. Woodbridge: Boydell, 1992.
Holman, Katherine. "Defining the Danelaw." In Graham-Campbell et al., *Vikings and the Danelaw*, 1–11.
Hooke, Della. *The Anglo-Saxon Landscape: The Kingdom of the Hwicce*. Manchester: Manchester University Press, 1985.
– "The Anglo-Saxons in England in the Seventh and Eighth Centuries: Aspects of Location in Space." In Hines, *The Anglo-Saxons*, 65–99.
– *The Landscape of Anglo-Saxon England*. London: Leicester University Press, 1998.
Hoskins, W.G. *Local History in England*. 2d ed. London: Longman, 1984.
– *The Making of the English Landscape*. London: Penguin, 1985 [1955].
Houwen, L.A.J.R., and A.A. MacDonald, eds. *Beda Venerabilis: Historian, Monk and Northumbrian*. Mediaevalia Groningana Series, 19. Groningen: Egbert Forsten, 1996.
Howe, John, and Michael Wolfe, eds. *Inventing Medieval Landscapes: Senses of Place in Western Europe*. Gainesville: University Press of Florida, 2002.
Howe, Nicholas. "An Angle on This Earth: Sense of Place in Anglo-Saxon England." *Bulletin of the John Rylands Library of the University of Manchester* 82.1 (2000): 3–27.
– "The Cultural Construction of Reading in Anglo-Saxon England." In *The Ethnography of Reading*, edited by Jonathan Boyarin, 58–79. Berkeley: University of California Press, 1993. Reprinted in *Old English Literature:*

Critical Essays, edited by R.M. Liuzza, 1–22. New Haven: Yale University Press, 2002.
– "The Landscape of Anglo-Saxon England: Inherited, Invented, Imagined." In Howe and Wolfe, *Inventing Medieval Landscapes*, 91–112.
– *Migration and Mythmaking in Anglo-Saxon England*. 2d ed. Notre Dame: University of Notre Dame Press, 2001.
– *The Old English Catalogue Poems*. Anglistica 23. Copenhagen: Rosenkilde and Bagger, 1985.
– "Rome: Capital of Anglo-Saxon England." *Journal of Medieval and Early Modern Studies* 34.1 (2004): 147–74.
– *Writing the Map of Anglo-Saxon England: Essays in Cultural Geography*. New Haven: Yale University Press, 2008.
Hudson, John. *The Oxford History of the Laws of England*, vol. 2: *871–1216*. Oxford: Oxford University Press, 2012.
Hunter, Michael. "Germanic and Roman Antiquity and the Sense of the Past in Anglo-Saxon England." *Anglo-Saxon England* 3 (1974): 29–50.
Hurt, James. *Ælfric*. New York: Twayne, 1972.
Iamartino, Giovanni. "San Guthlac: 'Militia Christi' e letteratura agiografica nell'Inghilterra Anglosassone." In *"Militia Christi" e Crociata nei secoli XI–XIII*, Miscellenea del Centro di studi medievali, 13, 785–822. Milan: Università Cattolica del Sacro Cuore, 1992.
Ingold, Tim. *Lines: A Brief History*. London: Routledge, 2007.
Innes, Matthew. "Danelaw Identities: Ethnicity, Regionalism, and Political Allegiance." In Hadley and Richards, *Cultures in Contact*, 65–88.
Irvine, Martin. "Medieval Textuality and the Archaeology of Textual Culture." In *Speaking Two Languages: Traditional Disciplines and Contemporary Theory in Medieval Studies*, edited by Allen Frantzen, 181–210, 276–84. Albany: SUNY Press, 1991.
Irvine, Susan. "The Anglo-Saxon Chronicle." In Discenza and Szarmach, *A Companion to Alfred the Great*, 344–67.
Jesch, Judith. "Scandinavians and 'Cultural Paganism' in Late Anglo-Saxon England." In *The Christian Tradition in Anglo-Saxon England: Approaches to Current Scholarship and Teaching*, edited by Paul Cavill, 55–68. Cambridge: D.S. Brewer, 2004.
– *The Viking Diaspora*. Abingdon, Oxon: Routledge, 2015.
John, Eric. "The Age of Edgar." In Campbell, John, and Wormald, *The Anglo-Saxons*, 160–91.
– *Land Tenure in Early England: A Discussion of Some Problems*. Leicester: Leicester University Press, 1960.
– *Reassessing Anglo-Saxon England*. Manchester: University of Manchester Press, 1996.

– "The Return of the Vikings." In Campbell, John, and Wormald, *The Anglo-Saxons*, 192–213.

Jones, Charles W. *Bede, the Schools and the* Computus. Edited by Wesley M. Stephens. Aldershot: Variorum/Ashgate, 1994.

– *Saints' Lives and Chronicles in Early England*. Ithaca: Cornell University Press, 1947.

Jones, Christopher A. "Ælfric and the Limits of 'Benedictine Reform.'" In Magennis and Swan, *A Companion to Ælfric*, 67–108.

– *Ælfric's Letter to the Monks of Eynsham*. Cambridge: Cambridge University Press, 1998.

– "Envisioning the Cenobium in the Old English *Guthlac A*." *Mediaeval Studies* 57 (1995): 259–91.

Jordan, Timothy R.W. "Holiness and Hopefulness: The Monastic and Lay Audiences of Abbo of Fleury's *Passio Sancti Eadmundi* and Ælfric of Eynsham's *Life of St. Edmund, King and Martyr*." *Enarratio* 19 (2015): 1–29.

Jordan, Victoria B. "Monastic Hagiography in Anglo-Saxon and Anglo-Norman England: The Cases of Edward the Confessor and St. Edmund, King and Martyr." Ph.D. diss., Boston College, 1995.

Jorgensen, Alice, ed. *Reading the Anglo-Saxon Chronicle: Language, Literature, History*. Studies in the Early Middle Ages Series, 23. Turnhout: Brepols, 2010.

Karkov, Catherine E. "The Body of St. Æthelthryth: Desire, Conversion and Reform in Anglo-Saxon England." In *The Cross Goes North: Processes of Conversion in Northern Europe, AD 300–1300*, edited by Martin Carver, 397–411. Woodbridge: Boydell and Brewer, 2003.

– *Imagining Anglo-Saxon England: Utopia, Heterotopia, Dystopia*. Woodbridge, UK: Boydell Press, 2020.

– "Post 'Anglo-Saxon' Melancholia." *Medium*, 10 December 2019. https://medium.com/@catherinekarkov/post-anglo-saxon-melancholia-ca73955717d3.

– "Postcolonial." In Stodnick and Trilling, *Handbook of Anglo-Saxon Studies*, 149–63.

– *The Ruler-Portraits of Anglo-Saxon England*. Woodbridge: Boydell, 2004.

Karkov, Catherine E., and Nicholas Howe, eds. *Conversion and Colonization in Anglo-Saxon England*. Tempe: ACMRS, 2006.

Kendall, Calvin B., and Peter S. Wells, eds. *Voyage to the Other World: The Legacy of Sutton Hoo*. Minneapolis: University of Minnesota Press, 1992.

Kennedy, Maev. "Detectorists Strike Gold as British Museum Reveals Record Haul." *The Guardian*, 4 December 2017. https://www.theguardian.com/culture/2017/dec/04/coin-laden-pot-pendant-british-museum-record-haul-2016-treasure-finds.

Kershaw, Jane F. *Viking Identities: Scandinavian Jewellery in England*. Oxford: Oxford University Press, 2013.

Kershaw, Paul J.E. "The Alfred-Guthrum Treaty: Scripting Accommodation and Interaction in Viking Age England." In Hadley and Richards, *Cultures in Contact*, 43–59.

– *Peaceful Kings: Peace, Power, and the Early Medieval Political Imagination*. Oxford: Oxford University Press, 2011.

Keynes, Simon. "An Abbot, an Archbishop, and the Viking Raids of 1006–7 and 1009–12." *Anglo-Saxon England* 36 (2007): 151–224.

– "Alfred the Great and the Kingdom of the Anglo-Saxons." In Discenza and Szarmach, *A Companion to Alfred the Great*, 13–46.

– "Appendix II: Archbishops and Bishops, 597–1066." In Lapidge, Blair, Keynes, and Scragg, *Wiley Blackwell Encyclopedia*, 540–66.

– *The Diplomas of King Æthelred 'the Unready,' 978–1016*. Cambridge: Cambridge University Press, 1980.

– "Edward, King of the Anglo-Saxons." In Higham and Hill, *Edward the Elder*, 40–66.

– "Ely Abbey 672–1109." In *A History of Ely Cathedral*, edited by Peter Meadows and Nigel Ramsay, 3–58. Woodbridge: Boydell, 2003.

– "England, 700–900." In McKitterick, *New Cambridge Medieval History*, 18–42.

– "King Alfred and the Mercians." In Blackburn and Dumville, *Kings, Currency, and Alliances*, 1–45.

– "The Kingdom of the Mercians in the Eighth Century." In Hill and Worthington, *Æthelbald and Offa*, 1–26.

– "The Power of the Written Word: Alfredian England 871–899." In Reuter, *Alfred the Great*, 175–97.

– "Rædwald the Bretwalda." In Kendall and Wells, *Voyage to the Other World*, 103–23.

Keynes, Simon, and Michael Lapidge, eds. and trans. *Alfred the Great: Asser's* Life of King Alfred *and Other Contemporary Sources*. London: Penguin, 1983. Reprint, 2004.

Kilbride, William. "Why I Feel Cheated by the Term 'Christianisation.'" In "Early Medieval Religion," edited by Aleks Pluskowski, special issue, *Archaeological Review from Cambridge* 17.2 (2000): 1–17.

Kilpatrick, Kelly A. "The Place-Names in Felix's *Vita Sancti Guthlaci*." *Nottingham Medieval Studies* 58 (2014): 1–56.

– "Places, Landscapes and Borders in the *Vita S. Guthlaci*." In Roberts and Thacker, *Guthlac*, 97–115.

King, Thomas. "Borders." In *One Good Story, That One*. Toronto: HarperPerennial, 1993. Reprinted in *Elements of Literature: Fiction, Poetry, Drama*, edited by Robert Scholes, Nancy R. Comley, Carl H. Klaus, and David Staines, 4th Canadian ed., 328–36. Don Mills, ON: Oxford University Press, 2010.

Kingsley, Charles. *Hereward the Wake, "Last of the English."* London: Macmillan, 1867. Reprint, London: Blackie and Son, n.d.

Kingsnorth, Paul. *Real England: The Battle against the Bland*. London: Granta UK, 2009.

Kirby, D.P. "Bede's Native Sources for the *Historia Ecclesiastica*." *Bulletin of the John Rylands University Library of Manchester* 48.2 (1966): 341–71.

– *The Earliest English Kings*. London: Routledge, 1992.

– *The Making of Early England*. London: B.T. Batsford, 1967.

– "Welsh Bards and the Border." In Dornier, *Mercian Studies*, 31–42.

Klaeber, Frederick (Friedrich) J. "Notes [to *Beowulf*]." In *Beowulf and the Fight at Finnsburg*, edited by Frederick Klaeber, 121–230. 3d ed. Boston: D.C. Heath and Co., 1950.

Klaniczay, Gábor. *Holy Rulers and Blessed Princesses: Dynastic Cults in Medieval Central Europe.* Translated by Éva Pálmai. Cambridge: Cambridge University Press, 2002.

Klein, Stacy S. *Ruling Women: Queenship and Gender in Anglo-Saxon Literature.* Notre Dame: University of Notre Dame Press, 2006.

Konshuh, Courtnay. "Constructing Early Anglo-Saxon Identity in the Anglo-Saxon Chronicles." In *The Land of the English Kin: Studies in Wessex and Anglo-Saxon England in Honour of Professor Barbara Yorke*, edited by Alexander James Langlands and Ryan Lavelle. 154-79. Leiden: Brill, 2020.

Kurtz, Benjamin P. "From St. Antony to St. Guthlac: A Study in Biography." *University of California Publications in Modern Philology* 12 (1926): 103–46.

Laistner, M.L.W. *Thought and Letters in Western Europe: A.D. 500 to 900.* London: Methuen and Co., 1931.

Lambert, Tom. "Frontier Law in Anglo-Saxon England." In *Crossing Borders: Boundaries and Margins in Medieval and Early Modern Britain: Essays in Honour of Cynthia J. Neville*, edited by Sara Butler and K.J. Kesselring, 21–42. Leiden: Brill, 2018.

Lapidge, Michael. *Anglo-Latin Literature 600–899*. London: Hambledon, 1996.

– *The Anglo-Saxon Library*. Oxford: Oxford University Press, 2005.

– "Æthelwold as Scholar and Teacher." In Yorke, *Bishop Æthelwold*, 89–117.

–, ed. and trans. *Byrhtferth of Ramsey: The Lives of St. Oswald and St. Ecgwine.* Oxford: Clarendon, 2009.

– "Felix." In Lapidge, Blair, Keynes, and Scragg, *Wiley Blackwell Encyclopedia*, 186.

– "Introduction." In *Byrhtferth of Ramsey: The Lives of St. Oswald and St. Ecgwine*, edited and translated by Michael Lapidge, xv-ciii.

– "The Saintly Life in Anglo-Saxon England." In Godden and Lapidge, *Cambridge Companion*, 251–72.

Lapidge, Michael, John Blair, Simon Keynes, and Donald Scragg, eds. *The Wiley Blackwell Encyclopedia of Anglo-Saxon England*. 2d ed. Chichester: John Wiley and Sons, 2014.

Lavelle, Ryan. *Alfred's Wars: Sources and Interpretations of Anglo-Saxon Warfare in the Middle Ages*. Woodbridge: Boydell, 2010.

– "Geographies of Power in the Anglo-Saxon Chronicle: The Royal Estates of Anglo-Saxon Wessex." In Jorgensen, *Reading the Anglo-Saxon Chronicle*, 187–219.

– *Places of Contested Power: Conflict and Rebellion in England and France, 830-1150*. Woodbridge: Boydell Press, 2020.

– "The Politics of Rebellion: The *Ætheling* Æthelwold and West Saxon Royal Succession, 899–902." In Skinner, *Challenging the Boundaries*, 51–80.

Lavezzo, Kathy. *The Accommodated Jew: English Antisemitism from Bede to Milton*. Ithaca: Cornell University Press, 2016.

– *Angels on the Edge of the World: Geography, Literature, and English Community, 1000–1534*. Ithaca: Cornell University Press, 2006.

Lawson, Graeme. "The Lyre Remains from Grave 32." In Filmer-Sankey and Pestell, *Snape Anglo-Saxon Cemetery*, 215–23.

Leader, Damian Riehl. *A History of the University of Cambridge*, vol. 1: *The University to 1546*. Cambridge: Cambridge University Press, 1988.

Lebecq, Stéphane, Michel Perrin, and Olivier Szerwiniack, eds. *Bède le Vénérable entre tradition et postérité*. Centre d'histoire de l'Europe du Nord-Ouest (France), Textes, images et spiritualité (Université de Picardie). Lille: CEGES, Université Charles-de-Gaulle, Lille III, 2005.

Lee, Christina. "Healing Words: St. Guthlac and the Trauma of War." In *Trauma in Medieval Society*, edited by Wendy J. Turner and Christina Lee, 259–73. Leiden: Brill, 2018.

Lees, Clare A., ed. *The Cambridge History of Early Medieval English Literature*. Cambridge: Cambridge University Press, 2013.

Lees, Clare A., and Gillian R. Overing. "Anglo-Saxon Horizons: Places of the Mind in the Northumbrian Landscape." In Lees and Overing, *A Place to Believe In*, 1–26.

–, eds. *Double Agents: Women and Clerical Culture in Anglo-Saxon England*. Philadelphia: University of Pennsylvania Press, 2001.

–, eds. *A Place to Believe In: Locating Medieval Landscapes*. University Park: Pennsylvania State University Press, 2006.

Leeser, Sarah. "On the Edge and in the Middle: The Dynamic and Territorial Context of St. Guthlac's Early Cult." In Roberts and Thacker, *Guthlac*, 138–56.

Le Goff, Jacques. *The Medieval Imagination*. Translated by Arthur Goldhammer. Chicago: University of Chicago Press, 1988.

Levison, Wilhelm. *England and the Continent in the Eighth Century*. Oxford: Clarendon, 1946.

Licence, Tom, ed. *Bury St. Edmunds and the Norman Conquest*. Woodbridge: Boydell, 2014.

– "The Cult of St. Edmund." In Licence, *Bury St. Edmunds and the Norman Conquest*, 104–30.

– "Introduction." In Herman the Archdeacon, *Miracles of St. Edmund*, xiii–cxxxiii.

– "The Origins of the Monastic Communities of St. Benedict at Holme and Bury St. Edmunds." *Revue Bénédictine* 116.1 (2006): 42–61.

Liddiard, Robert. "Introduction: The North Sea." In Bates and Liddiard, *East Anglia and Its North Sea World*, 1–14.

Liebermann, Felix, ed. *Die Heiligen Englands: Angelsächsisch und Lateinisch.* Hannover: Hahn'sche Buchhandlung, 1889.

– "Über ostenglische Geschichtsquellen des 12., 13., 14. Jahrhunderts, besonders den falschen Ingulf." *Neues Archiv der Gesellschaft für Ältere Deutsche Geschichtskunde* 18 (1893): 225–67.

Lobel, Mary D. *Cambridge*. Historic Towns series. Vol. 2, part 2. London: Scolar Press/Historic Towns Trust, 1974.

Lockett, Leslie. *Anglo-Saxon Psychologies in the Vernacular and Latin Traditions.* Toronto: University of Toronto Press, 2011.

Loomis, Grant. "The Growth of the Saint Edmund Legend." *Harvard Studies and Notes in Philology and Literature* 14 (1932): 83–113.

Love, Rosalind. "The Anglo-Saxon Saints of Thorney and their Hagiographer." In *Hagiography in Anglo-Saxon England: Adopting and Adapting Saints' Lives into Old English Prose (c. 950–1150)*, edited by Loredana Lazzari, Claudia Di Sciacca, and Patrizia Lendinara, 489–522. Textes et études du moyen âge, 73. Turnhout: Brepols, 2014; Barcelona: Fédération internationale des instituts d'études médiévales, 2014.

– "Folcard of Saint-Bertin and the Anglo-Saxon Saints at Thorney." In Brett and Woodman, *The Long Twelfth-Century View*, 27–45.

– "The Sources of Vita S. Guthlaci (L.E.2.1.)." 1997. *Fontes Anglo-Saxonici: World Wide Web Register*. http://fontes.english.ox.ac.uk/.

Lowe, Kathryn. "The Development of the Anglo-Saxon Boundary Clause." *Nomina: Journal of the Society for Name Studies in Britain and Ireland* 21 (1998): 63–100.

– "Linguistic Geography, Demography, and Monastic Community: Scribal Language at Bury St. Edmunds." In *Interfaces between Language and Culture in Medieval England: A Festschrift for Matti Kilpiö*, edited by Alaric Hall, Bethany Fox, Ágnes Kiricsi, and Olga Timofeeva, 147–78. Leiden: Brill, 2010.

– "The Nature and Effect of the Anglo-Saxon Vernacular Will." *Journal of Legal History* 19 (1998): 23–61.

Loyn, H[enry] R[oyston]. "Kings, Gesiths and Thegns." In Carver, *Age of Sutton Hoo*, 75–9.

– *The Vikings in Britain*. Oxford: Blackwell, 1994.

Lozovsky, Natalia. *"The Earth Is Our Book": Geographical Knowledge in the Latin West ca. 400–1000*. Recentiores: Later Latin Texts and Contexts Series. Ann Arbor: University of Michigan Press, 2000.

Luckhardt, Courtney. "Gender and Connectivity: Facilitating Religious Travel in the Sixth and Seventh Centuries." *Comitatus* 44 (2013): 29–54.

Lugli, Adalgisa. *Naturalia et mirabilia: Il collezionismo enciclopedico nelle Wunderkammern D'Europa*. Milan: Gabriele Mazzotta, 1983.

Lumley Prior, Avril. "*Pegeland* Revisited: St. Pega in the Post-Guthlac Fenland." In Roberts and Thacker, *Guthlac*, 326–41.

Lundgren, Timothy J. "Hereward and Outlawry in Fenland Culture: A Study of Local Narrative and Tradition in Medieval England." Ph.D. diss., Ohio State University, 1996.

Luscombe, David. "City and Politics before the Coming of the *Politics*: Some Illustrations." In *Church and City 1000–1500: Essays in Honour of Christopher Brooke*, edited by David Abulafia, Michael J. Franklin, and Miri Rubin, 41–55. Cambridge: Cambridge University Press, 1992.

Lutterkort, Karl. "Beda Hagiographicus: Meaning and Function of Miracle Stories in the *Vita Cuthberti* and the *Historia Ecclesiastica*." In Houwen and MacDonald, *Beda Venerabilis*, 81–106.

Lyon, Stewart. "The Coinage of Edward the Elder." In Higham and Hill, *Edward the Elder*, 67–78.

MacCarron, Máirín. "The Adornment of Virgins: Æthelthryth and Her Necklaces." In *Listen, O Isles, unto Me: Studies in Medieval Word and Image in Honour of Jennifer O'Reilly*, edited by Elizabeth Mullins and Diarmuid Scully, 142–55, 353–6. Cork: Cork University Press, 2011.

– "Æthelthryth and Hild in the *Historia Ecclesiastica*." Paper presented at the 20th International Medieval Congress, University of Leeds, 1–4 July 2012.

– "Christology and the Future in Bede's *Annus Domini*." In Darby and Wallis, *Bede and the Future*, 161–79.

Magennis, Hugh. *The Cambridge Introduction to Anglo-Saxon Literature*. Cambridge: Cambridge University Press, 2011.

– "Geography and English Identity in the Middle Ages." Review of Fabienne Michelet, *Creation, Migration, and Conquest*, and Kathy Lavezzo, *Angels on the Edge of the World*. *College Literature* 35.3 (2008): 180–90.

– "Warrior Saints, Warfare, and the Hagiography of Ælfric of Eynsham." *Traditio* 56 (2001): 27–51.

Magennis, Hugh, and Mary Swan, eds. *A Companion to Ælfric*. Leiden: Brill, 2009.

Marten, Lucy. "The Shiring of East Anglia: An Alternative Hypothesis." *Historical Research* 81 (2008): 1–27.

Martin, Lawrence T. "Bede and Preaching." In DeGregorio, *Cambridge Companion*, 156–69.

Martin, Toby F. *The Cruciform Brooch and Anglo-Saxon England*. Woodbridge: Boydell, 2015.

Marzinzik, Sonja. *The Sutton Hoo Helmet*. British Museum Objects in Focus. London: British Museum Press, 2007.

Maseres, Francis. *Historiae anglicanae circa tempus conquestus Angliae a Gulielmo Notho, Normannorum Duce, selecta monumenta*. London, 1807.

Mattéoni, Olivier. "Mirrors of Princes." In *Encyclopedia of the Middle Ages*, vol. 2: *L–Z*, edited by Andre Vauchez, Barrie Dobson, and Michael Lapidge, 959–60. Cambridge: James Clarke, 2000.

Matthews, Catherine R. "Token and Promise: The Saintly Role of Royal Bodies in Ælfric's Lives of Oswald, Æthelthryth and Edmund." Master's thesis, Harvard University Extension School, 2016.

Mattingly, David. *An Imperial Possession: Britain in the Roman Empire, 54 BC–AD 409*. London: Penguin, 2006.

Mayr-Harting, Henry. *The Coming of Christianity to Anglo-Saxon England*. 3d ed. University Park: Pennsylvania State University Press, 1991.

McClure, Judith. "Bede's Old Testament Kings." In Wormald, Bullough, and Collins, *Ideal and Reality*, 76–98.

McClure, Judith, and Roger Collins, ed. and trans. *The Ecclesiastical History of the English People; the Greater Chronicle; Bede's Letter to Egbert*, by Bede. Oxford: Oxford University Press, 1994.

McDougall, Ian. "Serious Entertainments: An Examination of a Peculiar Type of Viking Atrocity." *ASE* 22 (1993): 201–25.

McKeehan, Irene Pettit. "St. Edmund of East Anglia: The Development of a Romantic Legend." *University of Colorado Studies*, gen. ser., 15 (1925): 13–74.

McKitterick, Rosamond, ed. *The New Cambridge Medieval History*, vol. 2: *c. 700–c. 900*. Cambridge: Cambridge University Press, 1995.

McLeod, Shane. *The Beginning of Scandinavian Settlement in England: The Viking "Great Army" and Early Settlers, c. 865–900*. Turnhout: Brepols, 2014.

Meaney, Audrey L. "Felix's *Life of Guthlac*: History or Hagiography?" In Hill and Worthington, *Æthelbald and Offa*, 75–84.

– "Felix's Life of St. Guthlac: Hagiography and/or Truth." *Proceedings of the Cambridge Antiquarian Society* 90 (2001): 29–48.

Mehan, Uppinder, and David Townsend. "Nation and the Gaze of the Other in Eighth-Century Northumbria." *Comparative Literature* 53.1 (2001): 1–26.

Merrills, A.H. *History and Geography in Late Antiquity*. Cambridge: Cambridge University Press, 2005.

Merton, Thomas. *The Seven Storey Mountain: An Autobiography of Faith*. Fiftieth anniversary ed. Introduction by Robert Giroux, with Note to the Reader by William H. Shannon. San Diego: Harcourt, Brace, 1998.

Meyer, Marc A. "Queens, Convents and Conversion in Early Anglo-Saxon England." *Revue Bénédictine* 109 (1999): 90–116.

Michelet, Fabienne. *Creation, Migration and Conquest: Imaginary Geography and Sense of Space in Old English Literature*. Oxford: Oxford University Press, 2006.

Mignolo, Walter D. *Local Histories/Global Designs: Coloniality, Subaltern Knowledges, and Border Thinking*. 2000. Reissue, with a new preface by the author, Princeton: Princeton University Press, 2012.

Miller, Edward. *The Abbey and Bishopric of Ely: The Social History of an Ecclesiastical Estate from the Tenth Century to the Fourteenth Century*. Cambridge: Cambridge University Press, 1951.

Miller, James I., Jr. "Literature to History: Exploring a Medieval Saint's Legend and Its Context." In *Literature and History*, edited by I.E. Cadenhead, Jr., 59–72. University of Tulsa Monograph Series, 9. Tulsa: University of Tulsa, 1970.

Mitchell, Bruce, and Fred C. Robinson. *A Guide to Old English*. 8th ed. Chichester: Wiley- Blackwell, 2012.

Miyashiro, Adam. "Decolonizing Anglo-Saxon Studies: A Response to ISAS in Honolulu." *In the Middle*, 29 July 2017. http://www.inthemedievalmiddle.com/2017/07/decolonizing-anglo-saxon-studies.html.

Moilanen, Inka. "Writing the Order: Religious-Political Discourses in Late Anglo-Saxon England." Ph.D. diss., University of Bergen, 2011.

Molyneaux, George. "Did the English Really Think They Were God's Elect in the Anglo-Saxon Period?" *Journal of Ecclesiastical History* 65.4 (2014): 721–37.

– *The Formation of the English Kingdom in the Tenth Century*. Oxford: Oxford University Press, 2015.

– "The *Old English Bede*: English Ideology or Christian Instruction?" *English Historical Review* 124 (2009): 1289–323.

– "Why Were Some Tenth-Century English Kings Presented as Rulers of Britain?" *TRHS* 21 (2011): 59–91.

Moreland, John. "Ethnicity, Power and the English." In Frazer and Tyrrell, *Social Identity*, 23–51.

– "Land and Power from Roman Britain to Anglo-Saxon England?" *Historical Materialism* 19.1 (2011): 175–93.

Morris, Richard. *Time's Anvil: England, Archaeology and the Imagination*. London: Weidenfeld and Nicolson, 2012.

Mostert, Marco. "Abbo of Fleury." In Lapidge, Blair, Keynes, and Scragg, *Wiley Blackwell Encyclopedia*, 3–4.

– "King Edmund of East Anglia (†869): Chapters in Historical Criticism." Ph.D. diss., University of Amsterdam, 1983.

– *The Political Theology of Abbo of Fleury: A Study of the Ideas about Society and Law of the Tenth-Century Monastic Reform Movement*. Middeleeuwse Studies en Bronnen Series, 2. Hilversum: Verloren, 1987.

Muir, Richard. "The Landscapes of East Anglia." In Ravensdale and Muir, *East Anglian Landscapes*, 173–247.

Mynors, R.A.B. "Textual Introduction." In Bede, *Ecclesiastical History*, xxxix–lxxiv.

Naismith, Rory. "Kings, Crisis and Coinage Reforms in the Mid-Eighth Century." *Early Medieval Europe* 20.3 (2012): 291–332.

– "A New Type for Æthelberht II of East Anglia." *British Numismatic Journal* 84 (2014): 236–8.

Naismith, Rory, and David A. Woodman, eds. *Writing, Kingship and Power in Anglo-Saxon England.* Cambridge: Cambridge University Press, 2018.

Neidorf, Leonard. "*Beowulf* as Pre-National Epic: Ethnocentrism in the Poem and its Criticism." *ELH* 85.4 (2018): 847–75.

– "Germanic Legend, Scribal Errors, and Cultural Change." In *The Dating of* Beowulf: *A Reassessment*, edited by Leonard Neidorf, 37–57. Cambridge: Brewer, 2014.

Nelson, Janet L. "Alfred's Carolingian Contemporaries." In Reuter, *Alfred the Great*, 293–310.

– "Presidential Address: England and the Continent in the Ninth Century: II, The Vikings and Others." *TRHS*, 6th ser., 13 (2003): 1–28.

– "Royal Saints and Early Medieval Kingship." *Studies in Church History* 10 (1973): 39–44.

Nelson, Janet L., and Janet M. Bately. "Alfred the Great (849–899; r. 871–99)." In *Medieval England: An Encyclopedia*, edited by Paul E. Szarmach, M. Teresa Tavormina, and Joel T. Rosenthal. New York: Garland, 1998. Reprinted as *Key Figures in Medieval Europe: An Encyclopedia*, edited by Richard K. Emmerson and Sandra Clayton-Emmerson, 26–30. New York: Routledge, 2006.

Neville, Jennifer. *Representations of the Natural World in Old English Poetry.* Cambridge: Cambridge University Press, 2004.

Newman, David. "Borders and Bordering: Towards an Interdisciplinary Dialogue." *European Journal of Social Theory* 9.2 (2006): 171–86.

Newman, John. "The Late Roman and Anglo-Saxon Settlement Pattern in the Sandlings of Suffolk." In Carver, *Age of Sutton Hoo*, 25–38.

Newton, Sam. "The Forgotten History of St. Bótwulf (Botolph)." *Proceedings of the Suffolk Institute of Archaeology and History* 43 (2016): 521–50.

– *The Origins of* Beowulf *and the Pre-Viking Kingdom of East Anglia.* Cambridge: Brewer, 1993.

– *The Reckoning of King Rædwald: The Story of the King Linked to the Sutton Hoo Ship-Burial* Colchester: Red Bird, 2003.

Noetzel, Justin. "Monster, Demon, Warrior: St. Guthlac and the Cultural Landscape of the Anglo-Saxon Fens." *Comitatus* 45.1 (2014): 105–31.

North, Richard. *Heathen Gods in Old English Literature.* Cambridge Studies in Anglo-Saxon England, 22. Cambridge: Cambridge University Press, 1997.

– *The Origins of* Beowulf: *From Virgil to Wiglaf.*

O'Brien, Conor. *Bede's Temple: An Image and Its Interpretation.* Oxford: Oxford University Press, 2015.

– "A Quotation from Origin's *Homilies on Leviticus* in Bede's Commentary on Luke's Gospel." *Notes and Queries*, N.S. 60.2 (2013): 185–6.

O'Brien O'Keeffe, Katharine. "Guthlac's Crossings." *Quaestio: Selected Proceedings of the Cambridge Colloqium in Anglo-Saxon, Norse and Celtic* 2 (2001): 1–26.

Olsen, Alexandra Hennessey. *Guthlac of Croyland: A Study of Heroic Hagiography*. Washington, DC: University Press of America, 1981.

Olsson, Stefan. "Peace Agreements through Rituals in Areas of Confrontation in the Viking Age." *Temenos* 53.2 (2017): 265–84.

Oosthuizen, Susan. *The Anglo-Saxon Fenland*. Oxford: Windgather, 2017.

– "Culture and Identity in the Early Medieval Fenland Landscape." *Landscape History* 37.1 (2016): 5–24.

Orchard, Andy. "*Lege feliciter, scribe felicius*: The Originality of the *Vita S. Guthlaci*." In Roberts and Thacker, *Guthlac*, 25–54.

O'Reilly, Jennifer. "Islands and Idols at the Ends of the Earth: Exegesis and Conversion in Bede's *Historia Ecclesiastica*." In Lebecq, Perrin, and Szerwiniack, *Bède le Vénérable*, 119–45.

Otter, Monika. *Inventiones: Fiction and Referentiality in Twelfth-Century English Historical Writing*. Chapel Hill: University of North Carolina Press, 1996.

– "The Temptation of St. Æthelthryth." *Exemplaria* 9.1 (1997): 139–63.

Owen-Crocker, Gale R. "Dress and Identity." In Hamerow, Hinton, and Crawford, *Oxford Handbook of Anglo-Saxon Archaeology*, 91–118.

Page, Jeremy. "Is There an East Anglian Literature?" http://jeremypage.co.uk/Site/inside%20the%20shed.../5481C8CE-9791-40A8-B110-3C3B82ECBE2D.html.

Page, R.I. "Anglo-Saxon Aptitudes." Inaugural lecture, University of Cambridge, 6 March 1985. Cambridge: Cambridge University Press, 1985.

– "A Most Vile People: Early English Historians on the Vikings." London: Viking Society for Northern Research, 1987.

Parker, Rowland. *Men of Dunwich: The Story of a Vanished Town*. Bury St. Edmunds: Alastair, 1978.

Parks, Tim. *Italian Neighbours: An Englishman in Verona*. London: William Heinemann, 1992. Reprint, London: Vintage, 2001.

Paxton, Frederick S. "*Abbas* and *Rex*: Power and Authority in the Literature of Fleury, 987–1044." In Berkhofer, Cooper, and Kosto, *The Experience of Power*, 197–212.

Paxton, Jennifer. "Lords and Monks: Creating an Ideal of Noble Power in Monastic Chronicles." In Berkhofer, Cooper, and Kosto, *The Experience of Power*, 227–36.

Pearson, M. Parker, R. van de Noort, and A. Woolf. "Three Men and a Boat: Sutton Hoo and the East Saxon Kingdom." *ASE* 22 (1993): 27–50.

Pelteret, David A.E. "Bede's Women." In *Women, Marriage, and Family in Medieval Christendom: Essays in Memory of Michael M. Sheehan, C.S.B.*, edited by Constance M. Rousseau and Joel T. Rosenthal, 19–46. Kalamazoo: Medieval Institute Publications, 1998.

Pestell, Tim. "The Kingdom of East Anglia, Frisia and Continental Connections, c. AD 600–900." In *Frisians and Their North Sea Neighbours: From the Fifth Century to the Viking Age*, edited by John Hines and Nelleke IJssennagger, 193–222. Woodbridge: Boydell, 2017.

– *Landscapes of Monastic Foundation: The Establishment of Religious Houses in East Anglia c. 650–1200*. Woodbridge: Boydell, 2004.

– "Paganism in Early-Anglo-Saxon East Anglia." In Heslop, Mellings, and Thøfner, *Art, Faith and Place*, 66–87.

Petts, David. *Pagan and Christian: Religious Change in Early Medieval Europe*. London: Bristol Classical Press, 2011.

Phelpstead, Carl. "King, Martyr and Virgin: *Imitatio Christi* in Ælfric's *Life of St. Edmund*." In Bale, *Saint Edmund, King and Martyr*, 27–44.

Pinner, Rebecca. *The Cult of St. Edmund in Medieval East Anglia*. Woodbridge: Boydell and Brewer, 2015.

– "Thinking Wetly: Causeways and Communities in East Anglian Hagiography." *Open Library of Humanities* 4(2).3 (2018): 1–27.

Pitt, Georgina. "The Enigmatic Sutton Hoo Ship-Burial: Fresh Insights from Assemblage Theory." *Parergon* 36.1 (2019): 1–29.

Plunkett, Steven. *Suffolk in Anglo-Saxon Times*. Stroud: Tempus, 2005.

Pluskowski, Aleks. "The Archaeology of Paganism." In Hamerow, Hinton, and Crawford, *Oxford Handbook of Anglo-Saxon Archaeology*, 764–78.

Pohl, Walter. "Ethnic Names and Identities in the British Isles: A Comparative Perspective." In Hines, *The Anglo-Saxons*, 7–31.

– "Frontiers and Ethnic Identities: Some Final Considerations." In Curta, *Borders, Barriers, and Ethnogenesis*, 255–65.

Pohl, Walter, Ian Wood, and Helmut Reimitz, eds. *The Transformation of Frontiers from Late Antiquity to the Carolingians*. Leiden: Brill, 2001.

Poole, Russell. "Anglo-Scandinavian Language and Literature." In Lees, *Cambridge History*, 579–606.

– "Skaldic Verse and Anglo-Saxon History: Some Aspects of the Period 1009–1016." *Speculum* 62 (1987): 265–98.

Pope, John C. "Ælfric and the Old English Version of the Ely Privilege." In *England Before the Conquest: Studies in Primary Sources Presented to Dorothy Whitelock*, edited by Peter Clemoes and Kathleen Hughes, 85–113. Cambridge: Cambridge University Press, 1971.

– "Introduction." In *Homilies of Ælfric: A Supplementary Collection*, edited by John C. Pope, 1–190. EETS O.S. 259–60. Vol. 1. London: Oxford University Press, 1967.

Powlesland, Dominic. "Early Anglo-Saxon Settlements, Structures, Form and Layout." In Hines, *The Anglo-Saxons*, 101–24.

Pratt, David. *The Political Thought of King Alfred the Great*. Cambridge: Cambridge University Press, 2007.

Prestwich, J.O. "King Æthelhere and the Battle of the Winwaed." *EHR* 83 (1968): 89–95.

Pulsiano, Philip. "Blessed Bodies: The Vitae of Anglo-Saxon Female Saints." *Parergon* 16.2 (1999): 1–42.

Rabin, Andrew. "Holy Bodies, Legal Matters: Reaction and Reform in Ælfric's *Eugenia* and the Ely Privilege." *Studies in Philology* 110.2 (2013): 220–65.

Rackham, Oliver. *The History of the Countryside*. London: Dent, 1986.

– "The Medieval Countryside." In Howe and Wolfe, *Inventing Medieval Landscapes*, 13–32.

Raffield, Ben. "Bands of Brothers: A Re-Appraisal of the Viking Great Army and Its Implications for the Scandinavian Colonization of England." *Early Medieval Europe* 24.3 (2016): 308–37.

Rambaran-Olm, Mary. "Anglo-Saxon Studies [Early English Studies], Academia and White Supremacy." *Medium*, 27 June 2018. https://medium.com/@mrambaranolm/anglosaxon-studies-academia-and-white-supremacy-17c87b360bf3.

Ravensdale, J.R. *Liable to Floods: Village Landscape on the Edge of the Fens AD 450–1850*. Cambridge: Cambridge University Press, 1974.

– "The Themes of East Anglia." In Ravensdale and Muir, *East Anglian Landscapes*, 15–172.

Ravensdale, Jack, and Richard Muir. *East Anglian Landscapes: Past and Present*. London: Michael Joseph, 1984.

Reed, Michael. "Anglo-Saxon Charter Boundaries." In *Discovering Past Landscapes*, edited by Michael Reed, 261–306. London: Croom Helm, 1984.

Reed, Michael F. "Sculpture and Lordship in Late Saxon Suffolk: The Evidence of Ixworth." In Devlin and Holas-Clark, *Approaching Interdisciplinarity*, 38–46.

Reichardt, Paul F. "*Guthlac A* and the Landscape of Spiritual Perfection." *Neophilologus* 58 (1974): 331–8.

Remein, Daniel. "ISAS Should Probably Change Its Name." Paper presented at the International Congress on Medieval Studies, Kalamazoo, MI, 2017. https://www.academia.edu/34101681/_Isas_should_probably_change_its_name_ICMS_Kalamazoo_2017?fbclid=IwAR1xCT1ypVtg2OuMQgpLMB3mRc8jecr0xLulJpq7L_SCU5Lys8qv82i7q8A.

Reuter, Timothy, ed. *Alfred the Great: Papers from the Eleventh-Centenary Conferences*. Farnham, Surrey: Ashgate, 2003.

Reynolds, Andrew. *Later Anglo-Saxon England: Life and Landscape*. Stroud, Gloucs.: Tempus, 1999.

Reynolds, Susan. "The Idea of the Nation as a Political Community." In Scales and Zimmer, *Power and the Nation*, 54–66.

– *Kingdoms and Communities in Western Europe, 900–1300*. 2d ed. Oxford: Clarendon, 1997.

Richards, Julian D. "Anglo-Scandinavian Identity." In Hamerow, Hinton, and Crawford, *Oxford Handbook of Anglo-Saxon Archaeology*, 46–61.

– "Identifying Anglo-Scandinavian Settlements." In Hadley and Richards, *Cultures in Contact*, 295–309.

Richards, Julian D., and Dave Haldenby. "The Scale and Impact of Viking Settlement in Northumbria." *Medieval Archaeology* 62.2 (2018): 322–50.

Riché, Pierre. *Abbon de Fleury: Un moine savant et combatif (vers 950–1004)*. Turnhout: Brepols, 2004.

Ridyard, Susan J. "*Condigna veneratio*: Post-Conquest Attitudes to the Saints of the Anglo-Saxons." *Anglo-Norman Studies* 9 (1987): 179–206.

– *The Royal Saints of Anglo-Saxon England: A Study of West Saxon and East Anglian Cults*. Cambridge: Cambridge University Press, 1988.

Rigold, S.E. "Further Evidence about the Site of 'Dommoc.'" *Journal of the British Archaeological Association* 37 (1974): 97–102.

– "The Supposed See of Dunwich." *Journal of the British Archaeological Association* 24 (1961): 55–9.

Roberts, Jane. "Guthlac of Crowland and the Seals of the Cross." In *The Place of the Cross in Anglo-Saxon England*, edited by Catherine E. Karkov, Sarah Larratt Keefer, and Karen Louise Jolly, 113–28. Woodbridge: Boydell, 2006.

– *Guthlac of Crowland: A Saint for Middle England*. Fursey Occasional Paper, 3. Norwich: Fursey Pilgrims, 2009.

– "Hagiography and Literature: The Case of Guthlac of Crowland." In Brown and Farr, *Mercia*, 69–86.

– "An Inventory of Early Guthlac Materials." *Mediaeval Studies* 32 (1970): 193–233.

Roberts, Jane, and Alan Thacker, eds. *Guthlac: Crowland's Saint*. Donington, Lincs.: Shaun Tyas, 2020.

– "Introduction to Guthlac's Life and Cult." In Roberts and Thacker, *Guthlac*, xv–xlvi.

Roffey, Simon, and Ryan Lavelle. "West Saxons and Danes: Negotiating Early Medieval Identities." In *Danes in Wessex: The Scandinavian Impact on Southern England, c. 800-c. 1100*, edited by Ryan Lavelle and Simon Roffey, 7-34. Oxford: Oxbow, 2016.

Rogerson, Andrew. "Vikings and the New East Anglian Towns." *British Archaeology* 35 (June 1998): 12-13.

Rohl, Darrell J. "The Chorographic Tradition and Seventeenth- and Eighteenth-Century Scottish Antiquaries." *Journal of Art Historiography* 5 (2011): 1–18.

Rollason, D.W. (David). "Lists of Saints' Resting Places in Anglo-Saxon England." *Anglo-Saxon England* 7 (1978): 61–93.

– *Northumbria, 500–1100: Creation and Destruction of a Kingdom*. Cambridge: Cambridge University Press, 2003.

– *Saints and Relics in Anglo-Saxon England*. Oxford: Blackwell, 1989.

Rosser, Susan. "Æthelthryth: a Conventional Saint?" *Bulletin of the John Rylands University Library of Manchester* 79 (1997): 15–24.

Rouche, Michel. "The Early Middle Ages in the West." In *A History of Private Life. I: From Pagan Rome to Byzantium*, edited by Paul Veyne, translated by Arthur Goldhammer, 411–549. Cambridge, MA: Belknap, 1987.

Rowley, Sharon. *The Old English Version of Bede's* Historia Ecclesiastica. Cambridge: Boydell and Brewer, 2011.

Rumford, Chris. "Introduction: Theorizing Borders." *European Journal of Social Theory* 9.2 (2006): 155–69.

Rush, Michael Calvert. "Cultural Transition in East Anglia, c. 350 to c. 650, and the Origins of the Kingdom of the East Angles." Ph.D. diss., University of Birmingham, 2013.

Ryan, Martin J. "The Anglo-Saxons and the Vikings, c. 825–900." In Higham and Ryan, *The Anglo-Saxon World*, 232–83.

– "Sources and Issues 5a: *The Anglo-Saxon Chronicle*." In Higham and Ryan, *The Anglo-Saxon World*, 272–3.

Salway, Peter. *A History of Roman Britain*. Oxford: Oxford University Press, 1993.

Sauer, Carl Ortwin. "The Morphology of Landscape." In *University of California Publications in Geography* 2.2 (1925): 19–54. Reprinted in *Land and Life: A Selection from the Writings of Carl Ortwin Sauer*, edited by John Leighly, 315–50. Berkeley: University of California Press, 1983 [1963].

Sauer, Hans, and Joanna Story, eds., with the assistance of Gaby Waxenberger. *Anglo-Saxon England and the Continent*. AZ: ACMRS, 2011.

Sawyer, P.H. *The Age of the Vikings*. 2d ed. London: Edward Arnold, 1971.

Scales, Len, and Oliver Zimmer, eds. *Power and the Nation in European History*. Cambridge: Cambridge University Press, 2005.

Scarfe, Norman. *Suffolk in the Middle Ages*. Woodbridge: Boydell, 1986.

– *The Suffolk Landscape*. The Making of the English Landscape Series. London: Hodder and Stoughton, 1972.

Scheil, Andrew P. "Anti-Judaism in Ælfric's *Lives of Saints*." *ASE* 28 (1999): 65–86.

– *The Footsteps of Israel: Understanding Jews in Anglo-Saxon England*. Ann Arbor: University of Michigan Press, 2004.

– "Space and Place." In Stodnick and Trilling, *Handbook of Anglo-Saxon Studies*, 197–213.

Schulenburg, Jane Tibbetts. *Forgetful of Their Sex: Female Sanctity and Society, ca. 500–1100*. Chicago: University of Chicago Press, 1998.

Schütt, Marie. "Vom heiligen Antonius zum heiligen Guthlac: Ein Beitrage zur Geschichte der Biographie." *Antike und Abendland* 5 (1956): 75–91.

Scull, Christopher. "Before Sutton Hoo: Structures of Power and Society in Early East Anglia." In Carver, *Age of Sutton Hoo*, 3–23.

Scull, Christopher, Faye Minter, and Judith Plouviez. "Social and Economic Complexity in Early Medieval England: A Central Place Complex of the East Anglian Kingdom at Rendlesham, Suffolk." *Antiquity* 90 (2016): 1594–1612.
Scull, Christopher, and Tom Williamson. "New Light on Rendlesham: Lordship and Landscape in East Anglia, 400–800." *The Historian*, no. 139 (2018): 6–11.
Scully, Diarmuid. "Bede, Orosius and Gildas on the Early History of Britain." In Lebecq, Perrin, and Szerwiniack, *Bède le Vénérable*, 31–42.
Sellar, Walter Carruthers, and Robert Julian Yeatman. *1066 and All That*. Illustrated by John Reynolds. London: Methuen, 2009 [1930].
Semple, Sarah. "A Fear of the Past: The Place of the Prehistoric Burial Mound in the Ideology of Middle and Later Anglo-Saxon England." *World Archaeology* 30.1 (1998): 109–26.
– "Sacred Spaces and Places in Pre-Christian and Conversion Period Anglo-Saxon England." In Hamerow, Hinton, and Crawford, *Oxford Handbook of Anglo-Saxon Archaeology*, 742–63.
Seymour, John. *The Companion Guide to East Anglia*. 3d ed. Revised by John Burke. London: Collins, 1988.
Sharma, Manish. "A Reconsideration of the Structure of *Guthlac A*: The Extremes of Saintliness." *JEGP* 101.2 (2002): 185–200.
Sheppard, Alice. *Families of the King: Writing Identities in the* Anglo-Saxon Chronicle. Toronto: University of Toronto Press, 2004.
Shook, Lawrence K. "The Burial Mound in *Guthlac A*." *Modern Philology* 58 (1960): 1–10.
Siewers, Alfred. "Landscapes of Conversion: Guthlac's Mound and Grendel's Mere as Expressions of Anglo-Saxon Nation-Building." *Viator* 34 (2003): 1–39.
Sims-Williams, Patrick. *Religion and Literature in Western England, 600–800*. Cambridge: Cambridge University Press, 1990.
– "The Settlement of England in Bede and the *Chronicle*." *ASE* 12 (1983): 1–41.
Sisam, Kenneth. "Anglo-Saxon Royal Genealogies." *Proceedings of the British Academy* 39 (1953): 287–348.
Skeat, Walter W. "Preface." In *Ælfric's Lives of Saints*, ed. and trans. Skeat, vol. 2, vii–lxiii.
Skinner, Patricia, ed. *Challenging the Boundaries of Medieval History: The Legacy of Timothy Reuter*. Turnhout: Brepols, 2009.
Sklar, Elizabeth S. "Ælfric's *Life of Saint Edmund*: Constructing English Identity." *Medieval Perspectives* 17.2 (2003): 129–42.
Smith, Anthony D. *Chosen Peoples*. Oxford: Oxford University Press, 2003.
– *The Ethnic Origins of Nations*. Oxford: Blackwell, 1986.
Smith, Julia M.H. "*Fines Imperii*: The Marches." In McKitterick, *New Cambridge Medieval History*, 169–89.

Smith, Scott Thompson. *Land and Book: Literature and Land Tenure in Anglo-Saxon England*. Toronto: University of Toronto Press, 2012.

– "Marking Boundaries: Charters and the Anglo-Saxon Chronicle." In Jorgensen, *Reading the Anglo-Saxon Chronicle*, 167–85.

Smyth, Alfred P. *King Alfred the Great*. Oxford: Oxford University Press, 1995.

– *Scandinavian Kings in the British Isles 850–880*. Oxford: Oxford University Press, 1977.

Sneesby, Norman. *Etheldreda: Princess, Queen, Abbess and Saint*. Haddenham, Ely: Fern House, 1999.

Sobecki, Sebastian I., ed. *The Sea and Englishness in the Middle Ages: Maritime Narratives, Identity and Culture*. Cambridge: Brewer, 2011.

Söderbaum, Fredrik. "Introduction: Theories of New Regionalism." In Söderbaum and Shaw, *Theories of New Regionalism*, 1–21.

Söderbaum, Fredrik, and Timothy M. Shaw, eds. *Theories of New Regionalism: A Palgrave Reader*. Houndmills: Palgrave Macmillan, 2003.

Sot, Michel. "Pratique et usages de l'histoire chez Abbon de Fleury." In Dufour and Labory, *Abbon, un abbé de l'an mil*, 205–23.

Stafford, Pauline. "Church and Society in the Age of Aelfric." In *The Old English Homily and Its Backgrounds*, edited by Paul E. Szarmach and Bernard F. Huppé, 11–42. Albany: State University of New York Press, 1978.

– *The East Midlands in the Early Middle Ages*. London: Leicester University Press, 1985.

– "Kings, Kingships and Kingdoms." In W. Davies, *From the Vikings to the Normans*, 11–39.

– "The Making of Chronicles and the Making of England: The Anglo-Saxon Chronicles after Alfred." *TRHS* 27 (2017): 65–86.

– *Unification and Conquest: A Political and Social History of England in the Tenth and Eleventh Centuries*. London: Edward Arnold, 1989.

Stancliffe, Clare. "Kings Who Opted Out." In Wormald, Bullough, and Collins, *Ideal and Reality*, 154–76.

Stanton, Robert. *The Culture of Translation in Anglo-Saxon England*. Cambridge: D.S. Brewer, 2002.

Stenton, Doris Mary, ed. *Preparatory to Anglo-Saxon England: Being the Collected Papers of Frank Merry Stenton*. Oxford: Clarendon, 1970.

Stenton, Frank. *Anglo-Saxon England*. 3d ed. Oxford: Oxford University Press, 1971.

– "The East Anglian Kings of the Seventh Century." In *The Anglo-Saxons: Studies in Some Aspects of Their History and Culture Presented to Bruce Dickins*, edited by Peter Clemoes, 43–52. London: Bowes and Bowes, 1959. Reprinted in D.M. Stenton, *Preparatory to Anglo-Saxon England*, 394–402.

Stephenson, Carl. *Borough and Town: A Study of Urban Origins in England*. Cambridge, MA: Mediaeval Academy of America, 1933.

Stephenson, Rebecca. *The Politics of Language: Byrhtferth, Ælfric, and the Multilingual Identity of the Benedictine Reform*. Toronto: University of Toronto Press, 2015.

Stevenson, Francis Seymour. "St. Botolph (Botwulf) and Iken." *Proceedings of the Suffolk Institute of Archaeology* 18 (1924): 29–52.

Stevenson, Jane. "Brothers and Sisters: Women and Monastic Life in Eighth-Century England and Frankia." *Nederlands Archief voor Kerkgeschiedenis* 82.1 (2002): 1–34.

– "Christianity in Sixth- and Seventh-Century Southumbria." In Carver, *Age of Sutton Hoo*, 175–83.

Stock, Brian. *The Implications of Literacy: Written Language and Models of Interpretation in the Eleventh and Twelfth Centuries*. Princeton: Princeton University Press, 1983.

– *Listening for the Text: On the Uses of the Past*. Philadelphia: University of Pennsylvania Press, 1990.

Stodnick, Jacqueline. "Emergent Englishness." In *The Oxford Handbook of Medieval Literature in English*, edited by Elaine Treharne and Greg Walker with the assistance of William Green, 496–511. Oxford: Oxford University Press, 2010.

– "'Old Names of Kings or Shadows': Reading Documentary Lists." In Karkov and Howe, *Conversion and Colonization*, 109–31.

– "Sentence to Story: Reading the Anglo-Saxon Chronicle as Formulary." In Jorgensen, *Reading the Anglo-Saxon Chronicle*, 91–111.

– "What (and Where) Is the *Anglo-Saxon Chronicle* About? Spatial History." *Bulletin of the John Rylands Library of the University of Manchester* 86 (2004): 87–104.

Stodnick, Jacqueline, and Renée R. Trilling, eds. *A Handbook of Anglo-Saxon Studies*. Chichester: Wiley-Blackwell, 2002.

Strohm, Paul. *Theory and the Premodern Text*. Minneapolis: University of Minnesota Press, 2000.

Sturdy, David. *Alfred the Great*. London: Constable, 1995.

Styler, Ian David. "The Story of an English Saint's Cult: An Analysis of the Influence of St. Æthelthryth of Ely, c.670–c.1540." Ph.D. diss., University of Birmingham, 2019.

Swift, Graham. *Waterland*. London: Picador/Pan Books, 1984.

Symonds, L.A. "Territories in Transition: The Construction of Boundaries in Anglo-Scandinavian Lincolnshire." *ASSAH* 12 (2003): 28–37.

Szarmach, Paul E. "Æðeldreda in the Old English Bede." In *Poetry, Place and Gender: Studies in Medieval Culture in Honor of Helen Damico*, edited by Catherine E. Karkov, 132–50. Kalamazoo: Medieval Institute Publications, 2009.

–, ed. *Holy Men and Holy Women*. Albany: State University of New York Press, 1996.

–, ed. *Writing Women Saints in Anglo-Saxon England*. Toronto: University of Toronto Press, 2013.

Szarmach, Paul E., ed., with the assistance of Deborah A. Oosterhouse. *Old English Prose: Basic Readings*. New York: Garland, 2000.

Szerwiniack, Olivier. "L'*Histoire ecclésiastique* ou le rêve d'un retour au temps de l'innocence." In Lebecq, Perrin, and Szerwiniack, *Bède le Vénérable*, 159–76.

Taylor, Christopher. *The Cambridgeshire Landscape*. London: Hodder and Stoughton, 1973.

Taylor, Craig. *Return to Akenfield: Portrait of an English Village in the 21st Century*. London: Granta, 2006.

Taylor, Mark. *Edmund: The Untold Story of the Martyr-King and His Kingdom*. N.p.: Fordaro, 2014.

Tennyson, Julian. *Suffolk Scene: A Book of Description and Adventure*. Introduction by Ronald Blythe. Foreword by Sean Fielding. Bury St. Edmunds: Alastair, 1987 [1939].

Thacker, Alan. "Bede and History." In DeGregorio, *Cambridge Companion*, 170–89.

– "Bede and the Ordering of Understanding." In DeGregorio, *Innovation and Tradition*, 37–63.

– "Bede's Ideal of Reform." In Wormald, Bullough, and Collins, *Ideal and Reality*, 130–53.

– "Bede's Idea of the English." *Bulletin of the John Rylands Library of the University of Manchester* 92.1 (2016): 1–26.

– "Bede, the Britons, and the Book of Samuel." In Baxter, Karkov, Nelson, and Pelteret, *Early Medieval Studies*, 129–48.

– "Dynastic Monasteries and Family Cults: Edward the Elder's Sainted Kindred." In Higham and Hill, *Edward the Elder*, 248–63.

– "Guthlac and His Life: Felix Shapes the Saint." In Roberts and Thacker, *Guthlac*, 1–24.

– "Kings, Saints, and Monasteries in Pre-Viking Mercia." *Midland History* 10 (1985): 1–25.

– "*Loca Sanctorum*: The Significance of Place in the Study of the Saints." In *Local Saints and Local Churches in the Early Medieval West*, edited by Alan Thacker and Richard Sharpe, 1–43. Oxford: Oxford University Press, 2002.

– "The Social and Continental Background to Early Anglo-Saxon Hagiography." D.Phil. thesis, University of Oxford, 1976.

– "Why Did Heresy Matter to Bede? Present and Future Contexts." In Darby and Wallis, *Bede and the Future*, 47–66.

Thacker, Alan, and Richard Sharpe, eds. *Local Saints and Local Churches in the Early Medieval West*. Oxford: Oxford University Press, 2002.

Thomas, Gabor. "Anglo-Scandinavian Metalwork from the Danelaw: Exploring Social and Cultural Interaction." In Hadley and Richards, *Cultures in Contact*, 237–55.

Thomas, Hugh M. *The English and the Normans: Ethnic Hostility, Assimilation, and Identity 1066–c.1220*. Oxford: Oxford University Press, 2003.

Thompson, A. Hamilton, ed. *Bede: His Life, Times and Writings*. Oxford: Clarendon, 1935.

Thompson, Pauline A. "St. Æthelthryth: The Making of History from Hagiography." In *Studies in English Language and Literature – "Doubt Wisely": Papers in Honour of E.G. Stanley*, edited by Mary Jane Toswell and Elizabeth M. Tyler, 475–92. London: Routledge, 1996.

Thompson, Pauline A., and E. Stevens. "Gregory of Ely's Verse Life and Miracles of St. Æthelthryth." *Analecta Bollandiana* 106 (1988): 333–90.

Thornbury, Emily V. *Becoming a Poet in Anglo-Saxon England*. Cambridge: Cambridge University Press, 2014.

Tombs, Robert. *The English and Their History*. London: Penguin/Allan Lane, 2014.

Townend, Matthew. *Language and History in Viking Age England: Linguistic Relations between Speakers of Old Norse and Old English*. Turnhout: Brepols, 2002.

– "Viking Age England as a Bilingual Society." In Hadley and Richards, *Cultures in Contact*, 89–105.

Townsend, David. "Cultural Difference and the Meaning of Latinity in Asser's *Life of King Alfred*." In *Cultural Diversity in the British Middle Ages: Archipelago, Island, England*, edited by Jeffrey Jerome Cohen, 57–73. New York: Palgrave Macmillan, 2008.

– "Hagiography." In *Medieval Latin: An Introduction and Bibliographical Guide*, edited by F.A.C. Mantello and A.G. Rigg, 618–28. Washington, DC: Catholic University of America Press, 1996.

Treharne, Elaine. "The Authority of English, 900–1150." In Lees, *Cambridge History*, 554–78.

– "Borders." In Stodnick and Trilling, *Handbook of Anglo-Saxon Studies*, 9–22.

Trilling, Renée R. *The Aesthetics of Nostalgia: Historical Representation in Old English Verse*. Toronto: University of Toronto Press, 2009.

Tuan, Yi-Fu. *Space and Place: The Perspective of Experience*. Minneapolis: University of Minnesota Press, 1977.

Tugène, Georges. "L'Histoire 'ecclésiastique' du peuple anglais: Réflexions sur le particularisme et l'universalisme chez Bède." *Recherches augustiniennes* 17 (1982): 129–72.

– *L'idée de nation chez Bède le Vénérable*. Paris: Institut d'Études Augustiniennes, 2001.

Turner, James. *Rivers of East Anglia*. London: Cassell, 1954.

Turville-Petre, Thorlac. *England the Nation: Language, Literature, and National Identity 1290–1340*. Oxford: Clarendon, 1996.

Tyler, Damian J. "Offa's Dyke: A Historiographical Appraisal." *Journal of Medieval History* 37 (2011): 145–61.

– "Reluctant Kings and Christian Conversion in Seventh-Century England." *History* 92.2 (2007): 144–61.

"'Unique' Anglo-Saxon Coin Could Give Royal Murder Clue." BBC News. http://www.bbc.com/news/uk-england-27485772.

Upchurch, Robert. "A Big Dog Barks: Ælfric of Eynsham's Indictment of the English Pastorate and 'Witan.'" *Speculum* 85.3 (2010): 505–33.

van Court, Elisa Narin, "*The Siege of Jerusalem* and Augustinian Historians: Writing about Jews in Fourteenth-Century England." In *Chaucer and the Jews: Sources, Contexts, Meanings*, edited by Sheila Delany, 165–84. New York: Routledge, 2002.

van Houts, Elisabeth. "Hereward and Flanders." *Anglo-Saxon England* 28 (1999): 201-23.

Voth, Christine. "Three Tenth-Century Latin Manuscripts of Felix's *Vita S. Guthlaci*." In Roberts and Thacker, *Guthlac*, 116–37.

Waite, Greg. "The Preface to the Old English Bede: Authorship, Transmission, and Connection with the *West Saxon Genealogical Regnal List*." *ASE* 44 (2015): 31–93.

Wallace, David. "General Preface." In *The Cambridge Companion to Medieval English Literature*, edited by David Wallace, xi–xxiii. Cambridge: Cambridge University Press, 1999.

Wallace-Hadrill, J.M. *Bede's* Ecclesiastical History of the English People*: A Historical Commentary*. Addenda by Patrick Wormald and Thomas Charles-Edwards. Oxford: Clarendon, 1988.

Wareham, Andrew. *Lords and Communities in Early Medieval East Anglia*. Woodbridge: Boydell, 2005.

– "St. Oswald's Family and Kin." In *St. Oswald of Worcester: Life and Influence*, edited by Nicholas P. Brooks and Catherine R.E. Cubitt, 49–63. London: Leicester University Press, 1996.

Warner, Peter. *The Origins of Suffolk*. Manchester: Manchester University Press, 1996.

Waterhouse, Ruth. "Discourse and Hypersignification in Two of Ælfric's Saints' Lives." In Szarmach, *Holy Men and Holy Women*, 333–52.

Watt, Diane. "The Earliest Women's Writing? Anglo-Saxon Literary Cultures and Communities." *Women's Writing* 20.4 (2013): 537–54.

Weiss, Judith. "East Anglia and the Sea in the Narratives of the *Vie de St. Edmund* and *Waldef*." In Sobecki, *The Sea and Englishness*, 103–12.

Wentersdorf, Karl. "*Guthlac A*: The Battle for the *Beorg*." *Neophilologus* 62 (1978): 135–42.

West, Stanley. A *Corpus of Anglo-Saxon Material from Suffolk*. Ipswich: Suffolk County Council, 1998.

West, Stanley E. "A New Site for the Martyrdom of St. Edmund?" *Proceedings of the Suffolk Institute of Archaeology and History* 35 (1981–4): 223–4.

West, Stanley E., Norman Scarfe, and Rosemary Cramp. "Iken, St. Botolph, and the Coming of East Anglian Christianity." *Proceedings of the Suffolk Institute of Archaeology and History* 35 (1984): 279–301.

Weston, Lisa M.C. "Guthlac Betwixt and Between: Literacy, Cross-Temporal Affiliation, and an Anglo-Saxon Anchorite." *Journal of Medieval Religious Cultures* 42.1 (2016): 1–27.

– "Saintly Lives: Friendship, Kinship, Gender and Sexuality." In Lees, *Cambridge History*, 381–405.

Wetherbee, Winthrop. "Some Implications of Bede's Latin Style." In *Bede and Anglo-Saxon England: Papers in Honour of the 1300th Anniversary of the Birth of Bede*, edited by Robert T. Farrell, 23–31. British Archeological Reports, 46. Oxford: BAR, 1978.

Whatley, Gordon E. "Introduction to the Study of Old English Prose Hagiography: Sources and Resources." In Szarmach, *Holy Men and Holy Women*, 3–32.

White, Hayden. *The Content of the Form: Narrative Discourse and Historical Representation*. Baltimore: Johns Hopkins University Press, 1987.

Whitelock, Dorothy. *English Historical Documents c. 500–1042*. London: Eyre and Spottiswoode, 1955.

– "Fact and Fiction in the Legend of St. Edmund." *Proceedings of the Suffolk Institute of Archaeology* 31 (1967–9): 217–33.

– "The Pre-Viking Age Church in East Anglia." *ASE* 1 (1972): 1–22.

– "Wulfstan and the So-Called Laws of Edward and Guthrum." *EHR* 56 (1941): 1–21.

Whiteman, Robin (text), and Rob Talbot (photography). *East Anglia and the Fens*. London: Weidenfeld and Nicolson, 1996. Reprint, London: Cassell, 2002.

Wickham, Chris. *Framing the Early Middle Ages: Europe and the Mediterranean, 400–800*. Oxford: Oxford University Press, 2005.

Wickham-Crowley, Kelley M. "Fens and Frontiers." In *The Material Culture of Daily Living in the Anglo-Saxon World*, vol. 3: *Water and the Environment in the Anglo-Saxon World*, edited by Maren Clegg Hyer and Della Hooke, 68–88. Liverpool: Liverpool University Press, 2017.

– "Living on the *Ecg*: The Mutable Boundaries of Land and Water in Anglo-Saxon Contexts." In Lees and Overing, *A Place to Believe In*, 85–110.

Wieland, Gernot R. "*Aures lectoris*: Orality and Literacy in Felix's *Vita Sancti Guthlaci*," *Journal of Medieval Latin* 7 (1997): 168–77.

Wilcox, Jonathan. "Ælfric in Dorset and the Landscape of Pastoral Care." In *Pastoral Care in Late Anglo-Saxon England*, edited by Francesca Tinti, 52–62. Woodbridge: Boydell, 2005.

Williams, Ann. *The English and the Norman Conquest*. Woodbridge: Boydell, 1995.

Williams, Gareth. "Coins and Currency in Viking England, AD 865–954." In *Early Medieval Monetary History: Studies in Memory of Mark Blackburn*, edited by Rory Naismith, Martin Allen, and Elina Screen, 13–38. Ashgate, 2014. Reprint, Abingdon, Oxon: Routledge, 2016.

Williams, Howard. "Ancient Landscapes and the Dead: The Reuse of Prehistoric and Roman Monuments as Early Anglo-Saxon Burial Sites." *Medieval Archaeology* 41 (1997): 1–32.

– *Death and Memory in Early Medieval Britain*. Cambridge: Cambridge University Press, 2006.

– "Engendered Bodies and Objects of Memory in Final Phase Graves." In *Burial in Later Anglo-Saxon England c. 650–1100 AD*, edited by Jo Buckberry and Annia Cherryson, 24–36. Oxford: Oxbow, 2010.

– "Mortuary Practices in Early Anglo-Saxon England." In Hamerow, Hinton, and Crawford, *Oxford Handbook of Anglo-Saxon Archaeology*, 238–65.

Williams Boyarin, Adrienne. *Miracles of the Virgin in Medieval England: Law and Jewishness in Marian Legends*. Cambridge: Brewer, 2010.

Williamson, Tom. "East Anglia's Character and the 'North Sea World.'" In Bates and Liddiard, *East Anglia and Its North Sea World*, 44–62.

– *Environment, Society and Landscape in Early Medieval England: Time and Topography*. Woodbridge: Boydell Press, 2012.

– *The Origins of Norfolk*. Manchester: Manchester University Press, 1993.

– *Sutton Hoo and Its Landscape: The Context of Monuments*. Oxford: Windgather, 2008.

Wilson, David. *Anglo-Saxon Paganism*. London: Routledge, 1992.

Wilton, David. "What Do We Mean by Anglo-Saxon? Pre-Conquest to the Present." *JEGP* 119.4 (2020): 425-54.

Wolpers, Theodor. *Die englische Heiligenlegende des Mittelalters: Eine Formgeschichte des Legendenerzählens von der spätantiken lateinischen Tradition bis zur Mitte des 16. Jahrhunderts*. Tübingen: Niemeyer, 1964.

Wood, Ian N. "Before and After the Migration to Britain." In Hines, *The Anglo-Saxons*, 41–64.

– "The Foundation of Bede's Wearmouth-Jarrow." In Degregorio, *Cambridge Companion*, 84–96.

– "The Franks and Sutton Hoo." In *People and Places in Northern Europe: 500–1600: Essays in Honour of Peter Hayes Sawyer*, edited by Ian N. Wood and Niels Lund, 1–14. Woodbridge: Boydell, 1991.

– *The Merovingian Kingdoms 450–751*. London: Longman, 1994.

– *The Merovingian North Sea*. Alingsås, Sweden: Bokförlag, 1983.

– *The Missionary Life: Saints and the Evangelisation of Europe 400–1050*. Harlow, Essex: Pearson, 2001.

– "Monasteries and the Geography of Power in the Age of Bede." *Northern History* 45.1 (2008): 11–25.

Woolf, Alex. "A Dialogue of the Deaf and Dumb: Archaeology, History and Philology." In Devlin and Holas-Clark, *Approaching Interdisciplinarity*, 3–9.

Wormald, Patrick. "Anglo-Saxons: The Making of England." *History Today* 45.2 (1995): 26–32.

– "Æthelwold and His Continental Counterparts: Contact, Comparison, Contrast." In Yorke, *Bishop Æthelwold*, 13–42.

– "Bede and the Conversion of England: The Charter Evidence." In Wormald, *Times of Bede*, 135–66.

– "Bede, *Beowulf*, and the Conversion of the Anglo-Saxon Aristocracy." In *The Times of Bede: Studies in Early English Christian Society and Its Historian*, edited by Patrick Wormald and Stephen Baxter, 30–105. Oxford: Blackwell, 2006.

– "Bede, the *Bretwaldas* and the Origins of the *Gens Anglorum*." In Wormald, Bullough, and Collins, *Ideal and Reality*, 99–129. Reprinted in Wormald, *Times of Bede*, 106–34.

– "*Engla Lond*: The Making of an Allegiance." *Journal of Historical Sociology* 7.1 (1994): 1–24.

– *The Making of English Law: King Alfred to the Twelfth Century*, vol. 1: *Legislation and Its Limits*. Oxford: Blackwell, 2001.

– "The Venerable Bede and the 'Church of the English.'" In *The English Religious Tradition and the Genius of Anglicanism*, edited by Geoffrey Rowell, with foreword by the Archbishop of Canterbury, 13–32. Eugene, OR: Wipf and Stock, 1994.

Wormald, Patrick, Donald Bullough, and Roger Collins, eds. *Ideal and Reality in Frankish and Anglo-Saxon Society: Studies Presented to J.M. Wallace-Hadrill*. Oxford: Blackwell, 1983.

Wormald, Patrick, and Thomas Charles-Edwards. Addenda to Wallace-Hadrill, *Historical Commentary*, 203–47.

Wragg, Stephany J. "The Early Texts of the Cult of Saint Guthlac." *English Studies* 100.3 (2019): 253–72.

– "*Guthlac A* and the Cult of Guthlac." In Roberts and Thacker, *Guthlac*, 214–28.

– "Vernacular Literature in Eighth- and Ninth-Century Mercia." D.Phil. thesis, University of Oxford, 2017.

Wright, C.E. *The Cultivation of Saga in Anglo-Saxon England*. Edinburgh: Oliver and Boyd, 1939.

Yarrow, Simon. *Saints and Their Communities: Miracle Stories in Twelfth-Century England*. Oxford: Clarendon, 2006.

Yorke, Barbara. "Anglo-Saxon *Gentes* and *Regna*." In Regna *and* Gentes*: The Relationship between Late Antique and Early Medieval Peoples and Kingdoms in the Transformation of the Roman World*, edited by H.-W. Goetz, J. Jarnut, and W. Pohl, with the collaboration of Sören Kaschke, 381–407. Leiden: Brill, 2003.

– "Anglo-Saxon Origin Legends." In *Myth, Rulership, Church and Charters: Essays in Honour of Nicholas Brooks*, edited by Julia Barrow and Andrew Wareham, 15–29. Aldershot: Ashgate, 2008.

– "Æthelwold and the Politics of the Tenth Century." In Yorke, *Bishop Æthelwold*, 65–88.

–, ed. *Bishop Æthelwold: His Career and Influence*. Woodbridge: Boydell, 1988.

– "The *Bretwaldas* and the Origins of Overlordship in Anglo-Saxon England." In Baxter, Karkov, Nelson, and Pelteret, *Early Medieval Studies*, 81–95.

– "The Burial of Kings in Anglo-Saxon England." In *Kingship, Legislation and Power in Anglo-Saxon England*, edited by Gale R. Owen-Crocker and Brian W. Schneider, 237–58. Woodbridge: Boydell, 2013.

– *The Conversion of Britain: Religion, Politics and Society c.600–800*. London: Routledge, 2006.

– "Edward as Ætheling." In Higham and Hill, *Edward the Elder*, 25–39.

– *Kings and Kingdoms of Early Anglo-Saxon England*. London: B.A. Seaby, 1990. Reprint, London: Taylor and Francis e-Library, 2003.

– *Nunneries and the Anglo-Saxon Royal Houses*. London: Leicester University Press, 2003.

– "The Origins of Mercia." In M. Brown and Farr, *Mercia*, 13–22.

– "Political and Ethnic Identity: A Case Study of Anglo-Saxon Practice." In Frazer and Tyrrell, *Social Identity*, 69–89.

– "'The Weight of Necklaces': Some Insights into the Wearing of Women's Jewellery from Middle Saxon Written Sources." In *Studies in Early Anglo-Saxon Art and Archaeology: Papers in Honour of Martin G. Welch*, edited by Stuart Brookes, Sue Harrington, and Andrew Reynolds, 106–11. BAR British series, 527. Oxford: Archaeopress, 2011.

Young, Francis. *Edmund: In Search of England's Lost King*. London: Tauris, 2018.

– "St. Edmund, King and Martyr in Popular Memory since the Reformation." *Folklore* 126.2 (2015): 159–76.

Younge, George. "The New Heathens: Anti-Jewish Hostility in Early English Literature." In *Essays and Studies*, N.S. 68 (2015): *Writing Europe, 500–1450: Texts and Contexts*, edited by Aidan Conti, Orietta da Rold, and Philip Shaw, 123–45. Cambridge: D.S. Brewer, 2015.

Zacher, Samantha. *Rewriting the Old Testament in Anglo-Saxon Verse: Becoming the Chosen People*. London: Bloomsbury, 2013.

Index

Abbo of Fleury, 10, 16, 17, 24, 28, 34, 61, 153, 170, 171–7, 180–6, 188, 190–3, 195–204, 208–9, 210, 211, 212, 214, 216, 304n21; "*O Ramesiga cohors*," 184; *Passio sancti Eadmundi*, 5, 10, 16, 28, 34, 136, 171, 172, 174–209, 210, 211, 212, 214, 216, 290n112, 312n101, 312n103, 314n126, 317n147, 318n164, 321n185

Additamentum Nivialense de Fuilano, 71

adventus Saxonum, 22, 37–40, 175–6, 186, 202, 296n166

Agatho, Pope, 76, 254n36

Aimo of Fleury, *De vita et martyrio sancti Abbonis*, 183, 310n74

Alcuin of York, 271n51

Alde, 19

Aldhelm, 262n19, 271n52, 277n101

Alfred, 4, 5, 7, 14, 28–30, 127, 129–32, 136, 137, 139–58, 160–4, 167–70, 185, 194–5, 198, 203, 208, 217, 250n152, 321n186, 322n10

Alfred-Guthrum Treaty, 5, 28–30, 34, 128, 138, 141–52, 158, 162, 165, 166, 168, 191, 194, 216

Andreas, 123, 240n28, 281n134

Angeln, 21, 39, 71

Angilbert, 258n77

"Anglian Collection," 17, 23, 25, 59–60

"Anglo-Saxon" as demonym/ethnonym, 4

Anglo-Saxon Chronicle, 5, 17, 22, 24, 28, 34, 128, 131, 133–41, 145, 151, 152, 157, 158, 161, 166, 168, 171, 173, 176, 181, 182, 191, 196, 201, 203, 209, 216, 230n100, 239n19, 252n20, 285n42, 296n166, 296n168, 305n29, 315n138; "A" (Parker) recension, 22, 29, 63, 71, 72, 105, 126, 129, 133, 134, 137–8, 140–1, 143–4, 147, 152–4, 155, 156–7, 158–62, 163, 164–6, 170, 179, 252n18, 284n30, 291nn126–7, 303n15, 306n38; "B" recension, 131–32, 159, 161, 162, 284n31; "C" recension, 134–5, 160, 162, 284n31, 320n184; "D" recension, 162, 284n30, 301n246; "E" recension, 284n30; St. Neots Chronicle (see *St. Neots, Annals of*)

Anna, 24–5, 33, 60, 70, 71–2, 75–6, 88, 94, 98, 251n11, 263n135, 318n163

Annals of St. Gall (*Annales Alamannici*), 285n43, 286n61

anonymous queen of East Anglia, 26, 32, 33, 41–49, 51–56, 63, 69, 70, 77, 89, 191, 211
Antony, Saint, 72, 112
Asser, 49, 152, 271n52, 285n42, 293nn143–4
Augustine, Saint, *De civitate Dei*, 268n25
Æbbe, 74, 79–80, 81, 256n58
Ælfric of Eynsham, 6, 9, 17, 24, 28, 127, 153, 170, 193, 196–209, 210, 212, 214, 215, 218, 305n32, 307n50, 312n101, 315n127, 315n129, 319n165; *Catholic Homilies*, 317n148, 317n157, 320n176, 321n187; *De oratione Moysi*, 315n138; *De populo Israhel*, 320n181; Homily on Judith, 277n101; Homily on Maccabees, 320n181; *Life of Æthelthryth*, 87, 204, 223n35, 257n67, 259n89, 277n101; *Life of Edmund*, 5, 7, 32, 34, 127, 170, 171–3, 178, 181, 193, 197–209, 214, 216, 218, 297n183, 304n18, 307n50, 312n101, 313n117, 319n168; *Life of St. Swithun*, 315n127, 315n138, 320n178; *Lives of Saints*, 87, 196, 198, 199, 203, 204, 207, 277n101, 316n141, 317n147, 317n157, 319n171; Prayer of Moses, 108; *Sermo de memoria sanctorum*, 316n145; Sermon on the Assumption, 207
Ælfthryth, 167
Ælfwald, 6, 23, 33, 34, 95, 102, 105–9, 112, 115, 116–20, 122–6, 185, 186, 191, 206, 211, 216, 228n79, 267n18; Letter to Archbishop Boniface, 107–8, 128
Ælle, 39, 250n154
Æthelbald, 33, 102–5, 106–9, 116–19, 123–4, 216, 278n115
Æthelberht (king of Kent), 30, 31, 39–42, 47, 48, 49, 53, 58, 71, 191, 217–8, 249n131
Æthelberht I (king of East Anglia), 236n165
Æthelberht II (king of East Anglia), 72, 125–6, 133, 137, 172, 174, 211, 236n165, 304n19
Æthelburh (abbess of Barking), 74, 83
Æthelburh of Faremoutiers, 318n163
Æthelburh of Kent, 47
Æthelflæd, Lady of the Mercians, 167
Æthelflæd of Damerham, 12, 14, 166–7
Æthelfrith, 41–4, 61, 77–8, 191
Æthelhere, 71, 251n12
Æthelmær, 196, 200, 318n162
Æthelred (ealdorman of Mercia), 167
Æthelred (king of East Anglia), 236n165
Æthelred (king of Mercia), 72, 105, 108, 124–5, 268n27
Æthelred I (king of Wessex), 158, 160, 198, 212, 322n10
Æthelred II (king of East Anglia), 237n165
Æthelred II "the Unready" (king of Wessex and of England), 195, 197–200, 204, 218, 307n50; *II Athelred* (peace treaty), 290n115
Æthelstan (king of England), 130, 131, 164, 167, 174, 176, 181, 199–200, 201–2, 222n27, 298n191
Æthelstan I (king of East Anglia), 236n165, 282n3
Æthelstan II (Scandinavian king of East Anglia). *See* Guthrum
Æthelstan "Half-King" (ealdorman of East Anglia), 131, 132, 167, 186, 209, 310n76

Æthelthryth, Saint, 6, 7, 32–3, 47, 53, 60, 65, 68, 69–101, 102, 104, 106, 111, 112, 118–19, 121, 124, 140, 143, 172, 174, 189, 191–2, 193–4, 201, 202–5, 211, 222n26, 248n123, 276n100, 321n8
Æthelweard (author of *Chronicon*), 133, 138, 146, 196, 198, 200–1, 271n52, 285n42, 286n67, 316n141, 317n150
Æthelweard (king of East Anglia), 236n165
Æthelwine "Dei Amicus," 28, 183, 185–6, 209, 311n86
Æthelwold, Saint, 100, 181, 189, 197, 198, 200, 316n146, 318n161, 318n165
Æthelwold "Ætheling," 130, 158–63, 164, 166, 216, 283n19, 284n24

Baldwin, 192–3
Bartholomew, Saint, 105, 114, 115, 117
Battle of Brunanburh, 176
Battle of Maldon, 193, 306n35
Beccel, 105
Bede, 4, 5, 6, 9, 10, 11, 16, 17, 20, 21–2, 24, 25, 26–8, 29, 30–1, 32–3, 35–68, 69–101, 102, 103, 106, 109, 111–12, 118–19, 124, 125, 128, 137, 143, 152, 163, 168, 169, 170, 174, 175–6, 179, 180, 182, 188, 189, 191, 194, 201, 203, 208, 209, 211, 213, 215, 216, 218, 220n9, 221n20, 229n95, 266n12, 266–7n15, 268n25, 270n40, 273n69, 276n95, 276n99, 285n45, 289n110, 306n33, 309n63, 316n143, 320n176; *Chronica maiora* (included in *De temporum ratione*), 260n103; Commentary on Acts of the Apostles, 64; Commentary on Genesis, 51; Commentary on Proverbs (*Super parabola Salomonis*), 47, 65, 101, 242n54, 242n55, 245n78, 268n25; Commentary on 1 Samuel, 242n54, 244n76; *De templo*, 246n94; *Ecclesiastical History of the English People* (*Historia ecclesiastica gentis Anglorum*), 5, 10, 11, 16, 17, 20, 21, 22, 24, 25, 26, 28, 29, 32–3, 35–68, 69–101, 102, 103, 106, 109, 111–12, 118–19, 124, 125, 128, 137, 143, 152, 163, 168, 174, 175–6, 179, 182, 188, 189, 191, 194, 201, 208, 209, 211, 213, 215, 216, 220n9, 229n95, 266n12, 266–7n15, 268n25, 270n40, 273n69, 276n95, 285n45, 306n33, 316n143; *History of the Abbots*, 254n36; *In cantica canticorum*, 251n158; *Letter to Ecgbert*, 44; *Life of St. Cuthbert*, 53, 118, 245n90, 258n72, 276n99. *See also* Old English translation of Bede's *Ecclesiastical History* (Old English Bede); *Super parabola Salomonis*
Bedford, 142–3
Bedricesgueord/Bedricesweorth. See Bury St. Edmunds
Benedict Biscop, 76, 254n36
Benedictine Reform in England, 115, 170, 171–2, 173, 181–7, 190–1, 195–8, 201, 204–5, 206, 208, 276n93, 294n153, 311n100, 316n140, 318n161
Benedict of Nursia, Saint, 179–80, 273n67
Beonna, 236n165
Beowulf, 8, 18–19, 123, 227–8n79, 229n95, 240n28, 254n40, 276n92, 322n22
Bernicia, 41, 43, 44, 61, 78, 130, 191, 245n82
Bertha, 47, 49

Bible, 35, 207, 320n175; Acts, 54; Ecclesiasticus, 305n32; John, 246n96; Kings, 81, 223n35, 247n106; Luke, 56–7, 65, 246n96, 247n108; Mark, 246n96; Matthew, 207, 246n96; Proverbs, 47, 101; Psalms, 90, 120
Birinus, 244n77
Blythburgh, 24
Boniface, Saint, 107–8, 125, 280n127
Boniface V, 47
borders and border/frontier spaces, 16, 20, 27, 30, 54, 55, 85, 93, 103–4, 145, 147, 150, 151–2, 178, 226n60, 275n85, 281n134, 290n115, 292n133
Botwulf/Botolph, Saint, 60, 70, 72–3, 124, 172
Boudicca/Boadicea, 21
Bran (or Heydon) Ditch, 20
Brent Ditch, 20
Britons. *See* Romano-British cultures
Bures, 177–8
Burrow Hill, 18
Bury St. Edmunds (town), 171, 234n132, 313n109, 313n112, 321n2
Bury St. Edmunds Abbey, 14, 34, 104, 166–7, 171, 184–5, 186–7, 190, 192–3, 195, 196, 204, 212, 213–14, 296n177, 310–11n81, 314n126, 321n8
Byrhtferth of Ramsey, 184, 271n52, 309n64; *Vita sancti Oswaldi*, 174, 183–4, 309n64
Byrhtnoth, 193–4

Cælin (or Ceawlin), 39
Caistor-by-Norwich/Caistor St. Edmund, 15, 89, 230n94
Caister-on-Sea, 18
Cam, 272n60
Cambridge (*Grantacæstir, Granta/Gronta, Grantabrycg*), 20, 53, 84, 85, 110–1, 118–20, 138–40, 156, 165, 215, 258n69, 272n60
Cambridgeshire, 5, 11, 17, 20, 84, 135, 160, 178, 185, 217, 220n9, 233n132
Canterbury, 9, 71, 100, 197, 297n186
Catuvellauni, 122, 279n119
Cædmon, *Hymn*, 11, 250n146, 258n76
Centwine, 125
Ceolred, 106
Ceolwulf, 79, 125, 255n48, 268n25
Ceorleswyrth (Chelsworth), charter of 962, 12–14, 93, 166–7, 190
Cerdic, 157, 224n49
Cerdicings (West Saxon royal dynasty), 14, 28, 34, 127, 128, 130–2, 136, 137, 144, 146, 148–9, 152, 155, 156, 158–70, 171, 185–6, 190, 201–2, 209, 224n49, 296n166, 298n191
Cerne (Cerne Abbas), 171, 303n16, 318n162
charters, 12–14, 69, 92–3, 98, 151, 164, 166–7, 190, 226n60, 269n33, 274n79, 281n134
chorography, 8, 10–11, 16, 210
civitatula, 84–5, 87, 97, 140
Cnobheresburg (Burgh Castle?), 64, 71, 73–4, 86, 124
Cnut, 131, 132, 135, 184, 209, 244n71
Coenred, 120, 124, 278n115
Coifi, 55, 64, 241n44
Colchester, 21, 165, 170
Coldingham, 74, 75, 79–82, 100, 112
Constantinople, Council of, 245n80
"Count of the Saxon Shore," 21, 229n92
Cratendune, 71, 251n11
Crowland, 6, 53, 95, 103–4, 106, 111–12, 113–24, 186, 257n64, 257n68
Cuthbert, Saint, 53, 198, 201, 202, 203, 316n143; anonymous *Life of St. Cuthbert*, 258n72; Bede's *Life*

of St. Cuthbert (*see* Bede: *Life of St. Cuthbert*); monastic community in Bernicia, 132
Cynefrith, 87, 89, 90
Cynewulf (poet), 320n176; *Elene*, 277n101, 281n134
Cynewulf (king of Wessex) and Cyneheard, 299n217

Danelaw, 34, 128, 130, 131, 156, 166, 222n23, 237n166, 284n28, 285n42, 300n225
Deben, 19, 24, 25, 228n86
Deira, 41, 42, 61, 74, 130, 245n82
Devil's Dyke, 20, 117, 178–80, 186, 191, 307n46
Domnoc/Dummoc (Walton Castle), 25, 64, 69, 71, 124
Dorchester, 261n108, 267n16
Dunstan, Saint, 174, 181, 196, 197, 198, 199–200, 314n126, 316n146
dykes. *See* Devil's Dyke, Fleam Dyke, Offa's Dyke

Eadbald, 48, 243n62, 243n68
Eadbert, 125
Eadgyth, 131, 132
Eadwald (king of East Anglia), 237n165
Eadwald (possible real name of Felix), 269n36
Eadwold (named in 962 Chelsworth charter), 12, 14
ealdormanry, 28, 132, 284n34
Ealdwulf, 57, 80, 94, 103, 256nn52–3
East Anglia, bishopric, 6, 63–6, 69, 71–2, 135, 193; client-kingdom of Mercia, 103–5, 109, 112, 123, 125–6; ealdormanry under West Saxon control, 28, 34, 131, 132, 164–8, 170–1, 173, 182–3, 184–6, 190–1, 195–209; earldom, 132, 211–15; kingdom (of the East Angles), 6, 9, 15–34, 36–68, 69–83, 85–96, 98–101, 102–12, 116, 118–20, 121–2, 124–6, 127–8, 130, 137–8, 172, 174, 178–80, 187–9, 191–2, 195, 212–13, 217–18; region, 3–6, 9, 10–12, 14–15, 26, 32, 128, 141, 172, 176–8, 194, 196–7, 210–11, 214–18; royal court, 45–9, 51–6, 73, 80, 94, 104; royal genealogy, 59–60, 98; Scandinavian-held territory of the East Anglians within southern Danelaw, 6–7, 18, 29–30, 34, 127, 128–49, 150, 152–64, 168–70, 195. See also *gens Orientalium Anglorum*
Ecga, 106
Ecgberht (anchorite[?]; possible miswriting of "Ecgburh"), 268n32
Ecgbert (missionary), 44
Ecgburh, 102–3, 104, 106
Ecgfrith, 75–81, 98, 101, 256n55
Ecgric, 58–9, 60, 61, 71
Eddius Stephanus. *See* Stephen of Ripon
Edgar, 12, 14, 131–2, 166–7, 185, 189, 197–8, 200, 201, 252n19, 283n23, 298n191, 301n246, 303n11, 309n63, 319n165
Edmund, Saint, 6, 23, 28, 29, 34, 61, 127, 128, 130, 133, 134, 136–8, 153, 154–6, 166, 170, 171–4, 177–8, 179, 181, 182, 184–209, 210, 211, 212–14, 216, 217, 236–7n165, 285n42, 298n191, 304n19, 307n50, 309n69, 312n102, 312n103, 312n105, 317n154, 321n2
Edmund I (king of England), 166–7
Edward the Elder, 28, 30, 129, 130, 132, 152, 156, 158–60, 163–5, 167, 170, 171, 179, 296n168, 296n178, 298n191, 300n232, 307n47

Edwin, 32, 40, 41–5, 46, 47, 48, 55, 56, 58, 61, 62, 79, 249n131
Edwold, Saint, 318n162
Ely, 10, 33, 68, 72, 77, 79–80, 84, 90–3, 103, 121, 256n53, 259n95, 261n105, 267n16, 272n60, 311n100
Ely Abbey, 6, 7, 53, 68, 69, 70–2, 74, 75–8, 79–95, 97–100, 103, 111–12, 118–20, 124, 189, 192, 193–4, 202, 204, 205, 253n32, 253n33, 256n53, 259n94, 261n105, 267n16, 308n60, 311n86, 311n100, 318n161, 319n165, 321n8
Eni, 25
Eohric, 160, 296n178
Eorcenberht, 72, 99, 222n26
Eormenhild, 72, 94, 99
Eorpwald, 30, 33, 44–5, 58, 61, 70, 79, 88, 247n115
Essex (kingdom of the East Saxons), 5, 14, 16, 21, 24, 26, 28, 32, 37, 48, 55, 130, 144, 146, 156, 164–5, 177, 193, 194, 230n104, 232n118, 244–5n77, 246n98, 285n45
Ethandun (Edington), battle of, 129, 140, 141, 143, 145, 146, 160
Evagrius, *Vita sancti Antonii*, 111
Exning, 260n104

felicitas, 48, 64, 70, 82, 109, 249n136, 270–1n46
Felix (bishop of East Anglia), 6, 33, 60, 63–6, 68, 69–71, 85, 124, 211, 247n108
Felix (monk and author), 17, 20, 24, 33, 102–11, 118–19, 121, 123, 125, 128, 143, 152, 170, 180, 206, 209, 269n36; *Vita sancti Guthlaci*, 5, 7, 10, 20, 33, 53, 102–25, 128, 178, 191, 206, 216, 228n79, 240n27, 250n154, 257n64, 259n81, 308n55
Felixstowe, 64
Fens/Fenland, 3, 5, 7, 10, 16, 17, 20, 22, 28, 33, 53, 65, 71, 72, 75, 80, 84, 87, 88, 92–4, 101, 102–5, 110–24, 159, 160, 171, 177–80, 183–6, 206, 211, 216, 220n9, 233n132, 257n64, 267n24, 276n95, 277n101, 288n85, 308n60, 310n80, 311n82, 320n173, 322n22
Fleam Dyke, 20
foederati, 21, 229n94
Folcard of Saint-Bertin, author of *Vita sancti Botolphi*, 73
Francia, 71, 74, 131, 156, 163
freoðuwebbe (OE "peace-weaver"), 254n40
Fursey (Fursa), Saint, 6, 33, 36, 60, 61, 64–5, 70–4, 85, 86, 124, 172, 211, 252–3n22; anonymous *Vita virtutesque sancti Fursei*, 36, 118, 252n22, 273n65, 276n99

genealogies, royal, 17, 23, 25, 34, 51, 59–60, 71, 137, 143, 177, 226n65, 232–3n122, 236–7n165, 239n21, 247n116, 248n123, 274n76, 306n39
gens ("nation," "people"), 27, 40, 41, 95, 98–9, 270n40, 316n141
gens Anglorum, 35, 38–9, 41, 50–1, 95, 98–9, 121, 168, 211, 213, 221n21, 306n33
gens Orientalium Anglorum, 37–40, 43–5, 76–7, 81, 82, 88, 93, 95, 107, 109, 112, 122, 124, 127, 187–8, 189, 190, 192, 217
Geoffrey of Wells, 5, 177
"germanic" as ethnonym, 21, 22, 24, 26, 37, 46, 65, 70, 121, 175, 176–7, 220n7, 225n53, 227n75, 229n89, 229n93, 229–30n95, 231n107, 240n27, 241n49, 241n50, 279n118, 306n35
Gesta Herwardi, 92, 257n68, 260n100, 274n75. *See also* Richard of Ely

Gildas, *De excidio et conquestu Britanniae*, 22
Goscelin of Saint-Bertin: *Lectiones in festiuitate Sanctae Sexburge*, 222n26, 263n134; *Miracula sancte Ætheldrethe*, 253n32, 255n46; *Miracula sancti Eadmundi*, 321n8; *Vita sancte Werburge*, 261n12, 263n135; *Vita sancte Wihtburge*, 263n135
Granta/Gronta. *See* Cambridge
Grantabrycg. *See* Cambridge
Grantacæstir. *See* Cambridge
Great Army, 128, 283n11, 287n76
Great Ouse , 25–6, 142–3, 179, 272n60, 299n208
Great Summer Army, 128–9, 287n75
Gregorian mission, 45, 48, 53, 54, 72
Gregory I, "the Great," 53, 55, 66–7, 85, 86, 241n51, 246n91; *Regula pastoralis*, 194, 293n146
Gregory of Tours, 246n92
Guthfrith/Guthred, 132
Guthlac, Saint. *See* Felix (monk and author): *Vita sancti Guthlaci*
Guthlac A, 115, 123, 181, 206, 240n28, 264n1, 268n30, 271n55, 272n57, 273n66, 273n67, 274n74, 274n79, 274–5n81, 275n86, 275n92, 276n95, 278n115, 281n134, 308n61, 319n172
Guthlac B, 123
Guthlac, Life of, OE prose hagiography, 115, 264n1, 271n55, 275n83, 276n95, 280n123
Guthrum, 129, 145, 155, 157, 297n186
Gyrwe, 75–6, 77, 80, 104, 118, 259–60n95, 270n45, 276–7n100

Hadleigh, 296n177
Hálfdan, 128–9, 132, 138, 283n11, 283n13, 284n24,
Harford Farm, 15, 89
Hatfield (Hertfordshire), Council of, 57
Hatfield Chase (S. Yorkshire), 240n42
Hæglesdun (Hellesdon Wood), 192, 313n109
Headda, 106, 113, 267n20
Henry of Huntingdon, *Chronicle*, 257n68
Herbert de Losinga, 304n19
Hereward ("the Wake"), 92, 133, 274n75
Herman the Archdeacon, *Miracula sancti Eadmundi*, 212–14, 303n7, 305n32, 321n8
Heydon Ditch, 20
"hides" (*familiae*), 12, 13, 14, 91, 93, 94, 112, 260n97, 273n63
High Ditch, 20
Hild, Saint, 11, 53, 74, 83, 264n141
Hincmar of Reims, *De regis persona et regio ministerio*, 268n25
Historia Croylandensis, 269n33
Holme, 160, 164, 170, 299n210
Honorius, 63, 244n77
Horace, *Odes*, 189, 311n99
Hoxne, 304n19
Hoxne Hoard, 21
Hugh Candidus, *Chronicle of Peterborough Abbey*, 180, 257n68, 274n71, 308n55
Hulme, 184, 310–11n81
Humber, 7, 30, 31, 37–8, 40, 71, 109, 131
Huntingdonshire, 160, 185, 220n9, 299n210
Hwætred, 106

Icanhoe (Iken), 72, 252n20
Icel, 114, 274n77
Iceni, 20–1, 22, 23, 121–2
Iclingas, 124
Idle, 43

imperium ("overlordship"), 37–41, 42, 45, 55, 63, 65, 67–8, 77, 94, 109, 123–4, 127, 152, 158, 168, 187–8, 190, 204, 216, 234n140, 239n19, 240n30, 311n97
imperium-list (in Bede), 32, 37–41, 42, 60, 67–8, 137
Ingulph, 269n33
Isidore, Saint, 235n140
Ívarr the Boneless, 128, 288n94
Ixworth, 234n132, 286n51

John of Worcester, 177, 252n20
Jonas of Orléans, *De institutione regia*, 268n25

Kyneburga, 74

"Laws of Edward and Guthrum," 237
Laȝamon, *Brut*, 322n21
Lea, 142–3, 290n111
Leofstan, 194
Libellus Æthelwoldi, 263n138
Liber Eliensis, 24–5, 71–2, 80, 193–4, 239n26, 251–2n12, 253–4n33, 255n45, 256n52, 261n112, 268–9n32, 308n55, 313n112, 314n120
Lichfield, 106, 266n14
Life of St. Æthelwold, 7, 200
Life of St. Cuthbert, 258n72
Life of St. Edmund. *See* Abbo of Fleury: *Passio santi Eadmundi*; Ælfric of Eynsham
Life of St. Erkenwald, 174
Lincolnshire, 5, 185, 215, 220n9, 233n132
Lindsey, 43, 119, 240n35
locus amoenus, 92, 114, 179–83, 190, 193, 274n74, 310n75, 310n80
lyres, 18

manuscripts: Cambridge, Corpus Christi College, MS. 308, 126; Cambridge, Corpus Christi College, MS. 383, 142; Glasgow, Hunterian Library, MS. Hunter 86, 250n153; London, British Library, MS. Cotton Tiberius B.ii, 312n106; London, British Library, MS. Cotton Vespasian B.vi ("Anglian Collection"), 17, 23, 25, 59–60; London, British Library, MS. Egerton 1993, 256n55; London, British Library, Harley Charter 43 C 3 (Chelsworth), 12–14, 166–7, 190, 223n37, 225n50; London, British Library, MS Royal 13.A.xv, 250n154; London, British Library, MS. Royal 13.C.v, 250n154; Oxford, Bodleian Library, MS. Hatton 43, 67; St. Petersburg, National Library of Russia, Lat. Q.v.I.18 (St. Petersburg Bede), 66
Medehamstede. *See* Peterborough Abbey
Mercia (kingdom of the Mercians), 9, 16, 17–18, 20, 23, 24, 25, 28, 29, 33, 37–8, 43, 58–9, 69–72, 74, 77, 85, 93, 98, 99, 102–26, 127–8, 131–3, 135, 138, 144, 152, 159, 171, 177, 178, 184–7, 206, 211, 216, 228n79, 251n8, 261n108, 266n12, 266n14, 267n16, 267n18, 268n27, 270n44, 270n45, 271n49, 274n77, 275n81, 276n95, 276–7n100, 277n10, 278n115, 278n116, 279n112, 280n124, 288n94, 294n154, 296n170
Middle Anglia (kingdom of the Middle Angles), 5, 25, 38, 43, 81, 101, 103–4, 108, 114, 118, 20, 187, 212, 266n12, 266–7n15, 267n18, 270n44, 277n110

Mildenhall Treasure, 21
Monk of Whitby, *Earliest Life of Gregory the Great*, 238n14

"Nennius,", 22
Norfolk, 3, 5, 8, 15, 18, 20, 25–7, 59, 89, 135, 184, 185, 215, 217, 219n1, 220n9, 228n87, 229n90, 233n125, 248n119, 249n139, 259n95, 284n28, 306n41
Norman Conquest, 4, 8, 74, 214
North Elmham, 15, 25
Northumbria (kingdom of the Northumbrians), 6, 9, 16, 17, 24, 26, 32, 37–8, 40, 41, 43–5, 55, 75–81, 94, 98, 101, 109, 112, 125, 127, 128–32, 138, 156, 157, 158, 159, 161–2, 163, 169, 198, 211, 222n27, 233n128, 238nn10–12, 241n44, 242n61, 245n90, 246n98, 248n123, 252–3n22, 255n47, 256n51, 258n72, 263n135, 283n11, 283n19, 287n75, 288n94, 296n166
Norwich (diocese), 233n126
Norwich (town), 156, 229n94
Notitia dignitatum, 21

Ofa, 106
Offa, 17, 72, 124, 125–6, 137, 140, 281n132
Offa's Dyke, 17
Old English translation of Bede's *Ecclesiastical History* (Old English Bede), 27, 28, 30–1, 208, 289n110
Ordinance concerning the Dunsæte, 290n115
Oswald (king of East Anglia), 237n165
Oswald, Saint (archbishop of York), 28, 181, 183,197, 304n25, 318n161, 321n185
Oswald, Saint (king of Northumbria), 40, 62, 198, 201, 249n131, 263n135, 268n27, 316n143
Oswiu, 40, 245n77
Ouse. *See* Great Ouse

Pachomius, Saint, 113
Paulinus, 42, 45
Pega, Saint, 106, 123
Penda, 25, 61–2, 66, 69, 70, 71–2, 74, 103, 118, 119, 201, 240n42, 242n61, 247n115, 251n11, 251n12, 252n20, 266–7n15
Penwalh, 105, 270n44, 278n116
Peterborough Abbey, 74, 84, 103, 120, 186, 308n60
provincia (kingdom), 27–8, 30–1, 35, 47, 68, 71, 72, 90–1, 93, 98–9, 108, 137, 139, 144, 204, 209, 211, 212, 235n140, 236n160, 270n40
Pseudo-Ingulph, 269n33

Quadripartitus, 142

Ramsey Abbey, 28, 34, 103, 104, 171, 174–5, 181, 183–7, 190–1, 196, 204, 208, 257n68, 304n20, 304n21, 304n25, 305n29, 310n75, 310n80, 310n81, 311n86, 318n161, 321n185
Rædwald, 6, 23, 24, 25, 26, 32, 33, 36–49, 51–8, 59–61, 62, 63–8, 69–71, 74, 75, 76, 77–9, 81, 82, 86–7, 89–90, 99, 124, 143, 163, 174, 179, 182, 185, 187, 191, 211, 216
Rægenhere, 43, 44
regio ("region"/"district"), 91, 108, 135, 137, 139, 212, 213, 236n160, 270n40
regnal lists. *See* genealogies, royal
Rendlesham, 24, 55, 59, 73, 91, 225n56, 228n83, 231n107, 232n116, 233n131, 246n100, 285n45

Repton, 102, 104, 105, 112–13, 114, 119, 129, 138–9, 265n6, 265n7, 266n11, 266n14, 269n34, 273n67, 273n68, 287n75, 288n86
Ricberht, 58, 247n115, 247–8n117
Richard of Ely, *Gesta Herwardi/De gestis Herwardi*, 92, 180, 260n100
Richerus of Reims, *Historiarum libri quatuor*, 303n12
Romanitas, 23, 26, 73–4, 97, 118–19, 140, 192, 249n130, 258n72, 258n77, 258n79, 273n68
Romano-British cultures, 20–4, 35, 39, 40, 53, 84–6, 118, 119, 120–2, 175–6, 206, 229n89, 233n128, 242n57, 258n72, 278–9n116. *See also* Catuvellauni; Iceni; Trinovantes
Rome, 26, 41, 82, 85, 113, 119, 124, 192, 250n157, 254n36, 273n69

sarcophagi, 53, 82–8, 89, 90, 97, 118, 119, 258n72, 258n74, 258n77, 258n80
Sæberht, 48, 243n62
Seafarer, 250n149
Seaxburh, 72, 74, 83–7, 94, 99, 100, 204, 205, 222n26, 257n67, 259n94, 263n133, 263n134, 263n135
Sebbi, 125, 244n77
Secgan be þam Godes sanctum þe on Engla lande ærost reston, OE text (*Resting Places of the English Saints*), 72–3, 277n100
ship-burials, 15, 18–20, 24, 50, 51, 67
Sigeberht (king of East Anglia), 6, 30, 33, 58, 60–4, 70, 71, 72, 73, 82, 88, 125, 133, 174, 187, 189, 247n115, 313n112, 318n163
Sigeberht (king of Essex), 245n77
Sihtric, 131–2
Snape, 18–19, 24, 225n56, 233n131
Speculum principis/Fürstenspiegel, 105, 268n25
spolia, 73–4, 82–8, 124, 258n79, 259n81
Spong Hill, 15
St. Benet's Abbey, 184, 310–11n81
Stephen of Ripon, author of *Vita sancti Wilfridi*, 32, 94
St. Neots, Annals of, 161–2, 177, 296n177, 300n219, 306–7n42
Stour, 14, 177, 306n42
subregulus (subject king/client-king), 71, 105, 123, 125, 126, 137, 151, 152, 213, 237n165, 251n12, 265n9, 268n26
Suffolk, 3, 5, 11–20, 24–6, 55, 59, 64, 72, 91, 135, 164, 171, 177, 185, 217, 220n9, 224n41, 224–5n50, 228n87, 231n107, 232n114, 233n125, 233n129, 233n131, 248n119, 249n139, 259n95, 260n104, 284n28, 286n51, 286n51, 286n59, 296n177, 306n41, 306n42
Suidhelm, 55
Sutton Hoo, 15, 17, 18, 19–20, 24, 50, 67, 73, 225n54, 226–7n66, 228n86, 232n118, 233n131, 240n38, 244n71
Sweyn, 132, 213, 214
syncretism, 36, 39, 46–57, 59, 60, 67, 90, 128, 216, 238n9, 243n65

Tatwine, 113–14, 117
Tette, 105
Thames, 142–3, 144, 146, 159
Thetford, 29, 133–6, 139, 140, 156, 201
Thietmar of Merseburg, 250–1n157
Thorney Abbey, 186, 252n19, 257n68, 277n110
Tiddingford, 163
Tondberht, 76, 80, 82, 118, 251n11, 253–4n33, 256n53

Tribal Hidage, 25, 28, 91, 112, 266n12, 266n14, 273n63
Trinovantes, 21, 22, 23
Tytil, 59

Ubba (called "Hubba" by Abbo of Fleury), 128, 173
Ulfcytel, 134–5, 164

Vergil, 72, 86, 97, 280n129
vikings, 6, 7, 21, 28, 34, 127, 128–70, 172–3, 174, 176, 178, 182, 188–96, 197–8, 201–4, 208–9, 216, 217, 220n12, 237n166, 288n86, 290n113, 291n119, 296n168, 306n35, 313n110, 314n126, 317n150, 319n168, 320n179
Vitalis, Orderic, *Ecclesiastical History*, 106, 269n33, 272n58
Vita virtutesque Fursei, 249n139, 252n22

Walton Castle. See *Domnoc/Dummoc*
Watling Street, 142–3, 144
Wearmouth-Jarrow, 27, 53, 76, 79, 82, 252–3n22, 254n36, 254n37, 273n69
Welland, 278n112
Werburh (Waerburg; abbess of Ely), 94
Wessex (kingdom of the West Saxons), 7, 9, 12–14, 16, 17, 23, 28, 29–30, 37, 39, 48, 98, 125, 127–70, 178, 190, 202, 212, 216, 217, 236n163, 281n140, 293n147, 294–5n155, 296n168
Whittlesmere, 277n110
Widukind of Corvey, 251n157
Wigfrith, 113
Wilfrid, 78, 79–80, 87, 256n53, 262n119
William of Malmesbury, 300n232; *Gesta pontificum Anglorum*, 64, 172
Wimborne, 159
Winwæd, battle of, 72, 251n12
Witham, 164, 170
Wuffa, 25, 59, 192
Wuffings/*Wuffingas*, East Anglian royal dynasty, 23, 25, 33, 36, 55, 58–9, 73, 80, 90–2, 105, 124, 127, 186, 192, 241n48, 296n177
Wulfhere, 72, 99
Wulfstan of Winchester (*Vita sancti Æthelwoldi*), 7, 200
Wulfthryth, 158

www.ingramcontent.com/pod-product-compliance
Lightning Source LLC
LaVergne TN
LVHW040153080826
844660LV00014B/948/J

* 9 7 8 1 4 8 7 5 0 5 7 3 8 *